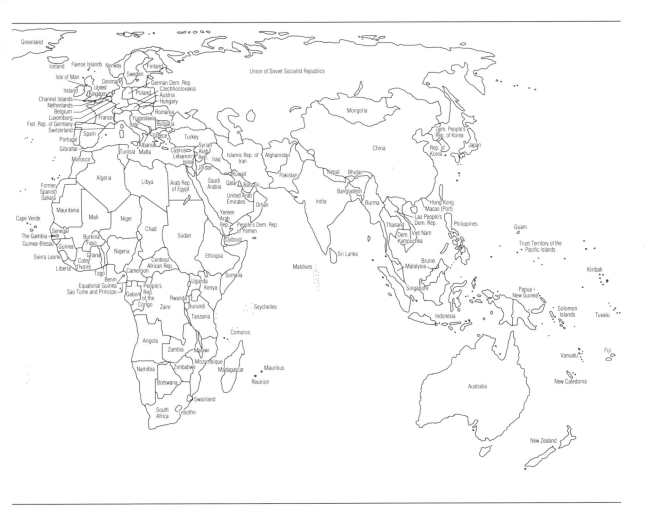

SOURCE: World Development Report, The World Bank, 1988

GLOBAL BUSINESS STRATEGY

A SYSTEMS APPROACH

A. G. KEFALAS

Professor of Management
The University of Georgia

G23
PUBLISHED BY
SOUTH-WESTERN PUBLISHING CO.
CINCINNATI   WEST CHICAGO, IL   CARROLLTON, TX   LIVERMORE, CA

Library of Congress Cataloging-in-Publication Data

Kefalas, Asterios G.
  Global business strategy: a systems approach/A. G. Kefalas.
    p. cm.
  Bibliography: p.
  Includes index.
  ISBN 0-538-07232-6
    1. International business enterprises—Management.   2. System
analysis.   I. Title.
  HD62.4.K44   1990
  658.4'012—dc20
                                                     89-90896
                                                        CIP

1 2 3 4 5 6 7 8 Ki 6 5 4 3 2 1 0 9

Printed in the United States of America

COVER PHOTO: © Jook Leung

To
Georgios, my father, who gave me life
and
Georgios, my son, who gave it purpose

PREFACE

Future historians of business will undoubtedly describe the 1990s as the dawn of globalization. Gradually but steadily, goods, services, money, and people are coming to be exchanged in a market that has virtually no national borders. This market is not simply an extension of the domestic markets that grew up after the end of World War II. Rather, the global market is a new phenomenon brought about by a convergence of the social, political, and economic systems of the peoples of the earth.

At the center of this globalization process is the interplay between the multinational corporation (MNC) and the nation-state, or country. The nation-state, responding to the political and economic cooperation among the great powers, has found that it must adopt a more cooperative attitude toward the MNC. Similarly, the MNC, faced with some new managerial challenges, has discovered that it needs the support of the nation-state. These challenges stem from changes in technology (primarily information technology), market forces, and people's attitudes toward work. Even among MNCs, conventional "go-it-alone" strategies, prevalent in the 1970s and early 1980s, are giving way to "cooperate-to-compete" strategies. Indeed, strategic alliances among some of the largest MNCs seem to be the norm rather than the exception.

Institutions of higher education, cognizant of this shift toward globalization, are developing curricula that aim at preventing American students, the business leaders of the future, from falling prey to "the backyard view." When one sees no light in any of the other windows in the neighborhood, it is all too easy to assume that everyone in the world is asleep—to forget that there is more to the world than one's own backyard. The business leader of the future must understand that from now on, business opportunities and challenges will be global ones; no single country will ever again have a monopoly on business or technological expertise.

THE APPROACH OF THIS BOOK

The greatest dilemma facing the author of a textbook on international business strategy is estimating readers' knowledge of the domain. Should the author assume that the student already comprehends such subjects as international economics, international trade, and international finance? Or should the book deal extensively with these subjects before tackling management issues?

After over fifteen years of teaching, I have come to recognize that the appropriate compromise is to provide a quick refresher on international economics, trade, and finance. For this reason, *Global Business Strategy: A Systems Approach* builds a good theoretical base before addressing the basic functions, or tasks, of global management. The philosophy underlying this work is that international managers are practitioners of economics and, in particular, its subdiscipline of international economics. Just as a good engineer must learn the science of physics before practicing engineering, and a physician the science of biology before practicing medicine, international managers must learn international economics before they can begin practicing global management.

STRUCTURE OF THE TEXT

The book is organized into three parts.

Part 1, The Subject, explores the field of international business (Chapter 1) and its main actors, the MNC (Chapter 2) and the nation-state (Chapter 3).

Part 2, Theoretical Base, presents in compact form all the background knowledge that students need to refresh their memories.

Part 3, The Management of Global Operations, is the main focus of the book. The material in this part describes the phases in the process of internationalization. Generally, a firm goes global by following a process of "creeping incrementalism." The first step in this process is to adopt the strategy involving the least commitment—exporting. Subsequently a firm moves into contractual arrangements such as licensing, franchising, or management contracts. If the firm's efforts prove successful, management commits more resources to the more risky entry mode of investment. Part 3 of the book contains seven chapters that correspond to the main tasks of management. The decision to participate, or enter the global market, is the subject of Chapter 7, Participation Strategy. Chapter 8 describes how the organization structure of an MNC is built. The next five chapters deal with the main functions of management. Financial management strategy is the subject of Chapter 9, production/sourcing strategy is dealt with in Chapter 10, and marketing strategy is explained in Chapter 11. Chapter 12, Human Resource Development, tackles the difficult subject of attracting, developing, and retaining good managerial personnel. Chapter 13, Communication and Control, explores the design of appropriate systems for monitoring and controlling global operations. Finally, Chapter 14, Consortia and Strategic Alliances, reviews the latest trends in the interplay between MNCs and between MNCs and nation-states, and speculates on some of the most likely developments in the global race.

FEATURES OF THE BOOK

Great care has been taken to make the book as effective a teaching aid as possible. The mixture of visual stimuli with text is one of the distinguishing characteristics of the book. At the beginning of each chapter is a flow diagram of the main concepts and subconcepts covered in the chapter. This diagram is accompanied by a list of learning objectives and a short overview, which serves as a prelude to the main part of each chapter. The body of each chapter contains a combination of text and graphical material. A recapitulation at the end of each chapter provides a concise summary of the main points. Finally, questions and exercises at the end of each chapter give students an opportunity to test their understanding of the material covered in the chapter.

The concept that ties the text together is the systems approach. This approach looks at an MNC as an open system that is in continual interaction with its external environment. The emphasis on the MNC's external environment is manifested in features called Emerging Issues. These sections describe factors in the external environment that are likely to have a marked impact on the strategies and structures of MNCs. The Emerging Issues allow the instructor to expose students to societal issues that are not usually textbook material. Six such issues have been included, one for each of the first six chapters.

The conciseness of the book is perhaps its greatest advantage. Most professors have pet topics or techniques that they like to emphasize in their courses—simulation exercises, the Pacific Basin and Japan, the European Common Market, or industry analysis, for example. This kind of special emphasis takes time. A lengthy text presents a problem for the instructor, who has to skip some material to accommodate his or her own interests.

SUPPLEMENTARY MATERIAL

The Instructor's Manual contains concise summaries of each chapter; chapter outlines; suggested multiple choice, true/false, and essay questions; suggested paper topics; sources of additional instructional materials such as films, speakers, and data bases; and a set of transparency masters of charts used in the book.

ACKNOWLEDGMENTS

The writing of this book took me across the Atlantic a dozen times during the last five years. In the process of learning about the workings of MNCs, I have had invaluable assistance and guidance from many people. It is virtually impossible to mention all of them here. However, I cannot fail to acknowledge the contributions of the following persons: Yohannan T. Abraham, Southwest Missouri State; Todd Barber, The Alexander Group, for his help with the software provided as an ancillary to the text; William Boulton, Roberto Friedmann, Margaret E. Holt, and William Megginson, University of Georgia; Philip L. Cochran, Penn State University; David Allen Cole, AMRO Bank of Holland, Chicago; Zaki F. El-Adawy, Pace University; Les Flynn, Strategic Management Alliance, Inc.; Juan Carlos Folino, Integra, Inc.; James D. Goodnow, Bradley University;

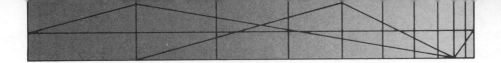

Chris Knoll, Small Business Development Center, University of Georgia; Demitrios Koutsounis, Design Data Ltd., Greece; Georgios Mantes and Demitrios Bourantas, TEAM Ltd., Greece; Reza Motameni, Fresno State; Panagiotis Pippas, A. C. Nielsen, Greece; P. J. Richardson, RACAL/Health and Safety Products, Inc., Frederick, Maryland; Erik Van Houweligen and Bart Zieleman, The Netherlands; Michael von der Heydt, Deutsche Bank, New York; Mark R. Zuccolo, Snapper Power Equipment, McDonough, Georgia; and the hundreds of students and executives in the United States, Venezuela, Argentina, the United Kingdom, and Greece who have gone through the pains of testing the material in the book. In addition, I must thank the International Intercultural Studies Program (IISP) of Georgia, which gave me the opportunity to write in Brussels and London; the London Business School, which generously gave me access to its library and computer facilities; and the ICBS, Greece, and its students for giving me the opportunity to test the globalization of business education. I am grateful as well to the chairman of the Management Department at the University of Georgia, Richard C. Huseman, and to Dean Albert Niemi, Jr. for their patience and support over the last five years. Finally, I thank Karen Turner, Melanie Blakeman, Nancy Fajardo, and Debra Sinclair, who passed repeated tests of their patience and typing skills with flying colors. All of these people, working in concert with the postal services on both sides of the Atlantic, the airline, and my loyal companion, a portable PC, made it possible for me to study and to practice what I preach—globalization.

Athens, Georgia   A. G. Kefalas
March 1989

CONTENTS

PART 1
THE SUBJECT

The global marketplace is reality. Money and ideas can and do move to any place on this planet in seconds, and there is no longer any place to hide from the judgments of others. . . .

Every day, a computer system called CHIPS in the New York Clearing House processes the debits and credits of London Eurodollar trading in a volume approaching some $200 billion. . . . This market is not just more of the same: it is something new in the world. . . . The global, information-intensive marketplace for ideas, money, goods, and services knows no national boundaries. . . .

Economic interdependence in no way lessens the importance of independent national initiative. . . . Each nation has to evolve its own system for bettering the condition of its people. . . .

The great global corporations are a new expression of the entrepreneurial thrust that thrives on the free exchange of goods, services, factors of production, technology, capital, and ideas. They are now the principal agents for the peaceful transfer of technology and ideas. . . . Since no country has a monopoly on industrial and agricultural skills, or on other knowledge, this transfer is necessary if we are to raise the world's living standards. . . .

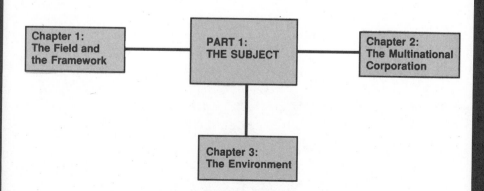

The reality of a global marketplace has pushed us along the path of developing a rational world economy. Progress owes almost nothing to political imagination....

The development of truly multinational organizations has produced a group of managers who really believe in one world.... They are against the partitioning of the world on the pragmatic ground that the planet has become too small, that our fates have become too interwoven for us to engage in the old nationalistic games which have so long diluted the talent, misused the resources, and dissipated the energy of mankind....

Economic chauvinism is obsolete in a world where the prosperity of all nations depends more and more on cooperation and free trade.

Walter B. Wriston

"The World According to Walter," *Harvard Business Review,* January–February 1986, 66, 67, 68.

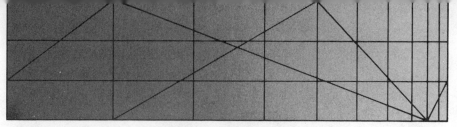

CHAPTER 1 THE FIELD AND THE FRAMEWORK

The beginning of wisdom is calling things by their right name.

Confucius

OVERVIEW

This chapter addresses two main questions: (1) What activities are involved in the field of international business? (2) How are these activities organized and executed? This combination of "know what" and "know how" is essential for understanding the field of international business.

Answering the first question involves study of the variety of activities typically performed by business organizations engaged in international business and of the nature of such organizations. Answering the second question requires study of the process used by an organization considering involvement in international business and how this involvement actually materializes (that is, entry strategies).

Finally, because organizations are made up of people who carry out the various decision-making activities involved in international business, the chapter delineates the basic tasks in setting global business strategy and the subsequent decisions and plans that must be made and carried out in implementing international operations.

LEARNING OBJECTIVES

After studying the material in this chapter, the student should be familiar with the following concepts:

(1) International business

(2) Exchange of goods

(3) Exchange of services and information

(4) Exchange of money

THE MAIN CONCEPTS | THE SUBCONCEPTS

The Field of International Business

- Exchange of Goods
- Exchange of Services and Information for Commercial Purposes
- Exchange of Money (Investment)

CHAPTER 1: THE FIELD AND THE FRAMEWORK

The Internationalization/ Globalization Process

- Phase A: Export/Import Entry Modes
- Phase B: Contractual Entry Modes
- Phase C: Investment Entry Modes
- Phase D: Global Consortia

Global Business Strategy: An Overview

- The Systems Approach
- A Brief Look at Strategic Management

The Challenging Task of the Global Manager

The Conceptual Framework: The Organization of the Book

Emerging Issue 1: The Internationalization of Uncle Sam

(5)   Portfolio (stock) investment

(6)   Direct foreign investment (USDFI)

(7)   Direct foreign investment in the United States (DFIUS)

(8)   The business enterprise

(9)   The business enterprise as an open system

(10)   The internationalization process

INTRODUCTION

Few people question the importance of a country's interaction with the rest of the world in fostering its economic, political, and social well-being. International business—a country's exchange of goods, money, services, and information—is a very important part of this interaction.

Because of the role the United States has played in world affairs during the last forty years, the average person's understanding of the importance of international business to U.S. prosperity is distorted. First, many assume that the amount of international business is quantitatively insignificant, as only a small percentage of the GNP is involved. Second, people assume that other nations depend on U.S. business more than Americans depend on others' business. This book subscribes to the proposition that the United States' dependence on the exchange of goods, money, services, and information with the rest of the world is neither small nor unimportant.

The misconception regarding the significance of international business for the United States stems from a lack of understanding of certain basic concepts and the supporting statistics. The ignorance of statistics is forgivable—few can claim that they fully understand the accounting procedures used by the U.S. Department of Commerce in keeping track of international transactions. The purpose of this chapter is to overcome the lack of understanding of the basic concepts by familiarizing the reader with the field of international business in general and international management in particular. After a brief description of the nature, magnitude, and importance of international business, the focus will shift to the main theme of this book, which is the role and function of private enterprise as the main carrier of a country's international transactions.

THE FIELD OF INTERNATIONAL BUSINESS

The term **international business** denotes all international dealings of a country that pertain to the exchange of goods, services and information for *commercial purposes,* and money. Exhibit 1-1 graphically depicts the field and its main activities. All international business activities are interrelated and interdependent.

Exhibit 1-1   International Business Activities

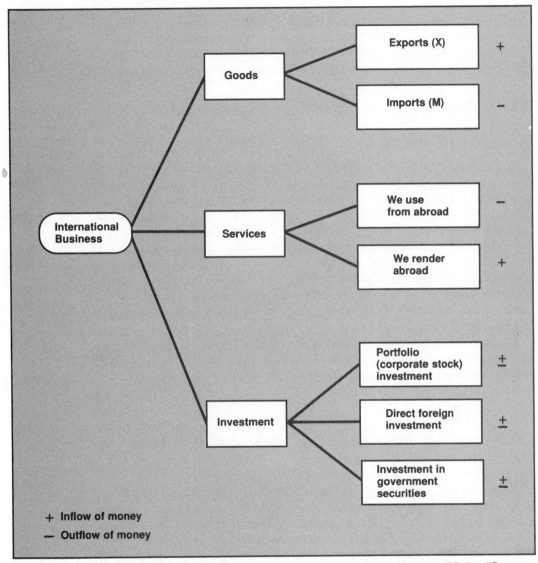

If industry produces more than people can consume, then the country will *export* (X) the difference:

$$SS > DD \longrightarrow X$$

If people consume more than industry can produce, then the country will *import* (M) the difference:

$$DD > SS \longrightarrow M$$

DD = Aggregate Demand   SS = Aggregate Supply

EXCHANGE OF GOODS

There are many reasons why goods are exchanged among countries. These reasons are referred to in the literature as theories of international trade. They will be explained in greater detail in Chapter 5, International Trade.

In general, the reasons for trading goods among countries can be classified into two categories:

Supply differences (that is, differences in countries' material or technological endowments)

Demand differences (that is, differences in consumer preferences)

Theoretically, when supply differences exist, a country may either *export* the excess of local production over local demand or, if local demand exceeds local supply, *import* enough products from abroad to satisfy local demand. Differences between demand and supply offer only a partial theoretical explanation for international trade, however. In reality, a country may export a portion of its domestic production even though domestic demand is unsatisfied. Similarly, foreign goods may be sold in domestic markets that are literally glutted with domestic products. The price difference between domestic and foreign products is only one factor to examine in these seemingly paradoxical situations. Customer preferences and tastes for foreign products are usually much more important explanations.

Whatever the reasons for the exchange of goods among countries, the volume and importance for human survival of exchange activities have accelerated beyond anyone's imaginings. Over one-fourth of the world's products are traded among its over 150 countries.

EXCHANGE OF SERVICES AND INFORMATION FOR COMMERCIAL PURPOSES

International services are defined as transactions by *private* individuals and/ or corporations that cross national boundaries. Thus, government services such as diplomatic, cultural, and scientific transactions among governments are *not* part of international services as defined here.

It must be pointed out at the outset that the exchange of services is closely linked to the exchange of goods, and vice versa. For example, shipping, one of the most important international services, is obviously the result of the exchange of goods, as are banking, insurance, communications, and aviation. Similarly, the exportation of machinery for a new factory in Brazil may be the result of the endeavors of a U.S. consulting, engineering, and construction firm.

Traditionally, services were restricted to the five main categories mentioned above: aviation, banking, communication, insurance, and shipping. The eighties have ushered in a new type of service, which is destined to be far more important for the United States than all other conventional services. This new service is the exchange of information and information technology. Because of its importance for contemporary and future international business, information technology is treated separately in Chapter 14, Consortia/Strategic Alliances.

A country's ability to export services will depend on, among other things, the level of the country's development. It is well established that a country evolves from an *agrarian society,* where the main source of its citizens' income is the production of primary products, such as agricultural produce and minerals, to an *industrial society,* where the production of secondary goods, such as machines and instruments, becomes the primary source of income for its citizens, to a *post-industrial society,* where tertiary activities, such as services, are the hallmark of the country's business activities.

The contribution of services to the United States' international transactions has been increasing steadily. For example, whereas in 1960 services amounted to a small percentage of the U.S. foreign exchange earned from exports, in 1984 services reached the $142.4 billion mark, an increase of 8% over the previous year. For 1988, services were expected to earn in the neighborhood of $150 billion. The United States has the largest share, about 20%, of services trade worldwide.

EXCHANGE OF MONEY (INVESTMENT)

Movements of money across national borders can take one of the following forms:

Private payments for the purchase of foreign goods and services

Government payments for the purchase of foreign goods and services

Government payments for aid, pensions, etc. (transfer payments)

Private payments for the purpose of investing in the private or government sector to derive earnings (interest, dividends, etc.)

This section is concerned with the last category of money exchanges—the movement of money across national boundaries for the exclusive purpose of earning money (that is, investment).

What holds true for exchanges of goods and services holds true for money also. A country may export money that is in excess of domestic demand, or, conversely, a country may import money (subject to laws and regulations) when the demand for it cannot be domestically satisfied.

Money available for international investment will go where the yield from its use (that is, interest payments or dividends) is the highest. In general, foreign investment will assume one or a combination of the following forms:

Portfolio investment (corporate stocks and bonds)

Direct foreign investment (facilities and other goods-producing assets)

Investment in government securities (for example, U.S. Treasury bonds)

Money invested in any of these three forms in foreign countries constitutes an *outflow* $(-)$ of money from the investing country (called the home country) and therefore signifies an increase in a country's fixed assets abroad. In other words, a country converts current (short-term, liquid) assets into fixed (long-term, nonliquid) assets.

For the country in which the money is invested (called the recipient, or host, country), the investment constitutes an *inflow* (+) of money and therefore signifies an increase in that country's long-term liabilities to foreigners. In other words, a country converts current (short-term, liquid) liabilities into long-term debt. The short-term liabilities stem from the country's demand for foreign goods and services that can now be produced locally because of another country's willingness to invest.

Whether the foreign money is invested in the private sector, in governmental stocks and bonds, or in brick and mortar facilities, the investment represents an exchange of short-term (liquid) assets of the home country for long-term (fixed) obligations of the host country. The investing country deprives its institutions of investment opportunities while boosting the host country's domestic money pool.

In the nomenclature of the U.S. Department of Commerce, U.S. money invested abroad in plant and equipment is called **direct foreign investment** (USDFI). Conversely, money invested in this country by foreigners is called **direct foreign investment in the United States** (DFIUS). Historically, foreign investment followed trade, which, of course, followed political hegemony and knowledge of business practices. Thus, Europe—primarily the United Kingdom, France, Spain, and Portugal, which had historically colonized most of the North and South American, Asian, and African continents—was the most important investor in foreign lands. Europe's investment was concentrated on primary products, especially raw materials and minerals needed to fuel its industrial revolution and economic development.

The end of World War II ushered in a new era of foreign investment. This new era was characterized by an increase in the variety of the investing countries as well as in the types of foreign investment. Among the new actors, the United States emerged in a very short period of time as the most important investor, largely because of the demand for reconstruction of the almost demolished European nations.

This hegemony of the United States in the international investment sphere was not the only novelty in post–World War II history. More significant than the skyrocketing of the volume of foreign investment was the change in the nature of investment away from investment whose purpose was to secure the uninterrupted flow of raw materials to the investing country (that is, for production purposes) and toward investment in the production of industrial and consumer goods (that is, for consumption purposes).

The reasons for and the rationale behind foreign investment are explored in Chapter 2, The Multinational Corporation. It will suffice to say here that foreign investment represents one of the most complex and least understood subjects of international business, in part because the complete impact of foreign investment decisions on the investing and recipient countries is not easy to assess.

THE INTERNATIONALIZATION/ GLOBALIZATION PROCESS

In the preceding section the basic international business transactions were explained using the concept of a country as an autonomous, sovereign state capable of making all the decisions necessary to carry out these economic transactions. In reality, however, countries or nations do not engage directly in any of the main activities of international business. Rather, the agent or main actor in this transnational interplay is *private enterprise* or *mixed enterprise* (private enterprise with substantial governmental participation).

The nature, structure, strategies, and role of private international enterprise are dealt with in Chapter 2. Here a brief explanation of the process of the internationalization of business enterprises is presented.

This book espouses the evolutionary theory of international business. According to this theory, firms become involved in international business by following a stepwise process.[1] This process represents a gradual involvement in international business, which begins with exporting and ends with direct foreign investment. The process is pictured in Exhibit 1-2. As the firm moves from left to right along the globalization line, it proceeds through several phases. Each step prepares the way for the next step.

In general, the potential benefits and risks for the firm increase as it upgrades its international involvement. Thus, the springboard, or base, of the stepwise globalization program (A. Export/Import Entry Modes) represents the lowest risk and, of course, the lowest control and benefit from international business activity. At the third step of the internationalization process (C. Investment Entry Modes), the opposite is true: the high benefits and control carry with them a rather substantial risk. Finally, at the extreme end of this process (D. Global Consortia Modes), the firm engages in "competitive cooperation" in the sense that it enters into "friendly ties" (agreements with competing firms and/or nation-states) and forms "strategic alliances."[2]

Once started in international business, a company will gradually change its entry mode decisions in a fairly predictable fashion. Increasingly, it will choose entry modes that provide greater control over foreign marketing operations. But to gain greater control, the company will have to commit more resources

---

[1]This view is endorsed by the majority of texts written in the field. Even though authors use different names such as internationalization, globalization, creeping incrementalism, degrees of corporate internationalization, and so on, all allude to a *gradual and purposeful increase in the firm's involvement in cross-national business.* One noted exception is the Industrial Organizations economists, who advance the so-called internalization theory. This theory holds that firms set up international subsidiaries that act as an expansion of the domestic market, because the transactional costs involved in operating in an open market are much higher than the costs of working in their own "internal markets." This theory, along with some others, will be explained in subsequent chapters.

[2]John Marcom, Jr., "Friendly Ties: More Companies Make Alliances to Expand into Related Business," *The Wall Street Journal,* November 8, 1985, 1.

Exhibit 1-2 The Globalization Process: An Evolution

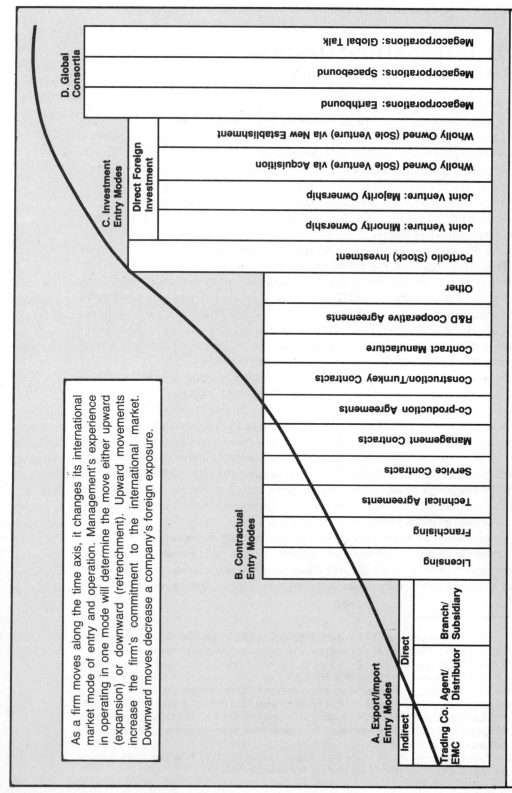

As a firm moves along the time axis, it changes its international market mode of entry and operation. Management's experience in operating in one mode will determine the move either upward (expansion) or downward (retrenchment). Upward movements increase the firm's commitment to the international market. Downward moves decrease a company's foreign exposure.

D. Global Consortia

Megacorporations: Global Talk

Megacorporations: Spacebound

Megacorporations: Earthbound

C. Investment Entry Modes

Direct Foreign Investment

Wholly Owned (Sole Venture) via New Establishment

Wholly Owned (Sole Venture) via Acquisition

Joint Venture: Majority Ownership

Joint Venture: Minority Ownership

Portfolio (Stock) Investment

B. Contractual Entry Modes

Other

R&D Cooperative Agreements

Contract Manufacture

Construction/Turnkey Contracts

Co-production Agreements

Management Contracts

Service Contracts

Technical Agreements

Franchising

Licensing

A. Export/Import Entry Modes

Indirect	Direct	
	Agent/Distributor	Branch/Subsidiary
Trading Co. EMC		

SOURCE: F. Root, *Foreign Market Entry Strategies* (New York: AMACOM, 1982), 7.

to foreign markets and thereby assume greater market and political risks. Growing confidence in its ability to compete abroad generates progressive shifts in the company's trade-off between control and risk in favor of control. Consequently, the evolving international company becomes more willing to enter foreign target countries as an equity investor.[3]

Of course, not all companies will follow this evolutionary, or graduated-commitment, type of strategy in going international. The model is, however, generally applicable, as traditionally most multinational companies have internationalized their business activities by moving along the export–wholly owned investment continuum. In general, a company will entertain the idea of going international for essentially two types of reasons:[4]

(1) Operational Necessities

    (a) To secure raw material
    (b) To secure equipment
    (c) To secure technology
    (d) To dispose of excess output

(2) Strategic Necessities

    (a) To assure its invulnerability to future changes in its external environment
    (b) To assure continued growth by
        (1) sustaining historical growth patterns
        (2) avoiding stagnation caused by saturation
        (3) increasing the volume of business
        (4) increasing the rate of growth
    (c) To assure and improve profitability

Although the emphasis in this book is on strategic management, keep in mind that strategic management concepts, once implemented, become operational necessities. For this reason, it is more appropriate to think of operational and strategic activities as interrelated and interdependent rather than as separate and discrete managerial functions.

A look at Exhibit 1-2 reveals four interrelated and identifiable phases:

Phase A: Export/Import Entry Modes

Phase B: Contractual Entry Modes

Phase C: Investment Entry Modes

Phase D: Global Consortia

A full description of the logic and managerial involvement in each of these

---

[3]F. Root, *Foreign Market Entry Strategies* (New York: AMACOM, 1982), 137–177.
[4]Igor H. Ansoff, *Implementing Strategic Management* (Englewood Cliffs, NJ: Prentice-Hall International, 1984), 152–172.

modes will be given in Chapter 7, Participation Strategy; only a brief introductory explanation is provided here.

PHASE A: EXPORT/IMPORT ENTRY MODES

As mentioned earlier, the main reason for exporting or importing a product
is to correct an imbalance between supply and demand. Since both continuously change, there will always be goods that are traded in international markets.

PHASE B: CONTRACTUAL ENTRY MODES

The majority of the contractual entry modes used by a company are responses to changes in the environment where a company operates. Alternatively, the contractual entry modes may be proactions on the part of
management.

Reactive contractual entry modes are usually responses to attempts by the
government of the host country either to restrict the volume of imports from
a particular country or to slow down the growth of its own exports. If a country
feels that its own industry needs some type of protection to develop (the
"infant industry" argument, usually used by the developing countries) or to
revitalize itself (an argument used by the U.S. car manufacturers), it will attempt
to limit imports either by increasing the cost of selling the foreign product in
its market (tariff barriers) or by imposing or negotiating voluntary quantitative
restrictions on the absolute amount of imports (quotas or other nontariff barriers).

When this situation arises (or before it arises, if management is being proactive), a firm, in order not to lose the revenue it has been deriving from the
exports, will enter into one or a combination of the nine contractual modes
listed in Exhibit 1-2.

PHASE C: INVESTMENT ENTRY MODES

Looking at an organization as an open system, one can easily see some of
the reasons why a firm might decide to go international by investing in the
stock of a company in another country, by buying up that company, or even
by building a brand new company from scratch (the so-called Greenfield
approach).

The international market is part of a domestic company's external business
environment. Although there are mutual effects, the company does not have
as much control over the external environment as it would like to have. A
company may decide to invest in another company's assets merely to learn
more about this environment—knowledge is the best surrogate for control.
Or a company may invest in another company's assets because it desires to
influence the other company's managerial decisions. Through investment a

company can eliminate the risk of being deprived of the opportunity to secure needed material (inputs), secure access to new technology (processes), and secure access to the market (outputs). Of course, the degree of control assumed by the investing company increases along with the investment commitment. Sole, or 100%, ownership is the type of direct foreign investment preferred by most U.S. companies. IBM, one of the world's most successful and best-managed companies, is notorious for its refusal to engage in anything but wholly owned ventures.

PHASE D: GLOBAL CONSORTIA

Certain projects require skills, resources, and distribution systems far beyond one single company's or country's capabilities. In such situations a number of companies may enter into an agreement to share knowledge and responsibilities while maintaining their own legal and managerial autonomy. These super-corporations will then attempt to enter into an agreement with a country that has the resources needed to jointly own and manage the enterprise while maintaining its own national sovereignty.[5]

These super-corporations, in their collaboration with nation-states, form a type of multinational industry that might be called a megacorporation (that is, a corporation of corporations). The conventional megacorporation has been involved in resource utilization—the mining, drilling, processing, transporting, etc., of raw materials such as oil, copper, bauxite, and zinc. ARAMCO, the Arabian American Company, is the classic example of that type of earthbound venture. In the future worldwide business will involve a plethora of space-based and earthbound super-corporations. Ventures such as the Columbia Space Shuttle and ocean exploration and seabed exploitation enterprises will be common. The increasing sophistication of telecommunications will bring a new breed of global corporations whose purpose will be to transmit spoken, written, and coded data via a huge network of global talk, or, as Joseph N. Pelton calls it, "telecomputerenergetics."[6]

Going international requires a company's gradual involvement in and devotion of organizational resources to international activities. The process begins with a low-involvement mode—exporting—and ends with a high-involvement mode—investing. Although most companies that become multinational start with exporting, it is conceivable that a company might find it extremely profitable to start at any step of the process. By the same token, it is also possible that a company might decide never to leave a given step in order to move to a higher-involvement step.

---

[5]H. V. Perlmutter and D. A. Heenan, "Cooperate to Compete Globally," *Harvard Business Review,* March–April 1986, 138–152.

[6]Joseph N. Pelton, *Global Talk: The Marriage of the Computers, World Communications and Man* (Brighton, U.K.: The Harvest Press, 1981), ix.

GLOBAL BUSINESS STRATEGY: AN OVERVIEW

The philosophy that underlies the model of an evolutionary globalization process is the systems approach. The systems approach emphasizes the relationship between the organization and its external environment. This viewpoint is particularly appropriate for the study of international business. It also fits the layperson's understanding of an international business transaction as something that involves going "outside" one's own national boundaries.

THE SYSTEMS APPROACH

Openness is one of the most important qualities of a managerial philosophy that fosters internationalization of a business's activities. The diversity and complexity of the international business environment require that a company's managers look upon the organization as an open, organic system that is in continuous communication with its external environment. It is the exchange of information with the external environment that guarantees the survival and prosperity of the organization. Thus, it follows that successful international managers use a systems approach.

Developing a systems viewpoint of an organization is primarily a matter of adopting a new philosophy of the world, of management's role within the organization, and of the organization's role in the world. The manager's philosophy advocated here is, of course, systems thinking.[7]

As Exhibit 1-3 illustrates, there are three main inputs to any organization: people, money, and physical resources. These three inputs are processed in accordance with certain economic principles (such as the least-cost combination). The results of this processing are three outputs: products, waste, and pollution. Input, processing, and output are coordinated by management through such functions as goal setting, decision making, and controlling. Management, in carrying out this combination of input, processing, and output functions, receives input from the external environment regarding scientific and technological development, governmental policies, and public attitudes.

The dotted line around the system in Exhibit 1-3 represents its boundary. The boundary separates the system from its external environment. The environment represents the totality of factors that have a marked impact on the organization's function but that are beyond its immediate control.

In order to survive, the open system depicted in the exhibit must maintain an internal order that is in tune with the order exhibited by the external environment. Not only must the management of the system have a very good knowledge of the internal workings of the organization; more importantly, it must learn as much as possible about the characteristics of the external en-

---

[7]The discussion of the systems approach draws heavily on material covered in Chapter 10 of P. P. Schoderbek, C. G. Schoderbek, and A. G. Kefalas, *Management Systems: Conceptual Considerations,* Third Edition (Plano, TX: Business Publications, Inc., 1984), 259–288.

Exhibit 1-3   The Organization as a System

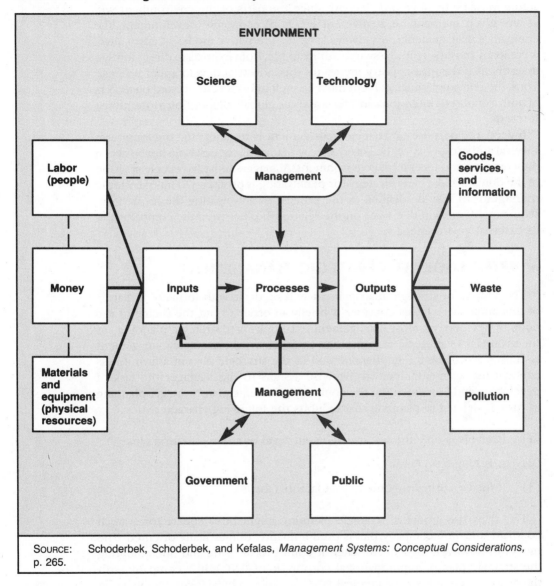

SOURCE: Schoderbek, Schoderbek, and Kefalas, *Management Systems: Conceptual Considerations*, p. 265.

vironment. It thus appears that the ultimate task of management is *to secure a harmony between the organizational objectives and the external environment's capacities.*

The implications for management of these demands for environmental and internal congruence are twofold. First, since the environment is multifaceted and changes continuously, the firm's management must remain intimately acquainted with it, consider as large a portion of it as possible, and make neither a conceptual nor an operational distinction between the home/domestic base and the foreign/international environment. Thus, management's thinking and acting must be truly *global.* Second, since the parts of the environment will at any given moment be at different levels of economic development, the company's management must always keep all alternative modes of entry alive. A company must be ready to switch, for example, from exports to direct foreign investment if the host country moves up the industrial development process. Thus, the company's management must be well-informed, interested observers of both a country's intentions/interests and the global competition's intentions/ interests.

Indeed, the purpose of strategic management is to guarantee the long-term survival and prosperity of the enterprise by managing the relationship between the company and its external environment. Managers must have a clear vision of the domain and a clear strategy for penetrating it profitably. Thus, **strategic management** may be defined as the process of anticipating the future consequences of present decisions on the relationship between the company and its external environment.

A BRIEF LOOK AT STRATEGIC MANAGEMENT

The subject of strategic management will be dealt with formally in Part 3 of this book. Here let us consider it briefly in order to put the theme of the book in perspective. Most management textbooks list "strategic planning" as the main task of strategic management. In other words, strategic management is considered to be the implementation of the strategic plan of a firm. International management literature likewise assigns to the manager the task of developing and implementing the company's strategic plan. Strategic planning in turn, is defined as planning that exhibits the following characteristics:

(1)   It involves only the top management level of an organization (locus).

(2)   It is long-term (time).

(3)   It focuses primarily on external factors (focus).

This tripartite model of strategic planning might be adequate for a small company and/or a company that is predominantly domestically oriented. The model is, however, inadequate when it comes to devising and implementing the strategic plan of a multinational corporation (MNC). In a company with the degree of complexity of a typical MNC, the hierarchical locus, the planning horizon (time), and the types of factors involved (focus) are difficult to pinpoint. For these reasons, strategic planning and management will be defined in this book by the following additional characteristics:

(1)   The contemplated actions involve the *integrated allocations of a significant portion of organizational resources.*

(2)   The contemplated actions involve *large uncertainties* about possible outcomes.

(3)   The contemplated actions *cannot be reversed,* except at great cost, increasing with time.[8]

The addition of these three characteristics to the definition of strategic planning is very important, for internationalization of a business's activities is a process that involves substantial resources, is exceedingly uncertain, and is not easily reversible.

Planning, one of the most important management activities, can be defined as thinking before action. More specifically, R. L. Ackoff defines **planning** as "the design of a desired future and of effective ways of bringing it about."[9] Designing a desired future for an organization is, of course, tantamount to predicting the organization's ability to survive in the future environment. Thus, the process of devising a strategic plan involves thinking about and analyzing the relationship between the organization and its external environment for some time into the future and then implementing effective ways of setting and accomplishing organizational goals. In short, organizational objectives and goals are set after a careful estimation of the environment's future state has been juxtaposed against the organization's strengths and weaknesses.

Exhibit 1-4 presents a list of the key questions one must ask when involved in strategic planning and a diagram of a corporate planning framework. The lower portion of the diagram (area III) depicts the three main elements of corporate planning: the environment, the corporation, and the stakeholders. The middle portion (area II) shows management as the process of thinking

---

Exhibit 1-4   Strategic Management

A. Key Questions and Descriptors

Questions	Descriptors
What are our objectives?	Objectives
What principal factors and changes may influence achievement of these objectives?	Scenarios
What choices do we have?	Options
How do we value these choices in light of perceived consequences vis-à-vis our objectives?	Consequences
How do we best allocate our resources?	Decisions
What do we monitor to improve the process by iteration?	Results

---

[8]Roy Amara and A. J. Lipinski, *Business Planning for an Uncertain Future: Scenarios and Strategies* (New York: Pergamon Press, 1983), 22.

[9]R. L. Ackoff, *A Concept of Corporate Planning* (New York: John Wiley, 1970), 1.

B. The Corporate Planning Framework

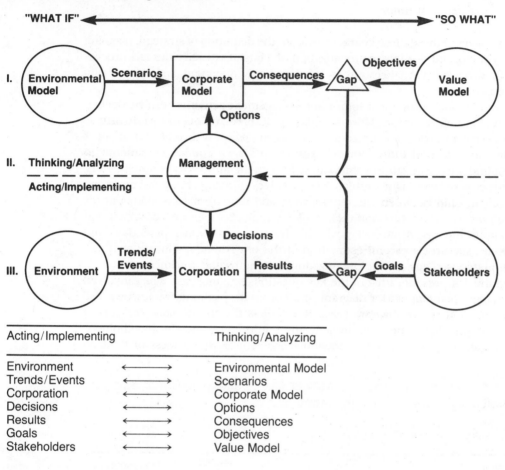

Acting/Implementing		Thinking/Analyzing
Environment	←——→	Environmental Model
Trends/Events	←——→	Scenarios
Corporation	←——→	Corporate Model
Decisions	←——→	Options
Results	←——→	Consequences
Goals	←——→	Objectives
Stakeholders	←——→	Value Model

SOURCE: Reprinted with permission from Roy Amara and A. J. Lipinski, *Business Planning for an Uncertain Future: Scenarios and Strategies* (New York: Pergamon Press, 1983), 4, 29. Copyright 1983, Pergamon Books Ltd.

about/analyzing the three main elements and acting on/implementing them. The upper portion (area I) illustrates management's modeling process. Thus, the environment is dealt with by management via the Environmental Model, the corporation via the Corporate Model, and stakeholders via the Value Model. Management's overall task is to make a statement that answers the what if's with so what's. In other words, management must estimate the future state of the environment (create scenarios), assess the corporate strengths and weaknesses (estimate the consequences), and then tell the stakeholders how their goals will be achieved (set objectives).

The entire strategy-setting process depicted in Exhibit 1-5 consists of management's attempt to maximize the quality of decisions—or, alternatively, to minimize the difference between intended/desired outcomes and actual outcomes, surprise factors, or unanticipated consequences. The quality of a decision is determined by the degree of congruence between intended and actual results.

Management's ability to produce quality decisions depends on three main sets of factors: the controllable (options or alternatives), the uncontrollable (states of nature or the environment), and the objectives (corporate goals). The controllable factors (X in Exhibit 1-5) represent the possible—the company's capabilities. The uncontrollable factors (Y in Exhibit 1-5) represent the probable—what is most likely to happen in the external environment. The goals and objectives (Z in Exhibit 1-5) represent the preferable—what management would like to see happen.[10] These factors might be called the "three Ps" of the strategic management process.

Exhibit 1-6 depicts the strategic management process as an interface between the multinational corporation and the nation-state (NS). Both the MNC and the NS have their unique structures; goals, interests, and shared values; and means of achieving them. These two subsystems are linked to each other in such a way as to form a synergistic relationship in which, ideally, the end result of the interaction is always greater than the sum of the individual parts. When this happens, the system has reached a state of homeostatic equilibrium that is ultrastable (stable under any disturbance). Let us take a closer look at the details of Exhibit 1-6. The two subsystems, the MNC and the NS, are the two main parts of a supersystem called the MNC-NS synergy. Each subsystem has its own organizational infrastructure and its own goals, interests, and shared values. The MNC must be ultrastable with respect to its stakeholders. They must be satisfied under any condition. (See Exhibit 1-7.) The NS, on the other hand, must make sure that its interaction with the MNC will not disrupt its ultrastability with the state's stakeholders (citizens, pressure groups, and nature).

Each subsystem can reach its goals or fulfill its interests either by depending on its own environment or by expanding its environment's physiological, cognitive, and economic limits through making an offer to interact with the other. Attempts to overcome the limits set by each subsystem's environment may result in cooperation or in conflict.

State A: Convergence. Suppose the managers of the MNC decided that by investing in the NS they could realize their goal of growth. If the NS saw this interaction as assisting in the accomplishment of its goals of development, growth (increase GNP), liquidity (saving foreign exchange for imports), and employment, the ultimate result would be cooperation.

State B: Divergence. If, however, wages paid to MNC employees were

---

[10]Amara and Lipinski, *Business Planning,* Chapter 4.

Exhibit 1-5   Strategic Management: Framework

$\boxed{X}$	$+$	$\boxed{Y}$	$\approx$	$\boxed{Z}$
Organization		Environment		Goal

Possible/Strategies	Probable/States of Nature	Preferable/Objectives
The organization (X) is the totality of *resources* that are	The environment (Y) is the totality of *factors* that are	The goal (Z) is the organization's *reason* for existence.
1. Relevant 2. Known 3. Controllable	1. Relevant 2. Unknown 3. Uncontrollable	The Preferable = What the firm would like to see happen
The Possible = What the firm can do	The Probable = What is likely to happen	*Task*: Assess potential outcomes of candidate strategies/state-of-nature combinations and evaluate consequences vis-à-vis objectives.
Task: Assess the firm's potential	*Task*: Assess the external business environment (EBE)	
Method: Firm scanning (Firmscan). Firmscan looks at the firm's performance in	*Method*: Environmental scanning (Enscan). Enscan conceives of the EBE as a set of emerging issues. Enscan does the following:	*Method*: Value modeling (Valmod). Valmod does the following:

A. Finance
  1. Balance Sheet
  2. P + L Statement
  3. Cash Flow
	1. Identification
	2. Evaluation
	3. Incorporation
	4. Transaction
		A. Generates and selects appropriate objectives
		B. Evaluates consequences
		C. Suggest modifications of objectives

B. Operations
  1. Production Capacity
  2. Sales
  3. Quality
	Outcome: Metascenario matrix	*Outcome*: Inferences matrix

C. People
  1. Labor
  2. Middle Management
  3. Top Management		

D. Diagnostics
  1. Ratios
  2. Z-Factor
  3. Company Value		

Outcome: Options/candidate strategies matrix		

The system = an organization (X) is an open, organic system that operates within an environment (Y) in search of a goal (Z).

Management = the process of anticipating and estimating the future consequences of its decisions to set certain goals and to deploy certain resources. The words "anticipating" and "estimating" are used because of the probabilistic nature of the second component in the identity X + Y = Z.

Exhibit 1-6   The MNC–NS Synergy

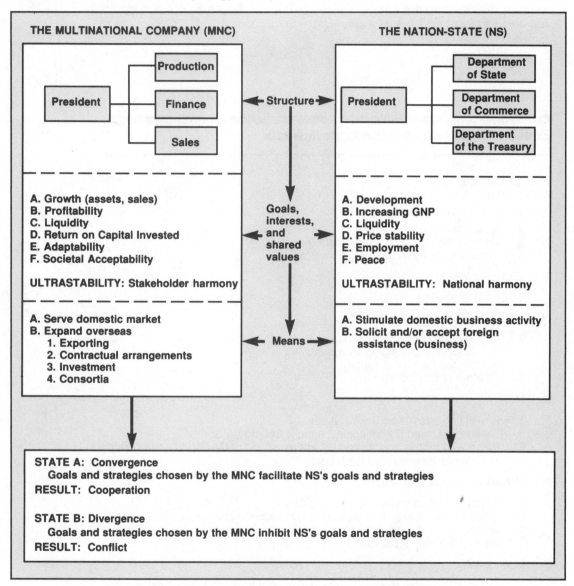

THE MULTINATIONAL COMPANY (MNC)   THE NATION-STATE (NS)

President — Production / Finance / Sales

← Structure →

President — Department of State / Department of Commerce / Department of the Treasury

A. Growth (assets, sales)
B. Profitability
C. Liquidity
D. Return on Capital Invested
E. Adaptability
F. Societal Acceptability

ULTRASTABILITY: Stakeholder harmony

Goals, interests, and shared values

← and →

A. Development
B. Increasing GNP
C. Liquidity
D. Price stability
E. Employment
F. Peace

ULTRASTABILITY: National harmony

A. Serve domestic market
B. Expand overseas
  1. Exporting
  2. Contractual arrangements
  3. Investment
  4. Consortia

← Means →

A. Stimulate domestic business activity
B. Solicit and/or accept foreign assistance (business)

STATE A: Convergence
  Goals and strategies chosen by the MNC facilitate NS's goals and strategies
RESULT: Cooperation

STATE B: Divergence
  Goals and strategies chosen by the MNC inhibit NS's goals and strategies
RESULT: Conflict

much higher than local wages, the MNC's decision to invest in the NS might be perceived as conflicting with the NS's goal of price stability. By the same token, the NS's decision to stimulate domestic business activity might be perceived as hindering the MNC's strategy of exporting to the NS. The ultimate outcome of this state of divergence would be *conflict.*

The majority of the criticism levied at MNCs for exploitative behavior and at NSs for unreasonable dictatorial actions would be eliminated if both parties accepted the necessity for interaction and perceived the game as a non-zero-sum/win-win game and not as a zero-sum/win-lose game.

Exhibit 1-7   Government-Corporate Interests

U.S. National Interests
A. Political

    1. U.S. unity
    2. U.S. democracy and liberty
    3. Democratic institutions throughout the world
    4. Individual liberty throughout the world

B. Economic Welfare

    1. Of U.S. citizens
        a. access to raw materials
        b. U.S. trade
        c. U.S. investments
        d. efficient world monetary system
        e. limited harmful pollution
    2. Of other nations' citizens

C. Military

    1. Preventing attacks on United States
    2. Defending United States against attacks that do occur
    3. Preventing military attacks on U.S. interests, and defending those interests when other means prove inadequate

D. Moral/Psychological/Cultural

    1. Safety of U.S. citizens
    2. U.S. citizens' access to diverse cultures, experiences, ideas, travel
    3. Amelioration of human suffering worldwide—genocide, war, starvation, slavery, political oppression

E. Managerial

    1. Credibility—global reputation for sincerity and ability to fulfill commitments
    2. Intelligence—access to information affecting U.S. interests and ability to attain those interests
    3. Good morale—sense of confidence, rectitude, effectiveness
    4. Effective U.S. organization

F. General
Whenever interests are being discussed on a regional or local basis, using the above list, it is always necessary to add an interest in facilitating attainment of U.S. interests elsewhere.

Key Corporate Interests

A.   Overall Profitability

B.   Assets

    1.   Equity position
    2.   Rights to land, minerals, etc.

C.   Organizational

    1.   Decision-making capability
    2.   Staffing capability
    3.   Safety and comfort of employees

D.   Operational

    1.   Access to equipment
    2.   Access to raw materials
    3.   Technology
    4.   Ability to import and export
    5.   Ability to transfer funds

E.   Markets

    1.   Continued access to existing markets
    2.   Access to new and growing markets

Source: W. Aschen and W. H. Overholt, *Strategic Planning Forecasting: Political Risk and Economic Opportunity* (New York: John Wiley and Sons, 1986), 23–24. Copyright © 1986 John Wiley & Sons, Inc. Reprinted by permission of John Wiley & Sons, Inc.

THE CHALLENGING TASK OF THE GLOBAL MANAGER

Management is the process of anticipating the future consequences of today's decisions. What kinds of decisions does a multinational manager have to make? What kinds of information does the manager need to make these decisions? What kinds of knowledge must the manager have in order to (1) find, organize, and evaluate the information; (2) use this information to determine the possible alternatives; (3) choose one possible state and name it the preferred state; and finally, (4) implement the programs and procedures that will enable the organization to reach its goals?

A search of the literature on international business in general and international management in particular yielded a list of twelve decisions multinational managers must make (see Exhibit 1-8). Given the number of subdecisions included in each, the number of different decisions that an international manager must make is mind-boggling. Managing a global company is indeed a very complex affair.

Exhibit 1-8   The Decisions Confronting the International Manager

(1) Should the firm enter a new country?

(2) What type of entry should it undertake: exporting, licensing, direct investments, management contracts, other arrangements?

(3) What are the opportunities/risks in various countries of different modes of entry?

(4) In what countries should the firm expand its existing plants, undertake new investments, make acquisitions?

(5) In what region or countries and when should the company expand its international commitments in funds, technology, management, know-how, and personnel?

(6) What should the company do about exchange risks, political vulnerability, and adverse governmental controls and regulations?

(7) Should the firm go into joint ventures with other private firms or government enterprises abroad, and under what conditions?

(8) Where should it raise funds for its worldwide operations?

(9) What product adaptations should it make and what new products should it introduce in various countries?

(10) To what extent should it change its marketing and product mixes in different countries?

(11) What management development programs should it undertake at headquarters and at its affiliates abroad?

(12) Should it disinvest or phase out business in certain countries?

SOURCE: Adapted from W. A. Dymsza, "Global Strategic Planning: A Model and Recent Developments," *Journal of International Business Studies*, Fall 1984, 169–170.

Global Business Strategy: A Systems Approach is designed to familiarize students with the basic principles of managing an international enterprise as "one integrated chessboard on which every move is planned for its strategic effect on the whole game."[11] In this global business framework, decisions made

[11]Ira C. Magaziner and R. B. Reich, *Minding America's Business: The Decline and Rise of the American Economy* (New York: Vintage Books, 1983), 137.

at the company's headquarters in, say, Peoria, Illinois regarding a new product or process must be evaluated for their possible impact on the company's sales office in Patras, Greece.

THE CONCEPTUAL FRAMEWORK: THE ORGANIZATION OF THE BOOK

The main actors in this book are the multinational corporation and the nation-state (the environment). These two entities are mutually interdependent. The MNC's survival depends on the survival of the nation-state, and vice versa.

The student of international business must comprehend the dynamics of the mutual interdependence between the MNCs and the nation-states of the world. A process of globalization is going on, as MNCs bid for the privilege of assisting nation-states in accomplishing their goals and thereby profiting. Similarly, nation-states are bidding for the privilege of assisting MNCs in accomplishing their goals and thereby profiting. As globalization continues, no nation-state can afford to erect unreasonable barriers to any MNC's desire to participate in the wealth-creating process and no MNC can afford to refuse a nation-state's reasonable request for assistance.

Understanding the exceedingly complex interactions among the thousands of MNCs and the hundreds of nation-states requires an equally complex scheme. The goal of Part 1 of this book, The Subject, is to provide the reader with a clear understanding of what the field is and who the main actors are (see Exhibit 1-9). The science of economics and its special field of international economics, with its emphasis on international trade and international finance, are the subjects of Part 2, The Theoretical Base: The Fundamentals. Part 3 is the heart of the book. The chapters in this part examine the initial decision to enter the global market and the main functions of management such as finance, production, personnel, communication and control, and marketing. The final chapter provides a glimpse into the future of the MNC.

International management is to international economics what engineering is to physics: the former creates mechanisms by applying knowledge created by the latter. The mechanism this book is concerned with is the MNC—a goal-directed enterprise run by people who look around the globe in search of profitable opportunities for satisfaction of human needs and creation of wealth. Although in the real world MNCs do not behave in the sequential form depicted in this book, analyzing managerial decisions and strategies in the sequence adopted here facilitates understanding.

Exhibit 1-10 provides a bird's-eye view of the material in this book. Accompanying a short summary of each chapter is the main question it addresses, along with a brief answer. The questions in Exhibit 1-10 fairly adequately represent the tasks that a multinational manager must master. The material covered in this book is not easy. An attempt has been made here to make it

Exhibit 1-9   The Book and Its Organization

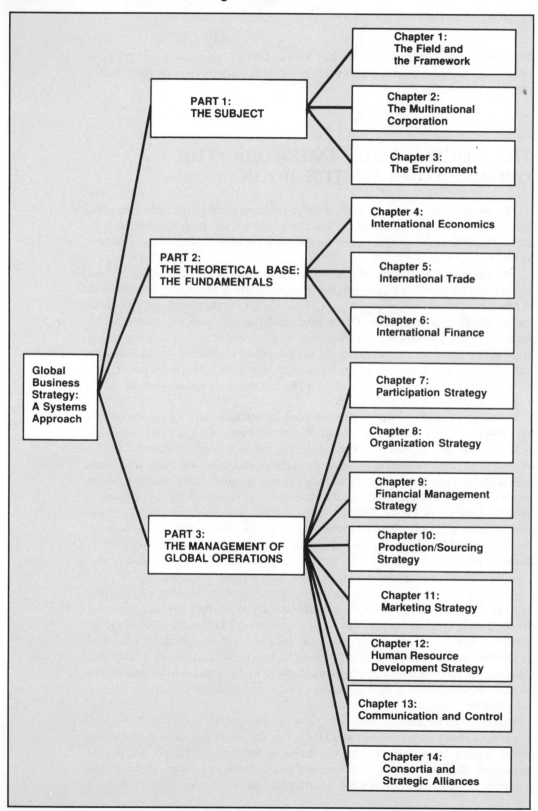

Exhibit 1-10   Key Questions and Answers about International Management

Question	Answer	Relevant Material in the Book
(1) What is global business all about?	The interaction between an MNC and its environments (i.e., the diverse sociopolitical and economic systems that affect the company's operations)	Chapter 2, The Multinational Corporation, describes the company's role in modern society and the controversies surrounding its existence and operations around the globe. Chapter 3, The Environment, presents material on the world within which the company operates.
(2) What background knowledge must students have to understand the company-environment (MNC-NS) interaction?	Students must possess an adequate knowledge of international economics, international trade, and international finance.	Chapter 4, International Economics, exposes students to the basics of economics, the "mother science" of the discipline. Chapter 5, International Trade, focuses on the pragmatic aspects of exports and imports and their meaning for the practicing manager. Chapter 6, International Finance, provides a working knowledge of the international monetary system.
(3) How should the company become involved in international business?	By following the "evolutionary approach to international market entry"	Chapter 7, Participation Strategy, explores the various entry modes and some of the analytic tools commonly used to evaluate the cost and benefits of each mode of entry.
(4) Once the company enters foreign markets, how should it organize its global activities?	The company should develop an adaptive (flexible) organizational structure.	Chapter 8, Organization Strategy, considers the many diverse organizational structures that enable the firm to accomplish its goals.
(5) How does the MNC find, protect, and dispense the financial resources needed to maintain the organizational structure designed to carry out the participation strategy?	Management must design a global financial strategy that minimizes the cost of financing global operations.	Chapter 9, Financial Management Strategy, examines the main tasks of international financial management—finding, using, and protecting financial resources.

Question	Answer	Relevant Material in the Book
(6) How should the company serve the global market?	The company must develop a global sourcing and production strategy that minimizes production and transportation costs.	Chapter 10, Production/Sourcing Strategy, explores the basic considerations of overseas production for the local, international, or home market.
(7) How do multinational companies market their products overseas?	Although selling products is pretty much a universal function, there are some differences in selling internationally that a multinational manager must deal with.	Chapter 11, Marketing Strategy, focuses on the nature of international marketing and the development of a global marketing mix.
(8) How do so many people from different cultural backgrounds manage to work together?	By learning the corporate culture and by practicing the formal corporate procedures and informal corporate rituals	Chapter 12, Human Resource Development Strategy, examines the process of finding, selecting, hiring, and developing personnel who will staff the various positions in the organizational structure.
(9) How does a company that is spread all over the world hold together?	An MNC is held together by a network of information flows among the different subsystems and between the subsystems and the "mother" company.	Chapter 13, Communication and Control, describes the types of financial controls an MNC uses to make sure that every single subsystem's performance contributes to the performance of the entire company.
(10) What is the future of international business and the MNC?	The field of international business management will permeate every aspect of business education and practice.	Chapter 14, Epilogue: Consortia/Strategic Alliances, summarizes the current trends toward new forms of global business and speculates about the future.

simple without making it simplistic. After studying the ideas in the following chapters, as well as the associated examples of life in the global village, the student will know a great deal about international business.

RECAPITULATION

The purpose of this chapter is to help the student of international business understand the main activities of the international business field and the basic conceptual framework that has been developed for carrying out these various

Exhibit 1-11   Education: Cornerstone of Competition

American education fails to prepare our citizens to compete and participate in the world marketplace.

We know neither the globe nor the cultures of the people who inhabit it. We cannot speak to potential customers, our friends, or our foes in a language they can understand. Our teachers have not been adequately prepared to discuss geography, cultures, languages, or world events.

Throughout most of our history, we have been endowed with many resources and a domestic market large enough to handle what our productive economy has been able to turn out. In addition, most other nations were far behind in the development of technology and the translation of that technology into products the world wanted. As a result, we could sell whatever we wanted overseas, almost anywhere.

We have been slow to notice the change. In some sectors, our economy can produce even more than Americans can consume. Other nations have caught up with us in the development of many forms of technology, and some have even surpassed our ability to turn that technology into products the world wants to buy.

We are no longer isolated by the large oceans on either side of our nation. Our economic and political future depends on the ability to communicate with and understand people across national boundaries.

Compounding the problem are two very simple realities:

Three decades ago, a worker in Virginia competed with a worker in South Carolina or South Dakota. Now, the competition comes from South Korea as well. It is not possible for us to compete with the relatively lower wages paid to workers elsewhere in the world. What we can—and must—do is give our workers the finest of equipment and the best of educations.

Three decades ago, there were sixteen Americans working for every one person on Social Security. By 1992, that ratio will be three to one. Those three working Americans must be well educated to be sufficiently productive. In a global economy, a well-educated individual, by definition, will need a firm grounding in international studies.

SOURCE: *Cornerstone of Competition: The Report of the Southern Governors' Association Advisory Council on International Education* (Washington, DC: Southern Governors' Association, November 1986).

activities. To assist the reader in knowing what and knowing how, the chapter provided a brief explanation of (1) the exchange of goods, services, and money, (2) the internationalization process and the various modes of entry into it, (3) global business strategy setting, and (4) the challenging tasks of the global manager.

Understanding the exceedingly complex field of international business requires an equally complex framework. This framework must blend the fundamentals of such diverse disciplines as sociology, the physical sciences, the political sciences, and economics, each of which has a plethora of highly specialized subdisciplines. Thus, a specialization in multinational management might be one of the greatest oxymorons. A person wishing to become a specialist in multinational management not only must claim expertise in the above disciplines—an expertise firmly grounded in international studies (see Exhibit 1-11)—but also must possess an extraordinary talent for applying this knowledge to several different and at times conflicting situations. This person must indeed be a Renaissance person.[12] Such a manager must be able to set and achieve organizational goals and objectives in a world where Greek sailors dance to American music with Japanese women, drinking Scotch whisky or German beer in French or Romanian glasses and munching Georgian peanuts— a true global village. Although it is by no means easy, developing these skills is not beyond the capabilities of the average human being. This book aspires to provide a small contribution toward easing the difficult task of globalizing management thinking and action.

REVIEW QUESTIONS

(1)   Define the term "international business."

(2)   What motivates people to trade goods and services across national boundaries?

(3)   Money movements across national boundaries can take three forms. What are they and how do they differ from one another?

(4)   What does the term "internationalization process" mean?

(5)   What are the two main reasons that compel a company to go international?

(6)   Briefly describe the systems approach as it relates to international management.

(7)   What is strategic management?

(8)   Write a short essay explaining the "three Ps" of the strategic management process.

(9)   Describe the strategy-setting process depicted in Exhibit 1-6, using the

---

[12]William Dymsza, "The Education and Development of Managers for Future Decades," *Journal of International Business Studies* 13 (Winter 1982): 9–18.

United States as the nation-state and a large Japanese company as the MNC.

(10)   Assess your own ability to make each of the twelve decisions of the international manager listed in Exhibit 1-8. Assign a 10 for a *Yes* answer and a 0 for a *No* answer. Then write a short essay on what you must learn to improve your management skills. Use this opportunity to set some personal goals in areas where you need improvement.

SUGGESTED READINGS

Ball, Donald, and W. H. McCulloch. *International Business: Introduction and Essentials,* Second Edition. Plano, TX: Business Publications, 1985.

Daniels, J. D., and L. H. Radebaugh. *International Business: Environments and Operations.* Reading, MA: Addison-Wesley Publishing Co., 1986.

Didsbury, H. F., Jr. (ed.). *The Global Economy: Today, Tomorrow, and the Transition.* Bethesda, MD: World Future Society, 1985.

Kidron, Michael, and Ronald Segal. *The New State of the World Atlas.* New York: Simon and Schuster, 1984.

Kolde, Endel-Jakob. *Environment of International Business,* Second Edition. Boston: Kent Publishing Co., 1985.

Korth, Christopher M. *International Business: Environment and Management,* Second Edition. Englewood Cliffs, NJ: Prentice-Hall, 1985.

Moyer, Reed. *International Business: Issues and Concepts.* New York: John Wiley & Sons, 1984.

Negandhi, Anant R. *International Management.* Boston: Allyn and Bacon, 1987.

Our Magnificent Earth, A Rand McNally Atlas of Earth Resources. New York: Rand McNally and Co., 1985.

Richman, B. M., and M. R. Copen. *International Management and Economic Development.* New York: McGraw-Hill, 1972.

Robock, Stefan H., and Kenneth Simmonds. *International Business and Multinational Enterprises,* Third Edition. Homewood, IL: R. D. Irwin, 1983.

Ronen, Simcha. *Comparative and Multinational Management.* New York: John Wiley & Sons, 1986.

Terpstra, Vern, and Kenneth David. *The Cultural Environment of International Business,* Second Edition. Cincinnati, OH: South-Western Publishing Co., 1985.

Vernon, Raymond, and L. T. Wells, Jr. *Manager in the International Economy,* Fifth Edition. Englewood Cliffs, NJ: Prentice-Hall, 1985.

Walter, Ingo (ed.). *Handbook of International Business.* New York: John Wiley & Sons, 1982.

The World Almanac and Book of Facts. New York: Newspaper Enterprise Association, 1986.

The World Bank Atlas 1985. Washington, DC: World Bank, 1985.

World Development Report. New York: Oxford University Press, 1984.

World Economic Outlook. Washington, DC: International Monetary Fund, 1986.

EMERGING ISSUE 1: The Internationalization of Uncle Sam

Whether by necessity or by desire, every country exchanges goods, services, and money with a number of other countries. Despite some short-term and even some long-term negative effects, internationalization benefits a country more than it harms it.

Most people tend to assign great economic benefits from internationalization to a country that exports more than it imports and invests/lends more than it borrows. By the same reasoning, countries that import more than they export and accept more investment/borrow more than they invest/lend abroad should experience severe economic costs.

The result of this conventional wisdom is the advocacy of "regulation" or "management" of the degree and nature of internationalization. The regulation mechanisms proposed by the advocates of "managed internationalization" include import tariffs, surcharges, and quotas; export subsidies; adjustment assistance to domestic firms and workers "hurt" by imports and foreign competition; and restrictions on the acquisition of capital and real assets.

The United States has until very recently been considered to be on the "winner's" side of the field. Jack L. Hervey, a senior economist at the Federal Reserve Bank of Chicago, describes the internationalization of the United States as follows:

> For well over two decades after the end of World War II the international trade of the United States was primarily viewed by Americans as a one-way street synonymous with rapidly expanding markets abroad for U.S. goods and services and the rapid acquisition of foreign assets by U.S. investors. Critics called it economic imperialism. By the late 1960s a hint of changes was in the wind. Import growth began to exceed export growth. The rate of increase in foreign direct investment in the United States outpaced that of U.S. direct investment abroad. By the late 1970s the growing presence of foreign goods and services and foreign investment on U.S. shores was beginning to force a reassessment of the U.S. place in the international economy.[13]

Exhibit E1-1, U.S. Internationalization, presents vividly the dramatic change in the openness of U.S. economic activity to the rest of the world. To illustrate more fully the importance of this growth in U.S. internationalization, Exhibit E1-2 presents the growth of international trade's share of the U.S. GNP. During the last fifteen years, the nominal value of the United States' international activity rose on average 14% per year, whereas the GNP grew at 9.5% per

---

[13]Jack L. Hervey, "The Internationalization of Uncle Sam," *Economic Perspectives* (Federal Reserve Bank of Chicago), May–June 1986, 3.

Exhibit E1-1   U.S. Internationalization

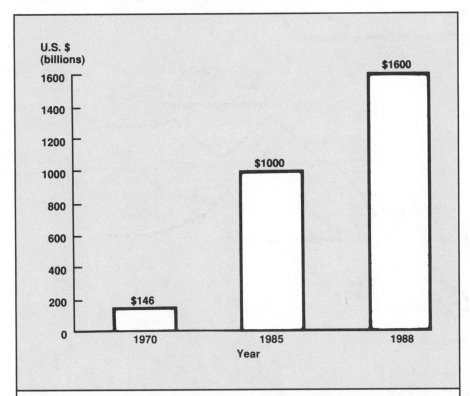

SOURCE: Jack L. Hervey, "The Internationalization of Uncle Sam," *Economic Perspectives* (Federal Reserve Bank of Chicago), May–June 1986, 3. 1988 estimates are based on data from U.S. Department of Commerce, *Survey of Current Business* (Washington, DC: Government Printing Office), June 1988, 78.

The sum of the absolute values of the various individual components of international transactions—exports and imports of goods and services (excluding military grant programs), unilateral transfers (excluding military grants), net acquisition of U.S. assets abroad by U.S. residents, net acquisition of U.S. assets by foreigners, the allocation of SDRs (special drawing rights) by the IMF, and unrecorded transactions ("statistical discrepancy")—is used here only as a relative gauge of internationalization of the U.S. economy. From an analytical view such a compilation includes substantial double counting; most obviously, to the extent that either exports or imports exceed the other, the offsetting entry on the capital account is counting the second side of the same coin. On the other hand, capital transactions and unilateral transfers are recorded as net inflows or outflows; thus, as a measure of the volume of transactions, the reported capital transactions are an underestimate.

Exhibit E1-2   Increase in U.S. International Trade Share During the 1970s

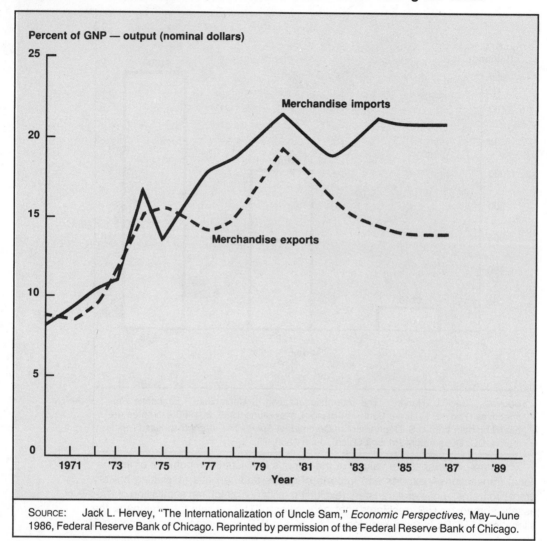

Source: Jack L. Hervey, "The Internationalization of Uncle Sam," *Economic Perspectives,* May–June 1986, Federal Reserve Bank of Chicago. Reprinted by permission of the Federal Reserve Bank of Chicago.

year. At the same time international trade's share of the U.S. GNP climbed from about 8.5% in 1971 to 23% in 1988.

This growth of U.S. international trade has not been in the United States' favor. As Exhibit E1-3 shows, the country has been importing considerably more than it has been exporting. As a result, the merchandise balance deteriorated to a deficit of almost $150 billion for 1985.

As the graph shows, the service portion of the United States' international trade of goods and services (what is known in balance-of-payments or international-transaction nomenclature as the *current accounts*) experienced a rather substantial growth over about the last fifteen years. This activity reached a peak in 1981 and then declined until 1983. It appears that it still pays for the United States to engage in trading services with the rest of the world.

A large percentage of the service trade consists of earnings derived from holdings of foreign assets by U.S. residents abroad and foreign residents in the United States. Receipts by U.S. residents from investments abroad are treated as exports of U.S. services. On the other hand, receipts by foreigners from holdings of U.S. assets, loans to U.S. banks and U.S. firms, and investments in corporate and government stocks and bonds are treated as imports of foreign services into the United States. In 1987, U.S. exports of services amounted to $163 billion, of which $104 billion (64%) were investment receipts ($58 billion portfolio and $46 billion direct foreign investment). Imports of services by the United States for 1987 totaled $141 billion, of which $83 billion (59%) were earnings from investments made by foreigners.[14]

Exhibit E1-3   U.S. International Trade Balances

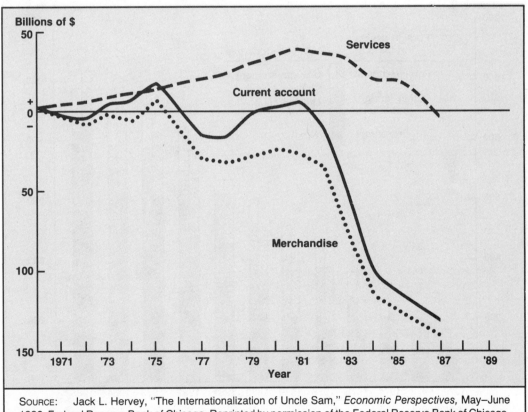

SOURCE: Jack L. Hervey, "The Internationalization of Uncle Sam," *Economic Perspectives,* May–June 1986, Federal Reserve Bank of Chicago. Reprinted by permission of the Federal Reserve Bank of Chicago.

[14]U.S. Department of Commerce, *Survey of Current Business* (Washington, DC: Government Printing Office), June 1988, 40–41.

Exhibit E1-4 identifies the international investments that created the streams of earnings described above. The graph clearly shows that the result of the United States' internationalization has been a change in the country's position from that of a net lender until 1985 to that of a net borrower in 1985. A close look at the bars shows that from 1970 until 1984 total foreign investment by Americans was greater than total investment by foreigners in the United States.

Although many factors are involved in the shift in the U.S. financial position around the globe, the most obvious explanation is a combination of U.S. economic recovery, acceleration in the national budget deficit accumulation, and a slowdown in European investment activity.

Exhibit E1-5 shows the United States' combined international transactions.

Exhibit E1-4   U.S. International Investment Position

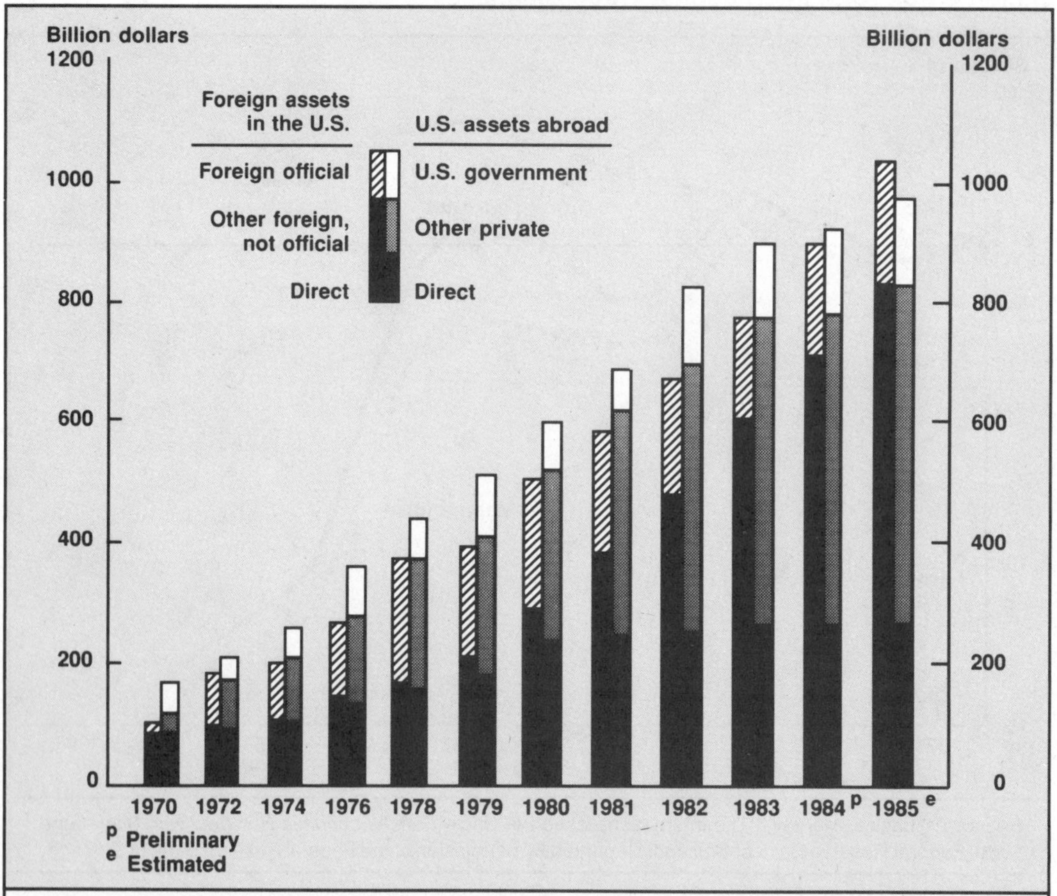

Exhibit E1-5   U.S. International Transactions (excluding military grant programs)

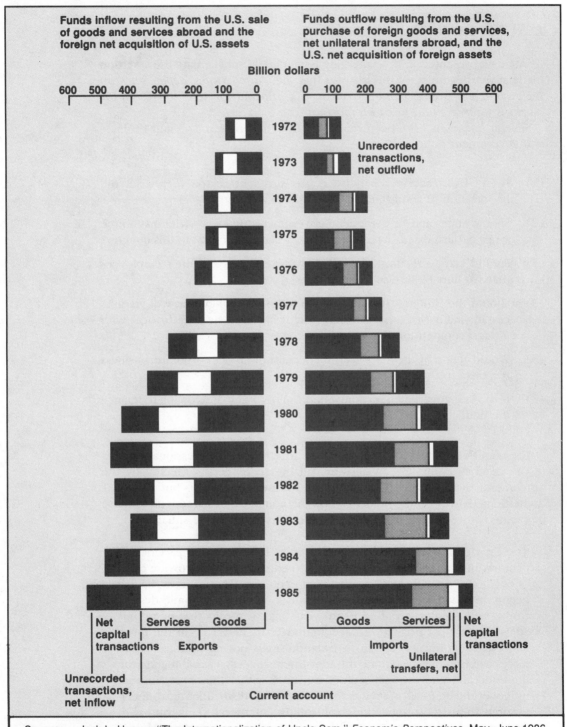

Funds inflow resulting from the U.S. sale of goods and services abroad and the foreign net acquisition of U.S. assets

Funds outflow resulting from the U.S. purchase of foreign goods and services, net unilateral transfers abroad, and the U.S. net acquisition of foreign assets

Billion dollars

600 500 400 300 200 100 0   0 100 200 300 400 500 600

1972
1973   Unrecorded transactions, net outflow
1974
1975
1976
1977
1978
1979
1980
1981
1982
1983
1984
1985

Net capital transactions   Services   Goods   Goods   Services   Net capital transactions
Exports   Imports
Unilateral transfers, net
Unrecorded transactions, net inflow   Current account

SOURCE: Jack L. Hervey, "The Internationalization of Uncle Sam," *Economic Perspectives,* May–June 1986, Federal Reserve Bank of Chicago. Reprinted by permission of the Federal Reserve Bank of Chicago.

ISSUES FOR DISCUSSION

The data presented in this Emerging Issue clearly substantiate the assertion made at the beginning of this chapter that *the United States' dependence on the exchange of goods, money, services, and information with the rest of the world is neither small nor unimportant.*

Several questions have been raised by academic researchers and business and government policy makers:

(1)   Is the U.S. trade/merchandise deficit sufficient reason to restrict the importation of goods and services into this country?

(2)   Should states and/or the federal government impose restrictions on the types of businesses that a foreigner may acquire or start in this country?

(3)   Should taxpayers' money be spent to assist firms and their employees that are hurt by foreign competition?

(4)   Should the United States develop an industrial policy that will "target" certain industries for assistance in developing a strategy to deal with foreign competition at home and abroad?

(5)   Would action by the U.S. government assist or hinder corporate/business response to the foreign challenge?

(6)   Is the U.S. government making good use of foreign borrowing to finance the budget deficit?

These and other questions will be at the forefront of congressional debates in the years to come. U.S. businesses will be tremendously affected by the outcome of these debates. Not only their overseas operations but also their domestic activities will be influenced by the competition's reactions to these emerging issues. Here is how Jack L. Hervey has assessed the situation:

The United States has been a world power for the better part of this century. But it has only recently begun to experience the growing pains of becoming a full-fledged international economy. That process, having begun, means the United States does not control its economic destiny to the same degree it did 15 or 20 years ago. It means that numerous adjustments must be made to accommodate its new role in the international economy. Reversion to isolationism is not an option. Market forces can effectively facilitate the adjustments necessary to integrate the domestic and international sectors, but only within the constraints set by government fiscal/monetary policy and the distortions introduced through the myriad regulations controlling commerce. Tinkering with trade cannot cure these ills, but it can make them worse. Instead, it is the basic issues associated with the distortions imposed on productivity

and competitiveness and the central issue of the influence of the fiscal/
monetary policy environment and the impact of regulatory distortions
on economic activity that must be addressed. If not soon, then indeed
the economy of the United States faces leaner times ahead as additions
to future real income are siphoned off to pay for the excesses of today.[15]

---

[15]Hervey, *Economic Perspectives*, p. 9.

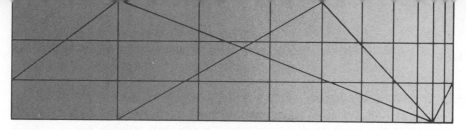

CHAPTER 2

THE MULTINATIONAL CORPORATION

Global corporations operate everywhere. They cross the frontiers of academic disciplines as easily as they cross national frontiers. Any serious attempt to understand what they are doing or the meaning of what they are doing involves a journey into politics, sociology, and psychology as well as economics.

Richard J. Barnet and Ronald E. Müller

"A Note to the Reader," in *Global Reach* (New York: Simon and Schuster, 1974), 2.

OVERVIEW

This book envisions international business as a process of continuous interaction between an organization and its external environment. Chapter 3 will deal with the external business environment in terms of human interaction with the natural habitat. This chapter deals with the first element of this organization-environment interaction: the organization. In the international business vocabulary, this organization goes under different names. Some writers refer to it as the multinational corporation (MNC). Others call it the transnational enterprise (TNE), and still others use the name multinational enterprise (MNE). In this book the term MNC will be used because it is the one most widely used in the U.S. literature.

The complexity and diversity of an MNC's activities make any kind of analysis of MNCs exceedingly difficult. There is no general consensus about either the nature or the role of an MNC. This chapter will summarize current views of this extremely controversial question: What is an MNC and what role does it play in humanity's struggle for survival?

LEARNING OBJECTIVES

After studying the material in this chapter, the student should be familiar with the following concepts:

(1) Multinational corporation (MNC)

(2) The reasons businesses become MNCs

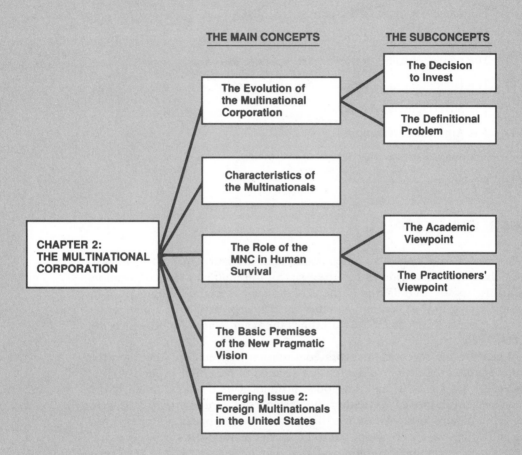

THE MAIN CONCEPTS

THE SUBCONCEPTS

The Evolution of
the Multinational
Corporation

The Decision
to Invest

The Definitional
Problem

Characteristics of
the Multinationals

CHAPTER 2:
THE MULTINATIONAL
CORPORATION

The Role of the
MNC in Human
Survival

The Academic
Viewpoint

The Practitioners'
Viewpoint

The Basic Premises
of the New Pragmatic
Vision

Emerging Issue 2:
Foreign Multinationals
in the United States

(3)   The size of the world's MNCs

(4)   Advantages of an MNC

(5)   Disadvantages of an MNC

(6)   The impact of an MNC on the host country

(7)   The impact of an MNC on the home country

(8)   The names of some of the largest U.S. MNCs

(9)   The names of some of the largest European MNCs

(10) The names of some of the largest Japanese MNCs

(11) The Dependencia School

(12) The Sovereignty at Bay School

(13) The American Challenge

(14) Five main issues in the debate about MNCs

(15) Benchmark study

INTRODUCTION

Few issues have caused so much sound and fury and remained so long in the public eye worldwide as has the issue of the multinational corporation. Its nature, its size, and its role in the economic and social development of its home country, its host country, and the world at large have been at the center of a long controversy. Exhibit 2-1 outlines the main issues around which the debate revolves.

In general, the seventies inaugurated a tension between the MNC and the nation-state. At the center of the tension seemed to be a huge groundswell of suspicion that the MNC had developed a mind of its own and fallen into a "Frankensteinian mode." As neither the designers of contemporary MNCs (in the United States, post–World War II government and business leaders) nor the individuals who were supposed to be served by the MNCs could comprehend very clearly the complex and frequent changes that the MNC was undergoing, they set off a series of MNC investigations worldwide. From Paris to Frankfurt, London to Pretoria, and Toronto to Washington to Tokyo, one after another, MNC executives took the stand at public hearings to explain their actions or inactions.[1] Some people interpreted the worldwide scrutiny as a modern-day witch hunt in which the MNC was made the scapegoat for

---

[1]U.S. Congress, Senate Subcommittee on Multinational Corporations, *Multinational Corporations and United States Foreign Policy,* Hearings, 93rd Cong., 2nd sess., June 1974; A. Sampson, *The Sovereign State of ITT* (New York: Fawcett Books, 1977).

Exhibit 2-1   The Debate on Multinationals: The Five Issues

Question	Yes	No
(1) *Are multinational companies exporting U.S. jobs?*	Thousands of jobs in such industries as apparel, radios, and bicycles have been lost to American workers because U.S. companies have shifted manufacturing or the production of component parts to such places as Taiwan, Singapore, or Korea, where labor costs are far lower. Between 1966 and 1969, 500,000 U.S. jobs were exported by such arrangements, says the AFL-CIO.	The charges are correct in general but misrepresent the total situation. When companies moved production abroad, the usual alternative was to lose sales—perhaps even in the domestic market—to foreign competitors. Says Reginald Jones, the chairman of General Electric: "As the last company in the United States to give up the manufacture of radios, we know exactly how tough the foreign competition has been." Moreover, U.S. multinationals export so much to their overseas affiliates that the net effect is that more jobs are created than are lost (but not necessarily in the same occupations or cities). Robert S. Stobaugh, professor of business administration at Harvard Business School, found in a recent study "using every bit of information available" that on balance U.S. corporate operations abroad add 700,000 jobs to the domestic economy and add an income of $7 billion a year to the nation's balance of payments. Some other studies have put the figures much higher.
(2) *Do multinationals create "export platforms" abroad to ship back cheaply made goods to the United States?*	One need only consider where TV sets and radios are being made nowadays. Companies shift manufacturing overseas to exploit cheap labor, to circumvent antipollution laws, and to avoid taxes.	Again, the balance runs in the other direction. Less than 10 percent of the products manufactured by overseas affiliates of U.S. companies are imported into the United States. But nearly a third of all U.S.-manufactured exports go to foreign affiliates of American companies. The Department of Commerce found that in 1972 majority-owned foreign affiliates of American companies sold 72 percent of their goods and

Question	Yes	No
		services in the country where they were produced. Another 22 percent of their sales went to other foreign countries; only 7 percent was exported to the United States, an increase from 6 percent in 1966.
(3) *Are multinationals the villains of currency crises?*	Companies have shifted "hot money" out of weak currencies and into strong ones in such massive amounts that past efforts to stabilize the dollar were weakened. By so doing, it has been argued by Andrew Biemiller, the AFL-CIO's chief lobbyist, that "corporations and banks put profits ahead of patriotism." Sometimes they do so to protect their holdings against anticipated exchange-rate changes and sometimes to engage in outright speculation.	Since the major currencies have been "floating"—that is, allowed by governments to fluctuate in value day by day in the international money market—the complaint is partly moot. After a long study, the U.S. Tariff Commission concluded in 1973 that while multinationals do have the "capacity for disruptive movements" of funds, few of them use it. The commission found that "only a small fraction" of corporate treasurers and bank vice-presidents speculate in currencies. (When the GATT tried to hedge against currency fluctuations in 1974, it miscalculated and lost more than $25 million.) The real cause of currency crises, as research economist Edward M. Bernstein told a U.N. inquiry, was the failure of governments to raise or lower the value of their currencies until long after it became clear to the world's financial experts that they must do so.
(4) *Do multinationals exploit the economies of underdeveloped countries?*	Critics, mostly from academia, complain that even when multinational companies have accelerated economic development, as, for instance, in Brazil and (in the late Sixties) Pakistan, the poor remain as poor as ever. Sometimes the multinationals preempt scarce local resources. Barnet and Muller contend that between 1957 and 1965 U.S.-based companies financed more than four-fifths	Governments, not multinational corporations, set the policies that determine whether all classes in a given country will share in economic advances. The poor of most newly rich Arab oildoms have received little of much of their countries' larger slice of the petroleum pie. Peru has been busy expropriating U.S. subsidiaries in the name of controlling its own economy, but there has been no transformation of class

Question	Yes	No
	of their operations in Latin America with local capital or reinvested earnings.	structure or the power of the elite. It is probable that some siphoning off of local capital did occur, though host governments could have prevented it at the time. In any case, it is becoming much more difficult to do so.
(5) *Do multinationals evade taxes abroad by rigging prices?*	In buying or selling goods within the confines of a company, but across national borders, companies manipulate prices so that they can avoid taxable profits in high-tax countries and inflate profits in low-tax countries. According to a U.N. study, such intracorporate trade within multinational companies accounts for nearly a quarter of the world's foreign trade in goods. It is concentrated in a few industries, including chemicals and autos. Some studies contend that overpricing in underdeveloped countries has ranged from 30 percent to 8,000 percent; underpricing, from 40 percent to 60 percent.	Some of this activity undoubtedly does, or at least did, go on. But most big companies require "arm's length" pricing of sales between subsidiaries or divisions. In the United States and Europe, tax collectors are zealous about auditing corporate books to prevent such practices. Apparently few executives would object if governments reached an international agreement setting uniform rules for tax purposes on all transfer pricing.

SOURCE: C. Breckenfeld et al., "Multinationals at Bay: Coping with the Nation-State," *Saturday Review,* January 24, 1976, 12–30, 57.

unrelated problems; others found the entire affair very useful. The latter group saw the occasion as a good opportunity to familiarize the general public with the vast richness of the MNC phenomenon.

This chapter is designed to provide a panoramic view of the evolution of the MNC by emphasizing the quantitative aspects of the phenomenon. My thirty years of experience with debates over MNCs among students, academicians, managers, and government officials have shown me that most people tend to grossly underestimate or overestimate the magnitude of the MNC global network, and for this reason exaggerate the MNC's positive or negative role.

THE EVOLUTION OF THE MULTINATIONAL CORPORATION

International business begins with the exchange of goods among nations (international trade). Its second stage is reached with the partial exchange of the physical corporate assets of one company for the capital assets of another (portfolio investment). The third stage evolves with the acquisition of an entire company or the establishment of productive facilities owned and managed by a firm with economic interests in more than one country (foreign direct investment). International business finally reaches its apex with the multinational corporation, which is involved in all three modes of international business: international trade, portfolio investment, and foreign direct investment (see Exhibit 1-2).

The literature on the subject of multinational corporations is reaching gigantic proportions. In general, the literature focuses on four main areas of investigation:

(1)   The various aspects of the decision to invest abroad

(2)   The definition of a multinational corporation

(3)   The growth of the multinational corporation

(4)   The impact of the multinational corporation's activities on the firm itself, on the home and host countries, and on world economic and political welfare

As a general rule multinational corporations can best be conceived of as business enterprises that are engaged in all activities of international business. As such, they share certain common characteristics:

(1)   They are large, usually having several billions of dollars in sales.

(2)   They have numerous affiliates in many countries.

(3)   They do most of their business inside the developed countries.

(4)   They are perceived as both a potential and a real threat to purely national companies, the labor force of home countries, the labor force of host countries, and the international economic order.

(5)   They are greatly distrusted by the public in both the investing and the recipient countries.

THE DEFINITIONAL PROBLEM

Academicians, businesspeople, and national and international agencies have expended considerable intellectual energy trying to provide a sound and workable definition of the multinational corporation.

THE ACADEMIC DEFINITIONS

Representative definitions from academia include the following:

An MNC is "a cluster of corporations of diverse nationality joined together by ties of common ownership and responsive to common management strategy."[2]

An MNC "owns and manages businesses in two or more countries. It is an agency of direct, as opposed to portfolio, investment in foreign countries, holding and managing the underlying physical assets rather than securities based upon these assets."[3]

An MNC is "a business organization that has its roots in one country and operations of various sorts in another."[4]

Finally, Charles Kindleberger, among others, distinguishes among national firms that carry on foreign operations, multinational firms that seek to integrate extensively into each national community in which activities are carried on, and international corporations that truly function as integrated, world economic units.[5]

THE BUSINESS DEFINITIONS

Although MNCs vary widely in their structure and operations, all must be concerned with most, if not all, of the following areas: management, ownership, financing, resourcing, manufacturing, and marketing.[6]

Sir David Barran of the Shell Centre, London, views the "international enterprise" as "incorporating everything from the very large-scale type of integrated enterprises to the single-product manufacturer based in one country who finds himself increasingly driven by the exigencies of the business into successive stages of involvement overseas."[7]

The most complete operational definition has been given by Jacques G.

---

[2]Raymond Vernon, *Sovereignty at Bay: The Multinational Spread of U.S. Enterprises,* (New York: Basic Books, 1971); also "Economic Sovereignty at Bay," *Foreign Affairs* 7, No. 1 (October 1986): 114.

[3]Neil Jacoby, "The Multinational Corporation," *The Center Magazine* 3, No. 3 (May 1970): 38.

[4]Seymour Rubin, "The International Firm and the National Jurisdiction," in C. Kindleberger, ed., *The International Corporation* (Cambridge, MA: MIT Press, 1970), 65–87.

[5]R. Farmer and B. Richmond, *International Business: An Operational Theory* (Homewood, IL: R. D. Irwin, 1966), 13; S. Robock and K. Simmonds, *International Business and Multinational Enterprises* (Homewood, IL: R. D. Irwin, 1985); N. S. Fatemi and G. W. Williams, *Multinational Corporations* (New York: A. S. Barnes and Co., 1984); C. Kindleberger, *American Business Abroad* (New Haven: Yale University Press, 1969).

[6]A. W. Clausen, "The International Corporation: An Executive Viewpoint," *The Annals of the American Academy of Political Science* 403 (September 1972): 12–21.

[7]David Barran, "The Multinationals: Sheep in Sheep's Clothing," *Journal of General Management* 1, No. 3 (1974): 13.

Maisonrouge, former president of IBM World Trade Corporation. He asserts that there are five criteria for identifying an MNC:[8]

(1)   It must do business in many countries.

(2)   It must have foreign subsidiaries with the same R&D, manufacturing, sales, services, and so on, that a true industrial entity has.

(3)   There should be nationals running these local companies; they understand the local scene better than anybody else, and this helps promote good citizenship.

(4)   There must be a multinational headquarters, staffed with people coming from different countries, so one nationality does not dominate the organization too much.

(5)   There should be multinational stock ownership—the stock must be owned by people in different countries.

THE INSTITUTIONAL DEFINITIONS

The U.S. Department of Commerce offers the most clear-cut definition of MNCs as "firms with direct investment outside the countries in which their headquarters are located."[9] For statistical purposes the Department considers direct investment to be ownership relationships between a company and an affiliate in another country in which the parent company has a 10% ownership.

The United Nations' Economic and Social Council, on the other hand, arrived at a more detailed quantitative definition of an MNC:

> In the broadest sense, any corporation with one or more foreign branches or affiliates engaged in any of the activities mentioned [assets, sales, production, employment, or profits of foreign branches and affiliates] may qualify as multinational. More strictly, a particular type of activity (e.g., production), a minimum number of foreign affiliates (e.g., six), or a minimum foreign share of activity (e.g., 25 percent of sales or assets) may be added as conditions for qualifying for the definition.[10]

THE DECISION TO INVEST

There is no general agreement among either academicians or practitioners as to the reasons MNCs choose to invest abroad. Traditionally, economists

---

[8]Jacques G. Maisonrouge, quoted in G. E. Bradley and E. C. Bursk, "Multinationalism and the 29th Day," *Harvard Business Review* 50, No. 1 (January–February 1972): 39.

[9]U.S. Department of Commerce, "1982 Benchmark Survey of Direct Foreign Investment," in *Survey of Current Business,* (Washington, DC: Government Printing Office), December 1985, 37.

[10]United Nations, *Multinational Corporations in World Development* (New York: United Nations, 1985): 6.

viewed foreign investment simply as a transfer of capital among countries, whereas practicing managers and government officials regarded it as just another business decision.

THE ACADEMIC VIEWPOINT

When international transfers of capital began to take the form of direct investment rather than portfolio investment, explanatory theories based on capital movements became inadequate. MNC investment is too complicated a process to be satisfactorily explained via the traditional capital movements theories.

There are three main categories of academic theories concerning the MNC decision to invest: financial theories, life cycle theories, and market imperfection theories.[11]

Financial Theories.   Financial theories of international investment are more or less straightforward extensions of the financial theories that are used to justify domestic investment. The basic principle that governs domestic investment decisions is the maximization of the worth of an asset. The worth of an asset is equal to the present value of all future cash flows associated with that asset, discounted at a rate that reflects the riskiness of such flows. A company can maximize the worth of an asset by either increasing the net cash flows (increasing revenues or decreasing costs) or decreasing risk (increasing product and area diversification) (see Exhibit 2-2). According to financial theories, international investment constitutes an attempt to decrease risk by combining investments whose future cash flow returns (revenues) are influenced by different environmental factors such as social, technological, ecological, political, and economic trends.

Life Cycle Theories.   Unlike the financial theories, product life cycle theories focus on direct foreign investment. These theories consider such investment to be a bona fide management strategy aimed at overcoming market saturation and/or product maturation (a product's loss of market and customer appeal).

Exhibit 2-3 depicts a typical product development process. A product goes through four phases of development:[12]

(1)   Pioneering/introduction characterized by

    (a)   high but declining price/unit ratio
    (b)   exponential increase in sales
    (c)   substantial losses (absence of profits)

---

[11]This portion of the text draws heavily on D. K. Weekly and R. Aggarwal, *International Business: Operating in a Global Economy* (Chicago, IL: The Dryden Press, 1986).

[12]Benton E. Gup, *Guide to Strategic Planning* (New York: McGraw-Hill, 1980).

Exhibit 2-2   Maximization of Asset Worth

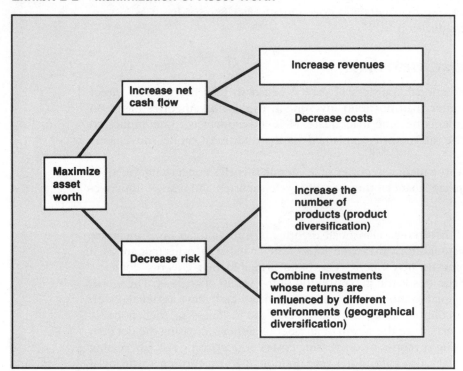

(2)   Expansion/growth characterized by

    (a)   smooth decline in the price/unit ratio
    (b)   smooth increase in sales
    (c)   profits (absence of losses)

(3)   Stabilization/maturation characterized by

    (a)   slightly increasing price/unit ratio
    (b)   leveling increase in sales
    (c)   declining profits

(4)   Decline characterized by

    (a)   increasing price/unit ratio
    (b)   decreasing sales
    (c)   declining profits

Firms exploit the local/domestic market during the pioneering phase, when high prices enable them to recover all development costs. Internationalization begins during the expansion phase (about where the X appears on the sales curve in Exhibit 2-3), when the presence of profits enables firms to inch their way into the world market. This is the stage of exporting via either an export agent or a small sales office. Slightly before the stabilization phase begins, the firm starts thinking about contractual agreements (such as licensing) and even direct investment. Finally, at the onset of the decline phase, the firm will have transferred most if not all of the productive capacity to a developing country for servicing of the international and to some extent its own domestic market.

Market Imperfection Theories. Market imperfection theories of the transfer of international investment focus on the firm as a whole rather than on a specific product.

Proponents of the Monopolistic Advantage Theory point out that a firm, in the course of its evolution in the home market, acquires certain capabilities and captures a rather substantial market share. The firm then uses these ca-

Exhibit 2-3 Product Life Cycle

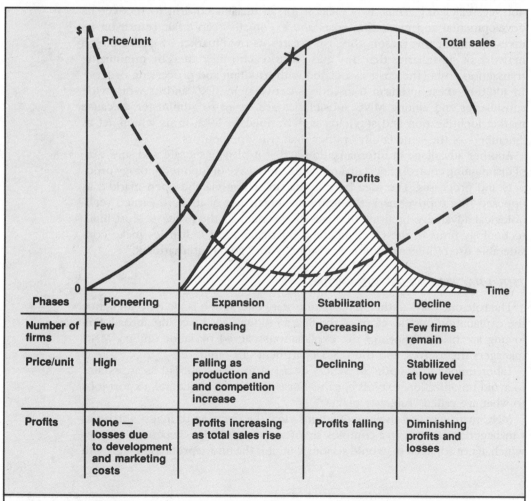

Phases	Pioneering	Expansion	Stabilization	Decline
Number of firms	Few	Increasing	Decreasing	Few firms remain
Price/unit	High	Falling as production and and competition increase	Declining	Stabilized at low level
Profits	None — losses due to development and marketing costs	Profits increasing as total sales rise	Profits falling	Diminishing profits and losses

SOURCE: Adapted from Benton E. Gup, *Guide to Strategic Planning* (New York: McGraw-Hill, 1980), 26.

pabilities to secure a leading position in the industry. This position enables the firm to produce and market certain products swiftly, thus depriving other firms of the opportunity to enter the market; to control the availability of existing raw material or the development of new substitutes; and to attract and retain superior managerial and employee talent in production, finance, and marketing. The Monopolistic Advantage Theory states that once the firm has established itself in the home market, it can further exploit the same monopolistic or oligopolistic advantage by reaching out into the world market. This way, production advantages that are due to superior R&D or product and process technology can be prolonged, bringing additional revenues into the company.

The Internalization Theory asserts that external markets (that is, other firms that use the firm's product either as an intermediate or as a final product) are not very efficient.[13] Thus, it is difficult for an unaffiliated firm to recover its developmental and marketing costs and eventually reap a fair return on its investment. For this reason, the firm creates its own market by developing a network of subsidiaries that buy and sell to each other, thereby minimizing transaction costs (the costs associated with handling and processing orders). In addition, these intrafirm transactions between an MNC and its worldwide subsidiaries and among MNC subsidiaries are easier to administer, because market identification and servicing is performed by local firms which act as "members of the same family" rather than true competitors.

Another advantage of internalization is that it provides a safe and sure way of maintaining control of certain knowledge-intensive or high-technology products and processes. The idea here is that in selling via the open market, as opposed to a captive market, a firm risks unfair use of its hard-earned technological advantage by firms that use the product or the process. Most high-technology firms in the electronic and pharmaceutical industries make considerable use of internalization as a strategy for "going international."

THE PRACTITIONERS' VIEWPOINT

The role one plays in the MNC–nation-state interaction is likely to influence the explanation one develops of the firm's rationale for investing abroad. Following are brief outlines of the explanations offered by labor unions, MNC managers themselves, and the U.S. Department of Commerce.

Labor unions look upon an MNC's decision to invest abroad as an excuse to avoid unionization, exploit cheap labor abroad, and, in general, export jobs to what are called "runaway plants."

MNC managers and their associations view the decision to invest abroad as a managerial response to a complex set of social, political and economic forces which, if not adjusted to, would seriously inhibit the future profitability, growth

---

[13]Alan M. Rugman, *Inside the Multinationals* (New York: Columbia University Press, 1981), 40–50.

and survival of the firm. After reviewing the findings of the Emergency Committee for American Trade (ECAT), the Williams Commission, the Department of Commerce, and the National Foreign Trade Council, the National Association of Manufacturers offered the following reasons for a firm's decision to invest abroad:[14]

(1)   MNCs make foreign investments to *get behind tariff and non-tariff* barriers which make it impossible for them to serve a foreign market from the outside. These barriers combined with the rate of domestic inflation and high transportation costs seem to be a major incentive for U.S. direct investment abroad, especially in the European Economic Community. For example, a U.S. pharmaceutical firm must produce in France or lose the French market since pharmaceutical standards are regulated in France through periodic inspection of the production process. This method of providing consumer protection has resulted in a virtual embargo on the importation of pharmaceuticals into France.

(2)   Many companies view international investment as a *means of serving a foreign market more effectively and more efficiently* than could be done through exportation. In addition to transportation and time savings, one of the main advantages of being close to the market being served is that the company can get a "better feel" of the market. This may enable them to tailor better their products to the purchasing patterns and customs of the local market and in this way increase sales over and above what would have been possible from export alone.

(3)   Direct foreign investment may also be part of *a defensive strategy* to diversify and protect the firm from the risks and uncertainties of domestic business cycles, strikes and threats to its source of supply.

(4)   Considerable foreign investment is made by MNCs in *response to increased foreign competition.* To meet the competition, a company may have to adopt a "follow thy competitor" strategy into the local market. In this case, direct foreign investment is made to prevent market pre-exemptions by competitors or to keep market outlets and sources of supply open. Today, with the challenge of Japanese products and increasingly large sophisticated European producers, this motivation is particularly strong. Service companies often invest abroad for defensive reasons because their customers have also done so. This is particularly true of banks, insurance companies, and management consulting firms as well as manufacturing firms.

(5)   Another motivation for direct investment abroad is the *reduction of transportation and production costs.* Many firms in the extractive in-

[14]"U.S. Stake in World Trade and Investment: The Role of the Multinational Corporation," National Association of Manufacturers, pp. 12–15 (italics added).

dustry are finding that given the rapidly rising cost of transportation it is cheaper to process raw materials on site and ship the processed, high value product than it is to ship relatively low value unprocessed raw materials.

Some manufacturing firms are able to reduce their cost of goods sold by combining U.S. technology with foreign labor and raw materials. In addition, production costs may also be reduced by spreading R&D expenses as well as certain other fixed costs between U.S. and foreign subsidiaries. The fact that the largest increase in U.S. direct investment over the last ten years has been in relatively high-wage, high-material-cost areas (Canada and Europe) indicates that this motivation, although important, is by no means the only factor which is considered when the decision is made to produce abroad.

(6)   Many MNCs which license abroad find they can take better advantage of their *technological advantage by manufacturing* rather than licensing. Often, licensees are limited by their ability to raise capital to expand their facilities to take advantage of expanding markets.

Further, by operating abroad, a MNC can better monitor the technical innovations of other countries. For example, in the recent National Foreign Trade Council survey, several large firms indicated their foreign operations often enabled them to acquire new technologies and products which frequently stimulated domestic manufacturing and sales. It is likely if U.S. firms were not operating abroad, other foreign MNCs would have reaped the benefits of these technological breakthroughs.

(7)   A number of experts, including Judd Polk, have argued that in order to *protect foreign investment already made,* many corporations are forced to continue to invest abroad in order to protect the value of the capital already employed. In other words, unless there is a continuous flow of foreign investment funds, the existing stock of capital would run down, jeopardizing the value in competitiveness of the whole foreign investment.

(8)   Many firms are attracted to invest abroad by *foreign incentives* such as tax holidays, unlimited remittances, 100% foreign ownership and duty-free import of needed materials and machinery. Although these incentives are often pointed to with disdain by groups which oppose MNCs, they demonstrate the importance which certain foreign countries attach to attracting foreign investment.

In addition to many of the reasons cited above, the Department of Commerce offers the following motivations for investing abroad:[15]

A need to diversify product lines to avoid fluctuations in earnings

---

[15]U.S. Department of Commerce, *The Multinational Corporation,* Vol. 1 (Washington, D.C.: Government Printing Office), March 1972.

A desire to avoid home-country regulations, such as antitrust laws in the United States

CHARACTERISTICS OF THE MULTINATIONALS

Although extreme caution must be exercised in drawing any major inferences from the abundance of quantitative data compiled by the U.S. Department of Commerce, the International Chamber of Commerce, the OECD, the World Bank, the International Monetary Fund (IMF), and the United Nations, certain statements can be made about MNCs. For example, there is a widespread agreement among researchers that the typical MNC is a large, complex, powerful, diversified, and, above all, important social institution that is here to stay. In this section we will construct an overall picture of the growth of MNCs by focusing exclusively on the quantitative aspects of world and U.S. MNCs. Later the MNC–nation-state interaction will be placed in perspective through an examination of the MNC's relationship to human survival and well-being.

With very few exceptions, the multinationals are a country's largest corporations. A comparison of the *Fortune* 500, the *Business Week* 1000, or the *Forbes* 500 with a list of the largest MNCs would reveal a great deal of overlap. Only a few of the largest U.S. companies would not appear on the list of MNCs: Lockheed, McDonnell Douglas, Boeing, AT&T, and perhaps USX (formerly U.S. Steel). Similar results would be obtained by comparing lists of the largest European and Japanese corporations with a list of the largest MNCs.

Most of the large corporations not included among the largest MNCs are among the largest exporters. *Business Week* magazine's April 19, 1986 list of the twenty-five largest U.S. exporters included the three aircraft companies mentioned in the preceding paragraph. The reason these large corporations have not evolved to the multinational stage is that the production processes employed require a certain level, or scale, of production to be cost effective. The final process of producing an aircraft, for example, must be performed at one location, although various parts can, of course, be manufactured at different locations and brought for assembly to the main plant.

In addition to being large, most MNCs are diversified with respect to both product and area. A measure of product diversification is the number of industries and product lines in which a given company participates. As the Harvard Multinational Enterprise Project found, the large MNCs do not ordinarily "belong" to just one industry.[16] An MNC's degree of geographical diversification is measured by the number of subsidiaries that it maintains. The 2,245 U.S. MNCs surveyed by the Department of Commerce in its 1982 benchmark study maintained some 34,000 affiliates all over the world (an average of 15 affiliates for each MNC).

What are the best-known multinational corporations? What countries do

---

[16]Raymond Vernon, *Storm over Multinationals* (Cambridge, MA: Harvard University Press, 1977).

they represent? To which industries do they belong? Exhibit 2-4 lists the world's fifty largest multinationals. An examination of the statistics on these fifty companies as a group or as individual economic units—their total sales, net income, and degree of internationalization (ratio of foreign sales to total sales)—reveals their tremendous importance. These fifty companies made over $1.5 trillion worth of sales in 1987. This figure is almost 10% of the world's total production and close to 30% of the U.S. gross national product.

The U.S. presence in the list of the world's top fifty corporations is obvious. Nineteen of the world's largest corporations are U.S. MNCs, and these nineteen account for 45% of total sales and 62% of total net income.

Exhibit 2-4   The World's Fifty Largest Multinationals

	Company	Home Country	Internationalization Ratio*	Sales	Net Income (millions of dollars)	Net Income as Percent of Sales
1	General Motors	U.S.	24%	101,782	1010	0.99%
2	Royal Dutch/Shell Group	U.K./Netherlands	62%	78,319	4726	6.03%
3	Exxon	U.S.	75%	76,414	4840	6.33%
4	Ford Motor	U.S.	33%	73,145	4625	6.32%
5	IBM	U.S.	54%	54,217	5258	9.70%
6	Mobil Oil	U.S.	61%	52,256	2033	3.89%
7	British Petroleum	U.K.	83%	45,206	2280	5.04%
8	Toyota	Japan	40%	41,455	1700	4.10%
9	IRI	Italy	—	41,270	147	0.36%
10	General Electric	U.S.	9%	40,515	4430	10.93%
11	Volkswagen	W. Germany	62%	39,393	242	0.61%
12	Daimler-Benz	W. Germany	60%	37,536	970	2.58%
13	Texaco	U.S.	50%	34,372	4625	13.46%
14	E. I. DuPont De Nemours	U.S.	38%	30,468	2100	6.89%
15	Hitachi	Japan	—	30,332	617	2.03%
16	Fiat	Italy	—	29,643	1830	6.17%
17	Siemens	W. Germany	55%	27,463	650	2.37%
18	Matsushita Electric Industrial	Japan	—	27,326	862	3.15%
19	Unilever	U.K./Netherlands	49%	27,129	1279	4.71%
20	Chrysler	U.S.	10%	26,277	2180	8.30%
21	Philips' Gloeilampenfabrieken	Netherlands	66%	26,021	317	1.22%
22	Chevron	U.S.	23%	26,015	3313	12.73%
23	Nissan Motor	Japan	66%	25,651	124	0.48%
24	Renault	France	45%	24,540	614	2.50%
25	ENI	Italy	—	24,243	484	2.00%
26	Nestle	Switzerland	97%	23,626	1225	5.18%
27	BASF	W. Germany	45%	22,384	585	2.61%
28	Philip Morris	U.S.	20%	22,279	4067	18.25%
29	CGE	France	—	21,204	305	1.44%
30	ELF Aquitaine	France	12%	21,186	690	3.26%

Company	Home Country	Inter-national-ization Ratio*	Sales	Net Income (millions of dollars)	Net Income as Percent of Sales
31 Samsung	South Korea	—	21,054	1010	4.80%
32 Bayer	W. Germany	75%	20,662	833	4.03%
33 Hoechst	W. Germany	37%	20,558	767	3.73%
34 Amoco	U.S.	21%	20,477	1360	6.64%
35 Peugeot	France	13%	19,658	1116	5.68%
36 ITT	U.S.	25%	19,525	1278	6.55%
37 Imperial Chemical Industries	U.K.	—	18,233	1246	6.83%
38 Honda Motor	Japan	30%	17,238	516	2.99%
39 United Technologies	U.S.	27%	17,170	592	3.45%
40 Procter & Gamble	U.S.	32%	17,000	327	1.92%
41 Atlantic Richfield	U.S.	16%	16,282	1224	7.52%
42 RJR Nabisco	U.S.	26%	15,766	2486	15.77%
43 Petrobras (Petroleo Brasileiro)	Brazil	—	15,641	172	1.10%
44 NEC	Japan	—	15,325	94	0.61%
45 Xerox	U.S.	32%	15,125	575	3.80%
46 Tenneco	U.S.	18%	14,790	735	4.97%
47 Nippon Steel	Japan	—	14,640	−70	−0.48%
48 Volvo	Sweden	45%	14,576	730	5.01%
49 Total	France	15%	14,488	242	1.67%
50 Lucky-Goldstar	South Korea	—	14,422	181	1.26%
Totals			1,494,294	73,542	4.9%

Regional Comparisons

Country/Region	No. of Firms	Percentage of Total	Sales (millions of dollars)	Percentage of Total	Net Income (millions of dollars)	Percentage of Total
United States	19	38%	677,937	45.37%	45,302	61.60%
EEC	19	38%	463,624	31.03%	14,380	19.55%
Japan	7	14%	171,966	11.51%	3843	5.23%
Other	5	10%	180,767	12.10%	10,017	13.62%
Totals	50	100%	1,494,294	100%	73,542	100%

*Foreign sales as a percentage of total sales.
SOURCE: "The World's 50 Biggest Industrial Corporations," *Fortune,* August 1, 1988, D3.

Exhibit 2-5 The Top Fifty U.S. Multinational Corporations

Company	Sales	Assets (millions of dollars)	Net Income	Net Income as Percent of Sales	Foreign Revenue (millions)	Foreign Revenue as Percent of Sales	Employment (thousands)	E/S Growth Rate 1977-87 (%)	ROI 1977-87 (%)
1 General Motors	101,782	87,241	1010	0.99%	24,091	23.67%	813.0	-1.4	6.9
2 Exxon	76,414	74,042	4840	6.33%	57,375	75.08%	101.1	9.8	20.9
3 Ford Motor	73,145	61,090	4625	6.32%	23,955	32.75%	350.3	11.1	20.1
4 IBM	54,217	63,688	5258	9.70%	29,280	54.01%	493.0	6.7	10.3
5 Mobil Oil	52,256	41,140	2033	3.89%	31,633	60.53%	163.3	2.6	16.8
6 General Electric	40,515	38,920	4430	10.93%	3799	9.38%	330.5	10.3	18.4
7 Texaco	34,372	61,090	4625	13.46%	17,120	49.81%	51.1	—	11.1
8 E. I. duPont de Nemours	30,468	28,209	2100	6.89%	11,651	38.24%	140.7	7.2	14.3
9 Chrysler	26,277	19,945	2180	8.30%	2591	9.86%	122.7	17.2	17.1
10 Chevron	26,015	34,465	3313	12.73%	5905	22.70%	51.4	-0.1	13.8
11 Philip Morris	22,279	19,145	4067	18.25%	4544	20.40%	191.8	18.7	23.4
12 Amoco	20,477	24,827	1360	6.64%	4400	21.49%	112.0	4.4	16.9
13 ITT	19,525	39,983	1278	6.55%	4891	25.05%	121.5	5.2	15.8
14 Occidental Petroleum	17,746	16,739	184	1.04%	1836	10.35%	50.8	-9.6	9.1
15 United Technologies	17,170	11,929	592	3.45%	4713	27.45%	111.7	4.8	11.2
16 Procter & Gamble	17,000	13,715	327	1.92%	5524	32.49%	73.9	-3.9	11.7
17 Atlantic Richfield	16,282	22,670	1224	7.52%	2605	16.00%	26.2	8.8	16.5
18 RJR Nabisco	15,766	16,861	2486	15.77%	4045	25.66%	121.4	10.4	21.0
19 GTE	15,421	28,745	1119	7.26%	2052	13.31%	161	-1.4	15.7
20 Xerox	15,125	23,462	575	3.80%	4852	32.08%	111.7	0.6	7.9
21 Tenneco	14,790	18,503	735	4.97%	3834	25.92%	102.5	—	10.1
22 Dow Chemical	13,377	14,356	2315	17.31%	7431	55.55%	52.2	8.0	18.8
23 Eastman Kodak	13,305	14,451	2132	16.02%	5265	39.57%	122.9	7.4	13.2
24 PepsiCo	11,485	9023	1321	11.50%	1970	17.15%	219.5	12.2	17.8
25 Allied Signal	11,116	10,226	515	4.63%	2140	19.25%	126.3	2.0	5.6
26 Goodyear	9905	8396	1076	10.86%	3997	40.35%	114.7	16.1	20.5
27 Kraft	9876	4888	910	9.21%	2335	23.64%	9.6	7.0	21.0
28 Unisys	9713	9958	1432	14.74%	4237	43.62%	102.6	5.9	7.9

29 Minn Mining & Mfg	9429	8031	1578	16.74%	3616	38.35%	82.1	8.5	15.1
30 Digital Equipment	9389	8407	1672	17.81%	4373	46.58%	46.8	19.9	19.3
31 Sara Lee	9155	4192	632	6.90%	2214	24.18%	—	12.4	25.4
32 Unocal	8446	10,062	181	2.14%	2093	24.78%	18.1	-2.3	11.8
33 Caterpillar	8180	6866	743	9.08%	2237	27.35%	53.8	-3.8	4.4
34 Hewlett-Packard	8090	8133	1181	14.60%	3968	49.05%	82.0	16.7	21.0
35 Johnson & Johnson	8012	6546	1406	17.55%	3845	47.99%	77.7	13.1	14.2
36 Aluminum Co. of America	7767	9902	677	8.72%	2521	32.46%	54.5	-2.1	11.8
37 Coca-Cola	7644	8356	1499	19.61%	4185	54.75%	22.7	10.6	17.5
38 Monsanto	7639	8455	764	10.00%	2756	36.08%	50.7	4.2	17.1
39 Union Carbide	6914	7892	232	3.36%	2136	30.89%	46.7	-1.4	15.7
40 TRW	6821	4378	589	8.64%	1755	25.73%	78.2	5.3	16.0
41 Motorola	6707	5321	578	8.62%	2937	43.79%	96.1	7.4	17.4
42 American Brands	6029	11,314	1071	17.76%	2835	47.02%	42.0	12.1	23.4
43 Colgate-Palmolive	5647	3228	294	5.21%	3161	55.98%	37.7	-9.3	12.2
44 NCR	5641	4187	751	13.31%	3081	54.62%	62.0	12.9	23.3
45 Texas Instruments	5595	4256	257	4.59%	1765	31.55%	77.6	7.7	10.6
46 Merck	5061	5680	1423	28.12%	2561	50.60%	30.9	13.2	22.5
47 Pfizer	4920	6923	1034	21.02%	2268	46.10%	40.4	12.6	16.8
48 CPC International	4903	3261	500	10.20%	2213	45.14%	35.1	12.0	19.3
49 HJ Heinz	4639	3364	593	12.78%	1859	40.07%	48	15.4	26.1
50 Gillette	3167	2731	535	16.89%	2001	63.18%	31.1	4.2	22.7
Totals MNCs	934,082	957,022	76,303		338,494		5663.6		
Averages MNCs	18,682	19,140	1526	10.32%	6769.88	35.75%	115.58	6.59	15.95
Totals Fortune 500	1,879,506	1,705,657	90,556						
Averages Fortune 500	3759	34,113	1811	48.18%					

SOURCE: Employment figures: *Forbes*, July 25, 1988; *Fortune*, April 25, 1988. Growth and ROI figures: *Fortune* (April 25, 1988). Remainder of figures: "The 100 Largest U.S. Multinationals," *Forbes* (July 25, 1988).

A CLOSER LOOK AT THE U.S. MNCs

Exhibit 2-5 shows the top fifty U.S. multinational corporations. Again, a quick look at the bottom portion of the table is revealing. In 1987 the top fifty U.S. MNCs accounted for over 50% of the *Fortune* 500's total sales, which amounted to almost 44% of that year's GNP. The average MNC's sales ($19 billion) were almost five times larger than the average *Fortune* 500 company's sales ($3.8 billion).

The last four columns of Exhibit 2-5 provide evidence of the MNCs' superiority in overseas performance. None of the MNCs posted losses (negative net incomes) in either overall or overseas performance. The average profitability from foreign sales (net income from foreign sales as a percentage of foreign sales) was over three times greater than the overall profitability (35.75% vs. 10.32%). Obviously it *pays* to be multinational.

How important are MNCs for the U.S. economy? At the risk of being accused of concentrating only on the quantitative aspects of business at the expense of qualitative considerations, I will use the U.S. Department of Commerce's framework to illustrate the importance of the MNCs. This framework is fairly well accepted not only in the United States but worldwide. To a certain extent the United Nations uses the same set of criteria in evaluating MNCs' performance and role in world development.

In compliance with the International Investment Survey Act of 1976, the Department of Commerce keeps track of the activities of U.S. and foreign MNCs by carrying out what are known as benchmark surveys. The data presented here are based on the benchmark study conducted in 1982.[17]

The benchmark surveys report data on the following aspects of the activities of U.S. MNCs and their foreign affiliates:

(1)   Assets, liabilities, investments, and owners' equity

(2)   Sales, net income, and profit

(3)   Employment and employment compensation

(4)   Imports and exports

(5)   Receipts of and payments for services and royalties

(6)   Distribution of profits and reinvestments

(7)   Geographical and industry concentration

(8)   Number of affiliates and their geographical distribution

(9)   Type of ownership and financial and management control

(10)   Type of entry strategy

---

[17]U.S. Department of Commerce, "1982 Benchmark Survey."

Exhibit 2-6 presents data on the number of reporting affiliates and their total assets by industry and geographical location (country). The tremendous importance of Western Europe and Latin America as host countries to U.S. MNC activity is reaffirmed by these data. Over 41% of the affiliates and over 43% of their assets are located in Europe. Latin America's importance for the U.S.

Exhibit 2-6   Number and Total Assets of U.S. MNCs (1982)

	Parents		Affiliates*	
	Number	Assets (thousands of dollars)	Number	Assets (thousands of dollars)
By Industry				
All Industry	2245	3,754,218	18,339	1,348,494
Petroleum	143	486,608	1801	195,210
Manufacturing	1215	1,017,645	7004	265,418
Wholesale Trade	168	43,418	3700	57,911
Banking	133	1,012,319	882	573,721
Finance, Insurance, and Real Estate	234	677,469	2423	182,813
Services	160	52,717	1336	20,991
Other	192	464,039	1193	51,961
By Location				
Developed Countries:			11,543	828,811
Canada			2075	120,357
Europe			7608	580,097
European Community (10)			6073	508,625
Other European			1535	71,472
Japan			704	75,092
Australia, N. Zealand, and South Africa			1155	53,265
Developing Countries:			6442	502,438
Latin America			3937	324,638
Other Africa			596	23,911
Middle East			419	52,292
Other Asia and Pacific			1490	101,597
International			354	17,245

*The total number of U.S. MNC affiliates is 33,650 (an average of 15 per MNC). Of these affiliates, 32,671 (97%) are nonbanks and 979 (3%) are banks. Although the number of affiliates that responded to the survey by filing the BE-108 form is small, their influence is substantial, as these 18,339 (54.5%) affiliates account for almost 99.0% of the assets, sales, and net income.

SOURCE: U.S. Department of Commerce, "1982 Benchmark Survey," 8, 36.

MNCs' affiliates is exemplified by the substantial percentages represented by that region's affiliates and their assets (21.5% and 24.1%, respectively).

Exhibit 2-7 contains data on the U.S. MNCs and their affiliates for the years 1977, 1982, and 1983. As the exhibit shows, the U.S. MNCs represent a rather substantial part of the U.S. economic scene. The total assets of the 2245 U.S. MNCs for 1983 were over $4.6 trillion. This level of total assets was 4.8% higher than for the previous year and 11.4% higher than for 1977. Some 20% of these assets belonged to the affiliates of the U.S. MNCs which are spread all over the world. These assets were used to produce some $3.3 trillion worth

Exhibit 2-7 Total Assets, Sales, and Employment of Nonbank U.S. MNC Parents and Foreign Affiliates, 1977, 1982, and 1983

	MNCs Worldwide	Parents	Affiliates	Affiliates as % of MNCs Worldwide
Total Assets (millions of dollars)				
1977	2,038,418	1,548,240	490,178	24.04%
1982	3,493,105	2,741,619	751,486	21.51%
1983	4,660,827	3,899,575	761,252	16.33%
Average Percent Change				
1977–1982	11.4	12.2	8.9	
1982–1983	33.4	42.2	1.3	
Sales (millions of dollars)				
1977	2,060,263	1,412,293	647,969	31.45%
1982	3,284,168	2,348,388	935,780	28.49%
1983	3,304,547	2,402,743	901,804	27.28%
Average Percent Change				
1977–1982	9.8	10.7	7.6	
1982–1983	0.6	2.3	−3.6	
Number of Employees (thousands)				
1977	26,082	18,885	7197	27.59%
1982	25,345	18,705	6640	26.19%
1983	24,959	18,408	6551	26.24%
Average Percent Change				
1977–1982	−0.6	−0.2	−1.6	
1982–1983	−1.5	−1.6	−1.3	

SOURCE: U.S. Department of Commerce, *Survey of Current Business* (Washington, D.C.: Government Printing Office), January 1986, 24.

of sales revenue, an amount almost equal to the 1983 U.S. gross national product. It must be noted that although the assets of the U.S. MNCs grew between 1982 and 1983 at a rate of 4.8%, their use created an increase in sales of only 0.6%. In addition, as the exhibit shows, all of the increase was created by the parents. The affiliates of these MNCs experienced a drop in sales over the 1982–1983 period. Increases in sales over the 1977–1983 period kept up with the increase in total assets over the same period. The MNCs included in the U.S. Department of Commerce's 1982 benchmark study employed some 26 million people all over the world in 1983. Just over one fourth (26%) of these employees (some 6.5 million) were employed by the affiliates of these MNCs.

One overwhelming fact is obvious from Exhibit 2-7: the growth in both assets and sales experienced by the MNCs over these years was entirely what is called "jobless growth." In other words, employment by these MNCs declined for all the companies (both parents and affiliates) and all the years.

Exhibit 2-8 presents data on the overall financial structure and operational and economic performance of the U.S. MNC parents by industry. Financial structure is measured by the usual balance-sheet items such as assets, liabilities, and owners' equity. Operational performance is measured by sales, expenditures for property and equipment, and employment.

Data for 1983 on U.S. MNC exports to their affiliates and imports from their affiliates appear in Exhibit 2-9. As the data show, overall, U.S. MNC affiliates served as good overseas customers for their parents in 1983. The U.S. MNC affiliates exported to their U.S. parents some $54.3 billion, $4.0 billion more than was exported by the U.S. firms. Similarly, U.S. MNCs exported $9 billion more to the developed countries via their affiliates than they imported from them. The picture is completely different when it comes to affiliates in the developing countries. U.S. MNCs imported some $6.2 billion more from these affiliates than they exported to them. In other words, the U.S. MNC affiliates in developing countries exported to their U.S. parents over 51.41% more than they imported from them.

THE ROLE OF THE MNC IN HUMAN SURVIVAL

This book does not treat the MNC as an isolated entity. Rather, the center of investigation is the relationship between the MNC and its environment. For practical purposes the environment is equated with the nation-state. Thus, the study of the MNC becomes the study of the interaction between the MNC and the nation-state. This interaction was explained briefly in Chapter 1 and was shown in Exhibit 1-6, The MNC–NS Synergy. Scholars in the field have been researching this interaction for years, as evidenced by the shelves of writings in both business and political science libraries. This section presents a brief summary of the main schools of thought on the MNC–nation-state interaction, using the two-level conceptual framework that was introduced earlier. At the first level, the academic level, are theories from economics and political science. At the second level, the practitioner level, are perspectives from business,

Exhibit 2-8   Selected Data for Nonbank U.S. Parents by Industry, 1983 (thousands of dollars)

	Total Assets	Liabilities	Owners' Equity (thousands of dollars)	Total Sales	Sales of Goods	Sales of Services	Expenditures for Property, Plant & Equipment	Employee Compensation	No. of Employees (thousands)
All Industries	2,899,575	1,894,754	1,004,820	2,402,743	1,850,344	552,399	163,622	522,045	18,407
Petroleum	490,559	281,005	209,554	536,413	505,250	31,163	45,421	42,788	1141
Manufacturing	1,058,891	576,001	482,890	1,080,485	1,002,750	77,735	60,437	313,086	10,390
Wholesale Trade	46,479	28,328	18,152	123,790	121,229	2561	2286	8811	396
Finance, Insurance, and Real Estate	755,818	670,868	84,950	206,188	11,675	194,513	5478	28,454	1005
Services	59,434	35,859	23,575	60,528	10,861	49,667	7417	20,814	1073
Other Industries	488,393	302,694	185,699	395,340	198,579	196,761	42,582	108,063	4401

SOURCE: U.S. Department of Commerce, *Survey of Current Business*, January 1986, 27.

Exhibit 2-9   International Trade Transactions of U.S. MNCs, 1983 (in millions of dollars)

	Exports Shipped to United States Affiliates	Imports Shipped by Affiliates	Net Trade (Exports − Imports)	Net Exports/ Exports (percent)
All industries	58,275	54,257	4018	6.89%
Developed countries	45,882	36,968	8914	21.61
Developing countries	12,078	18,287	−6209	−51.41

Source: U.S. Department of Commerce, "1982 Benchmark Survey," 129.

government, and leaders of international organizations. Exhibit 2-10 presents the two main levels of analysis of the MNC–nation-state relationship, along with the name of each school of thought, the entity that school designates as main actor in the interaction, and the main proponents of the school.

As the table shows, the first two schools of the academic level assign the protagonist role to the MNC, whereas the last one puts the nation-state at the center of the conceptual framework. At the practitioner level, the emphasis is on the MNC's ability and willingness to contribute to world development by instructing its managers to adopt new philosophies and policies that reflect new world realities. A new world economic order would entail a shift toward a more equitable distribution of the world's wealth. The quest for a more

Exhibit 2-10   Theories of the MNC–Nation-State Relationship

	School	Main Actor	Main Proponents
Academic Level	Sovereignty at Bay	MNC	Raymond Vernon
	Dependencia	MNC	Stephen Hymer
	Mercantilism	Nation-State	D. Calleo and B. Rowland
Practitioner Level	Optimists	MNC Manager	Henry Kissinger
	Pessimists	MNC Manager	Ronald Müller and Richard Barnet
	Meliorists	MNC Manager/ Government Leaders	A. G. Kefalas

equitable distribution of wealth calls for an increase in the participation of the developing nations in the creation of wealth via greater industrialization and local knowledge generation through such means as R&D.

THE ACADEMIC VIEWPOINT

The three academic views presented in Exhibit 2-10 are representative of the three prevailing schools of thought on political economy: liberalism, Marxism, and mercantilism, identified here by their more popular and to some extent more modern names.[18]

THE SOVEREIGNTY AT BAY SCHOOL

The Sovereignty at Bay school represents the liberal view of the role of the MNC in the MNC–nation-state phenomenon. The name of the school is derived from Raymond Vernon's classic work, published over fifteen years ago, entitled *Sovereignty at Bay.*[19] In this book Vernon argues that increasing economic interdependence and technological advances in communications and transportation are making the nation-state an anachronism.

These economic and technological developments are said to have undermined the traditional economic rationale for the nation-state. In the interest of world efficiency and domestic economic welfare, the nation-state's control over economic affairs will continue to give way to the multinational corporation, the Eurodollar market, and international institutions better suited to meet economic needs. In the words of Charles Kindleberger, "The nation-state is just about through as an economic unit." In this interdependent world, domestic national goals can only be understood in terms of their relation to domestic economic goals, which can only be accomplished through participation in the world. In this liberal vision of the future, the multinational corporation, freed from the shackles of the nation-state, is the critical transmitter of capital, ideas, and growth.

THE DEPENDENCIA SCHOOL

Unlike the happy world of "partners in development" envisioned by the Sovereignty at Bay school, the Dependencia school presents a conception of the world as a exploitive hierarchy. In this hierarchy, wealth and benefits are moving away from the base, which is occupied by the poor countries, and toward the center, which is occupied by the large multinational planners and decision makers.

Enabling the MNC to reap most of the benefits of its interaction with the nation-state are, according to Stephen Hymer, one of the most well-known

---

[18]Robert Gilplin, *U.S. Power and the Multinational Corporation* (New York: Basic Books, 1975).

[19]Raymond Vernon, *Sovereignty at Bay: The Multinational Spread of U.S. Enterprises* (New York: Basic Books, 1971).

proponents of the Dependencia school, the "two laws of development." These two laws are the Law of Increasing Firm Size and the Law of Uneven Development.

The Law of Increasing Firm Size, Hymer explains, describes the tendency, since the industrial revolution, for firms to increase in size "from the workshop to the factory to the national corporation to the multidivisional corporation and now to the multinational corporation." The Law of Uneven Development, he continues, "is the tendency of the international economy to produce poverty as well as wealth, underdevelopment as well as development." Together, these two economic tendencies would have the following consequences:

> ...a regime of North Atlantic Multinational Corporations would tend to produce a hierarchical division of labor between geographical regions corresponding to the vertical division of labor within the firm. It would tend to centralize high-level decision-making occupations in a few key cities in the advanced countries, surrounded by a number of regional sub-capitals, and confine the rest of the world to lower levels of activity and income, i.e., to the status of towns and villages in a new Imperial system. Income, status, authority, and consumption patterns would radiate out of these centers...and the existing pattern of inequality and dependency would be perpetuated. The pattern would be complex, just as the structure of the corporation is complex, but the basic relationship between different countries would be one of superior and subordinate, head office and branch plant.[20]

THE MERCANTILIST SCHOOL

Whereas the main actor in both the Sovereignty at Bay school and the Dependencia school is the MNC—the hero in the former and the villain in the latter—the protagonist in the mercantilists' play is the nation-state.

In a sense the Mercantilist school stands at exactly the opposite end of the spectrum from the Sovereignty at Bay school. Its essential idea is the priority of national economic and political objectives over considerations of global economic efficiency. Thus, according to this school of thought, a nation-state will pursue economic policies designed to satisfy domestic economic needs and external political ambitions, which in turn depend on its governing party's political ideologies and economic and societal aspirations.[21]

THE PRACTITIONERS' VIEWPOINT

Unlike academic observers, who regard the MNC as a subject of scientific inquiry, practitioners are concerned with the role of the MNC in national and

---

[20]Stephen Hymer, "The Multinational Corporation and the Law of Uneven Development," in J. N. Bhagwati, ed., *Economics and World Order: From the 1970s to the 1990s* (New York: Free Press, Macmillan Publishing Co., 1972), 113–135.

[21]D. Calleo and B. Rowland, *America and the World Political Economy* (Bloomington, IN: Indiana University Press, 1973).

international economic and social development. Thus, their main question is "What role does an MNC play in the world?"

Exhibit 2-11 provides a summary of three main viewpoints on the MNC's role and its future. These represent three points along a continuum describing the degree of optimism regarding the ability of MNCs to play a positive role.[22]

THE OPTIMISTS

At the extreme left-hand side of the continuum are the optimists. These are individuals who conceive of the MNC as the best thing that has happened since the industrial revolution. They envision the MNC as playing an ever more active role in both domestic and international affairs and see no conflicts between the nation-state's objectives and the MNC's goals.[23]

THE PESSIMISTS

At the other end of the continuum are the pessimists. These are individuals who would argue that, far from being the most elegant and useful creation of the twentieth century, as Senator Daniel Moynihan once baptized the MNC, it is instead one of the most dangerous beasts since the mythical many-headed Hydra. According to this view, not only is there a great conflict between the nation-state's objectives and the MNC's goals, but as a rule the MNC is indeed rendering the nation-state obsolete as a mechanism for economic and social development.

THE MELIORISTS

Those people espousing the third viewpoint in Exhibit 2-11 are given the name meliorists because they subscribe to *meliorism*: the doctrine, inter-

---

Exhibit 2-11   Three Viewpoints Regarding the MNC's Role and Its Future

Optimists	Pessimists	Meliorists
Nature The MNC is the most creative international institution, representing humanity's highest accomplishment in the art and science of organizing material and human resources.	The MNC is the most destructive mechanism ever invented. Its current structure and function represent humanity's worst accomplishment.	The MNC has the potential for becoming a very useful vehicle for improving the human condition all over the world.

---

[22]A. G. Kefalas, "The Multinational Corporation and the New International Order," in Anthony J. Dolman (ed.), *Global Planning and Resource Management* (New York: Pergamon Press, 1980).

[23]*The Wall Street Journal*, July 17, 1975, 18.

Optimists	Pessimists	Meliorists
Role The MNC must and will play a more active and more visible role in domestic and international human affairs. There is basically no incompatability between the nation-state's plan and the MNC's objectives and specific goals.	Because the MNC's existence in an area undermines the power of the nation-state to maintain political and economic stability within its sovereign territory, the MNC's role must diminish.	By its very existence the MNC will continue to play a very important role in human development. This is an organization-dominated and -dependent world and it will become more so.
The MNC and the world order The Third World's demand for a "new" economic order seems to be justified but must be accomplished by their "putting their own house in order" and not by handouts from the MNCs. They must create an environment conducive to more freedom for the MNC, not less. Those Third World nations that have made progress toward industrialization have done so through the offices of the MNCs.	The Third World's demand for a new economic order is not only legitimate and justified but a manifestation of the end of economic imperialism, which has through years of exploitation of the poor by the rich created a yawning gap in economic development between the rich and the poor. The new order will give the poor their just share.	The Third World's demand for a new economic order reflects certain changes in our conception of the earth's carrying capacities and of our own purpose in life. Specifically, humans are becoming more and more "limits-conscious" and adopting a long-range perspective. As a result, people are attempting to prolong the use of their finite resources so that future generations will have the minimum means of survival.
Future proposals The MNC should be left alone to evolve into a more effective and efficient wealth-creating mechanism. Do not kill the Golden Goose. Both the host and the home country will depend on the MNC to lay the golden eggs of a peaceful, prosperous, and viable world.	The MNCs must be controlled. Their objectives and goals are basically imcompatible with the aims of the nation-state (particularly in the Third World). One sees today that there are a few very visible multinational managers creating a world that is very pleasant for them but essentially unbearable for those who work for them and have to live with them. Nothing short of an international, supragovernmental agency will suffice.	The MNC must change drastically, in terms of its goals and objectives, its structure, and its policies and procedures. Although some degree of institutionalization of this change appears necessary, it is by no means sufficient. Both the MNC and the nation-state are much more diverse problems than Adam Smith and the Westphalian organizers had in mind.

SOURCE: A. G. Kefalas, "The Multinational Corporation and the New International Order," in A. J. Dolman (ed.), *Global Planning and Resource Management* (New York: Pergamon Press, 1980), 38.

mediate between optimism and pessimism, that affirms that *the world can be made better by human effort*. This viewpoint recognizes and accepts the evolutionary changes that have taken place over the last quarter of this century in the relationship between humans and nature.

The meliorist believes that the MNC is indeed a potentially useful instrument and can play a constructive role in the orchestration of a new world economic order. The meliorist's point of departure is that an unattended Golden Goose might lay eggs in too few or too many places and some of these might turn out not to be golden. On the other hand, a closely attended Golden Goose might not lay any eggs at all.

Although the meliorist's camp is composed primarily of Third World scholars, a number of First World intellectuals and practicing executives of MNCs are becoming proponents of this view. This change in the mood of the First World toward a meliorist attitude regarding the role of the MNC in a new world order is exemplified by some of the suggestions and opinions that have emerged in recent years.

Scholars have recommended maintaining minimal external institutionalized control over MNCs through such mechanisms as an international treaty, suggested by scholars such as Charles Kindleberger, Eugene Rostow, and Paul Goldberg; an international charter, proposed by Professor Kindleberger and former Undersecretary of State George Ball; procedures, codes, and international institutions, proposed by Professor Joseph Nye; the Sullivan Code for MNCs in South Africa; and the OECD Code of Conduct for member multinationals.[24] The views of high-ranking executives of some of the largest MNCs in the world appeared in a series of thirteen articles published in 1976 in the *Christian Science Monitor*. Condensed from a report by the International Management and Development Institute titled "Corporate Citizenship in the Global Community," these articles offered opinions on the role of the MNC in the world economy. Contributors included such figures as Henry Ford II, chairman of the Ford Motor Company; Reginald H. Jones, chairman and CEO of the General Electric Corporation; Walter B. Wriston from Citibank; Donald M. Kendall from Pepsi Cola; and U.S. Secretary of the Treasury William Simon; as well as the heads of UN agencies, the International Chamber of Commerce, and other influential corporate and governmental bodies.[25] Although the messages offered to the public by these corporate and public giants were basically the conventional ones to be expected from free enterprise "flag wavers," overt hints surfaced as to the graveness of the MNCs' present and future situation. The unreserved optimism of earlier decades had to some extent given way to a more cautious hopefulness.

---

[24]See references at the end of the chapter.

[25]"The Global Corporation: Views from the Top," *Christian Science Monitor*, reprinted in *Top Management Reports* (Washington, DC: International Management Institute), Summer 1977.

THE BASIC PREMISES OF THE NEW PRAGMATIC VISION

The MNCs are real; they are affecting people's daily lives and future plans. For this reason, it is advisable to think and talk about them in human terms rather than in terms of money and power. A better understanding of the role of MNCs as they affect individual lives can be gained by recognizing the quantities of resources consumed by the MNCs in their wealth-creation processes, the number of people who derive a livelihood from participating in the MNCs' activities, and the amount of output they generate, both useful and wasteful.

The presence of an MNC in a country is frequently a necessary condition for the country's economic development, but it is by no means sufficient. By the same token, the absence of an MNC from a country (which can come about as a result of expropriation of existing facilities, voluntary divestment, or a country's making new entries difficult) will not automatically lead to a country's economic and social development through domestic business concerns. France is an excellent case in point. During the Charles de Gaulle era, at the zenith of the period described in Servan-Schreiber's *American Challenge,*[26] MNCs (primarily U.S.-based MNCs) left France because of the "unfavorable and hostile climate." Having determined that this exodus was not beneficial to the economy, France today is attempting to generate a return of U.S. investments through image advertisements in *Business Week, Fortune,* and other business media. In one such advertisement, the chairman of DATAR began his invitation with "Dear American Friends." The same method has been used by Sweden, Spain, Italy, Japan, the United Kingdom, Mexico, Turkey, Egypt, and Zaire.

The post–World War II era has been characterized by a tremendous growth of economic activity all over the globe and a relatively stable political climate. The MNCs have played an important role in this economic activity. As a result, their agents, the people at the top and the bottom of the organizational hierarchy, have gained an unprecedented blend of knowledge about and experience in the intricate process of combining human and physical resources to create marketable products and services. It would be to the benefit of humanity to evaluate this vast storehouse of knowledge and determine what can be used and what can be improved upon.

If the goal of a new world economic order—that is, a more equitable distribution of material wealth—is to be accomplished, a rather complex and sophisticated process of needs assessment and needs fulfillment must be set in motion. It is the premise of this book that international business concerns are a potent and potentially valuable force that must be integrated into this process. Dismantlement, or breakup, of the MNCs is neither feasible nor desirable. The only viable and realistic strategy for transforming the global econ-

---

[26]J. Servan-Schreiber, *The American Challenge* (New York: Atheneum, 1968).

omy is enhancement of the MNC managers' understanding of their complex role and their responsibility to humanity beyond "bottom line" considerations.

In summary, the vision underlying this book's strategy for transformation of the MNC is a rather optimistic one. The nation-states of the world are assumed to have the goals of establishing world security, increasing world productivity, stabilizing the world populations, sustaining economic growth, creating equitable conditions for development, and promoting world monetary stability. The MNC is viewed as possessing great potential for facilitating the accomplishment of these goals. For this to be possible, two conditions must be satisfied:

(1)   The MNC must be recognized as a full-fledged partner in the design of this new world order. Its equitable participation will minimize the probability of resistance to change and the accompanying backlash that have characterized past attempts to regulate business enterprises at a national and international level.

(2)   The MNC corporate commonwealth must engage in a process of self-assessment in order to bring its philosophies, policies, and operating procedures in line with the idea of an interdependent world of diverse but unified societies.

RECAPITULATION

This chapter dealt with the first part of the MNC–nation-state interaction system: the corporation. The main objective was to provide an adequate answer to the following question: "What is an MNC and what role does it play in humanity's struggle for survival?"

To answer the first part of the question, the chapter reviewed the literature with respect to the definition of the term MNC, the size of the MNCs around the world, their decisions to invest, and the number of affiliates MNCs maintain around the globe.

The lists of the largest MNCs in the world and in the United States provided evidence that the MNC represents a rather substantial part of human life. These large, diversified, complex, and extremely efficient corporations use a very large portion of the earth's resources, provide employment for millions of people, supply economic resources to hundreds of governments, and, of course, yield profits and dividends to millions of investors all over the globe.

To answer the second portion of the question, the chapter examined the very complex issue of the match between the objectives of a nation-state and the goals of an MNC. In general, it appears that neither the nation-state nor the MNC is at bay. The likelihood that nation-states would be better off if they eradicated the MNC via nationalizations or confiscations is very small. By the same token, the probability that the MNC would be more profitable and would better serve the interests of its stockholders if it could eliminate the functions of the sovereign government of a nation-state is also close to zero.

This hypothesis requires no testing. The literature of the sixties and seventies is replete with examples of attempts by both MNCs and nation-states to eradicate each other. There are no success stories. Rather, what we do find is allegations of MNC misconduct without any conclusive evidence of results benefiting the corporation. On the other side are various nation-states' attempts to take over "what is justly ours"—nationalizations of MNC property—only to discover that the resurrection is much harder than the birth. Millions of jobs evaporated and billions of tax revenues were unnecessarily forfeited. If the goals of world stability, prosperity, and survival are to be realized, the MNC–nation-state interaction must be a non-zero-sum game: a win-win situation.

REVIEW QUESTIONS

(1)   Define the term "multinational corporation."

(2)   List and briefly explain the theories developed by academicians to explain the MNC decision to invest.

(3)   List and briefly explain the eight reasons for the MNC decision to invest offered by the National Association of Manufacturers.

(4)   Based on Exhibit 2-4, compare the position of the United States relative to those of Japan and Western Europe with respect to the activities of their MNCs.

(5)   Exhibit 2-5 presents data on the size, growth, profitability, and so on, of the top fifty U.S. MNCs. Is there a correlation between size and profitability?

(6)   In Exhibit 2-7, how would you explain the decline in both affiliate sales and employees for 1983 in view of the fact that affiliate assets increased by 1.3% that year?

(7)   Compare and contrast the Sovereignty at Bay school and the Dependencia school.

(8)   Exhibit 2-11 presents some proposals for maximizing the MNC's future role in promoting human survival. Choose one of the three proposals and either defend or refute it.

(9)   Using a multinational corporation that you are familiar with and the framework developed in Exhibit 2-1, describe a discussion that might take place between representatives of the MNC and local authorities who are in the process of reviewing an application from the company to set up a new plant in their community.

(10)   "What is good for the MNC is good for the country and you." Defend or refute this statement.

SUGGESTED READINGS

Doz, Yves L. *Strategic Management in Multinational Companies.* Oxford: Pergamon Press, 1986.

Fayerweather, John. *International Business Strategy and Administration.* Cambridge, MA: Ballinger Publishing Co., 1982.

Freeman, Orville L. *The Multinational Company: Instrument for World Growth.* New York: Praeger, 1981.

Gray, H. Peter. *Research in International Business and Finance.* Greenwich, CT: Jai Press, 1986.

Hennart, Jean-Francois. *A Theory of Multinational Enterprise.* Ann Arbor: University of Michigan Press, 1985.

Hladik, Karen J. *International Joint Ventures: An Economic Analysis of U.S.-Foreign Business Partnerships.* Lexington, MA: Lexington Books, 1985.

Negandhi, Anant R. *International Management.* Boston: Allyn and Bacon, 1987.

Rugman, A. M. *Inside the Multinationals.* New York: Columbia University Press, 1981.

Rutenberg, David P. *Multinational Management.* Boston: Little, Brown and Co., 1982.

Said, A. A., and L. R. Simmons. *The New Sovereigns: Multinational Corporations as World Powers.* Englewood Cliffs, NJ: Prentice-Hall, 1975.

U.S. Senate. Subcommittee on Multinational Corporations. *Direct Investment Abroad and the Multinationals: Effects on the United States Economy.* August 1975.

U.S. Senate. Subcommittee on Multinational Corporations. *Multinational Corporations and United States Foreign Policy.* Hearings, 93rd Cong., 2nd sess., June 1974.

U.S. Senate. Subcommittee on Multinational Corporations. *Multinational Corporations in the Dollar Devaluation Crisis: Report on a Questionnaire.* June 1975.

Walmsley, John. *Handbook of International Joint Ventures.* London: Graham and Trotman, 1982.

EMERGING ISSUE 2: Foreign Multinationals in the United States

There was a time when the word "multinationals" was used as a synonym for U.S. corporations overseas. Jacques Servan-Schreiber, a French journalist, created a name for himself with his 1968 bombshell *The American Challenge.* The main thesis of the book was that the U.S. multinational corporations, the MNCs (or as they are called in Europe, the "multis"), were rapidly becoming a very significant economic power in Europe with equally significant socio-economic repercussions. Schreiber's contention was that these corporations were controlling a substantial part of the European economy, thereby making it exceedingly difficult, if not impossible, for Europeans to start up, develop, and run their own corporations. If the situation continued unchecked, Schreiber argued, U.S. multinationals would become the third world power after the United States and the U.S.S.R. Schreiber concluded his book by advising European management to form alliances of the largest European corporations to compete with the U.S. MNCs.

The decade following the appearance of Schreiber's book witnessed numerous attacks on U.S. multinationals. These attacks came not only from the traditional "natural enemies" of the MNCs—the host countries—but from critics here at home. Indeed, in the seventies the U.S. Congress created a committee for the investigation of the behavior of the U.S. multinationals. The Church Committee, named after the late senator from Idaho, Frank Church, was originally charged with investigating allegations that ITT had conspired to overthrow the Chilean government, but it extended its mandate, taking upon itself an investigation of MNC dealings all over the world.

At the peak of these investigations, many MNCs mounted their own counterattacks. ITT, the original protagonist in this drama, commissioned Pierre Salinger to interpret for the company's own internal publication, *Profile,* a survey of public opinion on U.S. multinationals performed in the mid-seventies. The businesspeople and professionals who were polled in six European countries—Austria, Britain, France, Italy, Norway, and Spain—told reporters that even though they were overwhelmingly critical of MNCs, they did "like their money."

Similar publications and even educational films were produced and distributed to anyone concerned with the issue of MNC behavior by almost all U.S. and European MNCs, including Exxon, GMC, Ford, Sears, NCR, Mobile, Caterpillar, Union Carbide, Deere, Dow, Philips, Shell, Unilever, and Nestle.

The main objective of this corporate effort was to educate the general public and especially congresspeople and their staffs on the devastating effects of this "unnecessary concern" with the behavior of the MNCs on their ability to compete in world markets. Speaking to an audience at the 1975 World Trade Conference in Chicago, Lee Morgan, president of Caterpillar, said of the main thesis expressed by Barnet and Müller in *Global Reach,*

> It challenges the very premise on which we base our economy and our actions—the premise that free, private enterprise represents man's most

effective tool for identifying, producing, and distributing the world's economic assets, in a manner responsive to man's needs. . . . We have an
obligation to refute the inaccurate portrayal of our goals and behavior.
Let's convert this challenge to an opportunity, an opportunity to achieve
greater public knowledge about the *constructive role* we play in a changing interdependent world.

Preoccupied with what Professor Vernon called "the storm over multinationals," most Americans did not notice the gradual increase in the "U.S. in-
vasion" by foreign multinationals. Suddenly, at the beginning of the eighties,
stories began to appear in the media about a takeover of the United States by
multinational corporations from overseas. Virtually overnight the concept of
international investment in reverse became the subject of numerous conferences, workshops, and even congressional hearings.

A BRIEF LOOK AT FOREIGN INVESTMENT IN THE UNITED STATES

Direct foreign investment is only a fraction of international investment—
that is, money that foreigners invest in this country. Of the approximately $1.5
trillion worth of foreign investment in the United States for 1987, DFIUS ($262
billion) represented only about 17.5%; the remaining $1238 billion was in
U.S. Treasury securities, corporate stocks and bonds, commercial bank deposits,
and other foreign investments that do not qualify as DFI. The latter category
represents investments in physical assets of a company in which the foreign
investor has more than 10% ownership or equity interest.[27]

Although it has increased markedly in the last few years, DFIUS is not a
recent phenomenon. With the advent of the railroad and the development of
the West, foreigners took advantage of state, territorial, and railroad land promotions to buy extensive tracks of land and to take up cattle ranching, mining,
and agriculture. Europeans were not the only ones buying up U.S. land. The
Japanese were prominent landowners, primarily in Hawaii and California,
where by 1919 they held up to 75% of the land. In addition to land, foreigners
acquired a significant part of the resources industry. For example, about 25%
of the common stock and 9% of the preferred stock of the U.S. Steel Corporation was held by foreigners in 1914. During the next forty or so years, foreign
direct investment activity in the United States was rather small, primarily
because of the two World Wars. By the end of 1959, DFIUS was barely over
$3 billion.

DFIUS increased substantially during the first two decades following World
War II. In 1971, however, the United States experienced a net outflow of
money invested by foreigners, especially the Japanese. These investors re-

---

[27]U.S. Department of Commerce, *Survey of Current Business*, June 1988, 78.

moved their investments in anticipation of major problems with currencies that they anticipated would follow this country's refusal to honor foreign demands for dollar convertibility into gold.

Following the large increase in oil prices and the huge accumulation of U.S. companies' stock by the primarily Arab "petrodollar" owners, the Foreign Investment Act of 1974 was enacted. The act required two executive-branch agencies, the Department of Commerce and the Treasury Department, to undertake major studies on the extent, characteristics, and impact of direct (commerce) and portfolio (treasury) investment in the U.S. economy.

In 1974, the Commerce Department carried out its first benchmark survey of DFIUS and the Treasury Department its benchmark survey of portfolio investment. These surveys were updated in 1982 in compliance with the act, which requires studies of international investment activity in the United States, both USDFI and DFIUS, at least every five years.

The eighties witnessed a remarkable reversal of this country's role in foreign investment. The United States changed from a major investor in foreign countries to a principal recipient of foreign investment (see Exhibit E2-1). The 1982 U.S. Department of Commerce benchmark survey provides a wealth of

Exhibit E2-1   U.S. vs. Foreign Assets

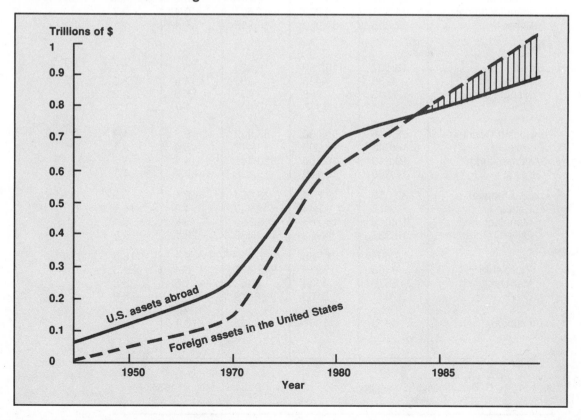

Exhibit E2-2   U.S. Direct Foreign Investment (USDFI) (in millions of dollars)

	1982	1983	1984	Percent Change 1983	1984
All Areas:	225,843	226,962	233,412	2.3	2.9
Petroleum	56,810	60,330	63,319	6.2	5
Manufacturing	90,609	90,171	93,012	− 0.5	3.2
Other	74,424	76,461	77,091	2.7	0.8
Developed Countries:	164,312	169,975	174,057	3.4	2.4
Petroleum	37,134	39,093	49,615	5.3	3.9
Manufacturing	71,399	71,771	72,866	0.5	1.5
Other	55,778	59,111	69,575	6.0	2.5
Canada:	46,190	47,553	50,467	3.0	6.1
Petroleum	10,357	10,883	11,614	5.1	6.7
Manufacturing	19,725	19,851	21,467	0.6	8.1
Other	16,108	15,819	17,386	4.4	3.4
Europe:	99,525	102,689	103,663	3.2	0.9
Petroleum	22,539	23,774	24,714	5.5	4.1
Manufacturing	44,131	43,962	43,661	0.4	0.7
Other	32,855	34,953	35,288	6.4	1.1
Japan:		8063	8374		
Other:	18,597	19,733	19,928	6.1	1.1
Petroleum	4239	4436	4288	4.6	3.3
Manufacturing	7543	7958	7738	5.5	2.8
Other	6815	7340	7901	7.7	7.7
Developing Countries:	56,618	51,430	53,932	2.3	4.9
Petroleum	16,040	16,903	18,417	5.4	9.1
Manufacturing	19,210	18,400	20,146	− 4.2	9.5
Other	17,369	16,126	15,368	− 7.2	− 4.7
Latin America:	32,655	29,674	28,094	− 9.1	− 5.3
Petroleum	6677	6944	5940	4.0	14.5
Manufacturing	15,640	14,766	15,665	− 5.6	6.1
Other	10,337	7963	6489	− 23.1	− 18.5
Other:	19,664	21,756	25,838	9.1	18.8
Petroleum	9363	9959	12,477	6.4	25.3
Manufacturing	3570	3634	4482	1.8	23.3
Other	7031	8163	8879	16.1	8.8
International	4913	5557	5423	13.1	2.4

SOURCE: U.S. Department of Commerce, *Survey of Current Business,* August 1985, 47.

data on both USDFI (see Exhibit E2-2) and DFIUS, or, as it is alternatively known, foreign investment in reverse (see Exhibit E2-3).

The Department of Commerce's records on both USDFI and DFIUS address the following items: (1) investment position—the book value of the foreign investor's equity in and net outstanding loans to its affiliates (a measure of the net claims of the foreign direct investor in its overseas affiliates); (2) income and rate of return on investment; (3) earnings and reinvestment; and (4) fees and royalties.

The USDFI position was consistent and stable in the years 1982 to 1984.

Exhibit E2-3 Direct Foreign Investment in the United States (DFIUS) (in millions of dollars)

	1982	1983	1984	Percent Change 1983	1984
All Areas:	124,677	137,061	159,571	9.9	16.4
Petroleum	17,660	18,209	24,916	3.1	36.8
Manufacturing	44,065	47,665	50,664	8.2	6.3
Wholesale Trade	18,397	21,031	24,042	14.3	14.3
Other	44,555	50,156	59,949	12.6	19.5
Canada:	11,709	11,434	14,001	−2.3	22.4
Petroleum	1550	1391	1419	−10.2	2.1
Manufacturing	3500	3313	3888	−5.4	17.4
Wholesale Trade	1058	1040	1120	1.6	7.7
Other	5601	5690	7573	1.6	33.1
Europe:	83,192	93,936	106,567	11.7	14.7
Petroleum	15,071	16,326	22,897	8.3	40.3
Manufacturing	33,032	36,866	38,684	11.6	4.9
Wholesale Trade	8952	10,124	11,396	13.1	12.6
Other	26,137	29,619	33,590	13.3	13.4
Netherlands:	26,191	29,198	32,643	11.4	11.9
Petroleum	8098	8646	9878	6.8	14.3
Manufacturing	9901	11,222	12,470	13.3	11.1
Wholesale Trade	1273	1435	1620	12.7	12.9
Other	6919	7879	8674	13.9	10.1
United Kingdom:	28,446	32,152	38,099	13	18.5
Petroleum	5444	5955	10,917	9.4	83.3
Manufacturing	8504	9221	9347	8.4	1.4
Wholesale Trade	3086	3685	3580	19.4	2.8
Other	11,412	13,290	14,256	16.5	7.3

	1982	1983	1984	Percent Change 1983	1984
Japan:	9677	11,336	14,817	17.1	30.7
Petroleum	113	408	178	*	*
Manufacturing	1624	1605	2262	1.1	40.9
Wholesale Trade	6126	7823	9696	27.7	23.9
Other	1814	2316	3037	27.7	31.1
Other:	20,099	21,356	21,187	6.3	13.3
Petroleum	926	900	778	2.8	13.3
Manufacturing	5909	5881	5830	0.5	0.9
Wholesale Trade	2261	2043	1829	9.6	10.5
Other	11,003	12,531	15,750	13.9	25.7

*Percent change is not defined because the position is negative.

SOURCE: U.S. Department of Commerce, *Survey of Current Business,* August 1985, 47.

The USDFI position grew at a rate of 2.3% from 1982 to 1983 and at a rate of 2.8% from 1983 to 1984. These growth rates are a small fraction of the growth rates of direct foreign investment in reverse over the same period of time.

DFIUS grew at a remarkable rate in the 1982–1983 period, and at an even greater rate in the 1983–1984 period. The growth rate of DFIUS for the 1982–1983 period was about four times that of USDFI for the same period (9.9% vs. 2.3%). The difference in growth rates between USDFI and DFIUS is considerably larger for the 1983–1984 period, when the DFIUS growth rate was almost eight times that of the USDFI (16.4% vs. 2.8%). This growth in the DFIUS was due in large measure to the activities of foreign companies operating in the United States, many of which are listed in Exhibit E2-4.

The Japanese were the greatest contributors to the growth rate of DFIUS. Over 64% of the Japanese investments in the United States from 1982 through 1984 were in wholesale trade. It appears that the Japanese are steadily increasing their wholesale and distribution investment in the United States. In 1984, Japanese manufacturing investment jumped by an unprecedented rate of 40%, after lying dormant during 1983.

Overall, the Europeans hold the majority of foreign investments in this country. European DFIUS surpassed USDFI in Europe by some $3 billion in 1984. Some 67% of the total foreign investments are by Europeans. During 1984 alone, Europeans increased their foreign investment position by almost 15%, to over $106 billion. Among the Europeans, the British were the heaviest investors during the 1982–1984 period. In 1983 there was a tremendous

Exhibit E2-4 Foreign Companies in the United States

Company	Country	Company	Country
Electronics		*Automotives*	
Mitsubishi	Japan	Renault-AMC (joint venture)	France
Matsushita		Honda	Japan
Sanyo		Nissan	
Hitachi		Toyota-GMC (joint venture)	Japan
Sharp		Volvo	Sweden
Toshiba		Volkswagen	W.
JVC		*Pharmaceuticals*	Germany
Gold Star		Chemdex	
Philips	Netherlands	Ron American Pharmaceutical	
Samsung	S. Korea	Novo Biochemical Industries	Bahamas
Tatung	Taiwan	Beecham Labs	Canada
Sampo		Rucker Pharmacal	Denmark
Semiconductors		ICI America	U. K.
Northern Telecoms	Canada	Chemical Manufacturing Co.	
Schumberger	France	Stuart Pharmaceuticals	
SGS-Ates	Italy	Burrough-Wellcome Co.	
NEC	Japan	Searle, G. D. (joint venture)	
Hitachi		Rhodia	
Toshiba		Norwich-Eaton	France
Fujitsu		Premo Pharmaceutical Labs	
Mitsubishi		Federal Pharmacal	
Oki		Cutter Labs	Germany
Hatori		Miles Labs	
Tonyo		American Home Products Corp.	
Mashei Kogyo		Hexagon Labs	
INMOS	U. K.	Towne Paulsen	
Siemens	W. Germany	Phillips Roxane	
Chemicals		American Hoechst Corp.	
American Petrofina		Ashford Labs Ltd.	
Soltex Polymer		Adria Labs	
E. I. du Pont		Warren-Teed	Hong Kong
Polysar	Netherlands	Eisai USA	Italy
Rhone-Poulenc	Neth./U. K.	Alpha Biochemical Co.	
W. R. Grace	Neth./U. K.	Abbott Labs (joint venture)	Japan
American Hoechst	S. Africa	Hepar Industries	
Mobay Chemical		Syntex Labs	
BASF Wyandotte	Switzerland	Astra Pharmaceuticals	Netherlands
Badische	U. K.	Biogen	Panama
Akzona		Ciba	Sweden
Shell Oil	Belgium	Alza	Switzerland
National Starch		S. J. Tutag	
Terra Chemicals	Canada	Hoffman–La Roche and Co.	
Engelhard Corp.		Alcon Labs	
Ciba-Geigy Corp.	France	Sandoz Pharmaceuticals	
Airco	Germany		
Standard Oil Ohio			

SOURCE: H. P. Gray, *International Business and Finance,* Vol. 5: *Uncle Sam as Host* (Greenwich, CT: JAI Press, 1986).

increase in British wholesale trade investment (19.4%). Then in 1984 the United Kingdom upped its holdings in the petroleum industry by some $10 billion, an 83.3% increase that reflected Shell Oil Company's acquisition of its U.S. affiliate.

ISSUES FOR DISCUSSION

If history is a predictor of the future, questions regarding foreign investors' role in U.S. society will soon emerge. The relationship between the foreign investor and the host country resembles the popular view of marriages: after an initial honeymoon, in which both partners enjoy the relationship, there comes a period during which at least one of the partners begins to question the benefits derived from the relationship. Finally, after considerable negotiation a settlement is reached, which may involve the termination of the relationship or the formation of a somewhat different arrangement. The honeymoon between this country and foreign investors is ending, and questions are beginning to be raised about foreign investors' presence in the United States. For example:

(1)   Should the U.S. government think about imposing some type of control over the amount, kind, and nature of direct foreign investment beyond the existing requirements?

(2)   Should the U.S. government demand that foreign multinationals be managed by U.S. citizens, a practice followed by most countries, including some rather economically and politically developed countries such as Canada?

(3)   Should the U.S. government set up screening procedures and establish agencies whose job it is to produce a sort of foreign investment impact statement?

(4)   Should the U.S. government forbid states from offering preferential treatment (incentives) to investors from overseas?

(5)   Should the U.S. government impose limitations on currency expatriation (that is, sending profits, fees, and commissions back to the homeland) by foreign MNCs, as do most countries?

(6)   Should the U.S. government impose conditions on technology transfer between the U.S. subsidiary and the headquarters?

Although no one can predict when or with what intensity, these and many other issues may surface in the years to come, and it behooves students of international business to think about them. Such forethought is precisely what proactive management is all about.

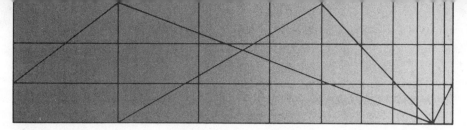

CHAPTER 3

THE ENVIRONMENT

Now that mankind is in the process of completing the colonization of the planet, learning to manage it intelligently is an urgent imperative. Man must accept responsibility for the stewardship of the earth. The word stewardship implies, of course, management for the sake of someone else. . . . As we enter the global phase of human evolution it becomes obvious that each man has two countries, his own and the planet earth.

Barbara Ward and Rene Dubois

Only One Earth (New York: Ballantine Books, 1972), xx.

OVERVIEW

This chapter discusses the concept of the environment.

The first part of the chapter, on the macroenvironment, presents a framework for considering how the various aspects of the world environment are organized. Here the biologist's approach to the environment is chosen as the most practical methodology. The biologist conceives of the universe as a continuous interaction between the living organism and its natural surroundings. For the international manager, the universe is a continuous interaction between the people of the world and their physical environment.

The second part of the chapter, on the microenvironment, looks more specifically at a particular organization's external business environment (EBE) and outlines practitioners' attempts to make use of this environment. Because the international EBE encompasses a collection of sovereign nation-states, international managers must be extremely cautious and very well prepared before they begin tinkering with it. The international manager's microenvironment is approached using the well-accepted methodology of environmental scanning. Scanning is a method of gaining knowledge about the external environment by searching it thoroughly and continuously, point by point, in order to form an image of it. This scanning process begins with a more or less casual glance and ends with structured research whose purpose is the solution of a specific problem.

In sum, a scan of the macroenvironment provides the so-called big picture or bird's-eye view, and a scan of the microenvironment zeroes in on the actual

THE MAIN CONCEPTS   THE SUBCONCEPTS

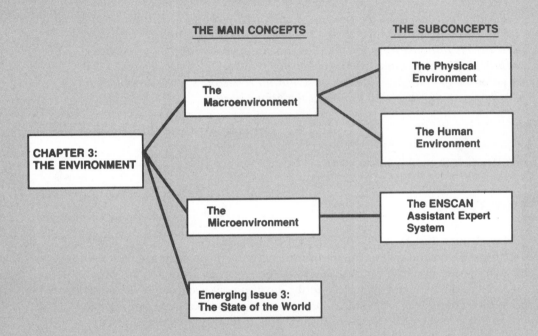

pragmatic question: How does the external environment affect managerial decision making?

LEARNING OBJECTIVES

After studying the material in this chapter, the student should be familiar with the following concepts:

(1)   Environment

(2)   Macroenvironment

(3)   Microenvironment

(4)   Food power

(5)   Mineral power

(6)   Oil power

(7)   Ecology

(8)   Major religions of the world

(9)   Politics and major political alliances

(10)   United Nations and its family

(11)   NATO and the Warsaw Pact

(12)   Economics and major economic alliances

(13)   OECD, COMECON, and the Group of 77

(14)   First, Second, and Third Worlds

(15)   Environmental scanning

INTRODUCTION

The environment represents the totality of factors that affect the firm and are beyond the immediate control of the firm's management. Most traditional books on international business deal with the environment by emphasizing either the economic structure or the political structure of the world. Some recent books focus on the sociocultural aspects of the world.[1] *Global Business*

---

[1]B. M. Richman and M. R. Cohen, *International Management and Economic Development* (New York: McGraw-Hill, 1972); Vern Terpstra and K. David, *The Cultural Environment of International Business,* Second Edition (Cincinnati, OH: South-Western Publishing Co., 1985); L. Copeland and L. Griggs, *Going International: How to Make Friends and Deal Effectively in the Global Market* (New York: Random House, 1985); S. Ronen, *Comparative and Multinational Management* (New York: John Wiley and Sons, 1986).

Strategy: A Systems Approach looks at two aspects of the external business environment: the macroenvironment and the microenvironment.

The study of the macroenvironment places emphasis on the relationship between humans and their natural habitats. The natural habitat is the set of interrelated and interdependent life support systems that provide the means of human survival. Human beings affect and in turn are affected by the life support systems of nature.

In this chapter the natural ecosystem will be examined in terms of

(1)   its ability to produce food and minerals (the so-called *reservoir* concept)

(2)   its capacity to absorb human and industrial waste (the so-called *sink* concept)

Human systems will be examined in terms of

(1)   the number of people on earth and the rates of growth (population/demographics)

(2)   the cultures of the peoples of the world (religious, political, and economic systems)[2]

The macroenvironment, with which most students are already familiar from courses in geography, religion, ecology or earth science, political science, and economics, is diagrammed in the upper portion of Exhibit 3-1.

The microenvironment is the particular environment within which an individual enterprise does business in a particular country or region. This book conceives of a business enterprise as an open system which is in continuous interaction with its external environment. Within such a system the people, both managers and workers, act as continuous scanners, seeking and receiving information about the environment. This information becomes input in the organizational decision-making process as the set of *uncontrollable variables,* or *states of nature,* in the strategic management framework (see Exhibit 1-5).

The literature on organizational environments, or external business environments, divides the variables that are relevant to the organization's objectives, goals, and functions but beyond its immediate control into three basic categories.[3] The first category, called the internal environment, includes all the factors in the work situation that are beyond the immediate or complete

---

[2]Different authors choose different names for the main parts of the macroenvironment. F. T. Haner, for example, uses the terms "physical variables" and "human variables" in *Global Business Strategy for the 1980s* (New York: Praeger Publishers, 1980).

[3]H. Smith, A. B. Carroll, A. G. Kefalas, and H. Watson, *Management: Making Organizations Perform* (New York: Macmillan, 1981), Chap. 3; P. P. Schoderbek, C. G. Schoderbek, and A. G. Kefalas, *Management Systems: Conceptual Considerations,* Third Edition (Dallas: BPI, 1985); L. Fahey and V. K. Narayanan, *Macroenvironmental Analysis for Strategic Management* (St. Paul, MN: Kent Publishing Co., 1986).

Exhibit 3-1 The International Environment

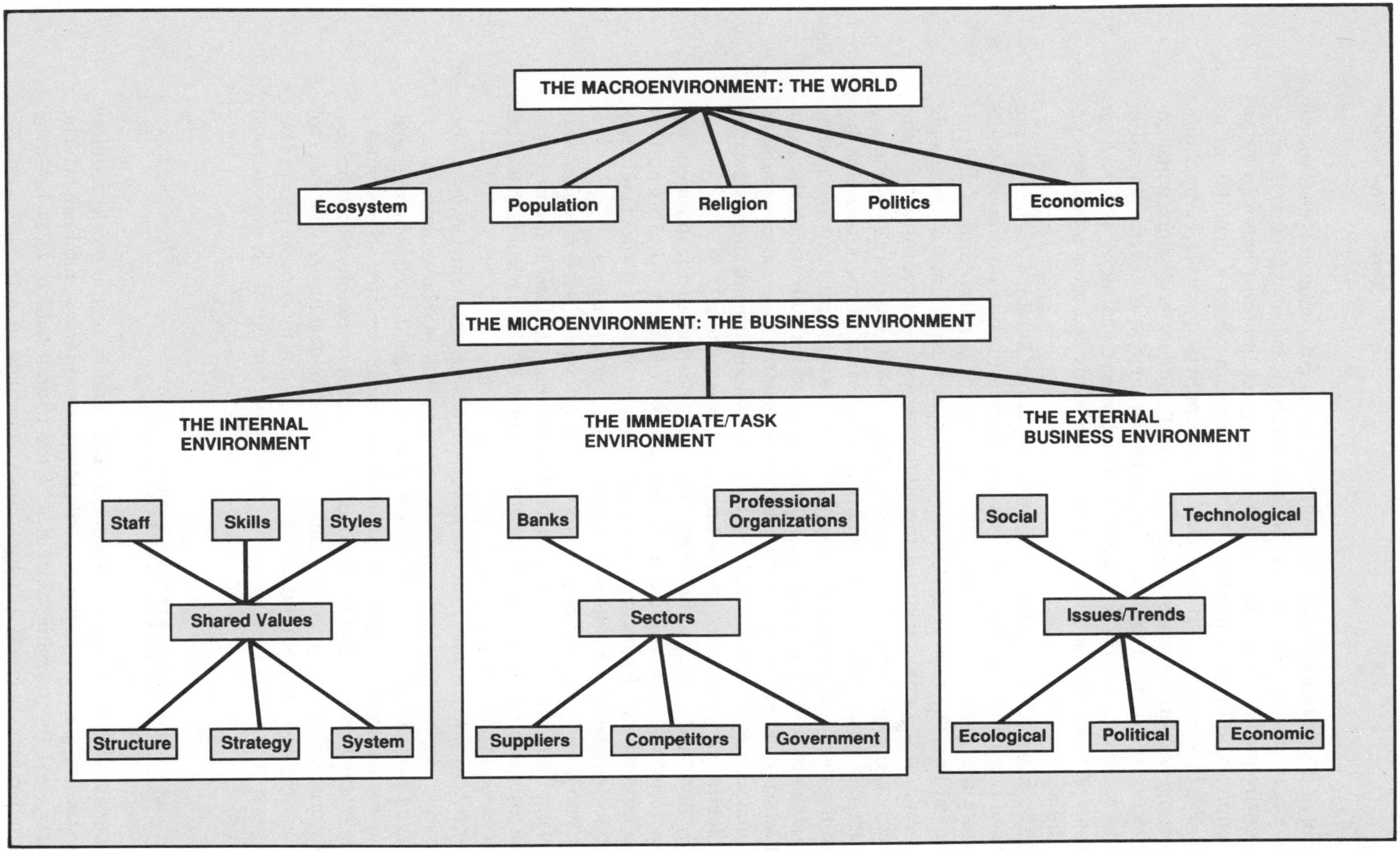

control of the jobholder (individual). The internal environment is also known as the organizational climate. The second category, called the immediate, or task, environment, represents the longstanding relationships between an organization and other organizations or individuals on which it depends for its day-to-day functioning, such as stockholders, suppliers, creditors, competitors, customers, and labor unions. Finally, the third category of organizational environments, the general external business environment, is usually defined in the literature very loosely as background factors such as social, political (or regulatory), economic, and technological conditions that affect a business organization.

This framework is presented in the lower portion of Exhibit 3-1. The extreme left-hand box represents the internal environment. In contemporary business literature this portion of the business environment is referred to as the corporate culture. The term refers to the accumulated experience of the people connected to the enterprise and the atmosphere and climate in which this experience is expressed. The middle box in Exhibit 3-1 represents the immediate/task environment. This environment consists of the interaction between the organization and other organizations to which it has longstanding commitments. Traditionally, these other organizations with which the organization has daily interractions are called sectors of the external environment. Five such sectors are identified here: banks, professional organizations (lawyers, consultants, etc.), suppliers, competitors, and government.

The third, and perhaps the most important, portion of the business microenvironment is represented in the third box in Exhibit 3-1. This portion of the business environment consists of various emerging issues, including social, technological, ecological, political, and economic issues.

Division of the environment into three main categories is a convenient way of making some sense of the uncontrollable variables. At least it focuses managerial attention on the uncontrollability of some of the variables that affect the decision-making process.

The framework is inadequate, however, when management wishes to become more sophisticated in strategy setting. As will be shown later, a very important part of strategic management is what is called environmental analysis. When performing environmental analysis, a manager must go beyond this simple distinction between the immediate, or task, environment and the general external environment. And the managerial task of dealing with the external environment and incorporating it into the strategic management process becomes significantly more difficult when the environment is an international one.

THE MACROENVIRONMENT

Understanding the macroenvironment of a country or the world requires understanding the relationship between humans and their natural habitat. The resources and the carrying capacities of the natural habitat affect both the quantitative aspects (such as population volume and growth rates) and the cultural aspects (such as social, political, and economic behaviors) of human life.

THE PHYSICAL ENVIRONMENT[4]

The earth is a life support system. It provides everything humans, plants, and animals need to survive: air, food, minerals, and so on. Until very recently, the earth was thought of as an unlimited reservoir of resources. During the last couple of decades, however, research on the finiteness of the earth's capacities both as a supplier of resources and as a depository of human and industrial waste has fostered a consciousness of the need to protect the natural environment. There is a growing suspicion that humans are approaching the physical limits of both the earth's ability to feed and maintain life and its capacity to absorb pollution.

The critical issue for the international manager is not whether the doom-sayers are right or wrong about environmental crises. It is that a great deal of managerial know-how must be exercised to accommodate people's attitudes about the environment. The international manager must realize that the physical conditions of an area may completely nullify its technological and/or economic advantages.

FOOD

The earth's capacity to produce enough food for the people who occupy it has long been the subject of considerable research. A lack of conclusive evidence has not prevented heated controversies.[5] At one extreme are the prophets of doom, sometimes known as Neo-Malthusians, who believe that the earth's carrying capacity is near exhaustion: croplands cannot be extended much further and land resources are being steadily depleted. At the other extreme are those who believe that enough food is available or could be made available to feed perhaps twice the world's current population. According to this view, what is needed is more arable land, better production methods, a better and more equitable distribution system, and a free marketplace for agricultural products.

Personal beliefs aside, there are certain cruel facts that an international manager must recognize.[6] First, hunger and sometimes famine are harsh realities for millions of people throughout the world. Second, because of good harvests during the sixties and the resulting great surpluses, the food shortages of the 1970s caught the world by surprise. Third, much of the agricultural

---

[4]This section of the description of the macroenvironment draws heavily on *Our Magnificent Earth: A Rand McNally Atlas of Earth Resources* (New York: Rand McNally and Co., 1985).

[5]See, for example, D. Meadows et al., *The Limits to Growth: The First Report to the Club of Rome* (New York: Universe Books, 1972).

[6]For a vivid presentation of these and other facts, see The Hunger Project, *Ending Hunger: An Idea Whose Time Has Come* (New York: Praeger Publishers, 1985).

activity in most of the world has more to do with making money than with supplying food to the people who need it. Fourth, one of the most disturbing aspects of Western agriculture is its heavy emphasis on the output of meat and dairy products. Almost one quarter of all the grain produced each year is consumed by livestock. Together the industrialized nations, including the USSR, allocate more grain to livestock than is consumed by all less-developed countries. A mere 10% of the grain fed to beef cattle in 1974 would have met the entire Asian shortfall for that year. Unfortunately, cereals and grain eaten by livestock lose about 90% of their original vegetable protein when they are converted into beef. Fifth, three-quarters of the world's grain trade consists of traffic from the United States, the biggest agricultural exporter of all, to Europe. Finally, because they consume space and agricultural resources, cash crops such as cotton, rubber, coffee, and cocoa bring relatively little benefit to the bulk of a country's indigenous population.

MINERALS

Unlike food, minerals are nonrenewable resources. Controversy about the adequacy of the existing supply of minerals to meet world demand is as heated as debates about the food crisis. On one hand, pessimists argue that the world's supplies of minerals cannot be indefinitely maintained. Thus, they recommend strict conservation of mineral resources. On the other hand, optimists claim that plenty of minerals remain in the crust of the earth for future generations. Although some materials occasionally appear to be in short supply, optimists assert that advances in science and technology will allow the supply to keep pace with the ever-increasing demand.

Again, the issue for the international manager is not whether the pessimists or the optimists will be proven right. What the international manager must realize is that a country's supply of natural resources will to a large extent determine its economic and political stability.

Most of the world's reserves of resources (defined as those identified resources that can be economically mined today using known technology) are in the southern hemisphere, or the developing countries. However, most of the flows of minerals (defined as additions to the marketable stocks due to the processing of raw resources) are in the northern hemisphere, or the developed world. Some of the most industrialized parts of the world, notably Japan and Western Europe, have no resources to speak of, yet are the heaviest producers of industrial material made of minerals.

ENERGY

There should be little doubt in anybody's mind that humanity's remarkable accomplishments over the last forty years would have been impossible without oil. Today, human society is excessively dependent on oil. Oil acccounts for some 40% of global power supplies. Because of the ease with which it can be extracted, refined, stored, transported, distributed, and used, oil has become virtually indispensable.

Most of the developed world, with the exception of Canada and Australia, is energy-poor. Japan consumes about nine times more energy than it creates. The situations of the United States and Western Europe, the other two industrial giants, though less severe, are similar.

In 1973, some of the Western countries experienced a taste of what it would mean to be without oil. After that, the price of oil skyrocketed to unimagined heights. Currently, an oil glut has developed, with the expected impact on price. Though most people are celebrating the fall of the OPEC cartel, others remain extremely wary.

ECOLOGY

There is disagreement as to whether the earth's "reservoir" of food, minerals, and energy is at a safe level. It is clear, however, that the earth's capacity to absorb human and industrial waste—its carrying capacity—has reached critical limits in many parts of the world. This is especially true for the industrialized countries of Western Europe, Japan, and the United States. All three types of conventional pollution—land, air, and water—are more pronounced in the developed world.

Occasionally people react negatively to the word "ecology." For these people the word implies an excessive or overzealous concern for the environment and the flora and fauna therein and evokes visions of a return to the "good old days" at the expense of any kind of progress. Ecology, however, is simply the study of ecosystems. This definition provides a unified framework for a discipline that integrates such areas as population ecology, community ecology, evolutionary ecology, environmental ecology, behavioral ecology, mathematical ecology, marine ecology, and human ecology. Like other disciplines, ecology has adopted the systems approach, which has unified and redefined the field by emphasizing a holistic viewpoint, wherein ecology is thought of as the study of populations and communities as a whole in relation to one another and to their total environment.[7]

Ecological awareness has changed managerial thinking about production processes and industrial growth. Waste treatment mechanisms, whether biological or chemical, have gradually become part of original plant construction blueprints and plans. The purpose of making managers aware of the natural environment is not to turn them into ecologists or earth scientists, but rather to make them aware of the issues they will face when constructing a new factory or expanding an old one.

This book assumes that for the next few decades the earth will have the capacity to provide most of the resources needed for industrial development, with the exception perhaps of copper, fresh water, and oil. The capacity of the land, air, and water to absorb human wastes, however, is an entirely different matter. The manager is strongly advised to exercise extreme caution and take

---

[7]Arthur S. Boughey, *Fundamentals of Ecology* (Scranton, PA: Intext Educational Publishers, 1971).

every measure necessary to make sure that plants are built and operated with the latest safety features. Managers must resist the temptation to forgo expenditures for pollution controls designed to ensure the safety of the people who work and live in close proximity to a factory. Union Carbide's accident in Bhopal, India should be adequate warning of the futility of compromising on ecological considerations even when local governments lack requirements.

THE HUMAN ENVIRONMENT

Both quantitative and qualitative aspects of the human environment are important to the international manager. The number of people and their social, economic, and political behavior are fundamental determinants of the success or failure of business activities. The international manager must be well informed in order to be able to allow for these human variables in formulating strategies.

POPULATION

Every minute of every day more than 250 babies are born into the world. The earth's population as of 1988 stood at about 5.2 billion people, and it continues to grow rapidly. If current trends continue, by the year 2050 there will be some 11 billion people on earth. Exhibit 3-2 vividly illustrates population dynamics. At the beginning of recorded history, there were about 300 million people on earth. World population then took more than 1500 years to double. That is a growth rate of much less than $\frac{1}{2}$%. At the beginning of the eighteenth century, the world's population started to rise steadily. By 1900, it had reached the 1.7 billion mark, the result of a growth rate of about $\frac{1}{4}$%.

The twentieth century saw a truly remarkable rate of population growth. During the first half of the century, the world's population, growing at 1% per year, reached the 2.5 billion level. Today, as a result of an absolutely devastating growth rate of some 2% per year for the first two decades of the second half of the century, world population has doubled again.[8]

The remarkable growth during the second half of the twentieth century took place almost exclusively in the developing countries. This fact is of major importance for international business managers. The contrast between the developed and the developing countries is evident. Most of the former experienced a slight rate of growth in population. Two countries, Britain and West Germany, actually experienced a decline in population over the last five years. While most of Europe, including the USSR and Japan, grew at an annual rate of less than 5%, the United States and Canada added to their populations at a rate of more than 5% per year.

---

[8] *Our Magnificent Earth*, p. 38.

Exhibit 3-2   Past and Projected World Population, A.D. 1–2150

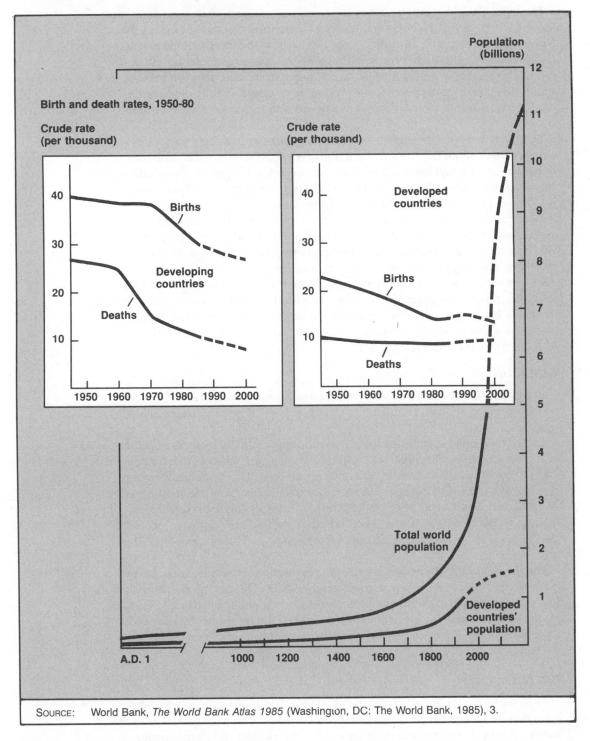

SOURCE: World Bank, *The World Bank Atlas 1985* (Washington, DC: The World Bank, 1985), 3.

RELIGION

Most people find religion an extremely difficult subject to discuss. In some societies it is considered blasphemy even to mention the name of one's god. Nevertheless, religion is an aspect of the culture that the international manager must consider. Although very few religions influence business activities directly, the impact of religion on human value systems and decision making is significant. More immediately, one's religion to some extent dictates one's consumption habits, both in terms of amount and in terms of types of goods consumed.

Religion is a socially shared set of beliefs, ideas, and actions that focus on a reality that cannot be verified empirically, yet is believed to affect the course of natural and human events. The world's main religions can be classified into six categories (see Exhibit 3-3): (1) nonliterate religions; (2) Hinduism; (3) Buddhism; (4) Islam; (5) Judaism; (6) Christianity.

Whereas most businesspeople who are briefed for a business trip abroad are advised about the eating and drinking habits of the people they plan to visit, few receive an organized introduction to the country's religions. Avoiding the social embarrassment that may be encountered as a result of not knowing another's religious beliefs and traditions is only one of the reasons to carefully study the religious makeup of a country in which one intends to do business. Religious holidays and preparations for major religious events can have tremendous implications for production schedules, delivery deadlines, unloading of ships, and other operating practices.

LANGUAGE

Language is the means of communication. In some countries, more than one language is spoken. In India, for example, over fifteen languages are recognized.

English is the language most widely used in international business dealings. It is estimated that more than 400 million people use English as their primary and official language, and some 700 million use English as a second language; one half of the world's newspapers are printed in English. For this reason most North Americans have developed the attitude that they can speak any language as long as it is English. When asked whether he had any language problem during his year in Egypt, a friend once responded, "I had no problem. They did."

For the manager who will work in another country, however, some knowledge of the languages spoken is an invaluable asset. The manager who has to live with the people in a foreign country must be concerned with their language for the simple reason that he or she must decide on the language of the everyday directives, training manuals, report systems, and all forms of spoken and written exchange.

POLITICS

Analysis of the political environment of international business can be approached on two levels. At the global level, attention is focused on the world's various political systems and their alliances—the subject of international pol-

Exhibit 3-3   The World's Religions: Adherents in Millions and as a Percentage of the World Population

	1900 Millions	1900 Percentage of World Population	1980 Millions	1980 Percentage of World Population	2000 (estimate) Millions	2000 (estimate) Percentage of World Population
Literate Religions						
Buddhist	127	7.84	274	6.29	359	5.73
Christian	558	34.44	1433	32.90	2020	32.27
Roman Catholic	272	16.79	809	18.58	1169	18.67
Protestant and Anglican	153	9.44	345	7.92	440	7.03
Eastern Orthodox	121	7.47	124	2.85	153	2.44
Other	12	0.74	155	3.56	258	4.12
Hindu	203	12.53	583	13.39	859	13.72
Jewish	12	0.74	17	0.39	20	0.32
Muslim	200	12.35	723	16.60	1201	19.19
New Religions	6	0.37	96	2.20	138	2.20
Other*	13	0.80	17	0.39	61	0.97
Nonliterate Religions						
Chinese Folk Religion	380	23.46	198	4.55	158	2.52
Tribalist and Shamanist	118	7.28	103	2.37	110	1.76
Nonreligious and Atheist	3	0.19	911	20.92	1334	21.31
World Population	1620	100.00	4355	100.00	6260	100.00

*Including Sikh, Confucian, Shinto, Bahai, Parsi

SOURCE: Vern Terpstra and K. David, *The Cultural Environment of International Business* (Cincinnati, OH: South-Western Publishing Co., 1985), 82. Reprinted by permission of the publisher.

itics or international relations. At the state or country level, the focus is on
the nature of the political system and of the government in which it is expressed
and on the government's attitudes toward private enterprise.

Currently there are almost 200 nations on earth. Most of these nations arose
in recent history, as shown in Exhibit 3-4. All of these nations—new as well
as old—share characteristics. They have legal authority over their territories
and people; they have armies and air forces; they send and receive ambassadors;
they collect taxes; and they seek to regulate their economies and maintain
order through parliaments, ministries and departments, courts, police, and

Exhibit 3-4   Formation of Nations Since the Eighteenth Century

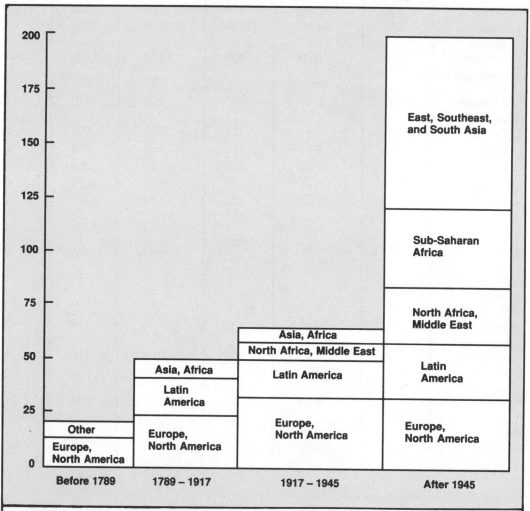

SOURCE: Data to 1945 are from Charles S. Taylor and Michael C. Hudson, *World Handbook of Political and Social Indicators,* Second Edition (New Haven, CT: Yale University Press, 1972), 26 ff.; data after 1945 are from *The World Almanac and Book of Facts* (New York: Newspaper Enterprise Association, 1978), 511 ff.

prisons. Almost all of them belong to the United Nations. But they also vary enormously in many different ways. The most important distinction that people make among the countries of the world is the degree of freedom that their citizens have to choose their own political leaders. The 1986 count by The Freedom House reported that the world contains fifty-seven free nations, fifty-seven partly free nations, and fifty-three unfree nations.[9] In the 1973 survey, half as many nations were classified as free.

Exhibit 3-5 provides a list of problems confronting most of the countries of the world. The international manager is strongly advised to study the list thoroughly and, when proposing to expand the business into another country, to incorporate into his or her proposals ideas that, if they do not contribute toward the solution of these problems, at least do not aggravate them.

Patterns of Political Alliances.   The possibility of these states' living together harmoniously is rather unlikely. Indeed, hardly any day passes without some incident involving one country's aggressive act against another. For this reason, throughout human history nations have tried to form alliances with one another to protect themselves from aggressors.

In general, there are three types of alliances: alliances for collective security, political alliances, and economic alliances. Each of these three categories includes both governmental organizations and nongovernmental organizations.[10]

Humanity's greatest accomplishment in forming alliances for collective security was establishment of the United Nations (U.N.), which succeeded and remedied some of the defects of the pre–World War II League of Nations. The U.N. was founded in San Francisco in 1945. Its original charter was signed on October 15, 1945 by fifty-one nations and took effect on October 24 of the same year.

The United Nations organization represents an attempt on the part of the earth's inhabitants to keep the earth in one piece. It is a global effort; almost all members of the human race belong to it. Although compliance with the United Nations' directives is not mandatory, almost all nations believe in and abide by its rules and directives. It is an apolitical alliance in the sense that any nation, whether democratic or autocratic, whether capitalist or communist, has the right to apply for membership and expect to be accepted in the world community.

A number of regional alliances with more stringent rules are also in existence today. These regional alliances are political to the extent that their members have more or less similar political systems and government selection procedures. In addition, the members share a uniform and coordinated defense strategy. The two most important regional political alliances tend to divide the world into two camps: the North Atlantic Treaty Organization (NATO) in the West and the Warsaw Pact in the East. Both the United States and the USSR have their own treaties or agreements with other nations outside of NATO and the Warsaw Pact.

---

[9]*The Map of Freedom* (New York: Freedom House, 1987).
[10]Terpstra and David, *Cultural Environment,* p. 79.

Exhibit 3-5   Policy Problems Confronting Industrial and Preindustrial Nations

Policy Problem	Industrial Nations	Preindustrial Nations
Governmental organization	*Maintaining and adapting* existing policy-making and implementing agencies (e.g., reform of parliament, reorganization of provincial and local government)	*Creating* effective governmental agencies; recruitment and training of governmental personnel
National unity	*Coping with* persistent tendencies toward ethnic and subcultural fragmentation	*Creating* national identity and loyalty
Economic development	*Maintaining* satisfactory growth rate through some combination of public and private investment and use of fiscal controls and incentives	*Accumulating* capital from domestic and foreign sources for investment in industry and industrial infrastructure (e.g., transportation, education)
Economic stability	*Combining* satisfactory growth rate with control of inflation; *maintaining* balance of payments equilibrium and adequate employment	*Coping with* fluctuations in demand for raw materials, extreme inflation resulting from rapid and uneven growth, and acute unemployment problems due to urban migration
Social welfare	*Maintaining* educational opportunity, medical care, old-age assistance, etc. in time of limited growth and taxpayer resistance	*Creating* educational and welfare systems
Participation	*Responding to* demands for popular participation and from disadvantaged racial, ethnic, status, age, and sex groups; *coping with* demands for greater participation in industry and local communities	*Creating* organizations for participation: political parties, interest groups, communications media, local community organizations

Policy Problem	Industrial Nations	Preindustrial Nations
Quality of life	*Coping with* problems of industrial growth, urban blight, and consumption of natural resources	*Coping with* environmental deterioration, the crowding caused by urban migration, and beginning conservation
Foreign and security policy	*Maintaining* national security through weapons development and alliance systems; *seeking to reduce* risks of war through disarmament negotiations and effective foreign trade diplomacy	*Dealing with* economic and security dependency through integration in Western or Eastern camp, or *maintaining* a neutral posture; *coping with* foreign trade and investment problems

SOURCE: Gabriel A. Almond and G. B. Powell, Jr., *Comparative Politics Today: A World View,* Second Edition (Boston: Little, Brown and Co., 1980).

ECONOMICS

The economic aspects of the international environment receive the greatest share of attention in most standard textbooks and other publications in international business, perhaps because statistics on the subject are easy to come by.

In the World Bank's annual *World Development Report,* the economies of the world are categorized as follows:

Category A: Low-income economies (some thirty-two countries)

Category B: Middle-income economies (some thirty-four countries)

Category C: Upper-middle-income economies (some twenty-two countries)

Category D: High-income oil exporters (five countries)

Category E: Industrial market economies (nineteen countries)

Category F: East European nonmarket economies (eight countries)

The disproportionate share of the world's wealth held by countries in the fifth category (the industrial market economies), specifically the United States, Japan, and Western Europe, is remarkable. Exhibit 3-6 shows the relationship between population and GNP per capita worldwide, and makes the extremely disturbing concentration of world wealth in relatively few hands starkly obvious.

Exhibit 3-6   World GNP and Population

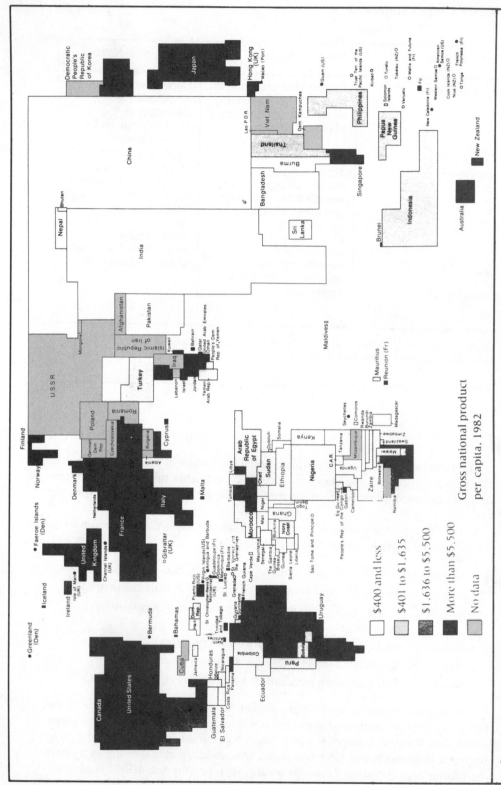

Gross national product per capita, 1982

$400 and less
$401 to $1,635
$1,636 to $5,500
More than $5,500
No data

SOURCE: World Bank, *The World Bank Atlas 1985* (Washington, DC: The World Bank, 1985), 20, 22.

Patterns of Economic Alliances.   As with the political systems of the world, so with economics: the peoples of the world have attempted to organize themselves so that there will never be another worldwide depression in which the world goes hungry. Since the end of World War II, many economic organizations have been set up, some of them more ambitious than others. Some have survived and prospered; others have disappeared. The world is divided into two major economic blocks. In the West is the Organization of Economic Cooperation and Development (OECD), and in the East is the Council for Mutual Economic Assistance (COMECON). Recently a rather loosely organized collection of developing and nonaligned countries was formed. Although the group now numbers more than 120, it is still called the Group of 77, or G77, after the original seventy-seven founding members.

THE MICROENVIRONMENT

The microenvironment has been defined as a particular organization's external business environment. As it is virtually impossible to thoroughly study the entire macroenvironment, managers are obliged to narrow their focus to that portion of the macroenvironment which either facilitates or hinders the organization's pursuit of profitable opportunities. Only then can they feasibly do something with it—that is, use it for the purpose of accomplishing organizational objectives.

The main reason for being concerned with the microenvironment stems from the necessity to provide an adequate answer to the following question: How does the macroenvironment affect the quality of particular managerial decisions? It was mentioned in Chapter 1 that the quality of managerial decisions is measured by the difference between the intended results and the actual results: The smaller the difference, the higher the quality of the decisions made by the management. The quality of managerial decisions is influenced by two sets of variables: the controllable variables (the possible) and the uncontrollable variables (the probable). The possible represents the organization's strengths and weaknesses; the probable represents the state of nature or the external environment. Organizational objectives (the preferable) are set by matching the possible with the probable—that is, by matching the organization's capabilities with the environment's capacities.

The manager assesses the company's strengths and weaknesses by performing an internal audit of its physical, monetary, and human resources or assets. This assessment is a relatively simple matter; most managers have considerable experience with this task. Assessing the external business environment, however is not as easy as assessing the firm's strengths and weaknesses. To begin with, the manager has much less control over the external environment. Second, because in the past the external environment could often be expected to play a positive role in the corporate strategy-setting process, many managers still tend to assume that "What is good for the company is good for the society." Today, assessing the impact of the environment on the firm's ability to survive and prosper is the most difficult task facing managers of every kind of organization.

Multinational corporations use a variety of methods to assess the external environment, or do what was called in the past environmental forecasting. These methods range from the so-called grand tours by a team of high-ranking executives to the "old hands approach" of having company experts prepare reports on an area's political, economic, and social conditions to the Delphi method of analyzing expert opinions, quantitative econometric models, and simulation exercises and role playing. Most MNCs limit their aspirations to simply obtaining some type of quantitative measure of the risk involved in venturing abroad.[11]

Though this book recognizes that an attempt to assess the risk of a foreign strategy is very important, its focus is the broader concept of environmental scanning. The purpose of **environmental scanning** is to gain an adequate understanding of the environment in which the MNC contemplates involvement, to enable the management of the company to minimize the potential political and economic risks as well as to detect opportunities for further profitable involvement.

This book will follow the well-established and accepted contemporary management practice of treating the external environment as a set of "emerging issues." This approach, known as **issues management,** was originally developed by the International Planners Association and was subsequently adopted and further refined by corporate executives and expert consultants as well as by academics. Joseph F. Coates, President of J. F. Coates, Inc., one of the pioneers and perhaps the best known consultant in issues management, describes the technique this way:

> Within the past decade, issues management, a new form of futures research, has taken hold in corporate America. It is rapidly spreading to trade and professional associations and is beginning to be effectively applied in federal, state, and local government planning. *Issues management* is the organized activity of identifying emerging trends, concerns, or issues likely to affect an organization in the next few years and developing a wider and more positive range of organizational responses toward that future. Business and industry, in adopting issues management, seek to formulate creative alternatives to constraints, regulations, or confrontation. Often in the past, the awareness of a trend, a new development, or the possibility of new constraints came too late to frame anything but a reactive response.[12]

---

[11]Charles W. Hofer and Terry P. Haller, "GLOBSCAN: A Way to Better International Risk Assessment," *Journal of Business Strategy* 1, No. 2 (Fall 1980). For a good treatment of country risk assessment and helpful advice on how to design a system to do it, see Ingo Walter, "Country Risk Assessment," in *Handbook of International Business* (New York: John Wiley and Sons, 1982), Ch. 21.

[12]J. F. Coates, *Issues Management: How You Can Plan, Organize, and Manage for the Future* (Mt. Airy, MD: Lamont Publications, 1986).

The remainder of this chapter will be devoted to a description of a computer package called ENSCAN, developed by the author.[13] The package is not intended to provide a foolproof or complete system for environmental scanning. Rather, its purpose is to help the manager become personally involved in performing an environmental scan. As with most managerial activities, there is no substitute for personal involvement in environmental scanning.

THE ENSCAN ASSISTANT EXPERT SYSTEM

The ENSCAN expert system is one of the least ambitious expert systems. It attempts to replicate an *assistant's* contribution to the problem of environmental scanning for a multinational corporation. For this reason the system focuses mostly on the mechanics of scanning. Most of the creative part of the scanning process is left to the individual manager who, alone or as a member of a group, constitutes the expert.[14]

Exhibit 3-7 diagrams the main components of the expert system: component A, the database; component B, the knowledge base; and component C, the inference engine.

COMPONENT A: THE DATABASE

The data for this expert system are the manager's perceptions of the external business environment. These perceptions should be expressed as a set of emerging issues. The user of this system has two ways of creating a set of emerging issues: mode A, which is structured, and mode B, which is unstructured.

Mode A: Structured.   In the structured mode the user scans the environment by responding to a number of questions chosen by the designer of the system and organized in a framework known as STEPE. The emerging issues are arranged along a continuum, starting with social issues and ending with economic issues. The basic theory behind this framework is that issues develop first in the social sphere. Social issues translate into technological issues, for social developments are often accommodated by the discovery of new ways of assisting humans via technological mechanisms. Technological developments will sooner or later create some ecological issues, as the use of technology creates additional demands on the ecosystem's life-support and waste-carrying capacities. Ecological issues will trigger political debates on the solutions and will, therefore, eventually develop into political issues. Finally,

---

[13]For a more detailed description of ENSCAN, see Schoderbek, Schoderbek, and Kefalas, Ch. 13.

[14]Literature on artificial intelligence and expert systems has grown to massive proportions. See, for example, E. Faigenbaum and P. McCormick, *The Fifth Generation* (Reading, MA: Addison-Wesley, 1983); Paul Harmon and David King, *Expert Systems: Artificial Intelligence in Business* (New York: John Wiley and Sons, 1985).

Exhibit 3-7   ENSCAN: An Assistant Expert System

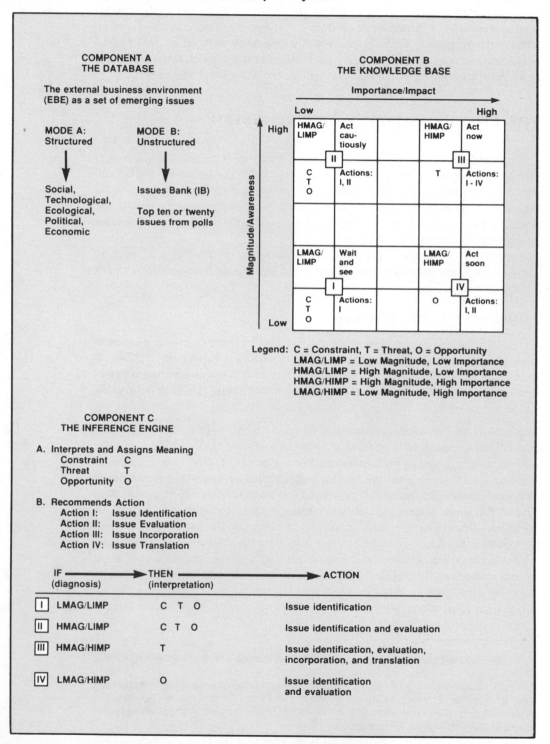

political issues are usually resolved via legislation, which will eventually create economic consequences; thus political issues become economic issues.[15]

Mode B: Unstructured.   In the unstructured mode the user has the choice of either inputting his or her own issues by listing them one after another or selecting a number of issues from an issue databank provided by the system. This databank contains the latest top ten or twenty issues identified by public polling companies, associations, newsletters, and other organizations specializing in issues management.

COMPONENT B: THE KNOWLEDGE BASE

The knowledge base consists of two types of information. Type A knowledge is the facts of the domain. Included here is the widely shared knowledge, commonly accepted among practitioners, that is expressed in textbooks and journals and discussed in classrooms, seminars, and workshops. Type B knowledge is often called heuristics. This knowledge encompasses good practices and good judgment in a field—the information gleaned from trial-and-error efforts by concerned theoreticians and practitioners. It is experiential knowledge, the art of good guessing that a human expert perfects over years of conceptual and empirical work.

ENSCAN uses knowledge from the domain of issues management and heuristics that have been developed by experts in the field. In the field of issues management, scanning the environment is conceived of as a four-step process involving identification, evaluation, incorporation, and translation.

Step One: Issue Identification.   In step one the main task is to make some sense of the environment by identifying a few relevant issues. This step is the easiest one because the efforts exerted by organizations thus far have concentrated on developing techniques for monitoring and identifying key issues.

Step Two: Issue Evaluation.   As one moves through the four steps of the process, the tasks become progressively more difficult. The evaluation step is, to some extent, the key to the entire process. Here issues that have been identified as being worthy of monitoring and assessing are judged for their relevance to the organization's short-term survival and long-term prosperity and growth.

Futures research is a field that offers considerable help with this task. Futures research has developed numerous methods for assessing the "importance,

---

[15]For an investigation of a similar framework, see J. J. O'Connell and J. W. Zimmerman, "Scanning the International Environment," *California Management Review* XXII, No. 2 (Winter 1979), 15-23; reprinted in Heidi Vernon Wortzel and L. H. Wortzel, *Strategic Management of Multinational Corporations: The Essentials* (New York: John Wiley and Sons, 1985). For a similar framework, see F. T. Haner, *Global Business: Strategy for the 1980s* (New York: Praeger, 1980); K. Ohmae, *The Mind of the Strategist: Business Planning for Competitive Advantage* (New York: Penguin Books, 1980), Ch. 13.

relevance, impact, weight, ... and so on"[16] of issues and trends for an organization's internal workings. ENSCAN employs a simple method known as MIM. Issues in ENSCAN are evaluated by asking users of the system to assess the following:

(1)   The *magnitude* of the issue (MAG)—the amount of attention the issue receives by the public media

(2)   The *importance* of the issue (IMP)—the perceived degree of impact the issue will have on the organization

(3)   The *meaning* of the issue—the perceived degree of urgency of the issue. Three degrees of urgency are used: Constraint (C), Threat (T), and Opportunity (O).

User evaluations of an issue are organized in an MIM matrix whose two dimensions are magnitude/awareness and importance/impact. Depending on the position of a given issue within the magnitude/awareness and importance/impact matrix, it is judged to be a constraint, a threat, or an opportunity. Finally, based on this judgment certain actions are recommended.

Step Three: Issue Incorporation.   Issues are incorporated into the strategic planning process in the form of scenarios depicting possible states of the environment and their impact on the corporation's goals and strategies. In this step of the process, the top five or ten issues are chosen as the basis for three scenarios. An *optimistic* scenario will represent the situation in which the environment is most favorable to the corporation's goal-seeking strategies. A *pessimistic* scenario will represent the worst situation, and a *most likely* scenario will describe a middle-of-the-road situation.

Step Four: Issue Translation.   Scenarios describing the nature of the environment and its impact on the organization must be translated into specific *consequences* for the organization. These consequences represent quantitative measurements of the environment's impact on the organization's *inputs* (resources), *processes* (production of the goods or services), and *outputs* (products or services). These quantitative measurements must be presented in the same language as is used in the internal audit of the company's strengths and weaknesses. Such translation of environmental scenarios into corporate language is manifested in projections with respect to the data contained in the corporation's main reporting instruments, such as income statements (P&L), balance sheets, and the various operating statements.

---

[16]See, for example, R. Amara and A. J. Lipinski, *Business Planning for an Uncertain Future: Scenarios and Strategies* (New York: Pergamon Press, 1983).

COMPONENT C: THE INFERENCE ENGINE

Inference engines in expert systems perform two functions: they interpret or diagnose the database using the knowledge base, and they recommend or prescribe actions. The inference engine is in reality a set of rules that translate into "if-then" statements, such as "If A is given, then B must be the case, and for this reason C is recommended."

As noted, in ENSCAN, issues are diagnosed in accordance with their position in the magnitude/awareness (MAG) and importance/impact (IMP) matrix. Issues at the lower left-hand side of the matrix are characterized by low MAG and low IMP. These are issues that have attracted little attention from the media or awareness on the part of the issue monitor; in addition these issues must be perceived as having a low impact on the organization. The inference engine assigns one of three meanings—C, T, or O—to such issues and recommends simply continuing to identify them. No further movement along the four-step process is recommended.

Issues that fall in the upper left-hand side of the matrix are high MAG, low IMP issues. They are at the center of media attention, but managers expect them to have a low impact on the organization's present and future objectives, strategies, and plans of action. These issues also are categorized as either constraints, threats, or opportunities. For such issues the inference engine recommends that the organization continue to perform only the first two steps of the process: identification and evaluation.

The third possibility is for an issue to fall in the upper right-hand corner of the matrix, when it is judged to have both a high MAG and a high IMP. Such issues are the hottest and the most urgent ones. The inference engine interprets them as threats and recommends immediate action along the four steps of the process: the identified issues should be more carefully evaluated using a well-known technique such as cross impact analysis, trend impact analysis, or the Delphi method and then incorporated and translated.

Finally, in the lower right-hand side of the matrix are issues that have a high IMP and low MAG. These issues are interpreted by the inference engine as opportunities, and continuation of actions I and II—identification and evaluation—is recommended.

RECAPITULATION

This chapter described the second half of the organization-environment interaction system. For the international manager, the environment consists of the interplay between humans and their natural habitats. Understanding the environment and its impact on MNCs' present and future survival requires that the international manager first comprehend the physical world which is the life support system of the humans who occupy it.

Under the heading Macroenvironment the chapter first described the physical world in terms of its resource-supplying capabilities (ability to supply food, minerals, energy, and oil) and its waste-carrying capacities (ability to absorb pollution). The human element of the macroenvironment was then discussed in terms of both its quantitative aspects and its cultural dimension.

The microenvironment is a particular organization's external business environment. In order to effectively assess the macroenvironment's potential impact on the organization, the manager must narrow his or her focus to the microenvironment. The recommended method of assessing the microenvironment, which will be used in subsequent chapters, is environmental scanning (ES). The environmental scanning approach to assessing the environment offers many advantages. It forces the international manager not only to keep an eye on developments that take place in the environment but also to try to evaluate them and incorporate the results of this evaluation into the strategic planning of the corporation. In addition, unlike the conventional approach of purchasing an environmental report and "plugging it into" the strategic-planning process, environmental scanning motivates the manager to become personally involved in the assessment, thereby becoming more knowledgeable.

Recent advances in artificial intelligence have allowed the development of systems that mimic and to some extent replicate the decision-making process of experts. The ENSCAN Assistant Expert System described in this chapter provides the international manager with a simple but adequate method for understanding and assessing the environment. The system uses issues management, a conceptual framework developed by corporate planners and public affairs officers of some of the world's largest and most progressive corporations.

REVIEW QUESTIONS

(1)   Define the term "environment."

(2)   Define and differentiate between "macroenvironment" and "microenvironment."

(3)   There is considerable controversy as to whether the earth can support the number of people occupying it. Neo-Malthusians make a case for the finiteness of the earth's carrying capacities and insist that soon most minerals will be depleted. Refute or support that argument.

(4)   With respect to the earth's pollution-absorption capacities, some people believe that the end is near. They argue that human and industrial waste cannot continue to pollute the earth and its atmosphere any longer without severe consequences which will have profound implications for humans and corporations. Make a case for or against this argument.

(5)   Most international managers are advised to avoid discussing the religion of those in a host country. Yet the case was made in this chapter that religion is a very important determinant of managerial decision making. How would you advise a manager to approach this sensitive aspect of international business?

(6)   Politics is another subject that international managers are advised not to talk about. Yet the manager must learn as much about a country's political system as possible, and some of this knowledge must come from discussions with citizens of the host country. What approach would you suggest a manager take in such discussions?

(7)   The data presented in this chapter clearly prove that the majority of the people of the world live below a subsistence level. Do you think that the multinational corporation has a responsibility to assist people in rising above a subsistence level? Imagine you are an officer of an MNC, and write a one-page speech to be delivered at the next annual meeting to help stockholders see that the MNC does have such a responsibility.

(8)   You have just been hired by a multinational corporation that is in the industrial safety equipment business. Develop a list of emerging issues you must monitor.

(9)   MNC, Inc. has decided to move its manufacturing facilities to a Third World country. Among the reasons that management offered to its employees for making the move is that the company must invest "sizeable sums of money for pollution abatement equipment as required by the new antismog law." Imagine you are an officer of the employees' union, and write a one-page speech to management explaining to them that the corporation may have to spend the same amount of money wherever it goes.

(10)   Students for Responsible Business Practices (SREBPS) have staged a sit-in in front of the main gate of your company. They are carrying signs saying "Get out of that fascist country," "Stop helping the minority government kill innocent people," and "Americans should not stand for that kind of corporate behavior. Get out now!" Write a short statement to be read to the students explaining to them that your company "stays out of politics."

SUGGESTED READINGS

Ball, Donald, and W. H. McCulloch. *International Business: Introduction and Essentials,* Third Edition. Plano, TX: Business Publications, 1988.

Boughey, Arthur S. *Fundamentals of Ecology.* Scranton, PA: Intext Educational Publishers, 1971.

Brown, L. R. *State of the World: 1987.* New York: W. W. Norton, 1987.

Cantor, Robert D. *Contemporary International Politics.* St. Paul, MN: West Publishing Co., 1986.

Chase, H. *Issues Management.* Stamford, CT: Issue Action Publications, 1986.

Disbury, H. F. *The Global Economy: Today and the Transition.* Bethesda, MD: World Future Society, 1985.

Kidron, Michael, and Ronald Segal. *The New State of the World Atlas.* New York: Simon and Schuster, 1984.

Kolde, Endel-Jakob. *Environment of International Business,* Second Edition. Boston: Kent Publishing Co., 1985.

Korth, Christopher M. *International Business: Environment and Management* Second Edition. Englewood Cliffs, NJ: Prentice-Hall, 1985.

Moyer, Reed. *International Business: Issues and Concepts.* New York: John Wiley and Sons, 1984.

Our Magnificent Earth: A Rand McNally Atlas of Earth Resources. New York: Rand McNally and Co., 1985.

Robock, Stefan H., and Kenneth Simmonds. *International Business and Multinational Enterprises,* Third Edition. Homewood, IL: R. D. Irwin, 1983.

Ronen, Simcha. *Comparative and Multinational Management.* New York: John Wiley and Sons, 1986.

Terpstra, Vern, and K. David. *The Cultural Environment of International Business,* Second Edition. Cincinnati, OH: South-Western Publishing Co., 1985.

Vernon, Raymond, and L. T. Wells, Jr. *Manager in the International Economy,* Fourth Edition. Englewood Cliffs, NJ: Prentice-Hall, 1981.

The World Almanac and Book of Facts. New York: Newspaper Enterprise Association, 1986.

World Bank. *The World Bank Atlas 1985.* Washington, DC: The World Bank, 1985.

EMERGING ISSUE 3: The State of the World: Crossing Some Perceptual Thresholds

"You know Jim," said Maggie, "I don't think this stuff here in my *Geography and Development* book is right ... at least not anymore. It might have been right back then, but it doesn't really make any sense. I mean, look at this Demographic Transformation Model. It says that a society goes through four stages of population transformation. In the first stage both birth and death rates are high, and for this reason population growth rates are low and the number of people is also low. Then in the second stage both birth and death rates decline. Death rates decline because of scientific developments which eradicate most of the infant diseases. The decline in the infant death rate results in an increase in the population growth rate and the population level. In the third stage the decline in the death rate levels off and the birth rate declines sharply, so there is an overall decline in the population growth rate. Finally, in the fourth stage birth and death rates level off and equal each other, causing the population growth rate to reach zero and the population level to stabilize."

Jim was looking at the graphical presentation (Exhibit E3-1) while he listened to what Maggie was saying. "Well," he asked, "what's wrong with it? It seems to me to make a lot of sense. I mean, that's exactly what happened in this country. I remember my grandmother's telling me that she had a bunch of brothers and sisters, something like ten or twelve. My mother came from a large family of five. I have only one younger sister. So I really think that this model is a rather good description of how societies develop. As the world makes technological and economic progress, most people reproduce less and less."

"That's just it," interrupted Maggie. "You said it: most people—not all people, but most. It seems to me it's the other way around. Most people in the world do not get past the first stage. They get trapped in the high birth rate and high death rate circle. The more babies they have, the more of them die, because they don't have the money to buy drugs and food for their children. I think they ought to have a stage in this model called the Demographic Trap. I think most of us here in the United States misunderstand things. Just because *we* developed that way, from an agrarian or rural society with high birth and death rates to a highly industrial and even post-industrial society, books lead us to believe that Asia and Africa will develop the same way. The truth is that people in Asia and Africa will never get out of this Demographic Trap. I saw some really horrid things on the tube about life in those parts of the world."

A few days later Jim came home with a ton of books under his arms. He had the last three years' issues of *World Development Reports* from the World Bank; the Worldwatch Institute's *State of the World* reports; The Hunger Project's *Ending Hunger: An Idea Whose Time Has Come;* the latest *Freedom at Issue* and the *Map of Freedom Report* from Freedom House; the latest reports of the World Resources Institute/International Institute for Environment and

Exhibit E3-1   Demographic Transformation Model

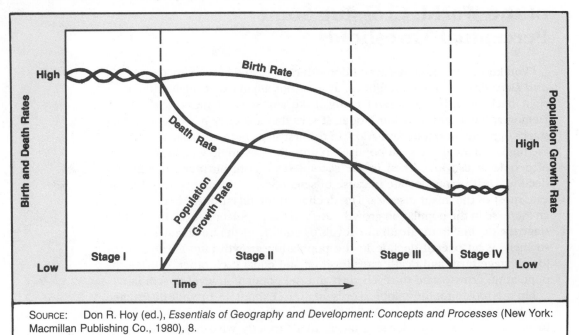

SOURCE: Don R. Hoy (ed.), *Essentials of Geography and Development: Concepts and Processes* (New York: Macmillan Publishing Co., 1980), 8.

Development; and several reports from the International Monetary Fund on the international debt crises.

The more Jim read on the state of the world and its physical and human systems, the more he began to realize that Maggie had a really good point with her Demographic Trap. As a matter of fact, he started identifying some other traps. In particular, Jim found *The State of the World 1987: A Worldwatch Institute Report on Progress Toward a Sustainable Society* extremely interesting. The back cover of the report highlighted some of the key issues.

Our relationship with the earth and its natural systems is changing, often in ways that we do not understand. The scale of human activities threatens the habitability of the earth itself. A sustainable society satisfies its needs without diminishing the prospects of the next generation. But by many measures, contemporary society fails to meet this criterion.

State of the World 1987 examines the counterpoint of urgency and uncertainty that has come to dominate world affairs in an age when the environmental consequences of human activities transcend national boundaries. . . .

The 1987 report assesses human-caused disruptions of global chemical cycles; evaluates the worldwide reappraisal of nuclear power after the Chernobyl accident; profiles the accelerating urbanization of the world's population; discusses the shift to reliance on markets in a growing number of countries; and advocates new initiatives in recycling materials and raising agricultural productivity.

Further reading elsewhere brought more facts to light:

Economic activity could be approaching a level where further growth in gross world product costs more than it is worth.

By 2000, three out of the five cities with populations of 15 million or more will be in the Third World.

More than half the cities in the United States will exhaust their current landfills by 1990.

Climate change could carry a global price tag of $200 billion for irrigation adjustments alone.

The existing scientific effort falls short of what is needed to assess the impacts of human activity on the global environment.

For some of the major adjustments facing humanity, a relatively small number of countries hold the key to success.

Jim was impressed and disturbed. He drew up a list of some traps he had identified and handed it to Maggie after their economics class. Jim divided the traps into three main categories.

Category A: Global Traps:

The Nuclear Trap

The Carbon Trap

The Acid Rain Trap

The Ozone Trap

The Deforestation Trap

The Desertification Trap

The Soil Erosion Trap

The Fresh Water Trap

The Trade Trap

The Slow Growth Trap

Category B: Developed World Traps:

The Overcapacity Trap

The Growth Engine Trap

The Dollar Trap

The Underreproduction Trap

Category C: Developing World Traps:

The Demographic Trap

The Hunger Trap

The Lack of Economic Development Trap

The Liquidity Trap

The Export Development Trap

The Cash Crop Trap

The Survival Trap

Maggie looked over Jim's list and got really upset, but since she had to write a paper on the general international business environment for her international business class, she decided to do some research on the positive things that are happening which might eliminate some of these traps.

For the next few days Maggie hit the library. She had found the term "perceptual thresholds" in one of Jim's references and liked it. A perceptual threshold was defined as the point where "enough people perceive the threat for a cogent response to emerge." Maggie thought that with all this talk about environmental conscience, the Green Party movement in Europe and other parts of the world, and the like, she might be able to identify some perceptual thresholds regarding the natural environment.

After a lot of research Maggie came up with enough evidence to write a paper highlighting humanity's concern for what she termed "A Better Global Habitability."

Maggie sat in front of her computer and started listing the evidence she would discuss in her paper:

Harvard University's National Forum on Biodiversity

International Geosphere-Biosphere Program

Global Change Program of the International Council of Scientific Unions (ICSU)

NASA's Global Habitability Project

United Nations' Fund for Population Activities (UNFPA)

World Future Society's Global Solutions

What Maggie noticed in her research was that the greatest turning point is the recognition that a rekindling of progress now depends on a careful integration of economics, population, and environmental policies. In addition, Maggie observed a trend toward greater cooperation between governments and the business world. In September of 1986, for instance, a chlorofluorocarbons (CFC) industry group, the Alliance for Responsible CFC Policy, announced that its 500 members were prepared to support international limits on CFC production. Maggie closed her preliminary list of perceptual thresholds and turning points with the following excerpt from *Trend Letter,* John Naisbitt's newsletter:[17]

From Nation State to Business State: Redefining Roles

We noticed recently one more indication of an interesting trend in the global economy: 16 major multinational companies, based in the U.S., Canada and Europe, banded together to provide free technical advice and to lend experts to foreign governments coping with critical environmental problems.

---

[17]*Trend Letter*, October 2, 1986 (Washington, DC: The Global Network, Inc.), 2–3.

Tenneco, Dow Chemical, Weyerhauser, USX and 3M are among U.S.-based firms involved in this global effort, sharing expertise under the umbrella of the newly formed International Environmental Bureau, based in Geneva.

. . . Now we're seeing examples of private-sector involvement with other nations—corporations interacting with foreign powers. . . . I think private enterprise, and even nonprofit organizations such as the International Environmental Bureau, will become increasingly involved in interactions across national borders. Joint research ventures like the Boeing-Japan development project, for example, will become commonplace. Boundaries between political entities and corporate bodies will be blurred.

Government diplomacy and treaties won't vanish, of course. But in both domestic and international affairs, the roles of government and business will be completely redefined.

The nation state–business state movement is particularly promising for the potential it has toward ensuring world stability. One country is less likely to attack another if their business communities are integrally involved.

The trend could be our best shot for peace.

ISSUE FOR DISCUSSION

Support or refute the notion that getting out of one's own trap is equivalent to providing somebody else with an opportunity—for example, the Overcapacity Trap can be solved by making excess capacity available to the people who are caught in the Hunger Trap.

Nothing is more practical than a good theory.

Albert Einstein

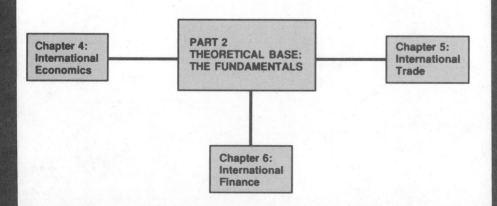

CONNECTIVE SUMMARY

The introductory chapters in Part 1 were designed to familiarize the reader with the field of international business and its main actors. As Chapter 1 demonstrated, the field of international business is very diverse, involving people and corporations that exchange goods and services across national boundaries and invest the profits of their efforts either by buying government and corporate stocks and bonds, real estate, and other types of property or by setting up new factories and offices. Although the main participants in these activities are individual citizens of a given country, a great deal of international business is conducted through interactions between large private or semi-private corporations and agencies of the governments of the countries involved. In international business nomenclature the corporation is known as a multinational corporation or an MNC, and the government agency represents the nation-state or the state. Thus the subject of inquiry in this book is the MNC–nation-state interaction system.

The three chapters that constitute Part 2, Theoretical Base, are designed to acquaint the reader with the fundamentals. Every human endeavor involves the application of basic knowledge. The construction of a large highway or a port, for example, is an expression of basic principles of physics; the civil engineer who supervises such a project must have learned the fundamentals of physics to be able to calculate the distances, curvatures, inclines and declines, and so forth. The science that serves as the basis for the international business discipline is **economics**—the study of scarce resources that have alternative uses. In its pure scentific mode, economics deals with a basic question at the center of international business: Why and how do people and their organizations make decisions to buy, sell, and invest in wealth-creating facilities?

The three chapters that follow aim at providing a brief exposure to the fundamentals of international economics. Chapter 4, International Economics, provides an overview of the workings of an open economy. The chapter focuses on the theoretical aspects of international economics rather than on the policy aspects. Chapter 5, International Trade, details the major characteristics of an exchange economy. Chapter 6, International Finance, is designed to familiarize the reader with the fundamentals of this complex subject. Few people can claim to fully understand the workings of international financial markets and their main players. Ironically, the miracle of the electronic revolution, the computer, which has helped most other human endeavors considerably, has made the acquisition, sale, exchange, and transfer of money almost unfathomably complex. Thus the aim of the chapter is to provide a basic exposure to the primary concepts and techniques which are the tools of the trade.

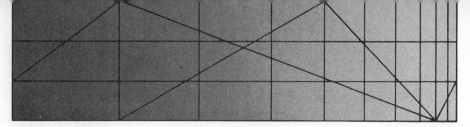

CHAPTER 4

INTERNATIONAL ECONOMICS

Economic deficits may dominate our headlines, but ecological deficits will dominate our future.

Lester Brown

The State of the World 1986 (New York: W. W. Norton, 1987).

OVERVIEW

International economics is the branch of economics concerned with the study of individual and organizational decision-making regarding the purchase and sale of *foreign* goods and services, investment in *foreign* corporate and government stocks and bonds, and the construction of new facilities or purchase of real estate in a *foreign* country. Thus, from the purely theoretical viewpoint, the first step in studying international economics is to develop a model of the economy as an open system. As such the economy will interact with other economies through the exchange of goods, services, money, and information.

In this chapter the conventional economic modeling process is used to describe first a closed economy and then an open economy characterized by a more or less free flow of goods, services, people, money, and information worldwide.

LEARNING OBJECTIVES

After studying the material in this chapter, the student should be familiar with the following concepts:

(1) International economics

(2) Circular flow diagram

(3) Basic components of aggregate demand

(4) Value added

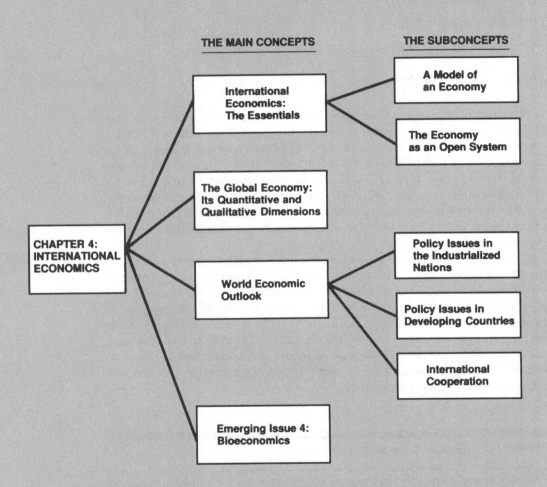

(5)   GNP = Y = C + I + G + N

(6)   OECD

(7)   *World Economic Outlook*

(8)   Development

(9)   Industrial countries

(10) Developing countries

INTRODUCTION

Traditionally, the international aspects of the United States economy have not been on the "most frequently discussed" list. Because the United States outstrips all other nations not only in the size of its economy but also in the abundance of its natural resources and the stability of its currency and government, people have tended to focus on the internal aspects of the economy. This lack of interest on the part of the general public does not mean, however, that the country's international position is not worthy of consideration. A view of the United States as self-sufficient and immune from international economic events is myopic.

The seventies ushered in unprecedented interest on the part of business in the United States' position in the world economy. Tremendous exposure by U.S. companies overseas (especially in the so-called Eurodollar market), coupled with substantial U.S. involvement in Vietnam, forced the U.S. government to abandon its traditional closed economy model and to adopt an open economy viewpoint. Since then the United States' vulnerability to external influences has been increasing. *The Report of the President's Commission on Industrial Competitiveness* (see Exhibit 4-1) makes it clear that concern with international economics in mounting.[1]

Exhibit 4-1   Global Competition

Americans are not used to the idea of comparing our economic strengths to those of our trading partners. Our unchallenged leadership position after World War II and our vast domestic economy have led us to ignore the competitive consequences of our actions—or our inaction.

Yet the environment in which American business operates has changed

---

[1] *Global Competition: The New Reality. The Report of the President's Commission on Industrial Competitiveness,* Volume 1 (Washington, DC: U.S. Government Printing Office, 1985).

dramatically over the past two decades. The interdependence of the U.S. economy with that of our trading partners, the rapid growth of opportunities in world markets, the transportability of technology, and the rise of aggressive new competitors—all these make improving our relative ability to compete in world markets an urgent priority.

Today, imports and exports represent twice as large a portion of our gross national product (GNP) as they did just two decades ago. Almost one-fifth of our industrial production is exported, and fully 70 percent of the goods we produce compete with merchandise from abroad. Quite simply, no longer is there a truly domestic U.S. economy. We are inextricably linked to our trading partners in countless important ways.

Since 1970, the total dollar volume of world trade has grown sevenfold. International trade is growing faster than the U.S. economy, and it represents a vast area of opportunity for American business. If we are to reap the benefits of this growth, our competitiveness is an urgent consideration.

The United States no longer commands an unchallenged lead. Our international competitors are closing the gap. Some slippage of our postwar dominance was both inevitable and desirable, since we need healthy trading partners. But we should be concerned about how rapidly the U.S. lead has diminished.

New competitors represent a final change in the global environment in which U.S. firms operate. Japan and the newly industrializing nations of the Pacific Rim—including Taiwan, South Korea, Singapore, Hong Kong, and Malaysia—now represent our major competitive arena. The United States now does more trade with these Pacific Rim countries than with all of Europe combined. If our trade in this arena continues to grow at its current rates, by 1995 America's trade with the Pacific Rim will be double the size of our European trade.

Technology is highly mobile, and these nations are aggressively applying it, along with their financial and human resources. They have benefited from governmental policies designed to nurture their export potential. These initiatives have distorted previous trade flows and constitute new rules of competition to which we have not yet responded effectively. Finally, our Pacific Rim competitors have focused attention on developing manufacturing expertise, and their products are often more attractive, in both price and quality, than our own.

SOURCE: *Global Competition: The New Reality. The Report of the President's Commission on Industrial Competitiveness,* Volume 1. (Washington, DC: U.S. Government Printing Office, 1985).

INTERNATIONAL ECONOMICS: THE ESSENTIALS

Three topics must be considered in any discussion of international economic matters: foreign buying, or imports; foreign selling, or exports; and foreign money exchange, or international financial transactions (international finance).

A MODEL OF AN ECONOMY

Economists think of an economy as a productive system that converts natural and human resources into products that are traded in an open market and are eventually consumed. Thus, the basic model of an economy consists of a production subsystem and a consumption subsystem. These two subsystems are at equilibrium when whatever is produced is actually consumed.

The basic concept used by economists to describe the production subsystem of an economy is the gross national product, or GNP.[2] The **GNP** is the sum of the money values of all final goods and services produced during a specific period of time, usually a year. The concept economists use to describe the consumption subsystem is aggregate demand. **Aggregate demand** is the total amount of money that all consumers, business firms, and government agencies wish to spend on all final goods and services. This aggregate demand disaggregates, so to speak, into its three constituent parts:

(1)   Consumer expenditures (consumption), designated by C

(2)   Investment spending (the sum of expenditures by business firms in new plants and equipment plus the expenditures of households on new homes), designated by I

(3)   Government purchases of goods and services, designated by G

A third main concept is national income. **National income** is the total income received by the citizens of a country for the services they perform. When taxes are excluded from national income, what remains is **disposable income**.

The interactions and relationships among these concepts are graphically represented in the circular flow diagram in Exhibit 4-2, which depicts the economic system as a set of tubes into which fluids are injected or from which they leak out. The three boxes in the center of the diagram represent the three main actors in the system—consumers, government, and business. The other two boxes represent the financial system, which accepts funds from consumers and pumps them into the aggregate demand, and investors, who channel the funds into the system to the firms that produce the gross national product.

---

[2]This discussion of essential concepts draws heavily on W. J. Baumol and A. S. Blinder, *Economics,* Third Edition (San Diego: Harcourt, Brace, Jovanovich, 1985).

Exhibit 4-2   The Circular Flow of Expenditure and Income

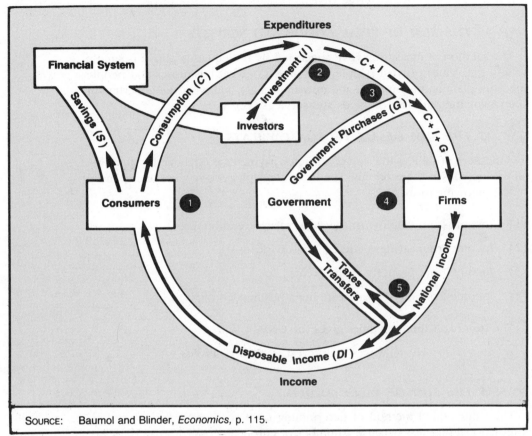

SOURCE: Baumol and Blinder, *Economics*, p. 115.

The upper half of this circular flow diagram depicts the flow of expenditures on goods and services, which comes from consumers (point 1), investors (point 2), and government (point 3) and goes to the firms that produce the output (point 4). The lower half of the diagram indicates how the income paid out by firms (point 4) flows to consumers (point 1), after some is siphoned off by the government in the form of taxes and part is replaced by transfer payments (point 5).

Ideally the system depicted in the diagram will be in equilibrium. That is to say, the production (supply) side will equal the consumption (demand) side:

$$Y = C + I + G$$

This equation states the first law of economics:

National product and national income must be equal.

Although there are no notable differences among definitions of the concept of GNP, there are quite a few differences in the ways nations measure this economic parameter. As a rule, however, most nations employ one of the following methods of measuring GNP.

GNP AS THE SUM OF FINAL GOODS AND SERVICES

The method of measuring GNP suggested by the equation above is simply to add the values of what people consume (C), what businesses and people invest in plant and equipment and new homes (I), and what the government spends for the purchase of goods and services (G).

GNP AS THE SUM OF ALL FACTOR PAYMENTS

A measure of GNP as the sum of all factor payments is obtained by summing all the incomes in the economy. The income people receive takes one or more of the following forms:

(1)   Income from employment (wages, salaries, and bonuses)

(2)   Income from savings (interest and dividends)

(3)   Income from property rental (rents)

(4)   Income from owning and running a business (profits)

The sum of all these incomes gives the GNP:

$$GNP = Wages + Interest + Rent + Profits$$

GNP AS THE SUM OF VALUE ADDED

The value added method of determining GNP is of particular interest to international business because a number of European countries use it for tax purposes. There is increasing talk of the United States' adopting this method of calculating GNP for taxation.

The **value added** by a firm is the revenues received from selling products, minus the amounts paid for goods and services purchased from other firms. According to the value added method of GNP estimation, the GNP is given by the sum of values added by all firms. Of course, what is added translates into the incomes received by the people and/or firms that participated in the process of successive additions of values. It follows, therefore, that

$$Value\ Added = Wages + Interest + Rents + Profits$$

so

$$GNP = Value\ Added = Wages + Interest + Rents + Profits$$

An example may help to illustrate the concept of value added. Suppose a farmer sells a bushel of soybeans for $3 to a miller, who grinds them and sells them for $4 to a factory, which makes soy sauce out of them and sells the soy sauce for $8 to a supermarket, which sells it to the consumer for $10. This product passes through three intermediate stages before it finally leaves the market by being consumed. In other words, in the course of the passage from the originator of the product (the farmer) to the end consumer (the customer), there are three points at which some value is added. These points are the miller's (value added = $1), the factory (value added = $4), and the supermarket (value added = $2). Add in the original value created by the farmer (value added = $3), to get the total value added of $10. The relationship between the price and the value added is illustrated in tabular form in Exhibit 4-3.

THE ECONOMY AS AN OPEN SYSTEM

As explained in the introduction to this chapter, North Americans have been used to treating the economy as a closed system. Traditionally the economy was considered to encompass only the goods and services produced by the people in a given country, which are then consumed by the same people. No interaction with the rest of the world was incorporated into the model; it was assumed that the people of the country, under the direction of the country's government, produce and consume whatever they need.

Today's economies, however, are not closed to external interactions. A rather substantial portion of the products and services produced in a country find their way to some other country. By the same token, a fairly large portion of the goods and services consumed by a country come from places several thousands of miles away.

To account for new sources of production and consumption—the international market—our model of the closed economy must be expanded on both sides of the equilibrium equation. In other words, our equilibrium condition

$$Y = C + I + G$$

Exhibit 4-3   An Illustration of Value Added

Item	Seller	Buyer	Price Paid	Value Added
Bushel of soybeans	Farmer	Miller	$ 3	$ 3
Bag of soy meal	Miller	Factory	$ 4	$ 1
Gallon of soy sauce	Factory	Supermarket	$ 8	$ 4
Gallon of soy sauce	Supermarket	Consumer	$10	$ 2
Total			$25	$10

SOURCE: Baumol and Blinder, *Economics*, p. 137.

**Exhibit 4-4   U.S. Gross National Product in 1987 as the Sum of
Final Demand**

Item	Amount (in billions of $)		Percentage of Total GNP
Personal consumption expenditures (C)	2967.8		66.1
Gross private domestic investment (I)	717.5		15.9
Government purchases of goods and services (G)	922.8		20.6
Net Exports (N)	−119.6		
Exports (X)		427.8	9.3
Imports (M)		547.4	12.2
Gross National Product (C + I + G + N)	4488.5		100.0

SOURCE: *Survey of Current Business*, May 1988, p. 4.

(output equals expenditures) must be changed so as to reflect the added source of output as well as the added source of consumers.

Closed Economy: Total Available Output = GNP = Y
                  Total Expenditures   = C + I + G

Open Economy: Total Available Output = GNP = Y + Imports (M)
                  Total Expenditures   = C + I + G + Exports (X)

In other words, imports (M) represent additions to the domestic output (payments) which increase the total available output. Exports (X), on the other hand, represent increases in the total expenditures (incomes). Thus, the final position of the GNP in an open economy will depend on the *net* effect of the transactions—that is, the difference between imports and exports.

The net effect of international transactions on domestic GNP can be represented as imports minus exports (M − X), or N. Thus, the GNP in an open economy is represented by the sum C + I + G + N.

Exhibit 4-4 shows the U.S. GNP for 1987. As the table shows, the end result of the international transactions of the United States for that year was negative (a deficit): − $119.6 billion. As a result of this deficit, the GNP was $4488.5 billion.

THE GLOBAL ECONOMY: ITS QUANTITATIVE AND QUALITATIVE DIMENSIONS

The global economy is the sum total of all the national economies. Just as national economies must be in some kind of equilibrium, so the global economy's product must equal the global economy's income. In other words, what is true for the national economy must be true for the global economy:

Global product and global income must be equal.

The global economy operates much like a national economy. Thus, the circular flow diagram shown in Exhibit 4-2 can also be used to represent the global economy. The main difference is, of course, the tremendous diversity among the three main actors in the global economy—namely, the consumers, the producers (the firms), and the governments. Although the functions performed by these main actors are the same on the global scale as they are on a national scale, their degree of participation in both the production and the consumption of their products varies.

Statistics used to provide a quantitative measure of the global economy and to explain some of its qualitative dimensions are not very reliable. Because the intention here is to promote an understanding of the magnitude of the phenomenon rather than to settle any conceptual or empirical questions or disputes, the reader should understand that the data to follow are not definitive but merely illustrative.

Researchers and practitioners who are concerned with gaining an accurate understanding of the world economy use three main concepts to do so: population, income, and resources. The logic behind this emphasis is that people are both the producers and the consumers of resources. Thus, when population increases so does the opportunity for greater production and consumption of resources.

Exhibit 4-5 summarizes data on the earth's people and their incomes for 1975 and gives projections for the year 2000. Between 1975 and 2000 the world's population is expected to increase 55%, from 4090 million to 6351 million; the world's GNP is expected to more than double, from $6025 to $14,677 billion in constant 1975 dollars. The areas of the world that are expected to show the greatest increases in per capita income are expected to have the smallest population increases. A line drawn approximately at the level of the equator would divide the world into two very different halves: the upper half rich in money and poor in people, and the lower half poor in money and rich in people.

The dynamic agent within the rich industrialized world is the OECD. As noted in Chapter 3, the twenty-four countries of the OECD are a vital part of the world economy. Exhibit 4-6 reveals that the OECD countries, which make up less than 15% of the world population, account for some 65% of the gross world product. Within the OECD a small number of countries, called the Group of 7 or G7, (the United States, West Germany, France, Britain, Italy, the Netherlands, and Japan) account for some 86% of the OECD's product and 56% of the world's product.

Exhibit 4-7 shows the changes in the basic components of aggregate demand for the industrialized countries between 1977 and 1984. Western Europe experienced the greatest decline in private consumption (− 3.5 points), and the United States the least decline (− 0.9 of a point). Overall, Europeans

Exhibit 4-5   Population and Gross Global Product: Past, Present, and Future

| | Population | | | | | Gross National Product | | | | |
| | Millions | | Percentage Increase by 2000 | Percentage of World Total | | Millions | | Percentage Increase by 2000 | Percentage of World Total | |
	1975	2000		1975	2000	1975	2000		1975	2000
World	4090	6351	55	100	100	6025	14,677	144	100	100
More Developed Countries	1131	1323	17	28	21	4892	11,244	130	81	77
Less Developed Countries	2959	5028	70	72	79	1133	3452	205	19	24
Major Regions										
Africa	399	814	104	10	13	162	505	212	3	3
Asia and Oceania	2274	3630	60	56	57	697	2023	190	12	14
Latin America	325	637	96	8	10	326	1092	235	5	7
U.S.S.R. and Eastern Europe	384	460	20	9	7	996	2060	107	17	14
North America, Western Europe, Japan, Australia, and New Zealand	708	809	14	17	13	3844	8996	134	64	61
Selected Countries and Regions										
China	935	1329	42	23	21	286	718	151	5	5
India	618	1021	65	15	16	92	198	115	2	1
Indonesia	135	226	67	3	4	24	99	313	0	1
Bangladesh	79	159	101	2	3	9	19	111	0	0
Pakistan	71	149	110	2	2	10	21	110	0	0
Philippines	43	73	70	1	1	16	52	225	0	0
Thailand	42	73	74	1	1	15	48	220	0	0
South Korea	37	57	54	1	1	19	61	221	0	0
Egypt	37	65	76	1	1	12	38	217	0	0
Nigeria	63	135	114	2	2	23	94	309	0	1
Brazil	109	226	107	3	4	108	353	227	2	2
Mexico	60	131	118	1	2	71	233	228	2	2
United States	214	248	16	5	4	1509	3530	134	25	24
U.S.S.R.	254	309	22	6	5	666	1377	107	11	9
Japan	112	133	19	3	2	495	1158	134	8	8
Eastern Europe	130	152	17	3	2	330	682	107	5	5
Western Europe	344	378	10	8	6	1598	3740	134	27	25

SOURCE: *The Global 2000 Report to the President* (Washington, DC: U.S. Government Printing Office, 1980), 9, 15.

Exhibit 4-6   The Significance of the OECD

Countries	1983 GNP (in billions of $)	Percent	1984 GNP (in billions of $)	Percent	Percentage Increase 1983–84
Australia	155.52	1.99	172.50	2.11	10.92
Austria	67.13	0.86	64.90	0.79	− 3.32
Belgium	80.09	1.02	76.30	0.93	− 4.73
Canada	324.00	4.14	334.10	4.08	3.12
Denmark	56.36	0.72	55.10	0.67	− 2.24
Finland	49.39	0.63	51.60	0.63	4.47
France	519.21	6.63	496.80	6.07	− 4.32
Germany	653.08	8.34	616.10	7.53	− 5.66
Greece	34.53	0.44	33.00	0.40	− 4.43
Iceland	2.26	0.03	2.30	0.03	1.77
Ireland	17.96	0.23	17.60	0.22	− 2.00
Italy	352.84	4.51	352.30	4.31	− 0.15
Japan	1155.98	14.76	1233.50	15.08	6.71
Luxembourg	3.19	0.04	3.10	0.04	− 2.82
Netherlands	131.99	1.69	123.80	1.51	− 6.21
New Zealand	23.01	0.29	21.80	0.27	− 5.26
Norway	55.06	0.70	54.80	0.67	− 0.47
Portugal	20.67	0.26	19.70	0.24	− 4.69
Spain	158.15	2.02	160.40	1.96	1.42
Sweden	91.88	1.17	96.01	1.17	4.49
Switzerland	97.12	1.24	92.10	1.13	− 5.17
Turkey	49.72	0.63	47.90	0.59	− 3.66
United Kingdom	455.08	5.81	426.30	5.21	− 6.32
United States	3275.73	41.84	3627.90	44.35	10.75
OECD Total	7829.95	100.00	8179.91	100.00	4.47
Seven's Total	6764.76	86.40	6787.00	86.63	
World Total	12,000.00		12,500.00		4.17
OECD Share of World GNP		65.24		65.44	0.20
Seven's Share of World GNP		56.37		54.30	− 0.04

SOURCE: *The OECD Observer* 133 (March 1985), 13–20. Reprinted by permission of the OECD.

experienced the greatest decline in all major components of the GNP, and as a result their GNP declined by the largest amount (− 3.8 points). The United States is the "engine of growth" or the "locomotive" for the rest of the world, as indicated by the fact that the United States' imports jumped some 14.4 points during the years shown.

The statistics in Exhibit 4-7 indicate that all the main components of demand

Exhibit 4-7   Major Industrial Countries: Cumulative Increase in the Components of Demand

	North America			Japan			Four Major European Countries			Seven Major Industrial Countries		
	1977	1984	Difference	1977	1984	Difference	1977	1984	Difference	1977	1984	Difference
Private consumption expenditures (C)	111.0	110.1	−0.9	107.3	105.5	−1.8	106.0	102.5	−3.5	108.8	106.8	−2.0
Gross fixed investment (I)	121.3	131.3	10.0	107.6	107.5	−0.1	105.7	103.3	−2.4	113.8	117.6	3.8
Government current expenditures (G)	102.0	103.8	1.8	108.7	105.5	−3.2	104.6	103.9	−0.7	103.8	104.3	0.5
Total domestic demand	112.3	114.7	2.4	108.3	106.4	−1.9	108.2	104.0	−4.2	110.3	109.8	−0.5
Exports (X)	110.7	106.4	−4.3	132.5	127.6	−4.9	116.6	111.3	−5.3	115.8	111.5	−4.3
Imports (M)	128.1	142.5	14.4	109.0	112.3	3.3	118.3	110.1	−8.2	121.9	126.4	4.5
Net Exports (N = X − M)	−17.4	−36.1		23.5	15.3		−1.7	1.2		−6.1	−14.9	
GNP (C + I + G + N)	111.3	111.8	0.5	111.5	109.8	−1.7	108.2	104.4	−3.8	110.3	109.1	−1.2

Note: For 1977 statistics, 100 = figure for first half of 1975. For 1984 statistics, 100 = figure for second half of 1982.

Source: International Monetary Fund, *World Economic Outlook* (Washington, DC: IMF, 1986), 121.

(private consumption, investment, government expenditures, and net exports) have increased over the last few decades. In addition, the other component of the economy—population—has shown encouraging signs of a slowdown in growth.

In general, the global economy is essentially run by about ten industrialized countries, which combined account for over 60% of the world's output but no more than 15% of the world's population. When these countries prosper economically, almost everybody else prospers. Most of the world depends on the financing and the demand generated by these industrialized countries.

WORLD ECONOMIC OUTLOOK

Each year the International Monetary Fund (IMF), the world's overseer of international financial matters, publishes *World Economic Outlook,* which reviews events of the previous few years. The details of the report address the usual economic issues of output, employment, inflation, debts, and related indicators, but the underlying theme is development. In this context, development encompasses more than continuous economic growth. Exhibit 4-8

Exhibit 4-8   A New Definition of Development

By "development" we mean a *sustainable* process geared to the satisfaction of the needs of the *majority* of peoples, and not merely to the growth of things to the benefit of a minority. As summarized in the 1975 Dag Hammarskjold Report, *What Now,*

> Development is a whole; it is an integral, value-loaded, cultural process; it encompasses the natural environment, social relations, education, production, consumption, and well-being. The plurality of roads to development answers to the specificity of cultural or natural situations; no universal formula exists. Development is endogenous; it springs from the heart of each society, which relies first on its own strength and resources and defines in sovereignty the vision of its future, cooperating with societies sharing its problems and aspirations. At the same time, the international community as a whole has the responsibility of guaranteeing the conditions for the self-reliant development of each society, for making available to all the fruit of others' experience and for helping those of its members who are in need. This is the very essence of [a] new international order.

SOURCE: Ann Mattis (ed.), *A Society for International Development: Prospectus* (Durham, NC: Duke University Press, 1983), xiii.

---

summarizes the broader definition proposed by the Society for International Development.

Reports analogous to the IMF's *World Economic Outlook* are issued yearly by the World Bank, the OECD, private banks such as Barclays Bank, and other financial institutions such as Price Waterhouse, as well as by the International Chamber of Commerce. A fundamental concern of all of these organizations is the international community's ability and willingness to create the conditions for, as the United Nations puts it, "a world economy that works." The international manager thus has a rather diverse array of sources in which to seek advice.

The IMF's *Outlook* begins by describing the current situation and the short-term outlook in terms of output and employment, inflation and interest rates, and external adjustment and debt. Next comes an analysis of the medium-term prospects, broken down into assumptions, implications for the industrial countries, and implications for the developing countries. The outlook for the medium term is based on a scenario of economic developments five years into the future. This scenario is not a forecast, but rather an assessment of the consequences of certain assumptions about exogenous economic conditions, given other assumptions about the behavioral relations that link these conditions to actual developments. Third, suggestions are made with respect to macroeconomic and structural policies and policy coordination plans for both the industrial and the developing countries. Finally, efforts at international coordination and the role of the IMF are summarized. Following is a summary of some of the key points made in recent editions of the IMF's *Outlook,* which can serve as a valuable guide to any student of international business.

POLICY ISSUES IN THE INDUSTRIALIZED NATIONS

MACROECONOMIC POLICIES

In the past economic policies in the industrialized nations have focused on the restoration of financial stability, control of government expenditures, reduction of fiscal deficits, and facilitation of the working of private markets for goods, services, and factors of production. Increasingly in the United States, macroeconomic policies will reflect the government's determination to deal effectively with the problem of the federal deficit. It is hoped that new policies will free savings which may be channeled into private investment to offset the initial dampening of demand that is bound to follow restraint in government expenditures. If the United States is successful in reducing its deficit, other countries are likely to experience declining interest rates, lower inflation, and softer demand in which to frame their macroeconomic policies. West Germany and Japan, for example, may grow slightly faster than the United States.

STRUCTURAL POLICIES

Structural policies relate to the roles of the labor market and government in influencing the behavior of private industry. In the medium term, real wages are expected to decline, as employees accept lower wage settlements to avoid massive firings. Employer flexibility in substituting capital for labor is expected to increase. Governments are likely to assist businesses by using tax deductions to stimulate investment and lower relocation costs.

POLICY ISSUES IN DEVELOPING COUNTRIES

MACROECONOMIC POLICIES

The overriding objective of the macroeconomic policies of the developing countries will be to strengthen both net exports and domestic sources of growth. The primary strategy will be to further reduce the absorption of national savings by governments. In addition, governments will make efforts to establish realistic foreign exchange policies.

STRUCTURAL POLICIES

The first and foremost change that must be made in the structural policies of the developing nations is a reduction in the dependence on international trade taxes as a source of budgetary revenues. Second, pricing policies must become more flexible. Third, the efficiency and productivity of state enterprises must be increased, perhaps by reducing the government's channeling of investment into large and inefficient state concerns. Finally, import liberalization must become an integral part of structural policies.

INTERNATIONAL COOPERATION

The largest industrial countries have committed themselves to the pursuit of policies aimed at promoting cooperation, reducing exchange rate misalignment, combatting protectionism, strengthening growth, buttressing the adjustment efforts of the developing countries, and reforming the international monetary system. One of the most encouraging developments to emerge from this cooperation of the major industrial countries is the debt initiative introduced by the Secretary of the U.S. Treasury in October of 1985. This initiative combines the efforts of three sets of agents in the debt situation: those of the indebted countries, to improve the functioning of their economies; those of the multilateral development banks, to increase their disbursements to heavily indebted countries; and those of the commercial banks, to step up lending to these same countries.

There seems to be a fresh air of optimism blowing around the world, and most experts applaud the initiative taken by the major industrialized nations. Although global cooperation has not yet reached the level needed to alleviate global economic disasters, there is evidence that a critical mass has been reached. Enough momentum has been gained to suggest that we are indeed at the cutting edge of a true conceptual revolution, a revolution that is causing political leaders all over the world to follow the World Future Society's motto, "Think globally, act locally."

RECAPITULATION

This chapter identified the concepts and laws that serve as the framework within which the discipline of international business functions.

The first portion of the chapter dealt with the conceptual framework that economists use to explain the way an economy works. The economy was defined as a productive system that converts natural and human resources into consumable products. These products and services are exchanged via the market system, which acts as a clearinghouse for the goods and services demanded and supplied.

The economist's modeling process begins with the idea of an economy that is completely self-sufficient—that is, its industrial systems produce whatever quantities and qualities of goods and services its citizens demand, and the citizens in turn consume the entire production. In such a model the economy's total output equals the total of the expenditures of its citizens, businesses, and government ($Y = C + I + G$).

In reality, however, most economies today are open, as countries exchange goods and services with the rest of the world. Some of their production goes abroad, and some of their consumption is satisfied with products and services from abroad. Thus a fourth factor—imports and exports—must be added to the three components of the original model: $GNP = C + I + G + N$, where N is imports minus exports.

The second part of the chapter provided an overview of the quantitative and qualitative dimensions of the global economy, with an emphasis on population, income, and resources.

Finally, the last part of the chapter described the reports of the International Monetary Fund (IMF) on developments in international finance. In addition to current statistics, *World Economic Outlook* includes projections and recommendations.

REVIEW QUESTIONS

(1)   What is "international economics"?

(2)   List and briefly explain the basic concepts used by economists in describing the functioning of an economy.

(3)   State and briefly explain the first law of economics.

(4)   Explain the concept of value added, and show how it is used to measure the GNP of a country.

(5)   Explain the basic equation for the GNP in an open economy.

(6)   Obtain the most recent figures for the U.S. GNP and compare them to the ones shown in Exhibit 4-4.

(7)   Based on the data shown in Exhibit 4-5, write a one-page essay on

whether or not the world in the year 2000 will be "better" for people all over the world.

(8)   If you had a chance to live anywhere in the world predicted in Exhibit 4-5, where would you like to live and why?

(9)   The world has changed considerably since the projections of *The Global 2000 Report to the President* were made. How close is the world today to the projections described in Exhibit 4-5?

(10)   The last few years the leaders of the major industrialized countries who attend the annual summit meetings have tried to convince West Germany and Japan to increase their domestic consumption and growth in an effort to take the pressure off the United States. How successful have they been? In other words, if you were to update Exhibit 4-7 by adding a column for 1989, how much different would the figures be from those given for 1977 and 1984?

SUGGESTED READINGS

Bacon, Donald C. "Poor vs. Rich: A Global Struggle. A Special Report," *U.S. News & World Report,* July 31, 1978, 55–60.

Baumol, W., and A. S. Blinder. *Economics,* Third Edition. San Diego: Harcourt, Brace, Jovanovich, 1985.

Block, Kenneth L. "International Business Strategies for the Eighties." *From the Podium,* a publication of Beta Gamma Sigma, Winter 1982, 1-2.

Brown, L. *State of the World 1986: A Worldwatch Institute Report on Progress Towards a Sustainable Society.* New York: W. W. Norton and Co., 1986.

Didsbury, H. F., ed. *The Global Economy: Today, Tomorrow, and the Transition.* Bethesda, MD: World Future Society, 1985.

Elbo, Ricardo G., and Richard Alm. "Is the U.S. Headed for Another Recession?" *U.S. News & World Report,* July 1, 1985, 44-46.

Federal Reserve Bank of Atlanta. *Economic Review* LXXI, No. 6 (June/July 1986).

Global Competition: The New Reality. The Report of the President's Commission on Industrial Competitiveness. Washington, DC: U.S. Government Printing Office, 1985.

The Global 2000 Report to the President: Entering the Twenty-First Century, Volume One. Washington, DC: U.S. Government Printing Office, 1987.

The Hunger Project. *Ending World Hunger: An Idea Whose Time Has Come.* New York: Praeger, 1985.

Malabre, Alfred L., Jr. "U.S. Economy Grows Ever More Vulnerable to Foreign Influences." *The Wall Street Journal,* October 27, 1986, 1, 33.

Peterson, P. G. *Economic Nationalism and International Interdependence: The Global Costs of National Choices.* The 1984 PFR Jacobsson Lecture, George Washington University. Washington, DC: GWU Press, 1984.

Stewart, M. *The Age of Interdependence: Economic Policy in a Shrinking World.* Cambridge, MA: MIT Press, 1986.

U.S. Department of Commerce, International Trade Administration. *International Direct Investment—Global Trends and the U.S. Role.* Washington, DC: U.S. Government Printing Office, August 1984.

Vansag, Carl. "Foreigners Put Their Money on America." *U.S. News & World Report,* July 29, 1985, 45.

World Bank. *World Development Report 1986.* New York: Oxford University Press, 1986.

EMERGING ISSUE 4: Bioeconomics: A Challenge to International Economics?

Increasingly, economics—the study of scarce resources and their alternative uses by the occupants of the "oikos" (the house)—is coming under attack. Paul Samuelson, one of its leading practitioners, said, "The malaise from which the mandarins of economics are suffering is not imaginary. It is genuine."[3] Samuelson and others believe that traditional economics cannot deal adequately with and explain the behavior of the economy. If that accusation is true with respect to national economies, it is indisputable with respect to the global economy.

Traditional criticism of conventional economics by economists themselves ranges from Karl Marx's hostile rejection of the capitalistic economic model to John Kenneth Galbraith's mild challenge of contemporary economic wisdom. Most of the self-criticism that has come from the contemporary economists' camp leaves the basic premises of economics intact. Thus, the basic circular flow diagram is still considered a good explanation of how an economy works, and government intervention is still considered to be an adequate tool for managing an economy—to correct temporary or cyclical excesses of productive capacity, production, or even demand, the government need only change fiscal and monetary policies.

Bioeconomics is a completely new approach that challenges the conventional economic framework. A major methodological development in economics, bioeconomics represents an amalgam of economic theory, biology, and physics, especially thermodynamics. The father of this new hybrid discipline is Nicholas Georgescu-Roegen, Distinguished Professor of Economics Emeritus at Vanderbilt University.[4] Bioeconomists challenge the basic premises upon which the entire edifice of economics is based. Bioeconomists have diverse educational backgrounds and political beliefs, but they all agree on the inadequacy of conventional economics and share a new vision of economics, which they consider superior in its conceptual elegance and practical usefulness.[5]

Bioeconomists' challenge of the four pillars of conventional economic wisdom begins with rejection of the "fundamental illusion" that *growth* is the answer to all economic problems and its logical corollary that growth can go on forever in a more or less exponential fashion.

The second pillar of economics that is beginning to show signs of severe cracks, according to bioeconomists, is the idea that the *scarcity* of the natural

---

[3]H. F. Didsbury, Jr. (ed.), *The Global Economy: Today, Tomorrow, and the Transition* (Bethesda, MD: World Future Society, 1985).

[4]Nicholas Georgescu-Roegen, *The Entropy Law and the Economic Process* (Cambridge, MA: Harvard University Press, 1971).

[5]William H. Miernyk, "Bioeconomics: A Realistic Appraisal of Future Prospects," in H. F. Didsbury (ed.), *The Global Economy*, pp. 334–352.

resources currently used to create economic wealth is only a matter of price and for this reason constitutes no real problem.

The third pillar of conventional economic wisdom that is beginning to crumble is belief in the *infiniteness* of natural resources that can be used in productive processes. This belief is a corollary of the principle of unlimited substitutability—the idea that one can always substitute one product, resource, or process for another—which is the centerpiece of traditional economic analysis.

Finally, the fourth pillar of conventional economic science being challenged by bioeconomists is the idea that an economy can be modeled in a rather scientific fashion as a system of equations that will eventually reach an equilibrium no matter what. Bioeconomists dispute the notion that economics, an essentially "soft" science, can reach the status and the prestige enjoyed by the "hard" sciences, such as physics and chemistry.

Bioeconomics attempts to explain economic phenomena by going outside the discipline of economics into biology and thermodynamics. The basic propositions upon which bioeconomics rest are that (1) all resources are scarce (finite) and (2) matter as well as energy is subject to entropic degradation (the Second Law of Thermodynamics).

The first and perhaps the most widely known exposure of the inadequacies of conventional economics came from a group of concerned world citizens who formed the Club of Rome in 1968. Under the leadership of an Italian industrialist, Aurelio Peccei, the Club of Rome commissioned Jay Forrester, a professor from the Massachusetts Institute of Technology's Systems Dynamics group, to create a model of the world that could be used to alert the world's decision makers to the devastating effects that continuing industrial growth would have on the earth's carrying capacities.

The group produced a computerized model of the world as an interactive system with five main components: population, food production, industrial production, nonrenewable resources, and pollution. The group presented the results of many simulated runs of the system and concluded that in the finite system of the earth, exponential growth of population, food, and industrial production was an impossiblity. The group reasoned that the physical system's life support capacities were growing at best linearly and as a result were imposing a limit on the exponential growth of the social systems of population, food, and industrial production. These limits to growth, the group asserted, were already visible in the area of energy production and energy use. The recommendation of the group is known as the "double zero solution": zero population growth (ZPG) and zero economic growth (ZEG).

The book that followed its initial presentation, *The Limits to Growth*,[6] earned for the Club of Rome the name Doomsday or Neo-Malthusian group. It spurred numerous responses both in the United States and abroad and was followed by many sequels by the Club itself as well as by others. In the United Kingdom

---

[6]Donna Meadows et al., *The Limits to Growth* (New York: Universe Books, 1972).

a group of concerned scientists signed a document entitled *Blueprint for Survival,* which espoused the Club of Rome view and provided some practical advice on how to implement the Club's recommendations.[7] In the United States the Council on Environmental Quality presented to President Carter *The Global 2000 Report to the President,* verifying and endorsing the main views of the Club of Rome.[8]

Herman Kahn and his Hudson Institute were the first to attack the Club of Rome both for its methodology and for its findings and recommendations.[9] Kahn's main contentions were that growth is good for everybody and that the argument that there are some natural limits to growth is nonsense. According to Kahn, the earth contains incredible amounts of resources which will last virtually forever. In addition, humans with their science and technology will continue to develop new and more efficient ways of doing things, so there is no reason to worry that growth will stop because of any limits on the "inputs" to the growth machine. Kahn did acknowledge, however, that there might indeed come a time when limits might develop on the demand, or output, side of the equation.

Julian Simon, a professor of economics at the University of Illinois, argued in *Science* magazine that all the talk about limits to growth and the deterioration of the world was a journalistic ploy to present only bad news.[10] Simon argued that the world is getting better and better and that population growth has positive effects on the well-being of everybody everywhere. In his book *The Ultimate Resource,*[11] Simon attempted to prove that rather than deleterious effects, the major economic consequences of population growth were augmentations of the stock of human knowledge. He also claimed that population growth is positively related to growth in per capita income.

Simon teamed up with Herman Kahn (who, as a physicist with knowledge of the physical aspects of the earth, could complete Simon's arguments on the positive impact of population growth) to refute *The Global 2000 Report to the President.* In their book, *The Resourceful Earth,*[12] they concluded, "If present trends continue the world in 2000 will be less crowded, less polluted, more stable ecologically, and less vulnerable to resource-supply disruption than the world we live in now." They also predicted "declining scarcity, lowering prices and increased wealth."

Regardless of who is right, the lesson for the international manager is that a study of international economics must nowadays take a holistic viewpoint,

---

[7]Edward Goldsmith et al., *Blueprint for Survival* (New York: New American Library, 1972).

[8]*The Global 2000 Report to the President: Entering the Twenty-First Century,* Volume 1 (Washington, DC: U.S. Government Printing Office, 1980).

[9]Herman Kahn, *The Next 200 Years* (New York: William Morrow, 1976).

[10]Julian Simon, "Resources, Population, Environment: An Oversupply of False Bad News," *Science* 208 (June 29, 1980): 1431–1437.

[11]Julian Simon, *The Ultimate Resource* (Princeton, NJ: Princeton University Press, 1981).

[12]Julian Simon and Herman Kahn (eds.), *The Resourceful Earth: A Response to Global 2000* (New York: Basil Blackwell, 1984).

one that combines the physical as well as the economic aspects of an economy. As Michael Stewart, from University College in London, wrote in his book *The Age of Interdependence,*

> The perception is that when governments make macroeconomic decisions they do so in a thoroughly myopic way. They look at the effects of their decisions on their own country, but not on the other countries. They look two or three years ahead, but no further. This limited horizon—both spatially and temporally—may once have been legitimate, but is so no longer. The world has become much more interdependent, and the decisions made by major industrial countries can have effects around the world. At the same time, man's activities have begun to have serious effect on the environment: decisions determined solely by the needs of the next few years can impose unwanted and irreversible constraints on future generations.[13]

ISSUE FOR DISCUSSION

In its *State of the World 1986,* the Worldwatch Institute presented a list of the effects of the depletion of various resources on the global economy.[14] Discuss the implications for the world economy and for MNCs of the depletion of the six resources listed in Exhibit E4-1.

Exhibit E4-1   Global Resource Depletion

Resource	Extent of Depletion
Forests	World's tropical forests disappearing at 2 percent per year. Far faster in West Africa and southeast Asia, where moist tropical forests will have virtually disappeared by end of century. Previously stable forests in temperate zone now suffering from air pollution and acid rain. Dead and dying forests plainly visible in West Germany, Czechoslovakia, and Poland.
Grasslands	Excessive pressure on grasslands, closely paralleling growing pressure on forests and soils, has led to deterioration, which is most advanced in Africa and Middle East. Herd liquidation in pastoral economies of Africa now commonplace.
Fisheries	Rapid growth in world fish catch during fifties and sixties now history; overfishing often the rule, not the exception. Fish catch per person, including from fish farming, down 15 percent since 1970.

---

[13]Michael Stewart, *The Age of Interdependence: Economic Policy in a Shrinking World* (Cambridge, MA: MIT Press, 1986).

[14]Lester R. Brown, William U. Chandler, and the Staff of Worldwatch Institute, *The State of the World 1986* (New York: W. W. Norton, 1987).

Resource	Extent of Depletion
	Biggest consumption cuts in Third World countries such as Philippines.
Soil	Soil erosion exceeding new soil formation on 35 percent of world's cropland. World losing an estimated 7 percent of topsoil per decade. Effects most evident in Africa, where 40 percent of people live in countries where land productivity is lower than it was a generation ago.
Water	Growing water demand exceeding sustainable supplies in many locations, leading to scarcity. Falling water tables now found on every continent and in key food-producing regions. In some areas, including portions of the United States, water being shifted out of irrigated agriculture to satisfy growing residential demands.
Oil	Increases in the price of oil, the principal commercial fuel, sharply reduced world economic growth since 1973. Part of decline is due to ill-conceived responses to oil price hikes, notably the heavy borrowing by Third World countries. Progress in developing renewable alternatives is lagging.

SOURCE: Brown et al., *The State of the World 1986,* p. 10.

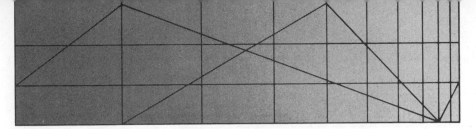

CHAPTER 5   INTERNATIONAL TRADE

No nation went bankrupt because of international trade.

Benjamin Franklin

OVERVIEW

The previous chapter presented an introduction to international economics, the foundation of international business. This chapter will focus on international trade. The term "international trade" denotes both an area of study and a human activity. Thus, this chapter will consider international trade both from the purely theoretical viewpoint and from the practical viewpoint.

The theoretical discussion will include an explanation of the main concepts and relationships that form the basis of the discipline, as well as an outline of the reasons for and the benefits derived from trading across national boundaries. The chapter will identify some policy issues surrounding governmental attempts to regulate international trade so as to maximize the benefits and minimize the negative effects on the domestic economy.

The second part of the chapter will discuss international trade as a human activity and will outline its quantitative and qualitative aspects in order to illustrate its tremendous importance for human survival.

LEARNING OBJECTIVES

After studying the material in this chapter, the student should be familiar with the following concepts:

(1)   The Principle of One Price

(2)   The Principle of Concentration

(3)   The Principle of Declining Share of Foreign Trade

(4)   Comparative advantage and the Ricardo and Heckscher-Ohlin Theorems

THE MAIN CONCEPTS

THE SUBCONCEPTS

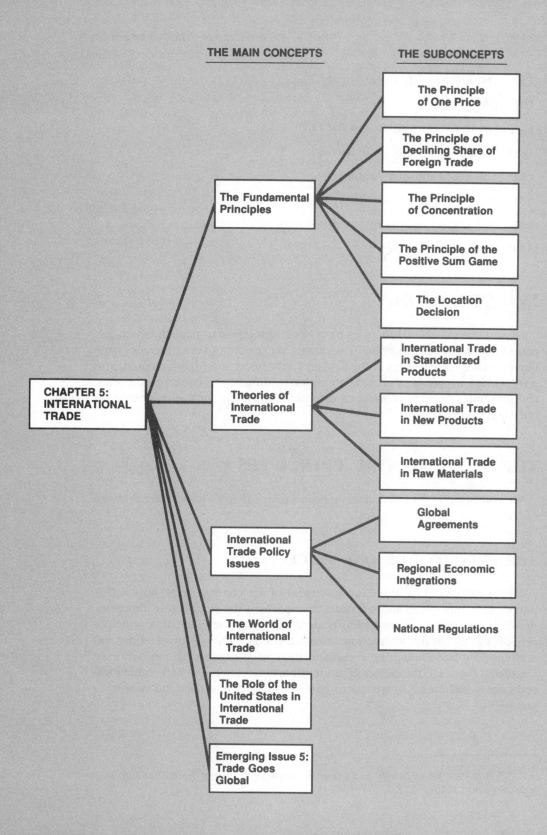

CHAPTER 5:
INTERNATIONAL
TRADE

The Fundamental
Principles

The Principle
of One Price

The Principle of
Declining Share of
Foreign Trade

The Principle
of Concentration

The Principle of the
Positive Sum Game

The Location
Decision

Theories of
International
Trade

International Trade
in Standardized
Products

International Trade
in New Products

International Trade
in Raw Materials

International
Trade Policy
Issues

Global
Agreements

Regional Economic
Integrations

National Regulations

The World of
International
Trade

The Role of the
United States in
International
Trade

Emerging Issue 5:
Trade Goes
Global

INTRODUCTION

Over the years several theories have been developed to explain why international trade occurs and how it is carried out. Some of these theories have been tested by researchers in the field and have become widely accepted. The goal of this chapter is to provide an understanding of the concepts, theories, and principles that are considered essential knowledge for the practicing international manager.[1]

THE FUNDAMENTAL PRINCIPLES

We will begin by examining some economic principles underlying theories of international trade.

THE PRINCIPLE OF ONE PRICE

The Principle of One Price is a statement of the commonsense notion that one should "buy cheap and sell dear." It is perhaps the single most important principle underlying international trade theory. In brief, what this principle proposes is that in the international market, goods, factors of production, and services flow from low-price regions to high-price regions. The Principle of One Price applies to the factors of production, taxes, governmental regulations, and even warehouses, as well as to commodities such as cars and consumer goods.

---

[1]This chapter draws heavily on Stephen P. Magee, *International Trade* (Reading, MA: Addison-Wesley, 1980).

Products will move from regions where they are abundant and cheap to regions where they are scarce and dear—whether the products are bananas, shirts, cars, or VCRs. Similarly, multinational corporations will move away from countries with high taxes and a lot of government regulations to countries with lower taxes and fewer regulations. Companies will also take advantage of lower costs in foreign countries in other ways; Japanese companies, for example, use U.S. ships and U.S. warehouses to transport and store their products destined for export because warehousing expenses are extremely high in Japan, where land is scarce.

THE PRINCIPLE OF DECLINING SHARE OF FOREIGN TRADE

The Principle of Declining Share of Foreign Trade says that as a country's population grows and its economic well-being increases, international trade tends to represent a smaller proportion of its GNP. The principle is an expression of a mathematical inevitability. A geographically larger country has a greater probability of possessing both the production capabilities to produce whatever is needed for consumption and a market of sufficient size to consume whatever is produced. A larger country will therefore have less need to supplement either its productive capacity or its markets than will a country with smaller area and population.

THE PRINCIPLE OF CONCENTRATION

The Principle of Concentration expresses the fact that developed countries have a much larger variety of imports and exports than do less developed countries. In other words, exports are more concentrated within certain categories of goods in developing countries than they are in developed countries. Less concentration in the developed countries not only reflects the greater variety of goods demanded by consumers but also attests to the greater innovativeness that results from higher research and development expenditures. Poorer countries understandably are less likely to devote a large percentage of their national income to researching and developing new products.

THE PRINCIPLE OF THE POSITIVE SUM GAME

The Principle of the Positive Sum Game explains why international trade is a "win-win" situation from which all parties obtain substantial benefits. The reason is that international trade by definition brings a commodity to a country at a price lower than the domestic price. In addition, international trade allows more efficient use to be made of all factors of production, such as people and raw materials.

THE LOCATION DECISION

Should production facilities for goods that use raw material inputs be located at the site of the raw materials or should they be located at the market? Decisions of this sort have tremendous implications for international trade. If, for example, a production facility is located at the raw material site, there will be more international trade in the final product. If, on the other hand, a production facility is located at the market, raw materials must be imported and thus there will be more trade in raw materials.

There are three important considerations in determining which production location will minimize total transportation costs:

(1)   The spatial distribution of the raw materials

(2)   The extent to which the production process is weight-losing or weight-gaining

(3)   The extent to which transportation costs per ton-mile differ for raw material inputs and the final product

If raw materials are *localized*—that is, if they exist only at a few places—production will occur in those places. If, on the other hand, raw materials are *ubiquitous*—that is, if they are widely distributed and available—production can take place anywhere and thus usually will be located close to the market. If the production process is a weight-losing one—for example, the conversion of pig iron into steel—production will take place at the raw materials site. The production of soft drinks, on the other hand, is a weight-gaining process and therefore is usually located at the market site. Finally, if, as is often the case, the transportation of raw materials is easier and cheaper than that of the finished products, production will tend to take place near the market. Transporting a Cadillac, for example, is much more costly than transporting the steel used to produce it.

Exhibit 5-1 presents the main theories used to explain production location decisions and their implications for international trade. International Trade Theory explains most of the reasons for and benefits of trading in commodities: a high cost for moving factors of production and a low cost for transporting commodities will result in heavy trade in commodities (cell G). Labor Migration Theory and Direct Foreign Investment Theory explain the main reasons for and benefits of moving people and capital to the markets: when the costs of moving the factors of production are low and the costs of moving commodities are high, production will locate at the markets (cell C).

These matters are at the heart of the international manager's job. They will therefore be taken up repeatedly throughout this book, especially in Chapter 10, Production/Sourcing Strategy.

Exhibit 5-1   Theories of Movements of Factors and Commodities

Cost of moving factors of production \ Cost of moving commodities	LOW	MEDIUM	HIGH
LOW	"Footloose": locate production anywhere (Location theory) **A**	**B**	International movement of factors only: locate production at market (Labor Migration theory and Direct Foreign Investment theory) **C**
MEDIUM	**D**	Produce at source of factors or market (Location theory) **E**	**F**
HIGH	International trade in commodities only: locate production at source of factors (International Trade theory) **G**	**H**	No international trade **I**

SOURCE: Adapted from Magee, *International Trade,* p. 8.

THEORIES OF INTERNATIONAL TRADE

It is not possible to provide a complete description and critique of all theories of international trade. Rather, the aim of this section is to give the student a fundamental understanding of the theoretical explanations of international trade and place international dealings in a proper perspective.

Theories of international trade are classified in accordance with whether they attempt to explain the reasons for international trade of standardized products, new products, or raw materials.[2]

INTERNATIONAL TRADE IN STANDARDIZED PRODUCTS

Theories of trade in standardized products are not very useful in explaining why international trade occurs. They are, however, the classics of the field and as such are considered a "must" for every student of international business to learn.

THE COMPARATIVE ADVANTAGE THEORY

There are two versions of the Comparative Advantage Theory: the one-factor theory, which assumes a single factor of production, usually labor, and the two-factor theory, which is based on two factors, usually labor and capital.

The Ricardo Model: The Labor Theory of Value (One-Factor Theory). **Ricardo's Labor Theory of Value** states that the value of any product is equal to the value of the labor time required to produce it. For example, if a computer requires one month to construct and an automobile requires one year to construct, the price of the car will be twelve times that of the computer. Over a century ago the British economist David Ricardo used this idea in constructing his version of the theory of comparative advantage. According to the principle of comparative advantage, a country will produce and export products that it can produce with less labor time than is used by foreign countries and will import those products for which it requires a greater amount of labor time than is used by foreign countries.

Exhibit 5-2 depicts hypothetical labor times required for the production of

Exhibit 5-2   Hypothetical Worker-Years Required for Production

	United States	Canada
One car	2 (0.5/year)	4 (0.25/year)
One truck	6 (0.17/year)	8 (0.125/year)
Price of truck/price of car	3/1	2/1

SOURCE: Magee, *International Trade*, p. 18.

---

[2]Magee, *International Trade*, Chaps. 2–4; and W. Baumol and A. S. Blinder, *Economics*, Third Edition (San Diego, CA: Harcourt, Brace, Jovanovich, 1985).

cars and trucks in the United States and Canada. In this example, the United States can produce one car with two worker-years, whereas Canada needs to spend twice as much labor time to produce the same car. On the other hand, the United States is only a bit more efficient than Canada in the production of trucks. Thus, according to Ricardo's theory, Canada will produce only trucks for its own consumers and for the United States, and the United States will produce only cars for its own customers and for the Canadians. Before international trade is instituted between the United States and Canada, the price of trucks relative to cars will be 3/1 in the United States, whereas it will be only 2/1 in Canada. But, as noted in the discussion of the Principle of the Positive Sum Game, one of the advantages of international trade is that it tends to reduce prices across international markets. Therefore, once international trade begins, prices of cars in Canada and trucks in the United States will begin to fluctuate downward until eventually they are pushed together in the two markets. That is, Canadians will sell their trucks to the United States, thereby pushing the price of U.S. trucks below the 3/1 ratio, and Americans will go to Canada to buy their trucks, thereby raising the price above the 2/1 ratio to, say, 2.7/1. These relationships will develop as long as each partner is sufficiently large to affect the prices in the other's market.

In this hypothetical situation the United States has a comparative advantage over Canada in the production of both products. As the exhibit shows, the United States is twice as efficient as Canada in the production of cars and $1\frac{1}{3}$ times as efficient in the production of trucks. In international trade language we say that the United States has an *absolute comparative advantage* over Canada. This situation might seem to suggest that it would pay the United States to produce both cars and trucks and not engage in international trade. Ricardo's major contribution was to debunk this myth of absolute advantage.

To prove that it is not advantageous to refrain from international trade, we need only demonstrate that workers in the United States are better off with international trade than without it. Without international trade an American worker who can produce one car in 2 years would have to work 12 years (and produce six cars) in order to purchase two trucks in the United States (since the ratio of trucks to cars is 3/1). With the same six cars, the U.S. worker can buy three trucks in Canada (where the ratio of trucks to cars is 2/1). Thus, even though U.S. workers are superior to Canadian workers in producing both products, it pays them to specialize in the item in which they have the greatest *relative advantage* (cars) and trade that item in Canada for trucks.

The Heckscher-Ohlin Theorem (***Two-Factor Theory***).   Despite its conceptual neatness and empirical verification, Ricardo's model cannot realistically be expected to explain all the complexities of international trade in terms of a single factor of production. The Heckscher-Ohlin model recognizes that more than one factor is needed to produce a given product and suggests that a country will export those products that require more of the factor it has in abundance. Capital-abundant countries will export products that use a lot of capital in their production—that is, *capital-intensive* products—and labor-abundant countries will export *labor-intensive* products. Cars are an example of a product that is more capital-intensive than labor-intensive. Chemicals are even more capital-intensive than cars. In both cases large sums of money must be invested in facilities and expensive equipment. Tomato growing, on the other hand, is a much more labor-intensive process than the production of either cars or chemicals.

Returning to the previous example of car and truck production in the United States and Canada, assume that cars are more capital-intensive than trucks: three units of capital are required to assemble a car, as compared to two units of capital to assemble a truck. Assume further that the United States has more capital per worker than does Canada. According to the Heckscher-Ohlin theorem, the United States will export its factor-abundant (capital-intensive) product, cars, and Canada will export its factor-abundant (labor-intensive) product, trucks.

Recall that in the Ricardo model, each country specializes in the production of only one product with which it has a relative comparative advantage. In the Heckscher-Ohlin model, *both* countries will produce *both* goods after free trade has been instituted. Thus, even though the United States is importing trucks from Canada, it will still satisfy some of its demand through local truck production. Canada will of course do the same for cars.

The Heckscher-Ohlin theorem has been studied by a number of economists, and some of the studies have corroborated the theorem. Stolper and Rosekamp, for example, found that West Germany, a capital-abundant country, exports capital-intensive goods; Bharadwaj found that, as would be expected, India exports labor-intensive goods. Other studies, however, have not supported the Heckscher-Ohlin theorem. Ichimura and Tatemoto found that Japan, a labor-abundant country, exports some capital-intensive goods; Wahl found Canada, a capital-abundant country, exporting labor-intensive goods.[3]

Despite the considerable amount of divergent evidence, the Heckscher-Ohlin theorem does appear at least partially to explain international trade. Some studies, for example, have found that the so-called Leontief paradox—the fact that the United States, a capital-abundant country, nonetheless exports products that are labor-intensive—disappears when one considers that the type of labor used in the production of these products is *skilled* labor. Thus it can be said that the United States exports *skill-intensive* products and imports *low-skill* products. Of course, it takes capital to convert unskilled labor into skilled labor, so the Heckscher-Ohlin theorem still holds.

---

[3]W. Stolper and K. W. Rosekamp, "An Input-Output Table for East Germany with Applications to Foreign Trade," *Oxford University Institute of Economics and Statistics Bulletin* 23 (November 1961): 379–392. R. Bharadwaj, "Factor Proportions and the Structure of Indo-U.S. Trade," *Indian Economic Journal* 10 (October 1962): 105–116. S. Ichimura and M. Tatemoto, "Factor Proportions and Foreign Trade: The Case of Japan," *Review of Economics and Statistics* 41 (November 1959): 442–446. D. F. Wahl, "Capital and Labour Requirements for Canada's Foreign Trade," *Canadian Journal of Economics* 27 (August 1961): 349–358. W. W. Leontief, "Domestic Production in Foreign Trade: The American Capital Position Re-examined," *Economia Internazionale* 7 (February 1954): 9–38.

ECONOMIES OF SCALE THEORY

The Economies of Scale Theory suggests that large countries will specialize in the production and exportation of products that can be mass-produced in large plants, and small countries will specialize in the production and exportation of products that require small plants and small runs. If, in addition to the size of a country, one considers the degree of sophistication of the economy, this theory makes a lot of sense. Indeed, Hufbauer correlated GNP per capita with economies of scale of exports and found an extremely strong fit.[4]

DEMAND SIMILARITIES THEORY

The Demand Similarities Theory differs from the previous ones in that it focuses on the demand side rather than the production or supply side of an economy. Linder, the major proponent of this theory,[5] speculated that countries tend to produce and export products of the quality demanded by most people within their borders, and to import products geared primarily to minorities, either the very rich or the very poor.

COMPENSATION THEORY

Basically, Compensation Theory argues that if an economy tends to export highly capital-intensive goods it will import highly labor-intensive products, and if it exports goods that require large plants and long production runs it will import goods that require small plants and short production runs.

In summary, the basic message of all these theories is that *it pays to specialize and to engage in international trade.*

INTERNATIONAL TRADE IN NEW PRODUCTS

The theories explained thus far implicitly take a classical macroeconomic view, which places considerable emphasis on the workings of the "free market system." Note that these theories all employ the concepts of *countries, resources, factors of production,* and *commodities.*

The following theories emphasize microeconomic concepts and place at the center of their conceptual frameworks the business enterprise as the main agent of international trade. The focus of these theories is the MNC, which is able to use a specific advantage to move factors of production and/or commodities around the globe.

---

[4]G. C. Hufbauer, "The Impact of National Characteristics and Technology on the Commodity Composition of Trade in Manufactured Goods," in R. Vernon (ed.), *The Technology Factor in International Trade* (New York: Columbia University Press, 1970), 145–231.

[5]Staffan B. Linder, *An Essay on Trade and Transformation* (New York: John Wiley and Sons, 1961).

Four different theories about multinational corporations as agents of international trade in new products will be explored in the next few pages:

(1)   The Comparative Advantage Theory

(2)   The Imperfect Competition Theory

(3)   The Appropriability Theory

(4)   The Product Life Cycle Theory

THE COMPARATIVE ADVANTAGE THEORY

The Comparative Advantage Theory as applied to new products states that a country will develop an advantage over others if it has a better quality of labor rather than merely more of it. Thus, in the case of high-technology goods, the Heckscher-Ohlin theorem implies that a country with a skilled labor force will export high-technology products (that is, products produced with the country's most abundant resource, skilled labor) and countries with unskilled labor forces will export low-technology goods (because that is what can be produced with their most abundant resource, unskilled labor).

THE IMPERFECT COMPETITION THEORY

Stephen Hymer, the main proponent of the Imperfect Competition Theory, argues that because of all the disadvantages the MNCs experience as a result of being in a foreign country, they can compete successfully only if they have advantages over the local firms. These advantages are generally superior technology and management abilities. Both of these advantages translate into superior product development, new and more efficient production processes, and better marketing methods. These advantages tend to distort the market mechanism and make it less perfectly competitive.

THE APPROPRIABILITY THEORY

According to the Appropriability Theory, the most serious threat facing innovative MNCs is the loss of their new technology to rivals and copiers. For this reason, MNCs prefer to transfer high technology worldwide from inside the firm rather than through the market mechanism. Because it is easier to copy or steal a less sophisticated technology than a more complex development, MNCs tend to prepare abroad those products and processes that are not very useful to the advancement of poor countries. In addition, they tend to price high-technology products at a level sufficiently low to discourage new competitors from entering the market.

THE PRODUCT LIFE CYCLE THEORY (PLC)

The Product Life Cycle Theory was developed originally by Raymond Vernon in the sixties. He theorized and later provided empirical proof that new products go through a life cycle of four stages: introduction, growth, maturation, and decline. In addition, Vernon observed that new products tend to be produced and consumed first in the United States and other high-income countries. As products mature, consumption and then production spread to other countries, with production ending finally in the developing countries as products become more standardized.

Why does the product life cycle originate in developed countries and only spread to less developed countries later? First, new product development requires large amounts of research and development funds and skilled labor. Second, new products require a sophisticated and affluent market—one both willing and financially able to try new products. Third, there must be quick and efficient communication between the producer and the consumer. Finally, patent protection is much more easily obtained and enforced in the developed world than elsewhere.

INTERNATIONAL TRADE IN RAW MATERIALS

Minerals in the earth's crust are not evenly distributed in all regions. Many regions that possess resources do not have the means to put them to economic uses, and other regions that have the means to bring about profitable uses do not have the resources. Thus, a substantial portion of international trade involves the movement of resources from countries that have them to countries that do not.

International trade in raw materials is influenced by two counteracting forces. First, industrialization and declining transportation costs have stimulated international trade. Second, scientific discoveries and the development of synthetic substitutes have minimized the use of some natural materials and eliminated the use of others completely, depressing international trade.

Although the end result of the interaction of these two forces has been favorable to the goods-producing countries, the future is not as certain as some observers tend to think. In addition to the limits to growth argument, which warns of the finiteness of most nonrenewable resources, there is the argument that the decline in prices of natural resources leaves the material-exporting countries with less revenue with which to buy products from the goods-producing countries.

THE RAW MATERIALS REVERSE LIFE CYCLE

In the discussion of Vernon's Product Life Cycle Theory, it was noted that new products tend to be developed, produced, and consumed in the developed countries first; then exported to the rest of the world; and finally produced in the developing countries. As the cost of production of these goods declines, countries with less sophisticated production processes begin to produce them for local consumption first and subsequently for exportation to the developed countries.

The raw materials development and consumption process follows the same pattern in reverse fashion. Raw materials are extracted and sold by developing countries first. When the use of the materials reaches a level sufficient to offset the higher labor cost of local production, developed countries begin to produce the materials synthetically, eventually reaching the point where they cease to import the materials altogether. Thus, the high price of the raw materials, a result of extensive demand for them, triggers a substitution process aimed at replacing natural raw materials with synthetic ones.

A perfect example of this process is the life cycle of rubber. The tremendous increase in demand for rubber that followed the invention of the automobile gave rise to the development of synthetic rubber. Today, over two-thirds of the rubber produced worldwide is synthetic, and many rubber plants are located in the industrialized countries, primarily the United States, Western European countries, and Japan. The same process of developing synthetic substitutes was followed in the areas of nylon yarns, industrial diamonds, paper, and other once indispensable natural raw materials.

In sum, the international trade in raw materials is not as stable as is the trade in consumer goods. Even though raw materials are much more indispensable to human survival than are goods (because without them there can be no production of consumer and capital goods), trade of raw materials is much more volatile than that of goods. The reason is that most of the raw materials are found in the developing world, and most of the users are in the developed countries. This situation has stimulated a number of attempts to stabilize both the production and the prices of raw materials via either bilateral or multilateral agreements or the development of cartels, which restrict the production and supply as well as determine the price of the materials. Examples of efforts of the first type are agreements concerning the exportation of coffee, sugar, rubber, and other primary products. The best-known example of the second type of effort was the 1973 oil embargo and price hike of the Organization of Petroleum Exporting Countries (OPEC).

INTERNATIONAL TRADE POLICY ISSUES

It is to nobody's benefit to try to restrict international trade. Yet the history of humanity is replete with trade wars aimed at preventing one country's exports from reaching another country's market. A complete account of such trade wars is beyond the scope of this chapter. However, students of international business need an adequate understanding of the logic of governmental attempts to regulate international trade by restricting imports and/or by promoting exports.

For convenience, attempts to regulate international trade are classified into three main categories:

(1)   Global agreements

(2)   Regional economic integrations

(3)   National regulations

GLOBAL AGREEMENTS

After World War II, policy makers attempted to develop international agreements on all political and economic issues in an effort to avoid a repetition of the 1930s. The most ambitious global agreement on international trade, signed in 1948, is known as the General Agreement on Tariffs and Trade (GATT). Exhibit 5-3 reviews the main outcomes of GATT discussions over the last forty or so years.

Exhibit 5-3   GATT at a Glance

Description
The General Agreement on Tariffs and Trade is both an agreement and an organization with a secretariat that operates from the Centre William Rappard on the Rue de Lausanne in Geneva. The secretariat employs about 150 persons. Its director general is a former Swiss diplomat, Arthur Dunkel.

Membership
The membership has grown from 23 founding "contracting parties" (governments) in 1948 to more than 90, representing four-fifths of world trade. The newest member is Mexico.

GATT Principles
The guiding principles of GATT include the following:

Trade without discrimination through application of Most Favored Nation principles;

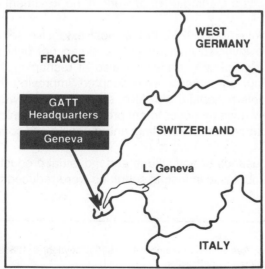

Reliance on tariffs rather than other commercial measures of protection, such as quotas, where protection of domestic industries is necessary;

Provision of a stable and predictable basis for trade through negotiated "bindings" of tariffs at fixed minimum levels;

Settlement of disputes through consultation, conciliation and, as a last resort, dispute settlement procedures.

Although parties agree to these principles, GATT recognizes the rules may have to be suspended.

Previous GATT Rounds

Geneva 1 (April–October 1947). Twenty-three countries, representing a volume of half the world's trade, were negotiating tariff cuts. The session gave legal status to the overall agreement. Some 45,000 agreements regarding the reduction and binding of individual tariff levels were made.

Annecy (1949). The session principally involved negotiations with nations that wanted to join. Some 5,000 concessions were made.

Torquay (1950–1951). Some 8,700 concessions were made, resulting in appreciable tariff reductions of 25 percent.

Geneva 2 (1955–1956). Twenty-five countries were represented, and there were negotiated reductions in tariffs affecting some $2 billion in international trade.

Dillon (May 1961–March 1962). Twenty-two nations and the entire European Community were represented. After the establishment of the E.C. in 1957, GATT gained more prominence. This round resulted in large-scale tariff negotiations involving nearly $5 billion in world trade, and some 4,400 concessions were made.

Kennedy (November 1963–May 1967). A one-third reduction in tariffs covering about $40 billion of world trade was made. An anti-dumping code was also established. The round was a starting point of work in the treatment of developing countries.

Tokyo (September 1973–November 1979). In the most extensive set of talks, over 90 countries were involved in negotiations aimed not only at eliminating tariff and non-tariff barriers to trade, but also at reshaping the multilateral trading system. Four agreements were adopted, improving the framework for the conduct of international trade. Also, six agreements were established. They covered new rules on government procurement, technical barriers to trade, customs valuation, import licensing, anti-dumping and countervailing measures.

Tariffs were reduced on thousands of agricultural and industrial products, and tariffs on manufactured products in industrial countries were reduced by about 34 percent.

REGIONAL ECONOMIC INTEGRATIONS

Although GATT is a noble effort, it cannot be expected to solve all real and potential problems in international trade. For this reason, countries have from time to time attempted to coordinate their regulatory efforts by developing schemes for economic integration. In general, economic integrations take one of the following forms:

(1)   Free Trade Area—an area in which members have no tariffs among themselves, but each has its own set of regulations with respect to the rest of the world.

(2)   Customs Union—a free trade area in which members have identical tariff rates on each product imported from outside.

(3)   Common Market—a customs union in which the factors of production can be moved freely from one member to another.

(4)   Economic Union—a single economy with one currency and unified fiscal and monetary policies.

As Exhibit 5-4 shows, the economic integration process is cumulative—each stage adds one more international trade–enhancing feature. Thus, the second stage, Customs Union, is as free as the previous stage, Free Trade Area, with the added advantage that members have identical tariff rates for the external world.

The benefits of economic integration include the following:

(1)   Increased efficiency of consumption as a result of lower prices

(2)   The breakup of monopolistic industry structures as a result of allowing all members to compete for formerly local markets

Exhibit 5-4   Stages of Economic Integration

I	II	III	IV
			Economic Union
		Common Market	One economy, one currency, uniform fiscal and monetary policies
	Customs Union	**Members: No tariffs, free movement of factors of production**	
Free Trade Area	**Members: No tariffs**		
Members: No tariffs	**World: One common tariff**	**World: Common tariff, coordinated industrial, agricultural, and commercial policies**	
World: Each member forms tariff policies on its own			

(3)   Better economies of scale as a result of the enlargement of markets, which permits plants to be larger and production runs to be longer

(4)   Increased efficiency of production as a result of the free movement of factors of production

---

Exhibit 5-5   The European Economic Community (EEC)

The European Community embraces 12 European countries that have joined together for these purposes:

to live in peace after the senseless wars of the past—a goal better achieved by a broad commitment to lasting cooperation than by specific agreements between individual States;

to avoid being mere pawns in the tough world of power politics and to be able, instead, to negotiate from strength in the protection afforded by a powerful Community;

to enable their economies to develop in conditions of fair competition;

to improve living conditions for their citizens and thus ensure social progress.

For an area stretching from Shetland to Crete, from Lisbon to Copenhagen, with all the different structures and traditions it encompasses, it is often hard to work out common objectives and to devise measures that will be equally effective for everyone. But the needs and aspirations of broad sections of the population are steadily growing closer, helping to bridge traditional differences. And the solutions to many of today's political and economic problems—of which the current state of the labour market is a reflection—are beyond the resources of any one nation alone.

The Treaty establishing the European Coal and Steel Community (ECSC) was signed in 1951, followed in 1957 by the Treaties establishing the European Economic Community (EEC) and the European Atomic Energy Community (Euratom). There were six founder-members: Belgium, France, Germany, Italy, Luxembourg and the Netherlands. Three more countries joined in 1973: Denmark, Ireland and the United Kingdom. In 1981 Greece became the 10th member, and with the accession of Portugal and Spain in 1986, the Community now numbers 12.

The institutions of the three Communities—ECSC, EEC and Euratom—were merged in 1967, and the term 'European Community' is now commonly used to mean all three together.

SOURCE: Commission of the European Communities, *A Journey Through the EC* (Brussels: EEC, 1986), 4.

There have been many attempts at economic integration, most of which were unsuccessful. Exhibit 5-5 presents information on the most successful economic integration today, the European Economic Community (EEC).

NATIONAL REGULATIONS

The greatest benefit of international trade is that exchanges bring about a decline in production costs, which results from the free movement of the factors of production; the decline in production costs in turn causes consumer prices to drop. Both of these changes, however, create a shock effect on local industries. Most smaller and marginal companies cannot sustain the losses in their market share and sales that are almost sure to result from unbridled competition with more experienced and more efficient foreign firms.

To avoid devastating effects on such small firms and their workers, governments usually devise artificial barriers to international trade. The effect of these barriers is to *increase* the price of the imported product and to cut down on the amount of imports. There are two main types of international trade barriers: tariff barriers and nontariff barriers.

TARIFF BARRIERS

Tariffs are taxes imposed by a government on imported goods as well as on exported and in-transit goods. The primary purpose of the tariff is to discourage the consumption of imported goods, thereby encouraging the consumption of domestic products; in addition, tariffs may be a good source of government revenue.

There are many reasons for imposing a tariff on imported products. Following are three of the more important arguments for imposing tariffs.

The Infant Industry Argument.   The oldest argument for the imposition of tariffs is the Infant Industry Argument. The logic behind this argument is that the young industries of a country will not be able to compete with older and more experienced foreign firms and will therefore go out of business, causing in the process a big unemployment problem. The imposition of a tariff on imported goods raises the price of the foreign product, in effect lowering the price of the domestic good and allowing local businesses to continue to operate.

The Employment Creation Argument.   According to the Employment Creation Argument, imposing an artificially created disadvantage (a tariff) on foreign competitors will allow the domestic industry to increase production and hire new workers. The increase in production will also create a need for more raw materials and other semi-finished goods produced by related industries. The ultimate result of this enhanced industrial activity will be a substantial increase in the number of people who are employed.

The Improvement of the Balance of Trade Argument.   Proponents of the Improvement of the Balance of Trade Argument believe that tariffs will cause the citizens of a country to purchase less of the imported product, thereby decreasing the importance of imports in the country's balance of payments.

NONTARIFF BARRIERS

The most commonly used nontariff barrier is the quota. A **quota** specifies the maximum amount of a good that may be brought into a country from abroad per unit of time. It is, in other words, a legal limit on the amount of a good that may be imported. Another commonly used nontariff barrier is the export subsidy. An **export subsidy** is a payment by a country's government to an exporter. This payment can take the form of a premium, a tax credit, or lower interest payments on loans made specifically for export production. Most countries that use export subsidies employ a combination of the above. In addition, paperwork, permits, quality verification, customs declarations, and other bureaucratic procedures can become much more effective nontariff trade barriers than any of the above-mentioned methods.

Exhibit 5-6   Quotas and Tariffs in International Trade

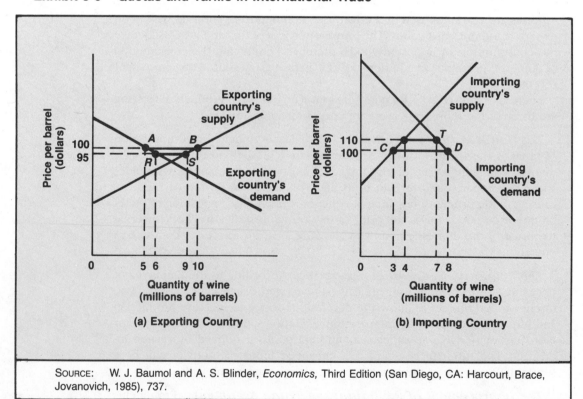

SOURCE: W. J. Baumol and A. S. Blinder, *Economics,* Third Edition (San Diego, CA: Harcourt, Brace, Jovanovich, 1985), 737.

Exhibit 5-6 illustrates the market adjustments that take place as a result of the imposition of a tariff and a quota. As the exhibit shows, both trade regulation methods have the same effect: a reduction in the quantity of a product imported. In the example illustrated, the equilibrium price of wine under free trade is $100 per barrel. At that price, the exporting country will send five million barrels of wine to the importing country. This exchange is represented by distance *AB* in part (a) and distance *CD* in part (b). If a quota of three million barrels is imposed by the importing country, the distance must shrink to three million barrels: distance *RS* for exports in part (a) and distance *QT* for imports in part (b). Exports and imports must remain equal, but the quota will force prices to be unequal in the two countries. Wine will sell for $110 per barrel in the importing country but for only $95 per barrel in the exporting country. A tariff achieves the same result in a different way. It requires that the prices in the two countries be $15 apart. As the graph shows, this requirement too dictates that exports and imports be at a level of three million barrels.

THE WORLD OF INTERNATIONAL TRADE

The previous sections considered the theoretical explanations of international trade and national, regional, and international attempts to regulate it. In this section we will consider the amount, distribution, and importance of international trade.

Exhibit 5-7 provides data on world trade (the total of imports and exports, which are listed separately in the exhibit) for the years 1985, 1986, and 1987. As the exhibit shows, in 1985 the industrialized countries accounted for over 74% of this trade, and the developing countries did not quite reach the 22% mark. Furthermore, the industrialized countries' share of world trade increased continuously over the three years shown; the developing countries' share declined from 25% in 1985 to 21.46% in 1987. Even though world trade increased by 36.43% for exports and 32.38% for imports over the three years, the developing countries enjoyed very little of this increase (18.54% and 11.31%, respectively).

Even within the developed world the growth in international trade was not shared equally. The largest increase in trade over the years shown was in Italy—a whopping 65.82% increase in exports (almost twice the world increase).

It is customary to report on world trade in terms of progressively larger groups labeled G-1 through G-7. Group 1, the single largest trader, is the United States, which accounted in 1987 for 12.24% of the world's trade. The three largest international trade powers, the United States, West Germany, and France, accounted in 1987 for over 30% of the world's trade. Group 5, the most widely known group, accounted for over 40% of 1987 world trade, and G-7 traded more than 50% of the world's goods and services. (See Exhibit 5-8.)

Exhibit 5-7   World Trade (Exports and Imports): Industrial Countries 1985–1987 (billions of dollars)

	Exports			
	1985	1986	1987	Percentage Change
World	1258.20	1463.80	1716.60	36.43
Industrial Countries	901.30	1084.10	1288.00	42.90
United States	211.90	236.40	254.80	20.25
Canada	60.90	61.60	75.70	24.30
Japan	43.90	51.80	60.50	37.81
Belgium-Luxembourg	48.30	62.00	75.50	56.31
France	80.90	102.10	127.50	57.60
Germany	111.70	141.80	170.20	52.37
Italy	50.9	66.4	84.4	65.82
Netherlands	57.30	68.80	83.10	45.03
United Kingdom	82.40	97.70	119.50	45.02
Developing Countries	303.10	319.10	359.30	18.54
Africa	39.10	39.90	42.30	8.18
Asia	104.10	113.70	133.20	27.95
Europe	34.70	41.90	50.90	46.69
Middle East	68.20	61.60	63.40	−7.04
Western Hemisphere	57.00	62.10	69.60	22.11
U.S.S.R.	27.90	28.80	29.90	7.17

SOURCE: International Monetary Fund, *Direction of Trade Statistics: Industrial Countries* (New York: IMF, June 1988), 6–7.

THE ROLE OF THE UNITED STATES IN INTERNATIONAL TRADE

The United States is the world's largest trader, importing and exporting more than any other country. What does this really mean? Does it mean that the United States depends more on trade with foreigners for its production, consumption, or employment? Although it is not a totally accurate measure, the proportion of a country's gross domestic product attributable to international trade does give a fairly good approximation of a country's dependence on international trade. Exhibit 5-9 illustrates the degree of openness of various countries to international trade. The data given confirm the Principle of Declining Share of Foreign Trade explained earlier.

Imports			Percentage Change	Totals	1987 Percentage of World Trade
1985	1986	1987			
1360.50	1529.50	1801.00	32.38	3517.60	100.00
944.90	1127.80	1322.30	39.94	2610.30	74.21
147.00	157.10	175.90	19.66	430.70	12.24
81.40	81.40	87.30	7.25	163.00	4.63
111.10	138.60	151.10	36.00	211.60	6.02
45.00	58.90	71.40	58.67	146.90	4.18
73.30	92.60	113.60	54.98	241.10	6.85
139.40	187.50	230.50	65.35	400.70	11.39
55.4	73.3	89.6	61.73	174.00	4.95
61.70	70.90	82.60	33.87	165.70	4.71
76.90	82.10	97.10	26.27	216.60	6.16
355.30	335.10	395.50	11.31	754.80	21.46
56.30	48.70	50.70	−9.95	93.00	2.64
109.10	118.30	150.30	37.76	283.50	8.06
28.30	34.10	42.50	50.18	93.40	2.66
76.10	57.10	66.90	−12.09	130.30	3.70
85.60	77.10	85.10	−0.58	154.70	4.40
28.60	28.70	29.80	4.20	59.70	1.70

The countries on the left side of the graph have one common characteristic—they are large in terms of population and GDP. The countries on the right side of the graph are small. Trade is a larger percentage of GDP for the countries on the right side of the graph than for those on the left. Belgium, for example, which has a rather small population of about ten million people, has the largest percentage of foreign trade. On the other hand, the United States, the country with the largest population, has the smallest dependence on foreign trade, with foreign trade accounting for less than 10 percent of the GDP.

The relative position of the United States is not as good as it appears, however. First, the United States' ratio doubled over the twenty years shown, while Japan's ratio increased by only 50%. Second, adding in international *financial* transactions increases the proportion of the U.S. GDP devoted to international business to about 25%.

Exhibit 5-8   World's Largest Traders
(Exports + Imports), 1987

| Top One (G-1) | | Top Three (G-3) | | |
Billions of $	Percentage of World Trade	Billions of $		Percentage of World Trade
United States 431	12.24	United States	431	12.24
		West Germany	401	11.39
		France	241	6.85
Totals 431	12.24		1073	30.48

SOURCE: International Monetary Fund, *Direction of Trade Statistics* (New York: IMF, June 1988), 6–7.

These documented quantitative changes in the United States' international trade position are less significant than some qualitative changes. The United States, formerly a leading exporter of industrial/manufacturing goods, has now become a leading importer of many of these goods. In addition, trade in services, in which the United States once had a healthy surplus, is beginning to decline.

Most people still hold high hopes for the United States' ability to compete in the world market in the so-called hi-tech area of industrial products. Yet the United States made little progress over the twenty years from 1960 to 1980 in enlarging its share in these markets. As a matter of fact, the country experienced losses in some of these markets, notably the electronic equipment and components and professional and scientific instruments categories. The data in Exhibits 5-10 and 5-11 show that the countries that have benefited from the deterioration of the United States' hegemony in the world's markets have been mostly the developed countries of Canada, Japan, and West Germany and the newly industrialized countries of Taiwan, South Korea, and Mexico.

The end result of this inability of U.S. business to compete in the world market—combined with a decline in the prices of primary products (agricultural products), which reduced import receipts, and fortified by the ever-increasing appetite of American buyers for foreign goods—has been a tremendous acceleration in the foreign trade deficit. The U.S. trade deficit quadrupled in the 1980–1986 period.

Top Five (G-5)			Top Seven (G-7)		
Billions of $		Percentage of World Trade	Billions of $		Percentage of World Trade
United States	431	12.24	United States	431	12.24
West Germany	401	11.39	West Germany	401	11.39
France	241	6.85	France	241	6.85
United Kingdom	217	6.16	United Kingdom	217	6.16
Japan	212	6.02	Japan	212	6.02
			Italy	174	4.95
			Netherlands	166	4.71
	1502	42.66		1842	52.32

RECAPITULATION

This chapter reviewed the subject of international trade. After a brief summary of the theories developed to explain the reasons for international trade and the benefits derived from it, some of the reasons for and forms of official intervention in international trade were identified. Despite both academics' and practitioners' assurances that restricting international trade is to nobody's benefit, governments have created and will continue to develop numerous schemes to minimize the exposure of their industries and their labor to external disturbances.

The chapter considered the importance of international trade for the world community. Though it is not a truly representative descriptor of the contemporary global scene, the ratio of international trade to GDP is considered to be a good measure of a country's dependence on the rest of the world.

The almost $3 trillion of international trade in goods and services is not equally shared among the countries of the world. A small number of countries, the so-called G-7, account for over half of the world's trade, even though combined they represent barely 15% of the world's population. This imbalance, coupled with the fact that international financial transactions and trade dominate global economic dealings, makes for an uncertain future.

Exhibit 5-9   Trade Importance

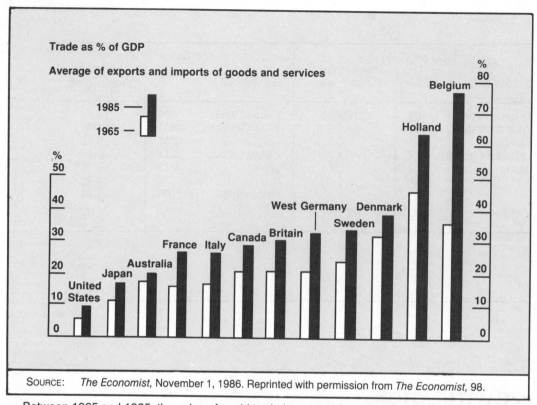

SOURCE: *The Economist*, November 1, 1986. Reprinted with permission from *The Economist*, 98.

Between 1965 and 1985, the value of world trade increased from $187 billion to $2 trillion a year. That means it more than doubled in volume terms, outpacing the growth of output in the industrial countries. Every country in the chart was much more open to trade (as measured by the average of exports and imports as a proportion of GDP) in 1985 than it was in 1965. The United States was the least open of the big industrial countries, though its ratio of trade to GDP increased from 5% to 9%, Japan, surprisingly, was still a closed economy by European standards; its ratio of trade to GDP increased from 10% to 15%. West Germany's ratio increased to 33%, Belgium's to 76%.

REVIEW QUESTIONS

(1)   Briefly explain the Principle of One Price, the Principle of Declining Share of Foreign Trade, and the Principle of Concentration.

(2)   What are some important considerations in determining which production location will minimize total costs?

Exhibit 5-10   Top U.S. Markets and Suppliers, 1987

	U.S. Domestic and Foreign Market Exports (in billions of $)		U.S. General Merchandise Imports (in billions of $)
Canada	59.8	Japan	88.1
Japan	28.2	Canada	71.5
Mexico	14.6	West Germany	28.0
United Kingdom	14.1	Taiwan	26.4
West Germany	11.7	Mexico	20.5
Netherlands	8.2	United Kingdom	18.0
South Korea	8.1	South Korea	18.0
France	7.9	Italy	11.7
Taiwan	7.4	France	11.2
Belgium and Luxembourg	6.2	Hong Kong	10.5
Italy	5.5	Brazil	8.4
Australia	5.5	China	6.9
Singapore	4.1	Singapore	6.4
Brazil	4.0	Venezuela	5.9
Hong Kong	4.0	Sweden	5.0
Venezuela	3.6	Saudi Arabia	4.9
China	3.5	Switzerland	4.4
Saudi Arabia	3.4	Belgium and Luxembourg	4.4
Switzerland	3.2	Netherlands	4.2
Spain	3.1	Nigeria	3.8
Israel	3.1	Indonesia	3.7
Egypt	2.2	Australia	3.3
Malaysia	1.9	Spain	3.1
Sweden	1.9	Malaysia	3.1
Ireland	1.8	India	2.7
World total	252.9	World total	424.1

SOURCE: U.S. Department of Commerce, *Business Week,* April 25, 1988, 6–7.

(3)   List and briefly explain the main theories of international trade in standardized products.

(4)   What are the main differences between the concepts of absolute and relative comparative advantage?

(5)   List and briefly explain the main theories of international trade in a new product.

Exhibit 5-11　U.S. Trade Balances, 1987 (Total: −$171.2 billion)

	U.S. Surplus Positions (in billions of $)		U.S. Deficit Positions (in billions of $)
Netherlands	+4.0	Japan	−59.8
Australia	+2.2	Taiwan	−19.0
Belgium and Luxembourg	+1.8	West Germany	−16.3
Egypt	+1.7	Canada	−11.7
U.S.S.R.	+1.0	South Korea	−9.9
Ireland	+0.7	Hong Kong	−6.5
Turkey	+0.6	Italy	−6.2
Israel	+0.4	Mexico	−5.9
Jordan	+0.4	Brazil	−4.4
Panama	+0.3	United Kingdom	−3.9
Bahamas	+0.3	Nigeria	−3.8
Morocco	+0.3	China	−3.4
Pakistan	+0.3	France	−3.2
Bermuda	+0.3	Sweden	−3.1
Jamaica	+0.2	Indonesia	−3.0
Paraguay	+0.2	Singapore	−2.3
Iraq	+0.2	Venezuela	−2.3
Leeward and Windward Islands	+0.1	Algeria	−1.7
Bahrain	+0.1	Iran	−1.7
Sudan	+0.1	Saudi Arabia	−1.5
French Guiana	+0.1	Angola	−1.3
Yemen, North (San'a)	+0.1	India	−1.3
Cayman Islands	+0.1	Switzerland	−1.2
El Salvador	+0.1	Malaysia	−1.2
Brunei	+0.1	Colombia	−1.0

SOURCE:　U.S. Department of Commerce, *Business Week*, April 25, 1988, 6–7.

(6)　Explain the Product Life Cycle Theory as it applies to raw materials.

(7)　What are the main forms and some benefits of economic integration?

(8)　Show how tariffs and quotas have the same effect on imports.

(9)　Some economists might argue that the United States has *not* lost its competitiveness, as its percentage of world trade increased from 12.2% in 1983 to 13.7% in 1985. Defend or refute that argument.

(10)　Explain why the percentage of the U.S. GDP for 1985 devoted to international business was actually closer to 25% than to the 9% shown in Exhibit 5-9.

SUGGESTED READINGS

Aliber, R. Z. *The International Money Game,* Second Edition. New York: Basic Books, 1976.

Bergsten, C. Fred. "The Trade Deficit Could be Ruinous." *Fortune,* August 5, 1985, 105–106.

Hervey, Jack L. "The Internationalization of Uncle Sam." *Economic Perspectives.* Federal Reserve Bank of Chicago, May/June 1986, 3–14.

Hufbauer, G. C. "The Impact of National Characteristics and Technology on the Commodity Composition of Trade in Manufactured Goods." In R. Vernon (ed.), *The Technology Factor in International Trade.* New York: Columbia University Press, 1970, 145–231.

Hymer, Stephen H. *The International Operations of National Firms: A Study of Direct Foreign Investment.* Cambridge, MA: MIT Press, 1976.

Ichimura, S., and M. Tatemoto. "Factor Proportions and Foreign Trade: The Case of Japan." *Review of Economics and Statistics* 41 (November 1959): 442–446.

Krugman, P. R. *Strategic Trade Policy and the New International Economics.* Cambridge, MA: The MIT Press, 1986.

Leontief, W. W. "Domestic Production in Foreign Trade: The American Capital Position Re-examined." *Economia Internazionale* 7 (February 1954): 9–38.

Linder, Staffan B. *An Essay on Trade and Transformation.* New York: John Wiley and Sons, 1961.

Meyer, Stephen A. *Trade Deficits and the Dollar: A Macroeconomic Perspective.* Philadelphia, PA: Federal Reserve Bank of Philadelphia, September/October 1986, 15–25.

Prindl, A. R. *Foreign Exchange Risk.* New York: John Wiley and Sons, 1976.

Wachter, Michael L., and Susan M. Wachter (eds.). *International Trade.* Reading, MA: Addison-Wesley, 1980.

Walters, Ingo. *Handbook of International Business.* New York: John Wiley and Sons, 1982, Parts 2 and 3.

EMERGING ISSUE 5: Trade Goes Global

"It is absolutely incredible," Rich said to his friend Judy as they were getting ready for their daily lunch ritual at the corner deli. "I've been involved in international banking for the last thirty years and I still can't seem to be able to make any sense of what I read in the daily newspapers. And most of the reports channeled up to me by the staff in the international department don't seem to make it any easier.

"Let me give you a few examples. Take, for instance, this business with the U.S. dollar. Way back during the Nixon and Ford administrations the dollar started to decline. I remember when my son went to Heidelberg for a short course in German at the Goethe Institute. I shelled out almost a whole dollar for each deutsch mark. Then when Reagan took over, the dollar began to rise. Suddenly, we were getting something like 2.5 DM for each dollar. I started feeling a bit better, particularly since my son decided to stay in Germany for further studies. Then I began seeing a lot of defaults in my accounts. Some of my good customers who were doing a lot of business overseas started complaining that they just could not sell anything. Their prices were just too high. They were accusing President Reagan of not caring for the country and were hoping that he would finally get the message and slam the door on all these cheap imports from low-labor countries and undervalued currencies like the Japanese yen.

"And I'm starting to believe these people are right. They do know what they are talking about. Look at our balance of payments: we managed to pile up some $170 billion in deficits in 1988. That's really a lot of money. And most of this deficit, some $80 billion, is with the Japanese."

Judy was listening to her friend very patiently. Judy wasn't in the banking business; she was the purchasing manager with a big department store in the city. Business the last few months had been absolutely great. She had managed to get the best buys ever. Her new supplier, the Yamoto Trading Company, had made great deals with producers in the Pacific Basin. The margins were absolutely superb; ladies' and men's shirts and shorts were coming in at prices that were a mere fraction of what she had to pay to the domestic suppliers; quality was great; payment arrangements were also very good. Just yesterday Judy had closed one of her largest deals ever: a huge order of $30 million. "It's terrific!" she exclaimed as she was explaining to Rich how she got hooked up with the Japanese trading company. "The deal just fell into my lap out of the blue."

"I don't know," interrupted Rich. "It just doesn't seem right. I see in the headlines that American companies are closing down because they can't get customers to buy from them, yet you seem to get a great deal of satisfaction out of the misery of all these people who are losing their jobs to foreigners. Because that's exactly what it is, you see. When you buy from overseas you put some people to work over there and you take some people off their jobs here at home. I learned in Econ 101 years ago that a purchase is consumption and consumption means production, which in turn means employment and

income, which goes back into consumption and purchases, and the cycle goes
on and on. When we purchase things made by people who are not employed
by American companies, we provide employment for them and not for our
own people. I bet you that by year's end the unemployment figures will sky-
rocket in this country. We might even see another 1930. I sure would like to
see some legislation on these cheap imports. We just cannot afford to have
our people jam the unemployment lines."

"I don't think things are that bad," said Judy. "Look, the deficit figure you
just gave me, that $170 or so billion, that's really peanuts. That isn't even 5%
of our GNP. Even if you were to add up everything that we buy from overseas
it wouldn't amount to 7% of our GNP. Besides, no country can afford to close
its borders to international trade. We are all interdependent. If we don't buy
from overseas they can't buy anything from us. What will happen to all these
farm products that our very efficient farmers produce? We have quite large
surpluses, you know. And what about our airplanes and all the sophisticated
military machinery that your friends are producing? Do you know how many
shirts the South Koreans have to sell to us to earn the foreign exchange to
buy one Boeing 747? I don't know myself, but I can guarantee you they must
load that 747 several hundred times over with nicely made silk shirts. Their
terms of trade are not that good, you know."

"If what you said is true," Rich answered, "how can we still buy things from
the Japanese even though we have such a large deficit? Are they giving us
credit because we are good guys, or what?"

"The Japanese are extending us credit, not because they think we are good
guys, but because they think we are a good risk," said Judy. "Besides, they
have to keep their people employed. Actually, the Japanese, the Germans, and
other people with whom we have a trade deficit not only extend us credit to
buy their products, but also loan us money to finance our own national debt.
Some of the money needed to cover the deficit in our federal budget will
come from American citizens like you and me. But a good portion of it will
come from overseas. Foreigners invest in U.S. Treasury bills more and more
every day. I just heard yesterday that when the Treasury Department auctioned
some bonds the Japanese were the first ones to put in a bid for $5–6 billion.
Just think— $6 billion in one day."

"That's another thing," Rich complained. "I've heard that foreigners own
some half a trillion dollars' worth of assets across the country. And that doesn't
include several hundred billion dollars' worth of commercial real estate and
farmland, including forests in Oregon and apartments, hotels, and office buildings in Miami, New York, Atlanta, and Los Angeles. That really bothers me a
lot. So many foreigners owning so much of the United States. . . . It seems like
we are selling off our heritage—going back to the colonial days when everything belonged to the Europeans."

"Well, things aren't really as tragic as you make them out to be," said Judy.
"So what if foreigners own that much land and other real estate? The United
States is still the largest single international investor in the whole world. I bet
if you were to add up all foreign investment in the United States it would not

be more than 15% of the U.S. GNP or, for that matter, a mere fraction of the investment that the United States has overseas. We have some of the world's largest multinational corporations, you know.

"I wouldn't really worry about that foreign debt. At least we can pay the debt in dollars. Our currency is still strong—it's acceptable worldwide. If we were Brazil or some other country, and had to pay the foreign bankers in dollars because they didn't like our cruzeiros or pesos, we might have to worry that some bureaucrat from the IMF would come in and force us to take 'drastic measures' to increase our exports and limit our imports. But we own most of the IMF's money; we are beyond any kind of control.

"A few years ago I read a good article in *The Wall Street Journal* by Herbert Stein. He was the chairman of the Council of Economic Advisers under presidents Nixon and Ford. He said that even though he worries about the national debt, it doesn't really bother him that foreigners own a large percentage of it. I really liked his rationale. He said that almost everybody is better off because of the willingness on the part of the foreigners to lend money to the United States and the United States' ability to convince them to keep lending money. U.S. companies find cheap money readily; merchants buy cheap foreign goods easily; workers are getting more productive because of investments made by the U.S. companies with the foreign money; the government can keep inflation very low; and, of course, U.S. banks and brokers make a pile of money trading all these billions."

But listening to Judy hadn't convinced Rich. "As much as I respect your intellectual capacities, Judy, I must say that this time you really went off the deep end," he insisted. Then he brought up several questions that had occurred to him as she talked. These are listed below as issues for discussion.

ISSUES FOR DISCUSSION

(1)   How can the national debt increase forever?

(2)   How can the foreign debt increase forever?

(3)   How can U.S. policy makers and bankers make such a big deal about the so-called international debt bomb and be oblivious to our own share of it? Is the United States beyond international economic controls, as Judy claims?

(4)   In 1971 President Nixon had to devalue the dollar by 10% against most foreign currencies. Should the United States be forced to do the same again soon?

(5)   Should the IMF force the United States to cut down on imports and beef up exports, as it does all other net debtors?

(6)   How can the government convince Detroit or North Carolina workers who lost their jobs because their companies couldn't compete with Korean and Chinese companies (whose workers earn only a dollar a

day) that it is good for the country and for them to have inexpensive goods coming into the country, and that without these goods they themselves would be worse off?

(7)   Why shouldn't Congress introduce some kind of legislation that would make it more difficult for other countries to export and invest in the United States unless they take steps to eliminate the large surpluses they have with us?

(8)   Are direct foreign investments in the United States (for example, factories that are either bought or built from scratch by foreigners) good for the country?

(9)   Are foreign investments in the United States a ruse for bringing more imports into this country? In other words, don't most of the parts that go into the production of Toyotas or Sonys come from overseas?

(10)   Should the United States take certain measures against Japan, similar to the nontariff barriers that country imposes on foreign goods?

CHAPTER 6

INTERNATIONAL FINANCE

Never before in the history of banking has so much been owed by so few to so few.

The Economist

Quoted in A. Sampson, *The Money Lenders: The People and Politics of the World Banking Crisis* (Middlesex, England: Penguin Books, 1981), 249.

OVERVIEW

The last chapter dealt with the exchange of goods and services across national boundaries. This chapter deals with the exchange of money that must follow each exchange of goods and services. Every purchase/sale of a good or service must be translated into some type of monetary transaction. Thus, all international trade transactions sooner or later become financial transactions. International finance deals with how exchanges of goods and services translate into monetary transactions.

Like the previous two chapters, this chapter will first address the theoretical aspects of the topic and then examine some policy issues. Finally, in the last part of the chapter the quantitative and qualitative aspects of international finance will be discussed. There are two main aspects of international finance that any student must understand: the International Monetary System and the international record-keeping system.

The International Monetary System (IMS) represents a set of rules and regulations aimed at facilitating the expansion of international trade without jeopardizing either individual national economies or the entire world economy. The key issue is the design of a system as "neutral and automatic" as possible, which is difficult for any single government to manipulate yet flexible enough to allow for temporary violations without great risk of disasters.

The international record-keeping system is another set of rules and regulations, governing the recording and reporting of financial transactions among countries. This record-keeping and reporting system is widely known as the balance-of-payments accounts or simply the balance of payments.

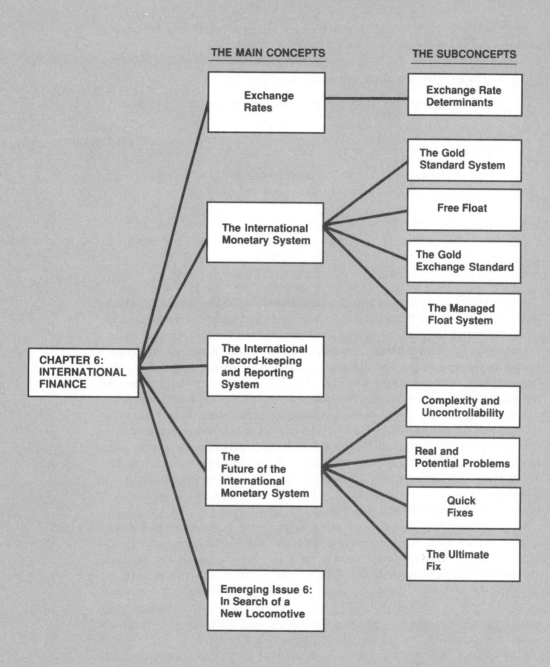

THE MAIN CONCEPTS

THE SUBCONCEPTS

Exchange Rates

Exchange Rate Determinants

The International Monetary System

The Gold Standard System

Free Float

The Gold Exchange Standard

The Managed Float System

CHAPTER 6: INTERNATIONAL FINANCE

The International Record-keeping and Reporting System

The Future of the International Monetary System

Complexity and Uncontrollability

Real and Potential Problems

Quick Fixes

The Ultimate Fix

Emerging Issue 6: In Search of a New Locomotive

LEARNING OBJECTIVES

After studying the material in this chapter, the student should be familiar with the following concepts:

(1)   Exchange rates and their determinants

(2)   The International Monetary System (IMS), its history and problems

(3)   Free float and managed float

(4)   The international record-keeping system (balance of payments)

(5)   EMS, ECU, and DEY

(6)   International debt

(7)   Optimal bankrupts

INTRODUCTION

International exchanges of goods and services must eventually be translated into monetary transactions between the buyers and sellers of goods and the users and suppliers of services. For example, when a U.S. citizen purchases a Japanese car for, say, $10,000, this money (minus the domestic merchant's profit) leaves the country and goes to Japan. Similarly, when a Japanese citizen buys an American computer for, say, 100,000 yen, this money (minus the Japanese merchant's profit) leaves Japan and comes to the United States.

These movements of money across national boundaries do not occur directly. In other words, the U.S. dollars do not actually travel to Japan, nor do the Japanese yen come to the United States. The individual people or organizations engaged in the goods transactions do not even perform the money transactions. The entire process is carried out through the intermediation of a financial institution, usually a bank, which is authorized by the government of the country to handle the process.

The Japanese car producer who sells a Japanese car to an American has little use for dollars; dollars cannot be used to pay the Japanese workers or the suppliers of the raw materials used to produce the car. What the Japanese producer needs is, of course, yen. The producer solves this problem by exchanging dollars paid by the purchaser for yen. The number of yen the Japanese producer gets for each dollar paid for the car is called the **exchange rate.** Many international financial problems are associated with the way exchange rates for the world's currencies are determined and maintained.

This chapter begins with a brief look at some theories of exchange rate determination. Then the chapter traces the evolution of the International Monetary System. After a short section on record-keeping and reporting of international financial transactions among countries, the concluding section presents the contemporary global financial scene and highlights some of the international financial problems that are of concern to the international manager.

EXCHANGE RATES

Ever since humans abandoned **barter**—the exchange of the fruit of one's own labor for the fruit of another person's labor—and adopted money as the generally accepted means of exchange, the issue of fairness in representing the correct value or worth of one's work has been central. How many units of money should a farmer receive for one unit of potatoes, and how many units of coffee should the farmer receive for these units of money? In other words, what is the exchange rate of potatoes for coffee?

For transactions within one economy, the market mechanism establishes the "fair" monetary value of all human activities. When national boundaries are crossed, however, national monetary units, or currencies, lose their universal acceptability. Every country in the world has its own currency, which is by law the only currency accepted and used by its own citizens and by foreigners who visit or do business with the country in question. Thus, if international trade is to take place, there must be a way of transforming one currency into another. The process of deciding how one currency will be converted into another is known as **exchange rate determination.** The end result of this process is a ratio expressing the number of units of one currency in terms of the other—the exchange rate.[1]

EXCHANGE RATE DETERMINANTS

What determines the number of units of one currency that a person is willing to give up for one unit of another person's currency? How, in other words, is it determined that one U.S. dollar will be exchanged for 150 Japanese yen or 0.80 British pound?

Exhibit 6-1 depicts the three main *theoretical determinants* of exchange rates. The exhibit assumes a more or less free market economy, in which direct governmental intervention is kept at a minimum. The theories deal with the short, medium, and long run. All three theories of exchange rate determinants assume that exchange rates are determined by the demand for and supply of a currency in the international market.

SOURCES OF DEMAND AND SUPPLY OF CURRENCIES

What causes people to demand a foreign currency? The main motivators are people's desires for foreign goods and services and for opportunities to

---

[1]The discussion of exchange rates draws heavily on W. Baumol and A. S. Blinder, *Economics,* Third Edition (San Diego: Harcourt, Brace, Jovanovich, 1985), Ch. 37.

Exhibit 6-1   Exchange Rate Determinants

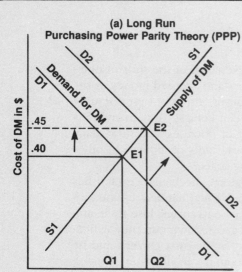

(a) Long Run
Purchasing Power Parity Theory (PPP)

Effect of a Rise in Inflation
Rate in the United States

Inflation increases the prices of all
goods, both foreign and domestic. In
effect, this price increase has the
same impact as a *real* increase in the
demand for DM and a decrease in the
DM/$ ratio.

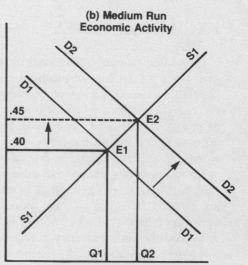

(b) Medium Run
Economic Activity

Effect of a Boom in U.S.
Economic Activity

An increase in economic activity creates an increase in consumption of
goods, both domestic and foreign. An
increasing demand for German goods
is translated into an increase in the
demand for DM and therefore a decrease in the DM/$ ratio.

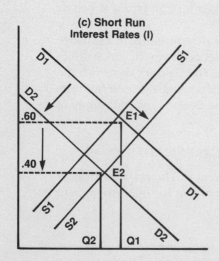

(c) Short Run
Interest Rates (I)

Effect of a Rise in U.S. Interest Rate

A rise in the U.S. interest rate attracts
German investors to the United
States. These investors increase the
supply of DM available for trading for
$. The increase in the supply of DM
and a decrease in the demand cause
the DM to drop in value.

make money in foreign markets. Thus, the demand for foreign currencies comes from the following:

(1)   International trade in goods and services. Suppose Ms. Shepart wishes to buy a French perfume in Topeka, Kansas. She goes to the local drugstore and exchanges dollars for the French perfume, leading her drugstore to place a new order with the French distributor. Thus, Ms. Shepart's demand for a French perfume leads to demand for francs.

(2)   International trade in financial instruments like stocks and bonds. Ms. Shepart reads in *The Wall Street Journal* that the British government is selling a portion of the British telephone company to the public, so she calls up her stockbroker and asks him to buy 1,000 shares of the British Telephone Company. Ms. Shepart's demand for British stock leads to demand for pounds.

(3)   Purchase of physical assets like real estate, factories, and machinery overseas. Ms. Shepart visits Greece on her summer vacation and likes the climate, so she decides to buy a villa in Rhodes. Ms. Shepart's desire for Greece's sunny beaches leads to demand for drachmas.

In sum, people's demand for foreign goods, stocks and bonds, or real estate creates a demand for foreign currencies. Similarly, people's desire to sell their products and services creates a supply of foreign currency.

LONG-RUN DETERMINANTS: THE PURCHASING POWER PARITY THEORY

Chapter 5 pointed out that international trade tends to equalize prices across the world because it equalizes the costs of the factors of production. Thus, as long as there is free trade, exchange rates should adjust so that the same product costs the same number of monetary units worldwide, except for differences in transportation costs and other added charges. This principle is the basis for the oldest and still the most accurate exchange rate determination theory, the Purchasing Power Parity (PPP) Theory, illustrated in part a of Exhibit 6-1.

The Purchasing Power Parity Theory holds that the exchange rate between any two national currencies adjusts to reflect differences in the price levels in the two countries. If, for example, an American car costs $10,000 and an equivalent German car costs 20,000 deutsche marks (DM), what must be the exchange rate between the dollar and the DM? Since 20,000 DM must be the equivalent of $10,000, each DM must be worth 50 cents ($10,000/20,000 = 0.50$). Why is that so?

To find the answer, we must figure out what would happen if the exchange rate were more or less than that dictated by the PPP theory. Suppose that one DM were worth 60 cents. Then a German car would cost $12,000 in the United States ($20,000 \times 0.60$), while the American car would still cost American buyers $10,000. This price difference of $2,000 would be enough to cause not only all Americans but also most foreigners, including Germans themselves, to come to the United States to buy American cars.

The result of these developments would be an adjustment in the exchange rate between the two countries. The DM would depreciate (one DM would buy fewer dollars), or the dollar would appreciate (one dollar would buy more DM). If the market mechanism failed to adjust the exchange rates, the government of one of the countries would do so. Germany would, for example, devalue its DM (decrease the *official* value of its currency), or the United States would revalue its dollar (increase the *official* value of its currency).

Indirectly, the PPP theory is a good predictor of the effects of a persistent increase in prices in one country (inflation) on exchange rates. Suppose that over a five-year period prices in the United States rose 33%, while in Germany they rose 60%. The PPP theory predicts that the DM would depreciate relative to the dollar (that is, one DM would buy fewer dollars). Further, the PPP theory predicts the amount of the currency depreciation (that is, how many fewer dollars a DM would buy or how many more DM a dollar would buy). Exhibit 6-2 shows the predicted effects of changes in prices on exchange rates in the two countries.

In general, the PPP theory states that differences in national inflation rates are the major cause of adjustments in exchange rates. Countries with faster inflation rates experience more frequent depreciations and devaluations than do countries with slower inflation rates. Though one can cite many exceptions to the above rule (primarily with respect to the relationship of the United States dollar to the currencies of Western Europe and Japan during the early 1980s), most economists believe that in the long run the PPP theory explains exchange rate determination rather well.

MEDIUM-RUN DETERMINANTS: ECONOMIC ACTIVITY

Economic activity is the totality of individual and business activities performed in a country. When economic activity increases, an economy experiences growth. When economic activity decreases, an economy undergoes a

Exhibit 6-2   Impact of Inflation on Exchange Rates

	United States ($) (33% inflation)		West Germany (DM) (60% inflation)	
	1986	1991	1986	1991
Prices of cars	10,000	13,300	20,000	32,000
Exchange rate	$1 = 2.0 DM	$1 = 2.42 DM	1 DM = $0.50	1 DM = $0.41
Change in exchange rate	The $ gained 0.42 DM		The DM lost $0.09	

recession. Growth has a positive impact on demand. Recession, on the other hand, has a negative impact on demand. Since economic activity in an open economy includes demand for foreign products, an increase in demand will lead to an increase in imports which, in turn, will lead to an increase in demand for foreign money. Because the demand for the national currency will remain the same or even decline, the supply of the national currency will increase. The end result will be a depreciation of the currency's value.

Part b of Exhibit 6-1 shows the effect of an increase in economic activity on the exchange rate. With demand represented by curve D1 and supply by curve S1, the cost of one deutsche mark will be $0.40. If an economic boom in the United States shifts demand to curve D2, the new equilibrium will be at point E2. Now the cost of one deutsche mark will be $0.45. Thus, the deutsche mark will appreciate by $0.05, as a result of the greater demand for marks and the accompanying greater supply of U.S. dollars.

In general, the Economic Activity Theory holds that a country's imports will rise quickly when the country experiences a boom and that this growth-stimulated increase in imports will lead to a depreciation of the country's currency, due to an increase in the demand for foreign currency to pay for the imports.

SHORT-RUN DETERMINANTS: INTEREST RATES AND EXCHANGE RATES

Money movements are, for the most part, triggered and channeled by the price one is willing to pay for the use of money or, alternatively, the benefit one is willing to accept for parting with it. This price is known as the *interest rate*. Thus, it follows that countries that are willing to offer a higher interest rate than the rest of the world will attract most of the available money. By the same token, countries whose interest rates are lowest will experience the greatest outflow of money.

Part c of Exhibit 6-1 shows that an increase in the interest rate of the United States will motivate the Germans to acquire stocks and bonds on the U.S. stock exchange. This German appetite for U.S. stocks and bonds will be translated into an increase in the supply of DMs within the United States, shown by the shift of the supply curve from S1 to S2. Unfortunately for the Germans, Americans may not have a similar appetite for German stocks and bonds. If not, there will be a shift in the demand for deutsche marks from D1 to D2. The result of these movements will be a drop in the value of the DM relative to the dollar. The DM will depreciate by some 20%.

In general, the following principles describe the short-term behavior of exchange rates:

(1)   Currencies generally *appreciate* in countries whose inflation rates are lower than those in the rest of the world (for example, Japan and West Germany after 1986).

(2)   Currencies generally *depreciate* in countries that experience lower economic activity than the rest of the world, because these countries import little (for example, the developing countries).

(3)   Currencies generally *appreciate* in countries with higher interest rates, because these countries attract capital from the rest of the world (for example, the United States during the early 1980s).

THE INTERNATIONAL MONETARY SYSTEM

The International Monetary System (IMS) is a catchall term for the various attempts to formalize financial transactions around the globe. The main objective of these attempts has been the development of a set of guidelines, rules, and regulations governing countries' fiscal and monetary policies.

As the previous section pointed out, exchange rate determination is neither an intuitively obvious nor a simple process. Under conditions of a free market system, exchange rates will be determined by one or a combination of the three main factors mentioned—inflation, interest rates, and growth. It is well known, however, that the "free market" is fiction. All national markets are more or less regulated markets in which governments intervene by means of fiscal and monetary policies. Fiscal policies manipulate taxes and government transfer; monetary policies deal with the money supply and interest rates. Obviously, taxes, money supply, and interest rates all affect the general economic activity, which in turn affects exchange rates.

Historically, the International Monetary System evolved from the rather simple and easy-to-administer *gold standard system* to today's very complex and virtually incomprehensible managed float system.[2] Exhibit 6-3 summarizes the evolution of the International Monetary System.

THE GOLD STANDARD SYSTEM

Gold has always fascinated humans. Thus, it is not surprising that the first attempts to develop an IMS used gold as the standard to which all countries linked their national currencies. Under the gold standard system national currencies were linked to gold at a *fixed parity*—that is, each nation defined its currency unit as equal to the value of a certain weight of pure gold. The weight of gold was determined by the number of grains. The U.S. dollar, for example, was defined as containing 23.22 grains of gold. There are 480 grains of gold in one troy ounce, so one troy ounce of gold was worth $20.67 (480/23.22).

---

[2]For more detailed descriptions of the International Monetary System, see H. S. Robock and U. Simmons, *International Business and Multinational Corporations,* Third Edition (Homewood, IL: R. D. Irwin, 1983), Ch. 5; A. Sampson, *The Money Lenders: The People and Politics of the World Banking Crisis* (Middlesex, England: Penguin Books, 1981); and R. Z. Aliber, *The International Money Game* (New York: Basic Books, 1975).

The British pound was defined as containing 113 grains of gold and was equal to $4.8665 (113/23.22). This dollar amount was termed the *par value* of the pound.

This simple system worked remarkably well until the First World War, simply because whatever international trade took place was between the big powers and the colonies. Since most of the gold was in the hands of the colonialists, they could make the rules. In addition, the system itself was very accommodating. It provided an easy and automatic mechanism for clearing international trade balances. Since countries had to sell gold to pay for their *deficits* whenever export earnings were not sufficient to pay for imports, their currencies would automatically *depreciate,* thereby making their exports cheaper. The added currency that was earned via the increase in exports would then eliminate the deficit.

In countries where export earnings were larger than import payments, the continuous *surpluses* would lead to an increase in the gold stock and hence in the money supply, which would provoke a general price rise. This increase in prices would increase the price of exports, causing export volume to decline, and increase the volume of imports. The accompanying increase in the demand for foreign currency (due to increasing imports) and decline in the demand for local currency (due to decreasing exports) would lead to an automatic elimination of the surplus.

FREE FLOAT: THE TURMOIL OF THE FIRST HALF OF THE TWENTIETH CENTURY

The years between the First World War and 1944 were marked by numerous attempts to restore the gold standard system, which had collapsed at the outbreak of the war, when Great Britain and the rest of the European colonialists lost their world hegemony. All of the attempts to restore the gold standard system failed. By the beginning of the 1930s it had become clear that the numerous and uncoordinated exchange rate manipulations were destined to bring the world to catastrophe. Indeed, just before the Second World War the entire economic system of the world went into a gigantic crisis, the Great Depression.

THE GOLD EXCHANGE STANDARD

At the end of the Second World War, the United States was virtually the world's sole wealth holder, consumer, and, most importantly, capital goods producer. The U.S. dollar seemed to be the only currency worth accepting in international transactions and holding as a reserve. So it surprised no one that the rest of the world enthusiastically accepted an American initiative to restructure the International Monetary System. Representatives of 44 nations met at Bretton Woods, New Hampshire, in 1944 and agreed to establish an International Monetary System that would be immune to individual countries'

Exhibit 6-3　The Evolution of the International Monetary System

The Era of Stability: British and Other European Colonial Hegemony (gold standard)	The Era of Turmoil: No Clear Leader (free float)	The Era of Stability Based on U.S. Hegemony (gold exchange standard)	The Era of Questioning U.S. Role (free float)	The Era of Soul-Searching (general float)	The Era of Reasoning (managed float)	The Era of Perplexity (free float again)
National currencies were linked to gold at a fixed parity—the value of a certain weight of pure gold. One U.S. dollar = 23.22 grains of gold and one troy ounce = 480 grains of gold, so one ounce of gold = 480/23.22 = $20.67. One British pound = 113 grains of gold; therefore one pound = 480/113 = £ 4.25 = 20.67/4.25 = $4.87.	There was no standard whatsoever. The world went through World War I, the Depression, and World War II. Many attempts to restore the gold standard failed.	National currencies were linked to gold. However, there was no obligation to exchange for gold. The U.S. dollar was the only currency convertible, at $35.00 per ounce. All other currencies had to have a dollar parity and maintain it at ±1%. All currencies were pegged to the dollar, and the dollar was pegged to gold.	Exchange rates were flexible. The United States refused to exchange dollars for gold. The EEC developed its own European Monetary Unit (EMU). Attempts via the Smithsonian Agreement to peg all currencies to the dollar without gold convertibility failed.	All major currencies were floating—confusion! Accumulation of external debt by developing countries was exponential.	There was a mixture of fixed currencies and floating (flexible) currencies: major countries had floating currencies, and developing countries had pegged currencies. The external debt of the less developed countries (LDC) increased explosively. West Germany and Japan accumulated foreign trade	The major G5 or G7 Plaza Agreement was signed. There was talk about pegging currencies to the dollar or DEY (dollar + European Currency Unit + yen). The LDC debt equaled $1 trillion. The U.S. external debt approached $1 trillion. The U.S. national debt equaled $2.2 trillion. The dollar depreciated by 30–35%

Members maintained values of gold by buying and selling gold.

Surpluses and deficits were eliminated automatically—when surpluses increased, prices went up, exports declined, and imports increased, thereby eliminating surpluses.

1927

1944

1971

1972

1976

surpluses. The United States experienced an explosive increase in national, trade, and external deficits and became a net debtor.

1985

against the yen and the DM.

currency manipulations and would guarantee a free flow of goods and money around the globe.

The Bretton Woods conference created the International Monetary Fund (IMF) and the International Bank for Reconstruction and Development (IBRD), commonly known as the World Bank. It was agreed that the IMF would guarantee stability in exchange rates, and the World Bank would provide financial and expert assistance to countries that needed capital for their economic development.

All participating countries agreed to try to maintain the value of their currencies within 1 percent above or below the official parity by selling foreign currencies or gold if necessary. If its currency became too weak to defend, a country could devalue it by up to 10 percent without formal approval from the IMF. Larger devaluations needed the official approval of the IMF.

The U.S. dollar was given special status as an *international reserve currency*. The United States agreed to convert dollars held by foreigners into gold upon request, at the official price of $35 per ounce. Thus, the fixed exchange rate system was essentially a system in which all countries "pegged" their currencies to the dollar and the dollar was pegged to gold. It is for this reason that the system is also known as the *adjustable peg system*. Although gold was still the king, so to speak, it was the dollar that was the pivot of the International Monetary System.

This system, which depended on the central role of the United States and its dollar, worked remarkably well for over 20 years. The postwar years were, however, unlike any previous era. The period witnessed dramatic economic activity in Europe and Japan and a substantial decline in the relative position of the United States in the world economy. This unprecedented expansion in international economic activity revealed one of the most obvious weaknesses of the Bretton Woods system. The system was designed essentially to prevent "sickness" and to assist "sick" currencies. The system did not provide for problems on the international financial scene that arose from some countries' being extremely "healthy" and accumulating surpluses that they did not have to "return" to the International Monetary System. Continuing surpluses drained needed funds from the system, thereby creating a large *liquidity shortage* in the international financial system. Thus, countries with deficits could not find dollars with which to pay. Even the IMF and the World Bank fell victim to this liquidity drought.

The hoarding of dollars by countries with surpluses, combined with the outflow of dollars in the form of direct foreign investment and the migration of dollars to the Eurodollar market, created a tremendous liquidity shortage in the United States. At the same time the war in Viet Nam strained the U.S. Treasury. The result was a loss of confidence in the United States on the part of European countries. This loss of confidence led to a massive unloading of the dollars held by countries with surpluses. The U.S. Treasury was unable to accommodate the sudden substantial increase in the demand for gold. By 1971 the U.S. gold stock had dropped to $11 billion, down from $24 billion in 1948. Then, since the United States had most of the gold, it decided to change the rules.

The first step in changing the rules of the fixed exchange-rate system was taken in 1968, when the United States suspended the sale of gold to industrial users. This step proved to be insufficient to solve the gold-drain problem, and on August 15, 1971 the United States was finally forced to stop selling gold altogether. This action drove the final nail into the coffin of the fixed exchange rate system.

THE MANAGED FLOAT SYSTEM

The warning the United States gave the world in 1968 triggered a number of attempts to save the fixed exchange rate system. To provide some international liquidity, the IMF issued what it called special drawing rights (SDR). The SDR is an international reserve asset, sometimes called *paper gold,* issued by the IMF and distributed to its members. SDRs can be used by IMF members to obtain a specific currency, settle a financial obligation, or secure a loan. The SDR was originally linked to gold. In 1974 SDRs became linked to a collection of five currencies—the U.S. dollar, the German deutsche mark, the British pound, the French franc, and the Japanese yen. By 1988 the average value of the SDR was $1.33, and SDRs accounted for only 10% of the total international reserves, excluding gold holdings.

In the early 1970s, the European countries attempted to stabilize their currencies by creating the European Monetary Union (EMU). The members of the EEC plus the United Kingdom and Denmark agreed that they would limit fluctuations among their currencies to within a small range, but that the value of the group of currencies as a whole could fluctuate against that of other currencies. Successive improvements of this initial scheme led to the development in 1979 of the European Monetary System (EMS).

All of these developments by the IMF and the EEC led finally to the total abandonment of the fixed exchange rate system in 1973. Obviously, the completely free floating system that followed the breakdown of the fixed exchange rate system could not continue to operate indefinitely. Free floating implies that the price of one currency relative to another is determined entirely by the daily market forces of demand and supply and not by the government of any country. In reality, most currencies are fixed in that they are tied to another currency, usually the currency of the country's major trading partner.

In April 1976, the IMF's Board of Governors approved a number of amendments to the IMF articles of agreement that legitimized the changes that had taken place, a move that led to official acceptance of the *managed float system.* Under the managed float system, the major industrialized countries' currencies float more or less freely against each other. The smaller countries peg their currencies to one of the major currencies. Most of the small countries peg their currencies to the U.S. dollar, the British pound, the Japanese yen, the Canadian dollar, or the French franc. (See Exhibit 6-4.)

The managed float system has substantially reduced the role of the IMF. The major countries have no need for it as a currency regulator, and the minor countries usually use it primarily as a consultant on international monetary

**Exhibit 6-4   Exchange Arrangements of IMF
Member Countries on April 30, 1985**

Type of Arrangement	Number of Countries
Currency pegged to:	
U.S. dollar	32
French franc	14
Other currency	4
SDR	12
Other currency composite	31
Exchange rates adjusted to set of indicators	6
Cooperative exchange arrangements	8
Other arrangements	40
Total	147

SOURCE: International Monetary Fund, *The Role and Function of the International Monetary Fund* (Washington, DC: IMF, 1985), 30.

reforms that have to be instituted to secure financial assistance from the major commercial banks.

In sum, after going through numerous changes over the past decade, the International Monetary System is in no better position today to guarantee financial stability in the international market that it was ten years ago. The good old days of the gold standard and the fixed exchange rate system seem to be gone forever.

THE INTERNATIONAL RECORD-KEEPING AND REPORTING SYSTEM

International transactions among countries are recorded in much the same way as company transactions are recorded, using double-entry bookkeeping methods. Every transaction is recorded twice: once as a debit and once as a credit. However, there is no requirement that the sums of the two sides of a *selected number* of balance-of-payments accounts be the same, as there is with the private sector balance sheet. As a matter of fact, it is more common for these accounts to show deficits and surpluses than to be balanced.

The technical details of balance-of-payments accounts are explained in Appendix 6A. This section will briefly explain the nature of and the reasons for deficits and surpluses, as well as the techniques for adjusting a country's exchange rates.

In a balance-of-payments account one simply computes the private demand for and supply of a country's currency and subtracts the quantity supplied (QS) from the quantity demanded (QD). When QS is greater than QD, the country experiences a balance-of-payments *deficit*. Balance-of-payments deficits arise whenever the exchange rate is pegged at an artificially high level—that is, when the currency is *overvalued*. When QS is less than QD, the country experiences a balance-of-payments *surplus*. The excess demand for a country's currency over its supply indicates that the currency is pegged at an artificially low level—that is, the currency is *undervalued*.

Overvalued currencies are offered at prices higher than customers are willing to pay. If there are no buyers, the currency's price—its exchange rate—will decline. To prevent the forced depreciation of a country's currency, the country's central bank usually steps in and acts as a buyer. The added demand for the currency stabilizes the exchange rate. The cost of stepping in is the amount the central bank spends to buy its own currency. Eventually, however, overvalued currencies do depreciate.

The pressure for the central bank to intervene in the foreign exchange market, which is characteristic of deficit-running countries, is not present in surplus-running countries. In such countries the central bank does not have to sell its currency to keep its value from rising even further.

Although there is tremendous international pressure to correct balance-of-payments deficits, there is very little that can be done to force a country to eliminate a balance-of-payments surplus. Thus, although the IMF, the World Bank, and some developed countries are devising various plans to assist the deficit nations (mostly developing countries) in eliminating their problems, there is no plan that aims at enticing developed nations to eliminate their rather substantial surpluses.

THE FUTURE OF THE INTERNATIONAL MONETARY SYSTEM

There does not appear to be any consensus on the International Monetary System's ability to perform its main role—namely, to facilitate international trade. Some people believe that the system has done a remarkable job of greasing the machinery of international financial markets by enabling borrowers to find funds and lenders to get the best returns ever on their assets. At the other extreme are people who would attribute to the post–World War II International Monetary System most, if not all, of the world's problems, from inflation to unemployment to external and internal debt crises.[3]

It can be argued that the International Monetary System performed extremely well until 1973, when the fixed exchange rate system collapsed. Since

---

[3]The discussion in this section draws heavily on Michael R. Sesit, Ann Mounof, and Peter Truell, "Prosperity and Peril in the Brave New Market," in "Global Finance and Investment: A Special Report," *The Wall Street Journal,* September 29, 1986, 1D, 40–46D.

then both the free floating system and the managed float system have performed rather poorly. The main criticism of floating exchange systems is that they encourage short-term speculative behavior at the expense of long-term economic growth and development projects. For this reason, critics would like to see the world return to some type of fixed exchange rate system or gold standard.

Most government officials outside of the United States still work under the assumption that even though the floating rate system is not completely faultless, it remains the only viable system. As Roland Leuschel, an economic advisor to Banque Bruxelles Lambert, put it:

> The floating rate system has helped produce the highest postwar unemployment in the Organization for Economic Cooperation and Development, but it is an honorable one; it is partly responsible for the accumulation of the highest nominal debt ever in the world, but it is an honorable system; it has created the highest current-account imbalances, but it is an honorable system; it has helped push up the real interest rates to perilous levels, but it is an honorable system; it has produced a rapid swing from high inflation to a deflationary environment, but it is an honorable system.[4]

On this side of the Atlantic, Robert Mundel from Columbia University warned as early as 1983, "The floating exchange rate system did not provide discipline or monetary restraint. On the contrary, it provided inflation, unrepayable debt and de facto bankruptcy."[5]

Although space limitations do not permit a thorough analysis and evaluation of the International Monetary System's performance, the following sections will point out some of the most obvious problems of the contemporary international financial scene.

COMPLEXITY AND UNCONTROLLABILITY

International finance, pointed out R. Z. Aliber, is a game with two sets of players: the politicians and bureaucrats in national governments and the presidents and treasurers of businesses of all sizes.[6] The government officials want to win elections and secure a niche in history. The corporate presidents and treasurers want to profit (or at least avoid losses) from the changes in exchange rates that are inevitable in a world with more than 200 national currencies and over a million firms. With so many players in the international financial game, the number of possible combinations is astronomical.

When a system that is inherently so complex undergoes frequent and drastic changes, its behavior becomes unpredictable. As Irwin D. Sandberg, Senior

---

[4]Ronald Leuschel, "Money's Riding on the Group of One," *The Wall Street Journal*, September 26, 1986, 30.

[5]Sesit, Mounof, and Truell, "Prosperity and Peril," p. 41D.

[6]Aliber, *The International Money Game*, p. 3.

Vice President of the Federal Reserve Bank of New York, put it, "The pace of innovation is so rapid and new products so complex that I have some concern whether the institutions themselves can manage it, much less the regulators, who always lag behind. These days, hardly anybody is safe from instant disasters."[7]

Indeed, the very elements of an integrated, worldwide financial market—huge sums of free-moving capital, high-speed communications systems, complicated new financial instruments, the opening of national markets to outside competitors—have made the system more vulnerable to unexpected shocks. Hans Baer, Chief Executive of Bank Julius Baer & Co. in Zurich, Switzerland, maintains that new financial instruments "aren't understood by central bankers, bank management or the people who trade them. We create things and then watch them with fascination. This is like being on the outer fringes of high-tech; you do it till it blows."[8] Nobody knows how many new financial instruments are created every day, and nobody knows which of those created are "sound international trade facilitators" and which are international "junk stock and bonds."

How big is the international financial market? Two U.S. payments systems—one operated by the Federal Reserve Bank and the other by commercial banks—together clear an average of $1.3 trillion in transactions daily, up from $175 billion in 1974. Advances in telecommunications have "obliterated all traditional concepts of time, space, geography and transaction capacity," noted Robert R. Bench, U.S. Deputy Comptroller of the Currency.[9]

REAL AND POTENTIAL PROBLEMS

The Bretton Woods system was designed to prevent foreign exchange shortages and exchange rate deterioration in the deficit countries. It never occurred to the designers of the system that there might be a global liquidity shortage due to the accumulation of huge surpluses by the developed countries. In addition, no one predicted that the mechanism for clearing the deficit markets by borrowing in the open market at the going interest rates would saddle the developing countries with a tremendous "external debt."

During the 1970s most of the developing countries experienced an exponential growth in foreign debt. This growth was the result of the convergence of several factors:

(1)   The inability of these countries to generate enough export-earned foreign currency

(2)   Ambitious development programs requiring massive importation of expensive capital goods

---

[7]Aliber, *The International Money Game*, p. 3.
[8]Sesit, Mounof, and Truell, "Prosperity and Peril," p. 40D.
[9]Sesit, Mounof, and Truell, "Prosperity and Peril," p. 40D.

(3)   Conspicuous consumption of imported goods as a hedge against inflation and currency devaluations

(4)   Accelerating global interest rates

(5)   The change in the policies of the lending countries, especially the United States, away from grants, which were referred to as "giveaway programs," and toward interest-bearing loans

The explosive increase in foreign debt has created some chilling monetary crises with potentially catastrophic consequences. Exhibit 6-5 shows that the external debt of the developing countries is approaching the $1.3 trillion level. Ten years ago it was barely over $500 billion. In 1955 foreign debt was just $10 billion.

Most people think that it is only the poor countries that have a gigantic problem. Lord Keynes would remind them, however, that the problem belongs to the international bankers who so freely loaned these monies. As Lord Keynes so elegantly put it, "If you owe a pound to the banker you are at his mercy. If you owe a thousand pounds he is at your mercy."

SOURCE: Don Wright, *The Miami News*. Reprinted with permission.

QUICK FIXES

Both the sheer size of the foreign debt and its growth rate have been the subject of numerous conferences, summits, and other get-togethers of the lending countries as well as of the recipient countries. The threats of newly elected leaders of developing countries to default on their loans or to pay only a small portion, usually a fixed percentage of their export earnings, have been

Exhibit 6-5   Total Foreign Debt

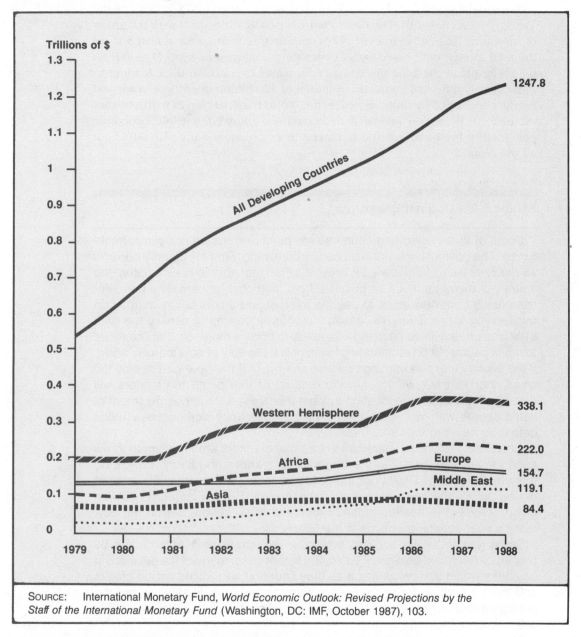

Trillions of $

All Developing Countries	1247.8
Western Hemisphere	338.1
Europe	222.0
Africa	
Middle East	154.7
	119.1
Asia	84.4

1979 1980 1981 1982 1983 1984 1985 1986 1987 1988

SOURCE: International Monetary Fund, *World Economic Outlook: Revised Projections by the Staff of the International Monetary Fund* (Washington, DC: IMF, October 1987), 103.

met at first by equally threatening rumors of freezing a country's assets in the United States and other lending countries. Eventually, the parties have usually worked out plans allowing the debtor nation to make "rollover" principal payments while borrowing enough to make the interest payments. But most schemes for rolling-over or rescheduling massive debts have merely turned the debtor countries into "optimal bankrupts" (see Exhibit 6-6).

The most ambitious attempt made by the lending countries to deal with the growing debt problem was the Baker Plan, named after U.S. Secretary of the Treasury James Baker III. The Baker Plan, devised in 1986, dealt with the group of seventeen leading borrowers who, combined, accounted for almost 50% of the total foreign debt owed by all developing countries in 1985 (see Exhibit 6-7). The plan called for the commercial banks to increase their lending to these heavily indebted countries by a total of $20 billion over three years, and for the multilateral institutions, led by the World Bank, to chip in with a further increase of $9 billion provided the countries followed sensible economic policies. But the banks refused to extend more credit, and the plan never got off the ground.

Exhibit 6-6   Optimal Bankrupts

Some of these borrowing countries are practicing the art of optimal bankruptcy. The optimal bankrupt lives well by borrowing. First the country borrows as much as it can from low-cost lenders; when that source is exhausted, the country borrows as much as possible from high-cost lenders. The borrower uses funds from new loans to pay the interest and amortization charges on outstanding loans. The only reason the country desires to service the debt at all is to protect its credit rating—its ability to borrow more. So it will continue to make payments on outstanding loans only if the flow of new loans is rising. If the country's export earnings decline sharply or if the new loan seems too small, the borrower will threaten to default. At that point, the lenders will usually offer a debt renegotiation to save themselves the embarrassment of being caught with worthless loans; the borrower may demand new funds before agreeing to the renegotiation.

Of course, the optimal bankrupt knows that creditors are reluctant to throw good money after bad. But the borrower also knows the injury it might do them by defaulting. The larger the possible damage, the larger the amount of new credits the borrower can probably secure. But the larger the volume of new credits the lenders extend today, the more severe will be the borrower's debt-service problems in the future.

Some lenders might seek to avoid the embarrassment of a default by placing all future aid on a grant basis. But in that case, many of the developing countries would borrow as much as they could on subsidized export credits and loans extended for political objectives; the debt would still rise and the process would be repeated. The only constraint on the amount they *do* borrow is the amount they *can* borrow.

The irony is that attempts to make U.S. financial assistance more businesslike have made it less businesslike. And the efforts to gain an advantage for U.S. exports and the balance of payments have been largely self-defeating, since other countries have adopted similar measures. If both lender and borrowers act under the presumption that a loan is on hard terms, less can be demanded of the borrower. Stricter conditions may be attached to the use of grants.

But it is naive to believe that changing the terms of aid could now make any great difference. The fact is that politicians in the aid-receiving countries do not have the same interests as the development planners in the donor countries and the international agencies; nor do they have the same constituencies. And so, even if the borrowers should promise—and keep their commitments—to use the external assistance wisely and frugally, domestic and other non-tied resources would still have to be used to accomplish their political interests. Why, then, do the lenders continue to be manipulated by the borrowers? The answer is that, on margin, continuing the game seems attractive: the cost of new loans always appears lower than the losses that would occur if the borrowers defaulted, for the point of no return has already been passed.

SOURCE: Aliber, *The International Money Game*, pp. 276–77.

Both the lenders and the borrowers are in a real predicament. The developing countries must borrow to increase their investment, which will produce the exports required to generate the foreign currency they need to repay the loans they have to make in order to import the capital goods necessary for the investment. The private banks, which account for an average of 80.8% of the debt outstanding, know that if this growth in exports does not materialize they stand little chance of ever receiving their money back. So they must lend more to make sure that they do not lose what they have already loaned, thereby aggravating the problem.

THE ULTIMATE FIX: THE NEW INTERNATIONAL MONETARY ORDER

The quick fixes thus far attempted have not solved the perennial problem of the accumulations of huge international debts by the developing countries and most recently by the United States. In addition, the schemes devised thus far have not convinced the two main surplus countries, Japan and West Germany, to eliminate their surpluses by increasing their buying overseas. It appears, therefore, that there is a need for a drastic new approach to the international debt and liquidity problem.

In the past most experts believed that bringing the debt accumulated by the developing countries under control was the key to resolving the international monetary problem. Today there is a groundswell of opinion that unless the U.S. national and international debt is brought under control, all other schemes are doomed to fail.

There are two main schools of thought on developing a permanent solution. Both of these schools set as a necessary condition removing the U.S. dollar from its position as the only reserve currency. In its place, the "American

Exhibit 6-7   The Focus of the Baker Plan:
Seventeen Heavily Indebted Countries

| Country | Debt Outstanding, 1985[a] | | Debt Service 1985–87[b] (billions of $) | | Ratio of Debt to Exports (%) | |
	Total (billions of $)	Of Which Private Source (%)	Total	Of Which Interest	1980	1984
Argentina	50.8	86.8	20.4	12.7	90.9	290.2
Bolivia	4.0	39.3	1.6	0.6	210.4	382.7
Brazil	107.3	84.2	39.7	28.0	171.3	219.8
Chile	21.0	87.2	9.2	5.0	75.5	225.1
Colombia	11.3	57.5	6.4	2.5	69.7	150.1
Costa Rica	4.2	59.7	2.4	0.9	139.5	270.8
Ecuador[d]	8.5	73.8	3.4	2.1	110.9	223.1
Ivory Coast	8.0	64.1	4.0	1.4	119.4	160.5
Jamaica	3.4	24.0	1.3	0.5	98.2	159.9
Mexico	99.0	89.1	44.4	27.2	136.7	213.5
Morocco	14.0	39.1	6.0	2.4	217.3	337.2′
Nigeria	19.3	88.2	9.1	3.1	15.7	95.4
Peru	13.4	60.7	5.2	3.1	127.1	247.0
Philippines	24.8	67.8	9.5	4.9	81.6	139.1
Uruguay	3.6	82.1	1.4	0.8	70.7	184.8
Venezuela[d]	33.6	99.5	17.8	7.8	48.9	91.4
Yugoslavia[e]	19.6	64.0	13.6	4.0	33.3	62.6
Total	445.9	80.8	194.9	106.9	106.9	203.1

[a]Estimated total external liabilities, including the use of IMF credit.
[b]Debt service is based on known long-term debt and terms at end-1984. It does not take into account new loans contracted or debt reschedulings signed after that date. Based on estimated interest actually paid on total external liabilities in 1985.
SOURCE: "Taking Up the Running: A Survey of the World Bank," *The Economist*, September 27, 1986, 24.

school" recommends using an asset that is not a liability to any nation—gold. The "European school" proposes using as a reserve currency a new currency called DEY, which would be a combined/weighted average of the dollar, the European Currency Unit, and the yen.

   The replacement of the dollar as a reserve currency with either gold or the DEY is only a necessary condition for solving the world debt crisis; it is by no means sufficient. Resolution of the crisis requires that the world's great powers make sure that their coordinated policies stimulate economic growth and foster international trade. At the very least, they must refrain from trade wars.

Trade Balance 1984 (billions of $)		Average Annual Growth Rates, 1980–84c (%)				
Total	Change from 1980	GDP	Exports	Imports	Investment	Per Capita Consumption
3.9	5.3	−1.6	3.6	−14.7	−16.8	−2.7
0.3	0.1	−4.7	−1.7	−15.8	−22.1	−7.8
13.1	15.9	0.1	10.8	−7.3	−8.6	−1.2
0.3	1.1	−1.4	0.7	−4.2	−11.6	−2.1
0.3	0.6	1.8	0.8	2.4	2.4	−0.1
−0.1	0.3	−0.4	1.1	−9.1	−9.4	−4.8
1.1	0.8	1.1	2.6	−13.7	−16.9	−2.3
1.3	0.9	−2.3	1.3	−8.8	−19.5	−6.6
−0.3	−0.2	1.3	−2.5	−2.1	9.5	−1.4
12.8	15.6	1.3	10.5	−14.5	−10.1	−1.4
−1.4	−0.1	2.5	4.1	−1.0	−2.7	−0.2
3.0	−8.2	−4.7	−13.3	−12.1	−19.3	−4.3
1.0	0.2	−0.7	−0.6	−10.8	−5.3	−3.7
−0.7	1.3	0.8	3.6	−4.8	−12.4	0.0
0.2	0.8	−3.7	2.2	−11.3	−20.2	−4.7
8.0	−0.2	−1.8	−3.8	−19.3	−15.6	−6.4
−1.2	3.7	0.6	−0.6	−8.1	−2.9	−0.5
41.6	37.8	−0.3	1.8	−9.2	−9.7	−1.8

cLatest year for which data are available. Growth rates are computed from time series in constant prices, using beginning- and end-period values.
dThe merchandise trade balance for 1984 is not available: the value shown is for 1983.
eAverage annual growth rates are for 1980–83, except for GDP which is for 1980–84.

THE AMERICAN SOLUTION

As noted earlier, the dollar continues to be used by most of the world as the main monetary reserve currency, despite the demonetarization of gold and the loss of U.S. hegemony in the global financial market. Reserves are the final asset that bridges the gap between sales and purchases of goods and services and stocks and bonds. When the dollar is used as a reserve currency, the official reserves of such countries as West Germany and Japan are held not in Bonn and Tokyo but in New York. This means, of course, that the ability of other countries to increase their assets by investing their reserves depends on the United States' willingness to accept an increase in its liabilities to offset the increase in its assets made possible by the foreign banks' investment. In other words, other countries can increase their reserves only if the United States increases its net reserve indebtedness with a balance-of-payments deficit.

This situation might seem harmless if it didn't have some side effects that exacerbate the problem. The dollar-reserve currency has two attractions. First, it allows other countries to earn interest on their reserves (which they could not do on gold reserves), thereby motivating them to accumulate dollar reserves. Second, it permits the United States to acquire foreign and domestic wealth with all the reserves lent to it by other countries, thereby promoting a false sense of national wealth or richness, and encouraging consumption of both domestic and foreign goods at the expense of domestic saving. Acquiring foreign goods requires, of course, more foreign currencies and more international indebtedness in the balance of payments. In other words, the dollar-reserve currency system makes the United States behave as if it were richer than it really is and the other countries as if they were poorer than they really are.

The "American solution" is for the world's three major trading partners (the United States, Japan, and West Germany), which combined account for over 45% of the world's exports and over 47% of its imports, to settle their accounts with one another, using gold as the medium of exchange. In addition to getting the United States off the hook, the gold-reserve system would solve the surplus problem plaguing the developed countries.

John Muller, economic advisor to U.S. Representative Jack Kemp (R-NY), put it as follows:

> Ending the dollar's official reserve currency role would make official reserves "portable" again; instead of being mechanically recycled to the U.S.—perpetuating the disadvantage for American farmers and manufacturers—part of the surpluses of West Germany and Japan would naturally be routed to growing nations with the most investment-friendly policies. These countries would, in turn, find more congenial Japanese and West German markets for their goods. If we are to restore an equilibrium of balances, noninflationary growth, we need to restore a money which is a real asset to the world: gold.[10]

THE EUROPEAN SOLUTION

European countries are extremely dissatisfied with the existing monetary system's inability to provide for adequate international liquidity and stability in exchange rates. They consider interventions from the Smithsonian Agree-

---

[10]John Muller, "Lifting the Reserve Current Curse," *The Wall Street Journal*, September 15, 1986, 6.

ment in 1971 to the Plaza Agreement in 1985 to have been short-lived and even fruitless attempts. Noting the relative success that the European Monetary System had in restoring stability to exchange rates within the European Economic Community, Europeans propose the implementation of a similar system on the global level.[11]

The tangible accomplishment of the EMS has been the emergence of the European Currency Unit (ECU) as a very robust currency (see Exhibit 6-8). The "European solution" calls for development of a similar currency for the global market. A combination of the U.S. dollar, the ECU, and the Japanese yen, the DEY would serve as the currency to which the rest of the countries would peg their own national currencies. The advantage of this arrangement is that there would be no incentive for any of the three main countries to accumulate foreign currencies. Variations beyond an upper or a lower limit would automatically trigger corrective intervention.

RECAPITULATION

This chapter described international finance as the more or less free flow of money to finance international trade transactions among the countries of the world. Most concern about international finance revolves around the determination of exchange rates—the price of one currency relative to that of another.

None of the many theories devised to explain the factors that influence the exchange rate between two currencies is totally satisfactory. In the past international trade seemed to explain exchange rate determination fairly adequately. A country that experienced a prolonged deficit in its balance of trade would also experience a deterioration in its exchange rates, since its demand for foreign currency to finance excess imports would be larger than other countries' demand for its currency. With the tremendous increase in the complexity of financial markets and the ease with which new and complex financial instruments can be created, exchange rate determination seems to have become more a function of the skills of the financial executives of a country than of its international trade position.

Various International Monetary Systems have evolved over the years from attempts to regulate exchange rates. They range from the relatively simple gold standard system of the pre–World War I years to the complex managed float system operating today. The resolution of the potentially very dangerous dilemma of international finance today requires a re-thinking of the role of the U.S. dollar as a reserve currency and the role of the United States as the world's banker.

---

[11]Clive Bergel, "Monetary Reform: A Global Model," *Europe*, July 1986, 24–25.

Exhibit 6-8   Trend of European, American, and Japanese Currencies Against the ECU

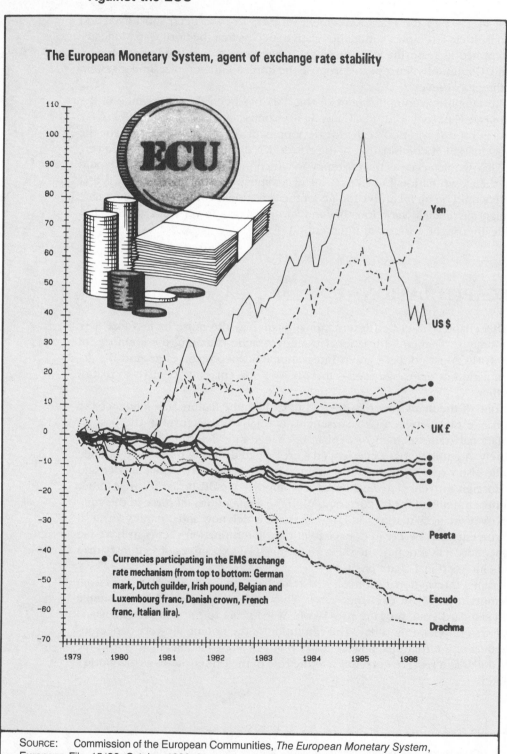

The European Monetary System, agent of exchange rate stability

Yen

US $

UK £

Currencies participating in the EMS exchange rate mechanism (from top to bottom: German mark, Dutch guilder, Irish pound, Belgian and Luxembourg franc, Danish crown, French franc, Italian lira).

Peseta

Escudo

Drachma

SOURCE: Commission of the European Communities, *The European Monetary System*, European File, 15/86, October 1986, 9.

REVIEW QUESTIONS

(1)   What is the exchange rate?

(2)   What are the sources of demand for foreign currency?

(3)   What are the main determinants of exchange rates in the short, medium, and long run?

(4)   What is the International Monetary System? Give a brief account of its historical development.

(5)   How was the dollar value of gold determined under the gold standard system?

(6)   Explain the terms "free float" and "managed float."

(7)   What were the major flaws of the Bretton Woods system?

(8)   What is an "optimal bankrupt"?

(9)   What was the Baker Plan? If you were an executive in a bank that had a large stake in the international debts of the nations covered by the Baker Plan, would you try to influence your congressperson to vote for it? Should the issue even be the subject of congressional debate?

(10)   What are two current schools of thought on devising a new monetary order?

SUGGESTED READINGS

Aliber, R. Z. *The International Money Game*. New York: Basic Books, 1973.

Alm, Richard, and Elaine Carey. "Will New Billions for Mexico Be Enough?" *U.S. News & World Report*, June 23, 1986, 34.

Baumol, William J., and Alan S. Blinder. *Economics: Principles and Policy*, Third Edition. San Diego: Harcourt, Brace, Jovanovich, 1985.

Bergel, Clive. "Commercial Bank Foreign Loans." *Savings Institutions*, November 1985, 33–35.

——. "Monetary Reform: A Global Model." *Europe*, July 1986, 24–25.

"Deficits: A Global Failure." *The New York Times*, September 17, 1986, D2.

Doan, Michael, Kenneth Smith, and Patricia M. Scherschel. "World Debt Bomb: Is It Being Defused?" *U.S. News & World Report*, October 10, 1983, 95–96.

Drucker, Peter F. "The Changed World Economy." *Foreign Affairs*, Spring 1986, 768–791.

Eiteman, D. K., and A. I. Stonehill. *Multinational Business Finance*, Fourth Edition. Reading, MA: Addison-Wesley, 1986.

Evans, T. G. *The Monetary Muddle: A Compilation of Wall Street Journal Articles*. New York: Dow Jones and Co., 1974.

Freund, William C. "First the Big Board, Now the Big Bang." *The Wall Street Journal*, October 27, 1986, 6.

Gall, N. "Will the U.S. Become a Pauper Nation?" *Forbes*, February 28, 1983, 18.

"Give Japan a Stronger Voice." *Business Week*, October 20, 1986, 142.

"How High the Yen?" *The Wall Street Journal*, September 29, 1986, 24.

International Monetary Fund. *The Role and Function of the International Monetary Fund*. Washington, DC: IMF, 1985.

————. *World Economic Outlook: Revised Projections by the Staff of the International Monetary Fund*. Washington, DC: IMF, October 1986.

Johnson, Thomas S. "Fixed Exchange Rates Will Not Work." *The New York Times*, February 20, 1986, D2.

Kristof, N. "That International 'Debt Bomb' Hasn't Stopped Ticking." *The New York Times*, March 31, 1985, D2.

Kuttner, Robert. "Why U.S. Allies Aren't Marching to Baker's Tune." *Business Week*, October 20, 1986, 16.

Larosiere, J. "Growth, Debt, and International Cooperation." Remarks before the Southern Center for International Studies. Atlanta, GA, October 28, 1986.

Leuschel, Roland. "Money's Riding on the Group of One." *The Wall Street Journal*, September 29, 1986, 30.

Lindley, H. Clark, Jr. "Do We Really Know What the Dollar Exchange Rate Should Be?" *The Wall Street Journal*, November 19, 1985, 31.

Lord, Mary, Mami Fukae, Alfred Zanker, Victoria Pope, John Lee, and John Collins. "Getting the Locomotives Back on Track." *U.S. News & World Report*, August 4, 1986, 44–46.

Mueller, John. "Lifting the Reserve Currency Curse." *The Wall Street Journal*, September 5, 1986, 6.

Sampson, A. *The Money Lender*. Middlesex, England: Penguin Books, 1981.

Scherschel, Patricia M., Alfred Zanker, Victoria Pope, John Lee, Mary Lord, and Robert F. Black. "Dollar Diplomacy at the Brink." *U.S. News & World Report*, October 13, 1986, 49–50.

Seidman, L. William. "A Time for Case-by-Case Control of Risk." *The Wall Street Journal*, October 27, 1986, 6.

Seist, Michael R. "Prosperity and Peril in the Brave New Market." *The Wall Street Journal*, September 29, 1986, 1D.

"Sell Some Gold." *The Wall Street Journal*, September 5, 1986, 6.

Silk, Leonard. "Stimulating Global Growth." *The New York Times*, May 16, 1986, D2.

————. "Capital Inflow and Trade Gap." *The New York Times*, October 10, 1986, D2.

Smith, Kenneth S. "As Third World Debt Nears the Trillion Mark." *U.S. News & World Report*, March 25, 1985, 47.

Sri-kumar, K. S. "Banks and IMF Offer Myopic Solutions to Latin Problems." *The Wall Street Journal*, May 10, 1985, 6.

Stabler, Charles N. "Making Debt Burden a Little Lighter." *The Wall Street Journal*, October 27, 1986, 1.

Stein, H. "My Foreign Debt." *The Wall Street Journal*, May 10, 1985, 35.

Stevens, Charles W. "Dollar Can't Continue Rise Without Signs of Stronger U.S. Economy, Traders Say." *The Wall Street Journal*, October 28, 1986, 35.

Wiener, Leonard, Alfred Zanker, Jim Jones, Mami Fukae, John Lee, and Richard L. DeLouise. "Investors Go for the Gold and Platinum." *U.S. News & World Report*, August 25, 1986, 8D.

Witcher, K. "Risky Medicine: Baker's Plan to Relieve Debt Crisis May Spur Future Ills, Critics Say." *The Wall Street Journal*, November 19, 1985, 1, 26.

————. "Baker Debt Plan Is Alive, but Is It Well?" *The Wall Street Journal*, September 29, 1986, 35.

EMERGING ISSUE 6: In Search of a New Locomotive

The last three chapters have concerned international economics, a discipline that deals with two distinct human activities: the exchange of goods and services (international trade) and the exchange of money (international finance). The material was separated into three chapters to facilitate explanation of international economic relations. In real life, of course, the world economy operates as an interrelated and interdependent network of trade and financial activities. The purpose of this Emerging Issue is to put it all together by focusing on the relationship between the world of goods and the world of finance.

International finance evolved as the facilitator, or "lubricant," of trade activities. This role implies a superior/subordinate relationship—one in which financial transactions follow and are subordinate to goods transactions. This was indeed the case until very recently. The exchange of goods was at the center of discussions among the countries of the world, and financial matters were introduced into the agenda only when they seemed to be hindering international trade.

One of the greatest fallacies of contemporary thought on international finance is that financial transactions continue to be subordinate to trade in physical goods. In recent years the international financial system has developed a "mind of its own," and it now operates on a scale and by means of a technology beyond the comprehension of most world leaders, both private and public. As Exhibit E6-1 shows, the volume of transactions in the symbolic economy is 37 times the volume of transactions in the real economy. This international financial system, far from serving simply as a trade facilitator, actually runs or dictates trade transactions. The fact that "the tail now wags the dog" has not yet sunk into the minds of most of the world's leaders. As a result, considerable time, effort, and money are being spent in tackling the wrong end of the relationship.

According to Peter Drucker, three fundamental changes have occurred during the last decade or so:

(1)   The primary-product economy has come "uncoupled" from the industrial economy.

(2)   Within the industrial economy, production has come uncoupled from employment.

(3)   Capital movements, rather than trade in goods and services, have become the driving force of the world economy. The two have not quite become uncoupled, but the link has become loose and, worse, unpredictable.[12]

---

[12]Peter Drucker, "The Changed World Economy," *Foreign Affairs*, Spring 1986, 768.

Exhibit E6-1 The New World Economy

The Real Economy	The Symbolic Economy
Exports and imports of goods and services	Capital movements, exchange rates, and credit flows
	(1) London Eurodollar Market: $75 trillion a year
	(2) Foreign Exchange: $35 trillion a year
$5 trillion a year	$110 trillion a year

SOURCE: Peter Drucker, "The Changed World Economy," *Foreign Affairs*, Spring 1986, 768–791.

The growth of external indebtedness has only exacerbated the first two problems Drucker lists. Because of the extent of their indebtedness, some countries have been obliged to change their internal fiscal, monetary, and developmental policies and plans to accommodate the servicing of their debt. As a result, developmental plans that would have resulted in an increase in employment and an improvement in the general welfare of the citizens have given way to "export cash crop" plans. To compete in an ever-changing world, countries have adopted production techniques that are contrary to their "comparative advantage." Thus, for example, countries with abundant labor have invested heavily in machinery (capital-intensive processes), the purchase of which requires massive borrowing of funds from abroad, thereby worsening an already critical indebtedness problem.

THE WORLD ECONOMIC OUTLOOK: THE IMMEDIATE FUTURE

Now that the United States no longer serves as the driving force, or locomotive, of economic growth around the globe, the International Monetary Fund is looking for a new *primus mobile*—a new vehicle for stimulating world economic growth and trade expansion.[13] It appears that West Germany and Japan are the most likely candidates for the role. Both of these countries are expected to drive down interest rates, thereby creating an environment conducive to investment and consumption. The increase in economic activity should lead to an increase in employment and incomes and, of course, greater demand for goods and services. Some of this increased demand, it is hoped, will be satisfied by imports from the United States and the developing world.

[13]International Monetary Fund, *World Economic Outlook: Revised Projections by the Staff of the International Monetary Fund* (Washington, DC: IMF, October 1986), 1–30.

The United States is likely to make the elimination of its budget deficit a top priority. With the U.S. government borrowing less money, international liquidity will increase, driving interest rates down further. The lower interest rates will make external debt servicing easier for the big debtors and will allow them to devote some cash to growth-producing projects. Greater growth will help these countries finance their own economies, thereby eliminating the need for further accumulation of external debt.

The biggest winner in this shift in the global consumption and trade patterns would be the United States. By decreasing the rate of growth of imports and increasing the rate of growth of exports, the United States could manage to arrest the increase in its current account deficit.

Whether this scenario comes true will depend on how quickly world leaders recognize the changes that have occurred during the past few years and institute appropriate national and global cooperation policies and procedures. Of particular importance is recognition of the transition of the world economy from a goods economy to a symbolic economy. World leaders must realize that world economic transactions involve information much more often than they do goods and services. Trillions of bits of information are transmitted daily through high-speed supercomputers to confirm decisions to buy, sell, hire, fire, invest in new plants, or close down existing factories or offices. These bits of data affect the lives of billions of people. Knowledge-driven and -directed global business is rendering obsolete the market mechanism that in the past equilibrated world markets.

ISSUES FOR DISCUSSION

1. Do you perceive any dangers inherent in the emergence of what Drucker calls the symbolic economy?

2. Discuss the three fundamental changes that Drucker believes occurred during the last decade.

3. Has the United States managed to cut its deficits since this book was published?

4. How has the dollar been affected?

5. Have Japan and West Germany grown as expected?

APPENDIX 6A • What Is the Balance of Payments?

A SHORT DEFINITION

A country's balance of payments is commonly defined as the record of transactions between its residents and foreign residents over a specified period. Each transaction is recorded in accordance with the principles of double-entry bookkeeping, meaning that the amount involved in each transaction is entered on each of the two sides of the balance-of-payments accounts. Consequently, the sums of the two sides of the complete balance-of-payments accounts should always be the same, and in this sense the balance of payments always balances.

However, there is no bookkeeping requirement that the sums of the two sides of a *selected number* of balance-of-payments accounts should be the same, and it happens that the (im)balances shown by certain combinations of accounts are of considerable interest to analysts and government officials. It is these balances that are often referred to as "surpluses" or "deficits" in the balance of payments.

This monograph explains how such measures of balance are derived and interpreted. Full understanding of the derivation requires a grasp of elementary balance-of-payments accounting principles, so these principles are outlined and illustrated in the first two sections.

RECORDING OF TRANSACTIONS: GENERAL PRINCIPLES

The double-entry bookkeeping used in accounting for the balance of payments is similar to that used by business firms in accounting for their financial positions. In ordinary business accounting the amount of each transaction is recorded both as a debit and as a credit, and the sum of all debit entries must, therefore, equal the sum of all credit entries. Furthermore, in business accounting it is recognized that the total value of the assets employed by the firm must be equal to the total value of the claims against the assets, that is, that all assets belong to someone. As is well known, the claims against assets are called the liabilities of the firm. (Assets of the firm not subject to the claims of creditors are, of course, the property of stockholders, so that, broadly speaking, the firm has two classes of liabilities: those due to creditors and those due

SOURCE: Norman S. Fieleke, *What Is the Balance of Payments?* Federal Reserve Bank of Boston Special Study, August 1985. Reprinted by permission. Fieleke is Vice President and Economist, Federal Reserve Bank of Boston.

to stockholders.) By accounting convention, *a debit entry is used to show an increase in assets or a decrease in liabilities, while a credit entry is used to show an increase in liabilities or a decrease in assets*. Since a debit entry is always accompanied by a credit entry, it follows that the value of total assets on the books of a going concern is always equal to the value of total liabilities (including the claims of stockholders).

These elementary principles can be applied to the recording of transactions in the balance of payments. For example, when a foreigner gives up an asset to a resident of this country in return for a promise of future payment, a debit entry is made to show the increase in the stock of assets held by U.S. residents, and a credit entry is made to show the increase in U.S. liabilities to foreigners (i.e., in foreign claims on U.S. residents). Or when a U.S. resident transfers a good to a foreigner, with payment to be made in the future, a debit entry is made to record the increase in one category of U.S. assets (U.S. financial claims on foreigners, i.e., U.S. holdings of foreign IOUs), and a credit entry is made to record the decrease in another category (goods).

These principles are illustrated in greater detail in the following section, which through a series of examples constructs a hypothetical balance-of-payments statement.

RECORDING OF TYPICAL TRANSACTIONS

The balance-of-payments accounts are commonly grouped into three major categories: (1) accounts dealing with goods and services; (2) accounts recording gifts, or unilateral transfers; (3) accounts dealing basically with financial claims (such as bank deposits and stocks and bonds). This section shows how typical transactions in each of these major categories are recorded.

COMMERCIAL EXPORTS: TRANSACTION 1

Suppose that a firm in the United States ships merchandise to an overseas buyer with the understanding that the price of $50 million, including freight, is to be paid within 90 days. In addition, assume that the merchandise is transported on a U.S. ship.

In this case U.S. residents are parting with two things of value, or two assets: merchandise and transportation service. (Transportation service, like other services supplied to foreigners, can be viewed as an asset that is created by U.S. residents, transferred to foreigners, and consumed by foreigners all at the same time.) In return for giving up these two assets, U.S. residents are acquiring a financial asset, namely, a promise from the foreign customer to make payment within 90 days. In accordance with the principles outlined above, the book-keeping entries required to record these transactions are as follows: (1) a debit of $50 million to the account "U.S. private short-term claims," to show the increase in this kind of asset held by U.S. residents; (2) a credit of $49 million to "Merchandise," and (3) a credit of $1 million to "Transportation," to show

Exhibit A6-1 Hypothetical Transactions between U.S. Residents and Foreign Residents (in millions of dollars)

Line	Account	Debits	Credits	Excess of Debits (−) or Credits (+)
1	Exports of goods and services		60	+ 60
2	Merchandise		(1) 49	+ 49
3	Transportation		(1) 1	+ 1
4	Income on U.S. investments abroad		(3) 10	+ 10
5	Other			
6	Imports of goods and services	50		− 50
7	Merchandise	(4) 45		− 45
8	Travel	(5) 5		− 5
9	Other			
10	Unilateral transfers	(6) 1		− 1
11	Changes in U.S. claims on foreigners[1]	320	71	− 249
12	U.S. official reserve assets			
13	Gold			
14	Special drawing rights	(9)200	(10) 10	− 190
15	Foreign currency balances			
16	Reserve position in IMF			
17	Other U.S. Government claims			
18	U.S. private claims			
19	Direct investments			
20	Other U.S. private "long-term" claims	(7) 60		− 60
21	U.S. private short-term claims	(1) 50 (3) 10	(2) 50 (4) 10 (6) 1	+ 1
22	Changes in foreign claims on U.S. (i.e., in U.S. liabilities to foreign residents)[2]	85	125	+ 40
23	Foreign official claims[3]	(10) 10	(8) 25	+ 15
24	Foreign private short-term claims	(2) 50 (8) 25	(4) 35 (5) 5 (7) 60	+ 25
25	Other			
26	Allocations of special drawing rights		(9)200	+200
27	Total	456	456	0
	Memoranda:			
28	Balance on merchandise trade (lines 2 & 7)			+ 4
29	Balance on goods and services (lines 1 & 6)			+ 10
30	Balance on current account (lines 29 & 10)			+ 9
31	Transactions in U.S. official reserve assets and in foreign official assets in the United States (lines 13–16 & 23)			− 175

[1]Including U.S. real property abroad.
[2]Including foreign real property in the United States.
[3]Here assumed to exclude U.S. Government liabilities associated with military sales contracts and other transactions arranged with or through foreign official agencies.

the decreases in these assets available to U.S. residents. These figures are entered on lines 21, 2, and 3 in Exhibit A6-1 and are preceded by the number (1) in parentheses to indicate that they pertain to the first transaction discussed.

PAYMENT FOR COMMERCIAL EXPORTS: TRANSACTION 2

To make payment in dollars for the merchandise he has received from the United States, the foreign customer might purchase from his local bank a demand deposit held by his bank in a U.S. bank, then transfer the deposit to the U.S. exporter. As a result U.S. demand deposit liabilities to foreign residents (i.e., foreign private short-term claims) would be diminished (debited). The payment by the foreign buyer would also cancel his obligation to the U.S. exporter, so that U.S. private short-term claims on foreigners would be reduced (credited). The appropriate entries, preceded by the number (2), are on lines 21 and 24 of the table.

RECEIPT OF INCOME FROM INVESTMENTS ABROAD: TRANSACTION 3

Each year residents of the United States receive billions of dollars in interest and dividends from capital investments in foreign stocks, bonds, and the like. U.S. residents receive these payments in return for allowing foreign residents to use U.S. capital which otherwise could be put to work in the United States.

Suppose that a U.S. firm has a longstanding capital investment in a profitable subsidiary abroad, and that the subsidiary transfers to the U.S. parent (as one of a series of such transfers) some $10 million in dividends in the form of funds held in a foreign bank. The U.S. firm then has a new (or enlarged) demand deposit in a foreign bank, as compensation for allowing its capital (and associated managerial services) to be used by its subsidiary. A debit entry on line 21 shows that U.S. private short-term claims on foreigners have increased, and a credit entry on line 4 reflects the fact that U.S. residents have given up an asset (the services of capital over the period covered) that is valued at $10 million.

COMMERCIAL IMPORTS: TRANSACTION 4

In the balance-of-payments accounts U.S. imports of goods and services have opposite results from U.S. exports. Residents of the United States are acquiring goods and services rather than giving them up, and in return are transferring financial claims to foreigners rather than acquiring them.

To take an illustration, assume that U.S. residents import merchandise valued at $45 million, making payment by transferring $10 million from balances that they hold in foreign banks and $35 million from balances held in U.S. banks.

A debit entry on line 7 records the increase in goods available to U.S. residents, while credit entries on lines 21 and 24 record the decrease in U.S. claims on foreigners and the increase in U.S. liabilities.

EXPENDITURES ON TRAVEL ABROAD: TRANSACTION 5

Residents of the United States who tour abroad purchase foreign currency with which to meet their expenses. If U.S. residents transfer balances of $5 million in U.S. banks to foreigners in exchange for foreign currency that they spend traveling abroad, the end result is that the account "Travel" must be debited $5 million to reflect U.S. purchases of this "asset," and "Foreign private short-term claims" must be credited $5 million to show the increase in U.S. demand deposit liabilities. Such expenditures on travel are classified under the general heading of "Imports of goods and services," since the expenditures go to purchase goods and services from foreigners.

GIFTS TO FOREIGN RESIDENTS: TRANSACTION 6

Many residents of this country, some of them recent immigrants, send gifts of money to relatives abroad. If individuals in the United States acquire balances worth $1 million that U.S. banks have held in foreign banks and then transfer these balances to relatives overseas, there must be a credit entry of $1 million showing the decrease in U.S. private short-term claims on foreigners. This transaction differs from the other transactions analyzed in that U.S. residents obtain nothing of material value in return for the asset given up. Yet if the books are to balance, there must be a debit entry of $1 million. The book-keeping convention followed in such cases is to debit an account called "Unilateral transfers" (line 10). In the official U.S. balance-of-payments presentation, this account is divided into several subsidiary accounts, some of which are used to record grants by the federal government under the foreign aid programs. These foreign aid grants, of course, have been much larger than gifts by private individuals.

LOANS TO BORROWERS ABROAD: TRANSACTION 7

A financial loan by a resident of the United States to a borrower in another country entails the transfer of money by the U.S. resident in exchange for a promise from the borrower to repay at a future time. Suppose that U.S. residents purchase $60 million in long-term bonds issued by Canadian borrowers. Also assume that the bonds are denominated in U.S. dollars, so that payment for them is made by transferring U.S. dollar demand deposits. A debit entry on line 20 records the increase in U.S. holdings of foreign bonds, and a credit entry on line 24 records the increase in demand deposits held by foreigners in U.S. banks.

In principle, direct investment abroad by a U.S. firm could have required the same accounting entries. For the $60 million bond purchase to qualify as a direct investment, the bonds would have to be the obligations of a Canadian firm in which a U.S. party (or affiliated parties) owned at least 10 percent of the voting securities. Typically, however, direct investment abroad by a U.S. firm takes some other form, such as a purchase of foreign equity securities or a simple advance of funds to a foreign subsidiary.

PURCHASES AND SALES OF DOLLAR BALANCES BY FOREIGN CENTRAL BANKS: TRANSACTION 8

At this point it is appropriate to examine the net result of the foregoing seven transactions on the short-term claims of U.S. residents and of foreign residents. As the table shows, these transactions have involved almost the same volume of debits as credits to U.S. private short-term claims on foreigners, with the net result that these claims have been diminished (credited) by $1 million (the figure on line 21 in the last column). By contrast, as shown on line 24, foreign private short-term claims on this country have risen by $50 million (excluding the effects of transaction 8, which remains to be discussed).

It happens that all of this $50 million is in the form of demand deposits, and private foreigners might not wish to retain all of these newly acquired dollar balances. Those who hold demand deposit dollar balances typically do so for purposes such as financing purchases from the United States (or from non–U.S. residents desiring dollars), and there is no guarantee that such motivations will be just strong enough to make the dollar-balance holders exactly satisfied with the $50 million increase in their holdings. For purposes of illustration, assume that foreign residents attempt to sell $40 million of this increase in exchange for balances in their native currencies, but that U.S. residents do not want to trade any of their foreign-currency balances for the proffered dollar balances at the going rates of exchange between the dollar and foreign currencies. In these circumstances the foreign-exchange value of the dollar (the price of the dollar in terms of foreign currencies) will decline.

However, some central banks might hold the view that the foreign-exchange value of their currencies was inappropriately high (i.e., that the foreign-exchange value of the dollar was inappropriately low), in which case they might sell foreign currencies in exchange for dollar balances in order to moderate the decline in the exchange price of the dollar. In the present case, suppose that foreign central banks purchased 25 million in dollar balances from commercial banks within their territories. The U.S. balance-of-payments accounts would register an increase of $25 million in U.S. liabilities held by foreign monetary authorities (line 23) and an equivalent decrease in short-term liabilities held by private foreigners (line 24).

It should be noted that such purchases of dollar balances by foreign central banks supply the commercial banks that sell the dollars with new reserves in their native currencies. In general, these reserves can be used by the banks to expand the loans and thus to inflate the money supplies in the countries concerned, if nothing else is changed.

RECEIPT OF ALLOCATION OF SDRs: TRANSACTION 9

Between 1970 and 1972 the International Monetary Fund (IMF) created and distributed the first issue of special drawing rights (SDRs) in order to enlarge the stock of international reserve assets. By international agreement SDRs are to be acceptable in settlement of debts between countries. They are created in limited internationally agreed amounts and are allocated to participating countries in proportion to their quotas in the IMF. In terms of currency an SDR is defined as a "basket" containing specified quantities of five major currencies—the U.S. dollar, the German mark, the French franc, the Japanese yen, and the U.K. pound.

To illustrate how the receipt of newly created SDRs is treated in the U.S. balance-of-payments accounts, assume that the IMF notified the U.S. authorities that $200 million in new SDRs had been credited to the U.S. account. A debit entry on line 14 would record the increase in this international reserve asset held by the United States. However, this transaction would involve neither a corresponding decrease in other assets nor a corresponding increase in liabilities; so to meet the requirement for an equivalent credit under the system of double-entry bookkeeping, a credit entry of $200 million would be made to a specially created account, "Allocations of special drawing rights" (line 26).

DEALINGS IN SDRs WITH FOREIGN CENTRAL BANKS: TRANSACTION 10

As a result of the foregoing transactions, the dollar holdings of foreign central banks have been enlarged by $25 million (as explained under transaction 8). But for a number of reasons these banks might not wish to hold exactly this additional amount of dollar claims for any length of time. In particular, they might fear a further depreciation of the dollar in the foreign-exchange markets. Whatever the reason, assume that the U.S. authorities wish to cooperate in supporting the foreign-exchange value of the dollar and that they therefore transfer SDRs valued at $10 million to the foreign central bankers in exchange for 10 million in dollar balances. U.S. liabilities held by foreign monetary authorities then decline by $10 million, and U.S.-owned SDRs decline by the same amount. If gold instead of SDRs had been transferred, the credit entry would have been made on line 13 rather than line 14.

STATISTICAL DISCREPANCY

At the beginning of this article it was noted that a country's balance of payments is commonly defined as the record of transactions between its residents and foreign residents over a specified period. Compiling this record presents difficult problems, and errors and omissions in collecting the data are sometimes made.

Take first the matter of coverage. In spite of attempts to gather data on them, some international transactions go unreported. One category of transactions that probably is often substantially underreported is purchases and sales of short-term financial claims; such unreported movements of short-term capital are widely believed to be a major component of total errors and omissions. No attempt is made to collect complete data on certain other transactions, which are estimated by balance-of-payments statisticians. The sample observations on which these estimates are based are sometimes of doubtful reliability, and even the best sampling and estimating techniques will not prevent errors of estimation.

Or take the matter of valuation. While import documentation, for example, may state a precise value for the merchandise imported, a different amount may eventually be paid the exporter. The discrepancy can arise for a number of reasons, ranging from default by the importer to incorrect valuation of the merchandise on the import documents.

Because of such problems total *recorded* debits do not equal total *recorded* credits in the actual balance-of-payments accounts in any given year. To provide a specific illustration of how this discrepancy arises, suppose that U.S. export documentation valued an item at $500, while in fact the terms of sale called for payment of only $400 by the foreign importer, who drew down his bank balance in the United States to make the payment. On the basis of the export documentation, balance-of-payments accountants would credit merchandise exports by $500; but when they turned their attention to U.S. short-term liabilities to private foreigners, they would find that U.S. banks had reported a decrease of only $400 (assuming no other transactions). Consequently, recorded credits would mistakenly exceed recorded debits by $100. In fact, of course, the credit entry should have been in the amount of $400.

It is to accommodate such discrepancies that the residual account, "Statistical discrepancy," was created. An excess of credits in all other accounts is offset by an equivalent debit to this account, or an excess of debits in other accounts is offset by an equivalent credit to this account. The account thus serves at least two purposes; it gives the balance-of-payments analyst an indication of the net error in the balance-of-payments statistics, so that he can have some idea of the reliability of the balance-of-payments data, and it provides a means of satisfying the requirement of double-entry bookkeeping that total debits must equal total credits. Of course, there is no need for the account in our hypothetical balance-of-payments table, which displays an equality between total debits and total credits (line 27).

MEASURES OF BALANCE

As noted at the beginning of this monograph, the balances shown by selected combinations of balance-of-payments accounts are of considerable interest to analysts and government officials. Four of these measures are shown on lines 28 to 31 of the table.

The first and simplest of these measures is the balance on merchandise trade, which is derived by computing the net excess of debits or credits in the merchandise accounts. In our hypothetical statement there is a net credit balance, or "surplus," of $4 million.

Similarly, by computing the net excess of debits or credits in the goods and services accounts, we obtain the balance on goods and services, which happens to be a credit (an excess of exports over imports) of $10 million. Such a credit balance indicates that the United States transferred more real resources (goods and services) to other countries than it received from them during the period covered by the statement, while a debit balance would indicate the reverse. The balance on goods and services is of interest not only as an approximation of such net transfers of real resources but also because it is defined in roughly the same way as the "net exports of goods and services" that comprise part of the nation's gross national product or expenditure; the main quantitative difference in definition is that interest payments by the U.S. government to foreign residents are not counted in tallying net exports of goods and services, on the rationale that government interest is not a payment for services used in the production process, while such interest payments are counted in striking the balance on goods and services.

The third measure, the balance on current account, is the net excess of debits or credits in the accounts for goods, services, and unilateral transfers, that is, the balance on all accounts other than the financial claims, or "capital," accounts. Because total debits must equal total credits in the balance of payments, the balance on the current accounts must equal the balance on the remaining, or capital, accounts. Thus, the current-account balance is an approximation of the change in the net claims of U.S. residents on the rest of the world; it is a major component of the change in the country's net international investment position, or "net worth," vis-à-vis the rest of the world.[14]

As a rule, it is much more difficult to interpret the fourth measure, "Transactions in U.S. official reserve assets and in foreign official assets in the United States." From a simple accounting perspective, this balance measures the difference between the change in U.S. official reserves and in foreign official claims on the United States. A debit balance, such as that shown in the statement, indicates that U.S. official reserve assets have risen more (or fallen less) than foreign official claims on this country, while a credit balance would indicate the reverse.

In some circumstances, however, this fourth measure summarizes considerably more information. For example, suppose that there had been no allocation of SDRs (no transaction 9), so that the balance on this fourth measure was a credit of $25 million rather than the debit of $175 million that is shown. From the description of transactions 8 and 10, it is clear that this $25 million credit arose from central bank operations in support of the foreign-exchange

---

[14]Other components include allocations of SDRs and accounting adjustments in the value of the assets concerned.

value of the dollar. The amount of this credit (support) *along with* any observed decline in the foreign-exchange value of the dollar would then provide a joint indication of the weakness of the dollar in the foreign-exchange markets during the period in question.

Such interpretations require knowledge of the details of transactions like 8 and 10, and the details are often difficult to come by. For example, foreign officials, such as those in some oil-exporting countries, sometimes acquire dollar balances for investment or reserve purposes (rather than as a result of supporting the dollar as in transaction 8). In such cases dollar purchases by foreign central banks testify to the desirability or strength of the dollar in the foreign-exchange markets, rather than to its weakness. Therefore, it is safest to interpret this fourth measure of balance from the simple accounting perspective outlined above.

This measure's first component, "Transactions in U.S. official reserve assets," is worthy of special attention in itself. To illustrate, when foreign central banks acquired $10 million in SDRs in transaction 10, they gave to the U.S. authorities (directly or indirectly) $10 million in U.S. commercial bank balances in return. The Federal Reserve authorities would collect this $10 million by deducting it from the reserve balances member banks hold with the Federal Reserve System, with the result that U.S. commercial banks would have less money to lend.[15] *If* the authorities took no measure to restore such sums to the commercial banks, the reduced lending capacity of the commercial banking system would tend to raise U.S. interest rates and attract more foreign investment into dollar-denominated assets, thereby bolstering the foreign-exchange price of the dollar.

In fact, of course, the Federal Reserve authorities commonly do act to offset any changes in commercial bank reserves stemming from international transactions unless such changes are in accord with Federal Reserve policy. Moreover, the volume of U.S. official reserve assets can be altered by transactions that lack even an initial impact on commercial bank reserves, such as allocations of SDRs. Therefore, "Transactions in U.S. official reserve assets" also must be interpreted with circumspection.

---

[15]Transfers by foreign central banks of their dollar balances from commercial banks to the Federal Reserve Banks would also reduce the lending capacity of the commercial banking system, but such transfers have always been inconsequential.

PART 3

THE MANAGEMENT OF GLOBAL OPERATIONS

Commit, I mean, really commit yourself to a global perspective. *Overseas business cannot be the antithesis of domestic business. In order to establish a truly global business, companies must view the world from a global perspective. People, systems, and organizational structure all must reflect this perspective. Unless organized correctly, the corporation will not become a true Triad power.... In a world growing closer and more complex, where competition is becoming more intense yet more cooperative, the customer more universal yet more distinct, the successful organization will be both more independent and more interdependent.*

Kenichi Ohmae

Triad Power: The Coming Shape of Global Competition (New York: Macmillan, 1985), 209–210.

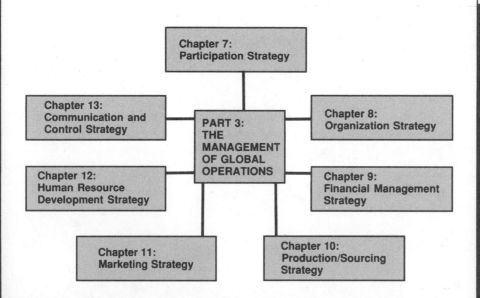

CONNECTIVE SUMMARY

The first two parts of the book set the foundation for Part 3: The Management of Global Operations. Part 1 presented international business as a diverse set of human endeavors resulting in the exchange of goods, services, information, and money across national boundaries for the purpose of obtaining financial benefits. It also examined the nature, motives, and importance of multinational corporations and described the business environment as a complex ecological system consisting of nature and humans.

Part 2 began with a summary of the basics of international economics. It then explored the fundamentals of international trade and considered the complex subject of international finance.

Part 3, The Management of Global Operations, describes the practical application of the art of international management. Managing a business enterprise as a global system requires a different mind set—a different view of the world—than does managing a business in one's home country. The manager of a global enterprise must subscribe to the dictum "Think globally and act locally."

Managing a global MNC begins with a conscious decision to participate in the global game. Chapter 7, Participation Strategy, assumes that the decision to participate in the international market has already been made. The question examined in this chapter is, what modes of entry into the global market are available, and how does a global manager go about choosing one?

After the basic entry strategy has been selected, the manager of an MNC must design the organizational structure that will most efficiently carry out the chosen strategy. Chapter 8, Organization Strategy, examines the various organizational structures used by MNCs in each phase of the internationalization process.

Once the MNC has an appropriate entry strategy and an appropriate organizational structure, the manager must find a way to finance the venture. Several possible approaches are dealt with in Chapter 9, Financial Management Strategy, as are the various financial reporting and control systems used by global managers. Production and marketing strategies are treated in Chapters 10 and 11, respectively. Selecting and developing managers for an MNC is the subject of Chapter 12, Human Resource Development. Communication with and control of an MNC's numerous affiliates are the focus of Chapter 13. Finally, Chapter 14 looks at the rise of important new actors in the global business environment—strategic alliances.

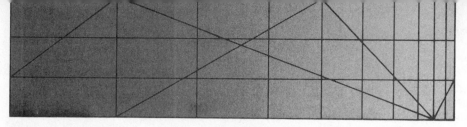

CHAPTER 7

PARTICIPATION STRATEGY

Some years ago, American industry began to move manufacturing offshore in a big way. Just as we were moving out, foreign manufacturers moved in. Indeed, it is estimated that by 1990 more than 2 million Japanese cars will be produced annually in North America, as are golf carts, word processors, compact discs, and a myriad of other products today.

Thomas R. Horton, President and CEO, American Management Association

"Memo for Management: The Global Marketplace and the Global Factory," *Management Review,* June 1987, 3.

OVERVIEW

Many government leaders believe that a nation of industrial workers is better off than a nation of salespeople. Politicians attach greater wealth-creation capabilities to a factory (investment) than to a sales office. Thus an MNC's exports to a country are usually tolerated in the hope that eventually the MNC will substitute domestic production for the imported goods. If the MNC decides to do so, the internationalization process moves into the second phase—the making of contractual agreements, such as those licensing local manufacturers. Alternatively, the MNC might opt to co-produce with a local firm or even to build a factory and then turn it over to a local private and/or state-owned firm.

The internationalization process generally proceeds in a piecemeal fashion until eventually MNC management recognizes that building many small plants all over the world is causing the MNC to lose the economies of scale potentially associated with its size. The MNC then begins a process known in the European literature as *rationalization* and in U.S. nomenclature *restructuring* or *globalization.* This restructuring, which is the last phase in the internationalization process, is an attempt to regain economies of scale through better organization and global management practices.

This chapter discusses the options available in designing an internationalization strategy and provides guidelines for choosing wisely among them.

220

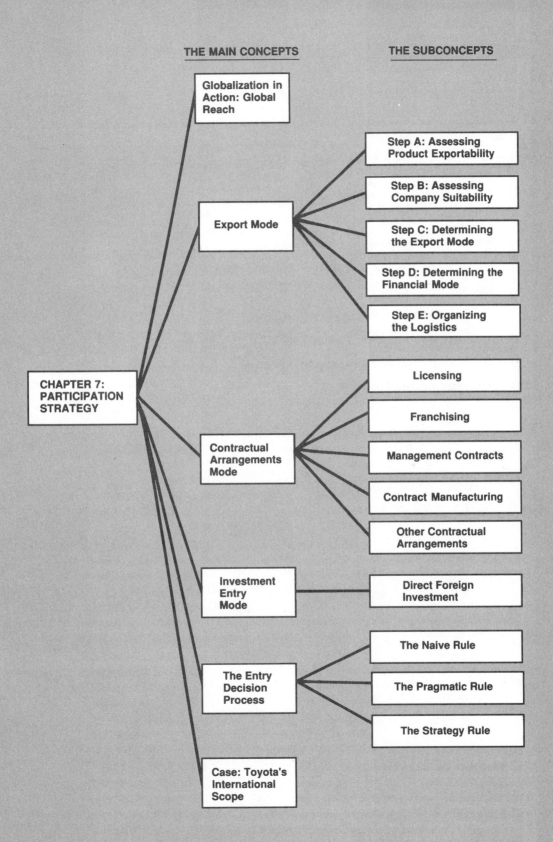

THE MAIN CONCEPTS

THE SUBCONCEPTS

Globalization in Action: Global Reach

CHAPTER 7: PARTICIPATION STRATEGY

Export Mode

Step A: Assessing Product Exportability

Step B: Assessing Company Suitability

Step C: Determining the Export Mode

Step D: Determining the Financial Mode

Step E: Organizing the Logistics

Contractual Arrangements Mode

Licensing

Franchising

Management Contracts

Contract Manufacturing

Other Contractual Arrangements

Investment Entry Mode

Direct Foreign Investment

The Entry Decision Process

The Naive Rule

The Pragmatic Rule

The Strategy Rule

Case: Toyota's International Scope

LEARNING OBJECTIVES

After studying the material in this chapter, the student should be familiar with the following concepts:

(1)   The internationalization process

(2)   The five steps in exporting

(3)   Contractual arrangements

(4)   International licensing and franchising

(5)   Management, manufacturing, and turnkey contracts

(6)   Knowledge agreements

(7)   Portfolio and direct foreign investments

(8)   Joint ventures and wholly owned subsidiaries

(9)   Evaluation of the foreign investment climate

(10) The entry decision process

GLOBALIZATION IN ACTION
Global Reach: Industry Is Shopping Abroad for Good Ideas to Apply to Products

As competition grows and as national differences decline in products ranging from cars to computers to consumer goods, companies scour the world for technology. Businesses without research centers in other countries are opening them. And companies are asking their overseas scientists to do more than adapt products to local markets. Today's objective is technology that can be applied world-wide.

REACHING ROUND THE WORLD

"We want to gain the strength and ideas of not only a few Japanese scientists, but of scientists from all over the world," says William Everitt, a vice president of the Kyocera International unit of Japan's Kyocera Corp. [In 1984] Kyocera, which makes computers, cameras and ceramic components for a range of products, announced it would open its first basic research center outside Japan ... in Vancouver, Washington.

"The risk of being blind-sided by new technology that could revolutionize the marketplace is going up all the time," says Arden L. Bement Jr., the vice president of technical resources for TRW Inc., a conglomerate that makes products ranging from satellites to seat belts. "You have to look outside your own alligator pit to see what's happening at the fringes of the swamp."

Sweden-based Ericsson Group intends not to miss out on new developments. In 1981, the maker of telecommunications equipment opened a research center in Garden Grove, California; the facility is now a joint venture with Honeywell Inc. [In 1984] Ericsson opened another facility in Richardson, Texas, to develop new telephone switching systems.

... Sumitomo Electric Industries Ltd., which has been manufacturing in the U.S. since 1979, opened its first U.S. research center in North Carolina. It will seek advances in fiber optics and other telecommunications fields. ... Nippondenso Co., which makes auto parts, [planned to] open a technical center near Detroit to specialize in new electronics and ceramics technologies for cars.

While companies everywhere are broadening their research activities, the trend may be most dramatic for U.S. businesses. With the notable exception of International Business Machines Corp., which began doing research in 1956, many American companies didn't systematically seek new technology overseas because they saw little need to. But they are coming to see virtues in foreign technology. (After all, foreign citizens got an estimated 43% of U.S. patents in

SOURCE: P. Ingrassia, "Global Reach: Industry Is Shopping Abroad for Good Ideas," *The Wall Street Journal,* April 29, 1985. Reprinted by permission of *The Wall Street Journal,* © Dow Jones & Company, Inc. (1985). All Rights Reserved.

1983, according to the National Science Foundation, up from only 23% in 1965.) Following are examples of U.S. companies that are conducting research and product development of an increasingly international scale.

DATA GENERAL CORP.

Until 1982, Data General's Japanese affiliate existed to adapt the parent company's U.S. computers for Japanese customers. Then Data General, based in Westboro, Mass., increased its stake in Nippon Data General to 85% from 50%; it also expanded the unit's role in world-wide product development. The payoff came . . . when the company introduced the first portable computer with a screen as big as those on desk-top computers.

"In Japan, they are masters of putting things into small packages," says Ronald W. Pipe, the project manager for the Data General/One portable computer. The device, which weighs less than 11 pounds, fits in a briefcase. The technology for the fullsize liquid crystal display screen came out of Japan's digital-watch industry. Just as critical was the "surface mounting" manufacturing technique developed in Japan's consumer-electronics industry. . . .

Robert C. Miller, a senior vice president of the company, knows the advantages of international research efforts but says they are not easy to bring off. "Managing R&D on an international scale is tougher than manufacturing, where you basically send your overseas plant a recipe," he says. "In research, there is no recipe, and you can't manage results day by day."

GOODYEAR TIRE & RUBBER COMPANY

Goodyear opened its International Technical Center in Luxembourg in 1957, with just three employees. Today, the Luxembourg operations has 1,000 workers and a big role in the company. The Akron, Ohio–based Goodyear had to scramble to compete with a foreign invention.

In the mid-1960s, Michelin, the big French tire maker, invaded the U.S. with its radial tire, which lasted far longer and provided better gas mileage then conventional bias-ply tires. Goodyear headquarters was caught napping. But its European operations had seen Michelin's success with radials early and had been making radials of its own.

"We took work done here on radials and built on that base in the U.S.," says Joseph M. Gingo, the director of the Luxembourg technical center. The base included tire-building machines and rubber compounds, which are different for radials than for bias-ply tires, and expertise in making steel-wire belts, which are not used at all in conventional tires.

More recently, Goodyear took technology it developed in Europe for high-performance tires and brought it to the U.S. . . . Now the company is trying to transfer its all-season tires developed in the convenience-minded U.S. market to Europe. . . .

[In 1984] Goodyear launched the first joint new-product effort between its Luxembourg and Akron researchers. The company wants a new radial truck tire that will last longer than 150,000 miles, while being light in weight and low in road friction. "We're working on the tread design," says Mr. Gingo, "while Akron is working on the bead"—the part that holds the tire to the wheel rim. . . .

To make such joint efforts easier, Goodyear is now installing direct desktop computer links between the Akron and Luxembourg technical centers.

TRW INC.

As differences between national markets decline, opportunities to transfer technology grow. That is why Cleveland-based TRW, which has owned a German seat-belt maker for 13 years, bought a U.S. seat-belt business. . . . TRW is betting that Americans will start to wear seat belts more, if only because laws are starting to require it. The company hopes the trend will create a U.S. market for such advances as the "pre-tension" seat belt developed by its Repa G.M.B.H. unit near Stuttgart.

The new belt . . . tightens around the wearer just before a crash. A mechanical device senses the car's rapid deceleration and sets off an electronic spark inside the belt's retractor. The spark ignites a tiny explosion that activates a wire cable, snapping the belt taut.

TRW has transferred auto technology among national markets before. Its Cam Gears division in England developed rack-and-pinion steering in the 1940s and introduced it to the U.S. (on the Ford Pinto) in 1970. Now Cam Gears, building on U.S. power-steering technology, has developed a power rack-and-pinion system that it says combines precise "road feel" at highway speeds—which Europeans demand—with ease of handling at low speeds, which Americans want. "We are aiming at a world-wide market," says D. J. Twiggs, a Cam Gears engineer. "The exchange of technology is increasing to a degree that is now quite dramatic."

INTRODUCTION

Even though not all MNCs start the internationalization process by exporting and end up getting into direct foreign investment, it is important for the international manager to be aware of the possible entry modes and the costs and benefits associated with each. In general, the choice of an entry mode is a strategic decision and thus can be approached using the XYZ framework presented in Chapter 1 (see Exhibit 1-5). The manager who is confronted with the task of recommending that the firm's management choose one entry mode over another must perform a careful analysis of the company's strengths and weaknesses (X); the environmental constraints, threats, and opportunities (Y); and the objectives and goals of the management of the organization (Z). After careful and thorough analysis of these three sets of variables, the manager will be prepared to select an entry mode.

As a general rule, movements to the right along the export-investment line (see Exhibit 1-2) are associated with greater risk, as well as greater potential benefits. Both the size of cash outflows and the uncertainty of cash inflows

Exhibit 7-1   Factors Influencing the Entry Mode Decision

Factor	Indirect and Agent/ Distributor Exporting	Licensing	Branch/ Subsidiary Exporting	Equity Investment Production	Service Contracts
External Factors (Foreign Country)					
Low sales potential	X	X			
High sales potential			X	X	
Atomistic competition	X		X		
Oligopolistic competition				X	
Poor marketing infrastructure			X		
Good marketing infrastructure	X				
Low production cost				X	
High production cost	X		X		
Restrictive import policies		X		X	X
Liberal import policies	X		X		
Restrictive investment policies	X	X	X		X
Liberal investment policies				X	
Small geographical distance	X		X		
Great geographical distance		X		X	X
Dynamic economy				X	
Stagnant economy	X	X			X
Restrictive exchange controls	X	X			X
Liberal exchange controls				X	
Exchange rate depreciation				X	
Exchange rate appreciation	X		X		
Small cultural distance			X	X	
Great cultural distance	X	X			X
Low political risk			X	X	
High political risk	X	X			X
External Factors (Home Country)					
Large market				X	
Small market	X		X		
Atomistic competition	X		X		
Oligopolistic competition				X	
Low production cost	X		X		
High production cost		X		X	X
Strong export promotion	X		X		
Restrictions on investment abroad	X	X			X

Factor	Indirect and Agent/ Distributor Exporting	Licensing	Branch/ Subsidiary Exporting	Equity Investment Production	Service Contracts
Internal Factors					
Differentiated products	X		X		
Standard products				X	
Service products		X		X	X
Service-intensive products			X	X	
Technology-intensive products		X			
Low product adaptation	X				
High product adaptation		X	X	X	
Limited resources	X	X			
Substantial resources			X	X	
Low commitment to internationalization	X	X			X
High commitment to internationalization			X	X	

SOURCE: F. Root, *Foreign Market Entry Strategies* (New York: AMACOM, 1982), 17–19.

increase as the company moves from the export mode to the investment mode. Investment decisions usually require a commitment on the part of the MNC to sizeable *certain* (present) cash outflows, in return for *potential* (future) cash inflows. An export decision, on the other hand, normally requires a small cash outflow and promises an almost certain cash inflow. Thus investment decisions will generally be scrutinized by many in top management, whereas an export decision may require less top management involvement. Exhibit 7-1 presents a sample of external (environmental) and internal (company) factors that may affect an MNC's choice of entry mode.

EXPORT MODE

Like every other management activity, designing an export strategy is a process made up of sequential steps:

Step A: Assessing product exportability

Step B: Assessing company suitability

Step C: Determining the export mode

Step D: Determining the financial mode

Step E: Organizing the logistics

STEP A: ASSESSING PRODUCT EXPORTABILITY

Not every product is exportable. Generally, people buy a foreign product because their own country does not produce that product (for example, Americans buy coffee from abroad because the United States' climate does not favor the production of coffee); because the foreign version is less expensive (for example, Chinese cloths are very popular in the United States), of better quality, more durable, or more dependable; or because of fashion or elitism (for example, in Europe it is fashionable to smoke American Marlboros or Winstons). So the first step in determining an export strategy is to see whether a particular product being considered for export is used in other countries. If so, the following questions should be answered:

How much is used?

How has the foreign market behaved?

Who are the major exporters?

What is the United States' market share?

In order to answer these questions, a manager must find out who is exporting to whom and who is importing from whom. There are several sources for such information.

(1)   Statistics on U.S. exports to the rest of the world are collected and published by the Department of Commerce. Data are fairly accurate and current.

(2)   World import statistics are collected and published by the United Nations. Data are fairly accurate but are a year to a year and a half old by the time they are published. World imports and exports are listed both by country and by Standard Industrial Classification number.

(3)   The Small Business Administration (SBA) has an export information system (called XIS), which provides data on imports and exports by more than 150 countries of all products included in the United Nations' Commodity Trade Data Base. In addition, the XIS provides data on the top twenty products imported by some sixty countries.

Using these data sources, an astute manager can develop an excellent market analysis for management scrutiny.

STEP B: ASSESSING COMPANY SUITABILITY

Assessing a company's suitability for exporting is a difficult process. The first step is to evaluate the company's philosophy, or world outlook.[1] One survey

---

[1]For a good example of a software package that is designed to assess a company's suitability for exports in terms of its management's attitudes and policies, see S. T. Cavusgil and M. Monaghan, *CORE: A Microcomputer Program to Assess Company Readiness to Export* (Peoria, IL: Bradley University Center for Business and Economic Research, 1987).

on U.S. businesses' attitudes toward exporting concluded that U.S. managers are "reluctant exporters."[2] Most U.S. managers view exporting as a "hard way of making a living." Unfamiliarity with foreign markets, customs, and procedures; fear of loss of revenues due to lack of funds on the part of the importing company; and longer break-even and pay-back periods are given by U.S. managers as some of the most important reasons for their reluctance to export.

The empirical evidence shows, however, that U.S. MNCs do export and import large quantities of goods and services. Much of this trade is done in the form of intercompany transfers. The process of exporting is the same, however, whether the importer is a subsidiary of an MNC or an independent company.

STEP C: DETERMINING THE EXPORT MODE

Essentially, there are two main modes of exporting: indirect and direct.

Exhibit 7-2 summarizes the particular export modes from which a company can choose.[3]

Indirect Exporting.   In indirect exporting the manufacturer does not undertake exporting singlehandedly. Rather, domestic intermediaries such as trading companies, export merchants, export management companies, and the like become involved in the process. Indirect exporting allows the company to get a feel for exporting without risking sizeable sums of money.

Direct Exporting.   When a company operates under the direct export mode, it maintains a chain of marketing agencies that links it to the final buyers (or users) of its product in the final target market. These agencies negotiate sales transactions, direct the physical movement and storage of the product, and provide the other services necessary to get the product to the buyers. The foreign agencies participating in a direct export channel may be independent intermediaries, or they may be owned by the manufacturer. It is important for manufacturers to conceive of the export channel as the full marketing channel rather than as a channel that stops with the foreign distributor or agent.

A **foreign agent** is an independent intermediary who represents the manufacturer in the target country. The agent does not take title to the manufacturer's goods and seldom holds any inventory or extends credit to customers.

A **foreign distributor** is an independent merchant who takes title to the goods and then resells them to other intermediaries or final buyers. The distributor also holds inventory, does promotion, extends credit to customers, and delivers and services the product. (See Exhibit 7-3 for sources of distributor leads.)

---

[2]R. Alm and R. F. Black, "The Yankee Trader: Death of a Salesman," *U.S. News and World Report,* April 8, 1985, 64–69.

[3]This section of the chapter draws heavily on F. Root, *Foreign Market Entry Strategies* (New York: AMACOM, 1982).

Exhibit 7-2   Principal Indirect and Direct Export Channels

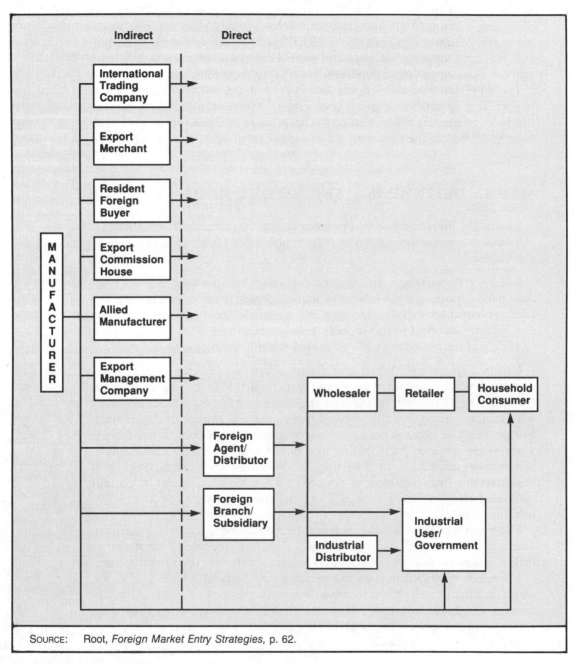

Source: Root, *Foreign Market Entry Strategies,* p. 62.

Exhibit 7-3   Sources of Distributor Leads

Country and regional business directories such as Kompass (Europe), Bottin International (worldwide), Nordisk Handelskalendar (Scandinavia) and the Japan Trade Directory are a good first sources.

Foreign yellow pages (available at libraries) can give you an idea of which companies are active at retail and wholesale levels. The Jaeger and Waldmann International Telex Directory is also useful.

Company lists by country, line of business or both can be ordered from the US Commerce Department, Dunn & Bradstreet, Reuben H. Donnelly, Kelly's Directory and Johnston Publishing.

Advertise in foreign trade publications.

Trade publications and exporters' associations sometimes help their subscribers and members find foreign dealers.

US firms can issue a new product press release and distributor request worldwide at minimal cost through the Commerce Department. Its Trade Opportunity Program (TOP) is available by subscription or online through the DIALOG data base.

Trade fairs are a good way to meet potential distributors, get lists of companies in your industry and pick the brains of "old hands."

Banks sometimes help good customers contact appropriate companies abroad.

Some of the more aggressive airlines, air cargo services and freight forwarders will make trade contacts; some publish trade leads.

Although most consulates and trade offices push their own exports, a few (for example, Japan's Jetro) can be very helpful with distributor leads.

National and international chambers of commerce can be very helpful, particularly if your company becomes a member or expatriate member.

Have a precise procedure to follow up unsolicited inquiries from overseas—reputable companies often see your advertising.

The best long-term investment in international business is a well-planned trip to selected markets.

SOURCE: *161 More Checklists* (New York: Business International, 1985), 89.

A **branch** or **subsidiary** is a unit of the exporting company. Such units range from small sales offices to sister companies engaged exclusively in exports.

STEP D: DETERMINING THE FINANCIAL MODE

There are essentially three steps that a company should take in deciding on the financial arrangements to be used in its exporting efforts:

(1)   Determine the foreign buyer's creditworthiness.

(2)   Choose the method of receiving payments.

(3)   Explore additional methods of issuing payments.

Most foreign concerns do not prepare audited financial reports as is customary in the United States. Although credit information is usually more difficult to obtain, it is by no means less important to business dealings. The following are a few ways of obtaining the credit information vital to a successful sale:

(1)   Request financial statements from the customer.

(2)   Have an international banker request credit information from the customer's bank overseas.

(3)   Ask the customer's commercial references for specific information.

(4)   Contact credit agencies such as Dunn and Bradstreet's International Division or the Foreign Credit Interchange Bureau (FCIB) in New York.

(5)   Look in government sources, such as the U.S. Department of Commerce's World Traders Data Reports (WTDRs), which provide descriptive, detailed background information on specific foreign firms.

To determine the safest and most feasible method of receiving payment for their exports, companies usually contact an international insurance company. The five basic methods of export financing are as follows:

(1)   Documentary letter of credit

(2)   Documentary draft for collection

(3)   Cash in advance

(4)   Open account

(5)   Consignment

A letter of credit is a written pledge on the part of a bank to honor drafts or other demands for payment under the conditions specified. A letter of credit is issued at the request of a buyer. The beneficiary is the seller who is entitled under the terms of the letter to draw or demand payment.

In relation to export trade, a collection draft is an unconditional written order, signed usually by the seller, requiring the foreign buyer to pay the amount of the draft upon presentation of the instrument or at some specified future date. Drafts are also referred to as "bills of exchange."

If the terms of the export transaction are cash in advance, the buyer must prepay either the entire shipment or a portion of it. This type of financing is recommended only in cases where there is serious risk of nonpayment. Prepayment may be required for shipments to countries that are experiencing serious political or economic problems. Under normal conditions, cash in advance is required only when the goods are manufactured to the buyer's specifications, at great expense to the manufacturer.

Open account sales are sales based on credit arrangements between the buyer and the seller. Such agreements offer little recourse to the seller should the buyer default, because they are difficult to enforce in foreign courts, where legal procedures are often complicated. Thus open account sales should be restricted to a foreign branch or subsidiary of the seller/supplier or to a long-standing customer.

Under a consignment contract, the exporter (consignor) retains title to the goods until the importer (consignee) sells them. Usually this type of financing is used with a U.S. company's overseas branch or subsidiary; it is not recommended for use with agents or other foreign customers.

The methods described above vary in the degree of protection they offer the seller and the degree of convenience they offer the buyer in making payments. Usually, the more protection the seller gets, the less attractive the payment terms are to the buyer. In determining which financing methods to use, the seller must compare the amount of protection desired with the need to make payment terms attractive in order to lure buyers. The following factors may help to determine the appropriate method of financing.

Buyer's creditworthiness

Amount of the transaction

Market conditions

Type of merchandise involved

Customs of the trade

Foreign currency availability

Applicable exchange controls in the foreign country

Political conditions in the foreign country

Terms offered by the competition

ADDITIONAL METHODS OF INSURING AND FINANCING

The Foreign Credit Insurance Association provides U.S. exporters with low-cost insurance against nonpayment by foreign customers due to either commercial or political reasons. Although the FCIA does not itself finance export receivables, the ability to assign the proceeds of the FCIA policy to a financing bank is a tremendous advantage to an insured exporter.

The Export Import Bank of the United States (EXIM) is an independent agency of the federal government whose primary function is to aid in financing and facilitating U.S. exports through dollar loans and assistance to exporters in the form of financing, guarantees, and insurance. It provides medium-term political and credit guarantees to financial institutions in the United States and to certain foreign financial institutions, and it cooperates with the FCIA in providing political and credit insurance for exporters. Anyone who is a purchaser of U.S. exports—including foreign private enterprises and foreign governments and their agencies—can borrow from EXIM if the money is spent in the United States and private capital is first sought.

Designed to finance large capital items such as aircraft, factories, and power plants, PEFCO (Private Export Funding Corporation) was formed by U.S. commercial banks and industrial concerns to mobilize supplementary capital from private channels. PEFCO purchases foreign buyers' debt obligations, financing these purchases through the sale of its own securities to private investors. This type of financing usually is for medium- to long-term maturities that carry an EXIM guarantee.

Founded by the Bretton Woods Economic Conference in 1944, the International Bank for Reconstruction and Development (World Bank) is owned jointly, but not equally, by 123 countries. The bank finances large projects in the less-developed countries over a period of years.

STEP E: ORGANIZING THE LOGISTICS

Once financial arrangements have been completed, the company's staff must do three things: document the export order, pack and mark the export shipment, and insure the export shipment. Many documents are used in ordinary international transactions (see Exhibit 7-4). These documents must be filled out completely and accurately to prevent delays in shipping and to assure payment for the goods.

For information on packing and marking export shipments, many companies consult foreign freight forwarders, marine insurance brokers, or professional export packing companies. Such companies may also provide insurance for the export shipments, as can an insurance broker or agent experienced in handling marine cargo insurance. Ocean marine cargo insurance covers losses or damages incurred in transit by mail, air, or ocean-going vessel. Either buyer or seller may arrange for insurance, depending on the agreement between the two. There are basically three types of policies offered: open cargo policies, contingent interest policies, and specialized policies.

CONTRACTUAL ARRANGEMENTS MODE

The contractual arrangements (CA) mode of entry is in most cases a stepping stone to international production. An MNC may move into that mode voluntarily (to test the waters, so to speak) or for purely defensive reasons (to prevent a competitor from entering the market or to preserve sales that oth-

Exhibit 7-4   **Principal Documents Used in Exporting**

A.   Required by foreign customer

    (1)   Pro forma invoice
    (2)   Acceptance of purchase order
    (3)   Ocean (airway) bill of lading
    (4)   Certificate (or policy) of insurance
    (5)   Packing list

B.   Required by exporting manufacturer

    (1)   Purchase order
    (2)   Letter of credit or draft (trade) acceptance

C.   Required by freight forwarder

    (1)   Shipper's letter of instructions
    (2)   Domestic (inland) bill of lading
    (3)   Packing list
    (4)   Commercial invoice (incomplete)
    (5)   Letter of credit (original copy)

D.   Required by U.S. government

    (1)   Export declaration
    (2)   Export license (strategic goods and shipments to Communist countries)

E.   Required by foreign governments

    (1)   Certificate of origin
    (2)   Customs invoice
    (3)   Consular invoice

F.   Required by exporter's bank

    (1)   Exporter's draft
    (2)   Commercial invoice
    (3)   Consular invoice
    (4)   Insurance certificate
    (5)   Ocean (airway) bill of lading

SOURCE: Root, *Foreign Market Entry Strategies*, p. 82.

erwise would be lost because of a government's change in policy). In either case, the MNC is taking a risk in sharing its hard-earned technological or product advantage with a potential competitor.

There are literally hundreds of contractual arrangements through which firms enter and/or maintain the international market. Because they all involve the transfer of knowledge (process, product, or management know-how) from the MNC to a local company, such agreements are also known as knowledge agreements. Knowledge agreements fall basically into nine categories:

Licensing

Franchising

Management contracts

Construction—turnkey contracts

Contract manufacturing

Technical assistance agreement

Service contracts

Co-production agreements

R&D cooperative agreements

Although the potential risks and benefits associated with each specific type vary, the general principle remains the same: the MNC is giving its proprietary expertise and intangible assets to a local firm in exchange for royalties and other fees.[4] According to the experts in the field, this type of entry mode is most appropriate in cases where a company's opportunities to export or to invest have been restricted or where MNC products have become very mature and have lost their lead over international competition. Or, as one expert put it, companies must become involved in contractual agreements as part of the process of "insiderization" into the huge global market of the OECD countries and especially the Triad, the "golden triangle" of the United States, Europe, and Japan.[5]

LICENSING

Broadly defined, international licensing encompasses a variety of contractual arrangements whereby domestic companies (licensors) make their intangible assets (patents, trade secrets, know-how, trademarks, and company name) available to foreign companies (licensees) in return for royalties and/or other forms of payments. Fees usually range from 2 to 5% of sales. Depending on the nature of the agreement, some technical assistance and training may be needed before and during the transfer, or even for the entire licensing period. In these cases the fees vary accordingly.

[4]Root, *Foreign Market Entry Strategies*, p. 78.
[5]Kenichi Ohmae, *Triad Power: The Coming Shape of Global Competition* (New York: Free Press/Macmillan, 1985).

The most obvious advantage of licensing is the circumvention of trade barriers such as tariffs, quotas, and other restrictions. The exporting company is replacing the exportation of finished products with the exportation of components and/or semifinished products, which are then assembled into final products by the licensee. In cases where the product requires extensive adaptation before it can be sold to the local market or extensive servicing once it has been sold, another advantage of licensing is that these functions can be performed by the licensee. Finally, by entering into a licensing agreement, a small firm that is relatively new to international business can acquire some knowledge of the international market with a relatively small investment.[6]

The most important disadvantage of licensing is that the licensing firm retains little or no control. No legal construct can prevent the licensee from making product and process modifications and then patenting the adapted product or process under a new name. In this case, the licensing firm has for all practical purposes helped create a new competitor for its own products. Some firms protect themselves against intrusions on the part of the licensee by reserving the right to export one major component or ingredient from their headquarters. Examples of this practice are numerous in the pharmaceutical and soft drink industries. Another significant disadvantage of licensing is that it generates less revenue than does production.

FRANCHISING

Franchising is a form of licensing in which a company (the franchisor) licenses a business system as well as industrial property to an independent company or person (the franchisee). Franchising permits various companies and individuals to take advantage of a highly publicized name, a well-respected set of procedures, and a carefully developed and controlled marketing strategy, to sell products and/or services. Fast food, soft drinks, home and car maintenance services, and hotels are the industries with the biggest franchisors.

Franchising has several advantages:

(1)   A company can expand rapidly into a foreign market with a small capital outlay.

(2)   A standardized method of marketing gives the product or service a distinctive image.

(3)   Franchisees tend to be highly motivated.

(4)   The political risks are low.

---

[6]F. J. Contractor, "Choosing Between Diverse Investment and Licensing: Theoretical Considerations and Empirical Tests," *Journal of International Business Studies,* Fall 1984, 110–136.

The key disadvantages of franchising resemble those of traditional licensing:

(1)   The franchisor's profit is limited.

(2)   Franchisors lack full control over the franchisees' operations.

(3)   Franchising may create competitors.

(4)   Many governments impose restrictions on the terms of franchise agreements.

MANAGEMENT CONTRACTS

Under an international management contract, an MNC manages the day-to-day operations of an enterprise in a foreign market. In addition, the MNC is usually responsible for long-range planning and goal-setting. The local enterprise maintains ownership and control of the organization. Large capital investment decisions are the prerogative of the host management.

There are several reasons for forming management contracts. For the MNC these may include the following:[7]

(1)   Licensing or franchising arrangements have turned out to be a disappointment because of the failure on the part of the licensee or the franchisee to manage the venture efficiently.

(2)   Fees for management services are easier to transfer back to the home office than are dividends, royalties, and the like.

(3)   The MNC has excess managerial talent, which for political and/or policy reasons it does not wish to dismiss.

(4)   Having a management contract with a foreign plant or company will allow the MNC to provide resources of some kind to one of its nearby operations.

(5)   Managing a going concern is a good way to get acquainted with a foreign market.

The host country may enter into a management contract for any of the following reasons:

(1)   The host country is dissatisfied with the performance of local management following the nationalization or expropriation of a foreign company. For example, after the Venezuelan takeover of foreign oil companies, most of the day-to-day operations of both the central Venezuelan

---

[7]M. Z. Brooke, *International Management: A Review of Strategies and Operations* (London: Hutchinson, 1986), 82.

oil company Petroven and its subsidiaries were performed by representatives of the so-called Seven Sisters (Shell, Exxon, Mobile, Chevron, BP,
Texaco, and Gulf).

(2)   Through a management contract, the government can acquire foreign
expertise without the loss of control and adverse publicity associated
with foreign ownership.

Management contracts are particularly common in the public sector, service
industries, food processing, and natural resource development. Most countries,
both developed and developing, reserve certain types of activities for the public
sector. In many countries electricity, gas, water, telephone, telegraph, television and other public services are run as state enterprises. Governments that
do not have the expertise necessary to continually update and modernize these
facilities may enter into international management contracts. Similarly, managing service industries—hotels, hospitals, airlines, subway projects—requires
a special type of talent that may not be readily available or easily developed
in the host country. The highly sophisticated techniques used in food processing, along with the undesirability of depending on a foreign-owned company to provide the basic means for survival, makes this industry a perfect
candidate for management contracts. Finally, searching for oil and minerals
and then developing these resources into commercial products is a very sophisticated task with which many countries seek assistance through international management contracts.

CONSTRUCTION-TURNKEY CONTRACTS

International construction-turnkey contracts are very similar to management
contracts in that ownership of the enterprise is retained by the host organization. In the case of construction-turnkey projects, however, the role of the
foreign company is to create the project. After successfully delivering the
project to the host enterprise ("turning over the key"), the foreign company
may enter into a management contract for a specified time. MNCs' reasons for
becoming involved in construction-turnkey contracts are pretty much the same
as their reasons for entering into management contracts: availability of expertise, excess talent, underutilized resources such as machinery and other equipment acquired to develop a project somewhere else, desire to get a foot in
the target market.

Host countries enter into international construction-turnkey contracts for
the same reasons they enter into international management contracts. Large
and ambitious projects designed to create the infrastructure necessary both
to service their own citizens and to attract foreign investors require resources
and technology not readily available within the home base. Projects that might
be carried out under construction-turnkey contracts include construction of
large highways, ports, schools, hospitals, and resource extraction and processing plants.

CONTRACT MANUFACTURING

International contract manufacturing is a cross between licensing and investment. It is an arrangement whereby a firm "hires" the production facilities of a foreign company to produce a specific product for a specified period of time. There are many reasons why an international company might decide to use a foreign company's facilities to produce its product.

(1)   The company's production facilities at home are overloaded, and thus the company cannot fulfill its obligation to supply foreign customers.

(2)   Changes in a foreign government's procedures are making it very difficult to supply products to foreign customers via the usual exporting channels.

(3)   The search for a local licensee or franchisee has proven unsuccessful.

(4)   The local manufacturer has excess capacity and is willing to produce at cost plus a small service charge.

(5)   The international firm wants to test the waters before jumping into an investment decision.

Contract manufacturing, also known as subcontracting, is widely used to supply products to world markets. For this reason, subcontracting will be dealt with in greater detail in Chapter 10 on Production/Sourcing Strategy.

OTHER CONTRACTUAL ARRANGEMENTS

The term technical assistance agreement (TAA) is used to refer to an agreement in which the nonhost party is an international agency (such as the U.N., the World Bank, or the IMF), a western government, or some other nonbusiness institution such as a university or a nonprofit foundation. A TAA may involve licensing, franchising, a management contract, or any of the other modes of entry. [The term industrial cooperation agreement (ICA) is used frequently to describe a relationship between a western company and government agency in a Communist country.]

Service contracts, co-production agreements, and R&D cooperative arrangements are all variations of the basic contractual agreements explained above. All of these types of agreements will be treated in Chapter 14.

INVESTMENT ENTRY MODE

The investment entry mode is the one that requires the most commitment on the part of a company, in terms of both management time and financial and human resources. A company that decides to enter the international market by investing equity in a foreign country is giving its stockholders a clear message that international business will be a substantial factor in its future survival and growth. In addition, management is communicating to its stock-holders that experience accumulated through previous involvement in exporting and international contractual agreements will now be put to use in pursuit of higher stakes.

There are two major types of foreign investment: portfolio foreign investment (PFI) and direct foreign investment (DFI). Both of these types of investment represent equity participation on the part of the international company. The difference between them is that with PFI the management of the investing company has no substantial involvement beyond that of the ordinary stockholder, whereas with DFI the investing company organizes and operates the enterprise.

Portfolio foreign investment will not be dealt with here; it is a straightforward financial transaction performed by top management with the assistance of staff and external consultants. This mode of entry into foreign markets has lately taken on a new twist with the creation of financial instruments known as junk bonds. A small group of top executives use the company's name and other tangible and intangible resources to create these extremely high risk bonds, worth much more than the company's market value. These junk bonds are then used to buy out the company in what is known as a leveraged buyout (LBO).

DIRECT FOREIGN INVESTMENT

Direct foreign investment (DFI) is an international business activity in which equity is accompanied by actual management. There are many reasons why an MNC might risk both money and management talent in a foreign operation. In general, a company invests overseas to obtain raw material (extractive investor); to acquire manufactured goods at a lower cost (sourcing investor), or to penetrate local markets (market investor).

JOINT VENTURE DFI

A joint venture takes place when a foreign and a domestic firm combine to form a new entity for a specific purpose, while each partner retains its independence in its other operations.[8] In a minority joint venture, the foreign partner holds less than 50 percent of the total equity; in a majority joint venture, the foreign partner holds over 50 percent of the total equity; and in a 50-50 joint venture, the partners share equally in the equity of the new company. Joint ventures may involve the partial acquisition of an existing company, which the foreign investor buys into, or they may be started from scratch. Exhibit 7-5 illustrates some of the reasons MNCs enter into joint ventures.

Joint ventures are not the mode of entry preferred by most U.S. companies.

---

[8]Peter Dicken, *Global Shift: Industrial Changes in a Turbulent World* (New York: Harper and Row, 1986).

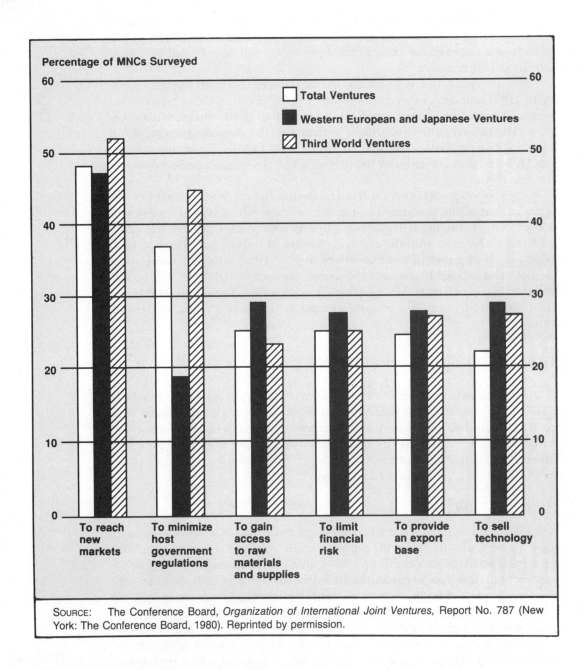

Percentage of MNCs Surveyed

Legend:
- ☐ Total Ventures
- ■ Western European and Japanese Ventures
- ▨ Third World Ventures

Categories (horizontal axis):
To reach new markets; To minimize host government regulations; To gain access to raw materials and supplies; To limit financial risk; To provide an export base; To sell technology

SOURCE: The Conference Board, *Organization of International Joint Ventures*, Report No. 787 (New York: The Conference Board, 1980). Reprinted by permission.

Research has indicated that Japanese and Western European MNCs are much more likely to become involved in joint ventures than are U.S. companies. Some firms, notably IBM, are philosophically opposed to the entire idea of joint ventures, which are considered to be a second-best type of arrangement. Management will give in to forming a joint venture only after all efforts to form a wholly owned business have failed.

A joint venture does offer some notable advantages. First, it permits expansion with limited capital outlay. Second, a suitable partner can provide expertise not possessed by the parent company. Finally, a joint venture can improve sales prospects, especially to governments; sometimes joint ventures provide captive markets.

The disadvantages of joint ventures are that one partner may lack adequate control; one partner may lack skills; or there may be disagreements between partners regarding such issues as dividends, trading areas, pricing and production policies, and competition.[9]

Joint ventures are very common in East-West deals. Some Communist countries that lack modern technology and managerial know-how have reached out to the West to form joint ventures in which the local firm or government agency provides the raw materials and/or the market and the foreign investor provides the know-how and some of the capital, as well as export channels.

WHOLLY OWNED SUBSIDIARIES

The wholly owned subsidiary is a manager's dream; it is the preferred type of DFI. For all practical purposes, it is an extension of the MNC's production and distribution system located in a country other than the MNC's home country. In discussions of the international management functions of organization, finance and accounting, production, marketing and sales, and personnel in later chapters, the wholly owned subsidiary will be used as the model.

THE ENTRY DECISION PROCESS

The basic alternative modes of entry into a foreign market have been defined. The remainder of this chapter is devoted to a description of the process of choosing one or a combination of these modes. Though a company's unique comparative advantage will generally dictate the choice of a specific entry mode, certain general principles are applicable to the process of identifying this mode.

Franklin Root has developed a useful, logical framework for deciding on a foreign market entry strategy. Acknowledging that the complexities and uncertainties involved in the decision-making process are of immeasurable proportion, Root recognized that the question of how managers should decide on the right entry mode for a given product and a given target country/market could not be answered by a mathematically neat computer program. Rather, what is imperative is that managers systematically examine and compare the different alternative modes.[10]

---

[9]Brooke, *International Management,* p. 104.
[10]Root, *Foreign Market Entry Strategies,* pp. 179–188.

Root identified three rules that managers tend to follow in deciding on the right entry strategy:

(1)   The naive rule

(2)   The pragmatic rule

(3)   The strategy rule

THE NAIVE RULE

According to Root, managers follow the naive rule when they consider only one way to enter a foreign market. Root thinks that managers who use the naive rule are guilty of "tunnel vision." Sooner or later they will be accused of either missing promising markets or entering appropriate markets using an inappropriate mode.

THE PRAGMATIC RULE

Most firms follow the pragmatic rule, which causes them to adopt a policy of "creeping incrementalism." In other words, companies start with low-risk, low-cost entry modes, such as exporting and contractual agreements, and then, provided their experiences have been rewarding, they move on to more complex modes of entry such as investment.

The advantage of this pragmatic approach, says Root, is that it saves the time and cost involved in gathering, analyzing, and assessing information on alternative entry modes. This approach is a safe one for managers, who are usually rewarded well for immediate successes (no matter how irrelevant they may be to the company's future) and punished for failures (no matter how important they may be to the learning process). But according to Root, the cost of lost opportunities associated with this rather timid type of management is great. Future prospects that might have been identified through systematic surveillance of the business environment are certain to be missed. Although some form of graduated entry is likely to be the best approach, the particulars of the strategy should be the product of long-term planning, based on an analysis of all the options.

THE STRATEGY RULE

The strategy rule is recommended here. Not only does it make the most sense, but it can be implemented in a short time with little cost.

Applying the strategy rule to choosing a foreign market entry mode is a three-step process:

Step A: Find the feasible modes out of all possible modes

Step B: Perform a comparative analysis of all feasible modes

Step C: Rank and choose the appropriate mode and implement it

This approach conforms with the XYZ framework shown in Exhibit 1-5, which requires that managers choose a foreign market entry strategy by matching up the company's goals (Z), the company's internal strengths and weaknesses (X), and the constraints of the external environment (Y). It also satisfies the requirements of the systems approach, which calls for managers to go through the following three steps: Conceptualizing the entire process, Measuring/quantifying the concepts and their relationships, and Computerizing the conceptual model developed in the first step and quantified in the second.

STEP A: FIND THE FEASIBLE MODES

The purpose of step A is to identify invariants. An invariant is a condition in the firm (X) and/or the environment (Y) that precludes one or many entry modes. An invariant within a firm might take the form of explicit statements, in the company's philosophy, policies, or standard operating procedures, that rule out a particular mode. For example, the company's management may have strong feelings about not doing business with the Communist world or about not being open on Sundays. Or, like IBM, the company may not wish to get involved in joint ventures. Governmental laws and restrictive policies are examples of environmental invariants that must be identified. Some possible environmental invariants are listed in Exhibit 7-6. The essential difference between constraints and invariants is that the former can be overcome by manipulating the firm's goals or resources, whereas the latter probably cannot be overcome.

STEP B: PERFORM A COMPARATIVE ANALYSIS

Conducting what is conventionally known as a feasibility analysis is step B. This analysis has three interrelated elements: a profit contribution analysis, a risk analysis, and a nonprofit objectives analysis. A two-tiered approach is followed. First, profit, risk, and nonprofit objectives are analyzed for each entry mode (vertical analysis). Then a comparative analysis is performed for all feasible modes (horizontal analysis).

Profit contribution is simply an expression of the difference between expected revenues and expected costs for an entry mode, adjusted to take into account the time value of money. All entry modes will bring two types of revenues: direct (primary) and indirect (secondary). All entry modes will subject the firm to two types of costs: direct (sunk) costs and operating costs. To estimate the net profit contribution, managers must identify and estimate all revenues and costs that are likely to arise from the use of the entry mode.

Risk refers to the likelihood of unanticipated changes that will have a negative impact on the firm's cash flow, value, or profitability. There are three types of macroeconomic risks. Financial risk refers to the likelihood of changes in interest rates and in the costs of different sources of capital in a particular currency. Currency risk refers to the likelihood of unanticipated changes in exchange rates and inflation rates (that is, in the value of foreign and domestic money). Country risk (which includes political risk) refers to the likelihood

Exhibit 7-6　Checklist for Evaluating the Investment Climate of a Foreign Country

A. General political stability

- **(1)** Past political behavior
- **(2)** Form of government
- **(3)** Strength/ideology of government
- **(4)** Strengths/ideologies of rival political groups
- **(5)** Political, social, ethnic, and other conflicts

B. Government policies toward foreign investment

- **(1)** Past experience of foreign investors
- **(2)** Attitude toward foreign investment
- **(3)** Foreign investment treaties and agreements
- **(4)** Restrictions on foreign ownership
- **(5)** Local content requirements
- **(6)** Restrictions on foreign staff
- **(7)** Incentives for and restrictions on foreign investment
- **(8)** Investment entry regulations

C. Other government policies and legal factors

- **(1)** Enforceability of contracts
- **(2)** Fairness of courts
- **(3)** Corporate business law
- **(4)** Labor laws
- **(5)** Taxation
- **(6)** Import duties and restrictions
- **(7)** Patent/trademark protection
- **(8)** Antitrust/restrictive practices laws
- **(9)** Attitudes of public officials

D. Macroeconomic environment

- **(1)** Role of government in the economy
- **(2)** Government development plans/programs
- **(3)** Size/growth rate of gross national product, population, per capita income
- **(4)** Distribution of personal income
- **(5)** Distribution of industry, agriculture, and services
- **(6)** Transportation/communications system
- **(7)** Rate of inflation
- **(8)** Government fiscal/monetary policies
- **(9)** Price controls
- **(10)** Availability/cost of local capital
- **(11)** Management-labor relations
- **(12)** Membership in customs unions or free trade areas

E.   International payments

    (1)   Balance of payments
    (2)   Foreign exchange position/external indebtedness
    (3)   Repatriation restrictions
    (4)   Exchange rate behavior

SOURCE: Adapted from Root, *Foreign Market Entry Strategies,* pp. 144–45.

---

of unanticipated changes in a country's productive development or in the
"rules of the game," including laws, regulations, and monetary and fiscal policies. In addition to these macroeconomic risks, one must consider a firm's
commercial risk, which refers to the likelihood of unanticipated changes in
firm-specific and industry-specific prices and demand conditions.

Nonprofit objectives include goals related to market share, sales volume
targets, concentration ratio, reversibility (ease of disinvestment), corporate
image, and so on.

STEP C: RANK, CHOOSE, AND IMPLEMENT

Once each entry mode has been subjected to the three kinds of analysis just
discussed and all the results have been brought together and compared, the
management team in charge of identifying and evaluating foreign market entry
strategies prepares a recommendation. This report should briefly summarize
and rank the findings for each individual mode as well as for combinations of
them. It should highlight the best mode, pointing out nonquantifiable advantages as well as disadvantages. Such a report supplies management with the
wherewithal to make and implement an informed decision.

The strategy approach to the choice of a foreign market entry mode is not
foolproof. But at least it forces the managerial team to become familiar with
all available modes and to think through all possible consequences of using a
particular mode. It thereby guards against adoption of a mode that is incompatible with either the company's philosophy or the external environment.
Entry modes that run counter to management philosophies or to the corporate
culture will fail. By the same token, entry modes and strategies that seem to
satisfy corporate objectives and top management wishes will not succeed if
they are in conflict with the external environment, especially the explicit or
implicit fiscal, monetary, political, and social policies pursued by a host government.

RECAPITULATION

Going international requires a substantial commitment of company resources. It affects the entire organization, and reversal of the decision is difficult and costly.

Despite its complexity, the task of choosing a specific foreign market entry mode (or a combination of modes) usually is a step-by-step process. Most firms internationalize their activities and operations through a process of "creeping incrementalism." A firm will begin by exporting some product. Gradually, because of environmental pressures, problems with the firm that the company has been doing business with, or a deliberate plan, the company will move into selling its knowledge and expertise via one of the many contractual agreements available.

Most traditional contractual agreements involve licensing the production of a product or the use of a process, franchising the entire production process, or a management contract. In all of these cases, the international company exchanges knowledge for fees, royalties, goods, or a combination of the above.

The most serious entry mode, in terms of both risks and benefits, is investment. Some companies begin the equity-sharing process with the acquisition of a foreign company's outstanding common stock. Usually this investment leads to more extensive involvement, with the investing company actually running the new venture. Finally, in a wholly owned subsidiary the investing company acquires a "home away from home" in the form of production and distribution facilities in a host country.

The last part of the chapter described a method for analyzing and comparing possible entry modes. In the first phase, the feasibility of each mode is examined. Here the emphasis is on identifying the existence of invariants—conditions that preclude a specific entry mode or combination of entry modes. Such invariants may be imposed by either the company or the environment. The second phase involves determining the suitability of a specific entry mode to a company's profit, risk, and nonprofit requirements. One can envision the profit, risk, and nonprofit requirements as a series of filters which become progressively finer as the management team moves through the entry mode analysis.

REVIEW QUESTIONS

(1)   Briefly outline the internationalization process.

(2)   Using the strategic approach developed by Root and the framework outlined in Exhibit 1-2, prepare a report for a small- to medium-size electronics manufacturing company that wishes to venture overseas. Choose three countries: a large developed country in Europe, a large developing country in the Pacific Basin, and a small developing country anywhere you wish. Use a scale from 1 (Very favorable) to 5 (Very unfavorable) to rank the three countries for each mode of entry. Your report should explain and justify your ranking of each country.

(3)   Assume that the company described above has decided to export its product, and develop an export business plan for the company. To obtain the necessary information, contact the Department of Commerce or the Small Business Administration or check your library's government document section.

(4)   Using some of the sources mentioned in Exhibit 7-3, recommend five distributors in five different countries for the company described in question 3.

(5)   Next Life Monument (NLM) Inc., of Atlanta, Georgia, has received an inquiry from a consulting firm on the west coast concerning getting involved in a licensing agreement with a Chinese state-owned company, China Marble and Granite (CMG) Company. The Chinese will provide all the raw marble and granite and will absorb 20% of the output. The remaining 80% of the output will be marketed by the British New Age and Life Improvement Company, Ltd. (NALI), of London, under the name New Age Monument. Upon approval of NLM, a small portion of the new product could be imported to the United States by NALI's wholly owned subsidiary, NALI, U.S.A., registered with the state of California. Draw up a licensing agreement between NLM and CMG.

(6)   The Japanese subsidiary of NALI in Tokyo has located a South Korean company that has recently discovered a huge deposit of marble. The Korean company lacks the capital and technology to exploit this new find. Its extraction equipment and processing technology are antiquated and completely inadequate for this large endeavor, and both processes require large sums of money. Draw up a minority joint venture agreement between the Korean material-rich company and each of the following: (1) a company that is rich in capital and poor in domestic investment opportunities; (2) a company in the same business (marble, stone, and cement extraction and processing) that has state-of-the-art technology; (3) a manufacturer of marble and stone machinery who cannot export.

SUGGESTED READINGS

Anderson, Erin, and Hubert Gatignon. "Modes of Foreign Entry: A Transaction Cost Analysis and Propositions." *Journal of International Business Studies* 17, No. 3 (1986): 1–26.

Artisien, Patrick F. R., and Peter J. Buckley. "Joint Ventures in Yugoslavia: Opportunities and Constraints." *Journal of International Business Studies* 16, No. 1 (1985): 113–136.

Barkas, James M., and James C. Gale. "Joint Venture Strategies: Yugoslavia—A Case Study." *Columbia Journal of World Business* 16, No. 1 (Spring 1981): 30–39.

Barrow, T. D. "International Business Strategies for the Eighties." *Vital Speeches* 46, No. 21 (August 15, 1980): 656–659.

Beamish, Paul W., and John C. Banks. "Equity Joint Ventures and the Theory of the Multinational Enterprise." *Journal of International Business Studies* 19, No. 2 (1987): 1–16.

Bello, Daniel C., and Nicholas C. Williamson. "Contractual Arrangement and Marketing Practices in the Indirect Export Channel." *Journal of International Business Studies* 17, No. 2 (1985): 65–82.

Betts, Paul. "Mr. Gomez Builds a High-Risk Empire." *London Financial Times,* July 24, 1987, 16.

Brown, Andrew. "Unilever Fights Back in the U.S." *Fortune,* May 26, 1986, 32–38.

Buxton, James. "Why Compaq Will Not Be Frozen Out." *London Financial Times,* July 24, 1987, 16.

Cao, A. D. "Social Pricing in Foreign Direct Investment Evaluation." *Business Economics* 15, No. 1 (January 1980): 53–60.

Chevalier, A., and G. Hirsch. "The Assessment of the Political Risk in the Investment Decision." *Journal of the Operational Research Society* 32, No. 7 (July 1981): 599–610.

Christopher, Robert C. *Second to None: American Companies in Japan.* New York: Crown Publishers, 1986.

Contractor, Farok. "A Generalized Theorem for Joint-Venture and Licensing Negotiations." *Journal of International Business Studies* 17, No. 2 (1985): 23–50.

Copeland, Lennie, and Lewis Groggs. *Going International: How to Make Friends and Deal Effectively in the Global Marketplace.* New York: Random House, 1983.

Deloitte, Haskins & Sells. *Expanding Your Business Overseas: An Entrepreneur's Guidebook.* New York: DHS, 1985.

Dicken, Peter, *Global Shift: Industrial Changes in a Turbulent World.* New York: Harper and Row, 1986.

Dixon, Hugh, and James Buchan. "Nat West Makes $820 Million Bid for New Jersey Bank." *London Financial Times,* August 6, 1987, 1.

Dodsworth, Terry. "Integration at a Gallop." *London Financial Times,* July 15, 1987, 12.

———. "A High Risk Rebalancing Act." *London Financial Times,* July 29, 1987, 11.

Dullforce, William. "An Iconoclast Who Inspired a Classic Regeneration." *London Financial Times,* July 20, 1987, 14.

Fisher, Andrew. "Bertelsmann: Going for the Bigger Steps in the U.S." *London Financial Times,* July 6, 1987, 14.

Globerman, Steven. *Fundamentals of International Business Management.* Englewood Cliffs, NJ: Prentice-Hall, 1986.

Heenan, David A., and Howard V. Perlmutter. *Multinational Organizational Development.* Reading, MA: Addison-Wesley, 1979.

Hill, Roy. "Philips over the Years: A Model of the Maturing Multinational." *International Management,* August 1986, 28–32.

Hills, S. M. "The Search for Joint Venture Partners." *Proceedings of the 38th*

Annual Meeting of the Academy of Management, August 1978, 277–281.

Hisey, Karen B., and Richard E. Caves. "Diversification Strategy and Choice of Country: Diversifying Acquisitions Abroad by U.S." *Journal of International Business Studies* 16, No. 2 (1985).

Hladik, Karen J. *International Joint Venture: An Economic Analysis of U.S.-Foreign Business Partnerships.* Lexington, MA: Lexington Books, 1985.

Lorenz, Christopher. "How Glaxo Moved into the Fast Lane." *London Financial Times,* July 17, 1987, 14.

Oram, Rod, and Nikki Tait. "Hanson Strategy Takes Leap Forward." *London Financial Times,* August 6, 1987, 19.

"Philips: An Electronics Giant Rearms to Fight Japan." *Business Week,* March 30, 1981, 86–89.

Root, Franklin R. *Foreign Market Entry Strategies.* New York: AMACOM, 1982.

————. *International Trade and Investment: Theory, Policy, Enterprise.* Cincinnati, OH: South-Western Publishing Co., 1984.

Servan-Schreiber, J. J. *The American Challenge.* New York: Atheneum, 1968.

United Nations Industrial Development Organization. *Manual on the Establishment of Industrial Joint-Venture Agreements in Developing Countries.* New York: United Nations, 1971.

Vernon-Wortzel, Heidi, and Lawrence H. Wortzel (eds). *Strategic Management of Multinational Corporations: The Essentials.* New York: John Wiley and Sons, 1985.

Walmsley, John. *Handbook of International Joint Ventures.* London: Graham and Trotman, 1985.

CASE ● Toyota's International Scope

Direct foreign investment (DFI) is the foreign market entry strategy requiring the most commitment from a company. When a company decides to invest capital in assets in a foreign country, its management has come to the conclusion that it will play the international business game for keeps. The decision to invest in physical assets (or, as these assets are commonly called, "bricks and mortar") is usually preceded by a great degree of deliberation and evaluation of a company's past experience with other, less extensive modes of operation in a foreign country (such as exports, imports, and contractual agreements).

As we have seen, the 1970s and 1980s witnessed a remarkable reversal of

SOURCE: This case was prepared by A. G. Kefalas, Professor of Management, and John Stein, Graduating Senior, College of Business Administration, the University of Georgia, as a basis for class discussion rather than to illustrate either effective or inefficient management practices.

the United States' role in the foreign investment game. The country changed from the major investor in foreign countries to a major recipient of foreign investment. While U.S. direct foreign investment abroad increased by a small amount (about 21% between 1980 and 1986), direct foreign investment in the United States more than doubled (from $83 billion to $209 billion). These foreign investments in the United States provided employment to almost three million people (about 3% of the total work force).[11]

Not surprisingly, trends in direct foreign investment in the United States follow social, economic, and industrial trends in the country. During the last two decades the United States experienced a massive shift of activity away from the Northern and Northeastern states and toward the Southeastern and Southwestern states. Indeed, statistics show that the Southeastern states received the lion's share of DFIUS. Exhibits C7-1 and C7-2 provide data on the regional shares of DFIUS, using as a measure the number of investment projects per thousand manufacturing employees. As Exhibit C7-1 shows, the Southeast ranks second among U.S. regions in the number of foreign manufacturing

Exhibit C7-1   Regions Ranked by Number of Foreign Manufacturing Constructions and Acquisitions per Thousand Manufacturing Employees

First Quarter 1978 through Fourth Quarter 1979		First Quarter 1980 through First Quarter 1982	
Region	Number per Thousand Employees[a]	Region	Number per Thousand Employees[b]
New England	.056	New England	.044
Southeast	.044	Southeast	.034
Far West	.043	Southwest	.031
Southwest	.040	Mid-Atlantic	.030
Mid-Atlantic	.037	Far West	.025
Rocky Mountains	.033	Rocky Mountains	.022
Great Lakes	.081	Great Lakes	.018
Plains	.015	Plains	.014

[a]Based on monthly average employment, 1978

[b]Based on monthly average employment, 1980

SOURCE: Based on data from the Conference Board, *Announcements of Foreign Investment in U.S. Manufacturing Industry,* 1978:I–1982:I; *Employment and Training Report of the President* (Washington, DC: U.S. Government Printing Office, 1979); and U.S. Bureau of Labor Statistics, *Employment and Earnings,* May 1982.

[11]U.S. Department of Commerce, *Survey of Current Business,* May 1987.

Exhibit C7-2   Regions Ranked by Number of Foreign Manufacturing Constructions (only) per Thousand Manufacturing Employees

First Quarter 1978 through Fourth Quarter 1979		First Quarter 1980 through First Quarter 1982	
Region	Number per Thousand Employees[a]	Region	Number per Thousand Employees[b]
New England	.032	Southeast	.019
Southeast	.028	Southwest	.015
Southwest	.026	New England	.012
Far West	.020	Rocky Mountains	.011
Mid-Atlantic	.017	Mid-Atlantic	.010
Rocky Mountains	.012	Far West	.007
Plains	.006	Great Lakes	.004
Great Lakes	.005	Plains	.004

[a]Based on monthly average employment, 1978

[b]Based on monthly average employment, 1980

SOURCE: Jane Little, "Foreign Investors' Location Choices: An Update," *New England Economic Review,* January–February 1983, 28–31.

constructions and acquisitions experienced during the period shown. When only new construction is considered, the Southeast is in first place for the latter part of the period (as shown in Exhibit C7-2). Although the New England region attracted the most DFIUS, the foreign capital invested there was for acquisition of existing facilities rather than for creation of new facilities and therefore new workplaces.

The implications of this shift toward investment by foreigners in more new construction in the Southeastern United States are tremendous, and it is no wonder that the competition among these states to attract foreign investment has increased tremendously. Governors are organizing foreign missions in collaboration with chambers of commerce, state and federal industry and trade offices, and other public and private interest groups. Political figures and even entertainment personalities have helped these efforts by using their contacts to set up meetings with their counterparts in foreign countries.

TOYOTA MOTOR CORPORATION[12]

Toyota Motor Corporation, which celebrated its fiftieth anniversary in 1987, is Japan's leading automobile manufacturer and one of the largest in the world.

---

[12]Much of the information in this section comes from the Toyota Motor Corporation's 1987 Annual Report.

The company was started in the early 1930s by Kiichiro Toyoda, the son of a successful inventor of an automatic weaving loom. In the face of widespread opinion that U.S. and other foreign auto makers were too firmly established and too far ahead technologically, Toyoda determined to catch up to them. He and a small team labored patiently to perfect an auto design that used Japanese components and technology. The team's first prototype was completed in 1935, and two years later the company was established. Today Toyota is principally engaged in the manufacture of passenger cars, trucks, and buses. The company also produces prefabricated housing, forklifts, and other industrial vehicles. In addition, it is moving into such new business areas as the provision of telecommunications services. Toyota's consolidated subsidiaries carry out a wide variety of production and sales activities, mainly related to the parent company's manufacturing operations. Toyota currently operates manufacturing plants in Japan and production and assembly facilities in twenty foreign countries. Its products are marketed in more than 140 countries through an extensive network of distributors and dealers. In fifty years Toyota has grown from a small automotive project set up in the corner of a loom factory to a corporation that has helped transform the global automotive industry and has firmly established itself as a world leader.

Toyota's Overseas Operations

Since the establishment of an assembly plant in Brazil in 1958, Toyota's overseas manufacturing network has grown to include twenty-seven production or assembly facilities in twenty countries. Toyota's California joint venture with General Motors was established in 1985 as an example of new industrial cooperation between Japan and the United States. The corporation is also establishing wholly or jointly owned manufacturing operations in the United States, Canada, and Taiwan. In the Federal Republic of Germany, the joint production of pickup trucks with Volkswagen started in 1989. In addition, Toyota cooperated in the establishment of a full-scale driving school in the People's Republic of China.

Toyota's international operations form a web of manufacturing plants, dealers, and sales outlets. In addition to manufacturing plants, the overseas network includes 155 importers and distributors and 6761 dealerships spread throughout Europe, the Middle East, Africa, Southeast Asia and Oceania, Latin America, and North America. Auto sales in Japan are handled through the Toyota, Toyopet, Corolla, Auto, and Vista facilities. These five channels consist of 318 dealers and 4333 sales outlets. In addition there are three divisions: the Industrial Vehicle division (consisting of thirty-one dealerships), the Parts Distribution division (consisting of thirty-one facilities), and the Toyota Rent-a-Car Company (consisting of sixty-one facilities).

Toyota entered the United States for the first time in 1957. Total world exports for 1957 were 6554 units, of which thirteen (eleven cars and two trucks) went to the United States. Toyota's first years in the U.S. market were far from easy. In 1957 two of the thirteen cars exported to the United States went to Los Angeles. But the company found that driving conditions on U.S. highways were too demanding for Japanese cars of that day. In fact, the first

Crowns were so heavy and underpowered that they could not make the steep climb to the Toyota dealership in Hollywood! Since 1957 Toyota's designs have obviously improved, and exports to the United States have increased steadily, to 609,908 in 1988. Toyota has used its facilities with staggering efficiency, surpassing Chrysler and closing the gap with Ford and GM in total sales.

Joint Ventures and Affiliates

Along with the numerous importers and dealers in the United States, Toyota has a number of joint ventures and affiliates. The establishment of Toyota Motor Sales, USA, Inc. in 1957 marked the beginning of the company's history in the United States. Total capital for the facility was $11 million; the company is 100% Toyota owned. In October, 1973, Toyota established Calty Design Research, Inc., an automotive design research center. The facility is 20% U.S. owned. In June, 1977, Toyota Technical Center, USA was established for auto testing, research, and information gathering; it is 10% U.S. owned. New United Motor Manufacturing, Inc. (NUMMI), in Fremont, California, is 50% GM owned. It was established in February, 1984, and can produce 250,000 Chevys and Toyotas annually.

Toyota's second plant in the United States is in Georgetown, Kentucky. It was scheduled to begin producing some 200,000 Camrys a year beginning in mid-1988. Of the two plants, the one in Kentucky is the more controversial. As with many DFI deals, Kentucky gave great concessions to lure Toyota to the state—including $125 million in subsidies and assistance, extravagant dinners for heads of the company, and great support from Governor Collins, who offered to buy the first car produced in the plant.[13]

Toyota's influence on and involvement in the U.S. economy is further illustrated by the numerous companies in the United States that supply Toyota with all sorts of products. In 1983, Japanese imports of foreign-made parts reached $146 million; Toyota imported $143 million worth of these products, a 30% increase from 1982. The various companies supplying Toyota in 1983 included

Collins and Aikman, carpet

Michelin Tire Company, radial tires

Chatham Manufacturing, fabrics

GE Company, headlights

GM-RDP, valve lifters

GM Delco Products, door lock actuators

GM New Departure-Hyatt, fuel caps

Eagle Ottawa Leather Company, upholstery

Bendix Corporation, disc brake pads

---

[13]Takeo Miyauchi, "The Man Who Lured Toyota to Kentucky," *Economic Eye,* March 1987, 23–27.

PPG Industries, Inc., laminated glass

Garrett Corporation, turbochargers

Milliken and Company, fabrics

Corning, catalyst carriers

Rockwell International, light alloy wheels

Clearly, Toyota uses the products of many domestic companies in its production processes, thereby creating new jobs and increasing demand for its products.

SOURCES

The Automotive Industry: Japan and Toyota. New York: Toyota Motor Corporation Public Affairs Department, 1987.

Duncan, William C. *U.S.-Japan Automobile Diplomacy: A Study in Economic Confrontation.* Cambridge, MA: Ballinger Publishing Co., 1973.

Japan 1986: An International Comparison. Tokyo: Japan Institute for Social and Economic Affairs, 1986.

Miyauchi, Takeo. "The Man Who Lured Toyota to Kentucky." *Economic Eye,* March 1987, 23–27.

"The Motor Industry: The Eye of the Storm." *Financial Times,* October 20, 1988, 1–28.

Sheard, P. *Automobile Production Systems in Japan.* (Melbourne, Australia: Monash University, 1983).

ISSUES FOR DISCUSSION

(1) What are some of the reasons that the Southeastern United States has been so successful in attracting foreign investors?

(2) Trace Toyota's internationalization course. Does it conform to the pattern described in this book?

(3) Research the decision-making process that led to Toyota's choice of Kentucky as a plant location. Was the choice the result of Kentucky's better fit to Toyota's strategic plan or was it because of the superior incentives offered by the state of Kentucky as compared with those offered by other states? In your opinion did Kentucky's Governor Collins go overboard with his support and enthusiasm for the project?

(4) Compare and contrast Toyota's New United Motor Manufacturing, Inc. (NUMMI) joint venture with GMC in California and its wholly owned plant in Kentucky. Is California getting a better deal from the Japanese connection than Kentucky? What does GMC bring to the joint venture with Toyota? What are Toyota's benefits from the NUMMI arrangement?

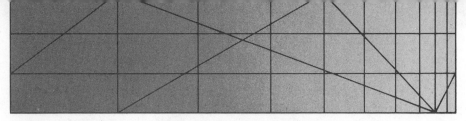

CHAPTER
8

ORGANIZATION STRATEGY

The concept of "organization" is not limited to boxes, lines and charts or the shape and size of units, departments and divisions. These form the skeleton. The flesh and blood, brain and heart of any organization are people (e.g., their selection, transfer and promotion, training and development, and style of leadership) and mechanical systems (e.g., planning, budget, performance measures, compensation and, especially, communication systems). An organization is the sum of these variables, all of which are interrelated.

Business International Staff

New Directions in Multinational Corporate Organization (New York: BIC, 1981), ii.

OVERVIEW

The previous chapter described how the management of a company chooses a foreign market entry mode—a participation strategy for entering the world market. The management team charged with executing this strategy must then begin to develop an organization structure that will enable the organization to achieve its goal of entering the foreign market. The view espoused in this book and accepted by most management scholars is that "structure follows strategy." In other words, management must first devise a framework (strategy), which it then uses to organize the company's resources into an efficient system (structure).

In the sciences the term "organization" refers to a system that is able to perform coordinated, useful work. In management literature the term "organization" is used very loosely to connote both an institution, such as an MNC, and the process of coordinating the organization's resources. This chapter describes the process that an MNC follows in creating a coordinating structure and summarizes attempts to develop an organization theory for international management.

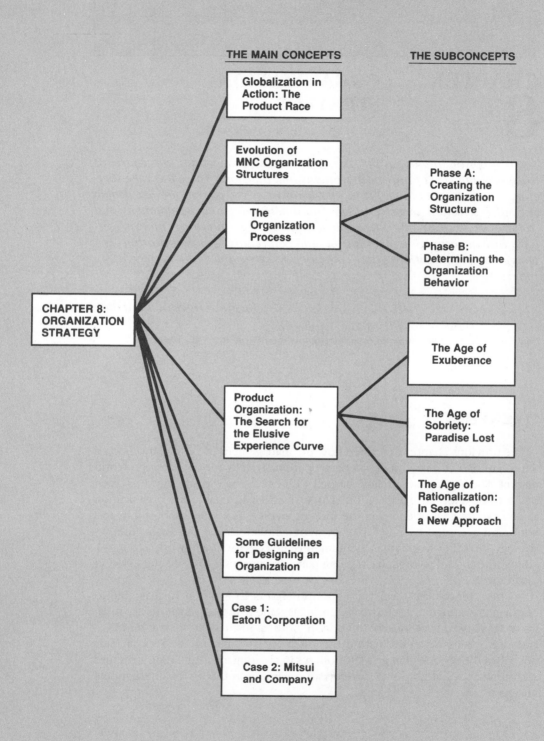

THE MAIN CONCEPTS   THE SUBCONCEPTS

Globalization in
Action: The
Product Race

Evolution of
MNC Organization
Structures

The
Organization
Process

Phase A:
Creating the
Organization
Structure

Phase B:
Determining the
Organization
Behavior

CHAPTER 8:
ORGANIZATION
STRATEGY

The Age of
Exuberance

Product
Organization:
The Search for
the Elusive
Experience Curve

The Age of
Sobriety:
Paradise Lost

The Age of
Rationalization:
In Search of
a New Approach

Some Guidelines
for Designing an
Organization

Case 1:
Eaton Corporation

Case 2: Mitsui
and Company

LEARNING OBJECTIVES

After studying the material in this chapter, the student should be familiar with the following concepts:

(1)   The meaning of the term "organization"

(2)   The "relay race" and "rugby" approaches to product development

(3)   The evolution of MNC organization structures

(4)   The two phases of the organization process

(5)   The main alternative forms of organization structure

(6)   Centralization vs. decentralization of decision making in an MNC

(7)   The experience curve

(8)   The meaning of the term "rationalization"

(9)   Some guidelines for designing an organization structure

(10)   "Product organization" as a future alternative

GLOBALIZATION IN ACTION
The Product Race: Rugby vs. Relay

"The procedural chart some companies used in the 1970s to design a coffee maker was complicated enough to put a rocket on the moon," says Steve Walleck, head of McKinsey & Co., the management consultancy. Now all that is changing, and not only in information technology, electronics and cars— sectors in which the Japanese challenge is greatest. Whether the prime competitor is from Japan or not, and whether the goal is to be first-to-market or a "fast follower," Western companies in industries as diverse as aircraft, food, drugs, and heavy engineering are also rushing to join the "product race."

> IBM nearly halved the personal computer industry's standard product development cycle of two years when it entered the market in 1981. It has since cut development times for typewriters and printers, as well as for its standard computers.
>
> Rolls Royce, the aero engine maker, has pruned the development-to-certification cycle on turbine blades from more than five years to as little as two and a quarter.
>
> Procter & Gamble has more than halved the development times for many of its household products.
>
> Allen-Bradley, a leading U.S. maker of engineering components, has cut the development cycle for electrical contractors from seven years to just two.
>
> General Motors, Ford, Volkswagen, and other mass motor manufacturers are starting to chase the Japanese industry's development time, currently at an average of three-and-a-half years and falling. They have a lot of catching up to do: the average U.S. time is five years, and some Europeans are even slower.

All these examples have one common characteristic: "scrum and scramble." "Scrum and scramble" is a variant of what is becoming known among insiders as the "rugby team" approach to product development. It has been practiced for over a decade by entrepreneurial Japanese companies such as Canon, Honda, and Sony, in preference to the more sluggish "relay race" tactics traditionally used by most of their bureaucratic competitors in Europe and the United States; only a few Western pioneers, such as Hewlett-Packard, are practiced users of "rugby" tactics.

In the traditional Western "relay race," one group of functional specialists "passes the baton to the next group," says Professor Hirotaka Takeuchi of Japan's Hitotsubashi University, who is one of the few academics or consultants to have studied Japanese product development in depth. Says Takeuchi, "The project goes sequentially from phase to phase: concept development, feasibility testing, product design, development, production design and tooling, pilot production, and full production." The various functions are compartmentalized from each other, "with different specialists carrying the baton at different stages of the race."

In the new "rugby approach" pressure is exerted on the engineers to do more group work in which specialists in marketing, industrial design, engineering and manufacturing work together on project teams.

There is a great temptation to suggest that this shift away from sequential attention to the various tasks of product development and marketing will render obsolete the conventional hierarchical structure of a business enterprise in favor of Apple founder Steve Jobs's "loose group of people." This type of organizational design is said to promote creativity and originality which, when coupled with organizational identification and dedication, leads to superior performance.

John Sculley pulled together Apple's fragmented product development program, which at times bordered on the chaotic, setting his engineers tough deadlines for new products. He merged and centralized Apple's different product divisions, which often operated as though they were autonomous companies. He laid down formal reporting procedures and strict financial controls. And to ram the message home, he closed plants, shed almost a quarter of the staff, and shook up his top management.

Sculley says, a little self-consciously, that the famous Apple style is alive and well. "We still have a great emphasis on having a work environment that is fun. We still do not have formal dress codes. We still have beer busts on Friday afternoon and parades and celebrations when we pass major milestones."

Yet beneath this California babble, Sculley has a deeper point to make. He believes that the lack of structure before he arrived, far from being a symptom of creativity, hindered innovation across a broad front. "There were great problems getting our products out of the door till we reorganized. We have increased the likelihood that innovative ideas will turn into shippable products." Citing People's Express and Atari as examples, Sculley argues that few U.S. companies have managed to combine their original entrepreneurial drive with the structures needed as they grew to that sort of size.

Unisys is another company that has been restructured. The aim of the new management structure, says Mias van Vuuren, Unisys's marketing director for Europe, is to make sure that centrally determined European strategies are hammered home at the local level.

Each national company formed by integrating the old rival teams is organized to sell machines in four broad product categories. These businesses—financial services, public sector and transportation, industrial and commercial, and indirect sales—are all fast-growing segments through which [Unisys's CEO] Blumenthal believes that the company can secure substantial market shares by concentrating its sales resources.

To bring this concentrated effort to bear, the manager of each of the product lines reports to a national chief executive, but also has a line of responsibility back to a headquarters-based European marketing manager, who is charged with reviewing and monitoring progress in each product area.

SOURCES: "The Product Race" (series), *Financial Times* (London), June 17, 19, 26, July 3, 10, 1987. The portion on Apple is from *Financial Times*, July 27, 1987. The material on Unisys is from *Financial Times,* July 15, 1987.

INTRODUCTION

The purpose of organization is to enable an MNC to perform useful work, by linking individuals, groups of individuals, firms, and groups of firms into a coherent and cohesive system that will facilitate decision making and decision implementation. Vernon describes the management task of organization as follows: "Organizations, it is evident, are created to link the behavior of individuals: to collect and pool information, skills, or capital; to engage in related actions towards the achievement of a set of goals; to monitor performance, initiate corrections, and define new goals."[1]

Brooke, on the other side of the Atlantic, has identified four main purposes of organization:

(1) To enable decisions to be taken efficiently and at the right time

(2) To provide a channel for the exercise of authority

(3) To provide a system for reporting and communication

(4) To provide a career structure[2]

The organization structure must facilitate decision making both vertically and horizontally. The number of ways of organizing even a small MNC, with five thousand employees, five products, and five subsidiaries, is astronomical.

The task of designing the appropriate organization structure is a very difficult one, and the choice of the wrong organization structure can be detrimental to an MNC's success. In a study performed at the University of Warwick in England, researchers attributed the superior performance of Japanese managers over both British and American managers to, among other factors, different organization structures. The Japanese subsidiaries examined by the researchers were organized by products, whereas both the U.S. and British companies were organized by functions.

[1]Raymond, Vernon and L. T. Wells, *Manager in the International Economy,* Fifth Edition (Englewood Cliffs, NJ: Prentice-Hall, 1986).

[2]M. Z. Brooke, *International Management: A Review of Strategies and Operations* (London: Hutchinson, 1986).

EVOLUTION OF MNC ORGANIZATION STRUCTURES

A company's choice of participation strategy—one of the controllable variables (X) in the familiar XYZ framework—is a very important determinant of organization structure. Thus changes in the organization structures of U.S. MNCs over the years have to a large degree paralleled changes in participation strategy.

U.S. MNCs evolved through five main stages. During the first two decades after World War II, the main entry mode was exports. To facilitate the export of U.S. products all over the world, most MNCs created an export department, the activities of which were confined mostly to the logistics of getting the product to the nearest port.

During the sixties contractual agreements and investments followed trade. One by one, U.S. MNCs set up factories and sales offices in Europe. At home they created international divisions to coordinate the activities of the subsidiaries overseas. Since most of the decision making was done at the headquarters, the task of the international division was fairly simple: to relay messages from home to the foreign subsidiaries.

The seventies ushered in the age of consolidation of the numerous plants created under the expansive management philosophy of the previous two decades. Exhibit 8-1 outlines the evolution and growth of international business and corresponding changes in organization structure. The typical multinational company went from a rather simple organizational design (Stage I) based on an export department to a very complex—and, at times, confusing—organizational design (Stage V) based on a combination of product and geographical factors.

THE ORGANIZATION PROCESS

The organization process can be divided into two phases:

Phase A: Creating an organizational structure that will allow the MNC to take full advantage of its global resources

Phase B: Determining the organizational behavior dictated by the required degree of coordination of the company's global activities

Phase A of the organization process involves dividing the MNC's domestic and foreign activities into departments. Phase B entails prescribing the decision-making rules that will be followed by the MNC headquarters and its overseas subsidiaries. The latter task requires choosing between centralization and decentralization. The organization process must result in a scheme that will satisfy two seemingly contradictory objectives. Obviously the desire to maximize the benefits of specialization must be weighed against the cost of

Exhibit 8-1   Structural Evolution of Multinational Corporations

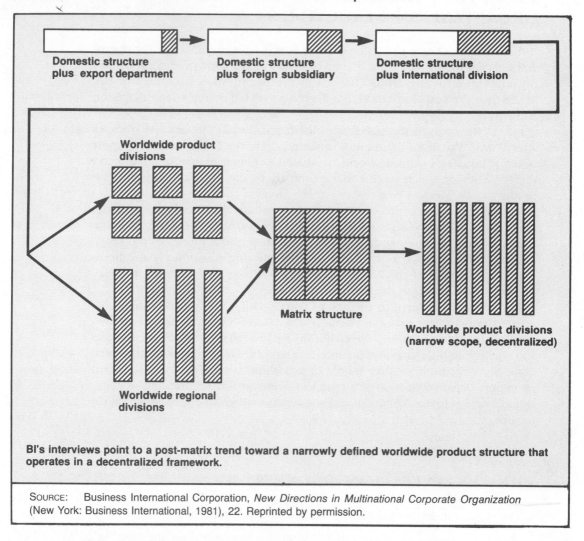

Domestic structure
plus export department

Domestic structure
plus foreign subsidiary

Domestic structure
plus international division

**Worldwide product
divisions**

Matrix structure

**Worldwide product divisions
(narrow scope, decentralized)**

**Worldwide regional
divisions**

**BI's interviews point to a post-matrix trend toward a narrowly defined worldwide product structure that
operates in a decentralized framework.**

SOURCE: Business International Corporation, *New Directions in Multinational Corporate Organization*
(New York: Business International, 1981), 22. Reprinted by permission.

the coordination necessary to prevent these specialized forces from pursuing
counterproductive objectives.

PHASE A: CREATING THE ORGANIZATION STRUCTURE

ORGANIZING FOR EXPORTING AND CONTRACTUAL AGREEMENTS

We have seen that exporting and contractual agreements are the least demanding modes of entry in terms of the amount of structure and coordination
required. Generally, companies engaged in such activities want to create an

office within the firm that will facilitate and stimulate international trade without disturbing the rest of the company. Many companies establish an office within the marketing department to handle export and franchising activity; other contractual arrangements are handled by an international office within the R&D department. Other companies assign the exporting function to a separate office, thereby awarding it slightly higher status within the company. Exhibit 8-2 shows two possible ways of incorporating international activities into the overall organization structure.

Usually appointments to international offices are made when things seem to be "getting out of hand." For most small firms that are beginning the internationalization process via exports or contractual agreements, either of the arrangements shown in Exhibit 8-2 is a very appropriate form of organization structure.

ORGANIZING FOR INVESTMENT

The organization structure appropriate for a company that is entering a foreign market at the investment level will depend on several variables. These variables include product, product line, geographical dispersion of the MNC's activities, company philosophy, and external environmental demands.

In general, a firm that engages in direct foreign investment will choose one of the following alternative forms of organization:

(1)   Organization by function

(2)   Organization by product

(3)   Organization by geographical area

(4)   Organization by combination (matrix)

Historically most MNCs started with an organization based on functions, one of which was international trade. Subsequently, as international activities picked up and the number of products produced and marketed overseas increased, the product and geographical forms of organization became very popular. In the seventies most progressive MNCs adopted the matrix form of organization structure. Recently mounting dissatisfaction with the matrix arrangement has led many MNCs to abandon it in favor of the product form of organization structure.

Organization by Function.   Exhibit 8-3 illustrates a functional organization. Firms that organize their global activities by function subscribe to the idea that management functions (production, finance, marketing, personnel, research and development, and public relations) are the same the world over, and functional expertise is more relevant than product knowledge. Thus, for example, once an executive has mastered the details of production capacity utilization, production runs, and the like at a Peoria, Illinois plant, he or she could conceivably hop on a jet plane and a few hours later "troubleshoot" a production line in Paris, France.

Exhibit 8-2   An International Organization: Two Options

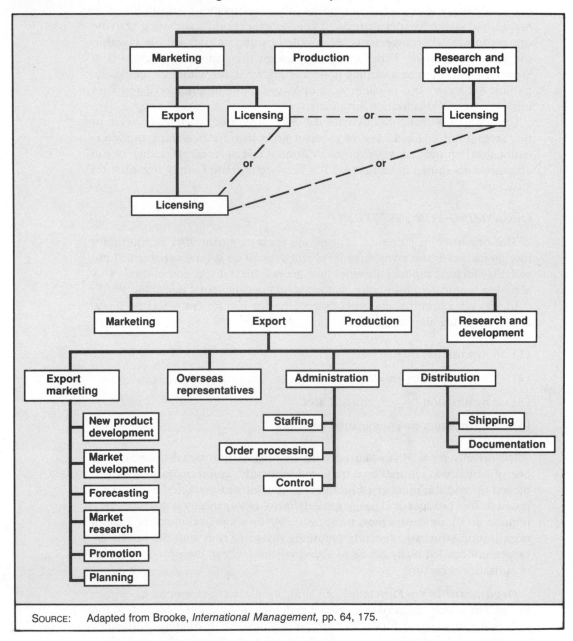

SOURCE: Adapted from Brooke, *International Management*, pp. 64, 175.

Exhibit 8-3   Functional Organization Structure

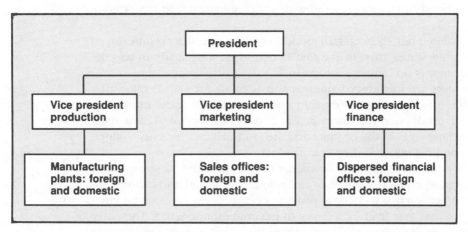

Organization by Product.   Exhibit 8-4 depicts a product-oriented organization. Under this type of organizational scheme, a single executive is put in charge of a specific product or product line. This executive, the product manager, is assisted by a "multifunctional team." Many European companies (Philips in the Netherlands and Volvo in Sweden, for example) have switched over to product organization.

The rationale behind product organization is that because of the tremendous increase in the rate at which products become obsolescent, today's managers must continually improve current product design and invent new products and processes in order to stay ahead of the competition. When the technical life of products was longer, the functional organizational structure was more

Exhibit 8-4   Product-Oriented Organization Structure

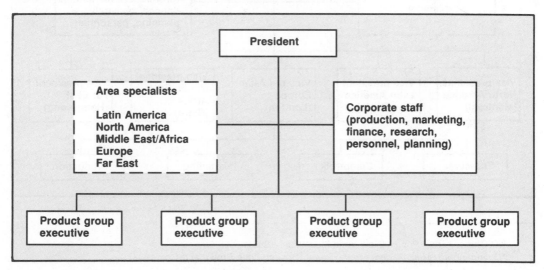

appropriate. But now that the life cycle of most products has been shortened considerably, the advantages associated with a technological lead have diminished.

As Ohmae pointed out, the waterfall model, whereby a product is introduced first in the United States, then in the OECD countries, and finally in less developed countries, is no longer appropriate.[3]

Today products are introduced simultaneously in all the OECD countries. Thus there often is little time to explain the product to finance, marketing, personnel, and production managers before production begins. Teams must first "learn the language" of the product and then must think the same product, dream the same product, live the same product.

Therein lies what some observers consider to be one of the most important disadvantages of a product-oriented organization: people's identification with the product. When carried to excess, product centeredness takes on an emotional overtone that may lead executives to become ethnocentric. They may come to believe in the inherent superiority of their own country as much as they do in that of their product.[4]

Organization by Geographical Area.   Executives who organize their firms' activities by geographical region believe that different regions call for different styles of management and, therefore, different skills and talents. As Exhibit 8-5 shows, under this approach one manager is put in charge of one

Exhibit 8-5   Geographical Organization Structure

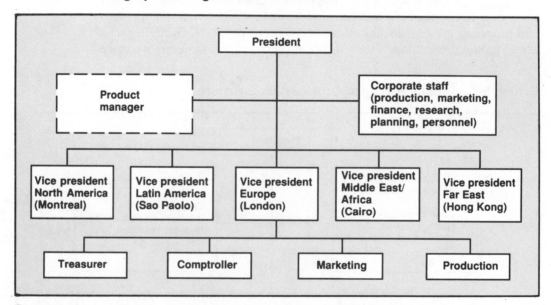

[3]K. Ohmae, *Triad Power* (New York: Macmillan, 1985).
[4]D. Rutenberg, *Multinational Management* (Boston: Little Brown and Co., 1981).

geographical region. Usually, the manager reports directly to the president at the headquarters. A geographical organization structure is generally selected only by firms that produce consumer goods, which depend on stable and well-known technology but demand considerable marketing ability. It stands to reason that a company would want to give a local manager considerable responsibility to market such a product. The activities of all these regional managers are often coordinated by a product specialist located at the headquarters or some other central point.

Organization by Combination (Matrix). The matrix organization structure evolved out of the desire to combine product, geographical, and functional expertise into a harmonious whole without sacrificing clear lines of authority. Firms that espouse the matrix organizational form are said to have a geocentric management philosophy. Even though the matrix organization structure has lost some of its glamour, it still has the potential to solve some dilemmas in MNC management. Much of the disillusionment seems to have been due to the failure of firms to provide the superimposed administrative structure (a superstructure) needed to manage the matrix organization.

Rutenberg describes most eloquently the basic facets of a matrix organization.[5] Structurally, there is a dual rather than a single chain of command. Some managers report to two individuals rather than to the traditional single boss. Behaviorally, there is lateral (dual) decision making and a chain of command that fosters conflict management and a balance of power.

Matrix organizations usually contain three key positions, as depicted in Exhibit 8-6. At the top is the top leadership—the general executive—whose role is similar to that of the CEO in traditional organizations. The *matrix managers*, who share common subordinates, are located on the sides of the diamond. In an MNC's international operations, one of the matrix managers is

Exhibit 8-6 Matrix Roles

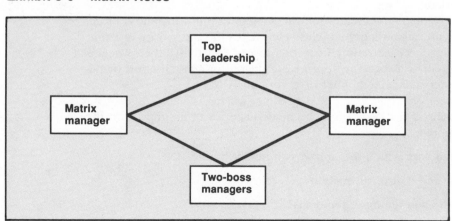

[5]Rutenberg, *Multinational Management*, p. 23.

likely to be a product-oriented manager and the other an international, regional, or country manager. In a pure matrix organization, matrix managers are fairly equal in power and importance. Jointly, they hammer out business plans and are responsible for meeting the goals set by the top leadership.

Two-boss managers report to both matrix managers, which means that they must learn to accommodate simultaneous—and sometimes competing—demands. The two-boss managers are each responsible at the regional or country level for the normal functions of the business, such as general management, manufacturing, marketing, and finance. Thus, they are each at the apex of their own pyramid, which they manage in traditional ways. The matrix format, therefore, does not affect everyone in an organization; in fact, only a small number of people are affected.

Matrix organization is intended to bring together expertise in geographic, product, and function areas. Decisions are made jointly by representatives from the national offices and function and product representatives from headquarters. Each product or product line is a revenue/profit center; the functional activities of finance, production, and so on are the cost centers. The functional areas sell their services to the profit centers.

PHASE B: DETERMINING THE ORGANIZATIONAL BEHAVIOR

The formal organization structure shows MNC employees the routes that organizational decision making theoretically must follow. It may or may not provide a clue to the locus of the authority to initiate the decision-making process. Where the majority of the decisions are made (at the headquarters level, the regional level, or the national subsidiary level) will depend on the company's attitude toward the question of centralization vs. decentralization of decision making.

Despite the voluminous research on the subject of the distribution of decision making, no single theory conclusively proves the superiority of either centralization or decentralization. Instead, a sort of "relativity" theory seems to govern decision making. The appropriate degree of centralization or decentralization depends on a number of factors, such as

(1)   The weight of the decision to be made in terms of its impact on the overall company

(2)   The speed with which the impact will be felt by the MNC

(3)   The ease and cost of reversibility

(4)   The nature and timing of the decision

Exhibit 8-7 illustrates the possible ways that decision-making prerogatives can be shared between the headquarters of an MNC and its foreign subsidiaries. The shaded area indicates the proportion of the decision-making authority held by the subsidiaries. As one moves from top to bottom, the amount of decision-

Exhibit 8-7   Decentralization and Centralization of Decision Making

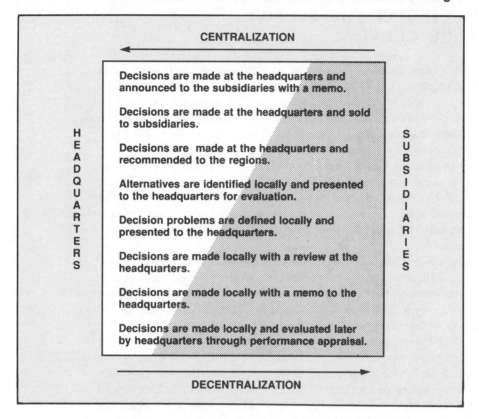

CENTRALIZATION

H
E
A
D
Q
U
A
R
T
E
R
S

Decisions are made at the headquarters and announced to the subsidiaries with a memo.

Decisions are made at the headquarters and sold to subsidiaries.

Decisions are made at the headquarters and recommended to the regions.

Alternatives are identified locally and presented to the headquarters for evaluation.

Decision problems are defined locally and presented to the headquarters.

Decisions are made locally with a review at the headquarters.

Decisions are made locally with a memo to the headquarters.

Decisions are made locally and evaluated later by headquarters through performance appraisal.

S
U
B
S
I
D
I
A
R
I
E
S

DECENTRALIZATION

making authority held by the subsidiaries increases. Note that in no case does the decision-making authority of either party reach zero. Thus, at the level of greatest decentralization, decisions are made by the local subsidiary and then evaluated by headquarters through a performance appraisal at the end of the year or other prearranged intervals. At the next level, the local manager makes the decision and informs the headquarters in a memo. At the other extreme, decisions are made at the headquarters and communicated to the subsidiaries via a memo. In between these two extremes one could arrange hundreds of possible combinations of shared decision-making privileges.

Most financial decision making is centralized, for financial decisions generally have an immediate impact on the entire company and are extremely difficult to reverse. Likewise, expensive R&D projects are usually centralized. Most MNCs resist decentralizing their R&D activities. (For example, IBM pulled out of India and Mexico when their governments insisted on setting up R&D facilities in their countries.)

Decision making about production, marketing, and logistics, on the other hand, is usually decentralized, because problems in such areas require immediate solutions. The need to wait for headquarters to make or approve these types of decisions can severely and unnecessarily constrain managerial effectiveness.

THE AGE OF PRODUCT ORGANIZATION: THE SEARCH FOR THE ELUSIVE EXPERIENCE CURVE

No matter what organizational philosophy an MNC follows, two goals guide the design and implementation of its organization structure: realizing economies of scale and spreading the risk. Economies of scale are realized by running large-scale, concentrated operations. Risk is spread by operating in different environments, so that adverse events in one environment are likely to be offset by favorable events in another.

Research by the Boston Consulting Group (BCG) in the early 1960s demonstrated that, in some firms, for every doubling of the output produced there is a decrease of 25 to 40% in the per-unit cost of production. Thus, the researchers argued, a firm can slide along a downward-sloping curve of per-unit production cost by increasing its output. They named this curve the experience curve.

Unfortunately, this rather solid principle of economics was widely misinterpreted. First of all, it was assumed that the decline in the per-unit cost is due solely to the learning that occurs as employees and management repeat the same activities over and over again. In fact, the decline represents the combined effects of four related factors: learning, specialization, investment, and scale.[6] Second, managers concluded that any strategy that further reduced per-person labor costs would enhance the effect. This idea led quite a few MNCs to embark on a quest for cheap labor, which in turn led to costly decisions to move entire production facilities to countries in which wages were very low. Soon these managers discovered, much to their surprise, that rigid employment, educational, and training habits of some labor forces made improving productivity extremely difficult. They realized that it is easier to continually train and upgrade labor in a country where the labor force is educated and there is a good state or private adult education system.

During the past forty years or so, most MNCs, both American and European, have been searching for workable economies of scale that would contribute to declining experience curves. The three main stages in this search can be conceived of as the "Age of Exuberance," the "Age of Sobriety," and the "Age of Rationalization."

THE AGE OF EXUBERANCE

Part I of Exhibit 8-8 illustrates experience curves for the Age of Exuberance. During the 1950s and 1960s, MNCs, primarily U.S.-based manufacturing companies, were operating at full capacity. These companies were enjoying a sharp

---

[6]Bruce D. Henderson, "The Experience Curve—Reviewed, IV," in *The Growth Share Matrix of the Product Portfolio* (Boston: The Boston Consulting Group, 1973).

Exhibit 8-8   The Evolution of Globalization

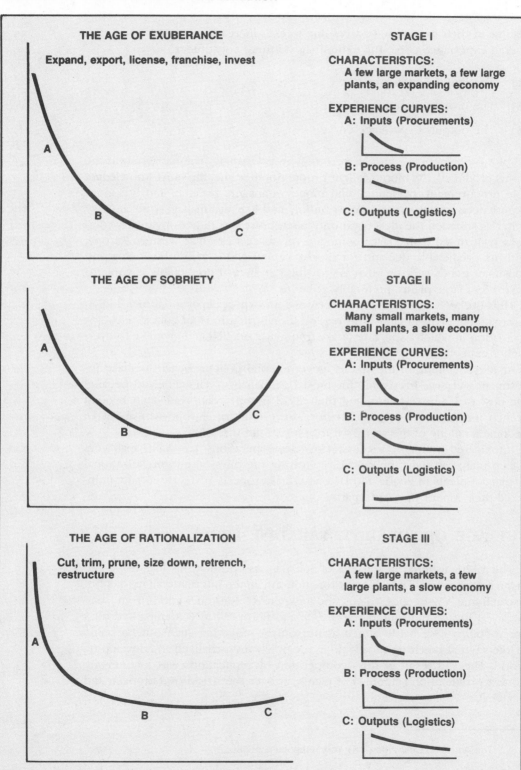

THE AGE OF EXUBERANCE

Expand, export, license, franchise, invest

A
B
C

STAGE I

CHARACTERISTICS:
A few large markets, a few large plants, an expanding economy

EXPERIENCE CURVES:
A: Inputs (Procurements)

B: Process (Production)

C: Outputs (Logistics)

THE AGE OF SOBRIETY

A
B
C

STAGE II

CHARACTERISTICS:
Many small markets, many small plants, a slow economy

EXPERIENCE CURVES:
A: Inputs (Procurements)

B: Process (Production)

C: Outputs (Logistics)

THE AGE OF RATIONALIZATION

Cut, trim, prune, size down, retrench, restructure

A
B
C

STAGE III

CHARACTERISTICS:
A few large markets, a few large plants, a slow economy

EXPERIENCE CURVES:
A: Inputs (Procurements)

B: Process (Production)

C: Outputs (Logistics)

decline in their experience curves due to ever-increasing outputs. Below the overall experience curve the exhibit shows three constituent curves:

(1)   The inputs experience curve

(2)   The process experience curve

(3)   The outputs experience curve

All of these experience curves were downward sloping. The more output the plants produced, the more efficient production became, the more knowledgeable procurement, personnel, and money managers became, and the more experienced inventory, sales, distribution, and logistics managers became.

In this situation the ideal organization structure was rather obvious. A company confronted with a large homogeneous market (such as Western Europe, with its predictable demand for mostly capital goods at the beginning and consumer goods later on) that is growing rapidly and predictably is going to have a few large plants, preferably at home.

Thus the MNCs of the 1950s developed an export department first and an international division later. This organization structure is, of course, ideal for a situation in which expectations are frequently fulfilled and give rise to ever-higher expectations.

At the beginning of the sixties, governmental policies began to make investment overseas irresistible for most U.S. managers. First England became the host to U.S. investment, and then all of Europe was invaded. In 1966, a French journalist, J. Servan-Schreiber, suggested that Europe was about to become a colony of the world's third power, the U.S. MNC.[7]

Intoxicated by highly successful overseas operations, U.S. MNC managers set up plants all over the world, replicating the physical and organizational designs of plants in Peoria and Detroit. The European MNCs essentially mimicked their American counterparts.

THE AGE OF SOBRIETY: PARADISE LOST

The 1970s ushered in the Age of Sobriety, as corporations in Europe and Japan became formidable competitors not only in the international market but also at home. VW Beetles, Volvos, and inexpensive consumer goods from Japan began to invade the United States. U.S. and European MNCs embarked on a fierce competitive battle aimed at not only conquering each other's home markets but also getting a foothold in the newly industrialized and developing world. The end result of this "competition by replication" was a nonevolutionary proliferation (cloning) of plants all over the world by European and U.S. MNCs.

---

[7]*The American Challenge* (New York: Atheneum, 1968).

Part II of Exhibit 8-8 depicts the experience curves characteristic of MNCs during these years. The replacement of a few large plants with a number of smaller plants, designed to satisfy the local markets, nullified the economies of scale. The inputs experience curve continued to decline sharply, primarily because the existence of many small plants close to both the factor and the product markets facilitated the sourcing process. The production experience curve still exhibited a slight decline, attributable to the low wages and salaries. (This effect was a temporary one which tended to disappear when labor forces became accustomed to the idea of being employed and began to understand their position within the MNC.) The outputs experience curve, however, became a sort of "negative experience curve." The existence of numerous small plants all over the globe made distribution of outputs exceedingly complicated. Millions of customers in small markets had to be researched, and thousands of distributors had to be investigated, negotiated with, and supplied. A huge administrative and support system had to be developed. The costs associated with the maintenance of this administrative system outweighed any decrease in the production experience curve.

Under such conditions the design and implementation of an organization structure becomes a very challenging task, to say the least. Billions of dollars in management and consultant time must be spent drawing and redrawing organizational charts, writing job descriptions, and reshuffling personnel from one area to another and from one function to another. Huge computer departments must be staffed and equipped with the latest in hardware and software to keep track of the daily business activities.

During the seventies and early eighties, MNCs were searching for an adequate response to the challenge of organizational design. New gurus were appearing every day. To decentralize or not to decentralize was not the question. The question was how to decentralize without ending up with inadequate control. Some consultants recommended trimming down, pruning, cutting back, "sticking to the knitting," and so on. Others went for the simplicity of the *One Minute Manager*. Still others proposed "Theory Z," a sort of Japanization of MNC management styles. Academics and consultants were busy developing new buzzwords, and MNC managers all over the world were struggling with a "change of heart."

THE AGE OF RATIONALIZATION: IN SEARCH OF A NEW APPROACH

Today growth through replication or through elimination of competition is no longer feasible. The new world realities dictate that MNCs seek evolutionary growth through cooperative competition. To survive, the MNC must grow by cooperating with its competitors. Past organizational design techniques produced too many firms all over the globe, which competed in an ever-shrinking economy. As Michael Dixon put it, "Companies faced by sharpening competition and rapid change are turning from empire-building to empire demolition."[8]

The word that best describes the various new organizational approaches being invented and implemented daily by MNCs worldwide is "rationalization." (Most American writers use the term "restructuring," but rationalization is a more encompassing concept, of which restructuring is a part.) The Oxford English Dictionary defines rationalization two ways. In the area of mathematics, rationalization is "the process of clearing from irrational quantities." In economics, it is "the scientific organization of industry to ensure the minimum waste of labor, the standardization of production, and the consequent maintenance of prices at a constant level." Both the mathematical definition and the economic definition fit the process being followed by contemporary designers of future MNC organizational structures. The new organizational designs aim both at clearing the MNC of "irrational" activities (for example, unrelated companies and offices) and at minimizing waste of labor, standardizing production, and maintaining reasonably constant prices.

Part III of Exhibit 8-8 depicts conditions that characterize the present Age of Rationalization. The strategies being used by MNCs to accomplish this rationalization include

(1)   Unifying production lines around the globe

(2)   Making parts wherever manufacturing is most economical

(3)   Selling where markets are growing

(4)   Forming global strategic alliances

The emerging organization structures will be dealt with in detail in Chapter 14.

SOME GUIDELINES FOR DESIGNING AN ORGANIZATION

Clearly, the task of designing the organization of an MNC goes far beyond drawing neat boxes that represent positions within a hierarchy. Rather, the challenge is to develop a coherent system of communication and control which will provide an appropriate foundation for efficient decision making. To provide such a foundation, an organization structure must group organizational tasks into logical units of mutually supporting activities; provide for sufficient coordination and integration among units; and allow for proper staffing, with the right people in the right places. Environmental constraints, threats, and opportunities influence the organizational process. Peter Drucker (among others)

---

[8]Michael Dixon, "Learning from the Dinosaurs," *Financial Times,* July 19, 1987, Section Two, 7.

recommends that organizational design specialists perform the following three kinds of analysis:[9]

(1)   Activity analysis

(2)   Decision analysis

(3)   Relations analysis

Activity analysis clarifies what work has to be performed, what work belongs together, and how each activity should be emphasized in the organizational structure. *Decision analysis* determines what kinds of judgments are needed, where in the organization they should be made, and how each manager should be involved in them. *Relations analysis* reveals each manager's necessary contribution to programs, the people with whom he or she must work, and the assistance other managers must give him or her. Exhibit 8-9 lists some specific questions that an organizational decision specialist might address to uncover vital information.

RECAPITULATION

Organization structure is the framework that allows an MNC to carry out its strategy for international involvement. Classical organization theories hold that structure determines strategy. Consequently, managers spend considerable amounts of time and organizational resources designing elaborate organizational structures and equally sophisticated organizational development systems aimed at instilling the organizational behavior that will allow the MNC to accomplish its stated objectives.

The term "organization" refers to three key concepts: (1) a system's ability to perform useful work, (2) the process of becoming organized, and (3) the end result of the organization process—the institution. In this chapter, the process of becoming organized was treated as a two-phase task. In phase A the organizational skeleton—the structure—is created. In phase B the organizational behavior is established and the desired degree of centralization or decentralization of decision making is determined.

There is no question that an MNC's style of organization matters. What preoccupies academics and practitioners alike is the nature of the ideal organization structure. Business International, a well-known consulting company, made a ten-year study of organization structures. In its report on the results of this study, the company suggested that "the ways in which companies organize to achieve the international business objectives are fundamental to

---

[9]Peter F. Drucker, "New Templates for Today's Organizations," *Harvard Business Review,* January–February 1974, 47. See also Drucker, *Management* (New York: Harper and Row, 1974) and Business International Corporation, *New Directions in Multinational Corporate Organization* (New York: BIC, 1981), 153.

Exhibit 8-9   Formulating an Organizational Design: Some Essential Questions

What does management want the company or unit to do?

What internal and external resources are available to accomplish the above mandate?

What must be done to transform the resources into finished products or services?

Which resources will be contained in which units?

What are the critical tasks that the organization must do well in order to survive and prosper (for example, high-quality manufacturing, sales, technological development)?

What kinds of management decisions are crucial to the success of the enterprise? How often must they be made, and at what organizational level?

In what ways do the company's structure, policies and regulations enhance or impede the pursuit of its strategy as well as the work environment of individuals and groups?

How does work move through the organization? As it flows through, who initiates a piece of work?

Who is the decision-maker?

To what extent can work, information flows, coordination and control systems, and the like be standardized?

To what degree should the firm attempt to specialize?

How adaptable can and should the organization be to the external environment?

To what extent should operating units be "self-contained," with their own complete line and staff operations?

What degree of decentralization is best?

How much accountability for results is given to the managers of each unit?

Which executives should be close to headquarters rather than scattered about in various regions or countries?

What formal and informal mechanisms should be created for the purpose of feedforward control? (Examples include budgets, forecasts, plans and projections.)

What formal and informal mechanisms should be created for the purpose of feedback control? (Examples include written reports, periodic meetings with senior management and special audits.)

How should managers be motivated to work toward common objectives? What reward systems—such as compensation, promotion and commendation—are appropriate?

What are the strengths/weaknesses of the key managers and what are their career goals? How will each fit into a new organization?

What are the CEO's personal interests [and] goals? Which functions does [this person] want to supervise directly?

What are the estimated costs of implementing and living with a new structure?

What specific organizational alternatives can be developed from the foregoing analyses? Which of these should be adopted? Why?

SOURCE: Business International Corporation, *New Directions in Multinational Corporate Organization,* pp. 154–155. Reprinted with permission.

---

their success." The report offered some recommendations to corporate planners:

> Emphasize planning, evaluation, control, and integration *systems,* rather than an organization structure. Over the past decade these kinds of systems have evolved to a greater extent than has organizational design.

> To preserve the strengths of the worldwide product or worldwide regional frameworks while overcoming their respective weaknesses, use a matrix structure, which places equal managerial emphasis on product, geographic, and functional elements.

For a time it appeared that corporations were moving toward matrix overlay or even pure matrix forms of organization structure. The difficulties associated with the matrix format, however, are such that some companies have rejected it. Many experts have speculated on what to expect in the "post-matrix" future. The following are some possible scenarios:[10]

(1)   A return to the worldwide product format, with strong mechanisms to assure country/regional inputs

(2)   The establishment of more vigorous management controls from headquarters, achieved structurally through the addition of a multidivisional group or sector level, the creation of an office of the president, and/or the strengthening of certain headquarters functions such as finance and strategic planning

(3)   An overall decentralization of international operations (the reverse of scenario two), along with more emphasis on nonequity business options, such as licensing and management service contracts

---

[10]Business International Corporation, *New Directions in Multinational Corporate Organization,* pp. i–ii.

(4)   The use of temporary, flexible mechanisms (such as committees, task forces, and career pathing) to supplement the firm's basic structure, in order to address specific organizational problems

REVIEW QUESTIONS

(1)   Explain the terms "organization" and "organization structure."

(2)   Compare and contrast the main purposes of organization advanced by Vernon with those proposed by Brooke. Do you see any particular national biases in the American view (Vernon) and the British view (Brooke)?

(3)   Study the annual reports of a large U.S. MNC to determine whether the company followed the evolutionary stages depicted in Exhibits 8-1 and 8-8. If you have access to the necessary annual reports, do the same for a large foreign MNC.

(4)   Using annual reports or other documents on a company of your choice, determine whether the company's organization structure seems to fit its main strategies. Write a report describing and explaining your conclusions.

(5)   RDS, Inc., a medium-size computer accessories and software company in your area, started its overseas business five years ago with a small export order. Now the money coming in from international transactions represents some 45 to 55% of the company's income. In addition to a large number of distributors overseas, the company has recently acquired a small manufacturer of diskette cases in Mexico and a manufacturer of IBM clones in Taiwan. Thus far the company's CEO has been taking care of the international business, with the help of an assistant with an undergraduate degree in journalism and a minor in business. The CEO believes that the time has come to set up a formal organization structure to handle the international business activity. You have been chosen to give the staff a 45-minute presentation on "Organizing for International Business." Your presentation should end with a specific recommendation for organizing RDS, Inc.

(6)   A few days after your presentation, the CEO calls you up and says, "Hey, I think I've found the answer. We're going to go matrix. I think matrix organization is for us—it's the latest word in organizational design." Develop a proposal for or against matrix organization for RDS, Inc.

(7)   Some members of the local chamber of commerce read the London *Financial Times* series cited at the beginning of this chapter and were impressed with what is going on in Europe. They have invited you to give a 45-minute presentation on "The Product Race." Include in your

speech examples of U.S. and Japanese MNCs that seem to be following the European lead.

(8)   Explain the concept of "rationalization." Give some examples of U.S. MNCs that seem to be pursuing this goal.

SUGGESTED READINGS

Ball, Donald A., and Wendell H. McCulloch, Jr. *International Business: Introduction and Essentials,* Second Edition. Plano, TX: Business Publication, 1985.

Boston Consulting Group Staff. *Perspectives on Experience.* Boston: The Boston Consulting Group, 1968.

Brooke, Michael Z. *International Management: A Review of Strategies and Operations.* London: Hutchinson, 1986.

Brown, Andrew. "Unilever Fights Back in the U.S." *Fortune,* May 26, 1986, 32–38.

Business International Corporation. *New Directions in Multinational Corporate Organization.* New York: BIC, 1981.

Capon, Noel, Chris Christodoulou, John U. Farley, and James M. Hulbert. "United States and Australian Corporations." *Journal of International Business Studies* 18, No. 1 (1987).

Conference Board. *Organization of International Joint Ventures,* Report No. 787. New York: The Conference Board, 1980.

Davidson, William H. *Global Strategic Management.* New York: John Wiley and Sons, 1982.

——, and Philippe Haspeslagh. "Shaping a Global Product Organization." *Harvard Business Review* 60, No. 4 (July–August 1981): 39–43.

Davis, Stanley M. *Managing and Organizing Multinational Corporations.* New York: Pergamon Press, 1979.

Deal, Terrence E., and Allen A. Kennedy. *Corporate Cultures: The Rites and Rituals of Corporate Life.* Reading, MA: Addison-Wesley Publishing Co., 1982.

Doyle, P., J. Saunders, and L. Wright. "A Comparative Study of U.S. and Japanese Marketing Strategies in the British Market." Mimeograph, Warwick University, Warwick, England, July 1987.

Doz, Yves Y. "Multinational Strategy and Structure in Government Controlled Businesses." *Columbia Journal of World Business* 15, No. 3 (Fall 1980): 14–25.

Dymsza, William A. *Multinational Business Strategy.* New York: McGraw-Hill, 1972.

Globerman, Steven. *Fundamentals of International Business Management.* Englewood Cliffs, NJ: Prentice-Hall, 1986.

Gooding, Kenneth. "Daimbler-Benz: Looking at Everything Again." *Financial Times,* July 22, 1987, 10.

Heenan, D. A. "The Regional Headquarters Decision: A Comparative Analysis." *Academy of Management Journal* 22, No. 2 (June 1979): 410–415.

——, and Howard V. Perlmutter. *Multinational Organizational Development.* Reading, MA: Addison-Wesley Publishing Co., 1979.

Hill, Roy. "Philips over the Years: A Model of the Maturing Multinational." *International Management,* August 1986, 28–32.

Kelley, Lane, Arthur Whatley, and Reginald Worthley. "Assessing the Effects of Culture on Managerial Attitudes: A Three Culture Test." *Journal of International Business Studies* 19, No. 2 (1987).

Kindleberger, Charles P. *American Business Abroad: Six Lectures on Direct Investment.* New Haven, CT: Yale University Press, 1969.

Kogut, Bruce. "Designing Global Strategies: Profiting from Operational Flexibility." *Sloan Management Review,* Fall 1985, 27–38.

Menzies, H. D. "Westinghouse Takes Aim at the World." *Fortune* 101, No. 1 (January 14, 1980): 48–53.

Moyer, Reed. *International Business—Issues and Concepts.* New York: John Wiley and Sons, 1984.

Negandi, Anant R. *International Management.* Boston: Allyn and Bacon, 1987.

Ohmae, Kenichi. *The Mind of the Strategist.* Harrisonburg, VA: R. R. Donnelly and Sons, 1983.

Pascale, Richard Tanner, and Anthony G. Athos. *The Art of Japanese Management: Applications for American Executives.* New York: Warner Books, 1981.

Phatak, Arvind V. *Managing Multinational Corporations.* New York: Praeger Publishers, 1974.

Robinson, Richard D. *International Business Management.* New York: Dryden Press, 1984.

Robock, Stefan H., and Kenneth Simmonds. *International Business and Multinational Enterprises,* Third Edition. Homewood, IL: Richard D. Irwin, 1983.

Rutenberg, David P. *Multinational Management.* Boston: Little, Brown and Co., 1982.

Sampson, Anthony. *The Sovereign State of ITT.* New York: Fawcett Books, 1977.

Schnitzer, Martin C., Marilyn L. Liebrenez, and Kondrad W. Kubin. *International Business.* Cincinnati, OH: South-Western Publishing Co., 1985.

Sethi, S. Prakash, and Jagdish N. Sheth. *Multinational Business Operations: Environmental Aspects of Operating Abroad.* Pacific Palisades, CA: Goodyear Publishing Company, 1973.

Stopford, J. M., and L. T. Wells, Jr. *Managing the Multinational Enterprise: Organization of the Firm and Ownership of the Subsidiaries.* New York: Basic Books, 1972.

Ten Years of Multinational Business. Economist Intelligence Unit Special Report No. 79. London: Spencer House, 1980.

Toffler, A. *The Third Wave.* New York: William Morrow and Company, 1975.

Tsurumi, Yoshi. *Multinational Management,* Second Edition. Cambridge, MA: Ballinger Publishing Company, 1984.

Vernon, Raymond, and Louis T. Wells, Jr. *Manager in the International Economy,* Fifth Edition. Englewood Cliffs, NJ: Prentice-Hall, 1986.

Vernon-Wortzel, Heidi, and Lawrence H. Wortzel (eds). *Strategic Management of Multinational Corporations: The Essentials.* New York: John Wiley and Sons, 1985.

Walter, Ingo, and Tracy Murray (eds). *Handbook of International Business.* New York: John Wiley and Sons, 1982.

CASE 1 ● Eaton Corporation

CORPORATE OVERVIEW

Eaton is a manufacturer of highly engineered and technologically advanced products serving world markets in the fields of transportation, industrial automation, electronic and electrical systems, and materials handling. Of $3.3 billion in 1979 sales, $787 million or 23% were outside the US. The company employs over 60,000 people in 23 countries.

Eaton is organized in five worldwide product groups, all reporting to the president:

(1) automotive components;

(2) industrial;

(3) investments and diversified products;

(4) materials handling; and

(5) truck components.

Three staff services groups—engineering and corporate development, finance and administration, and law and corporate relations—report directly to the chairman.

Eaton created an international division in the early 1960s, following several overseas acquisitions. Because of product diversity, the division was structured along product, rather than geographic, lines. A direct link was thus forged between each domestic product group and its overseas activities. In fact, the link shortly became strong enough to drop the international division and move to a global product structure. Since then, Eaton has found that a worldwide product format best meets the needs created by its product and customer diversity. As one executive stated, "Our customers are becoming world

SOURCE: Business International Corporation, *New Directions in Multinational Corporate Organization* (New York: BIC, 1981), 64–67. Reprinted with permission.

customers. This means that the company must be able to provide a world perspective on Eaton products and services, which can best be done at headquarters."

While worldwide product structure has proven to be an acceptable format, it was felt that some amount of geographic input was required when, in the 1970s, Eaton had to respond to such common environmental issues as political conditions, codetermination, taxes, labor relations, joint ownership, energy conservation and inflation. Another executive noted, "In a country where there are many company operations and diversified corporate representatives, where there is a variance in performance among the units, and where the government imposes price controls and import restrictions and is somewhat inhospitable to MNCs, a need for corporate assessments and strategies exists." One solution, utilized in Europe and South America, was to create coordinating committees (examined below). While these increased communication among all units, it was still felt that monitoring and assessment of the issues from a corporate perspective was required.

In 1976, therefore, Eaton created the position of vice-president, international, reporting to the executive vice-president, engineering and corporate development. [See Exhibit C8-1.] His duties are to keep track of Eaton's investments and evaluate the potential for additional investment outside the US; further the growth of worldwide export sales; represent the company in international organizations and institutions; and maintain direct international coordinating responsibility for Canada and Mexico. He does not have operating responsibilities but serves in an advisory capacity to the company's worldwide operations.

Reporting to the vice-president, international, are several regional coordinators, the head of Eaton-Japan, an international planning director (who also reports administratively to the head of corporate planning), and a political/economic information and analysis unit. The regional coordinators have three major responsibilities:

(1)   to represent Eaton Corporation as a whole within a country or region in various national and international activities and associations, including government and the media;

(2)   to assist in planning and investment studies and review consolidated plans and profit results for the vice-president, international; and

(3)   to provide for intercompany cooperation and communication on matters peculiar to one unit but having a potential impact on others, such as labor relations, legal affairs and accounting.

Some of the coordinators perform these duties on a full-time basis; others work part-time, depending on the region and the company's needs. The part-time coordinators are mainly line operations managers who are expected to spend about 10% of their time on their coordination duties.

Since it was created . . . , the international organization has been able to increase the amount of coordination and communication among diverse prod-

Exhibit C8-1   Eaton Corporation

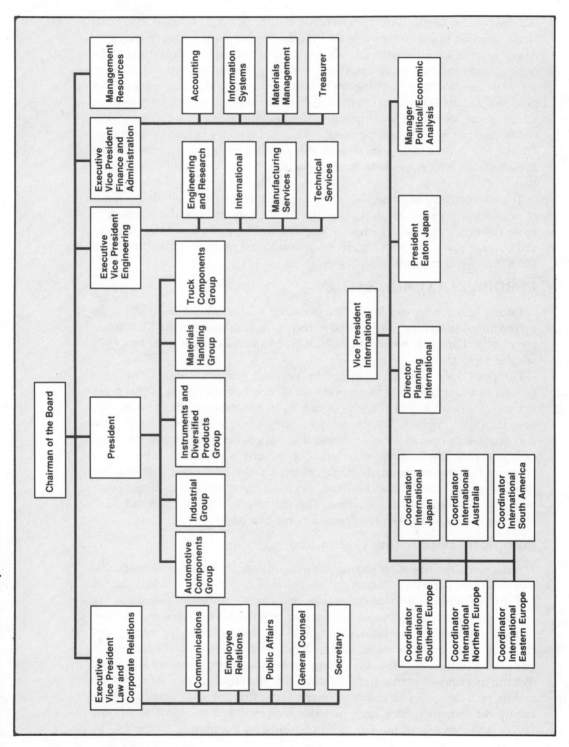

uct operations; factor more comprehensive international elements into functional strategic plans; and provide for better company representation overseas. A key issue is effective planning so that optimal decisions can be made for overseas markets: "Environmental factors are complex and important for Eaton; we must see that they are properly considered in the planning and strategy process." As noted above, an international planner reports to the vice-president, international, as well as to corporate planning. In addition, the company now holds quarterly worldwide operating reviews, at which executives from Asia, Europe and Latin America meet with the product group executives and the president. Such meetings help further the goals of planning and communication.

The international organization is still evolving. Since the need for the kinds of services it provides is increasing, the future may require the creation of more full-time regional coordinator positions. Also, more extensive regional and country plans may come from overseas regional planners rather than from the office of the international planner.

EUROPEAN COORDINATION

Eaton's first investment in Europe occurred in the late 1940s, when it acquired minority interests in axle and transmission producers in the UK. Eaton's presence in Europe is now substantial, with 35 manufacturing units and 1979 sales of $535 million.

European operations are managed by product group, . . . with a European general manager reporting to a worldwide director of operations for his product group. The center of Eaton's operations in Europe is in the London area, near Heathrow Airport. With some 150 employees, it houses the European data-processing operations base; financial and accounting personnel, including cash and credit administration; the legal department and directors of personnel, communications and materials management; and the marketing staff for some product groups. Each staff and service operation reports to its functional counterpart at headquarters in Cleveland. The only world headquarters staff functions not represented are planning and corporate development.

European Coordinating Committee

A need for coordination among Eaton's various European businesses and functions was perceived during the energy crisis of 1973–74, when the UK was forced to adopt a three-day workweek. Eaton's president asked the European managing directors and the director of finance—all based in the UK—to meet regularly to see what could be done about conserving energy and exchanging information about energy requirements among the different organizations in the UK. When the energy crisis passed, the president suggested that the meetings continue to be held not less than four times a year, that the agenda include topics of common interest and that the chairmanship rotate among the four members. Each member was expected to attend in person. This was the genesis of the European coordinating committee.

The committee's purpose was to enhance coordination function; it gave members a chance to exchange useful information. Meetings were held on a monthly basis, and detailed minutes were kept and sent to corporate head-quarters in Cleveland. Each of the operating executives delivered a 10-minute report on the state of his particular business and any significant related issues. The director of finance gave a financial forecast and discussed important common financial matters. A different corporate officer (staff or line) always attended and reported on a specific corporate topic. His presence also assured that committee messages would be transmitted back to Cleveland by him personally. The remainder of the agenda was open so that special subjects could be addressed if necessary. The agenda was circulated well ahead of the meeting so that such topics could be included.

After several years of meetings, the European coordinating committee became moribund in the summer of 1979, when a corporate study recommended that it meet on an "as needed" basis. The major reason for this was that the operating divisions did not find it useful. Also, the committee's charter did not include the authority to make decisions or recommendations, just to meet. Finally, the historical independence of the product divisions and their marketing differences make regional coordination via a committee impractical. The international division and the corporate planning unit today perform many of the coordination and information functions that the committee was originally intended to handle.

Country Coordinating Committees

Shortly after the European coordinating committee (ECC) began to function, country coordinating committees (CCCs) were established in most of the European nations in which Eaton had major interests. The CCCs are similar to the ECC in purpose (coordination of and communication among diverse activities) but are more narrowly focused on a specific country basis. The membership includes the head of each product group in the country, senior staff managers and the relevant international coordinator. The chairmanship rotates among the operating executives. . . .

Unlike the ECC, the CCCs are flourishing. Country executives think they are helpful. In fact, one European manager told BI, "If ours were disbanded, we would still meet informally." Meetings are held bimonthly and are well attended, although no attendance requirements have been imposed by corporate management. The minutes are circulated in Europe and Cleveland.

The following is a typical CCC agenda:

(1)   a report on the country's economic conditions;

(2)   a division-by-division and a countrywide Eaton cash flow report (this provides each manager with an idea of Eaton's present country cash position, which in turn helps them to understand corporate allocations and local bank borrowing);

(3)   the treasurer's report on the overall financial status of Eaton's country operations; . . .

(4)   a discussion (led by a communications executive) of specific items such as a new Eaton movie, the issuance of a worldwide personnel directory, who should receive the in-house management magazine and the extent to which a new acquisition is to be publicly identified with Eaton over the next few years;

(5)   a purchasing report; and

(6)   the business report of each of the product groups. . . .

FUNCTIONAL MEETINGS

While product coordination is Eaton's main concern in Europe, some of the European staff functions also hold coordinative meetings. Eaton has two employee relations/management resources directors for Europe, who report respectively to the vice-presidents of personnel and management resources in Cleveland. The personnel coordinators and immediate staff meet about four times a year to review developments in legislation, pensions, salaries, hiring and firing policies, etc. In addition to these, two other types of personnel coordinative meetings are held. About five sessions per year involve the country personnel managers and cover very specific personnel issues in some depth (e.g., policies, legislation and trends in the area of benefits). Also, there is an annual conference to which personnel managers from all plants are invited. Guest speakers from corporate headquarters also participate.

As a second functional example, the European finance director brings together various country financial managers. The meetings are not scheduled as formally as their personnel counterparts but are held as needed.

ISSUES FOR DISCUSSION

(1)   When this case was written, Eaton's global, or worldwide, product format was found to be serving the company very well. Since the inception of this format in the 1970s, the world had changed quite a lot, and so had Eaton's products. How had Eaton's organization structure been adapted to accommodate these changes?

(2)   Obtain a copy of Eaton's latest annual report. Does it still reflect a product-oriented organizational design?

(3)   Why do you suppose the operating divisions might have found the European coordinating committee "not useful"?

(4)   Where are most of Eaton's product centers located? Are they in "appropriate" places? If not, where should they be? Where will they be five or ten years from now?

CASE 2 ● Mitsui and Company

CORPORATE OVERVIEW

Mitsui & Co is Japan's oldest, most experienced trading house. Older than either the House of Rothschild or the Bank of England, it has played a leading role in Japan's industrial and commercial development since the latter half of the 17th century.

Beginning as a small, family operation, Mitsui prospered and expanded throughout Japan, eventually winning national recognition as a mercantile and banking house. After the Meiji Restoration in 1868, the mercantile company evolved into a trading company, and the banking function became the Mitsui Bank. With these two vehicles, Mitsui invested vigorously in other industries, such as mining and manufacture of a wide variety of products. Then the new trading company set out to provide its many services to businesses abroad.

Mitsui opened its first office outside Japan in Shanghai in 1877 and followed it one year later with offices in Paris and Hong Kong. Its New York office opened in 1879. By World War II, Mitsui had become the largest trading organization in Japan. After the war, the Mitsui family-owned industrial combine was dissolved into over 100 smaller companies, by order of occupation authorities. As Japan's industry recovered and international trade grew, the new Mitsui opened representative offices throughout the world. More recently, the company has accelerated its global business plan in the following ways:

(1) transferring control over foreign investments and extending loans (with certain limitations) to overseas offices;

(2) transferring existing joint ventures to the accounts of incorporated subsidiaries overseas;

(3) establishing and strengthening the primary control system of joint ventures by incorporating subsidiaries overseas and speeding the autonomy of overseas offices through establishment of fund-raising bases; and

(4) backing up global business from domestic divisions and offices.

In 1979, consolidated net sales were approximately $43 billion.

Mitsui's fundamental goal today is to promote the expansion of free trade and provide an impetus for continued international economic development. Although the company's numerous functions are closely interrelated, they can be classified into two general types: (1) basic trading services and (2) services

SOURCE: Business International Corporation, *New Directions in Multinational Corporate Organization* (New York: BIC, 1981), 145–148. Reprinted with permission.

for commercial development. Basic services include four primary functions:

(a) *Conduct of transactions.* Mitsui offers a broad range of support services for companies interested in exporting to or importing from Japan or engaging in trade transactions among the company's worldwide network of offices.

(b) *Arranging for the distribution systems,* including insurance, for each transaction. In some cases, distribution can be arranged using Mitsui's own vessels and warehousing facilities around the world.

(c) *Financing.* To augment the financial resources of client firms, Mitsui provides extensive trade credit for companies in the domestic market. It also purchases equity, makes direct loans, guarantees client obligations and provides assistance in obtaining finance from other financial institutions. The company's services in this area center around encouraging the flow and development of trade and commercial activity and therefore extend beyond those provided by financial institutions. Leasing services are also available. However, unlike conglomerates and merchant bankers, Mitsui makes such financial arrangements mainly in connection with trading activities to stimulate trade flows and the market—not for handling funds per se.

(d) *Information.* Through its network of domestic and overseas trade affiliates, the company is in a position to obtain basic information on virtually any market or business opportunity.

These services are augmented by four additional activities:

(1) Mitsui has been an active partner in joint ventures in Japan and elsewhere. The [company's] president, Toshikuni Yahire, . . . stated: "We plan to continue to improve the position of our subsidiaries in Japan and overseas. The company's purchase and leasing of grain storage facilities in the US and other investments in this area are one example of the types of investments in key businesses that Mitsui will undertake."

(2) The company has invested extensively in resource development.

(3) To assist in industrial development at home and abroad, particularly in the developing nations, Mitsui is an active intermediary in the export and import of technology, combining this activity with assistance in transactions and finance for new industries set up through technology transfer.

(4) The company also plays the composite role of organizer, in which it draws upon its full range of services—from marketing to finance to technology transfer—to put together major industrial projects.

In sum, Mitsui cannot be categorized as a company in the traditional mold, divided between domestic and foreign operations. It is a true multinational enterprise.

ORGANIZATION

The organizational structure of Mitsui & Co may be portrayed as [in Exhibit C8-2].

The head office is very important in Mitsui. The staff divisions—corporate secretary, personnel, legal, planning, finance and systems—gather necessary

Exhibit C8-2   Mitsui & Co

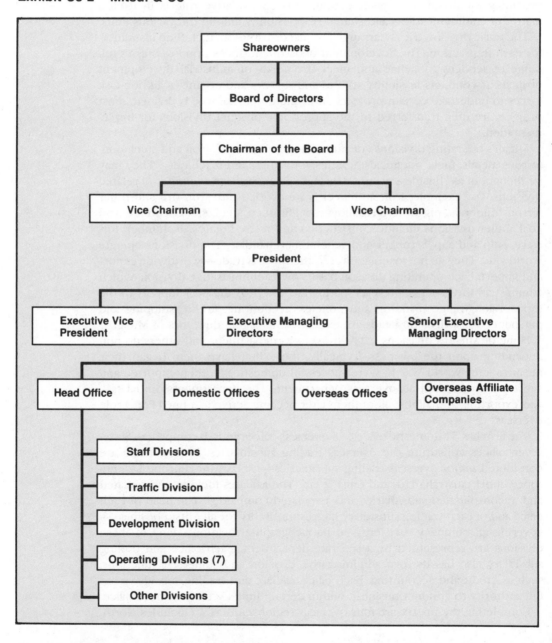

information (information-gathering is a high-priority activity in Japanese companies), draft corporate policies and see that they are approved via the *ringi* decision-making system, and coordinate policies and information for the operating divisions and geographic regions worldwide. The overseas planning division at headquarters is crucial for Mitsui's worldwide business. It coordinates the international policies, plans and operations of each of the divisions and overseas subsidiaries. It aims to eliminate conflict and duplication while providing for broad, synergistic action. This coordinative role is in itself a matrix of communications and shared responsibility among the various units.

The traffic division tries to arrange optimal distribution, including insurance, for each transaction. The development department draws upon the firm's full range of services to define and meet the needs of industrial development projects. It conducts feasibility studies and surveys and organizes ad hoc task forces to undertake certain projects. After the corporate role is defined, most projects are then transferred to the appropriate product divisions for implementation.

Mitsui's operating divisions (or business groups) cover: iron and steel; nonferrous metals; fuels; chemicals; textiles; foodstuffs; and machinery. They may be thought of as "business groups," because each contains a number of related divisions. For example, iron and steel is subdivided into iron ore and other ferrous minerals, pig iron, ferroalloys, semifinished steel, steel products and coal. Other divisions include construction and related materials, lumber, forestry, pulp and paper, rubber and general merchandise. The divisions operate worldwide. They do not manufacture: . . . their role is trade—worldwide export and import. Each operating division has its own administrative division, which administers the group's interests worldwide and provides staff support in the form of long-range planning and policies, accounting, credit, shipping and personnel. Most division heads are executive managing directors of Mitsui.

Some of Mitsui's divisions have an overseas department and others do not, depending upon the business. Typically, those that have them began their business after World War II, were successful domestically, then exported and subsequently created an overseas department. The departments' initial task was exporting, and almost all of them later became active in a line (P&L) role overseas.

The firm has 51 domestic offices, 75 overseas offices and 28 companies. Sixty-seven offices constitute the overseas trading subsidiaries. Five of these are considered *major* overseas trading subsidiaries—. . . USA Inc, Europe Ltd, Europe GmbH, Australia Ltd, and Canada Ltd. The affiliates include consolidated and unconsolidated subsidiaries and associated companies. The head of each office and of each trading subsidiary has responsibility for all Mitsui business—covering all company divisions—in his geographic location. Many of these divisions are represented by a separate department. Each office and trading subsidiary also has its own administrative division and some staff functions, such as credit and accounting. Each office, affiliate and trading subsidiary has full authority to conduct business, within certain limits set by the head office.

Completing the matrix are four overseas regions: America (includes North,

Central and South America), Europe, Mideast, and Oceania (Australia and New Zealand). Management of Asia as a region is diffused throughout all head office operations. The executive officer of each region is responsible for all Mitsui operations in that region and is delegated authority to conduct business, within certain limits. The regional executive officers of America, Europe and Oceania are either executive vice-presidents or executive managing directors of the parent organizations. The head of Mideast is at a lower level, but has special management authority.

Finally, the shareowners of Mitsui differ from those of many Western firms in two respects. First, they are companies rather than individuals. Over the years, Mitsui has helped to create many Japanese companies and owns shares in them. The companies, along with other commercial enterprises, simultaneously own shares in Mitsui. Second, these corporate shareowners are primarily interested in long-term business development, compared with the unremitting focus on short-term return on investment commonly found in the West.

ORGANIZATIONAL COORDINATION

Mitsui is a vast and diverse company. Coordination can prove difficult enough in much smaller, homogeneous firms. Mitsui executives [say] that there are several important keys to their attainment of organizational coordination:

(1) the communications network of the trading company, including telexes, computers, special departments, procedures and personal contacts;

(2) delegation of authority to domestic and overseas units (for example, Mitsui & Co USA Inc has been delegated responsibility for more than 40 business items from the head office; the US subsidiary, in turn, delegates responsibility to its regional organizations in the US and to its Latin American operations); and

(3) education and lifetime employment. For the first three years following employment, a college graduate is given assignments that help him learn a great deal about the company. From that point, programs such as delegation of responsibility, on-the-job training and job rotation continue the education process. Internationally, about 50 employees each year receive a scholarship to study at a foreign college for a year, followed by a work assignment at company operations within that country. In these ways, over periods of time, many managerial employees are exposed to different aspects of Mitsui business.

ISSUES FOR DISCUSSION

(1) Mitsui's business activities involve international trade rather than international production. Organizing a service firm is obviously different from

organizing a manufacturing company. In your opinion, which is more difficult and why?

(2)   What kinds of problems might develop in the relationship between the head office's staff divisions (whose purpose is to gather information and draft and coordinate policies and information for the operating and geographic regions) and the operating divisions worldwide?

(3)   Is Mitsui involved in Africa?

(4)   Does Mitsui & Co: USA Inc issue its own annual report? How does it differ from that of Mitsui & Co?

(5)   How does Mitsui manage to coordinate its vast number of companies around the globe?

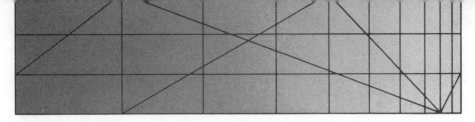

CHAPTER 9

FINANCIAL MANAGEMENT STRATEGY

Exchange-rate instability means no more "American" or "German" or "French" businesses—only Americans or Germans or French managing world-economy businesses.

Peter Drucker

"Insulating the Firm from Currency Exposure," *The Wall Street Journal,* April 30, 1985, 23.

OVERVIEW

Once an international enterprise has a strategy for going international and an organizational structure for carrying out the strategy, managers must begin to arrange the resources the business will use to achieve the stated objectives and goals. The first resources a manager must secure are financial resources. These resources will be combined with human resources and material and equipment to produce products, which will then be sold to secure the additional financial resources needed to fuel the ongoing process of wealth creation.

The task of the international financial manager is to ensure a continuous flow of funds among the various subsidiaries and between the subsidiaries and the headquarters sufficient to carry out the MNC's operations. Translating human efforts and goals into financial plans is always a very difficult task; at the international level it is inordinately complicated. Nevertheless, the job must be done and done well, as firms and managers rise and fall on the basis of their performances, which are put under the financial magnifying glass at the MNC's headquarters.

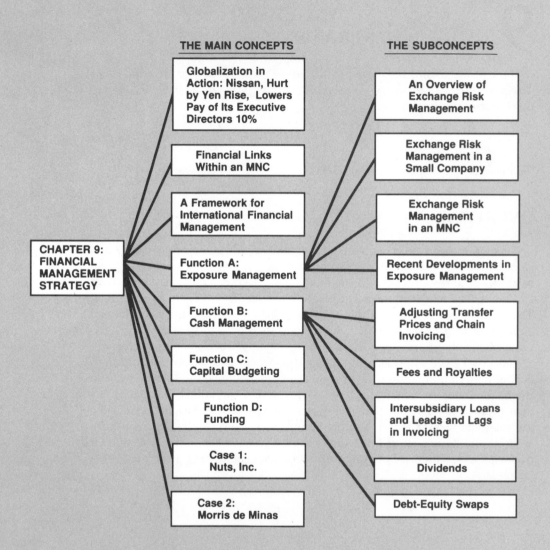

THE MAIN CONCEPTS

THE SUBCONCEPTS

CHAPTER 9:
FINANCIAL
MANAGEMENT
STRATEGY

Globalization in
Action: Nissan, Hurt
by Yen Rise, Lowers
Pay of Its Executive
Directors 10%

Financial Links
Within an MNC

A Framework for
International Financial
Management

Function A:
Exposure Management

Function B:
Cash Management

Function C:
Capital Budgeting

Function D:
Funding

Case 1:
Nuts, Inc.

Case 2:
Morris de Minas

An Overview of
Exchange Risk
Management

Exchange Risk
Management in a
Small Company

Exchange Risk
Management
in an MNC

Recent Developments in
Exposure Management

Adjusting Transfer
Prices and Chain
Invoicing

Fees and Royalties

Intersubsidiary Loans
and Leads and Lags
in Invoicing

Dividends

Debt-Equity Swaps

LEARNING OBJECTIVES

After studying the material in this chapter, the student should be familiar with the following concepts:

(1)   Financial links within an MNC

(2)   Exposure

(3)   Foreign exchange risk

(4)   Macroeconomic exposure of an MNC

(5)   Hedging as a means of protecting a company's assets

(6)   Spot and forward rates

(7)   Swaps

(8)   Options

(9)   Price transfers, fees, and royalties as means of cash transfer

(10) Leads and lags in invoicing, loans, and dividends as means of cash transfer

(11) Capital budgeting

(12) Funding of foreign operations

GLOBALIZATION IN ACTION
Nissan, Hurt by Yen Rise, Lowers Pay of Its Executive Directors 10%

Tokyo—Nissan Motor Co. said it has decided to cut salaries of executive directors by 10% next month because of the yen's sharp rise. Japanese exporters have been trying to overcome the yen's appreciation—33% against the U.S. dollar since last fall—by various means, but Nissan is the first major Japanese auto maker to opt for cutting compensation of its executive directors. Executive directors are senior members of the company who at the same time serve on the board of directors.

It is also the first time Japan's second largest auto maker has cut compensation for executive directors since its founding in 1933. It isn't known yet if other auto makers will follow, but officials at other auto companies said they are conducting a "very strict review of spending plans" because of the sharp appreciation of the yen.

"We haven't decided yet to go so far [as Nissan], but review of [previously approved] budgets [at each section] is underway," said an official at Honda Motor Co. "We have never experienced such a strict tightening as this one before," he added. A spokesman for Mazda Motor Corp. said that the company currently doesn't plan to follow Nissan, but added that "if the yen would be further appreciated, naturally it [such a plan] will come up."

The higher yen erodes earnings of Japanese companies unless they boost prices. But it isn't easy for most Japanese exporters to fully offset the adverse effect through price increases because higher prices make their product less competitive in international markets.

Nissan raised prices on its cars for the U.S. market an average of 4% last December, but officials said the boosts weren't high enough to offset the sharp appreciation of the yen. Because of the yen's gain, Nissan said it expects its recurring profit for the year ending March 31 to decline 16% from a year earlier, to the equivalent of $696.4 million on sales of 21 billion, up 3.6%.

Early this week, the Ministry of International Trade and Industry decided to ask major companies to try to absorb the adverse effect of the yen's appreciation by increasing prices, rather than by passing on the loss to their subcontractors. The decision is based on a recent government survey in which 14%, or 640, of subcontractors polled replied that they had received price reduction demands from companies they supply.

According to the survey, some majors forced subcontractors to take back goods, citing as an excuse the yen's appreciation. Among subcontractors in various export-oriented industries, those in transport equipment, including autos, and precision instruments were prominent with complaints of "bullying" by the larger concerns.

Meanwhile, corporate bankruptcies stemming from the yen's appreciation continue to grow. According to Tokyo Shouko Research Ltd., a major private credit research agency, such corporate failures (counting only those with bad debts of $56,000 or more) totaled 39 in the four months ended February 28. The number is expected to increase "considerably" toward this summer. Akira Akiyama, a senior analyst at the agency, said, "For the time being, the number of such bankruptcies would increase at a considerable pace."

INTRODUCTION

All subsidiaries of an MNC are linked together by a plethora of common interests and activities: objectives, goals, production processes, managerial philosophies, styles and policies, data banks, patented technologies, name brands and trademarks, and so on. Although they might want to do so, individual managers cannot treat their own subsidiaries as "the" company. Host governments, however, do consider the subsidiaries as their own national units, subject to regulation with respect to taxation, public disclosure, accountability, positive contributions toward national goals, and good corporate citizenship.

Thus, MNC managers must become accustomed to having a sort of split personality. Like the proverbial Janus, looking inward, they are a separate national unit responsible to the host country's laws and regulations; looking outward, they are part of a larger whole, the MNC, whose headquarters imposes certain rules and regulations that must be obeyed by all subsidiaries. It is understandable that conflicts should arise between the home and the host countries and between the MNC and its subsidiaries. No other area is affected more by these multidimensional relationships than finance. The investing, raising, retaining, reinvesting, dispensing, accumulating, and spending of money are influenced not only by the intersubsidiary and intra-MNC relationships but also by the host and home governments' rules and regulations.

FINANCIAL LINKS WITHIN AN MNC

In an MNC with many subsidiaries, both the money for the purchase of inputs and the money from the sale of outputs may come from within the MNC. In general, financial exchanges between an MNC and its subsidiaries, as well as those between subsidiaries, take one of the following forms (see Exhibit 9-1):

Link A: Investment or equity (dividends)

Link B: Services and technology (fees and royalties)

Link C: Merchandise or goods (accounts payable)

Link D: Credit or loan repayments (principal and interest)

Exhibit 9-1   Financial Links Between a Parent and a Subsidiary

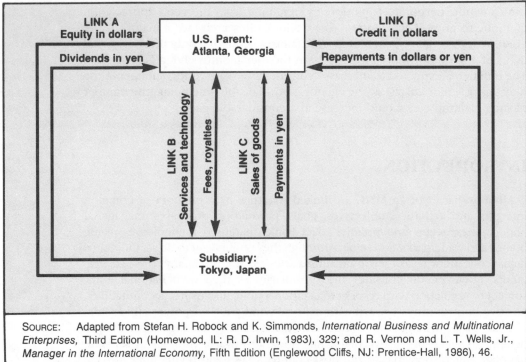

SOURCE: Adapted from Stefan H. Robock and K. Simmonds, *International Business and Multinational Enterprises,* Third Edition (Homewood, IL: R. D. Irwin, 1983), 329; and R. Vernon and L. T. Wells, Jr., *Manager in the International Economy,* Fifth Edition (Englewood Cliffs, NJ: Prentice-Hall, 1986), 46.

The links go both ways—from the parent to the subsidiary and from the subsidiary to the parent. The direction indicated by the larger arrowhead, however, is much more likely than the one indicated by the smaller arrowhead. For example, it is much more common for a parent to make an equity investment in a subsidiary than for a subsidiary to make an equity investment in the parent.

As Exhibit 9-1 indicates, transfers from the parent to the subsidiary are denominated in the currency of the parent company (in the hypothetical case illustrated in the exhibit, dollars), and returns to the parent from the subsidiary are denominated in the subsidiary's currency (for example, yen). This factor is a critical one in international financial management.

Managing and keeping track of interaffiliate transactions is a very complex process. Some observers fail to see the need for any record keeping and managing of these activities. "After all," they argue, "it's all in the family." This is true—it is all in the family. There are, however, many reasons why clear, meticulous, and consistent records must be kept. These reasons stem from the nature of the claims the MNC's various stakeholders have on its resources and outputs.

First, of course, there is the MNC itself. Headquarters must estimate fairly accurately each subsidiary's performance in order to determine whether the operation is achieving the goals set for it. Second, there are the home country taxing authorities. Profits of the MNC's subsidiaries, even though they are generated in the four corners of the world, are taxable at home. So the head-quarters' consolidated balance sheets and profit and loss statements must include all the financial activities of the MNC's subsidiaries. Third, there are the host country taxing authorities. Every subsidiary of an MNC operating within the sovereign jurisdiction of a foreign country is subject to taxation by that country, just as any domestic corporation is (except the tax havens of Bahrain and Liechtenstein). Finally, there are the stockholders. Some MNC subsidiaries are engaged in joint ventures with either local companies or other MNC subsidiaries. Profits generated by these subsidiaries serve as the basis for the declaration and distribution of dividends.

These demands, both external and internal, necessitate a rather complex and costly process of recording, reporting, and evaluating the results of managerial activity all over the globe. This process creates a number of problems for the MNC manager, but at the same time it provides numerous opportunities for global transferring of financial and other resources from one subsidiary to another and from the subsidiaries to the parent company so as to minimize foreign exchange risks and taxes.

The task of the international financial manager of an MNC is a very complex one. For this reason it is recommended that a systems approach be used in setting up the financial systems and procedures for an MNC. A complete description of such an approach will be presented in Chapter 13 when the subject of control and communication is considered. Here a brief description is offered.

A FRAMEWORK FOR INTERNATIONAL FINANCIAL MANAGEMENT

As Exhibit 9-1 shows, the two-way interactions between a parent and its subsidiaries can take quite a complicated form, with various links in different currencies. The overall objective of the system is, of course, securing adequate funds for the operations of the MNC and all its subsidiaries. This objective is accomplished by synchronizing all policy tools available to each subsidiary and to the parent. Thus the MNC and its subsidiaries form a system of inter-related and interconnected units, each of which depends on the others for its operation and survival.

Within this system the task of the international financial manager can be visualized as depicted in Exhibit 9-2. Four interrelated functions constitute the heart of international financial management:

Function A: Exposure management—protecting the company's assets

Function B: Cash management—maneuvering liquid assets

Function C: Capital budgeting—evaluating fund uses (projects)

Function D: Funding—finding funds for projects

Exhibit 9-2   A Framework for International Financial Management

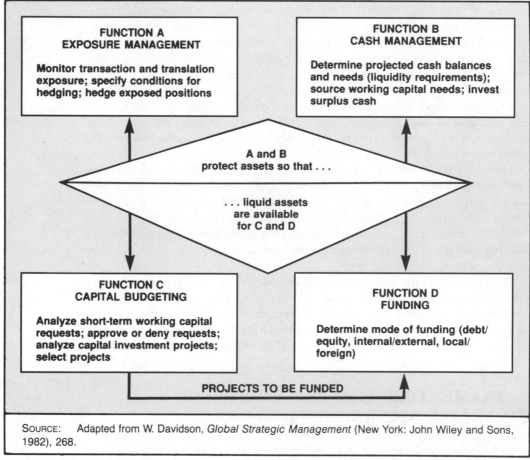

FUNCTION A
EXPOSURE MANAGEMENT

Monitor transaction and translation
exposure; specify conditions for
hedging; hedge exposed positions

FUNCTION B
CASH MANAGEMENT

Determine projected cash balances
and needs (liquidity requirements);
source working capital needs; invest
surplus cash

A and B
protect assets so that . . .

. . . liquid assets
are available
for C and D

FUNCTION C
CAPITAL BUDGETING

Analyze short-term working capital
requests; approve or deny requests;
analyze capital investment projects;
select projects

FUNCTION D
FUNDING

Determine mode of funding (debt/
equity, internal/external, local/
foreign)

PROJECTS TO BE FUNDED

SOURCE: Adapted from W. Davidson, *Global Strategic Management* (New York: John Wiley and Sons, 1982), 268.

Financial managers estimate, record, and protect the firm's assets via external exposure management (function A) and internal cash management tools (function B). They also plan, propose, and evaluate projects (function C) which must be funded (function D) to create the cash flows that must be managed to start the cycle again.

FUNCTION A: EXPOSURE MANAGEMENT

Risk managers are confronted with two types of risk: commercial risk and macroeconomic risk. Within the category of commercial risk are industry-specific risk and firm-specific risk. Industry-specific risk is caused by uncertainty about the demand for one industry's products relative to that for other industries' products. Firm-specific risk, on the other hand, arises as a result of uncertainty about the demand for a firm's specific product relative to that for other firms' similar products. These two forms of risk are addressed in standard financial management texts.

The three types of macroeconomic risk to which every MNC is exposed are listed in Exhibit 9-3. Financial risk refers to the magnitude and likelihood of unanticipated changes in interest rates and costs of different sources of capital in a particular currency. Currency risk refers to the magnitude and likelihood of unanticipated changes in the value of foreign and domestic money; it encompasses exchange rate risk and inflation risk. Country risk (including political risk) refers to the magnitude and likelihood of unanticipated changes in a country's productive development and "rules of the game," such as tax laws, investment incentives, and business climate.

Exhibit 9-4 illustrates the causal chain that links the sources of risk to the effects on the firm's cash flows. The sooner a manager recognizes a potential disturbance, the easier it is to convert it into an anticipated event for which a remedy can be found. A corollary to this rule is that MNCs must be risk averters. For example, management must be willing to pay money to protect the firm's assets from exchange rate risk, discussed in the next section.

AN OVERVIEW OF EXCHANGE RISK MANAGEMENT

In Chapter 6, International Finance, the term "exchange rate" was defined as a ratio expressing the value of one currency in terms of another. When the exchange rate between, for example, the British pound (£) and the U.S. dollar

---

Exhibit 9-3   Macroeconomic Risks

Risks	Refers to the Magnitude and Likelihood of Unanticipated Changes in
Financial risk	Interest rates Cost of capital
Currency risk	Exchange rates Inflation rates
Country risk	Productive development Rules of the game

SOURCE: Adapted from L. Oxelheim and C. Wihlborg, *Macroeconomic Uncertainty: International Risks and Opportunities for the Corporation* (New York: John Wiley and Sons, 1987), 12.

Exhibit 9-4   Sources of Risk

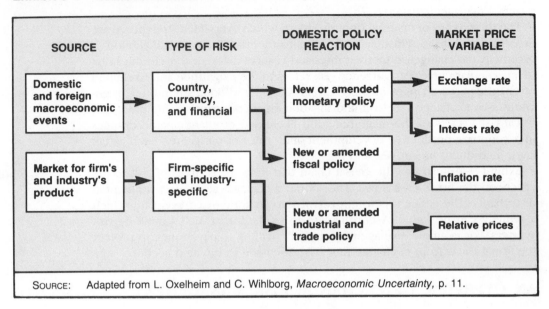

SOURCE: Adapted from L. Oxelheim and C. Wihlborg, *Macroeconomic Uncertainty*, p. 11.

($) is 1.6050, it takes $1.6050 to obtain one British pound. Although exchange rate fluctuations are common, they are not easy to understand or to predict. In general, there are three main exchange rate determinants:

(1)   The rate of price increases in a country (inflation)

(2)   The degree of economic activity (economic growth or stagnation)

(3)   The cost of money (interest rates)

The manager's task is to understand the forces that directly or indirectly affect exchange rates; assess the potential impact of these forces in terms of magnitude, likelihood, and timing; and devise means to protect the firm's assets from possible losses emanating from exchange rate fluctuations. In brief, the manager's job is *the minimization of the company's exposure to exchange rate risk*.

Although practitioners and academicians have been studying exchange rate risk for years, there is no consensus as to how to measure and manage it.[1] This section will give a brief introduction to measuring and managing exchange rate risk. More detailed treatments can be found in the sources listed at the end of the chapter.

---

[1]L. Oxelheim and C. Wihlborg, *Macroeconomic Uncertainty: International Risks and Opportunities for the Corporation* (New York: John Wiley and Sons, 1987).

As used in international finance, risk is a measure of the potential magnitude and the likelihood of unanticipated events. This definition of risk suggests the approach the international financial manager should take to evaluating exchange rate risk. First, the manager should concentrate on unanticipated events. Events that can be anticipated are presumably accounted for in the company's planning process. Second, the manager must make an effort to provide estimates of the magnitude of the events that may occur. Third, the manager must provide estimates of the probability (likelihood) of these events.

In evaluating the exchange rate risk to the firm's daily cash flows and final value, an international financial manager must look at

(1)   The macroeconomic structure

(2)   The policy regime followed by authorities in the home and host countries

(3)   The nature of the firm's assets

In examining the macroeconomic structure, the manager should concentrate on the three exchange rate determinants—inflation, economic growth (expansionary or contractive economic policy), and changes in interest rates. The impact of governmental policies on these factors then must be anticipated. Finally, the sensitivity of the firm's assets to any disturbances in exchange rates must be assessed.

The bulk of a financial manager's time is spent protecting the firm from potential harmful effects of exchange rate changes on its liquidity, profitability, and value. Three basic measures of exchange rate exposure are

(1)   Transaction exposure

(2)   Translation exposure

(3)   Economic exposure

Transaction exposure derives from uncertainty about the value in domestic currency of a specific future cash flow in a foreign currency. Thus, this type of exposure arises in the daily transactions between MNC subsidiaries and between each subsidiary and the headquarters. Most of these transactions are contractual—they take the form of agreements between one subsidiary, or one customer, and another to buy and sell products and/or services. In terms of the standard accounting recording, most of these transactions are reflected in the current assets portion of the balance sheet.

Translation exposure relates to the net balance sheet in foreign currency. Translation exposure is basically an accounting concept, as it is not felt until (or unless) the firm merges its activities into one consolidated balance sheet at the end of the reporting period, usually quarterly or annually. For all practical purposes, then, translation exposure is a latent risk which becomes real when and if the firm either consolidates at the end of the period or liquidates. Translation gains and losses due to exchange rate fluctuations have no cash flow effect; they are not realized over the reported period.

Economic exposure refers to the sensitivity of the firm's economic value to changes in exchange rates. The economic value of the firm depends, of course, on its expected ability to produce cash flows in the future. Usually, economic exposure does not come into question unless the firm is up for sale. Only very infrequently will a financial manager be asked specifically to protect the firm against economic exposure. Good transaction and translation exposure management should suffice to minimize the negative impact of exchange rate fluctuations on the value of a firm.

EXCHANGE RISK MANAGEMENT IN A SMALL COMPANY

AMTEC, Inc. is a hypothetical computer software company located in Atlanta, Georgia. Its latest product, DOWUPLOAD, is designed to make it easy for office microcomputer users to gain access to databases stored and run by large mainframe computer systems. The president of AMTEC, Dunken Sharp, realizes that he must tap the international market. So he takes a trip to London. He knows London rather well, for he attended a summer-abroad program there some time ago.

As Sharp is explaining his program to some old London chums in a pub on Goodge Street, his friend Sean O'Malley interrupts him: "You know, that program would be perfect for my chaps at the office. They have been complaining that they just can't do the job I've given them. They have to use the city's largest databases to estimate the square yardage of old houses so that we can determine how much to import of the various materials we use in renovating them. I'm telling ya, mate, your program will save me a lot of money."

Upon returning to Atlanta, Sharp calls in Jim Young, AMTEC's sales manager, and says, "Jim, I've made my first sale to the U.K. Ship the order and bill my friend 90 days net, just like all our good customers. We agreed on a price of 3,000 British pounds."

During lunch Sharp tells a banker friend how easy it is going to be to export the new computer software package. He thinks that the deal he made with Sean opened the door.

His friend says, "Listen, I really hate to tell you this, but we at the bank don't think much of the pound. I personally think that by the time you get your 3,000 pounds you'll have lost quite a lot on the deal."

"I don't understand," says Sharp. "He's my good friend."

"No, no, I don't mean that Sean isn't going to pay you. No doubt he will. What I mean is that when you bring the 3,000 pounds to the bank for deposit they aren't going to buy you the dollars that you expect. The pound has been depreciating drastically. A week ago the rate was $1.660 to a pound. Today it's down by as much as $0.30. For 90 days it sells at a hefty discount. Let me protect your exposure. Why don't you send over your accountant or sales manager and let me take care of this for you."

What are AMTEC's options for avoiding losses from currency fluctuation? Exhibit 9-5 summarizes the main tools available to lessen AMTEC's transaction exposure. Internal group/company tools refer to the ways a firm can change its own credit and payment procedures to minimize its exposure. External group/company tools refer to contractual arrangements that can be made with outside organizations, such as banks and other financial institutions specializing in international financial services.

Forward, or exchange market, hedging is the technique most commonly used to minimize transaction exposure. It is the most appropriate tool for a small company that is new in the international business game. A forward contract is an agreement between an importer or exporter and a third party, such as a bank, in which the former promises to deliver a certain amount of foreign currency to the latter on a specified future date in return for a fixed

---

Exhibit 9-5   Tools for Lessening Transaction Exposure

Internal Group/Company Tools

(1)   Change in contract currency

(2)   Matching of revenues and costs in current operations (structural matching)

(3)   Total matching of revenues and costs in current operations with revenues and costs in the financial side of the group

(4)   Change in payment rhythm internally (leads/lags between parent company and subsidiary)

(5)   Change in payment rhythm externally (leads/lags between parent company and other foreign stakeholders)

(6)   Advance payments in other forms

(7)   Allocation of responsibility for borrowing and payments between parent company and foreign subsidiary

(8)   Structural changes in debts/claims among currencies (weak currencies versus strong)

(9)   Maintenance of currency reserves (for example, with internal forward hedging)

(10)   Export financing arrangements in the group

(11)   Internal pricing routines (transfer pricing)

(12)   Adjustment in level of inventories

(13)   Change in credit conditions for foreign suppliers or foreign customers

(14)   Cross-matching based on correlation

(15)   Change in prices in export markets

(16)   Change in prices in local markets

External Group / Company Tools

(17)   Forward market transactions

(18)   Foreign loans

(19)   Swap arrangements (parallel loan/deposit)

(20)   Sales of future receivables

(21)   Arrangements for financing exports

(22)   Factoring

(23)   Leasing

(24)   Currency options

(25)   Financial futures

(26)   Interest rate options

SOURCE: Oxelheim and Wihlborg, *Macroeconomic Uncertainty* © 1987 by John Wiley & Sons, Ltd. Reprinted by permission of John Wiley & Sons, Ltd.

---

amount of another currency. In AMTEC's case the company and the bank would sign a contract stating that in 90 days AMTEC will sell 3,000 pounds for a stated number of dollars.

Why should the bank get involved in a contract of this nature, knowing full well that the pound may depreciate or the dollar may appreciate? The answer is, of course, that the bank will make a commission. AMTEC's protection from the depreciation of the pound will cost it some money. Being "risk-averse," the company is willing to pay money to ensure against possible decreases in the dollar value of the 3,000 pounds in accounts receivable.

The amount of money the bank charges AMTEC will depend on the difference between today's exchange rate (the **spot rate**) and the exchange rate for currency to be delivered 90 days from the date on which the contract is signed (the **forward rate**). When the forward rate is higher than the spot rate, the pound is said to be selling at a premium. In the opposite case, the pound is said to be selling at a discount.

Credit, or money market, hedging is much simpler than forward hedging. A company wishing to protect its cash flow from exchange rate fluctuations simply takes out a bank loan in the foreign currency and then immediately converts that money into local currency, which is either deposited or used. In the case of AMTEC, the company would borrow 3,000 pounds from the bank at the spot rate, convert them immediately into dollars, and then either deposit the dollars in the bank or use them to increase its working capital. AMTEC is then protected against any exchange rate fluctuations, since it can simply use the 3,000 pounds in accounts receivable to pay off the loan principal. Should the pound depreciate to the point where the decrease in the dollar value of 3,000 pounds exceeds the cost of borrowing from the bank (the interest), AMTEC will have made a smart move. If the pound appreciates, AMTEC will have spent money on interest unnecessarily.

Should AMTEC do nothing, borrow, or use the forward market? It all depends on the anticipated magnitude of the exchange rate fluctuation, the likelihood of fluctuation, the cost of hedging in the forward market, and the cost of borrowing in the credit market.

EXCHANGE RISK MANAGEMENT IN AN MNC

An MNC is, of course, a much more complicated system than is a simple exporter. Intuitively one might guess that an MNC manager would have a much more difficult job to do than would an export manager of a small company. The MNC manager does have a much more complex job to do, but at the same time there are a lot more options available to an MNC than to a small company. For the small company, the two basic hedging techniques explained in the last section are the only means available for managing foreign exposure.

For the MNC, hedging is merely a small portion of the entire process of risk exposure management. Hedging is usually used only for residual risk coverage—to cover transactions that cannot be handled through internal procedures. Most of the MNC's internal tools will be dealt with in the next section on cash management. Here we will consider the use of hedging by an MNC to manage translation exposure.

Whereas transaction exposure arises out of day-to-day cash flow movements, translation exposure results from uncertainty about foreign assets' value in domestic currency on a consolidation date on which the balance sheets are made public. Although translation exposure does not affect the company's liquidity and profitability, a company's legal responsibility to its stockholders requires that it be minimized. Before beginning to evaluate different options available for hedging, the international financial manager at headquarters must determine the balance sheet entries that are "exposed."

Which assets and liabilities are exposed depends on the legal system of the home country. In the United States the Financial Accounting Standards Board (FASB) sets out the guidelines managers must use to determine the types of assets and their exposure. The following brief example will demonstrate the use of both forward, or exchange market, hedging and credit, or money market, hedging.

Suppose a U.S. company is faced with the following situation:

(1)   Its exposed assets are 500 FC (foreign currency).

(2)   The exchange spot rate is $1/FC.

(3)   The end-of-year forward rate is $1.05/FC.

The problem: because the exposure is positive (that is, because accounts receivable are vulnerable), the company must hedge by using either the foreign exchange market or the credit market. Exhibit 9-6 illustrates what can happen in this situation. The far left column shows some possible exchange rates on the day of delivery, 12/31. In the next column are the corresponding translation gains (losses). The third column gives the gain realized by entering into a forward contract that must be fulfilled on 12/31. Finally, the right-most column shows how the gain realized under the forward contract compares to the translation gain under the different scenarios.

As the first row shows, if the exchange rate turns out to be \$1.10/FC (a \$0.10, or 10%, increase over the spot rate when the exchange was agreed upon), the translation gain will be \$50 (500 × \$0.10). Because of the forward contract, however, the gain realized will be only \$25. Thus the company will suffer a cash loss of \$25—the difference between the forward rate (\$1.05/FC) and the actual rate (\$1.10/FC). The bottom row depicts the situation in which the exchange rate on 12/31 is \$0.05 lower than the original spot rate and \$0.10 lower than the forward rate. In this case, there will be a cash gain of \$50. The gain actually realized, however, will still be \$25, as in all the other cases. It is important to note that the balance sheet value of the foreign asset is locked in at the forward rate of \$1.05/FC.

RECENT DEVELOPMENTS IN EXPOSURE MANAGEMENT

FUTURES

A number of currencies are traded, like other commodities, on a daily basis. These are the British pound, the Canadian dollar, the deutsche mark, the Dutch gilder, the French franc, the Japanese yen, the Mexican peso, and the Swiss franc. Futures are used by banks that buy (put) and sell (call) large quantities of foreign currencies.

Exhibit 9-6   A Hedge: Selling 500 FC on January 1 for Delivery on December 31 (spot rate = \$1/FC; forward rate = \$1.05/FC)

Exchange Rate on 12/31	Translation Gain (Loss) on 500 FC Exposure	Gain Realized on Forward Contract	Cash Gain (Loss) on Forward Contract
\$1.10/FC	\$50	\$25	\$(25)
\$1.05/FC	\$25	\$25	—
\$1.00/FC	—	\$25	\$25
\$ .95/FC	\$(25)	\$25	\$50

OPTIONS

Unlike forward contracts, options offer a firm an opportunity to make money, for a firm can call its option whenever the "striking price" that it paid for the currency falls behind the spot price. For example, suppose a firm purchases a 30-day option to buy British pounds at a "striking price" of $1.05 each. If the pound reaches $1.06, the firm will exercise its option and then sell the pounds in the spot market, earning a one-cent profit on each pound. Should the price drop to $1.04, the firm does not have to exercise its option.

KEY CURRENCIES

IMF-issued special drawing rights (SDR) and the European Community's european currency unit (ECU) are international financial instruments that will play a much larger role in international finance in the future. For the time being, however, they are used more in government-to-government transactions than by private MNCs.

SWAPS

Swaps are transactions in which a firm simultaneously buys and sells two different currencies. Swaps are designed to avoid exchange controls, alleviate political risks, and overcome informational problems in capital markets. Although swaps are usually thought of as protection against transaction and translation risks, they are more frequently used as a means of transferring and/ or raising capital for investment purposes. In the latter case, interest rate and debt-equity swaps are usually used; these will be treated later in the chapter. What follows is a brief explanation of the use of swaps to transfer capital.

Spot and forward market swaps are usually employed to alleviate financial difficulties stemming from foreign exchange regulations. For example, suppose a U.S. MNC's subsidiary in Spain needs 10,000 Spanish pesetas to finance its production. To avoid exchange problems, the U.S. parent company will *buy* the 10,000 pesetas in the spot market and *lend* them to its affiliate or subsidiary for, say, three months at the going interest rate. At the same time, the parent will sell the same number of pesetas for delivery in three months (the duration of its loan to its affiliate). The parent company will receive dollars for the pesetas, and its short position will be covered with the pesetas it will collect from the repayment of the loan to its Spanish subsidiary. This way the parent receives its dollars and the Spanish subsidiary its pesetas without violation of any foreign exchange regulations.

BACK-TO-BACK LOANS

A back-to-back loan is used to avoid foreign exchange or cross-border transactions, as well as any foreign exchange risks. Back-to-back loans involve an agreement between MNCs in different countries to lend money to each other's subsidiaries in the subsidiaries' local currencies. For example, a German subsidiary in the United States that needs $20,000 will receive the money from a U.S. MNC with a subsidiary in Hamburg, West Germany. The U.S. subsidiary in Hamburg will in turn receive 40,000 deutsche marks (the dollar equivalent) from the German parent company in Hamburg. The result is that both subsidiaries receive the needed funds with no cross-border or foreign exchange transactions and, therefore, no risks.

BANK SWAPS

Unlike the two previous transactions, in which the dealings are between two or more corporations, bank swaps involve a third party—a bank. This type of swap evolved from the traditional bank-to-bank swap through which two commercial banks in different countries would acquire temporarily needed foreign currencies. Such swaps were prevalent in dealings with developing countries whose currencies were not freely convertible or accepted. Today MNCs make frequent use of bank swaps.

The procedure is similar to those described above. A U.S. MNC in San Diego, for example, will deposit $10,000 to the credit of a Mexican bank. The Mexican bank will lend the equivalent number of pesos ($10,000 × 1,500 = 15,000,000, at the current exchange rate) to the U.S. MNC's subsidiary in Mexico, which will use the money to expand its facilities. At an agreed-upon future date, the Mexican bank will repay the $10,000 and the U.S. subsidiary will repay the 15,000,000 pesos. Because U.S. dollars are lent and repaid and Mexican pesos are lent and repaid, there is no cross-border transaction and, therefore, no foreign exchange risk; yet both parties obtain the foreign currency they desire.

FUNCTION B: CASH MANAGEMENT[2]

The previous section dealt with various tools designed to minimize the impact of external environmental changes on a firm's financial assets. Usually a firm does not hope to realize any financial benefits by using these tools; the main objective is to avoid losses. Most of the time there is at least one external party involved, such as a bank or another firm.

This section explores the variety of internal tools available to a firm. Although the main objective in using these tools is to minimize exposure risks, there is plenty of opportunity to realize financial benefits by minimizing taxes and optimizing cash generation and cash uses among a firm's subsidiaries.

There are many ways an MNC can maneuver liquid assets to accomplish cash management objectives without violating tax laws and/or foreign ex-

---

[2]The discussion in this section is based on D. Rutenberg, *Multinational Management* (Boston: Little, Brown and Co., 1981), 70–105.

change regulations. The cash management goals of an MNC are

To secure liquidity

To minimize financial costs

To minimize taxes

These overall objectives translate into various specific tasks that must be performed by the financial manager:

(1)   Estimate net cash flow for each subsidiary

(2)   Set minimum levels of bank deposits

(3)   Set minimum levels of liquid assets holdings

(4)   Select a method of maneuvering liquid assets:

    (a)   Adjusting transfer prices
    (b)   Charging fees and royalties
    (c)   Making intersubsidiary loans
    (d)   Handling intercompany dividends

Although most large MNCs have their own financial institutions, which for all practical purposes perform the financial transactions formally handled by a bank, for purposes of illustration a bank will be considered to be the vehicle through which all financial transactions are handled. The bank acts as a clearinghouse for all transactions among a firm's subsidiaries and between the parent company and each of the subsidiaries. The bank sets a minimum balance requirement for the year, as well as a minimum bank deposit for each subsidiary. The total of all subsidiaries' deposits can be used to satisfy the bank's minimum balance requirement. Once these requirements have been met, each subsidiary can use any of the four methods listed above to maneuver liquid assets.

ADJUSTING TRANSFER PRICES AND CHAIN INVOICING

Transfer prices are the prices an MNC subsidiary charges a sister subsidiary for goods and services. According to economic theory, transfer price equals marginal costs. An MNC wishing to move funds from subsidiary A to subsidiary B would raise the transfer prices on the items shipped from subsidiary A to subsidiary B. Because of variations from country to country in tax structure, foreign exchange regulations, and foreign investment policy, some subsidiaries will be better profit generators than others.

An MNC that desired to use transfer pricing as a means of moving funds from one subsidiary to another would increase the transfer price by the amount of the duty imposed by the country for which the funds were destined. Exhibit 9-7 gives an example of a transfer price increase situation. Products 1, 2, and 3 are subject to noticeably higher duty fees (20%, 15%, and 10%, respectively),

Exhibit 9-7   Transfer Pricing

Product	Duty	Price from Factory	Quantity Sent	Cash Flow	Price + Duty	New Price	New Cash Flow	Change
1	20%	10	100	1000	12.00	N/C	1000	0
2	15%	15	400	6000	17.25	N/C	6000	0
3	10%	20	300	6000	22.00	N/C	6000	0
4	8%	8	200	1600	8.64	8.64	1728	+128
5	5%	6	100	600	6.30	6.30	630	+30
Totals			1100	15,200			15,358	+158

Result: $158 moves from subsidiary A to subsidiary B.
N/C = No change.

so their prices are not raised in an attempt to incorporate duties. Therefore the new prices remain the same as the original factory prices. Products 4 and 5, however, are subject to lower duties (8% and 5%, respectively), and thus their prices can be increased from the original factory prices relatively inconspicuously.

An alternative way of moving funds from one subsidiary to another is to invoice the goods through a chain of subsidiaries, each of which adds its commission. This "chain invoicing" is less suspect than transfer price increases and therefore is subjected to less scrutiny by government authorities. Exhibit 9-8 illustrates chain invoicing.

FEES AND ROYALTIES

Managerial advice offered by headquarters, headquarters overhead, royalties on patents and trademarks, international computer hookups, ongoing costs of corporate R&D facilities, and other services rendered by the parent company

Exhibit 9-8   Chain Invoicing: Adding a 30% Commission at Each Stage

Location	U.S. Factory	U.S. FSC*	Bahamas	Switzerland	France	Algeria
Price	$2.50	$3.25	$4.23	$5.50	$7.15	$9.30

*Foreign Sales Corporation.

or by one subsidiary to another are very difficult to price. For this reason they can be suitable conduits for moving funds from one place to another.

Fees for licensing and other contractual arrangements, as well as payments for services, can take any one of the following forms:

(1)   A specific price per unit of product and/or pound of output

(2)   A specific percentage of sales price

(3)   A fixed sum per year (perhaps combined with one of the above two fees)

Rutenberg recommends that a financial manager take the following steps:[3]

(1)   Prepare a list of every conceivable fee, royalty, or service charge.

(2)   Eliminate those that are not tax-deductible in either of the countries involved.

(3)   Calculate the tax costs (income + withholding tax) and list the flows in descending order by total tax cost.

(4)   List the flows again in terms of the probability that their omission would be noticed by the officials in either country.

INTERSUBSIDIARY LOANS AND LEADS AND LAGS IN INVOICING

Just as a parent may pay a child ahead of time for cutting the lawn or defer repayment of a loan for a long period of time, an MNC may advance payment of its accounts payable to a subsidiary or defer collection of its accounts receivable from a subsidiary. Postponing repayment of a large obligation has the same effect on a subsidiary's cash flow and working capital as does granting a cash loan: it increases the funds available for production.

Because of MNCs' liberal use of this method of maneuvering liquid assets, tax authorities have set certain conditions. For example, loan agreements must specify an interest rate and date of maturity; otherwise the loans are "deemed dividends"—that is, considered to be taxable income. There are, of course, certain drawbacks to these methods of maneuvering liquid assets. Because loans and accounts receivable and payable are exposed assets, there is always the risk that exchange rate changes will create losses that wipe out the gains.

DIVIDENDS

Dividends are the price a company pays for the use of stockholders' money. The portion of a company's after-tax profit that will be declared as dividends

---

[3]Rutenberg, *Multinational Management*, p. 91.

depends on management's perception of the company's financial and investment needs. For example, if management plans to expand the company's productive capacity and wishes to self-finance this expansion, a larger portion of the profits will go into retained earnings and less will be declared as dividends.

Dividends represent taxable income in most countries. Thus MNCs, one of whose main objectives is to maximize shareholders' wealth, try to distribute dividends so as to minimize the tax burden. Because dividends may be taxed every time they enter and leave a country, the MNC must determine how much of a proposed dividend payment would accrue to each subsidiary and how much would get back to the parent.

Suppose an MNC has a subsidiary in Liechtenstein, which in turn has a subsidiary in West Germany, which in turn has a subsidiary in Belgium, which declares a dividend of 100 units. Exhibit 9-9 shows the tax implications of this dividend declaration.

The Belgian government has a withholding tax of 18.2%, so 81.80 units arrive in West Germany from the Belgian subsidiary. The West German business tax, based on the entire dividend of 100, is 13.50%, so income net of business tax is 86.50. Company income tax is 15% of income net of business tax. (This rate is for income that will be used for dividends; income retained within the firm is taxed at 51 percent.) At this point, however, credit is granted for the Belgian withholding tax of 18.20 units. Thus the company income tax is -5.23, or $(86.5 \times 15\%) - 18.20$. Combining this tax credit with the West German business tax of 13.50 units brings the total tax to 8.27 units. That is to say, only 73.53 units of the 100-unit dividend declared by the Belgian subsidiary get to its West German parent.

Exhibit 9-9   Dividends Declared and Received

Country	Dividends Declared	Dividends Received (Income)	Business Taxes	Income Taxes	Withholding Taxes on Dividend Leaving	Total Tax
Belgium	100	—	0	0	18.20 (100 × 18.2%)	18.2
West Germany	73.53	81.80 (100 − 18.20)	13.50 (100 × 13.5%)	−5.23 [(86.50 × 15%) − 18.20]	18.38 (73.53 × 25%)	26.6
Liechtenstein	—	55.15 (73.53 − 18.38)	0	0	0	0

The West German subsidiary uses this dividend to declare a dividend of 73.53 units to its parent in Liechtenstein. But the government of West Germany imposes a 25% withholding tax on dividends leaving West Germany, so only 55.15 units arrive at the parent in Liechtenstein. That nation levies no taxes on dividends received from abroad, so the parent receives the entire 55.15 units—just over half of the original dividend declared by the Belgian subsidiary.

FUNCTION C: CAPITAL BUDGETING

The tasks explained thus far, which are aimed at external exposure management and cash management, constitute one aspect of the international financial manager's job. The other aspect consists of capital budgeting (deploying financial resources) and funding (determining and evaluating funding options).

Capital budgeting is a process of balancing the advantages to be gained from possible uses of funds against the costs of alternative ways of obtaining the needed resources. Before capital budgeting can begin, the location of decision-making responsibility must be established. Financial decision making is one area in which corporate headquarters imposes strong controls via policies, procedures, and standards. Corporate headquarters generally specifies discretionary budgets, return requirements, and methods for evaluating and selecting projects. The actual evaluation of international investment proposals is a rather complicated process. A multitude of tax rates, exchange rates, inflation rates, and political risks must be carefully examined to establish an investment portfolio that maximizes stockholder wealth. Exhibit 9-10 outlines some of the complexities of international capital budgeting.

Most MNCs follow a three-stage process in their appraisal of international projects.

Stage A: At the subsidiary level estimated cash flows from proposed disbursements and receipts are adjusted to account for exchange rate risks and political risks.

Stage B: At the headquarters level a plan is made regarding the amount, form, and timing of the transfer of funds; taxes and other expenses related to the transfer; and incremental revenues and costs that will occur elsewhere in the MNC.

Stage C: At the headquarters level the project is evaluated and compared with other investment projects on the basis of incremental net cash flows accruing to the system as a return on investment.[4]

Capital budgeting is one area of international finance in which there has been a tremendous proliferation of analytical techniques, ranging from simple

---

[4]Robock and Simmonds, *International Business,* p. 519; D. K. Eiteman and A. I. Stonehill, *Multinational Business Finance,* Fourth Edition (Reading, MA: Addison-Wesley Publishing Co., 1983), 265–302.

Exhibit 9-10   Complexities of Foreign Capital Budgeting

Capital budgeting for a foreign project uses the same theoretical framework as domestic capital budgeting: project cash flows are discounted at the firm's weighted average cost of capital, or the project's required rate of return, to determine net present value; or, alternatively, the internal rate of return that equates project cash flows to the cost of the project is sought. However, capital budgeting analysis for a foreign project is considerably more complex than the domestic case for a number of reasons:

Parent cash flows must be distinguished from project cash flows. Each of these two types of flows contributes to a different view of value.

Parent cash flows often depend upon the form of financing. Thus cash flows cannot be clearly separated from financing decisions, as is done in domestic capital budgeting.

Remittance of funds to the parent must be explicitly recognized because of differing tax systems, legal and political constraints on the movement of funds, local business norms, and differences in how financial markets and institutions function.

Cash flows from affiliates to parent can be generated by an array of nonfinancial payments, including payment of license fees and payments for imports from the parent.

Differing rates of national inflation must be anticipated because of their importance in causing changes in competitive position, and thus in cash flows over a period of time.

The possibility of unanticipated foreign exchange rate changes must be remembered because of possible direct effects on the value to the parent of local cash flows, as well as an indirect effect on the competitive position of the foreign affiliate.

Use of segmented national capital markets may create an opportunity for financial gains or may lead to additional financial costs.

Use of host government subsidized loans complicates both capital structure and the ability to determine an appropriate weighted average cost of capital for discounting purposes.

Political risk must be evaluated because political events can drastically reduce the value or availability of expected cash flows.

Terminal value is more difficult to estimate because potential purchasers from the host, parent, or third countries, or from the private or public sector, may have widely divergent perspectives on the value to them of acquiring the project.

Since the same theoretical capital budgeting framework is used to choose among competing foreign and domestic projects, a common standard is critical. Thus all foreign complexities must be quantified as modifications to either expected cash flow or the rate of discount. Although in practice many

firms make such modifications arbitrarily, readily available information, theoretical deduction, or just plain common sense can be used to make less
arbitrary and more reasonable choices.

SOURCE: D. K. Eiteman and A. I. Stonehill, *Multinational Business Finance*, Fourth Edition
(Reading, MA: Addison-Wesley Publishing Co., 1983), 330–331.

---

quantitative models to sophisticated large-scale computerized simulations. The
model that has received the greatest attention in financial management literature is the Capital Assets Pricing Model (CAPM). This approach to capital
budgeting allocates funds to projects on the basis of *risk-adjusted returns,*
where returns are calculated from discounted cash flows. A complete treatment
of the CAPM is beyond the scope of this book. What follows is a brief explanation.

Before any future cash flows are calculated for a project, management must
make explicit its assumptions about the political risk and the exchange rate
risk, as well as about the business climate in general. (Management's ways of
dealing with these requirements will be explored in subsequent chapters when
the investment decision is treated in more detail.) Much effort must go into
formulating these assumptions.

Most managers adhere to some general principles when estimating, adjusting,
and discounting cash flows. In estimating future exchange rates, managers
usually use the Purchasing Power Parity Principle.[5] As explained in Chapter
6, purchasing power parity (PPP) refers to the equality of goods' prices across
countries when measured in one currency. Movements in internal price levels
correspond to movements in exchange rates:

$$\frac{e_{12}^{t}}{e_{12}^{t-1}} = \frac{P_1^t/P_1^{t-1}}{P_2^t/P_2^{t-1}}$$

where

e_{12}^{t} = the spot rate (currency in Country 1/currency in Country 2) at
    time t

e_{12}^{t-1} = the spot rate at time $t - 1$

P_1^t = the price level in Country 1 at time t

P_1^{t-1} = the price level in Country 1 at time $t - 1$

P_2^t = the price level in Country 2 at time t

P_2^{t-1} = the price level in Country 2 at time t

---

[5]Oxelheim and Wilhborg, *Macroeconomic Uncertainty,* pp. 89–100.

In other words, the rate of change in the equilibrium exchange rate is proportional to the rate of change in the price levels in the two countries concerned.

Alternatively stated, if prices in Country 1 rise to 10% more than those in Country 2, Country 1's exchange rate can be expected to depreciate by 10%, so that a particular amount of money will buy the same amount of goods in both countries. Boyd described this principle in 1801 by saying that exchange rates are in equilibrium when a buyer at a random point in time receives the same amount of goods for his or her money, regardless of which country he or she buys them from. The principle can be expressed as

$$e^{12} = \frac{P_1}{P_2}$$

where

e_{12} = spot rate (currency in Country 1/currency in Country 2)
P_1 = price level in Country 1
P_2 = price level in Country 2

Exhibit 9-11 presents an example of projected cash flows under PPP.

In estimating the impact of interest rates on exchange rates, the relationship most commonly used is the so-called Fisher Open. This relationship, which was developed by Irving Fisher in 1896, is also known as Fisher's International Effect. It is based on the equality, across countries and currencies, of both expected returns on financial investment and borrowing costs. The Fisher Open expresses the equilibrium in international interest rates after adjustment for

Exhibit 9-11   Projected Cash Flows Under PPP (assuming an inflation rate of 10% per year)

	Year 1	Year 2	Year 3	Year 4
Project revenues (pesos)	1000	1100	1200	1300
Project costs (pesos)	600	660	720	780
Cash flow (project revenues minus project costs)	400	440	480	520
Exchange rate (pesos/dollars)	10/1	11/1	12/1	13/1
Cash flow (dollars)	40	40	40	40

SOURCE: Davidson, *Global Strategic Management*, p. 220.

expected exchange rate movements:

$$\frac{e_{t+1}^* - e_t}{e_t} = \frac{i_t^D - i_t^F}{1 + i_t^F}$$

where

e_t = spot rate at time t

e_{t+1}^* = market expectations at time t regarding future spot rate at time $t + 1$

i_t^D = domestic interest rate for one period at time t

i_t^F = foreign interest rate for one period at time t

According to the Fisher Open, the expected change in the exchange rate is reflected in the interest differential ($i_t^D - i_t^F$) for assets under equal financial risk in two countries. This relationship is expressed in the principle of interest rate parity (IRP), which says that the forward premium on one currency relative to another reflects the interest differential between the currencies. This relationship can be written as

$$\frac{f_t - e_t}{e_t} = \frac{i_t^D - i_t^F}{1 + i_t^F}$$

where f_t is the forward rate at time t for delivery of currency at time $t + 1$.

Effective capital budgeting involves more than just financial criteria. The results of applying the Capital Assets Pricing Model must be supplemented with environmental analysis and strategic assessments. Exhibit 9-12 provides a summary of the three main subsystems of the capital budgeting system.

FUNCTION D: FUNDING

Funding is essentially a two-step process. In step one management makes the basic funding decisions. For example, management must decide on the amount of funds to be borrowed and the amount to be exchanged for equity participation—the debt-to-equity ratio. Traditionally, U.S. management has preferred equity to debt. European and, to a much greater extent, Japanese MNCs tend to choose debt financing.

Contemporary financial markets are in a state of extreme turbulence. Financial institutions are daily creating new financial instruments and techniques that offer numerous opportunities for funding. Exhibit 9-13 presents a sample of the options available and suggests some of the advantages and disadvantages associated with each class of options. An MNC will most likely decide to use a combination of funding techniques and a portfolio of currencies. Step two, which involves actually finding and delivering the funds, is then handled by the company treasurer. One of the treasurer's tasks is determining the cost of funding. Detailed treatment of the various approaches to this complex task is

Exhibit 9-12   Elements of the Capital Budgeting System: Project Selection Decisions

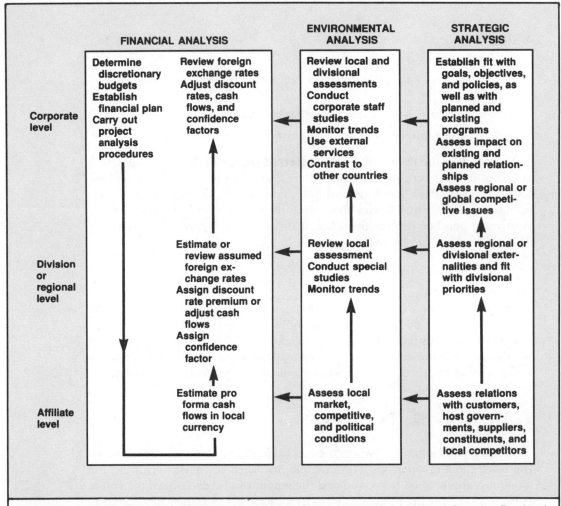

SOURCE: W. H. Davidson, *Global Strategic Management;* Copyright © 1982, John Wiley & Sons, Inc. Reprinted by permission of John Wiley & Sons, Inc., p. 228.

beyond the intent of this book. Exhibit 9-14 demonstrates the basic idea of estimating financing costs in different currencies.

As the exhibit shows, there are two main components of the total cost: the prime rate and the exchange cost.[6] There is an inverse relationship between the prime rate and the change in the exchange rate: high-prime-rate currencies sell at a discount; low-prime-rate currencies are forwarded at a premium. Thus

---

[6]Davidson, *Global Strategic Management,* p. 236.

Exhibit 9-13   Funding Options and Their Advantages and Costs

Options	Principal Advantages	Costs and Risks
Debt (long term, short term, fixed rate, or floating rate)	No loss of control; fixed payments good at growth times; tax deduction	Fixed payments bad at no-growth times

Internal
 Parent
 Sister
 Direct
 Holding Company
 Bonds
 Receivables
  Local Currency
  Foreign Currency
  Dollar
  Eurodollar
  Euroyen
  ECU
  Third Country
  Hedged
  Unhedged
	Repatriation; economies of central borrowing; access to low-cost funds	Affiliate exchange risk

External
 Trade
 Bank
 Bond/Paper
 Local Source
 Foreign Source
 Secured
 Unsecured
  Local Currency
  Foreign Currency
		Political and exchange risk; availability of funds

Equity (common or preferred)		
Internal Parent Sister	Debt capacity; managerial flexibility; economies of central borrowing; access to low-cost funds	Translation exposure; repatriation; expropriation
External Local Foreign		

SOURCE: Adapted from Davidson, *Global Strategic Management*, pp. 230–233.

Exhibit 9-14   Financing Costs in Different Currencies

Currency	Prime Rate	Spot Rate	Rate One Year Forward	Exchange Cost[a]	Total Cost[b]
British pound	10%	1.6620	1.6500	(.72)%	9.28%
French franc	15%	.1460	.1260	(13.69)%	1.31%
Deutsche mark	6%	.5548	.5670	2.19%	8.19%
Japanese yen	4%	.0070	.0080	14.28%	18.28%
Swiss franc	5%	.6707	.6890	2.72%	7.72%

Numbers have been rounded to facilitate calculations.

[a]Exchange cost = (Forward − Spot)/Spot. For example, (1.6500 − 1.6620)1.6620 = (.72%).

[b]Total cost = Prime rate ± Exchange cost

( ) Discount (when the forward rate is less than the spot rate)

England and France, for example, have high prime rates and discounted currencies. Losses in the exchange market are deducted from interest cost, and gains are added to it.

DEBT-EQUITY SWAPS: A NEW FUNDING INSTRUMENT

The year 1987 could be called the year of "the big chill" for the banking industry in general and for big international banks in particular. It finally became obvious to bankers that most developing countries could not service their debts. Large banks in the United States and Europe, starting with Citicorp, began setting aside billions of dollars as security against losses due to decisions on the part of some large debtors to defer or even refuse to pay their obligations. International debt by developing countries reached the trillion dollar mark, of which some 64% was private. The average ratio of interest service to exports reached the 10% level; the average ratio of total debt service to GNP climbed from 3.9% in 1980 to 5.5% in 1986. The average ratio of debt volume to GNP jumped from 20.6% in 1980 to 35.4% in 1986.

Under these circumstances banks had to invent something new. Debt-equity swaps are designed to bail out both bankers and developing country debtors, as well as some cash-laden investors in developed countries. Exhibit 9-15 explains debt-equity swaps in detail.

RECAPITULATION

Designing an optimal international financial strategy is perhaps the most difficult task facing contemporary MNC managers. Thousands of business op-

---

Exhibit 9-15   Debt-Equity Swaps

The existing exposure of commercial banks to developing countries is a key constraint to new spontaneous lending. Recently, a secondary market trading developing countries' debt instruments at a discount has emerged. The volume of transactions was initially quite limited, and price quotations on the discounted debt have been regarded as rather artificial in view of the thinness of the market. The market is becoming better organized, participation has widened, and the variety of transactions has increased. New interpretations of accounting and banking regulations in the United States have contributed to this development. A bank taking a loss on a sale or swap of a loan to a developing country would not be required to reduce the book value of other loans to that country, provided the bank considers the remaining loans collectible.

A few of the debtor countries whose liabilities are being traded at a discount have utilized the existence of the discount market to encourage a flow of private investments and to gain other advantages. The popular term for the conversion of discounted debt into local currency assets is a "debt-equity swap." "Debt conversion" would be a more appropriate term, since conversion of external debt instruments into domestic obligations can take place not only for foreign direct investment purposes, but also for more general purposes by residents or nonresidents of the debtor country. In essence, a foreign investor wishing to buy assets in a debtor country can, through a debt-equity swap, obtain local currency at a discount. The foreign investor, in effect, obtains a rebate on the purchase of the currency equivalent to the discount on the loan less the transactions costs of the debt-equity swap.

Chile has a well-developed legal framework for the conversion of external debt into domestic assets. There is a similar procedure for the conversion of debt using foreign currency holdings by domestic investors. The figure shows the detailed steps involved in the debt conversion. Although they seem complicated, the central steps are conceptually simple.

Debt-equity swaps are open only to nonresidents who intend to invest in fixed assets (equity) in Chile. The first step is to locate and buy at the going discount a Chilean debt instrument denominated in foreign currency. Next, with the intermediation of a Chilean bank, the foreign investor must obtain the consent of the local debtor to exchange the original debt instrument for one denominated in local currency and the permission of the central bank to withdraw the debt. Finally, the foreign investor can sell the new debt instrument in the local financial market and acquire the fixed assets or equity with the cash proceeds of the sale.

The main difference between the debt-equity swap and the straight debt conversion is that the debt conversion is available to resident or nonresident investors with foreign currency holdings abroad. Also, once the conversion has taken place, the investor faces no restriction on the use of the local currency proceeds.

The debt conversion scheme allows the debtor country first to reduce the

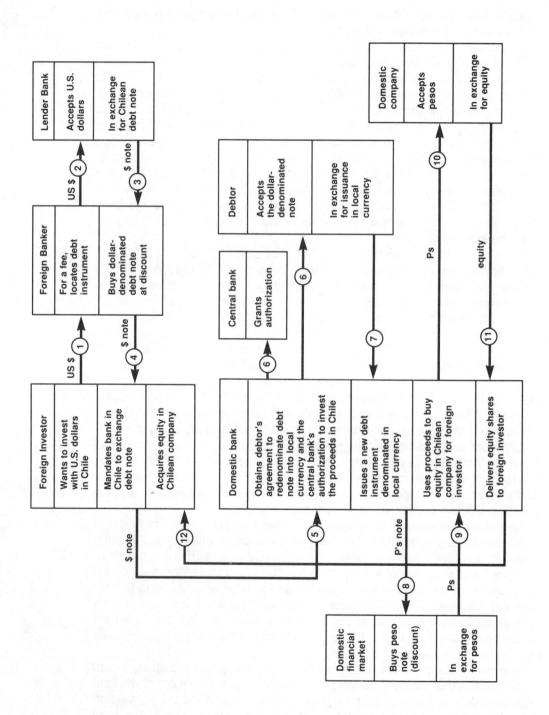

stock or the rate of growth of external debt. Second, it is a means to attract flight capital as well as foreign direct investment. Third, debt-equity swaps imply a switch from the outflow of interest and principal on debt obligations to the deferred and less certain outflows associated with private direct investment.

For the commercial banks the swaps provide an exit instrument or a means to adjust the risk composition of their portfolio. For banks that wish to continue to be active internationally, losses on the outstanding portfolio can be realized at a time and on a scale of the bank's own choosing and by utilizing a market mechanism.

The emergence of an active market in debt instruments of developing countries offers opportunities to both debtors and lenders. There are, however, obstacles to its development. Debtor countries must ensure that transactions take place at an undistorted exchange rate, otherwise the discounts on the debt may be outweighed by exchange rate considerations. In addition, long-term financial instruments in the domestic markets are needed to ensure that the conversion into domestic monetary assets does not increase monetary growth above established targets. The incentives for foreign investors will be nullified if the broader domestic policy environment is not conducive to inflows of foreign investment. Finally, a minimum regulatory framework is required. Documentation for debt restructuring must be adjusted to allow for prepayment for debt conversion purposes. Clear rules will facilitate the transactions. Overregulation, particularly in the form of administrative procedures for investment approval, would be a deterrence.

SOURCE: World Bank, *World Development Report* (New York: Oxford University Press, 1987), 22–23. Reprinted by permission.

---

erations must be converted into their monetary equivalents and denominated in various currencies. Each currency is subject to fluctuations arising from governmental and social factors. In spite of the complexity of the task and the uncertainties involved, the international financial manager must assure the company's stakeholders that their interests in the company have been protected and that their investments have been put to optimal use.

To make good on this promise, the international financial manager must, first and foremost, strive to minimize the impact of changes in the macroeconomic environment on the company's daily cash flows, annual financial performance, and long-term economic or market value. Given that an MNC, with its affiliates around the globe, interacts with numerous macroeconomic environments, the MNC financial manager must be able to comprehend and anticipate the intentions and actions of many governments with diverse political and economic systems. A manager must be able to assess not only the intentions of the British government with respect to an appreciation of the pound, but also the magnitude and the likelihood of a potential appreciation of the yen against the dollar.

Until the beginning of the seventies, governmental policies generally had very little impact on a country's currency, primarily because a very robust international monetary system buffered business activities from sudden and unexpected changes in regime. The seventies, however, ushered in an epoch of unprecedented uncertainty. When, in 1971, President Nixon refused to honor the United States' obligation to exchange dollars for gold, he triggered a series of changes in the international monetary system that led to today's total confusion and turmoil.

Because of the complexity and uncertainty of the international capital markets that are the international financial manager's daily preoccupation, the first two functions of the international financial framework—exposure management and cash management—must be given precedence over the other two functions of capital budgeting and funding. Even the best capital budgeting and funding plans will be to no avail if inadequate attention is paid to the tremendous effects that external macroenvironmental changes can have on exchange rates, or to the potential impact of these changes on the company's cash flows, consolidated balance sheet, and economic value. It is the job of the international financial manager to anticipate or minimize these effects.

REVIEW QUESTIONS

(1)   Interview the international financial manager of a large company in your area and identify the main financial links of the company. Outline the main sources and uses of funds (where the money comes from and where it goes) and the currency in which each income and/or expenditure stream is denominated. Use Exhibit 9-1 as a guide.

(2)   Write a one-page essay explaining the main functions of an international finance department.

(3)   Explain the following concepts:

Exposure to macroeconomic risks

Macroeconomic structure

Policy regime

Commercial risk

Firm- and industry-specific risk

Country risk

Currency risk

Financial risk

(4)   Leona DiPascali is president of LDP, Inc., a U.S. firm that operates a chain of small specialty stores selling ethnic coffees, candies, ice creams, and other gourmet foods. She recently ordered five Subitomacina machines

from an Italian firm. The machines are designed to make and dispense Italian-style ice cream, which is a huge success in Europe. Subitomacina is produced by Subitolabori of Milan, a company owned by Ms. DiPascali's distant cousin. The Italian cousin is willing to lag LDP's accounts receivable, because he wants to be nice to his cousin and get a foot in the U.S. market. Ms. DiPascali not only wants to make sure that she does not lose any money from the fluctuations of the Italian lira against the dollar, but also wishes to make some exchange profits on the deal. What are LDP's options? Explain how Ms. DiPascali and LDP, Inc. can avoid translation losses.

(5)   An international manager who is an alumnus of your college returns to campus to deliver a speech on "Joint Ventures and Other Type of Investment with Debtor Countries: The Only Solution to the International Debt Problem." The message is clear: there is no way the developing countries in Latin America can pay back the money they owe. At the same time, U.S. banks cannot continue carrying these nonperforming loans on their books without jeopardizing their financial positions. The visiting lecturer recommends debt-equity swaps as a viable solution. Pick a company in your area that might be willing to consider the idea of investing in a debtor country by buying bank paper in the United States and investing in real assets in the debtor country. Create a business plan for that company. If possible, get advice from a local bank official. Before exploring the debt-equity swap funding strategy, briefly examine the other funding options shown in Exhibit 9-13. Would any of these options be preferable to a debt-equity swap? If so, which ones, and why?

SUGGESTED READINGS

Aliber, Robert Z. *The International Money Game,* Second Edition. New York: Basic Books, 1976.

Anti, B., and A. C. Henry. "The Cost and Implications of Two Hedging Techniques." *Euromoney,* June 1979, 82–87.

Baker, James C. "Evolutionary Change in MNC Foreign Exchange Risk Management." *Baylor Business Studies* 12, No. 2 (May–July 1981): 23–33.

Bamber, D. "How Alcan Makes Financing Simple." *Euromoney,* April 1981, 79–88.

Bergsten, Fred C. "Crisis and Reform: The International Monetary System." *Vital Speeches of the Day,* November 13, 1986, 281–288.

Cooper, John C. B. "The Foreign Exchange Market." *Management Accounting* 59, No. 5 (May 1981): 18–23.

Dufey, Gunter, and Ian H. Giddy. *Fifty Cases in International Finance.* Reading, MA: Addison-Wesley Publishing Co., 1987.

Feskoe, Gaffney. "Reducing Currency Risks in a Volatile Foreign Exchange Market." *Management Accounting* 62, No. 3 (September 1980): 19–24.

Haner, F. T. "Rating Investment Risks Abroad." *Business Horizons* 22, No. 2 (April 1979): 18–23.

Hekman, Christine R. "A Financial Model of Foreign Exchange Exposure." *Journal of International Business Studies* 16, No. 2 (1985): 83–99.

Kwok, Chuck C. Y. "Hedging Foreign Exchange Exposures: Independent vs. Integrative Approaches." *Journal of International Business Studies* 19, No. 2 (1987): 33–51.

Lieberman, Gail. "A Systems Approach to Foreign Exchange Risk Management." *Financial Executive* 46, No. 12 (December 1978): 14–19.

Mascarenhas, Briance, and Ole Christian Sand. "Country-Risk Assessment Systems in Banks: Patterns and Performance." *Journal of International Business Studies* 16, No. 1 (1985): 19–35.

Negandi, Anant R. *International Management.* Boston: Allyn and Bacon, 1987.

Nigh, Douglas, Kang Rae Cho, and Suresh Krishnan. "The Role of Location-Related Factors in U.S. Banking Investment Abroad: An Empirical Examination." *Journal of International Business Studies* 17, No. 3 (1986): 59–72.

Oxelheim, L., and C. Wihlborg. *Macroeconomic Uncertainty: International Risks and Opportunities for the Corporation.* New York: John Wiley and Sons, 1987.

Park, Y. S. "Currency Swaps as a Long-Term International Financing Technique." *Journal of International Business Studies* 15, No. 3 (Winter 1984): 47–54.

Price Waterhouse & Co. *Guide for the Reader of Foreign Financial Statements,* Second Edition. New York: January 1985.

Price Waterhouse & Co. *Foreign Exchange Information: A Worldwide Summary.* New York: 1985.

Price Waterhouse & Co. *Capital Formation: International Survey and Analysis.* New York: 1985.

Prind, A. R. *Foreign Exchange Risk.* New York: John Wiley and Sons, 1976.

Root, Franklin R. *International Trade and Investment: Theory, Policy, Enterprise.* Cincinnati, OH: South-Western Publishing Co., 1984.

Rosett, Claudia. "Taiwan's Midas Touch." *The Wall Street Journal,* June 2, 1987, 25.

Rutenberg, David P. *Multinational Management.* Boston: Little, Brown and Co., 1981.

Sampson, Anthony. *The Money Lenders: The People and Politics of the World Banking Crisis.* New York: Penguin Books, 1981.

Stulz, R. M. "Pricing Capital Assets in International Setting: An Introduction." *Journal of International Business Studies* 15, No. 3 (Winter 1984): 55–73.

Swanson, Peggy E., and Stephen C. Caples. "Hedging Foreign Exchange Risk Using Forward Foreign Exchange Markets: An Extension." *Journal of International Business Studies* 18, No. 1 (1987): 52–65.

Vernon, Raymond, and Louis T. Wells, Jr. *Manager in the International Economy,* Fifth Edition. Englewood Cliffs, NJ: Prentice-Hall, 1986.

Vernon-Wortzel, Heidi, and Lawrence H. Wortzel (eds.). *Strategic Management of Multinational Corporations: The Essentials.* New York: John Wiley and Sons, 1985.

Walter, Ingo, and Tracy Murray (eds.). *Handbook of International Business.* New York: John Wiley and Sons, 1982.

Weston, Fred J., and Bart W. Sorge. *Guide to International Financial Management.* New York: McGraw-Hill Book Co., 1977.

CASE 1 ● Nuts Inc.

Nuts Inc. manufactures salted nuts and other snacks, which are sold through wholesalers to department stores and other shops and directly to airlines and companies operating cruise ships. About 50% of sales are to British Airways and British Caledonian Airways and are paid for in pounds.

Sales are seasonal. The demand of wholesalers peaks at the end of the year (Thanksgiving and Christmas); high level of sales is also reached during the summer months, because of increased demand from airlines and the tourist industry. Sales drop off sharply in January and again in August and September, after which they start to build up again.

The budget officer of Nuts Inc., Sarah Feldstein, is attempting to estimate the financial needs of the company for the first six months of 1989. Unit sales for the last three months in 1988 were (in number of cartons)

October	100,000
November	150,000
December	200,000

Ms. Feldstein makes the following sales forecasts for the first half of 1989, expressed in terms of percentages of actual October sales:

January	50%
February	60
March	60
April	70
May	80
June	120
July	125

Source: Information in this case study was prepared by D. Engberg, in the Graduate School of Business Administration at New York University. Used with permission of Prof. D. Engberg.

Collections in previous years have been erratic. But the collection procedure has been changed, and now customers must pay 20% of the total amount in cash immediately and 50% of the remainder in the month following the sale. The other half of the remainder is collected two months after the sale. The firm has negligible bad-debt losses.

Half a kilo of raw materials is needed to produce one carton of the final product. One-third of the raw materials are purchased in Gambia, West Africa, and paid for in British pounds. Raw materials are delivered in the month prior to sale, but are paid for in the month after sale. Labor costs are 50% of the total cost of the product and are paid for in the month of sale. The profit margin for Nuts Inc. is 20% of sales before depreciation and interest expenses. Sales, administrative, and other expenses are 16% of sales and are paid for in the month of sale. All goods are manufactured in the month of sale, but a base stock inventory of finished goods worth $20,000 is held in addition to raw materials.

New shelling and roasting equipment with a twelve-year life and no salvage value will be delivered and paid for in May. The cost of the equipment, installed and ready to run, will be $144,000, on which depreciation of $1,200 will be charged at the end of June.

Semi-annual interest charges on $235,833 worth of long-term bonds (12% coupon) are due in March. There are 15,000 shares of common stock (par value $10) outstanding; they are traded fairly actively in the over-the-counter market, typically at between ten and eleven times earnings per share (EPS). Quarterly common stock cash dividends of $10,000 are paid in March and June. Income tax prepayments of $8,000 are made in March.

Cash on hand on December 31, 1988, is $60,000, and a minimum cash balance of $50,000 should be maintained. All short-term borrowing is repaid as soon as cash is available. The interest rate on short-term borrowing is 12%. All borrowing and repayments take place on the first day of the month. Interest payments are due the first day of the month following the borrowing.

Fixed assets (net) as of the end of the year have a book value of $200,000 with an average life of ten years. All depreciation is taken biannually on a straight line basis. The tax rate is 40%. Retained earnings at the end of 1988 were $84,167. There were no accruals or notes payable.

Based on figures for 1988, Ms. Feldstein prepares a pro forma income statement for the first six months of 1989. She then prepares a cash budget for the first six months of 1989, indicating the estimated amount of excess cash or the estimated amount of financing required to maintain the $50,000 minimum cash balance.

When Ms. Feldstein presents her financial forecasts to the Vice President for Finance she learns that two additional one-year contracts with major American airlines are about to be closed. Each contract will involve monthly delivery of $10,000 worth of snacks and salted nuts, starting in the month of March. Both of the contracts will be settled in dollars.

ISSUES FOR DISCUSSION

(1)   What effects will the two new contracts have on the following?

The pro forma income statement for the first six months of 1989

The estimated amount of excess cash or the estimated amount of financing required to maintain the $50,000 minimum cash balance

The stock market price of the common stock of Nuts Inc. (assuming that the earnings multiple does not change significantly)

(2)   Management would like to know how sensitive the cash budget for the first six months of 1989 will be to changes in the exchange rate between the dollar and the pound. The foreign sales and purchases have been translated into dollars at the current spot exchange rate of $1.35 = 1 pound sterling. What would happen to the financial statements of Nuts Inc. if, as of January 1, (a) the dollar depreciated by 10%, to $1.48 = 1 pound; or (b) the dollar appreciated by 10%, to $1.22 = 1 pound? Assume that there is *only* a dollar/sterling spot market, and no forward, futures, or options market.

CASE 2 ● Morris de Minas

It was August 1984 in New Jersey and the management of Morris Mini Mainframe Computer Company was looking for the most desirable alternative to finance the working capital needs of its Brazilian affiliate, Morris de Minas Ltda. The total need was for 82,650 million cruzeiros, or US $39,320,000 at the then-prevailing exchange rate of 2,102 cruzeiros per United States dollar.[7] The

SOURCE: Prepared by Geraldo Valente and Ian Giddy, © 1985 Ian H. Giddy, New York University, from Dufey/Giddy, *50 Cases in International Finance,* © 1987, Addison-Wesley Publishing Co., Inc., Reading, Massachusetts. Reprinted with permission.

[7]The cruzeiro (Cr$) is the Brazilian currency. Its exchange value was set in relation to the US dollar, and exchange rates against other currencies were determined from their rate relative to the US dollar. For instance, while the Cruzeiro/US dollar exchange rate remained fixed until it was adjusted, the Cruzeiro/Deutsche mark exchange rate varied daily, according to the free-market fluctuations of the Deutsche mark/US dollar exchange rate. Under the minidevaluation system that had been prevailing in Brazil since 1968, the cruzeiro was continually devalued by small amounts at frequent intervals in order to take account of the chronically higher inflation rate in Brazil than in most of its trading partners. Prior to the introduction of the minidevaluation policy, the cruzeiro came to be overvalued as a consequence of prolonged high inflation periods without adjustments in the exchange rate. Expectations of large devaluations

Exhibit C9-1   Morris de Minas Selected Financial Data (Cr$ million)

	Fiscal (August 31)		Forecast for first 6 months of fiscal	
	1982	1983	1984	1985
Total Sales	36,246	86,593	158,916	166,194
Time Sales	30,954	75,865	142,548	152,063
Ending Balance Time Sales Receivables	18,525	49,236	92,484	175,134
Net Earnings Before Foreign Exchange Loss	4,952	6,321	14,927	15,964
Return on Net Worth Before Foreign Exchange Loss	13%	8%	11%	
Return on Investment After Foreign Exchange Loss	3%	1%	5%	

Working Capital Needs: Cr$ 82,650 Million
                                          US$ 39,320 Thousand (Cr$2,102/US$1)

Equity: Cr$16,530 million   *Debt:*   Cr$66,120 million
                 US$ 7,864 thousand   US$31,456 thousand

funds were required to meet competition by providing installment credit for increased sales forecast for the first half of Morris de Minas' fiscal year (Exhibit C9-1); this was a level of sales that the company felt it could sustain in the future.

BACKGROUND

Morris was a manufacturer of "supermini" computers based in Hacketts-town, New Jersey. It had gone international a long time ago and by 1983 about

were built up, encouraging the delay of exports, anticipation of imports, and, more important, eroding the competitive position of Brazilian goods in international markets. On the other hand, to the extent that the magnitude of the smaller and periodical devaluations reasonably matched inflation, this policy of minidevaluations avoided the occurrence of destabilizing speculation, especially in the form of capital outflows. Furthermore, it guaranteed the competitive advantage of the Brazilian exports. At least on two occasions, however, the Brazilian government had failed to adjust the cruzeiro exchange rate adequately by minidevaluations. Thus in December 1979 and in February 1983 two minidevaluations of 30 percent (each) had broken the continuity of the minidevaluation policy, raising, as a consequence, some doubts about the credibility of this exchange rate system. *Sources:* Financing Foreign Operations (FFO), "Domestic Financing: Brazil," June 1984. Peat, Marwick, Mitchell & Co., "Banking in Brazil," 1982.

two-thirds of its revenues were earned outside the United States. Morris (USA) entered the Brazilian market in 1971 by assembling and distributing computers in Belo Horizonte, in the state of Minas Gerais. Late in the 1970s, after it became known for the high quality of its products, Morris (USA) expanded its operations in Brazil to manufacture and distribute a line of superminis, which included a full line of disk drives, printers, and other peripherals. Sales in Brazil focused on medium-sized enterprises, foreign and domestic, and were made on a revolving and installment credit basis. Such sales had amounted (excluding financial charges) to 36,246 million cruzeiros (Cr$) in fiscal year 1982, 86,593 million cruzeiros in 1983, and 158,916 million cruzeiros in 1984 (Exhibit C9-1). Morris was beginning to feel the pinch of competition from the North American minicomputer manufacturers, who, having been excluded from the Brazilian market in their principal products by severe import controls, had moved aggressively into the one segment, halfway between minis and mainframes, that remained the principal domain of foreign producers.

Past experience in several countries, including the United States, had shown that the availability of credit was fundamental to maintaining a market position. This aspect was even more important in Brazil, where companies frequently

Exhibit C9-2   Morris de Minas Balance Sheets (Cr$ million)

	Fiscal (August 31)		
	1982	1983	1984
Assets			
Cash and Marketable Securities	2,658	3,597	7,086
Accounts Receivable	4,282	6,046	14,513
Time Sales Receivable	18,525	49,236	92,484
Inventory	7,947	16,319	29,486
Total Current Assets	33,412	75,198	143,569
Net Fixed Assets	16,452	43,341	121,485
Total Assets	49,864	118,539	265,054
Liabilities			
Accounts Payable	4,795	16,286	59,239
Accrued Taxes	1,846	5,211	13,180
Other Liabilities	3,652	9,142	45,236
Total Current Liabilities	10,293	30,639	117,655
Notes Payable	2,311	5,341	16,462
Capital Stock	29,325	70,986	111,469
Retained Earnings	3,149	5,135	9,152
Reserves	4,786	6,456	10,316
Total Liabilities	49,864	118,539	265,054

incurred indebtedness in the hope of benefiting from the chronically high inflation rate. Therefore, to assure sales, Morris de Minas would need to extend its investment in receivables from time sales for the foreseeable future.

Until recently, Morris (USA) had followed a policy of financing its growth almost entirely from its own cash flow without resort to external borrowing. For subsidiaries operating in countries with high inflation rates and soft currencies, that policy had sometimes led to heavy foreign exchange losses, as reflected in Morris de Minas' profitability in years 1982 and 1983, when equity was by far the most significant source of the affiliate's funds (Exhibits C9-1 and C9-2). However, during the fall of 1983, in a move aimed at limiting exposure to exchange losses, Morris (USA) management had set new equity participation limits for all subsidiaries potentially subject to high foreign exchange risk. According to the new policy the parent company would commit equity capital to its Brazilian affiliate only to the extent of 20 percent of its present working capital needs. The implication was that Morris de Minas would have to obtain Cr$66,120 million from outside sources in this instance.

David Albuquerque, the vice-president of finance for the Latin American Division, was in charge of exploring possible financing arrangements and preparing a financing plan. Albuquerque realized that both the Brazilian expected inflation rate and tax legislation, as well as the future behavior of the exchange rate, would play major roles in his analysis. These were difficult to predict; nevertheless he regarded this as a good opportunity to stack up the company's financing choices against one another in a systematic fashion and perhaps also to give some thought to the total financial structure of the Brazilian subsidiary. . . .

THE FINANCING ALTERNATIVES

After a few phone calls to Brazil and discussions with financial officers of other multinational corporations operating under similar conditions, several options to meet the financing needs of Morris de Minas had emerged. In order to make his task easier, Albuquerque divided the alternatives into those not involving exchange risk and those doing so. Two options, a Eurodollar loan to Morris de Minas and the establishment of a financing subsidiary, fell into the latter category, while another, a back-to-back loan, bore only partial exchange risk. Albuquerque thought he should begin with two widely used financing techniques that involved no foreign exchange risk.

Discounting of Receivables at Brazilian Commerical Banks

Traditionally, the most prevalent form of short-term financing for a company such as Morris was to discount receivables, with recourse, at Brazilian commercial banks.

The normal range of terms on trade bill discounts was 30 to 120 days, although occasional 180-day operations were observed. The range of nominal rates was 9 to 11 percent per month, including a 0.125 percent tax on financial transactions, all of which would be tax deductible. However, with the prevailing practice of charging upfront commitment fees and requiring compensating balances of 25 to 35 percent, the effective rate was approximately 395 percent per annum. Given the fact that firms need some balances to back up their day-to-day operations, the effective rate of interest would be less because the actual required compensating balance was not quite as high as it seemed to be.

The major drawback with this method, however, was that local banks did not have an abundant supply of cruzeiros. Because of the tight monetary policy of the Brazilian government, both in the form of a 35 percent reserve require-ment and other restrictions on the use of demand deposit funds, commercial banks often had a limited amount of funds they could make available to a client for the discounting of receivables. Compounding the problem was the fact that foreign-owned subsidiaries in Brazil faced official restrictions on lending, since the Brazilian government reserved 75 percent of commercial bank loan portfolios for privately owned local firms, which forced foreign-owned com-panies to compete with state agencies for the remaining 25 percent of the domestic credit supply. As a result, firms with large sales volumes and large working capital needs, as in the Morris de Minas case, would find it extremely difficult, if not impossible, to set up such large discount lines, even considering the use of a large number of banks. Adding to this, Albuquerque felt that the local subsidiary should not enter into discount agreements with more than twenty local banks because of the complications that almost certainly would arise from this expedient. In consequence, he felt that the firm should not count on raising more than half the required amount in this manner.

It was also possible to discount Morris' receivables with recourse at local private finance companies, which were the normal sources of credit to con-sumers, and which were somewhat less constrained by government regula-tions.

Albuquerque's assistant had computed the cost of discounting the receiva-bles to be, on the average, approximately equal to 494 percent per annum. All of this cost would be deductible in computing profits subject to Brazilian corporate taxes, which for Morris de Minas would be approximately 45 per-cent.

Loan from Local Investment Banks

As another alternative without currency risk, the Brazilian subsidiary would borrow its cruzeiro requirement from local investment banks. The six-month investment bank loan rate was regarded as the Brazilian prime rate and was related to the banks' CD rate, which had a minimum term of six months, according to Central Bank regulations.

A legal rate control imposed by the Central Bank of Brazil prevented large banks from charging more than 20 percent per annum over monetary correc-tion on a six-month loan. Taking into account semiannual compounding, this came to 9.54 percent for six months. For small banks, the limit was 24 percent per annum. But as in other high-inflation countries, it was very difficult, if not impossible, to control interest rates in Brazil. Bankers were accustomed to living with interest rate controls and had quickly developed a number of ingenious ways to circumvent them on both CDs and term loans, such as discounts for CDs and commitment fees and/or compensating balances for loans. Thus the old trick of charging a commitment fee up front had become general practice in recent years. Although fees varied, the most common charge was 5 percent for a six-month loan. There was also an upfront financial transactions tax of 0.125 percent per month on principal plus interest. Therefore, in order to obtain 100 cruzeiros, for example, one would have to borrow approximately 106 cruzeiros. Albuquerque's assistant calculated this as follows:

$$
\begin{aligned}
\begin{matrix} \text{Borrowing} \\ \text{requirement} \\ \text{for Cr\$100} \end{matrix} &= \frac{100}{1 - \text{Upfront fee}\,(\%) - \text{Upfront taxes}\,(\%)} \\[2ex]
&= \frac{100}{1 - \text{Upfront fee}\,(\%) - (\text{Prin.} + \text{Interest}) \times \text{F.T. tax}} \\[2ex]
&= \frac{100}{1 - .05 - (1 + .0954) \times 6 \times .125/100} \\[2ex]
&= 106.18
\end{aligned}
$$

From this, the effective loan rate, before indexing, could be calculated by figuring that for each Cr$100 obtained, Morris would have to pay the 9.54 percent interest rate on Cr$106.18. This effective interest charge, plus the ORTN monetary correction, would be fully deductible in computing profits subject to Brazilian corporate taxes.

However, because of current tight local credit conditions, Morris might have to use a large number of banks, perhaps ten, to meet its working capital needs in full.

Resolution 63 Eurodollar Loan[8]

The first of the alternatives bearing currency risk would be a Eurodollar loan under Resolution 63 of the Central Bank of Brazil. In general, the cost of a six-month Resolution 63 loan included the six-month LIBOR (London Interbank Offered Rate), which in late August was quoted at 12.25 percent per annum, plus a spread of 2.25 percent per annum over LIBOR, plus an upfront local commission of 7 percent per annum, and plus an upfront tax (Financial Transactions Tax) of 0.25 percent on principal plus financial charges. The

---

[8]Resolution 63 loans were medium to long-term foreign currency credits extended by a foreign bank to a Brazilian bank, which passed them on to local borrowers, in cruzeiros, as foreign currency-denominated loans. As for all incoming foreign loans, the term and rate structure of Resolution 63 loans were regulated by the Central Bank of Brazil. In August 1984 these repass loans had a minimum term of three months, whereas the minimum term of credits granted by a foreign bank was eight years. While the Brazilian bank was liable for the foreign credit and bore the credit risk when it passed the funds on, the ultimate borrower, among other costs, assumed the foreign bank's credit charges and the exchange risk as well. The Central Bank of Brazil, however, assured that exchange was available when needed for paying off the loan.

remittance of interest on foreign loans was subject to an effective withholding tax of 20 percent of the sum of LIBOR plus any spread. Financial charges (including any foreign exchange losses) on Morris de Minas borrowing, however, were deductible in computing profits subject to the Brazilian corporate profits tax.

Back-to-Back Loan[9]

A second alternative involving minimal exchange risk was a back-to-back loan, also known as a cash-collateralized loan. The back-to-back loan was a financial arrangement between the Bank of Brazil and the United States parent company. Morris (USA) would make a dollar deposit equal to Morris de Minas' funds needs in the New York Branch of the Bank of Brazil. In return, the Brazilian bank would lend the countervalue in cruzeiros, at the prevailing exchange rate, to Morris de Minas.

At the maturity of the loan, the parent company's dollar funds would be returned simultaneously with the repayment of the loan in cruzeiros by the Brazilian subsidiary. The exchange risk would be borne by the Bank of Brazil, because the exchange rate of cruzeiros for dollars would remain the same both when the parent currency is converted for local lending and when it is returned to the parent at maturity.

The parent company's dollar deposit in New York would earn interest at the prevailing market rate of 11 percent per annum. On the other hand, the Bank of Brazil would charge an interest rate equivalent to 20 percent p.a. over indexing on the loan in cruzeiros. Interest and monetary correction on this cruzeiro loan to Morris de Minas would be tax deductible.

It was the Morris (USA) policy to charge 13 percent p.a. payable in dollars in all loans made to its subsidiaries. Since the back-to-back loan would tie up Morris dollar funds, a 13 percent interest charge per year, payable in dollars, would be required of Morris de Minas on the dollars deposited in New York. However, since the parent company would receive interest of 11 percent p.a. on its dollar deposit with the Bank of Brazil, the Brazilian affiliate would only be charged for the remaining 2 percent p.a. interest. This interest payment would not be tax deductible in Brazil because the dollar deposit was not loaned directly to Morris de Minas. In addition, it would be subject to a 20 percent withholding tax applied to all interest remittances on foreign loans.

Another alternative, possibly cheaper, would be a direct loan from the parent company, Morris (USA). In recent months Morris (USA) had made similar dollar-denominated loans to foreign subsidiaries at an interest rate of 13 percent p.a. However, Brazilian regulations stipulated a minimum term of eighteen months on such foreign loans made directly by foreign companies to its affiliates in Brazil, and there was no assurance that the foreign exchange would be

---

[9]This exchange financing technique is generally used, when possible, to extend financing to a company's affiliates in countries that have high interest rates and/or restricted capital markets.

available to repay the loan, or at what price. For this reason Albuquerque felt that a surcharge of perhaps 2 percent would have to be added to the rate normally charged for subsidiary loans.

A Window: Resolution 63 Loan with No Exchange Risk[10]

Yet another alternative was a variation on the Resolution 63 loan. In this type of financing, the Circular 767 of the Central Bank of Brazil allowed the lending bank to charge a fixed rate for the expected devaluation of the cruzeiro against the U.S. dollar as a part of the loan's cost. In practice this meant that the bank would charge a sort of "currency premium" in addition to monetary correction. Because the bank would substitute a fixed charge for the actual devaluation of the cruzeiro over the term of the loan, the foreign exchange risk was shifted away from the borrower towards the lending bank. Furthermore, reflecting the aggressive Brazilian foreign exchange policy of devaluating the cruzeiro at the same rate as inflation, which made unnecessary a one-shot maxidevaluation, the effective cost, including the premium, over monetary correction was as low as 20 percent per annum, compared with common cruzeiro denominated loans costing 35.3 percent per annum over monetary correction.

However, this window might not continue to be open for long because banks were getting increasingly concerned about the government policy toward inflation, devaluation, and monetary correction after the January 1985 presidential election. To use it, the firm would have to move quickly.

Establishing a Finance Company in Brazil[11]

The final alternative consisted of establishing a finance company (financeira) in Brazil to assure consumer sales financing. There were four types of finance companies operating in Brazil: financeiras pertaining to financial conglomerates, financeiras related to industrial groups, financeiras linked to retail groups,

---

[10]Financing Foreign Operations (FFO), "Brazil: Financial Update Bulletin", October 1984.

[11]Authorization for the establishment of finance companies in Brazil was granted by the federal government, through the Central Bank, via the issuance of a "carta patente" (registration certificate). Since no new cartas patente had been issued for a number of years, the market value of an existing registration certificate was very high. Assuming that Morris de Minas could find a registration certificate for sale in the Brazilian financial market, it would have to pay about US$3 million for it. Furthermore, because the foreign ownership of financial institutions was restricted and carefully supervised in Brazil, Morris de Minas would still have to get the necessary Central Bank approval of the purchase, what should only be expected if it could convince the Brazilian authorities that its entry would bring very expressive benefits to the financial market in general. The Central Bank's manner of thinking toward this issue could be inferred from its manifest preference to intervene in failed institutions, assuming their losses, but keeping their control in hands of nationals, or even to liquidate the institution rather than authorizing the transfer of their control to foreigners. Nevertheless, if the purchase of the registration certificate by Morris de Minas were carried out successfully, all of the US$3 million investment (plus capital gains if any, from the resale of the carta patente) would be repatriated when the finance company was eventually collapsed always assuming that the authorities would continue to allow such funds to be remitted.

and independent financeiras. All of them were subject to the same government regulations, which were fairly loose. They differed basically in terms of the market segment they attended. Funding was obtained through the issuance and sale of "letras de cambio"[12] in the money markets. However, contrary to the common practice, financing would have to be extended to consumers prior to the sale of the drafts in the market.

In a typical consumer sales financing transaction, the customer signs promissory notes and a credit contract with the finance company, which would pay cash directly to the seller. The finance company, then, would issue letras de cambio which would be sold to investors on the Brazilian money market, where such drafts were actively traded. Presently, six-month letras de cambio were being discounted at a rate equivalent to 295 percent per annum in Belo Horizonte.

Despite the minimum required investment of approximately U.S. $3 million in the proposed finance company, which would issue and guarantee the letras de cambio, it was felt that Morris might not be able to obtain the total amount of funds to attend its immediate working capital needs due to factors such as timing, and most important, legal constraints on the ratio "outstanding loans (and consequently, outstanding letras de cambio) to equity" of finance companies in Brazil. Since the company would exist on paper only, Albuquerque felt that the cost of running it would be minimal, apart from start-up legal expenses.

As usual, Morris de Minas would have to pay 13 percent p.a. to its U.S. parent for the investment in the finance company which would tie Morris (USA) funds. In addition, Morris de Minas would incur the cost related to the discounting of the letras de cambio. All these costs were assumed to be tax deductible, since the funds would be advanced to Brazilian corporations. As before, the remittance of interest on foreign loans would be subject to a withholding tax of 20 percent.

FINAL REMARKS

Having gathered all the background information needed to properly evaluate the various financing methods that had been identified, David Albuquerque began to work on his plan. He knew that anticipations about Brazilian inflation and its effects on the behavior of exchange rates would be the key variables in the choice of the appropriate financing strategy. But overall he wanted to make a recommendation that would meet the company's needs, enable Morris to overcome government and monetary regulations, and minimize costs and risks while leaving the door open to future Morris visits to the Brazilian money markets.

---

[12]A letra de cambio was a form of draft. It was an instrument in which the finance company promised to pay a certain sum of money to the bearer at a definite future time. In August 1984, the minimum term of a letra de cambio was six months. In general, letras de cambio were sold at a discount.

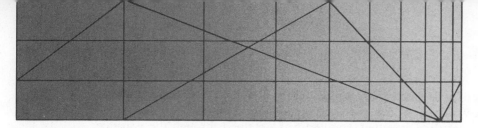

CHAPTER 10

PRODUCTION/SOURCING STRATEGY

Modernization involves a lot of things happening at once at the company's thirty plants around the globe. Old fashioned assembly lines and their large inventories of parts are being replaced with highly automated clusters or cells that produce components for final assembly. The company is "outsourcing" a lot of noncritical parts, such as sheet-metal stampings, to suppliers, finding that it can save a lot of money by shopping the world carefully for the lowest-cost providers. The main objective is to sharply cut inventory costs. This has to be done through advanced logistics, getting delivery of needed parts to the manufacturing cell "just-in-time," to quote the modern jargon. To make the entire world-wide process flow, a computerized network, using software still being improved, controls what is happening in company and supplier plants.

George Melloan

"Caterpillar Rides the Economic Policy Bumps," *The Wall Street Journal*, Tuesday, April 5, 1988, 26.

LEARNING OBJECTIVES

After studying the material in this chapter, the student should be familiar with the following concepts:

(1) Production/sourcing in international business

(2) The main components of a production/sourcing strategy

(3) Industrialization and the three industrial revolutions

(4) Lessons from industrialization experiences

(5) Types of global sourcing

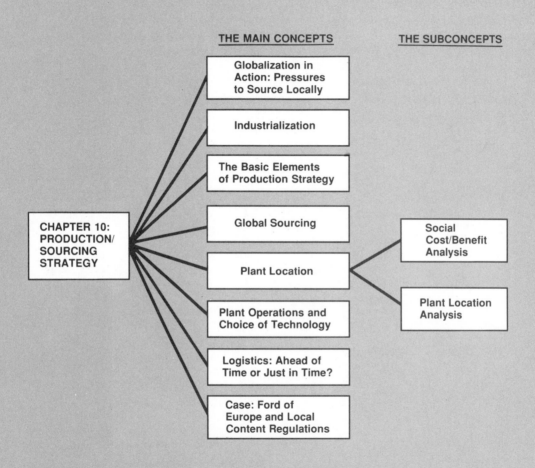

THE MAIN CONCEPTS

THE SUBCONCEPTS

CHAPTER 10: PRODUCTION/ SOURCING STRATEGY

Globalization in Action: Pressures to Source Locally

Industrialization

The Basic Elements of Production Strategy

Global Sourcing

Plant Location

Plant Operations and Choice of Technology

Logistics: Ahead of Time or Just in Time?

Case: Ford of Europe and Local Content Regulations

Social Cost/Benefit Analysis

Plant Location Analysis

(6)   International subcontracting

(7)   Social cost/benefit analysis in locating plants

(8)   International logistics

(9)   Just-in-time materials handling

(10)   Local content regulations

GLOBALIZATION IN ACTION
Pressures to Source Locally

Throughout the Third World, MNCs face growing pressures to source locally. In some cash-poor countries, they have no option if operations are to continue. Below, BI presents three cases where firms are meeting Nigeria's requirements in ways that may prove useful to others.

In a recent survey, BI's Africa Group found that, unless the government substantially increases imports, most manufacturers in Nigeria can run their plants at present low levels only until the end of the month. But Nigeria's 1985 budget actually calls for a 30% import cut.

For MNCs in Nigeria, there are three points to consider. First, those planning to continue operations can expect increasing pressure for local sourcing. Second, the government is planning to establish sector-by-sector local-sourcing targets within the next year, along with specific penalties for noncompliance. Third, most local-sourcing opportunities will be in agriculture and related industries. Nigeria offers tax incentives to promote investment in this sector; agro-industry imports also receive favored treatment. So what should companies do? Consider the following examples:

> Johnson Wax Nigeria Ltd. Insecticide represents a major portion of the company's business and, until recently, all raw materials were imported. Chukwuji Chizea, technical manager of the US subsidiary, notes that Johnson has invested heavily in both local and overseas R&D to develop local inputs. Chizea asserts that, without it, the company "couldn't have developed any local raw materials." The process requires "imagination, initiative and extensive local knowledge." One result: Johnson found it could use local propellent and so "adjusted the formula to fit this local material."
>
> The key imported element in insecticide is the active ingredient and, though used in very small quantities, it is the most expensive input. Chizea states, "If and when the petrochemical industry comes on stream, we may be able to find a synthetic active ingredient." But meanwhile, in conjunction with Nigerian universities, Johnson identified certain organic materials, mainly herbal, that have insecticidal properties and may be suitable local substitutes for the active ingredient. "However, prospects can only be long term."
>
> In another example, Johnson previously imported HTH (high-test hypochloride) to get chlorine for bleach, but thought that with some adjustment to the processing procedure it could make the bleach from salt. The company found a local salt lake and was prepared to set up an extraction process. However, Nigeria started a salt factory, which will meet Johnson Wax's local salt needs.

SOURCE: Business International Corporation, *101 More Checklists* (New York: BCI, 1985), 47. Reprinted by permission of Business International, Inc.

Union Carbide. This Connecticut-based firm, which has 46 battery plants worldwide, including six in Africa (Egypt, the Sudan, Kenya, the Ivory Coast, Nigeria, Ghana), actively pushes local content in its medium-tech production to cut costs. In their annual planning submissions, Union Carbide requires plants to provide an "operational improvement program" that addresses ways to increase both local and regional content. In Nigeria, for instance, it actively seeks ways to complete more production steps at the plant.

Recently, it cut imports by increasing the production stages of semifinished supplies that go into its battery manufacture. In addition to exploring useable local inputs, Union Carbide uses regionally available supplies, such as manganese from adjacent Ghana, if they meet quality standards. Oswald K. Weaver, treasurer of Union Carbide Africa & Middle East Inc., asserts: "More needs to be done to aggressively search out available local raw materials, even though it may involve additional processing to reach an appropriate quality control level."

Texaco Agro-Industrial (Nigeria) Ltd. Texagri produces and processes cassava into gari, a local staple food. The company considered buying on the local market, but not only would this have defeated the company's aims of helping Nigerian agriculture, it also gave no assurance of sufficient supply. Texagri now runs its own plantation. E. I. Nwizu, general manager of Texaco (Nigeria) and director of Texagri, states that the processing plant now produces around seven tons of gari per day. "About 70% of this goes to Texaco's service stations and 30% to the open market. To an extent," he continues, "this controls the price of our product to the final consumer and also ensures a wide distribution."

OVERVIEW

The previous three chapters described how managers of an MNC choose a mode of entry to the international market (Chapter 7) and then design the appropriate organizational structure (Chapter 8) and financial strategy (Chapter 9). At that point the MNC is ready to begin its main function: transforming raw materials into marketable products. This process is called *production*.

The aim of the present chapter is to study the process of securing the necessary inputs to the production process and delivering the resulting outputs to the marketplace. The production strategy–setting process goes beyond the customary function of the production department. Thus it would be more appropriate to call the production strategy the "supply strategy," as some authors do. The term "supply strategy," however, has recently acquired a specific meaning because of the Reagan administration's economic policy, known as "supply side economics." For this reason the more conventional term "production strategy" will be used here.

Issues addressed in the production strategy–setting process range from sourcing and subcontracting for parts and components to distributing the final products to the world markets. In between these two basic functions of providing for input acquisition and output delivery are the tasks of determining plant location, plant layout, and plant operations. Thus, the main function of the international production department of an MNC is to organize and coordinate the production functions of all of its plants around the globe so as to guarantee a worldwide supply of the goods and/or services that the MNC has contracted to deliver.

INTRODUCTION

The decision to produce overseas is dictated by pressures from the external environment as well as from within the organization itself. Most governments around the globe would rather a foreign investor acquire a local factory or set up a new one than open a sales office or a distribution center. Factories create "visible" employment and revenues, which can be used by politicians as evidence of the success of their policies. At the micro level, the firm's evolution dictates that at some time it must seek gains somewhere outside its immediate and original market. As we have seen, products tend to follow a life cycle; an MNC can postpone the decline of a product by having it "migrate" to a new environment. Products that have reached the mature stage at home can be "reborn" in a country where demand is sufficient to justify local production.

The existence of both external and internal pressures to move overseas is a necessary condition for overseas production. It is by no means sufficient, however. First, the firm's management must identify viable production opportunities abroad; second, management must possess the necessary attitude and know-how to take advantage of these opportunities. The firm must have a competitive advantage both in its product or technology and in its managerial know-how.

The first task in understanding the widely studied and discussed phenomenon of international production is to examine the role of the MNC in industrialization, a process that accomplishes the nation-state's goal of economic growth, and the role of the nation-state in international production, a means of accomplishing the MNC's goal of profit-making and capital accumulation (growth). Once the mutual interdependence of the MNC and the nation-state has been considered, the emphasis will shift to the production strategy per se. As noted, in international business, the production function encompasses much more than is conventionally implied by the term. In addition to the traditional process of manufacturing (that is, making usable things out of resources), production strategy incorporates the entire range of activities that must be performed in order to secure inputs for the manufacturing process and deliver the resulting outputs to appropriate markets.

Exhibit 10-1 shows the main elements of a production strategy. The factory is the place where the transformation process takes place. The greater the number of items produced, the lower the production cost. The factory does not necessarily have to belong to the MNC. The MNC may subcontract to

Exhibit 10-1   The Main Components of a Production Strategy

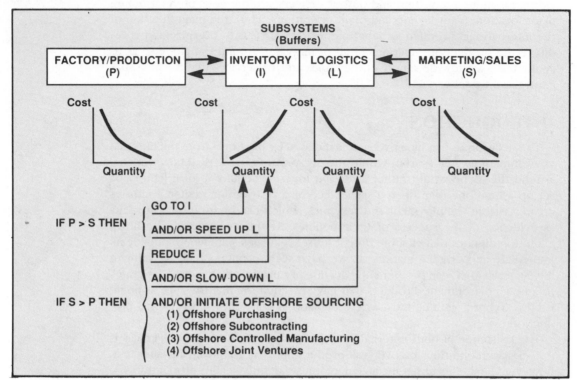

Adding to or depleting inventory (I) and speeding up or slowing down logistics (L) entail costs. These costs, however, pale in comparison to the costs of erratically increasing the capacity of the production system (P) by acquiring or constructing plants or decreasing it by selling or closing down plants. The same reasoning applies to minimizing sales losses via better management of the logistics buffer.

another company a portion of the production process or even the entire process. Or a subsidiary of an MNC may contract with another affiliate or with the MNC to do some of its production through a so-called sourcing contract.

The market is the place where buyers and sellers meet to exchange their goods and services. The marketing department of an MNC operates under the same principle as does the production department. Usually, but not always, the more efficient the marketing department is, the more it sells and the more quickly it sells it. Thus the marketing department would like always to have readily available quantities to sell.

The quantities of the product needed by the marketing department are procured through the inventory subsystem and delivered through the logistics subsystem. When quantities produced by the production department (the factory) cannot be sold quickly by the marketing department, they are temporarily put into the inventory subsystem. The functioning of the logistics subsystem can be slowed down or speeded up so as to accommodate the marketing department without frequent or unexpected jolts to the production line. The inventory and logistics subsystems thus act as buffers within the system.

Recognizing the importance of a continuous production line and large production runs, the Japanese have created a network of warehouses around the globe from which they feed their assembly plants and final markets. Since production interruptions can cause large set-up costs and delays, and since warehousing inventories in Japan is an expensive affair, given the skyrocketing cost of land and buildings, big Japanese trading companies regularly use ships, airplanes, port facilities, and free trade zones to guarantee an uninterrupted production process at home.

In sum, an international production strategy must provide answers to the following questions:

(1)   From where should the firm supply the target market?

(2)   To what extent should the firm *itself* undertake production (degree of integration)?

(3)   What and where should it buy from others?

(4)   Assuming that a firm opts to do at least some manufacturing, how should it acquire facilities?

(5)   Should the firm produce in one plant or in many? Should the plants be related or autonomous?

(6)   What sort of production equipment (technology) should the company use?

(7)   What site is best?

(8)   Where should research and development be located?[1]

This chapter begins with a macro view of the subject of industrialization: its meaning, status, forms, shifts, and future prospects. Subsequently, the chapter switches to a micro view, examining the various tasks that a manager must perform in setting up an international production strategy. The overriding objective of an international production strategy is to guarantee worldwide organization and coordination of an MNC's affiliates' production plans so as to ensure a steady growth in profits.

INDUSTRIALIZATION

Industrialization is the process of creating wealth via the transformation of primary products, such as agricultural products and minerals, into marketable

---

[1]R. D. Robinson, *Internationalization of Business: An Introduction* (Chicago: Dryden Press, 1984), 58.

Exhibit 10-2   The Three Industrial Revolutions

First (1820–1870)	Second (1870–1913)	Third (1950–)
Scientific inventions and agricultural applications	Scientific inventions and commercial applications	Scientific inventions and commercial applications
(1) Increased productivity in agriculture	(1) Increased productivity in industry	(1) Increased productivity in services/ information
(2) Raised income, creating demand for industrial products, which triggered industrial development	(2) Raised income, creating demand for services, which triggered the creation of the service industry	(2) Raised income, creating demand for leisure, which triggered the birth of the leisure and information industry
(3) Freed labor (a) Unskilled (b) Women (c) Skilled (d) Clerical	(3) Freed labor (a) Those with low skills (b) Women (c) Professionals	(3) Freed labor (a) Skilled (b) Women
which moved to big urban centers and fed the factories	which moved to big urban centers and fed the offices	which moved to rural and big urban financial centers and fed the information/leisure business

SOURCE: The World Bank, *World Development Report, 1987* (New York: Oxford University Press, 1987), 38–50.

products. Although industry, broadly defined, includes manufacturing, mining, construction, the production of electricity, and the supplying of gas and water, this chapter focuses on manufacturing—the largest and most volatile industrial sector.[2]

Industrial developments usually follow scientific discoveries. By applying these discoveries to satisfy human needs, humans are able to do more with less. When the industrial application of scientific discoveries reaches the point of affecting life to a large degree, an industrial revolution is said to have occurred. Thus far, humanity has undergone three industrial revolutions (see Exhibit 10-2).

---

[2]The World Bank, *World Development Report, 1987* (New York: Oxford University Press, 1987).

The First Industrial Revolution started in Britain early in the nineteenth century, when innovations in the processes of spinning and weaving cotton greatly boosted productivity and output. This revolution is erroneously attributed to the introduction of machinery. The true source of the increases in productivity and output, however, was the emphasis on Adam Smith's principles of specialization and division of labor. Scientific discoveries in physics (such as the steam engine, which sparked the transport and mechanization revolution) came later. The First Industrial Revolution is generally defined as the period between 1820 and 1870.

The Second Industrial Revolution spanned the years from 1870 to 1913. During that time technological advances became more dependent on scientific research conducted by firms and universities specifically for commercial application. Germany (which was at the time a unified country) and later the United States led the way. The revolution focused primarily on the production of consumer goods, demand for which was fueled by the increase in liquidity (disposable income) created by the increase in productivity in the agricultural sector. Fed with supplies from overseas, the Second Industrial Revolution created two worlds: the industrial league, made up of the countries engaged in heavy industrial production, and the suppliers of raw materials, consisting primarily of the colonies of European countries and the United States.

The fifties ushered in a new era of industrialization. Postwar reconstruction and growth in manufacturing were fueled by an explosion of new products and new technologies, liberalization of international trade, and increasing integration of the world economy. This Third Industrial Revolution, which began with mass assembly, synthetic raw materials, nuclear energy, jet aircraft, and electronic devices for entertainment and business use, is currently reaching a climax with supersonic travel, superspeed computers, and superconductive processes. By creating an electronic network that provides instant connectedness, the Third Industrial Revolution has led to the globalization of industrialization. Now the world is divided into two types of manufacturing industries: the so-called traditional industries and the high-technology industries.[3]

The traditional industries have generally been associated with fairly labor-intensive technologies. Because of the low wage rates in the Third World and the relatively low cost of establishing facilities, these industries have been on the leading edge of export manufacturing in developing countries.

The high-tech industries, on the other hand, depend on access to the specialized resources required for research and development and for highly complex production processes. These industries have therefore been located in the industrial countries. As products mature, technology diffuses and production moves to more competitive locations abroad. (This phenomenon corresponds to the product-cycle theory of international trade first advanced by Raymond Vernon in 1966.)

---

[3]Joseph Grunwald and Kenneth Flamm, *The Global Factory: Foreign Assembly in International Trade* (Washington, DC: The Brookings Institution, 1985).

Three main developments have marked the pattern of global industrialization in the postwar period:

(1)   The appearance of a nonmarket alternative to industrialization—a service and information industry—in Eastern Europe and elsewhere

(2)   Decolonization in Asia, Africa, and the Caribbean

(3)   The rise to prominence of the multinational corporation in world production and trade of manufactured items

The last four decades of experience with industrialization have taught the world some very important lessons. It is imperative that the student of international business and the international manager understand these lessons well, for they represent the canvas on which the tapestry of international production strategy is woven (see Exhibit 10-3).

Exhibit 10-3   Lessons from Industrialization Experiences

What are the lessons to be drawn from experiences of countries that have followed a successful path to industrialization?

(1)   Initial Conditions. A country with a large domestic market is in a better position to establish industrial plants that take advantage of the economies of scale. A larger *geographical size* and large *population* can, together, produce a large domestic market, unless *agricultural productivity* is exceptionally low. A rich endowment of natural resources may provide a country with the financial resources to import technology and with the high incomes to support a large domestic market for industrial products.

(2)   Domestic and Foreign Trade Policies. Many of the countries that industrialized successfully in the nineteenth century first acquired technology through imports, then rapidly moved to producing manufactures for export. Policies that allowed opportunities on foreign markets to be communicated to domestic producers, that allowed domestic resources to move freely in response to the opportunities, and that complemented existing resources through education, training, and infrastructure all contributed to the success.

(3)   Education, Skills, and Technology Adaptation. The transition from a primarily agricultural and trading economy to an industrial economy has required, at least in the initial stages, an increase in the skills of the labor force. To use foreign technology effectively, producers must examine the choices available, make intelligent selections, and adapt them to local conditions. All of this calls for education.

(4) Transportation and Communication Networks. One of the better known aspects of nineteenth century industrialization is the importance of railways. Transportation and communications networks integrated and expanded domestic markets and increased their efficiency. They also integrated domestic markets into the global economy, making it easier for exporters to compete. But transportation and communication networks are capital-intensive, and therefore expensive, especially during the early stages of industrialization.

(5) Stable Institutional and Macroeconomic Policies. Laws and institutions that allow markets to function efficiently—property rights, standardized weights and measures, patent laws and so forth—have helped to promote rapid and efficient industrialization. Laws and institutions should provide a stable environment that promotes long-term investments and risk taking. Yet they should also be flexible enough to allow institutional innovations. Industrialization requires large investments in machines and infrastructure, especially in its early stages. Macroeconomic policies in the countries industrializing in the nineteenth century encouraged domestic savings.

SOURCE: The World Bank, *World Development Report, 1987*, pp. 54–57.

THE BASIC ELEMENTS OF PRODUCTION STRATEGY

The post–World War II era witnessed a decline in the role of the production department. Management in the United States was guided by the marketing function. European scholars attributed the tremendous success of U.S. MNCs to their marketing orientation, which they contrasted to the traditional European production orientation. U.S. MNCs, they asserted, produced "what the market wanted," whereas the Europeans, primarily the Germans, "marketed what they produced."

Recently this attitude toward production has come under severe attack. Wickham Skinner, a leading authority on production management, summarizes the situation as follows:

> Part of the problem can be traced back to the time manufacturing managers were ousted from the corporate hierarchy. Starting about 1960, demoralization and discouragement gradually grew in the manufacturing world. Manufacturing managers were not in the top echelons of their companies; they were not in the key strategic planning cycles; they were left out, discouraged, and our plants got older. Now, after all these years, we are turning back to our manufacturing people and saying, "We're

SOURCE: Danziger in The Christian Science Monitor © 1987 TCSPS.

sorry we forgot you for so long; sorry we listened to Professor Galbraith at Harvard, who said in 1958 that our productivity problems were over; sorry we listened to some of my colleagues in 1960 who said, 'Don't mess with manufacturing—there's no intellectual talent left there. We've solved the problems of manufacturing.'" Now, we're turning back to manufacturing managers and saying, "We need you to turn things around, to improve quality, to speed up product development, to invest in the right equipment. We'll write blank checks for whatever you want."[4]

Currently, MNCs are trying to improve productivity by designing production strategies based on General Electric's 40-40-20 rule. According to this rule, only 20% of the total improvement in the productivity of production processes will come from cost-cutting techniques, efficiency improvements, and getting

---

[4]Wickham Skinner, "A Strategy for Competitive Manufacturing," *Management Review*, August 1987, 54–56.

more out of the labor force. Another 40% will be the result of changes in technology, equipment, and processes, and the remaining 40% will come from changes in manufacturing strategy. One of the most promising of the possible changes in manufacturing strategy is a switch to **global sourcing**—buying or making parts or products in foreign countries.

GLOBAL SOURCING

The basic decision that management must make when contemplating global sourcing is the so-called buy vs. make decision. Should the firm buy the product from another company, or should it make the product itself, in an offshore plant acquired or built by the company?

For global corporations the buy vs. make decision is not a simple either/or proposition. In general, an MNC has a far greater range of alternatives to choose from than does a domestic company or a small international company.

Exhibit 10-4 provides a simplified picture of the numerous connections among the main actors in the global business game. As has been pointed out, the systems approach dictates that the study of the functions of a global company focus on the relationships between the firm and its external environment. Thus the two main systems depicted in Exhibit 10-4—the private sector (firms) and the public sector (nation-states)—each include subsystems. The private sector's subsystems are the MNCs and national firms (NFs). The public sector consists of state-owned enterprises (SOEs) and mixed firms (MFs), which have a mixture of public-sector and private-sector equity. Business transactions among NFs, MFs, and SOEs fall into the category of national transactions or within-border transactions and therefore are not dealt with here. Business transactions between MNCs and the three other types of enterprises are international transactions and are the subject of this chapter. As Exhibit 10-4 shows, an MNC interacts with the other three actors both directly and via its affiliates (shown at the bottom of the figure).

The basic decision of a production management team as to whether to buy or make determines the basic nature of the global sourcing arrangement—equity or nonequity.

(1) Nonequity arrangements include

    (a) Offshore purchasing

    (b) Offshore international subcontracting

(2) Equity arrangements include

    (a) Offshore joint-venture manufacturing

    (b) Controlled offshore manufacturing

Exhibit 10-5 depicts the most widely used forms of international sourcing.

The version of global sourcing most often reported by the professional

Exhibit 10-4   The Main Actors in Global Business

Transactions	Arm's-Length Transactions (ALT)	Exports – Imports (X – M)	Contractual Arrangements (CA)	Joint Ventures (JV)	Subcontracting (SUBC)	Sourcing
Between two MNCs or between an MNC and an NF, MF, or SOE	X	X	X	X	X	
Between an MNC and one or more of its affiliates		X	X	X		X
Between an affiliate and an NF, MF, or SOE	X	X	X	X	X	
Interaffiliate	X	X	X	X		X

business periodicals is offshore purchasing. Buying parts somewhere abroad is very popular with big manufacturing companies such as Ford and General Motors. Japanese Sogoshoshas introduced American buying groups to this practice, which has been largely responsible for elevating the countries of Singapore, Taiwan, Hong Kong, and South Korea to the status of newly industrialized

Exhibit 10-5   Basic Forms of Global Sourcing

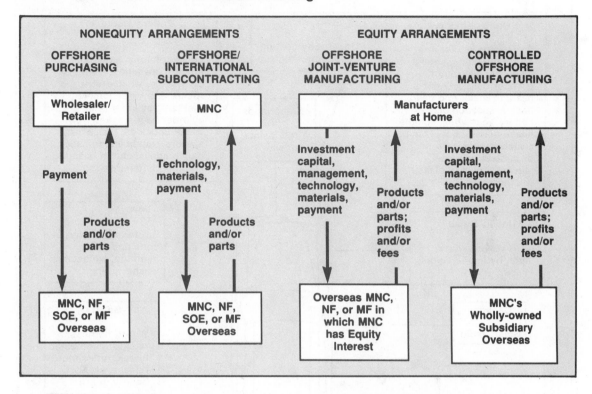

countries (NICs). Since this type of international business transaction is an arm's-length transaction, it will not be further treated here. Exhibit 10-6 shows where Ford purchases the various parts for the European Escort.

The two types of global sourcing currently at the forefront of academic, government, and management attention are offshore subcontracting and controlled offshore manufacturing. Offshore, or international, subcontracting is viewed by most government officials as the best way to develop indigenous industry without substantial long-term borrowing from abroad. Controlled offshore manufacturing is considered by MNC management as the best means of smoothing or rationalizing global production and by governments as the best way of keeping labor from migrating to other countries. The intermediate strategy of offshore joint-venture manufacturing offers some of the advantages of each of the other strategies.

The United Nations and most national governments pay considerable attention to international subcontracting because of its importance to national firms in developing countries and to small businesses in developed countries. The United Nations distinguishes between two main types of international subcontracting: industrial and commercial. This distinction is based on the general classification of goods into industrial products (such as parts and components), which are used for further processing, and commercial products, which are ready for final consumption.

Exhibit 10-6 Global Manufacturing: The Component Network for the Ford Escort (Europe)

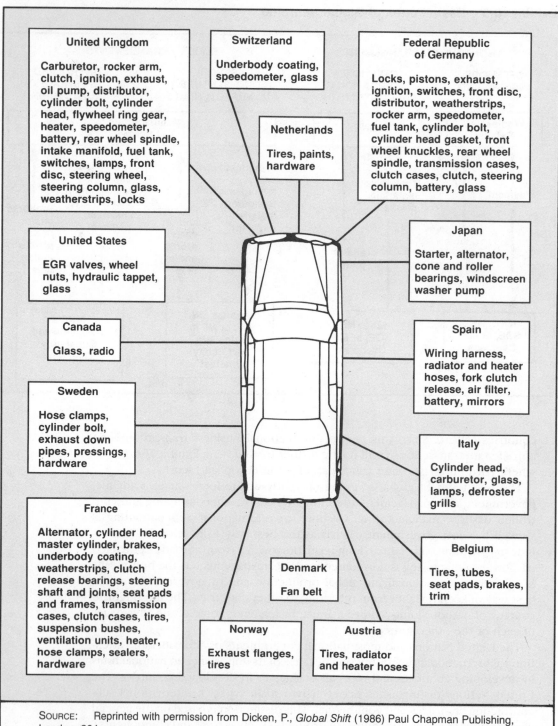

United Kingdom

Carburetor, rocker arm, clutch, ignition, exhaust, oil pump, distributor, cylinder bolt, cylinder head, flywheel ring gear, heater, speedometer, battery, rear wheel spindle, intake manifold, fuel tank, switches, lamps, front disc, steering wheel, steering column, glass, weatherstrips, locks

Switzerland

Underbody coating, speedometer, glass

Federal Republic of Germany

Locks, pistons, exhaust, ignition, switches, front disc, distributor, weatherstrips, rocker arm, speedometer, fuel tank, cylinder bolt, cylinder head gasket, front wheel knuckles, rear wheel spindle, transmission cases, clutch cases, clutch, steering column, battery, glass

Netherlands

Tires, paints, hardware

United States

EGR valves, wheel nuts, hydraulic tappet, glass

Japan

Starter, alternator, cone and roller bearings, windscreen washer pump

Canada

Glass, radio

Spain

Wiring harness, radiator and heater hoses, fork clutch release, air filter, battery, mirrors

Sweden

Hose clamps, cylinder bolt, exhaust down pipes, pressings, hardware

Italy

Cylinder head, carburetor, glass, lamps, defroster grills

France

Alternator, cylinder head, master cylinder, brakes, underbody coating, weatherstrips, clutch release bearings, steering shaft and joints, seat pads and frames, transmission cases, clutch cases, tires, suspension bushes, ventilation units, heater, hose clamps, sealers, hardware

Denmark

Fan belt

Belgium

Tires, tubes, seat pads, brakes, trim

Norway

Exhaust flanges, tires

Austria

Tires, radiator and heater hoses

SOURCE: Reprinted with permission from Dicken, P., *Global Shift* (1986) Paul Chapman Publishing, London, 304.

The United Nations' Industrial Development Organization (UNIDO) definition of subcontracting applies essentially to industrial subcontracting.

> A subcontracting relationship exists when a firm (the principal) places an order with another firm (the subcontractor) for the manufacture of parts, components, subassemblies or assemblies to be incorporated into a product which the principal will sell. Such orders may include the treatment, processing or finishing of materials or parts by the subcontractor at the principal's request.[5]

Subcontracting is a kind of halfway point between engaging in arm's-length transactions on the open market and setting up brick and mortar facilities in each market. It offers the obvious advantage of a low fixed investment. In addition, perhaps its greatest advantage is the degree of flexibility or maneuverability it offers. Usually, but not always, there is a dependent relationship between the initiating company and the subcontractor. Particularly where one large firm subcontracts to several small firms, the small subcontractors may perform the "shock-absorbing," or buffering, function described at the beginning of the chapter. By using small subcontractors instead of warehousing raw material and final products, a large firm can externalize some of the risks involved in buying large quantities of raw materials and components and carrying large inventories of finished products. As small business advocates and United Nations officials point out, from the MNC's point of view small subcontractors are "expandable and expendable."[6]

Exhibit 10-7 presents a picture of a hypothetical company's global sourcing relationships. A U.S. computer manufacturer in Los Angeles, COMPLA, INC., receives the next quarter's sales forecast from its sales office, NLCO, in Amsterdam, calling for 150,000 computers. This transaction, labeled #1, is an international transaction of the arm's-length type. COMPLA subcontracts to the Atlanta-based company ATLBRD, Inc. the supplying of 150,000 main boards (transaction #2, domestic subcontracting). ATLBRD subcontracts to a Taiwanese board manufacturer, TWANG Ltd., the production of 150,000 boards (transaction #3, international subcontracting).

The 150,000 boards are distributed from Taiwan as follows: 50,000 boards are shipped to COMPLA's joint-venture subsidiary in Brazil, COMPLABZ, S.A., for assembly (transaction #4, offshore joint-venture manufacturing equity arrangements); 50,000 are shipped to COMPLA's wholly owned subsidiary in Hong Kong, COMPLAHG, Ltd., to be assembled into final products (transaction #5, international sourcing); the remaining 50,000 boards are shipped to COMPLA's across-the-border maquiladora in Mexico, COMPLAMEX, S.A. (transaction #6, international sourcing).

---

[5]Dimitri Germidis, *International Subcontracting: A New Form of Investment* (Paris: OECD, 1980), 13–15.

[6]Peter Dicken, *Global Shift: Industrial Change in a Turbulent World* (New York: Harper and Row, 1986), 189.

Exhibit 10-7 Hypothetical Global Sourcing Transactions

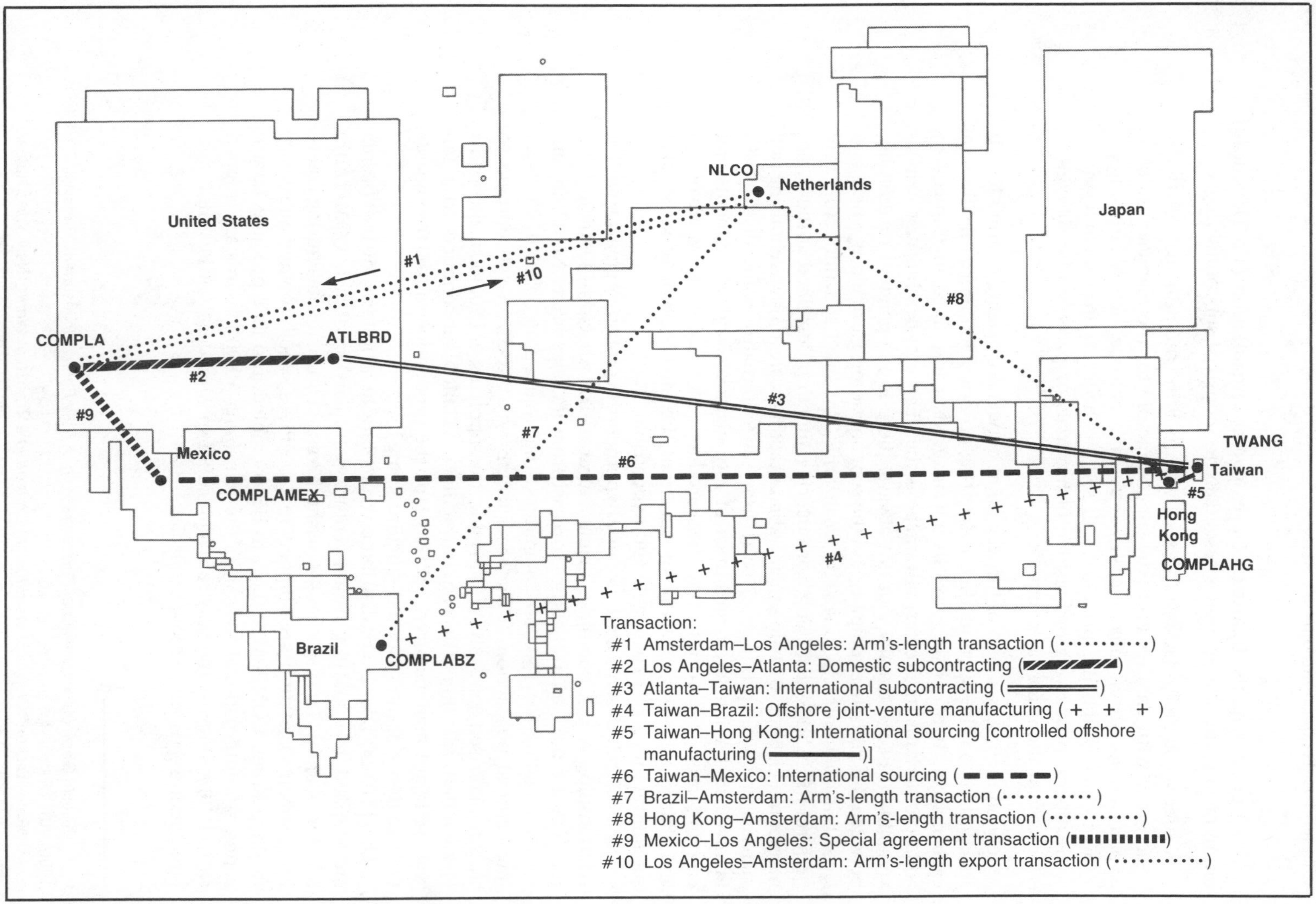

Transaction:

#1 Amsterdam–Los Angeles: Arm's-length transaction (·········)
#2 Los Angeles–Atlanta: Domestic subcontracting (▨▨▨▨)
#3 Atlanta–Taiwan: International subcontracting (━━━━)
#4 Taiwan–Brazil: Offshore joint-venture manufacturing (+ + +)
#5 Taiwan–Hong Kong: International sourcing [controlled offshore manufacturing (━━━━)]
#6 Taiwan–Mexico: International sourcing (━ ━ ━)
#7 Brazil–Amsterdam: Arm's-length transaction (·········)
#8 Hong Kong–Amsterdam: Arm's-length transaction (·········)
#9 Mexico–Los Angeles: Special agreement transaction (▮▮▮▮)
#10 Los Angeles–Amsterdam: Arm's-length export transaction (·········)

The finished computers are supplied to the Amsterdam COMPLA's sales office as follows: Brazil ships 50,000 computers directly to Amsterdam (transaction #7, arm's-length export transaction); Hong Kong ships 50,000 computers to Amsterdam (transaction #8, arm's-length export transaction); the remaining 50,000 computers produced by COMPLAMEX are reexported from Mexico into the United States (transaction #9, maquiladora 406-407 U.S.-Mexico, a special agreement transaction) and exported to the Netherlands (transaction #10, arm's-length export transaction).

PLANT LOCATION

Direct foreign investment—investment in land, plants, and equipment—is the most serious foreign entry strategy. From the nation-state's viewpoint, factories bring jobs, which create incomes. When spent by the local population, this money creates more jobs, and when saved, it creates the capital pool needed for further industrialization. In addition, the investing company brings technology, which is made available to indigenous companies. From the MNC's viewpoint, brick and mortar investment is the best global sourcing strategy. An affiliate overseas can not only secure most of the needed inputs but also dispose of some, if not most, of its output. Furthermore, an overseas factory provides opportunities to generate further revenues from obsolete technology and products.

On the surface it would seem that both the MNC and the nation-state would find plant construction extremely attractive. Both national authorities and MNC managers, however, must convince themselves that this arrangement is indeed a win-win situation. Both must perform some type of cost/benefit analysis and must end up with more benefits than costs.

Thus far it seems that for host nation-states, direct investment by foreign firms is in fact beneficial. For this reason, there is currently a global competition among governments of the world for potential investors. Offering generous incentives to lure MNCs to their country used to be a tactic of developing countries. Recently, however, countries that traditionally have been investors have become the greatest competitors for MNC investment. For example, the United States and Britain, two of the largest investors in the world, are competing for investment by Japanese manufacturing companies. The competition has become so intense that the OECD and the European Economic Community (EEC) have issued guidelines on how many and what kinds of incentives a country can offer to lure an investor. The EEC has even set up an agency that monitors and enforces these guidelines, giving punitive sentences to violators.[7] (See Exhibit 10-8.)

---

[7]*International Investment and Multinational Enterprise: Investment Incentives and Disincentives* (Paris: OECD, 1983).

Exhibit 10-8   Brussels Set to Drop Daimler Inquiry

The European Commission is today expected to call off a controversial investigation into state aid for a DM 1.8 billion car plant to be built by Daimler-Benz, the West German motor manufacturer.

This will end what has been an embarrassing episode for the West German Government, ironically known as a tough campaigner for ending national industrial subsidies. The Commission opened proceedings against Bonn last autumn under EC competition rules outlawing national aid likely to give its recipients unfair advantages over Community competitors.

It suspected that the Rastatt and Baden-Wuerttenberg authorities were planning to sell the site to the car group for between DM 170 million and DM 200 million below market value. It also questioned whether the state government's proposal to spend DM 100 million on preparing the site—an area of open farmland partly owned by the Rastatt town authorities and unsuitable for industrial use in its present form—for Daimler-Benz.

The new package, details of which should be released today, is understood to allow the state authorities to pay 80 percent of the cost of preparing infrastructure for the site—such as gas and water supplies—leaving it up to Daimler-Benz to pay for the foundations and the rest of the construction.

Theoretically, the Commission can block illicit national assistance or force companies to repay aid—a power which it has used several times in the past year. Because of the investigation, the car group cannot start building the plant until it receives the green light from Brussels. Construction is due to start next summer and lead to the creation of 7,000 jobs.

SOURCE: W. Dawkins, "Brussels Set to Drop Daimler Inquiry," *Financial Times*, July 22, 1987, 26.

SOCIAL COST/BENEFIT ANALYSIS

Although industrialization has enough benefits that an MNC's decision to invest in a country may be welcome right from the start, often the MNC manager must assist government officials in their effort to prove that the benefits of the proposed plant location outweigh the costs. Thus it is imperative that the manager understand the way host governments evaluate MNC proposals.

The cost/benefit evaluation framework developed by Vernon and Wells will be briefly explained here.[8]

---

[8]R. Vernon and L. Wells, *Manager in the International Economy* (Englewood Cliffs, NJ: Prentice-Hall, 1986).

As applied by governments, project evaluation is intended to help analysts determine whether the real value of a project's output is greater than the real value of its inputs. The key to this three-step process is to value the outputs and inputs at undistorted prices.

Step A: Estimate the value of the project's output to the economy. This value can be thought of as the cost of acquiring the output, usually from abroad, in the absence of the proposed facility.

Step B: Estimate the value of the project's inputs. This value is the total of the values of labor (L), capital (C), and material (M) that will be used by the plant.

Step C: Estimate the value of the project's externalities. This value reflects the costs and benefits of the project that are not captured in the economy's normal national statistical records.

Exhibit 10-9 presents Vernon and Wells's summary of the four basic methods used by governments in evaluating proposals. The World Bank and the United Nations have developed their own methods, which are too detailed to be treated here.

PLANT LOCATION ANALYSIS

Subsidiary managers like to have a plant as close as possible to the markets they serve. Nearby factories offer many benefits, such as delivery flexibility, government support, and freedom from trade and/or exchange restrictions. On the other hand, the size of the market, the technology, the quantity of raw materials and skilled labor available, and the general quality of the infrastructure in the host country might not justify the construction of a plant of a size sufficient to offer the necessary economies of scale. An MNC wishes to avoid what is called a "miniature replica effect"—too many plants, none of world scale.[9]

Each firm knows that there are considerable advantages to be gained by the first firm to make the move. Government incentives will be more generous as the host country struggles to develop a new industry. Latecomers must work hard to overcome the leader's cutthroat prices and cost-of-entry strategies. The follower must deal with smaller market shares, rising entry costs, and fewer government incentives, all of which work to the benefit of the leader. As managers know, however, premature plant construction can prove as fatal as late arrival.

There are no foolproof techniques for determining the right time to build a plant at a given location. Trying to anticipate the competitor's move is, of course, the essence of managerial life. There are some sources of information, however, that may provide a manager with some hints as to what the com-

---

[9]D. Rutenberg, *Multinational Management* (Boston: Little, Brown and Co., 1982), 128.

Exhibit 10-9   Principal Forms of Social Profitability Calculations

Method	Formula	Test
I. Social return (SOR)	Social benefits *minus* social costs for inputs other than capital, *divided* by relevant amount of capital	Should exceed the yield that the capital would bring in alternative uses
SOR =	$(SB - SC)/RAC$	> Alternative yields
II. Net benefits (NB)	Social benefits *minus* social costs for all inputs	Should exceed zero
NB =	$SB - SC_{inputs}$	> 0
III. Benefits/costs ratio (B/C)	Social benefits *divided* by social costs for all inputs	Should exceed one
B/C =	SB/SC	> 1
IV. Implicit exchange rate (E)	Social costs for all local inputs, denominated in local currency, *divided* by the difference between social benefits of the project and the social costs of all foreign inputs, both denominated in foreign currency	Should be equal to or better than a "shadow exchange rate," that is, a rate that the analysts believe reflects the value to the economy of an additional dollar of foreign exchange
E =	$SCI_{LC}/(SB_{FC} - SC_{FC})$	$\geq$ Shadow exchange rate

SOURCE: Raymond Vernon/Louis T. Wells, *Manager in the International Economy,* © 1986, p. 110. Reprinted by permission of Prentice-Hall, Inc., Englewood Cliffs, New Jersey.

petition is up to. U.S. firms that wish to expand abroad must file certain reports with the Department of Commerce, the Department of the Treasury, and the Department of Justice. Thus a search through the files of these offices will often prove beneficial. Shipments of products and technologies thought to be vital to national security are monitored by the Department of Commerce. Other business activities such as capital transfers, distribution of dividends, and accumulation of income are monitored by the Department of the Treasury and the IRS for their impact on money transfers. The Department of Justice monitors foreign payments and potential antitrust violations.

Large multinational banks and insurance companies are also good sources of information, as are potential host governments, which generally require that firms intending to invest in that country register their plans with a government office or offices. The firms most likely to engage in plant construction are those that have had years of experience with a given market—MNCs that currently export and/or import or are involved in contractual agreements.

PLANT OPERATIONS AND CHOICE OF TECHNOLOGY

Though operating a plant overseas is not much different from running a plant at home, there are certain special considerations that must be attended to. After personnel practices—the subject of Chapter 12—the most important consideration is the choice of the technology to be used. This problem is a very thorny one, because it can be a no-win situation.

From the MNC's viewpoint, it is best to choose the latest technology, which usually is capital intensive. This way the MNC not only exploits the efficiency associated with capital-intensive equipment and processes, but also lessens the problems that can arise from the human factor—labor. From the nation-state's viewpoint, the use of capital-intensive technology deprives the country of the job opportunities it had hoped for. Thus most developing countries would like to see labor-intensive rather than capital-intensive technology. The problem is that labor-intensive production processes, which create jobs for the host country, often increase the cost of a product, making it less competitive on the global market. Thus, many states find themselves in the peculiar position of welcoming high-tech industries that will enable them to compete and generate needed foreign currency, knowing full well that a low-capital, labor-intensive production technology would be more appropriate, given the local labor force. That is the paradox of appropriate technology.

LOGISTICS: AHEAD OF TIME OR JUST IN TIME?

At the beginning of this chapter, the inventory system was described as the buffer, or shock absorber, for the production function; the logistics subsystem performs the same role for the marketing function. The necessary raw materials are put into the raw material inventory (RMI). As needed, they are transferred to the work-in-process (WIP) inventory, and upon conversion into finished products, they are stored in the finished goods inventory (FGI). This buffering system of successive inventories, combined with an equally well-run logistics system, is every manager's paradise. No machine runs out of raw materials, and no retailer faces stockouts because of breakdowns in the production process.

This smoothing of the purchasing-production-delivery chain, however, is achieved at very high inventory cost. The large fixed investment for space and equipment and the large inventory carrying costs associated with this "com-

Exhibit 10-10   A Comparison of Ahead-of-Time and Just-in-Time Production Systems

Ahead-of-Time (AOT)	Just-in-Time (JIT)
Large-scale production	Small-scale production
Long production runs	Short production runs
Large inventories	Small inventories
Long lead times	Short lead times
Fewer switchovers	Frequent switchovers
Long set-up times	Short set-up times

fortable" production strategy have created a great demand for new and creative ways of trimming material and product handling costs.

The Japanese "just-in-time" (JIT) scheme has been heralded as the most innovative and efficient method of lowering material and finished goods handling costs.[10] Exhibit 10-10 compares the conventional Western "ahead-of-time" (AOT) system to the "just-in-time" scheme. JIT is characterized by smaller production runs, frequent changes in the production set-up, and closely synchronized operations, which transform raw materials into fabricated parts, fabricated parts into subassemblies, subassemblies into finished goods, and finished goods into sales. In order for JIT to be less costly, there must be a way of making up for time lost as a result of the frequent set-ups. In addition, there must be a way of ensuring the timely arrival of the needed materials or parts. In other words, external disturbances such as changes in vendors' schedules must be internalized and problems internal to the production line must be externalized. These principles are the key to the success of JIT. Good relationships with external vendors convert them into "family" members, and changes in the assembly line that are necessary for the new set-up are performed "externally" (that is, while machines are running) so as not to interrupt the flow of production.

In very simple terms, the main idea behind JIT is to purchase, produce, and deliver finished goods *just in time* to be sold, subassemblies *just in time* to be assembled into finished goods, fabricated parts *just in time* to go into subassemblies, and raw materials *just in time* to be transformed into fabricated parts.[11] The JIT philosophy evolved from the need to reduce production

---

[10]The discussion of JIT draws heavily on Byron J. Finch and James F. Cox, "An Examination of Just-in-Time Management for the Small Manufacturer: With an Illustration," *International Journal of Production Research* 24, No. 2 (1987): 329–342; and on Sumer C. Aggarwal, "MRP, JIT, OPT, FMS?" *Harvard Business Review*, September-October 1985, 8–12, 16.

[11]R. J. Schoenberger, *Japanese Manufacturing Techniques: Nine Hidden Lessons in Simplicity* (New York: Free Press, 1988).

costs, eliminate waste, and recognize workers' abilities. The objectives of the JIT system are

(1)   To minimize the work-in-process (WIP) inventory

(2)   To minimize fluctuations in WIP so as to simplify inventory controls

(3)   To minimize production instability by preventing fluctuations in demand from one process to another

(4)   To provide better control by decentralizing process supervision and moving it to the shop floor

(5)   To reduce defects

The main elements of JIT are

(1)   A focused factory

(2)   Reduced set-up times

(3)   Group technology

(4)   Total preventive maintenance

(5)   Cross-trained employees

(6)   Uniform work loads

(7)   Just-in-time delivery of purchased parts and/or components

(8)   Kanban

The *focused factory* concept requires that the production system be specifically designed for a limited number of product lines.

Reduction in set-up time is critical to the JIT philosophy. In order for production of parts in small lots to be economically feasible, set-up times must be short. The JIT approach requires that a set-up take less than ten minutes. The following four strategies comprise the Japanese approach to reducing set-ups:

(1)   Separate internal set-ups from external set-ups, internal set-ups being those that cannot be done while a machine is running and external set-ups being those that can.

(2)   Convert internal set-ups to external set-ups whenever possible.

(3)   Eliminate the adjustment process. Adjustments to machines usually take 50 to 70% of the total set-up time; minimizing adjustment time is therefore critical.

(4)   Abolish the set-up step whenever possible. Standardize parts within and across product lines or produce various parts on small, rather than large, machines.

Group technology is an engineering and manufacturing philosophy that emphasizes "sameness' in parts, equipment, and processes. Machines are grouped according to the destination of the parts they produce rather than according to their function.

Given the interdependence of work centers in a JIT system, a machine malfunction can necessitate the shutdown of an entire line (a problem magnified by the lack of buffer stock between work centers). Thus *preventive maintenance* is critical. Japanese workers are very knowledgeable about their machines' maintenance needs and are trained to do many repairs themselves.

Because only required items are produced in a JIT system, machines may become idle. Therefore, workers are *cross-trained* so that they can be moved to other machines. In addition to increasing efficiency, this practice lessens the monotony and boredom that characterize the traditional assembly line.

If products and components are to be produced at, or close to, the market rate by a limited number of work centers, *uniform work loads* must be established. Production of the same product mix daily ensures a smooth supply of products and components.

Purchased parts are delivered to the assembly area *just in time* for assembly into the finished products. More frequent deliveries of raw materials and purchased components reduce the amount of inventory needed, and therefore the space used for storage, and increase production flexibility. JIT delivery requires that businesses maintain good relationships with vendors and share information with vendors and customers.

Finally, *kanban* refers to a visible record, typically in the form of a card, that authorizes production and/or transfers parts from one work center to another.

RECAPITULATION

In this chapter production strategy has been defined in its most general sense—as the process of supplying a target market, whether through buying the needed goods or producing them. An MNC supplies a target market via a combination of sourcing tactics. The overriding objective is, of course, to minimize the cost of supplying the target market.

From the nation-state's viewpoint, factories are preferable to sales offices because they bring jobs, incomes, consumption, savings, houses, tax revenues, technologies, import substitutions and/or exports, and, in general, progress. From the MNC's point of view, the more closely it is involved in the production process, the more money it makes. Thus, both the MNC and the nation-state stand to gain considerably from manufacturing. Most U.S. MNCs would rather set up factories abroad than establish any other arrangement. The Japanese, who have in the past preferred joint ventures and other contractual agreements, seem to have developed an appetite for wholly owned subsidiaries, through which considerable control can be exerted over the long-term as well as the short-term plans of an enterprise.

An MNC has a variety of ways of smoothing out the entire supplying strategy. For example, the MNC can (1) use the inventory-logistics system to buffer sudden and unexpected changes in either production or marketing systems; (2) turn inward, resorting to overtime or layoffs; (3) subcontract to other business entities; or (4) source from its own minority joint ventures or wholly owned subsidiaries overseas. Last but not least, the MNC can rationalize its own internal procedures for handling material and/or final products. Just-in-time (JIT) production and inventorying techniques can be substituted for conventional methods of moving raw materials and products.

REVIEW QUESTIONS

(1) Define the term "production strategy."

(2) Industrialization has been heralded as the solution to many developing countries' economic and social problems. What are some of the necessary conditions for industrialization? Why is it that some countries have not managed to industrialize even though they meet most of these requirements?

(3) What are some of the characteristics of the Third Industrial Revolution? Speculate on what the Fourth Industrial Revolution might entail.

(4) Two foreign investors have applied for a permit to set up a business in your hometown. Investor A intends to establish an office to sell insurance and other financial services. Investor B plans to take over a factory that has been experiencing financial troubles. Investor B hopes to lessen the local company's troubles by streamlining its procurement, production, and distribution systems. You have been asked to help the local city council choose between the two proposals. Develop a cost/benefit plan for each proposal and recommend one.

(5) The president of a local textile plant just delivered a speech to the community Rotary Club in which he complained about "the unfair and un-American responses by some American manufacturers to foreign competition"—that is, U.S. manufacturers' sourcing abroad for cheaper parts and components. Such practices, he asserted, take jobs away from American workers and give them to foreigners. Refute or defend this argument.

(6) Write a two-minute speech on global sourcing. What steps are involved in the search for an offshore sourcing partner? What criteria should a men's dress shirt manufacturer, for example, establish for assessing the suitability of potential partners?

SUGGESTED READINGS

Bhote, Keki R. "Improving Supply Management." *Management Review,* August 1987, 51–53.

Brandt, Richard. "Seagate Goes East—And Comes Back a Winner: Its Asian-Made Disk Drives Are Clobbering the Competition." *Business Week,* March 16, 1987, 94.

Brooke, Michael Z. *International Management: A Review of Strategies and Operations.* London: Hutchinson, 1986.

Bylinsky, Gene. "GM's Road Map to Automated Plants." *Fortune,* October 28, 1985, 89–102.

———. "A Breakthrough in Automating the Assembly Line." *Fortune,* May 27, 1987, 64–66.

Cuashman, Robert F., and Herbert A. Morey (eds.). *A Guide for the Foreign Investor.* Homewood, IL: Dow Jones–Irwin, 1984.

Curtin, Frank T. "Global Sourcing: Is It Right for Your Company?" *Management Review,* August, 1987, 47–49.

Davidson, William H. *Global Strategic Management.* New York: John Wiley and Sons, 1982.

Dicken, Peter. *Global Shift: Industrial Changes in a Turbulent World.* New York: Harper and Row, 1986.

Dunning, John H. "Toward an Eclectic Theory of International Production: Some Empirical Tests." *Journal of International Business Studies,* Spring/Summer 1980, 9–25.

———. *International Production and the Multinational Enterprise.* London: Allen and Unwin Publishers, 1981.

Germidis, Dimitri. *International Subcontracting: A New Form of Investment.* Paris: Organization for Economic Cooperation and Development, 1980.

Globerman, Steven. *Fundamentals of International Business Management.* Englewood Cliffs, NJ: Prentice-Hall, 1986.

Hefler, Daniel F. "Global Sourcing: Offshore Investment Strategy for the 1980s." *Journal of Business Strategy* 2, No. 1 (Summer 1981): 7–12.

"Improving the Push for Quality: To Beat Imports, the U.S. Must Improve Its Products. That Means a Whole New Approach to Manufacturing." *Business Week,* June 8, 1987, 130–144.

Ohmae, Kenichi. *Triad Power: The Coming Shape of Global Competition.* New York: Macmillan, 1985.

Schonberger, Richard. "Frugal Manufacturing." *Harvard Business Review,* September-October, 1987, 95–100.

Selington, Mitchell A., and Edward J. Williams. *Maquiladoras and Migration Workers in the Mexico–United States Border Industrialization Program.* Austin, TX: The University of Texas Press, 1981.

Stobough, Robert, and Piero Telesio. "Match Manufacturing Policies and Product Strategy." *Harvard Business Review,* March/April 1983, 113–120.

Vernon, Raymond, and Louis Wells, Jr. *Manager in the International Economy,* Fifth Edition. Englewood Cliffs, NJ: Prentice-Hall, 1986.

Vernon-Wortzel, Heidi, and Lawrence H. Wortzel. *Strategic Management of Multinational Corporations: The Essentials.* New York: John Wiley and Sons, 1985.

Walter, Ingo (ed.). *Handbook of International Business.* New York: John Wiley and Sons, 1982.

CASE ● Ford of Europe and Local Content Regulations

In mid-1983, the Management Committee of Ford of Europe (the company's senior decision-making committee) was once again examining the trends, opportunities, and threats offered by the European market. The principal threat perceived by management was the growing Japanese presence in Europe. Japanese manufacturers had increased their car sales in Western Europe from 750,000 units in 1979 to almost one million units in 1983 and they were beginning to establish a manufacturing foothold in Europe. Nissan, for example, was just beginning to produce automobiles in Italy, it would soon increase its production of vehicles for Europe from a Spanish plant, and, most worrisome, the company was expected to announce imminently a decision to proceed with a previously shelved plan to construct a new and very large assembly plant in the United Kingdom. Although Ford competed very successfully against the other European producers—and for the first time had captured the number one European market share position in the second quarter of 1983—Japanese producers' plants in Europe would constitute a new and severe challenge. What especially worried Ford was the possibility that Nissan's new U.K. plant would import major automobile components into Europe from Japan, assemble them into finished vehicles, and then claim that the vehicles were European in origin and thus not subject to any existing European–Japanese trade agreements or understandings.

This worry had led Ford executives back in 1981 to consider seriously local content regulations as a way of reducing this risk and helping to stem the growth of the Japanese producers' share of the European market. Local content regulations, most commonly employed by developing countries against multinational firms based in developed countries, defined the percentage of a product that must be produced in a specified geographical region as a precondition of sale in that region.

SOURCE: This case study was developed after discussions with certain Ford personnel but it does not necessarily reflect the actual scope or manner of deliberations undertaken by Ford management or the conclusions of Ford management. H. Landis Gabel and Anthony E. Hall, "Ford of Europe and Local Content Regulations" (Fontainebleau, France: INSEAD), 1985. All rights reserved.

Although local content regulations had been discussed occasionally in the Management Committee for the past two years, no conclusions had been reached, and pressure was building to push the discussion through to a definitive policy stance. If the Committee were to decide to favor local content regulations, it would then have to decide on strategy and tactics. Regulations could take various forms, some of which might be more advantageous to Ford than others. And, of course, Ford would have to decide how to represent its position to the governmental bodies that would have to introduce, monitor, and enforce the regulations. . . .

LOCAL CONTENT REGULATIONS

Local content regulations have long been a device used by developing countries to force multinational companies to increase the rate at which they transfer technology and employment to their local operations. With respect to automobiles, these regulations typically require that a certain percentage of a vehicle's content be produced in the country of sale. This percentage may be defined by value or by weight. Weight is generally thought to be a stricter criterion because it is not susceptible to manipulation by transfer pricing. Yet it can lead to only low-technology, high-weight items being produced locally (e.g., steel castings and chassis components).

Although simple in concept, local content regulations can often be quite complicated in practice. The treatment of overhead and profit is often a problem. Some countries apply the regulations on the basis of fleet averaging, others to specific models. Mexico, where at least 50 percent of the value of all cars sold must be produced locally, strengthened its regulations by also requiring that the value of all component imports must be matched by component exports for each assembler. This led to a flurry of investments by Chrysler and Ford in engine facilities in Mexico.

Until recently, Spain had a 95 percent domestic content rule. All component imports were assessed a 30 percent customs duty, and 50 percent of all local manufacturing operations had to be Spanish owned. All this was changed in the 1975 negotiations between the Spanish government and Ford over Ford's "Bobcat" (or "Fiesta") project in Valencia. Contemplating the attractive prospect of a plant producing 225,000 cars annually, the Spanish government settled for 100 percent Ford ownership, 75 percent Spanish content, and 5 percent import duty on component parts. Concessions on import duty were also granted for machine tools and equipment unavailable in Spain. But two-thirds of automobile production had to be exported from Spain, and Ford's sales in Spain could not exceed 10 percent of the previous year's total Spanish market size. General Motors arranged a similar deal for a plant in Zaragoza, Spain, producing 280,000 small "S cars" ("Corsas") annually. Spanish accession to the EEC would phase out much of its protective legislation.

[In mid-1983] local content regulations did not exist in any EEC or European

Free Trade Association (EFTA) country except Portugal and Ireland. (The European Community's trade regime did have a scheme for defining local assembly with the EFTA countries for the purpose of trade classification—60 percent of value added had to be locally produced.) Nevertheless, there was a variety of statutory powers in the EEC and the General Agreement on Tariffs and Trade (GATT) that could protect specific industries. For example, Regulation No. 926 of the EEC allowed for the protection of specific industries and could be triggered by the Commission of the EEC after advice from the Council of Ministers.

At the GATT level, any member country could ask for temporary protection from imports from another member (under Articles 19–23) if those imports severely endangered national industry. These "escape clause" articles were difficult for EEC countries to use, however, because each country delegated responsibility for all trade negotiations to the EEC Commission in Brussels. Thus the European automobile industry would have to coordinate campaigns in a number of EEC member countries before it could approach the EEC Commission. Even then, there was no guarantee that the Commission would agree to take a case to the GATT. Not surprisingly, existing import restrictions were essentially bilateral diplomatic agreements—varying widely from country to country—rather than statutory enactments.

FORD'S DELIBERATIONS

At least on the surface, informal local content regulations in Europe looked very attractive to Ford's executives. The Japanese threat was surely very real. Production levels in Europe in 1980 were about the same as they had been in 1970, and in the last decade, while European exports to non-European markets fell 42 percent, Japanese worldwide exports rose 426 percent. Ford's market analysts forecast slow growth for the European market in the future, indicating that higher Japanese sales in Europe would come directly from those of the established European producers. The existing structure of voluntary agreements to limit Japanese imports into individual European countries was fragile. Although "voluntary" was clearly a euphemism, any cracks in the agreements could quickly lead to more Japanese imports before new and possibly more lenient agreements were negotiated. West Germany and Belgium were thought to be the weak spots.

If a European local content rule were to be established on the basis of local sales (i.e., if a specified percentage of each manufacturer's European sales had to be produced in Europe), then the existing system of individual national voluntary trade agreements would become redundant. Alternatively, if a local content rule were to be applied to local production (i.e., if a specified percentage of the content of each manufacturer's cars assembled in Europe had to be sourced in Europe), then some controls on automobile imports would still be needed. A local content rule of this type would prevent the Japanese from circumventing the intent of import controls by importing the bulk of their components from Japan while establishing only token assembly operations in Europe.

Yet there were many potential negative consequences for European producers if local content regulations spread across Europe. It was not obvious that European producers should object to Japanese imports, even at a substantially higher level than at present, if the alternative was to be new Japanese greenfield plants in Europe. Even if they complied scrupulously with local content rules, these new plants, employing the most advanced production technology and work methods, could be tough competitors, unshackled from any form of constraint. At the very least, they would add production capacity to a market already suffering from 20 percent excess capacity. A price war was certainly not impossible to imagine. And Ford, among others, was worried about the impact that these plants could have on fleet sales, particularly in the high-margin U.K. market, if nationalistic customers began to think of Nissan, for example, as a "national" producer.

Another problem was that local content rules could limit Ford's own manufacturing flexibility. The key new concept in the automobile industry in the 1970s was that of a "world car." A world car is assembled in local markets (tailored to local consumers' tastes) from a common set of components. Each component is produced in very high volume at one site, where it can be done least expensively, and then shipped around the world to the scattered assembly plants. Local content rules and world cars were seemingly incompatible.

Ford's "Erika" project (the 1981 "Escort") was the first of the world cars. In actual practice, the world car concept was of questionable success. The Escort that was marketed in the United States differed so much in style and design from its European sibling that there was little parts commonality, and transportation costs ate away at the efficiency gains from large-scale production of the common parts. The result was that although there was some international trade in components within Ford, most movement of parts was either within Europe or within the United States.

General Motors had similar problems with its "J car" (the Vauxhall "Cavalier" in the United Kingdom and Opel "Rekord" in West Germany) and "X car" (the Vauxhall "Royale" in the United Kingdom and Opel "Senator" in Germany). General Motors seemed to have been more successful than Ford, however, in standardizing components, and whereas Ford had primarily maintained an approach of European sourcing for European markets, GM had already moved to exploit its global reach.

To make matters even more complex, Ford had a 25 percent share in Toyo Kogyo (Mazda) and thus an option of working with Mazda to import inexpensive Japanese vehicles. Indeed, a Mazda pickup truck was sold in the United States and Greece as a Ford truck, and the very successful Ford "Laser" in the Far East was a version of the Mazda 626 made in Japan. (In July 1983, Ford was threatening such a policy to counteract the proposed GM–Toyota production plant in California.)

TECHNICAL ASPECTS OF LOCAL CONTENT REGULATIONS

If the management of Ford of Europe were to support local content regulations, they felt they would have to answer four technical questions:

(1)   How should "local" be defined geographically?

(2)   How was local content to be measured?

(3)   To what should local content regulations be applied—individual cars, models, or a producer's entire fleet?

(4)   What should the minimum percentage of local content be?

The company had already done some thinking about each question.

Of all the producers, Ford was the most geographically integrated in Europe. It would therefore be important to encompass most or all of Europe in the term "local." A definition restricted to the EEC would exclude Ford's big Valencia plant in Spain and a 200,000-unit per year plant contemplated for Portugal. These plants represented critical low-cost sources for small cars for the other European markets. (Both Spain and Portugal had applied for admission to the EEC, however.) Ford regarded a nation-state definition as impractical and intolerable.

Defining local content was a very difficult task. One proposal was to define content by weight. This had the advantage of being difficult to manipulate by transfer pricing, but it might allow the importation of high-value, high-technology components that were light in weight.

The other common definition of local content was by value. Essentially the percentage of local content was established by subtracting the value of the imported components as declared on customs documentation from 1) the distributor's price, 2) the ex-works price, or 3) the ex-works price minus the labor and overhead content of the car. Then the local content residue was divided by the corresponding denominator.

Clearly the percentage of the imported components gets larger from 1) to 3) as the value of the domestic content gets smaller. Ford had not decided its position with regard to this issue, except that it did not want specific components identified for mandatory local production. It was also possible to devise other hybrid methods of valuing local content, but they were generally not under discussion.

Regarding the question of to what should the local content rules be applied, Ford favored applying them to the average of a producer's entire line of cars, rather than to each individual car or model. The [latter] would jeopardize Ford's current importation from South Africa of small quantities of their P100 pickup truck (based on the "Cortina").

There was also a related question of whether automobile production or regional sales should form the basis of measurement. Ford preferred that a specified percentage of a producer's European sales be made in Europe, since such a rule was insurance against circumvention of the current import quotas. A production-based local content rule would only prevent circumvention of the intent of import quotas by token local final assembly.

Finally there was the question of what the appropriate percentage should be. Figures currently under discussion ranged from 60 to 80 percent, although the percentage clearly depended on the format of the specific proposals. Of particular significance in terms of these percentages was that a 60 percent rule might allow importation of engines and major parts of the drive train that would all be excluded by an 80 percent rule. Also, it might be very difficult for the Japanese to start up a new plant with an immediate 80 percent local content (even if that percentage were to be achieved with more time). Start-up at 60 percent would be substantially easier.

THE POLITICAL OPTIONS

Should Ford decide to support local content regulations and then find answers to the technical questions, it would still have to determine the best way to carry its case to the appropriate government body. And here again, the way was not clear.

Ford definitely did not want to act on its own. It would be much better to act in concert with the other European producers. (Despite the all-American image of the founder and his name, Ford of Europe unquestionably considered itself "European.") Not only was this desirable on general principles, but for one quite specific reason Ford preferred not to lobby the EEC directly. It had recently fought and was currently fighting other battles with the European Commission. . . .

Although Ford preferred to have a common industry position to press on the governmental authorities, there was little likelihood of unanimity among the European producers even on the most basic question of whether local content rules were desirable. General Motors was an almost certain opponent to local content rules despite the fact that it too might welcome relief from Japanese competition. Fiat, Renault, and British Leyland, on the other hand, might be strong allies who could perhaps rally the support of their respective governments. They appeared to have much to gain from local content rules because they had most of their operations in Europe and they purchased most of their components locally.

There were a number of sourcing arrangements, however, which could undermine the support of some of these firms. Japanese cars assembled in Australia were entering the United Kingdom with a certificate of origin from Australia. British Leyland's Acclaim was of questionable origin. Fiat was bringing in "Pandas" from Brazil, and Volkswagen "Beetles" came into Europe from Mexico. Renault had extensive operations in the United States that could alter the company's outlook. And on July 27, 1983, the *Wall Street Journal* reported that Fiat was being indicted by the Italian authorities for selling cars made in Spain and Brazil under the guise of Italian manufacture. Fiat denied the charge.

Ford executives believed, nonetheless, that with the exception of GM, Ford was likely to find general support within the industry. In fact, in a 1981 draft paper, the CLCA[12] stated:

> The establishment of Japanese motor vehicle manufacturing plants should be subject to the following durable conditions:
>
> a.   the CIF value of the components not originating from the EEC should not exceed 20 percent of the price ex-works of the vehicle.
> b.   the manufacturing and assembly of mechanical components (engines, gearboxes and drivetrain) should be performed within the EEC.

THE EUROPEAN COMMISSION

Ford executives believed that the European Commission was prepared to take some action on the automobile imports issue. In January 1983 the Commission had held discussions with the Japanese in Tokyo and had obtained a nonbinding commitment to moderate vehicle exports to the EEC. The Commission was currently monitoring the agreement. Beyond this it was unclear what action the European Commission was considering. In principle, the EEC should be expected to favor relatively free trade between its member countries and the rest of the world. The history of international trade since World War II—a history in which the EEC featured prominently—was one of declining tariffs (from an average of 20 percent on manufactured goods in the 1950s to 8 percent in the mid-1970s), dramatically growing trade volumes, and greater interdependence of national economies. Two other principles dear to the EEC were that all member countries maintain a *common* trade policy vis-à-vis non-EEC countries, and that there be no barriers to trade between member countries. Clearly, the existing set of nonuniform bilateral trade agreements with the Japanese offended these principles.

Although the principles underlying the EEC were relatively unambiguous, the EEC often resorted to protective policies, and it was not immune to pressures to maintain jobs in the automotive sector. But granted this observation, it was still not evident just how job preservation might best be achieved. Formal local content rules would be inconsistent with EEC law and would violate the GATT. Thus any local content measures would have to be informal such as those that currently existed between the Japanese and the British. Would the EEC prefer to see a uniform (albeit informal) external quota and internal production-based local content rule? Or would it rather see a uniform internal sales-based content rule and no quota? Would its preference in either case be less restrictive than the status quo, shaky though it might be? And was it realistic to expect that an informal negotiating process could create a com-

---

[12]Comité de Liaison des Constructeurs Associations. The CLCA was basically a political liaison committee of the national automotive trade associations of France, the United Kingdom, Germany, Belgium, Holland, and Italy.

mon position among the different EEC member states? A weak, contentious, and nonuniform set of local content rules established and enforced by each EEC member country could be the worst of all the imaginable alternatives.

The Japanese, of course, would have some influence on EEC thinking on this matter. Any EEC action would probably come in the context of trade negotiations—not simply unilaterally imposed trade sanctions. And what position might the Japanese take? It is conceivable that they might agree to some reasonable export restraints into the EEC in return for open markets within the EEC. That would give them access to the two big markets from which they were currently virtually excluded—France and Italy. But would those two countries agree? Each would face greater Japanese competition in its home market but less in its export markets in other EEC countries.

The executives on the Management Committee considered their alternatives. If they were to have any role in determining the public policies that would undoubtedly have a significant impact on their company, they would have to act quickly.

ISSUES FOR DISCUSSION

(1)   You are a consultant to the Management Committee of Ford of Europe. Make a case for local content legislation by showing that Japanese auto manufacturers do, in fact, threaten European companies. You might construct a table of the market shares and/or production volumes of all auto manufacturing companies for the years 1973 through 1983, to highlight Ford's "suffering" from Japanese competition.

(2)   You are a consultant to the European Economic Community. In order to help the EEC's Commission answer the questions raised in the last section of the case, present a picture of how the rest of the world copes with the problems facing the EEC. You might make a list of what is allowed by the GATT and what is not allowed, as well as a list of the costs and benefits of the various alternatives mentioned in the final three paragraphs.

(3)   You are a consultant to the governor of your state. A local manufacturer who is a substantial employer in your state followed Ford's example and filed an official request for local content legislation for Japanese car manufacturers. Advise the governor of the merits and/or perils of the proposed legislation.

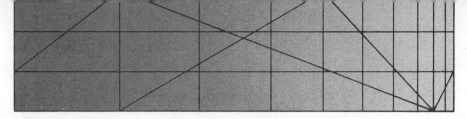

CHAPTER 11   MARKETING STRATEGY

A powerful force drives the world toward a converging commonality, and that force is technology. Gone are accustomed differences in national or regional preference. Gone are the days when a company could sell last year's models—or lesser versions of advanced products—in the less-developed world. And gone are the days when prices, margins, and profits abroad were generally higher than at home.

Theodore Levitt

"The Globalization of Markets," *Harvard Business Review,* May–June 1983, 94.

LEARNING OBJECTIVES

After studying the material in this chapter, the student should be familiar with the following concepts:

(1)   Globalization, multinationalization, and triadization

(2)   The seven Os, five Ws, three Hs, and four Ps

(3)   Convergence

(4)   The two main elements of a global marketing strategy

(5)   The four main decisions, and four main phases of a global marketing strategy

(6)   The marketing mix management process

(7)   Gray markets

(8)   Countertrade

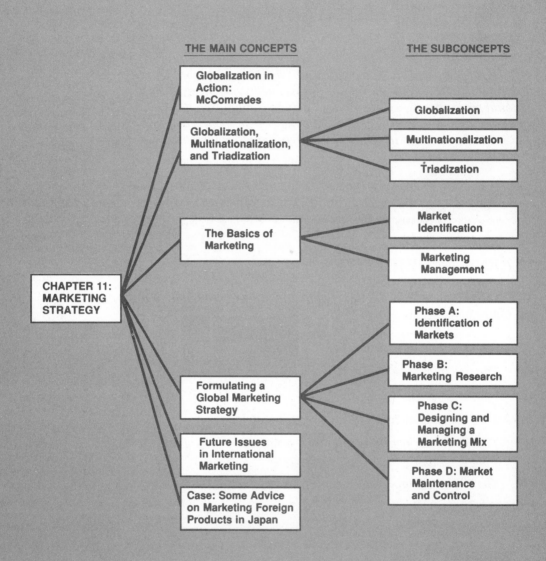

GLOBALIZATION IN ACTION
McComrades

It is something of a McTriumph: last month McDonald's opened a branch in Belgrade, its first in the communist half of Europe. The really hard part was not getting approval from a communist government; it was growing the potatoes and finding the ketchup.

Although Yugoslavs produce tomato paste, tomato puree and tomato sauce, they had never heard of tomato ketchup. Yugoslavs also grow potatoes, but McDonald's potatoes are an Idaho variety called Russets. Russets make fantastic French fries, but are difficult to grow. They need to be planted in even, spaced rows and watched over with care.

To break into Belgrade, McDonald's turned to Genex, a Yugoslav farming-tourism group. The two set up a joint venture in which each side owns 50% of the equity. Since Yugoslav dinars cannot be converted into hard currency, McDonald's agreed to receive its profits in the form of Yugoslav foodstuffs for its West European restaurants.

McDonald's sees Eastern Europe and the Soviet Union as a growth market. Elsewhere the fast-food market is reaching the point where McDonald's is left looking for new outlets in unusual sites such as hospitals. Communist Europe, however, has millions of frustrated fast-food freaks. This month McDonald's is opening its first branch in Budapest. Moscow could be next. Within two years, there could be as many as 18 McDonald's outlets in Yugoslavia alone.

For that to happen, Yugoslav farmers must produce McDonald's-quality products. So far they have managed with meat and cheese. The Russet potatoes proved harder. It took three growing seasons to get something close to the original, and too many still turn out soggy. Ketchup was even worse. McDonald's prefers a sugary recipe, and Yugoslavs have not yet managed to master the right mix. Hungarian ketchup, on the other hand, is said by McDonald's men to be excellent. In both countries, one product was easy to find: Coca-Cola. It has been on the East European market for years.

SOURCE: "McComrades," *The Economist,* April 16, 1988, 58. Reprinted with permission.

OVERVIEW

Despite the increasing tendency toward globalization of the buying needs, habits, and attitudes of consumers, there are still enough differences among international markets to make selling to them extremely challenging. For example, although Coca-Cola has had tremendous success in selling essentially the same dark drink all over the world, some people outside the United States still drink it with no ice at all—a fact that has implications for the size of the glass, the need for refrigeration, and the price of a Coke.

Most of the basic tasks of marketing overseas are the same as the ones performed by a manager attempting to enter domestic markets. The "four Ps"—product, price, promotion, and place—are relevant whether one is selling bread in the United States or rice in Japan. The specific combination of these Ps, however, varies with the particular socioeconomic and cultural setting. Customer responsiveness to promotional tactics is different in different countries. Thus the main decision international managers must make is between the so-called global and multidomestic marketing strategies. In other words, should a company develop a "one name, one message, one voice" marketing strategy, or should it tailor its marketing efforts to local or regional socioeconomic and cultural conditions?

Obviously neither extreme holds the answer. In most cases an adaptive marketing strategy will evolve. That is, a marketing manager will start with some common elements, and then modify the strategy to accommodate local or regional demands.

This chapter will first summarize the basic concepts and techniques of marketing and then outline the main elements of an international marketing strategy.

INTRODUCTION

Marketing is the process through which a company familiarizes potential customers with its products and tries to get them to make purchases. A company can sell only what customers will buy, so managers must continually ask themselves, "What do customers want and what will customers buy?" A lesson multinational managers have learned over years of trying to answer this question is that *equating customer wants with customer purchases is dangerous.* Marketing textbooks are replete with anecdotal and documented incidents of marketing blunders. A mismatch between what the firm thinks the customers want and what the customers actually buy can be caused either by the firm's misjudging market trends (bad marketing research) or by the customers' changing their buying habits for psychological, economic, or political reasons. In either case, a mismatch between what the company offers and what the customers buy results in large inventories of unwanted products and/or large losses of customers to competitors.

The international marketing manager's task is to assess customers' needs and purchases and inform production managers as to the types, quantities, and qualities of products most likely to be sold. Often hundreds of markets worldwide must be researched, analyzed, and targeted. Subsequently, a multitude of strategies for market segmentation, product introduction, pricing, and promotion must be coordinated so as to avoid missed sales in one area and inventory buildups in another.

GLOBALIZATION, MULTINATIONALIZATION, AND TRIADIZATION

Currently a key issue for every MNC marketing manager is the choice among globalization, multinationalization, and triadization.[1] In a nutshell, MNCs must select one of the following three strategies:

(1)   *Globalization,* in which the world is viewed as one giant market and superficial regional and national differences are ignored

(2)   *Multinationalization,* in which the world is seen in terms of a number of large and small markets whose differences dictate considerable product and marketing mix adaptation

(3)   *Triadization,* in which attention is concentrated on the huge, homogeneous, and predictable market of the Triad—the United States, Western Europe, and Japan

GLOBALIZATION

The doctrine of globalization asserts that the world is a homogeneous global village, where people live in a "Republic of Technology [whose] supreme law . . . is *convergence,* the tendency for everything to become more like everything else"[2] Technology seems to be able to cross the barriers that legal and ideological differences erect across the globe. Telecommunications in particular bring into everybody's living rooms ideas, events, products, lifestyles, working conditions, and life in general from places tens of thousands of miles away. Thus a marketing effort to sell a product in Atlanta, Georgia creates a demand for the same product in Hamburg, West Germany; Sydney, Australia; and Buenos Aires, Argentina.

The managerial implications of this globalization of people's needs and wants are many. In Theodore Levitt's words, "the commonality of preferences leads inescapably to the standardization of products, manufacturing, and the institutions of trade and commerce. Small nation-based markets transmogrify and expand. Success in world competition turns on efficiency in production, distribution, marketing, and management, and inevitably becomes focused on price."[3]

---

[1]The terms globalization and multinationalization are used by Theodore Levitt in his article on "The Globalization of Markets," *Harvard Business Review,* May–June 1983, 92–102. The term triadization is used by Kenichi Ohmae in *Triad Power: The Coming Shape of Global Competition* (New York: Macmillan, 1985).

[2]Levitt, "The Globalization of Markets," p. 93.

[3]Levitt, "The Globalization of Markets," p. 96. For an opposing view and descriptions of some unsuccessful experiences with globalization, see Joanne Lipman, "Marketers Turn Sour on Global Sales Pitch Harvard Guru Makes," *The Wall Street Journal,* May 5, 1988, 1, 9.

MULTINATIONALIZATION

Multinationalism is a way of thinking that dictates that firms operating in many diverse places must adjust their products and practices in each—a costly practice. According to Levitt, "multinational companies that concentrated on idiosyncratic consumer preferences have become befuddled and unable to take in the forest because of the trees."[4] In their eagerness to tailor their marketing mix strategy to many distinct markets, managers who espouse a philosophy of multinationalism are likely to miss the great benefits of product and technique standardization. National and/or regional differences are mistakenly viewed by such managers as constraints or invariants that must be accommodated and not tampered with.

TRIADIZATION

The godfather of the notion of triadization is Kenichi Ohmae, the managing director of the Tokyo office of McKinsey and Company, a well-known international consulting firm. In his book *Triad Power: The Coming Shape of Global Competition*, Ohmae asserted that "there is an emergence of the Triadians, or the residents of Japan, [North] America, and the European community.... These are the people whose academic backgrounds, income levels (both discretionary and nondiscretionary), lifestyle, use of leisure time, and aspirations are quite similar."[5]

According to Ohmae, for a firm to survive and grow, it must attempt to become an "insider." To do so it must abandon the so-called United Nations model, which enticed management to neglect the significance of the Triad and treat the world as if it consisted of hundreds of equally important markets. If firms are to succeed, says Ohmae, they must develop products and techniques that will capitalize on the similarities of these three markets and yet accommodate their differences. The cost of adapting to the local peculiarities of only three markets is much less than that of adapting to hundreds of markets and is offset by the large volume that the large markets can accommodate. It is much more efficient to adapt a product or a technique to a market with six hundred million potential customers with large disposable incomes than to adapt it to several small markets each composed of only a few thousand potential customers with diverse tastes and marketing awareness levels and low incomes.

This book views the world, as Buckminster Fuller did, as a "spaceship earth." On this spaceship humans live in Peter Drucker's "global village," which is experiencing a converging commonality. This converging commonality has

---

[4]Levitt, "The Globalization of Markets," p. 92.
[5]Ohmae, *Triad Power*, p. xvii.

created "a new commercial reality—the emergence of global markets for standardized consumer products on a previously unimagined scale of magnitude.[6]

Proponents of Levitt's philosophy of globalization advise their listeners to concentrate on the standardized products everyone wants rather than worry about the thousands of different products that customers in different markets might—or might not—like. It is possible to get the impression that managers can assume that what is appropriate for the home country is appropriate for the whole world. Nothing is further from the truth. Rather, the manager is advised to "think globally and act locally." Product design and marketing techniques should be guided by the converging commonality. An understanding of this superforce of converging commonality, however, requires considerable study of many diverse forces in operation in many distinctly different countries with unique sociocultural, economic, and political attitudes and systems. It is only after careful examination of these "globes" that a truly global strategy can be designed and successfully implemented.

Unity in diversity is indeed the main principle of general systems theory. The world can be looked at as an open system composed of many subsystems, each of which has its own images, aspirations, inspirations, objectives, and goals to accomplish. A global marketing strategy incorporates the common attributes of a number of these subsystems. Attempting to sell a product globally simply because it has successfully satisfied the home country's needs is not globalism; rather, it is ethnocentrism—the self-centered and mistaken assumption that what is good for one's own nation or people, the "ethnos," is good for the rest of the world.

THE BASICS OF MARKETING

Although the marketing function of an organization is essentially the same whether the market is domestic or international, there are many adaptations that must be undertaken when certain key concepts and/or techniques are carried overseas. The American Marketing Association, cognizant of the changes that have taken place in the concept of marketing, has recently approved a new broader definition of marketing. Marketing is defined as "the process of planning and executing the conception, pricing, promotion, and distribution of ideas, goods, and services to create exchanges that satisfy individual and organizational objectives."[7]

Two concepts stand out in this definition. First, there is the idea that the planning and execution relate not only to products but also to ideas and services. The new definition emphasizes that marketing involves much more

---

[6]Levitt, "The Globalization of Markets," pp. 92–102.
[7]"AMA Board Approves New Marketing Definition," *Marketing News,* March 1, 1981, 1.

Exhibit 11-1   The Basics of Marketing

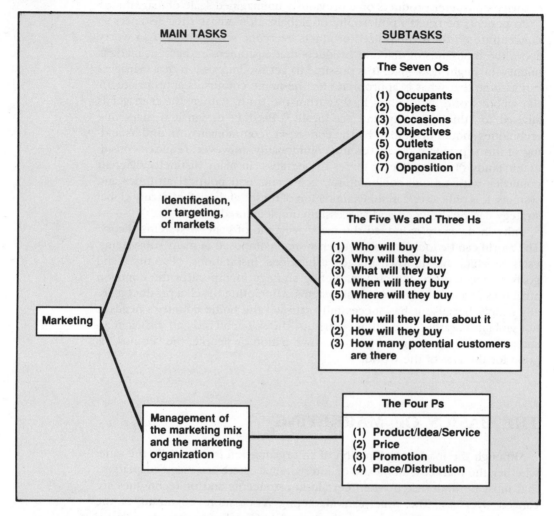

than just selling goods. Second, there is the notion that the modern marketing function is indeed a strategic matter in that it contributes to the overall strategic mission of the organization.

The overriding objective of the marketing manager is to ensure a long-term competitive advantage for the company. To accomplish this objective, the manager must perform two distinct but interrelated tasks:

(1)   Market identification via marketing research

(2)   Marketing management via development of a marketing mix

In Exhibit 11-1 these two tasks are subdivided into a number of subtasks. A review of the literature on marketing reveals a rather remarkable uniformity of opinion as to the main subtasks that should be mastered by the person who is given the responsibility of devising an international marketing strategy.[8]

MARKET IDENTIFICATION

Identifying, or targeting, markets is a task that requires considerable managerial effort. Most MNCs have within the marketing department a marketing research office, whose prime function is to identify markets. Market researchers use the "seven Os" framework to identify primary customers and their responses to products, prices, promotions, and places to buy.

(1)   *Occupants* are the targets of the marketing effort. The marketer must define the customers to be approached along numerous dimensions, such as demographics (age, sex, and nationality, for example), geography (country or region), psychographics (attitudes, interests, and opinions), product-related variables (usage rate and brand loyalty, for example), and customer types (industrial or final, for example).

(2)   *Objects* are what is being bought at present to satisfy particular needs. Included in this category are physical objects, services, ideas, organizations, places, and persons.

(3)   *Occasions* are the times when members of the target market buy the product or service. This information is important to the marketer because a product's consumption may be tied to a particular time period— for example, imported beer may be consumed in quantity only at a once-a-year festival.

(4)   *Objectives* are the factors motivating customers to purchase or adopt the product. A computer manufacturer markets not hardware but solutions to problems, because it is the desire to solve a problem that motivates a customer to buy a computer. Many customers are motivated in part by the "hidden value" in the product they purchase, which may be a function of, for example, the national origin of the product or its brand name.

(5)   *Outlets* are the places where customers expect to be able to procure a product or to be exposed to messages about it.

(6)   *Organization* refers to how the buying or acceptance of a new idea or product takes place.

---

[8]See, for example, Subhash C. Jain, *International Marketing,* Second Edition (Boston: Kent Publishing Co., 1987); Michael R. Czinkota and Ilkka A. Ronkainen, *International Marketing* (Chicago: The Dryden Press, 1988); Philip Kotler, *Marketing Management: Analysis, Planning and Control* (Englewood Cliffs, NJ: Prentice-Hall, 1982); and Yoshi Tsurumi, *Multinational Management: Business Strategy and Government Policy* (Cambridge, MA: Ballinger Publishing Co., 1984).

(7)   *Opposition* refers to the company's competition, as well as to groups
      antagonistic to the firm's product or goal. In the case of the tobacco
      industry, for example, the opposition would include nonsmokers who
      are opposed to cigarettes and other tobacco products.

An alternative way of obtaining the data needed to design a marketing
management strategy is to collect information about the "five Ws" and "three
Hs."

THE FIVE Ws

(1)   *Who is going to buy the product or service?*

(2)   *Why will the customer buy the product?* How does it fit into the cus-
          tomer's consumption pattern? For example, a product may meet a con-
          sumer need, in which case it may be considered a necessity, a conven-
          ience, or a luxury; or it may fill a manufacturing or other industrial need.

(3)   *What sort of product is it, and in what form would customers prefer
          it?* A washing detergent, for example, may be in the form of a powder
          or a liquid.

(4)   *When will the consumer buy the product?* The main issue here is fre-
          quency of purchase. Coffee, for instance, is bought more frequently than
          stereo systems; raw materials for industrial processes are bought more
          frequently than heavy machinery and equipment.

(5)   *Where will the consumer buy the product?* Obviously, fancy stationery
          belongs in a department store or a stationery store, not in a grocery
          store. In most cases, industrial consumers prefer buying directly from
          the producer over dealing with an intermediary.

THE THREE Hs

(1)   *How do consumers learn about the product?* Who are the opinion
          leaders, market leaders, and sources of authoritative recommendations?
          Recommendation by word of mouth is said to be the most persuasive
          form of advertising in most cultures. How can word-of-mouth endorse-
          ments be encouraged? What promotional strategies can be used to per-
          suade industrial consumers to prefer a particular product?

(2)   *How do customers buy products?* What are a customer's requirements
          for service at the time of purchase (help in selection, credit, delivery)
          and, particularly in the case of industrial consumers, after the purchase?

(3)   *How many potential customers are there?* Once consumers have been
          analyzed, they should be counted. The count should be broken down
          on both a geographical and an economic basis.

MARKETING MANAGEMENT

Marketing management is the process of designing and executing a marketing program for the targeted markets. The goal is to design organizational policies and procedures that will lead to a combination of the best product, the best price, the best promotion, and the best place of distribution for the targeted markets.

Product policy covers all of the elements that make up the product, service, or idea, including tangible characteristics (such as the core product and its packaging) and intangible characteristics (such as brand name and warranties). Many products are a combination of a concrete product and a service; for example, in buying an IBM computer, the purchaser receives not only the product but also an extensive service contract.

Pricing policy determines the cost of the product to the customer. Price is the only revenue-generating element of the marketing mix. An important consideration in pricing policy is the channel of distribution; profits to be made by the distributors who assist in the marketing effort must be taken into account, as must functional, quantity, seasonal, and cash discounts and promotional allowances.

Promotion (communications) policy relates to the use of promotional tools such as advertising, sales promotion, personal selling, and publicity to reach customers, distributors, and the public at large. Promotion is the most visible and sensitive of the marketing mix elements.

Distribution (place) policy covers channel management and logistics management. Channel management encompasses setting up and operating the contractual organization, which may consist of various types of wholesalers, agents, retailers, and facilitators. Logistics management focuses on providing the product at appropriate times and places in the marketing channel. Place is the most permanent of the marketing mix elements—it is the one that is most difficult to change in the short term.

Blending the various elements into a coherent program (the "marketing mix") requires consideration of the type of product or service being offered, the stage in the product's life cycle, the resources available for the marketing effort, and the type of customer to whom the marketing efforts will be directed.

FORMULATING A GLOBAL MARKETING STRATEGY

The decision facing any company that wishes to survive and prosper in today's turbulent global village is not whether to enter the international game but rather how to enter it. Once a mode of entry has been selected, a means of penetrating and maintaining the markets must be devised. The latter task is the domain of international marketing.

International marketing decisions are strategic decisions in that they affect the entire organization, require substantial organizational resources, are made

Exhibit 11-2   A Framework for Global Marketing Strategy

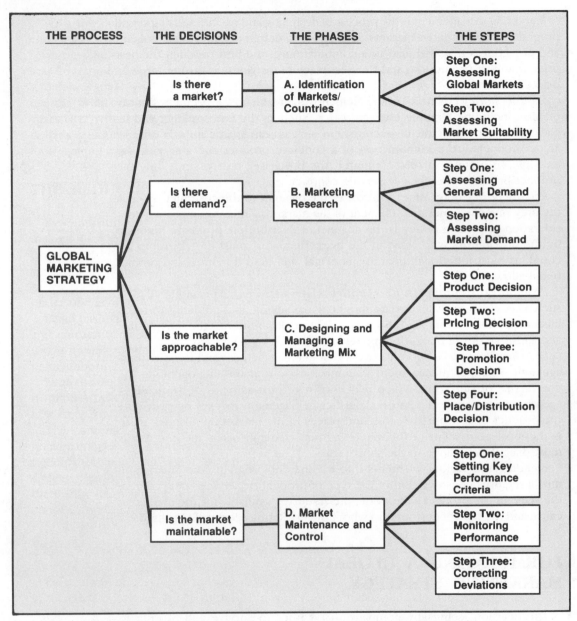

by top management, and are not easily reversed. Exhibit 11-2 presents the phases in designing and implementing an international marketing strategy. The international marketing process is a sequential one. It begins with Phase A, identification of markets/countries. The main objective here is to develop a panoramic view of the global market for the company's product or service. If the global market is deemed substantial in terms of size and volatile in terms of growth patterns, management may decide to devote organizational resources to in-depth marketing research (Phase B). If the result of the marketing research is favorable, the firm will move into Phase C, designing and managing a marketing mix to penetrate the market. Finally, in Phase D, the firm must devise systems to keep and control the market.

PHASE A: IDENTIFICATION OF MARKETS/COUNTRIES

The purpose of the first phase in the formulation of a global marketing strategy is to sensitize management to the global imperative: the need to take in the forest (the global market) and not just the trees (the local market and competition for it). There seems to be an overwhelming tendency among practicing managers to be overly domestically motivated. When management does look at the international market, it concentrates on its own country's exports. Phase A of international marketing involves consideration of the world's purchases of the product the company produces. The aim is to identify opportunities—to conduct "opportunistic surveillance."

As Exhibit 11-3 indicates, there are two steps in Phase A. Step One aims at assessing the quantitative dimensions of the global market for the company's products and/or services. Step Two zeroes in on the qualitative aspects of the identified markets. Certain large and growing markets might not be suitable for a particular company if the firm cannot meet the demands imposed by the government or overcome the market imperfections resulting from competition.

Exhibit 11-3   Global Marketing Strategy, Phase A: Identification of Markets/Countries

---

Step One
Assessing global markets and their growth by studying world exports, imports, re-exports, and the like.
Sources: United Nations Yearbooks, Predicast, OECD Worldcast, U.S. Department of Commerce, SBA's XIS.

Step Two
Assessing market suitability: the general business environment of the country, in social, technological, ecological, political, and economic areas. In particular, the political risk must be carefully assessed.
Sources: Business Environment Risk Index (BERI), Frost & Sullivan Political Risk Assessment Services, The Economist's Intelligence Unit's country studies, and Business International Corporation's country and area studies. The ENSCAN framework explained in Chapter 3 should prove very useful.

STEP ONE: ASSESSING GLOBAL MARKETS AND THEIR GROWTH

There are essentially two ways of acquiring data on the global market. The first—the one favored by most U.S. managers—is to focus on U.S. exports of a product. The second—favored by Japanese managers—is to focus on United Nations or OECD data on world exports, imports, and re-exports.

Exhibit 11-4 illustrates the kinds of information that are useful in Phase A of the marketing process. The exhibit shows a report generated by the Small Business Administration's Export Information System (XIS). The report provides three sets of data on imports of a particular product. The upper portion of the report gives the top twenty-five importers of the product; each importer's growth/decline pattern, expressed as a deviation from a base index (100); the major exporter to each importing country; the size of the global market; and total U.S. exports of the product. The middle section of the report presents data on the ten markets in which the United States has the highest share. The percentages of each market held by the United States and by its major competitors are given for the past five years. The bottom section of the report provides similar data on the markets in which the dollar value of U.S. sales is greatest. The XIS system contains information on over 2,500 products and 160 countries.

STEP TWO: ASSESSING MARKET SUITABILITY

There are many reasons why a certain quantitatively promising market might not be suitable for a particular company. Ascertaining a market's suitability goes under many names, including country risk analysis, political risk analysis, and environmental scanning. The main objective of all of these processes is to give management an adequate understanding of a country's general environment and of its receptiveness to the company's particular product or service. There are as many environmental scanning schemes as there are experts in international business. Chapter 3 presented a brief outline of ENSCAN, an environmental scanning software package.[9]

PHASE B: MARKETING RESEARCH

The markets identified in Phase A must be further scrutinized to more definitively determine the relationship between their potential and the firm's capabilities. The aim of Phase B is to assess the particular market's total potential demand and the firm's potential market share. The two main steps in this process are assessing general demand and assessing market demand (Exhibit 11-5).

---

[9]See Warren J. Keegan, "Multinational Scanning: A Study of the Information Sources Utilized by Headquarters by Executives in Multinational Corporations," *Administrative Science Quarterly*, September 1974, 411–421. For more on ENSCAN, see Asterios G. Kefalas, "Linking Environmental Scanning to the Strategic Plan Parts I and II," *Strategic Planning Management*, April and May 1987, 25–36.

Exhibit 11-4 XIS Product Report

```
*************************************************************************
***            SITC NUMBER: 752    AUTOMTIC DATA PROC EQUIP          ***
*************************************************************************
***               TOP 25 IMPORTING COUNTRIES (1986 FIGURES)         ***
   COUNTRY               DOLLAR VALUE   TREND (1982=100)    PRIMARY
   IMPORTING    QUANTITY  IN THOUSANDS (83) (84) (85) (86)  EXPORTER
   --------------------------------------------------------------------
```

COUNTRY IMPORTING	QUANTITY	DOLLAR VALUE IN THOUSANDS	(83)	(84)	(85)	(86)	PRIMARY EXPORTER
USA	243.374 W	5,718,650	195	358	406	564	JAPAN
GERMANY, FR	47.692 W	4,079,453	119	144	173	237	USA
UNTD KINGDOM	56.747 W	3,844,516	122	143	156	177	USA
FRANCE	41.243 W	3,187,705	106	126	143	192	USA
CANADA	NR	2,139,172	110	151	134	138	USA
ITALY	25,501 W	1,918,467	107	150	186	227	USA
NETHERLANDS	22,485 W	1,735,693	126	152	173	240	USA
JAPAN	7,411 W	1,143,340	105	142	158	176	USA
SWITZERLAND	11,147 W	1,038,380	112	138	171	251	GERMANY, FR
AUSTRALIA	NR	992,959	116	165	206	227	USA
BELGIUM-LUX	10,449 W	903,248	111	138	152	212	GERMANY, FR
SWEDEN	8,455 W	739,290	147	143	163	184	USA
NORWAY	452,658 N	528,572	119	174	206	289	USA
KOREA REP.	7,004 W	473,394	128	155	177	297	JAPAN
DENMARK	5,473 W	473,372	122	144	150	206	USA
AUSTRIA	4,533 W	445,451	117	139	164	238	GERMANY, FR
FINLAND	3,865 W	346,434	122	145	157	197	USA
SINGAPORE	1,401,143 N	320,887	115	188	187	195	USA
HONG KONG	638,169 N	301,093	131	310	242	243	USA
IRELAND	3,856 W	273,848	83	92	111	134	USA
ISRAEL	NR	245,170	135	139	148	138	USA
NEW ZEALAND	NR	190,663	110	177	224	247	USA
PORTUGAL	1,659 W	126,921	NR	NR	NR	NR	USA
GREECE	1,975 W	75,750	120	172	244	372	UNTD KINGDOM
ICELAND	330 W	24,886	160	309	491	615	USA
WORLD TOTAL	3,027,890	31,395,599	116	159	178	212	
TOTAL US EXP	428,031	9,428,881					

```
*************************************************************************
***             TOP 10 U.S. MARKETS BY MARKET SHARE                 ***
   COUNTRY    U.S. MARKET SHARE (%)      PRIMARY    COMPETITOR'S SHARE (%)
   IMPORTING (82) (83) (84) (85) (86)  COMPETITOR (82) (83) (84) (85) (86)
```

COUNTRY IMPORTING	(82)	(83)	(84)	(85)	(86)	PRIMARY COMPETITOR	(82)	(83)	(84)	(85)	(86)
CANADA	93.6	90.5	91.6	88.9	86.4	JAPAN	2.0	4.5	3.2	3.2	4.7
JAPAN	76.4	80.2	80.2	78.0	76.6	BRAZIL	9.5	6.9	7.5	6.8	5.9
ISRAEL	44.7	45.6	51.0	53.9	55.8	UNTD KINGDOM	10.4	9.6	8.5	10.4	9.7
NEW ZEALAND	63.3	53.7	53.4	47.1	50.9	JAPAN	18.2	22.7	17.1	18.9	20.3
IRELAND	66.1	61.6	59.1	54.4	49.3	UNTD KINGDOM	11.7	15.8	18.8	21.0	17.2
SINGAPORE	53.0	60.0	52.1	53.5	43.5	JAPAN	19.7	16.5	17.2	18.5	26.4
AUSTRALIA	57.4	52.3	52.9	44.5	43.1	JAPAN	19.8	24.0	21.3	24.0	27.5
FRANCE	48.4	45.7	47.9	40.8	37.7	GERMANY, FR	15.2	16.4	12.2	12.6	12.5
SWEDEN	44.5	35.8	41.7	38.0	35.7	JAPAN	4.9	7.2	10.5	12.4	15.1
NORWAY	43.2	37.0	38.8	33.9	33.7	UNTD KINGDOM	11.5	10.4	12.7	12.3	14.0

```
*************************************************************************
***   TOP 10 U.S. MARKETS BY SALES VOLUME (IN MILLIONS OF DOLLARS)  ***
   COUNTRY    U.S. MARKET VOLUME ($)     PRIMARY    COMPETITOR'S VOLUME ($)
   IMPORTING (82) (83) (84) (85) (86)  COMPETITOR (82) (83) (84) (85) (86)
```

COUNTRY IMPORTING	(82)	(83)	(84)	(85)	(86)	PRIMARY COMPETITOR	(82)	(83)	(84)	(85)	(86)
CANADA	1449	1547	2143	1851	1850	JAPAN	31	77	76	67	101
FRANCE	802	809	1005	974	1203	GERMANY, FR	253	290	256	301	400
UNTD KINGDOM	1047	1137	1284	1154	1160	JAPAN	77	190	267	305	480
GERMANY, FR	687	704	818	858	1063	JAPAN	107	208	301	458	784
JAPAN	495	548	742	799	876	BRAZIL	61	47	70	69	68
NETHERLANDS	253	354	366	365	479	GERMANY, FR	112	135	167	194	276
AUSTRALIA	251	266	382	401	428	JAPAN	86	122	153	216	273
ITALY	249	239	317	354	402	GERMANY, FR	193	228	259	287	363
SWEDEN	178	211	240	249	264	JAPAN	19	43	61	81	111
SWITZERLAND	134	140	169	211	199	GERMANY, FR	97	109	124	155	251

Exhibit 11-5   Global Marketing Strategy, Phase B:
Marketing Research

Step One: Assessing General Demand

(1)   Potential need (physically determined)
Climate; natural resources; land use; population (demography); occupational breakdown; life expectancy; topography; overall level of wealth
Key question: Is there a potential need?

(2)   Felt need (culturally determined)
Existence of linking products and services; values and institutions (class structure, influence on elite, lifestyle); market exposure (means of communication and transport, literacy, mobility, urbanization)
Key question: What effort (cost) is required to transform a potential need into a felt need of significant intensity and aggregate size to be attractive (profitable)?

(3)   Potential demand (economically determined)
Disposable income level; income distribution; consumption as a function of income; family budget; traditional trading patterns (external and internal)
Key question: Are there economic and organizational factors beyond the firm's influence that will block the development of a felt need into a potential demand?

(4)   Effective demand (politically determined)
"Buy national" restrictions; foreign exchange restrictions; import duties; import quotas; imposition of national law regarding public health, sanitation, safety, security, pollution; conflict with locally owned rights (pat-

ents, copyrights, trademarks); taxation; rationing; subsidy programs; price and wage controls; special external trade relations (such as bilateral trade treaties); effectiveness of commercial law; extent of law and order; relative importance of the government sector in total consumption; government control over communications; state planning
Key questions: To what extent are market factors permitted to operate? To what extent can the firm circumvent or change politically imposed restraints?

Step Two: Assessing Market Demand

(1) Market demand (commercially determined)
Cost or availability of internal distribution (degree of market dispersion, market organization, credit facilities, insurance, transport costs, special storage and handling facilities); advertising and promotion facilities and effectiveness
Key question: Can the firm get its product or service to the customer at reasonable cost relative to other products and services for which there is also effective demand?

(2) Specific demand: sales potential (competitively determined)
Appropriateness of the firm's and competitors' product or service in terms of quality, design, sizing, packaging, and pricing; credit terms; currency accepted (source of product); delivery time; service and warranties offered.
Key questions: Can the firm meet the terms offered by competitors in the supply of the same or similar products and services? What is its likely market share?

SOURCE: Adapted from R. Robinson, *Internationalization of Business: An Introduction* (Chicago: The Dryden Press, 1984), 37.

STEP ONE: ASSESSING GENERAL DEMAND

The purpose of Step One is to get a general idea of the potential size of the market and of other factors relevant to the marketing of the firm's products and/or services. The marketing research team's job at this point is to collect secondary data relating to the national business and market environment, internal company data relating to past sales and performance, and estimates of projected sales and market potential.[10]

---

[10]Susan P. Douglas and C. Samuel Craig, "Information for International Marketing Decisions," in Ingo Walter (ed.), *Handbook of International Business* (New York: John Wiley and Sons, 1982), 29.3–29.33.

STEP TWO: ASSESSING MARKET DEMAND

Often top managers are reluctant to authorize primary research into specific markets; they question the usefulness of research generally and balk at the tremendous expense involved in conducting in-depth research into foreign markets. As statistical techniques such as Bayesian analysis show, however, the benefits that well-designed and well-executed research can bring to a firm far outweigh the costs.

The dilemma facing an international marketing research team is whether to apply the domestic approach to international marketing research or to design a different type of research for every single country. The answer probably lies between these two extremes: some parts of the research package can be applied across the globe; others must be adapted to fit the peculiarities of the local market.

In general, there are four types of international marketing research:

(1)   Single-country research

(2)   Independent multicountry research

(3)   Sequential multicountry research

(4)   Simultaneous multicountry research

Single-country research is undertaken in one country by a foreign company; independent multicountry research is undertaken by subsidiaries of a multinational organization in different countries but is not coordinated across countries. Sequential multicountry research is conducted first in one country and then in other countries. This approach is attractive in that lessons learned in one country can be applied in another—the key findings of earlier studies influence the focus of later ones, increasing the efficiency of the research. In addition, costs are spread over a longer period. Simultaneous multicountry research is conducted at the same time in different countries and is coordinated across countries. This is the most difficult type of marketing research to undertake. Organization and coordination tend to be costly and relatively time-consuming. Consequently, although such studies are beginning to be undertaken in greater numbers, they are still relatively rare.

PHASE C: DESIGNING AND MANAGING A MARKETING MIX

Once the firm has identified the markets it wishes to service, the next step is to select a marketing mix that will enable the firm to penetrate the market and capture a profitable niche within it. The well-known principle of economies of scale applies to the marketing mix management process. The more markets that can be reached via the same marketing mix, the more the "sunk" costs of marketing can be spread out. The result—lower prices—benefits both the firm and the customer. (See Exhibit 11-6.)

Exhibit 11-6   Global Marketing Strategy, Phase C: Designing and Managing a Marketing Mix

Step One: Product Decision

(1)   What products and product lines should the company sell, and how broad and deep should the product line be for this market?

(2)   To what extent should the company adapt and modify products for this market to cultural, sociological, and national characteristics?

(3)   What improvements of existing products should be undertaken, and should the firm introduce a new product or products in this market?

(4)   How should products be packaged and labeled in this market? (Includes a review of existing packaging and labeling laws.)

(5)   What warranties and guarantees, if any, are desirable or must be offered, and what other services (such as repair service) are required in this market?

Step Two: Pricing Decision

(1)   What tariff and dumping laws are applicable in this market?

(2)   Should the firm establish (or attempt to establish) uniform base prices?

(3)   What specific pricing approach (such as cost-oriented, computer-oriented, or customer-oriented) should be used in the market?

(4)   Are there any regulations regarding pricing (that is, price fixing and cartel arrangements) in this market?

(5)   What pricing approach do competitors use in this market?

Step Three: Promotion Decision

(1)   To what extent should advertising themes and campaigns in this market be differentiated to accommodate cultural, sociological, and national characteristics?

(2)   Should a local advertising agency or a branch or subsidiary of the firm's international advertising agency be used in this market?

(3)   What media are available, and what are their costs and unusual requirements? How reliable are media circulation or audience data?

(4)   What regulations on media advertising would affect the firm's strategy in this market? What are the regulations on point-of-purchase and in-store materials?

(5) What roles do channel members play, and what advertising assistance, such as cooperative advertising, in-store promotion, and point-of-purchase materials, do channel members expect?

Step Four: Place/Distribution Decision

(1) What is the typical retail and wholesale structure for comparable products in this market?

(2) Should the firm use existing channels of distribution or attempt to alter the established distribution patterns in this market?

(3) Does the firm wish to sell directly to the retailer or through intermediaries in this market?

(4) Should the firm attempt to obtain wide distribution at the retail level or rely on exclusive dealerships or outlets in this market?

(5) What is the quality of the available transportation and warehousing? What are the firm's other physical distribution needs in this market?

STEP ONE: PRODUCT DECISION

The choice of the product to be introduced into a market is the most important decision made by a marketing management team. Product conception, testing, prototype development, market testing, and so on may be expensive, but they are vital, as the other three elements of the marketing process can do little to salvage a defective, ineffective, or useless product.

By and large, industrial products (products destined for further use in the production process as intermediate products or as machinery) are relatively standardized. There are, of course, occasions on which adaptations must be made, either because of environmental conditions or because of customer habits, but for the most part there is much less difference among models of industrial products (say, beer bottling machines) than among commercial products (for example, the brands of beer put into the bottles). Commercial products, which are consumed as they are, often are differentiated through packaging (different beers in different bottles), brand naming, color, flavor, services, quality of performance, and so on. The more commercial the markets a firm wishes to reach, the higher the probability that the product will have to undergo considerable modification and adaptation to local requirements. Warren Keegan has outlined five product strategies that can be used to expand international markets.[11]

---

[11]Warren Keegan, *Multinational Marketing Management* (Englewood Cliffs, NJ: Prentice-Hall, 1980), 385–389.

(1)   Product and promotional extension (dual extension) is the easiest marketing strategy to implement and probably the most profitable one. The strategy entails selling exactly the same product, with the same advertising and promotional themes and appeals, in every country in which the company operates. Pepsi Cola, for example, has been successful in selling the same product with standard promotional themes in a variety of markets. Pepsi has estimated that tailoring promotions to each foreign market would substantially raise the cost of doing business.

(2)   Product extension with promotional adaptation involves selling the same product in foreign markets but tailoring the promotion to local conditions. U.S. firms marketing analgesics in Japan sell essentially the same product as they do in the United States, but use a somewhat different advertising theme. Colgate has put its Irish Spring formula to use in Mexico in a new soap called Nordiko. The name Nordiko was chosen because it brings to mind the north ("el norte") and thus (Colgate hopes) projects a fresh and cool image to Mexican consumers.

(3)   Product adaptation with promotional extension is an approach in which the original promotional strategy is retained, but the product is adapted to local conditions. Exxon, for example, adapted its gasoline to suit different climatic conditions in foreign markets, but used its famous "Put a tiger in your tank" promotion in nearly all areas.

(4)   When the sociocultural and economic conditions in various markets are such that using the same product and/or promotion in all of them is impossible, a strategy of dual adaptation—adaptation of both the product and the communications efforts—is required. When the military government in Brazil imposed a heavy tax on all imports it considered "superfluous," liquor manufacturers came up with a score of new brands, all bottled (and some even distilled) in Brazil, and promoted them as thirst-quenching, cooling drinks.

(5)   Perhaps the riskiest market expansion strategy is to try to invent something to meet the special needs of overseas customers. Seeing a potential market in the estimated 600 million people in the world who wash clothes by hand, Colgate developed an inexpensive plastic, hand-powered washer that has the tumbling action of a modern automatic machine. This product has sold well in Mexico and could help expand the demand for Colgate's laundry detergent.[12]

STEP TWO: PRICING DECISION

Traditionally pricing decisions are made after careful costing of the product and determination of the level of profit or consumer surplus the firm may be

---

[12]Samuel Rabina, "International Marketing Mix," in Walter, (ed.), pp. 32.1–32.26.

able to realize. This approach is appropriate under the classical economic conditions of a free market characterized by many more or less equally competent suppliers, none of which is able to dominate the market. In such a setting the price will be set equal to the average cost of producing each unit, which is the sum of fixed costs, variable costs, overhead, and profit. (See Exhibit 11-7.)

In international business, pricing is not simply an exercise in costing out a product. Rather, pricing is an exceedingly important element of the marketing mix, to the extent that the firm uses prices as a competitive weapon. Usually one large producer has a competitive advantage, which allows it to become the so-called price setter. "Price takers" are the companies that exist under the "price umbrella" of the dominant competitor.

Because of the significant competitive advantage it holds, the price-setting firm has the opportunity to manipulate the umbrella, lowering it when it wishes to wipe out existing competitors and/or discourage newcomers and raising it when it wants to let the marginal competitors survive. In the absence of competition, the price setter may adopt a price skimming strategy, setting the initial price for its product high enough that the firm can quickly recover most, if not all, product development and marketing sunk costs. IBM, as the largest mainframe computer manufacturer, has been accused of using a price skimming strategy.

As technology becomes familiar and competitors gain experience, the dominant firm begins to slide down the experience curve, gradually cutting manufacturing costs. If the product has become well known, it may be possible to considerably reduce marketing costs as well. With costs at a minimum, the firm is in a position to adopt a penetration or predatory pricing strategy.

Predatory pricing involves discrete, short-term cuts intended to financially weaken the competition rather than to expand the market. After the price cuts have produced their effect and competitors have been eliminated, prices are

---

Exhibit 11-7   Two Ways of Setting Prices: Full Costing versus Incremental Costing

The following is an illustration of the full costing and incremental costing methods. The Natural Company is selling 15,000 units of its product per year. The regular market price is $15.00 per unit. The variable costs are $5/unit for materials and $4/unit for labor, for a total of $9/unit. The fixed costs are $40,000 per year. The income statement reflecting the situation would appear as follows:

Income Statement

Sales (15,000 @ $15.00)		$225,000
Less Costs: Variable costs (15,000 @ $9.00)	$135,000	
Fixed costs	40,000	− 175,000
Profit		$ 50,000

Suppose the company has the opportunity to sell an additional 3,000 units at $10.00 per unit to a foreign firm. (This is a special situation and will not have an adverse effect on the price of the product in the regular market.) If the Natural Company uses the full costing method to make its decision, the opportunity will be rejected, because the price of $10.00/unit does not cover the full cost of $11.67/unit ($175,000/15,000 = $11.67). By using the full costing method as a decision criterion, the company would actually be giving up $3,000 in additional profits.

If the incremental costing method is used, the opportunity will be accepted. The incremental costing method compares additional costs to be incurred with the additional revenues that will be received if the offer is accepted.

Additional revenue (3,000 @ $10.00)	$30,000
Less additional costs (3,000 @ $9.00)	−27,000
Additional Income	$ 3,000

The difference between the two decision methods results from the treatment of fixed costs. The full costing method includes the fixed cost in the cost-per-unit calculation. The incremental cost method recognizes that no additional fixed costs will be incurred if additional units are produced. Therefore, fixed costs are not considered in the decision process.

The following is an income statement comparing the results of accepting and rejecting the foreign offer:

Income Statement

	Rejecting the offer	Accepting the offer
Sales (15,000 units @ $15.00)	$225,000	$225,000
(3,000 units @ $10.00)	—	30,000
Total sales	$225,000	$255,000
Costs: Variable (@ $9.00/unit)	$135,000	$162,000
Fixed	40,000	40,000
Total costs	$175,000	$202,000
Net Income	$ 50,000	$ 53,000

Note: An important factor in such a decision is a consideration of the effects of accepting the offer on regular market price. For purposes of illustration, this example specified that the regular market price would not be affected by the sale of extra units at a lower price. In the real world, however, if the additional sales were made in the regular market at the $10.00 price, it could depress the regular market price below $15.00. This would severely hamper operations in the future.

Source: From Subhash C. Jain, *International Marketing Management,* 2nd ed. (Boston: PWS-KENT Publishing Company, 1987), Exhibit 13.1, pp. 459–469. © by Wadsworth, Inc. Permission granted by PWS-KENT Publishing Company, a division of Wadsworth, Inc.

returned to oligopolistic levels. *Penetration pricing* involves setting prices below existing equilibrium levels in order to maximize unit volume. Lower prices increase total sales, and the firm using penetration pricing acquires a significant share of the market. Japanese companies have captured sizeable shares of the U.S. color TV and automobile markets by using penetration pricing strategies to their limit.

According to Robinson, there are essentially three pricing policies: standard worldwide pricing, dual pricing (domestic/export), and market-differentiated pricing.[13] Any of these policies may, of course, include a discount system. (Depending on the priorities of foreign buyers, performance warranties, claims for services, payment in certain foreign currencies, or delivery within a specified time may take the place of a discount based on quantity, terms of payment, or purchase of associated goods or services.) In establishing a standard worldwide base price, management is most likely to use the full-cost pricing method, including an allowance for manufacturing overhead, general overhead, and selling expenses.

Dual pricing refers to the practice of quoting one price for the domestic market and a second price for exports. The latter is often the lower of the two. Various issues must be taken into consideration in establishing a dual pricing policy. For example, the export price cannot be set below the cost of production or else the firm may be subject to "antidumping" suits. Also, if the firm is exporting out of a country with a value-added tax (VAT) into a country that has no VAT, the tax on the exported product may be lower than the tax on the product sold domestically to the extent that the VAT is rebated by the exporting country.

The assumption underlying a market-differentiated pricing policy is that the head office knows enough about the target market to set the correct price for that market. The best approach in some circumstances is for headquarters to set a price floor and give local management full discretion to price above that point. A variation of this approach is to allow local management to set prices a certain percentage above or below a base price established by headquarters.

In some markets, the price an MNC can charge is restricted by the government. Some countries (such as Egypt), in order to protect the local small producer, set a floor price below which MNCs cannot sell their products. Some others (such as Japan), in order to accommodate local customers, set a maximum price above which the MNC cannot sell its products. The best advice that one can give to a newcomer in the international business game is to follow the leader and make sure that the cost structure allows for a respectable return on the invested capital.

STEP THREE: PROMOTION DECISION

Promotion is essentially a communication process aimed at drawing the customer's attention to the firm's products and services. Again, publications

---

[13]Richard D. Robinson, *Internationalization of Business: An Introduction* (Chicago: The Dryden Press, 1984), 49–51.

on international marketing are replete with stories of real blunders. They range from Chevy's use of the name "Nova" in Latin America, where "no va" means "no go," to Esso's multimillion-dollar expenditures to change its name, to P&G's ordeal over (and eventual abandonment of) the half-moon and five-star corporate symbol.

The major decision a firm must cope with in planning a promotional strategy is whether to go with "one name, one message, one voice"[14] or to develop promotional schemes tailored to the local audience. The main goal here is, again, to take advantage of economies of scale: the more people who are reached with the same promotional instrument, the lower the cost of promoting the product, the smaller the contribution of promotional expenses to the overall cost of the product, and the lower and more competitive the price of the final product.

There have been numerous successful attempts to carry one message internationally. Esso was able to use its advertising theme "Put a tiger in your tank" with considerable success in most countries in the world. In French, however, the word for "tank" is *reservoir,* which in the context of the phrase could have been highly suggestive, so the word *moteur* was substituted. And in Thailand, where the tiger is not a symbol of strength, the campaign was not understood. In England, a U.S.-designed advertising campaign built on the slogan "Don't spend a penny until you've tried . . ." had to be modified because the phrase "spend a penny" in Britain is the equivalent of "go see a man about a dog" in the United States.[15]

STEP FOUR: PLACE/DISTRIBUTION DECISION

The last P of the marketing mix management kit—place—has been replaced by the broader concept of distribution, which includes activities such as transportation, storage, order processing, inventory management, packaging, and customer and product service. Some of these activities were dealt with in Chapter 10 as integral parts of production/sourcing strategy. Others were treated in Chapter 7 on participation strategy.

In general, there are two main sets of managerial functions and staff activities that must be planned and carried out as part of an effective distribution strategy.[16] Logistics management involves

(1)   Carrier selection

(2)   Facilities location

(3)   Fleet management

---

[14]Myron Magnet, "Saatchi & Saatchi Will Keep Gobbling," *Fortune,* June 23, 1986, 26–45.

[15]Stefan H. Robock and Kenneth Simmonds, *International Business and Multinational Enterprises* (Homewood, IL: Richard D. Irwin, 1983), 445.

[16]William H. Davidson, *Global Strategic Management* (New York: John Wiley and Sons, 1982), 159.

(4) Establishment of inventory policy

(5) Establishment of delivery schedules and routes

(6) Order processing

Channel management involves

(1) Sales force management

(2) Establishment of trade margins

(3) Establishment of credit terms

(4) Agent selection and use

(5) Outlet selection

(6) Establishment of channel promotion policy

When cost savings from the application of technology to the production process begin to taper off, management's attention switches to improvements in the distribution system. It is estimated that almost 40% of the cost of doing business falls under the category of information cost, most of which relates to distribution. Thus the distribution function is no longer viewed as something that the truckers are supposed to take care of; rather, it is seen as a bona fide managerial activity.

Exhibit 11-8 shows channel configurations for consumer products, industrial products, and services. Choosing the right channel configuration is the most

Exhibit 11-8 Channel Configurations

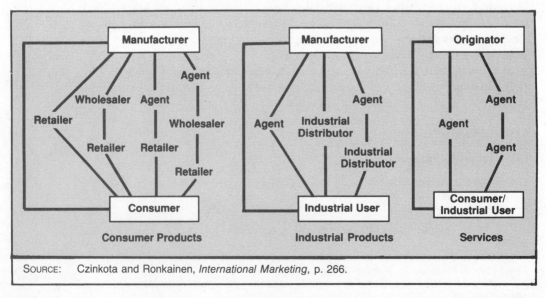

SOURCE: Czinkota and Ronkainen, *International Marketing,* p. 266.

difficult part of establishing a distribution strategy. Every country has its own distribution systems. In the United States, products are generally handled by a few distributors with a lot of resources. The entire Toyota distribution system in the United States consists of just three importers and 1,248 dealers. In Europe, where Toyota sells far fewer cars, there are nineteen importers and 3,182 dealers. Toyota's own headquarters is notorious for its complicated distribution system, which seems to be the greatest stumbling block to U.S. exporters.

Of the myriad of problems that surround this rather complicated element of the marketing mix, two stand out. The first is the complexity inevitably created by diverse ownership of the channels of distribution, geographic and cultural distances, and different legal systems.[17]

The second problem is known as the gray market. Although for the time being the gray market is strictly a U.S. phenomenon, its success is bound to cause it to spread over the globe. The phrases *gray market* and *parallel importation* refer to the trade in

> authentic and legitimately manufactured trademark items that are pro-
> duced and purchased abroad but imported or diverted into the United
> States by bypassing designated channels. These goods can be sold for
> less money than if they had been purchased from U.S. subsidiaries or
> authorized distributors of the foreign manufacturers because of currency
> fluctuations and other factors such as the absence of manufacturer's war-
> ranty. Gray markets ride on the coattails of the legitimate channel's efforts
> to build demand. Gray-market products steal market share from their
> legitimate counterparts simply because they cost less; many 35 mm cam-
> eras, for example, can be sold for 10 percent below list price.[18]

Exhibit 11-9 shows how the gray market affects the distribution of the Seiko watches marketed by K. Hattori & Co., Ltd.

International marketers are looking into taking legal action against the gray marketers because they drive down prices, steal sales, and damage the image of the product and of legitimate dealers. In addition, marketers have instituted various programs to protect both their distributors and consumers. Some have introduced improved warranties to preserve their sales and the goodwill of customers toward the brand—goodwill that is eroded when the repair of a gray good is not covered by the usual manufacturer's warranty accompanying products purchased from authorized dealers. For example, Hasselblad, the Swedish camera manufacturer, offers rebates to purchasers of legally imported, serial-numbered camera bodies, lenses, and film magazines.[19]

---

[17]For a detailed treatment of this issue, see Czinkota and Ronkainen, *International Marketing,* pp. 286–287.

[18]Czinkota and Ronkainen, *International Marketing,* p. 288.

[19]Czinkota and Ronkainen, *International Marketing,* p. 289; see also Gay Jervey, " 'Gray Market' Hits Camera, Watch Sales," *Advertising Age,* August 15, 1983, 3, 62.

Exhibit 11-9　Gray Markets: Authorized and Unauthorized Channels of Distribution

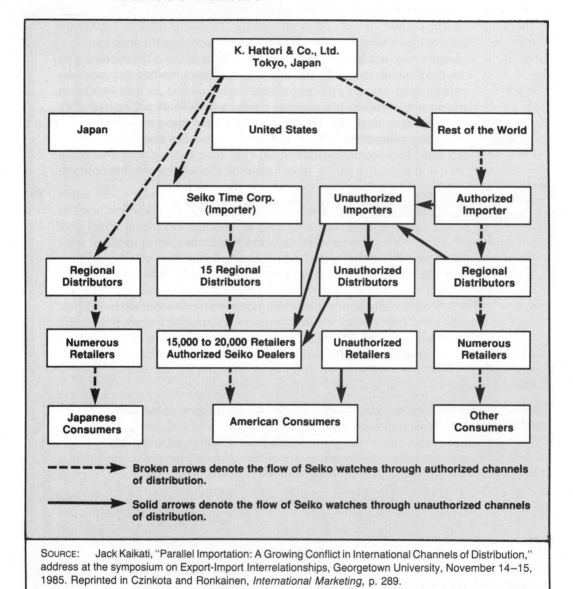

SOURCE:　Jack Kaikati, "Parallel Importation: A Growing Conflict in International Channels of Distribution," address at the symposium on Export-Import Interrelationships, Georgetown University, November 14–15, 1985. Reprinted in Czinkota and Ronkainen, *International Marketing,* p. 289.

PHASE D: MARKET MAINTENANCE AND CONTROL

Maintenance and control are managerial activities designed to help the firm hold on to markets that it has spent organizational resources developing. The subject of organizational control will be treated in detail in Chapter 13. Briefly, the process involves choosing, designing, and implementing an appropriate organizational structure. Marketing managers at headquarters must first choose the performance criteria and standards to be met by the company's overseas affiliates. Next they must set up a monitoring system which will detect deviations from these standards. Finally, managers must develop a set of organizational policies which spell out the guidelines for timely and effective corrective actions to eliminate deviations from the standard performance criteria.

FUTURE ISSUES IN INTERNATIONAL MARKETING

Two issues will occupy multinational managers' time in the near future. The first is the changes resulting from the Soviet policies of *glasnost* (openness) and *perestroika* (restructuring) of the economy. Close to half a billion people will be affected by Mikhail S. Gorbachev's breaks with traditional communist thinking.[20] Currently most western ventures in "nonmarket," or planned, economies involve a private enterprise dealing with a state-owned enterprise. This situation may very well change, however; the possibility will be explored in Chapter 14 on consortia, a new type of corporate global scheme. (See Exhibit 11-10.)

The second issue is "countertrade," or "barter trade." Countertrade transactions link exports and imports of goods or services to something other than financial settlements. Exhibit 11-11 provides an idea of the tremendous popularity that this concept has gained. Clearly, the popular view of countertrade as a way for developing or communist countries to deal with the lack of foreign currency to pay for imports is wrong. Indeed, a look at the right-hand side of the figure reveals that quite a few developed countries are making use of this method of trading. Exhibit 11-12 outlines the main types of countertrade and gives some examples.

RECAPITULATION

Levitt's landmark article on the globalization of markets initiated a great debate. Now "globalization" has become one of the buzzwords of the eighties, and globalization as a marketing strategy is here to stay. Even the definition of the term "global marketing" has undergone a change. What once meant

---

[20]Peter Galuszka, Bill Javetski, John Pearson, and Rose Brady, "Reforming the Soviet Economy," *Business Week,* December 7, 1987, 76–88.

Exhibit 11-10   Perestroika to Pizza

Pizza Huts in the land of Pushkin? Oreo cookies in Omsk? Big Macs in Belgrade? Yes, all that—and more. Maybe.

American companies have long viewed doing business with the Soviet Union as a dubious proposition, given the stormy politics of the superpower relationship. But under *perestroika,* General Secretary Mikhail Gorbachev's campaign to revitalize his country's economy, the Soviets are trying to attract American know-how to help step up the tempo of development. Encouraged by their overtures, dozens of U.S. companies—among them Honeywell, Occidental Petroleum and Archer Daniels Midland—are forming joint ventures in the Soviet Union. . . .

The official warming trend even revived the often sleepy U.S.–U.S.S.R. Trade and Economic Council, a group of 315 U.S. companies and 150 Soviet enterprises and ministries, which staged a four-day conference in Moscow in April to talk about prospective joint ventures. In a display of Madison Avenue glitz, council members from the U.S. gave their Soviet counterparts a crash course in marketing that included razzle-dazzle TV commercials for Diet Coke, NutraSweet and the American Express Card. . . .

Several industrial agreements have been signed since November. In the first of these ventures, Connecticut-based Combustion Engineering will provide machinery and software for managing petroleum production at refineries. Minnesota's Honeywell will equip Soviet fertilizer plants with high-tech manufacturing equipment. Occidental Petroleum will build two factories to supply plastics for food packaging, vinyl floors and other uses. Chevron is discussing an oil-exploration venture, while Monsanto is negotiating joint production of a weed-killing herbicide.

Economic detente with the Soviets has spawned consumer-oriented ventures as well. For the past two weeks, Muscovites have been lining up to buy slices of the first American pizza in the Soviet Union, for 1.25 rubles ($2.10) each at the AstroPizza truck that makes stops around the city. The 18-ft. mobile pizzeria is operated under a joint venture of New Jersey-based Roma Food Enterprises (1987 sales: $100 million) and the City of Moscow.

SOURCE: Janice Castro, "Perestroika to Pizza," *Time,* May 2, 1988, 52–53.

"marketing on a worldwide basis" has come to mean "marketing with a universal, standardized approach worldwide." As the Global Media Commission of the International Advertising Association explains in the foreword to its *Global Marketing* report:

It's the breakthrough tool of the '80s, and it's going to transform the advertising and television industries in the decades to come.

Exhibit 11-11   Countries Requesting Countertrade Privileges with the United States: 1972, 1979, and 1983

15 Countries by 1972	27 Countries by 1979	88 Countries by 1983				
PRC	North Korea	Singapore	El Salvador	Ivory	Belgium
USSR	Iraq	Vietnam	Guatemala	Coast	Netherlands
DDR	Iran	Korea	Honduras	Egypt	Greece
Poland	Israel	Philippines	Panama	Kenya	France
CSSR	Libya	Thailand	Chile	Togo	Germany
Hungary	Argentina	Hong Kong	Paraguay	Uganda	Norway
Rumania	Brazil	Malaysia	Peru	Upper	Denmark
Bulgaria	Colombia	Indonesia	Venezuela	Volta	Italy
Albania	Ecuador	Burma	Mexico	Zaire	U.K.
Cuba	Uruguay	Bangladesh	Algeria	Zambia	Mozambique
Yugoslavia	Switzerland	Pakistan	Nigeria	Zimbabwe	Portugal
India	Austria	Sri Lanka	Angola	South	Morocco
New Zealand		Trinidad	Cameroon	Africa	Liberia
Australia		Jamaica	Ethiopia	Sweden	Guinea
USA (CCC		Dominican	Ghana	Canada	Tunisia
Program)		Republic		Finland	
		Costa Rica		Turkey	
				Spain	

SOURCE: Adapted from Willis A. Bussard, "Countertrade: A View from U.S. Industry," *Countertrade and Barter Quarterly,* May 1984, 54. Reprinted in Czinkota and Ronkainen, *International Marketing,* p. 545.

Global marketing is a simple name for a complex new approach to worldwide business. Some experts think the concept spells the end of multinational corporations as they know them today. Global marketing means selling inexpensive, high-quality, reliable products. Selling the same products in all the nations of the world. And selling them with highly unified marketing techniques. No longer will there be a different advertising campaign for each country or each language of the world. Increasingly, products and their marketing support systems will be truly global.

Why now? Why should business practices that always have been theoretically possible seem so urgently in need of development? Because of television, the undisputed heavyweight champion of advertising.[21]

---

[21]Quoted in Dean G. Van Nest, *Developing Global New Products: Challenges to U.S. Competitiveness* (Ann Arbor, MI: UMI Research Press, Research for Business Decisions, 1987), 9.

Exhibit 11-12   Common Forms of Countertrade

Counterpurchase

Counterpurchase refers to a set of parallel cash agreements in which the supplier sells a service or product and orders unrelated products to offset the costs to the buyer. Here are some examples:

Canada is buying McDonnell Douglas F-18 aircraft worth $2.4 billion. In return, the company will help Canada find customers for goods and services worth $2.9 billion.

Yugoslavia requires automakers to buy Yugoslav goods equal in value to components they ship to Yugoslav auto plants. Fiat buys autos from its Yugoslav licensee.

Brazil asked bidders on a $130 million space satellite for pledges to export Brazil's goods. Canada's Spar Aerospace won jointly with Hughes Aircraft and will arrange imports of Brazilian products of equal value into Canada.

Russia is buying construction machinery from Japan's Komatsu and Mitsubishi. The Japanese are taking Siberian timber.

Colombia is asking equipment suppliers to buy its coffee. A Spanish government company did so in return for Colombia's purchase of buses from Spain's ENESA.

Switch Trading

In a switch-trading arrangement, additional parties are brought into the picture and some of the exchanged goods are shifted to the new party, often for cash. When one party has an unwanted balance of goods to be received from a second party, a third party in need of the goods offered by the first party is found to purchase the available goods, with the proceeds going to the second party. For example:

Greece has accumulated the equivalent of $1 million of credit in Rumania through its sales of cotton and fresh oranges, but it has agreed to take Rumanian goods, which it does not want, as payment. It asks a bank in Vienna to act as its switcher. The bank offers the equivalent of $700,000 in hard currency for the overvalued Rumanian credit position. The Greeks accept the offer and purchase aircraft parts from Boeing in Seattle, something they wanted all along. The switcher finds a customer in Africa who is willing to accept the Rumanian canned goods if the price is right. If the switcher has done a good job, the prices will be acceptable to the Africans, and everyone will benefit.

Clearing Agreement

The objective of the clearing agreement is to balance the exchange of products over time between two governments without having to transfer funds, by using an agreed-on value of trade, tabulated in nonconvertible "clearing account units." The contracting parties establish an exchange ratio of their respective currencies to determine the amount of goods to be traded. Usually, the exchange value is figured in U.S. dollars. For example:

> Morocco and the Soviet Union agree to exchange capital equipment and fresh oranges for a new phosphate plant. Morocco might prefer to buy the equipment elsewhere, but it has little foreign exchange, so it buys from the country that will take oranges in payment rather than hard currency. But Morocco needs the equipment more than the Soviets need the oranges. At settlement date, Morocco corrects the deficit by either paying the difference in hard currency or hoping the Soviets will enter a new agreement and permit the deficit to be carried over to the next contract.

> Russia rationed hard currency for copier imports. So Britain's Rank Xerox is making copiers in India for sale to Moscow under Russia's clearing agreement with India.

Buyback Barter

Under a buyback barter, one party's purchase of capital equipment (plant, process) is paid for through the output made feasible by the capital equipment. Examples:

> Russia is buying phosphates from Occidental Petroleum. In a $20 billion deal, Oxy helped the Soviets build ammonia plants and is buying part of the output.

> China awarded a $500 million contract to Italy's Tecnotrade to expand coal mines and modernize a railroad. Tecnotrade agreed to buy coal for sale abroad.

SOURCE: Adapted from S. Jain, *International Marketing,* pp. 630–633.

Evidence of the phenomenon of converging commonality (which Levitt attributes to widespread accessibility of communication, transportation, and travel) is widespread. Futurists, of course, had long been warning everybody about "global shrinkage." For example, a report on *Science and Future of Mankind,* a study done at the Stanford Research Institute in 1960, twenty years before Levitt's article, concluded as follows:

> In a few generations, man's world has shrunk from a vast expanse, whose area was still incompletely known and whose peoples were relatively distant from one another, to a continuous neighborhood. No man is more than a few hours journey from all other men, and communications between men may be almost instantaneous. Man-made satellites circle this

neighborhood many times in one day, and the repercussions of major events affecting any part of the human family are swiftly felt throughout the whole world.[22]

What was true twenty and thirty years ago is even more evident today. Ours is a global neighborhood, and the challenge confronting the international marketing manager is to determine how best to use the resources of the firm and the tools of the marketing profession to reach the inhabitants of this global neighborhood.

SUGGESTED READINGS

"The Controversy Grows." *Advertising Age,* Special Global Marketing Edition, June 25, 1984.

Czinkota, Michael R., and Ilkka A. Ronkainen. *International Marketing.* Chicago: The Dryden Press, 1988.

Davidson, William H. *Global Strategic Management.* New York: John Wiley and Sons, 1982.

Harrell, Gilbert D., and Richard O. Kiefer. "Multinational Strategic Market Portfolios." *MSU Business Topics,* Winter 1981.

International Advertising Association. *Global Marketing—From Now to the Twenty-First Century.* New York: Global Media Commission, IAA, 1984.

Jordan, Robert D. "Multinational Brand Marketing." Lecture presented at the Center for Business, Pace University, New York City, May 9, 1984.

Jain, Subhash C. *International Marketing,* Second Edition. Boston: Kent Publishing Co., 1987.

Kayanak, Erdener. "Global Marketing: Theory and Practice." *Journal of Global Marketing* I, Nos. 1, 2 (Fall/Winter 1987): 15–29.

Keegan, Warren J. *Multinational Marketing Management.* Englewood Cliffs, NJ: Prentice-Hall, 1980.

Keegan, Warren J., Richard R. Still, and John S. Hill. "Transferability and Adaptability of Products and Promotion Themes in Multinational Marketing—MNCs in LDCs." *Journal of Global Marketing* 1, Nos. 1, 2 (Fall/Winter 1987): 85–104.

Robinson, Richard D. *Internationalization of Business: An Introduction.* Chicago: The Dryden Press, 1984.

Root, Franklin. *Entry Strategies for International Marketing.* Lexington, MA: Lexington Books, 1987.

Saatchi & Saatchi, Compton Worldwide. *The Opportunity for World Brands* New York: 1984.

Tsurumi, Yoshi. *Multinational Management: Business Strategy and Government Policy.* Cambridge, MA: Ballinger Publishing Co., 1984.

---

[22]John McHale, *The Future of the Future* (New York: Ballantine Books, 1969), 65.

Van Nest, Dean G. *Developing Global New Products: Challenges to U.S. Competitiveness*. Ann Arbor, MI: UMI Research Press, 1987.

Walter, Ingo. *Handbook of International Business*. New York: John Wiley and Sons, 1982.

REVIEW QUESTIONS

(1)   Define the terms "globalization," "multinationalization," and "triadization."

(2)   Define and briefly explain the term "marketing" as it is used by the American Marketing Association.

(3)   List and briefly explain the two main sets of tasks of the marketing manager.

(4)   Prepare a report on the subject of "Some Myths about the Lack of Data on International Markets."

(5)   Use the XIS product report shown in Exhibit 11-4 to prepare a ten-minute report to be submitted to the president of a company that produces automatic data-processing equipment, making a case for marketing the company's product overseas.

(6)   The president, pleased with the research report you submitted, hires you to develop a marketing mix management program. You start by locating some distributors in Europe and Latin America; the European distributor will also service the Far East market. Now for the next step— put together a marketing mix package for the data-processing equipment manufacturer's entry into the overseas market. (If possible, secure a good computer package with good graphs and a good world map.)

(7)   Your European distributor has just informed you that "the Russians are extremely interested in our product. The new agreement between the United States and the USSR on declassifying some electronic equipment makes our project just right. We do have to barter, however. The Russians engage in countertrade only." The company's president asks, "What's countertrade, anyway?" Prepare a ten-minute presentation on countertrading with a state-owned enterprise.

CASE ● Some Advice on Marketing Foreign Products in Japan

A long-standing axiom holds that cultural differences oblige the international marketeer to alter his marketing mix. Japan presents a very different environment, and a standard marketing framework cannot be transposed directly from Europe or the United States.

It is often stated that the Japanese distribution system conspires, intentionally or not, to discriminate against imported products. Apparent upon most elementary examination, however, is that a number of U.S. and European firms hold major positions in a wide variety of products. This offers sufficient evidence that the distribution system in Japan, whatever its peculiarities, can be made to serve importers as well as it does local manufacturers. It is worth noting, for example, that this same distribution system has been used quite effectively to introduce Southeast Asian manufactured products in direct competition with some domestic industries that would often be protected in other industrial countries.

Far from being a rigid structure that leaves the foreign firm no room for manoeuvre or innovation, as some critics claim, the Japanese distribution system is essentially dynamic. In general, the foreign exporter or investor finds that his options in Japan are not dissimilar from those in other industrial countries. The problem is to identify and understand these options.

Ing. C. Olivetti & C. SpA is a case in point. Over the past two decades, presidents of Olivetti Japan, equipped with a working ability in the Japanese language, have developed a network designed to fit the company's special needs. Portable typewriters, once sold through the traditional office machinery wholesale channels, were switched to a direct-to-the-retailer sales organization. Olivetti thus established a comfortable 40% share of the portable typewriter market against strong competition.

Direct sale to the retailer is also one of the main features in the success of Estée Lauder Cosmetics Ltd.'s penetration of the men's cosmetics market. The company takes charge of product distribution from arrival in its Yokohama warehouse to selling at its own retail counters strategically located on the men's floor of major department stores. In doing so, it cuts distribution costs far below those of its major competitors. As a result, Estée Lauder was able to establish a share of over 40% of the total men's cosmetics business in department stores throughout Japan.

SOURCE: This is a condensation of a study written by Gunter A. Pauli at Sophia University's Institute of Comparative Culture in Tokyo. Copyright 1983 by Sophia University. This condensation appeared in *International Management,* September 1985, 121–123. Reprinted by special permission from *International Management.* Copyright © 1985. McGraw-Hill Publications Company. All rights reserved.

Taking a somewhat different route, Nihon Philips Corp. and Melitta-Werke Bentz & Sohn both introduced coffee-makers into the Japanese market, calling on coffee-bean wholesalers and retailers rather than on appliance channels largely controlled by Japanese makers. Practically speaking, the competition has been limited to the two European manufacturers. Although some Japanese appliance makers have since introduced electric coffee-makers, neither retailers nor customers appear to have taken them seriously.

If such innovation in distribution is possible in Japan, it does not mean, however, that existing channels are either closed or useless to foreign exporters. Nestlé S.A. has captured and held approximately 75% of the instant coffee market while using the traditional wholesale network. Lipton's has become a household word in Japan, synonymous with black tea, marketing its product through a joint venture with Mitsui & Co. and Toshoku, a major tea wholesaler. Similarly, Johnson & Johnson consolidated its position as a leading supplier of health-care products by working through the complicated traditional distribution system.

PREVENTING PRICE-CUT COMPETITION

Tampax Inc., under the guidance of its general agent, Chuo Bussan, also sells its products through existing wholesale channels and is now the leading brand, with a 30% market share. It demonstrated, moreover, that foreign firms are by no means at the mercy of established channels. To prevent the sale of its products at cut-rate prices, Tampax allows only a 5% margin. But because of customer loyalty, assured through mass advertising and promotion, Tampax can exercise as much influence over its distribution channels as any major Japanese manufacturer.

Some foreign firms have found that the best entry into the market is provided by the distribution networks of Japanese manufacturers, who may or may not use traditional channels. Pez, the Viennese maker of peppermints packaged imaginatively to appeal to young people, gained a meaningful position in the Japanese market through Morinaga & Co., a leading confectionery company. Sony Corp. distributes Whirlpool appliances and Dutch-made Bruynzeel kitchen cabinets through its domestic trading company.

The problem confronting foreign firms doing business in Japan is clearly not the unavailability of proper distribution channels. In general, the difficulties are of a more subtle kind and derive largely from the foreign company's approach to the market. Assuming that a foreign company has "something special" about its products and services that makes them competitive in quality and/or price, it will succeed in the long run only if it makes a serious marketing effort. If this appears an excessively obvious statement, it should be noted that many agents or executives of foreign companies in Japan are frustrated simply because the home office refuses to take seriously the differences observed in the Japanese market.

A most striking difference is price strategy. This aspect of marketing has generated considerable debate. Allegations of dumping practices are perhaps to be explained by divergence in pricing.

Western corporations guided by profit optimization set their price according to production costs, profit estimation, product definition and distribution strategy. The following equation prevails: $P + C = SP$, where P stands for profits, C for costs, and SP for sales price. P and C are largely determined within the company. It could be argued that to a large extent these firms decide price on the basis of internal parameters.

UNCOVERING SLACKNESS AND WASTE

On the contrary, the Japanese enterprise tends to accept the market price as a given parameter over which it has no control; management will only be in a position to generate profits if it can control costs effectively. The Japanese equation symbolizes a fundamentally different pricing strategy: $SP - C = P$. The parameter SP, from where the strategy evolves, is determined outside the company. Whereas the Japanese develop their strategy starting from given market conditions. Western firms prefer a competitive strategy based on internal parameters.

It has been noticed in recent years that the Japanese, by "accepting" market prices in the United States and Europe, are able to operate quickly at a profitable margin, thus uncovering a certain slackness and waste originally accepted by Western industries. It is not surprising that after some time they establish a considerable market share by lowering prices of high-quality goods and reaping the full benefits of the experience-curve principle. (If the volume of production increases the cost per unit decreases; it is then possible to determine today's sales prices on the basis of next month's cost. A close monitoring of the downward trend of costs not only ensures profitability, but guarantees an expanding market share as well.)

The foreign product or service in Japan can be positioned at a high price, and successfully, if it has an *image* all its own. This is not the image found in the foreigner's mind; it is found in the mind of the Japanese public, distributors as well as users. For marketing purposes, it is obviously this Japanese image of foreignness that must be taken into account, be it consonant with reality or not.

A product introduced from outside their world is appreciated for its novelty. It incorporates features that Japan does not yet master or perhaps will never master. So, this extraordinary item justifies an "extra" price, until the day when enough experience, ideas and information have accumulated to generate the same or even a better product locally. Then the extraordinary (foreign) product becomes an "ordinary" product, and the price is again a given parameter of the market. Meanwhile, the Japanese are indeed willing to pay a premium for this extraordinary product, but they also realize its ambiguity: "Will the product be available on time? Is there replacement in case of defect, and when? What is the after-sales service?"

This Japanese image of foreignness must be recognized by the foreign exporter, whatever his own view of the product may be. The development of a marketing strategy with image as a key variable may help overcome the uncertainties created by such foreignness. Image has three dimensions: the product, the corporation, and the country of origin.

The product image should testify to quality and reliability. Foreign products in Japan, and in other markets versus the Japanese, may suffer on these two counts. Japan is considered to be the champion of quality, and Western mass media reinforce this image, often to the detriment of Western industries.

The second dimension of the image, the corporate one, has to complement the first. Both could offset the damaged outlook for European and U.S. products and convey to the Japanese public strength in innovation and continuity in quality and service, notwithstanding rapid technological change undermining the attractiveness of an existing product. Unfortunately, foreign corporations operating or wishing to operate in Japan are in a weak position for two main reasons.

First, the number of foreign firms with investment and/or representative offices in Japan is very limited. Out of the more than one million enterprises in Japan, fewer than 2% are foreign affiliated. Many marketing managers are at a disadvantage, simply because they lack a corporate presence in the market itself.

FOCUS ON CORPORATE IMAGE

A second pitfall stems from the basic concept of managing a company. The West considers management of a company as management of assets.

In Japan, the running of an enterprise stands for management of people. People, their craftsmanship and intelligence, make the company what it is. Management of people results in innovative research and development, smooth and efficient production, and correct marketing appreciation. The image of the corporation stands for the image of its personnel. It stresses that the product image alone is too weak and buffeted by R&D and competitive actions. Goods change so fast that it becomes imperative to focus on corporate image and integrate product image into this broader picture.

The general level of education of the Japanese and their wide spectrum of interests make them very receptive to national images. In addition, it must be noted that they are very proud of their own nation; consequently, their frame of reference will be more pronounced in terms of country of origin. The high level of information on history and current affairs, combined with sensitivity to nationalism, opens new ways for developing a marketing mix adapted to Japan.

When the Japanese encounter on their market a product based on advanced design and technology, it is to be expected that they will not only imitate it, but in the long run improve it. As a result, it is to be feared that foreign technology and quality, even carefully translated into image, will quickly lose appeal. However, when a foodstuff company such as Lipton's Tea (Unilever plc) states that it is the sole "Purveyor to the Royal Court of Great Britain," not even the Japanese can imitate this. This success points to new opportunities and not the least for small and medium-sized companies that have been excluded from the Japanese market because of geographic distance and related costs. Indeed, several characteristics of the national image, already recognized or still to be communicated, can be identified and integrated into the marketing mix.

WORLDWIDE INFORMATION NETWORK

The marketing mix of the foreign company in Japan as influenced by image will have to be managed in a special way. The strategy must be global, coordinated and continuous.

The Japanese business community has developed a worldwide information network that efficiently feeds headquarters with all relevant data that can be gathered on target markets. The latest telecommunications and computer innovations speed up this information-processing system. This implies that a non-Japanese company or institution will have to be consistent in its message and strategy to all target groups around the world. Different or contradictory data, emitted to separate markets, will be quickly confronted with each other at the main offices in Tokyo.

For example, the Diamond High Council of Antwerp (Belgium) spent a considerable amount of money to create the image "Antwerp: Diamond Capital of the World". Problems arise when the Japanese, arriving in Zaventem, the national airport of Belgium, find no confirmation of this image. However, the nearby Dutch international airport of Schiphol (Amsterdam) sells diamonds with certificates in its tax-free shops. This not only confuses the Japanese but could generate a negative image.

When companies use a national characteristic in their marketing strategy, it is clear that it should be coordinated with respective authorities and other export-oriented firms. If the notion "Purveyor to the Royal Court" provides one company with a competitive edge over the Japanese, this effect can be reinforced when several British companies pool their efforts around the same characteristic. This could open up some possibilities for producers who would otherwise not be in a position to face the initial investment. The effort should be undertaken with business and government acting in tandem. After all, such a government-business relationship has long been recognized as one of the major strengths of the Japanese.

Finally, the marketing strategy can only succeed if it has continuity. The creation of an image does not materialize overnight through some fortuitous event. It is a laborious undertaking that will undergo many tests in the marketplace.

Several Western companies operating in Japan have succeeded remarkably well in coordinated efforts at the national level. Although it must be recognized that not all the examples were in fact marketing strategies in which the image variable was taken up consciously, the market dynamics responded spontaneously to image as part of the effort.

National sports heroes are the first image references that can be applied on a large scale, as is done in the United States and Europe extensively, but nearly exclusively for consumer goods. In March 1981, Japanese television channels showed a movie on Swedish industry entitled *Advantage... Sweden*. In this 15-minute program, a series of impressions on the industry followed rapidly the sounds of a tennis ball hitting a racket; at each smashing of the ball, another industry appeared on the screen. Without mentioning the name of Björn Borg, the Swedish world tennis champion, the movie took a free ride on Borg's image of superiority. Some Swedish companies with investments in Japan combined their promotion budgets with the governmental one and bought prime time for advertising, reaching approximately 2.3 million households. Belgium and Spain, two countries with hardly any investment in Japan and a low-key image there, could combine efforts at a national level to create an image of quality around "Purveyor to the Royal Court". The success of Lipton's Tea proves that there is a market niche.

PLAYING OFF THE NATIONAL IMAGE

The *sogo shosha* (large trading houses) regularly utilize aspects of the image of the country of origin for products they import into Japan. Löwenbrau, with Mitsubishi Corp. as sole agent, is marketed under the slogan, "the oldest beer from Germany". A tiny Belgian manufacturer of cookies—De Strooper—employing no more than 20 persons, exports to Japan through Americo Co. as "The Pride of Belgium".

The theory and application to Japan of image as a key element in the marketing mix needs further study. But already, at this stage of the research, it is obvious that image is a key element. The examples illustrate the comparative advantage national image can have through its uniqueness and related characteristics which are beyond any form of imitation. It allows foreign interests to capitalize on Japan's high level of education and information. It is up to the respective nations and their companies to select, with expert help, the appropriate and coherent strategy.

Image in marketing is a learning process for all interested groups. After all, not long ago Japanese products had the image of second-class, cheap imitations. Today the label "Made in Japan" conveys quality and novelty, whatever the real qualifications.

It is clear that any approach to the Japanese market has to be carefully planned in order to channel individual initiatives into a coherent total picture. New marketing strategies are a necessity. The alternative is the recourse to classical methods that have proven unsuccessful.

ISSUES FOR DISCUSSION

(1) The Japanese pricing system, at least in the opinion of the case writer, is quite different from the Western European and the U.S. pricing system. What is the major difference? In your opinion, which system is more efficient in terms of market penetration? Which one is more appropriate for market maintenance? Which one is more "appropriate" or "just" from the customer's viewpoint?

(2) You have just been hired by a local manufacturer of new and very different microcomputer software and hardware. Using the advice offered by the case writer, develop a marketing mix plan for penetrating the Japanese market.

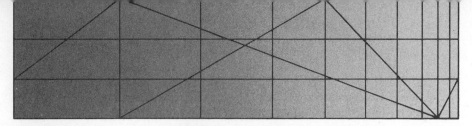

CHAPTER 12 HUMAN RESOURCE DEVELOPMENT

"We hire people for technical skills. We fire them for personality faults."
It is a pity that the personnel director who spoke those words insists on being anonymous. Few people can have made a more trenchant comment on recruitment and employment practices.

"Personal Chemistry Proves Hard to Define," *Financial Times,* July 16, 1987, 5.

LEARNING OBJECTIVES

After studying the material in this chapter, the student should be familiar with the following concepts:

(1) Quantitative and qualitative forecasting

(2) Ethnocentric, polycentric, regiocentric, and geocentric staffing policies

(3) International compensation packages

(4) Allowance phaseout

(5) Mobility premiums

(6) Cultural sensitivity

(7) Outplacement assistance

(8) Industrial democracy

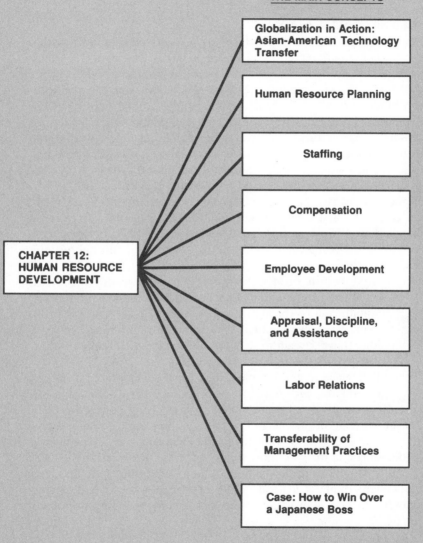

THE MAIN CONCEPTS

**CHAPTER 12:
HUMAN RESOURCE
DEVELOPMENT**

Globalization in Action:
Asian-American Technology
Transfer

Human Resource Planning

Staffing

Compensation

Employee Development

Appraisal, Discipline,
and Assistance

Labor Relations

Transferability of
Management Practices

Case: How to Win Over
a Japanese Boss

GLOBALIZATION IN ACTION
Asian-American Technology Transfer

Consumer Products, Inc. (a fictitious name) is a multinational consumer product company with subsidiaries around the world, including various Asian countries. ConP has maintained a centralized R&D operation in its headquarters in the Midwest and has transferred its technology to various subsidiaries around the world.

In one Asian country, a popular product began to be manufactured with a defect, which was being detected by consumers. The Asian subsidiary's marketing people communicated this recurrent problem back to the subsidiary's technology people, the same individuals who had been trained in the technology from headquarters.

The Asian technologists did not convey the problem to their American counterparts. The Asian cultural proclivity to be deferent to authority inhibited their communicating bad news to the American "bosses." Within months, the American management for the region began to discover that sales were slipping. Upon investigation they discovered the product defect.

Headquarters' top management decided to take steps to rectify the problem, since this was not the first time that communications difficulties between a foreign subsidiary and headquarters had resulted in impaired business performance. They were concerned about similar difficulties throughout the worldwide organization.

First, they directed that the product be corrected, and it readily was. Next, they decided to help the Asian technology group and its American counterpart improve their communications through a team-building process, so the problem would not recur. They also decided, if possible, to build upon the work with this technology transfer team to develop international technology-transfer/team-building processes throughout the company.

The team building began with the top organizational development manager, the head of R&D, and the president of the international product division agreeing that they would oversee the entire process. They engaged a management consultant team of one Asian from the country in question and one American. The Asian spoke both English and the local language. The thinking behind this decision was that the most timely and effective way for the consultants to gain trust with both groups would be to represent both. To cross a cultural boundary requires a local guide, as Margaret Mead had said in explanation of her success in crossing boundaries in cultures highly suspicious of Westerners.

SOURCE: "Asian-American Technology Transfer," *Management Review*, June 1987, 35. Reprinted, by permission of the publisher, from *Management Review*. Copyright © 1987. American Management Association, New York. All rights reserved.

The consultants worked with the Asian technologists and American technologists separately at first. They created interactive seminars in which the participants could acknowledge that their problems in dealing with their foreign counterparts were cross-cultural in origin. They then guided the groups into explicitly discovering their own cultures, their own assumptions, and their own individual personality and management styles. The training was focused on empathy skills—how to treat people as they would want others to treat them. To achieve this, individuals had to learn how to "suspend their own selves"—to act and listen in a manner detached from the "software program" of their own cultures, as much as possible.

Next, the Asian and American technologists were brought together to exchange their cultural learnings. They were also trained in communications skills. The result of the seminars was the development of open, collaborative norms of working and communicating in teams among the Asian and American technologists. The relationship became more productive and profitable, since the team developed the ability to spot problems before they became disasters and could now correct them together.

Based on the success of the Asian-American technology-transfer/team-building project, the top management group formed an international, multi-functional task force to enhance international technology transfer throughout the organization—employing international team-building techniques. The task force was trained in a manner similar to the Asian-American technology transfer group. In turn, it provided the training program to various technology-transfer teams of American and foreign technologists throughout the company.

The consensus today is that the rate of successful product adaptation to local markets is higher than it has ever been, and technologists' professional development and morale have received a significant boost worldwide. Suspicions that the American headquarters R&D people are authority-oriented and arrogant has abated significantly as well.

The international team building that began in the technology-transfer area has begun to expand to marketing and finance. The worldwide organization is continuing to evolve in the direction of more networks and international teams.

OVERVIEW

It has often been said that a company's greatest asset is its people. As we have seen, the second half of the eighties ushered in a new era of rationalizing, restructuring, or sizing down. At the center of organizational activity in this era has been better utilization of company assets. Assets are evaluated, and excess assets are sold, eliminated, or redeployed, as unused assets cost money to maintain. Like any other asset, people must be used efficiently: if they are too many, the excess must be "disposed" of in some way, and if they are too few, more must be acquired. All levels of the corporate structure, from the headquarters to the smallest plants in the four corners of the world, are under attack. In the United States the searchlight is on the corporate headquarters staff especially. As Robert Tomasko, author of the book *Downsizing*,[1] put it, "Corporate staff is becoming an endangered species."[2]

Recent staff reductions have been motivated largely by two related forces. The first and most important is, of course, the slowdown in economic growth within the developed world. The second is technology. It is becoming easier to use machines—particularly computers—to do what humans used to do. A lean, computerized organization nevertheless depends on people, and every MNC must develop policies to govern its use of its human resources.

INTRODUCTION

Establishing an efficient human resource strategy is a complicated process. The complexity inherent in assessing the current and future human resource needs of the organization and securing the appropriate personnel to fill these needs is augmented by significant differences between the country and corporate cultures of the headquarters and those of the numerous affiliates or subsidiaries.

Any attempt to understand the basics of building an international human resource strategy must begin with a thorough understanding of the major activities that go into human resource/personnel management. Scarpello and Ledvinka[3] have identified the main activities listed in Exhibit 12-1.

HUMAN RESOURCE PLANNING

There are two main tasks in human resource planning. The first is the assessment of the firm's future managerial and nonmanagerial personnel needs. The second is the choice of a feasible combination of personnel management and development programs that will enable the organization to accomplish its stated objectives.

Assessing future management needs is a two-step process. In the first step, a quantitative forecast is made of the number of managers needed to staff the organization for the foreseeable future. Subsequently a *qualitative* forecast is made of the skills these people will need to carry out their tasks. These forecasts permit managers to match managerial personnel to the future growth patterns of the firm.

---

[1]Robert M. Tomasko, *Downsizing: Reshaping the Corporation for the Future* (New York: American Management Association, 1987).

[2]Robert M. Tomasko, quoted in Thomas Moore, "Goodbye, Corporate Staff," *Fortune* December 21, 1987, 65.

[3]Vida Scarpello and James Ledvinka, *Personnel/Human Resource Management: Environments and Functions* (Boston, MA: Kent Publishing Co., 1987).

Exhibit 12-1   Major Activities of Personnel/Human Resource Management (1 indicates low involvement, 5 indicates high involvement)

Activity	Headquarters					Subsidiary				
	1	2	3	4	5	1	2	3	4	5
1. *Planning*										
Human resource planning and forecasting				4			2			
Career management				4			2			
Work scheduling	1									5
Job design	1									5
2. *Staffing*										
Recruiting		2						3		
Selection	1								4	
Placement	1								4	
3. *Compensation*										
Pay		2						3		
Benefits		2						3		
4. *Employee development*										
Training		2						3		
Career path planning		2						3		
5. *Labor relations*										
Collective bargaining		2						3		
Labor-management cooperation (codetermination)			3				2			
6. *Performance management and control*										
Performance appraisal		2						3		
Discipline	1								4	
Counseling and employee assistance	1								4	
Personnel policy and program evaluation	1								4	

In general, managerial work requires three categories of skills.[4]

(1) Technical skills: an understanding of and proficiency in specific kinds of methods, processes, procedures, or techniques. Technical skills involve specialized knowledge, analytical ability within that specialty, and facility in the use of the tools and techniques of the specific discipline.

---

[4]Robert L. Katz, "Skills of an Effective Administrator," *Harvard Business Review,* September-October 1974, 90–102.

(2)   Human skills: an ability to work effectively as a group member and to build cooperative effort within a team. Human skills are demonstrated in the way the individual perceives (and recognizes the perceptions of) his/her superiors, equals, and subordinates, and in the way he/she behaves subsequently.

(3)   Conceptual skills: the ability to visualize the relationship of the individual business to the industry, the community, and the political, social, and economic forces of the nation as a whole. An administrator must recognize these relationships and perceive the significant elements in any situation if he/she is to act in a way that advances the overall welfare of the organization.

The most difficult task in forecasting is to predict the conceptual skills that will be needed in the future. Of the three categories of skills, conceptual skills are the ones most vulnerable to changes in both technology and culture. The problem is twofold. Not only will future executives face environments different from the ones today's executives have become accustomed to dealing with, but changes in the external environment will not be the same the world over. Thus whatever training an individual underwent in his or her attempt to keep up with domestic job demands may not be appropriate for an overseas job.

Most, if not all, of today's management training and development efforts concentrate on technical and human skills. Conceptual skills, on the other hand, are supposed to be "picked up along the way." But increasingly organizations will have the responsibility for removing impediments to the individual's growth in *all three* skills areas, as well as providing the appropriate opportunities for growth.

Though an individual can acquire technical, human, and conceptual skills through formal education, prior to joining the organization, it is *experience* that converts abstract and theoretical knowledge into practical know-how. For this reason, any forecast of the future skills of a manager must take into consideration his or her on-the-job experience. Rutenberg described the ideal "experienced cosmopolitan executive for the year 2010."

(1)   She or he must have managed at least four different types of products (one competitively dominant and one competitively weak, each in a high-growth industry and in a stagnant industry).

(2)   She or he must have assimilated the pressures of *different managerial positions* (line manager, project integrator, and staff analyst) and experienced different types of business relationships (mergers, joint ventures, divestments).

(3)   She or he must be competent in accounting and treasury operations, manufacturing and labor relations, marketing and negotiating.

(4)   She or he must have lived in at least five nations: exposure to different

types of national behaviors, each affected by economic wealth, political sympathies, and cultural attitudes, is invaluable.[5]

STAFFING

Once an organizational structure has been constructed, management must fill the various positions of the organizational chart with the appropriate people. Staffing is the process of attracting and selecting job candidates and placing them in positions.

As we have seen, the staffing process begins with a review of the firm's human resource requirements. This review is essentially a headquarters activity. Subsidiaries are surveyed about their human resource needs, but ultimately the headquarters staff has the responsibility of putting it all together. Subsidiaries are brought into the staffing process as the specifics of job analysis, job design, work schedules, and career management are further scrutinized. The ultimate objective is, of course, a perfect match between job requirements and applicants.

Recruiting is the process of identifying people who will fit the requirements of a job. The first step in the recruiting process is job analysis and design—identifying the nature of the job and the factors crucial to success. Hays classifies overseas jobs into four major categories:[6]

Category 1: Chief executive officer (CEO), whose responsibility is to oversee and direct the entire operation

Category 2: Structure reproducer or functional head (FH), whose job is to establish functional departments in a foreign affiliate

Category 3: Troubleshooter (TS), whose function is to analyze and solve specific cooperational problems

Category 4: Element or rank-and-file members (operative).

Unfortunately, there is no general consensus on the variables that contribute to the success or failure of an executive's operations abroad. Some studies identify technical competence as the universal characteristic of a promising manager; others emphasize personality traits, such as the ability to adapt to cultural differences. An IBM World Trade study summarized the necessary qualities of successful executives as follows:[7]

(1)   Self-confidence to manage change

(2)   Organization to think clearly

---

[5]D. Rutenberg, *Multinational Management* (Boston: Little, Brown and Co., 1982), 361–362.

[6]R. D. Hays, "Expatriate Selection: Insuring Success and Avoiding Failure," *Journal of International Business Studies* 5 (1974): 25–37.

[7]Quoted in Rutenberg, *Multinational Management,* p. 363.

(3)   High activity or energy level

(4)   Ability to influence or persuade

(5)   Communication abilities

(6)   Interpersonal sensitivity, ability to develop the confidence of subordinates while exercising authority

The survey results in Exhibit 12-2 show that the characteristics MNC personnel managers look for in job applicants are different for each of the four major job categories. Attributes like "adaptability, flexibility in new environment" and "communicative ability" are more frequently considered "very important" for jobs that require extensive contact with the local community (for example, CEO and FH) than for technical or short-term jobs.

Once the jobs have been analyzed and the qualities desired in an applicant have been pinpointed, the human resource manager can begin to assemble a pool of candidates. At this point, the MNC must decide on the "mix" it wishes to achieve in its management team. In other words, the company must decide whether it should staff key management positions with individuals from the home country, host-country nationals, or some combination of the two.

The choice of the nationality of the management team is a function of both the host country's and the MNC's policies. Some countries, such as the United States, are fairly liberal in their immigration, naturalization, and employment laws. Other countries maintain some rudimentary restrictions. The United Kingdom, for example, stamps on the passport of every new arrival that employment is prohibited. Still other countries are more restrictive, requiring, for example, that the head of a subsidiary of a foreign enterprise be a citizen of the host country. Canada, Mexico, the USSR, and most developing countries fall into the latter category.

There are basically four different philosophies with respect to staffing overseas subsidiaries:

(1)   The ethnocentric view is that the primary positions in the subsidiary should be held by citizens of the parent (home) country.

(2)   The polycentric view is that the primary positions in the subsidiary should be filled by nationals (of the host country).

(3)   The regiocentric view is that the primary positions in the subsidiary should be staffed by regional citizens.

(4)   The geocentric view is that competence rather than nationality should be the determining factor in staffing subsidiary positions.[8]

---

[8]Howard V. Perlmutter, "The Tortuous Evolution of the Multinational Corporation," *Columbia Journal of World Business,* January-February 1969, 9. Also, H. V. Perlmutter, "How Multinational Should Your Top Management Be?" *Harvard Business Review,* November-December 1974, 121–132.

Exhibit 12-2   Selection Criteria Used for Different Job Categories [percentage of respondents evaluating each criterion as "not as important" (NI), "important" (I), and "very important" (VI)]

Criteria	Chief Executive Officer			Functional Head			Troubleshooter			Operative		
	NI	I	VI	NI	I	VI	NI	I	VI	NI	I	VI
Experience in company	1	16	83	1	31	68	11	31	58	39	24	37
Technical knowledge of business	0	21	79	1	8	91	0	11	89	11	21	68
Knowledge of language of host country	24	50	26	7	51	42	13	62	25	16	38	46
Overall experience and education	1	12	87	2	17	81	10	21	69	7	41	52
Managerial talent	0	4	96	0	14	86	30	54	16	41	41	18
Interest in overseas work	6	29	65	10	28	62	17	43	40	16	25	59
Initiative, creativity	5	11	84	5	13	82	4	14	82	16	32	52
Independence	11	25	64	16	37	48	10	33	57	30	48	22
Previous overseas experience	24	51	25	23	55	22	31	56	13	45	43	12
Respect for culture of host country	24	8	68	22	8	70	25	25	50	18	11	71
Sex	68	19	14	69	22	9	75	23	2	74	19	7
Age	70	20	10	64	31	5	80	14	6	70	20	10
Stability of marital relationship	33	32	35	42	24	34	59	25	16	49	22	29
Spouse's and family's adaptability	11	28	61	13	24	63	37	23	40	22	29	49
Adaptability, flexibility in new environment	5	12	83	5	19	76	16	38	46	7	31	62
Maturity, emotional stability	1	9	94	1	1	98	8	17	75	1	11	86
Communicative ability	5	8	97	7	8	85	9	32	59	5	42	53
Same criteria as other comparable jobs at home	8	16	76	6	16	88	12	20	49	5	24	71

SOURCE: Rosalie L. Tung, "Selection and Training for Overseas Assignments," *Columbia Journal of World Business*, Spring 1981. Reprinted in Phillip D. Grub, F. Ghadar, and D. Khambata (eds.), *The Multinational Enterprise in Transition* (Princeton, NJ: The Darwin Press, 1986), 221. Reprinted with permission.

Most personnel managers would like to follow an ethnocentric policy, employing home-country nationals (expatriates) to manage foreign subsidiaries. The reason, of course, is that both the personnel managers (who are charged with selection) and the line executives (who will work with and supervise the new managers) are better able to judge the technical, human, and conceptual skills of the home-country recruits, since they are familiar with the educational institutions and the culture that formed them. Often the expatriate has had experience with the company's philosophy and procedures, in which case there may be no need for job-related training.

The rate of failure experienced by expatriates, however, is high. International business literature is filled with accounts of problems experienced by MNCs that staffed their affiliates with expatriates. This failure is often attributable to the expatriate's inability to adapt to the local culture. In addition, expatriate MNC managers have been the focus of attacks by nationalistic governments.

To minimize personnel problems and to shed their "foreign" image, some companies employ host-country nationals. This type of personnel policy can protect the MNC from hostile treatment by the government. More important, of course, is the fact that the host-country national brings to the job a knowledge of the local market, people, and government policies.

Recently more MNCs have been taking a geocentric approach—hiring third-country nationals. A number of large MNCs use these "world professionals," or "international grade executives," extensively. For example, almost every major bank has some Dutch or Swiss personnel.

MNCs tend to move gradually toward internationalization in their staffing policies. Most MNCs will start their experience in a given country by transferring parent-country nationals to the foreign country. As the firm gains experience and becomes known in the country, it may begin to staff its positions with host-country nationals. Finally, as the firm's experience and presence in the world market widen, it may begin to adopt a more geocentric policy, staffing its operations with a mixture of nationalities. This evolutionary geocentrism is not confined to the staffing of foreign affiliates. Some MNCs (the more progressive ones) adopt the same hiring and staffing policies for the headquarters as well. (See Exhibit 12-3).

COMPENSATION

Designing a fair compensation system is one of the touchiest issues in international human resource management. It is difficult to establish a salary scale that will motivate employees in one country without discouraging those in another country. In addition to fluctuations in exchange and inflation rates and differences in the costs of living in different countries, the compensation system must take into account the cultural, political, and economic shocks that most employees experience upon taking on jobs in foreign countries. Thus a compensation system for overseas assignments must cover not only the salaries of PCNs, HCNs, and TCNs, but also how the company will ease the transition both for managers sent abroad and for managers brought back home.

Exhibit 12-3   Staffing Policies of MNCs Around the Globe (percentage of senior-, middle-, and lower-level positions)

Countries or Regions	U.S. MNCs			European MNCs			Japanese MNCs		
	Senior	Middle	Lower	Senior	Middle	Lower	Senior	Middle	Lower
United States									
PCN				29	18	4	83	73	40
HCN				67	82	96	17	27	60
TCN				4	0	0	0	0	0
Western Europe									
PCN	33	5	0	38	7	4	77	43	23
HCN	60	93	100	62	93	96	23	57	77
TCN	7	2	0	0	0	0	0	0	0
Canada									
PCN	25	1	3	28	11	0	33	33	17
HCN	74	99	96	67	89	100	67	67	83
TCN	1	0	1	5	0	0	0	0	0
Middle/Near East									
PCN	42	27	9	86	50	7	67	83	33
HCN	34	63	82	14	29	86	33	17	67
TCN	24	10	9	0	21	7	0	0	0
Eastern Europe									
PCN	15.5	8	0	100	100	100			
HCN	69	92	100	0	0	0			
TCN	15.5	0	0	0	0	0			
Latin/South America									
PCN	44	7	1	79	37	0	83	41	18
HCN	47	92	96	16	58	100	17	59	82
TCN	9	1	3	5	5	0	0	0	0
Far East									
PCN	55	19	2	85	25	5	65	41	18
HCN	38	81	96	15	75	95	35	59	82
TCN	7	0	2	0	0	0	0	0	0
Africa									
PCN	36	11	5	75	35	0	50	0	0
HCN	47	78	90	15	65	95	33	100	100
TCN	17	11	5	10	0	5	17	0	0

PCN = Parent-country national
HCN = Home-country national
TCN = Third-country national

SOURCE: Sincha Ronen, *Comparative and Multinational Management* (New York: John Wiley and Sons, 1986), 511–512.

Most companies set the salaries of parent-country-national and third-country-national management at more or less the same level. With respect to host-country nationals, however, the MNC must obey the wage and salary guidelines issued by the host country for local firms. In some cases, MNCs have been known to be extremely "creative" in devising ways of compensating their managers, especially top management personnel.

The vast majority of MNCs design a single compensation system for all home-country nationals working overseas. Such a system usually is made up of the following components:[9]

(1)   Base salary tied to salary range for comparable domestic position.

(2)   Premiums and inducements to work abroad. Such premiums are offered to encourage mobility and to compensate employees for the hardships of living abroad.

(3)   Allowances designed to permit those assigned to foreign posts to maintain their previous lifestyles. The most common of such allowances are for cost of living, housing, education, and tax protection.

Exhibit 12-4 illustrates the so-called balance sheet approach used by Volkswagenwerk, the well-known German auto company with subsidiaries in various countries, including Belgium, France, Brazil, Mexico, the United States, Canada, and South Africa.

The kinds of data needed by a personnel director charged with designing an international compensation package for a given type of worker are shown in Exhibit 12-5. Such data can be obtained from a number of sources. Every three years the Union Bank of Switzerland (UBS) publishes a booklet called *Prices and Earnings Around the Globe,* which contains very detailed data on cost of living and wages and salaries for some forty-nine cities throughout the world. Towers, Perrin, Foster and Crosby, a consulting group headquartered in New York, and the U.S.-based Wyatt Actuaries and Management Consultants (in conjunction with its subsidiary, Executive Compensation Services, in Brussels) offer their services all over the world. The Hays Group maintains offices in virtually every country of the world, providing job classification and compensation systems for both hourly employees and executives.

An important problem that should be addressed in designing a compensation policy is how to minimize the economic shock experienced by returning employees upon the discontinuation of the premiums and allowances of the overseas package. Overseas executives generally suffer an economic "letdown" upon returning to the home country. Although this letdown is more pronounced for executives who return to a country with a high inflation rate and a weak currency (for example, executives returning to England or the United

---

[9]Stanley Davis, "Career Paths and Compensation in Multinational Corporations," in *Managing and Organizing Multinational Corporations* (New York: Pergamon Press, 1977), 177–192.

Exhibit 12-4   Volkswagenwerk's Approach to Compensating Home-Country-National Managers

Salary Components	Sums in DM per Month	
	Place of Transfer A	Place of Transfer B
1. Basic salary	4500.00	4500.00
2. Overseas allowance (15% of base salary)	+675.00	+675.00
3. Conditions of living allowance (a percentage of base salary, depending on country)		+450.00
4. Cost-of-living allowance	+600.00	−150.00
5. Residence allowance	+400.00	−100.00
6. Overseas gross salary (before taxes)	6175.00	5375.00
7. Assumed taxes (on base salary) in Germany	−1200.00	−1200.00
8. Contribution to company pension plan	−333.00	−333.00
9. Statutory payments in country of assignment		+200.00
10. Net sum paid out monthly to individuals during overseas assignment (after taxes)	4642.00	4042.00

SOURCE: Peter Frerk, "International Compensation: A European Multinational's Experience," *The Personnel Administrator* 24 (May 1979): 33. Reprinted with permission from the May 1979 issue of *Personnel Administrator,* copyright 1979, The American Society for Personnel Administration, 606 North Washington Street, Alexandria, VA 22314.

States from West Germany or Japan), most executives find that their new salaries do not allow them to live up to the standards they became accustomed to during their overseas tour. The premiums, allowances, and other "perks" associated with overseas assignments, such as generous expense accounts for home and office entertainment, may be greatly missed by the returning executive.

MNCs use several procedures to minimize this shock. One approach is the so-called allowance phaseout, in which the overseas allowance is phased out while the employee is still overseas, the assumption being that after a certain number of years in a given location managers and their families adjust to the local cost of living and do not need the extra allowance. Another approach is the single-payment mobility premium. This approach ties the premium to the move instead of to the assignment. In other words, the executive receives a premium each time he or she is assigned to a new location, whether it is in the home country or overseas. As a rule, single-payment mobility premiums

Exhibit 12-5   Paycheck Power

Workers' pay buys more in America than in any other country, with one exception: Switzerland.

Union Bank of Switzerland, in a survey of wages and prices in cities throughout the non-Communist world, ranked Zurich slightly ahead of Los Angeles as the place where a typical paycheck has the greatest buying power. The bank's last previous survey, in 1982, put Los Angeles first, slightly ahead of Zurich.

The new study was conducted in the first half of 1985, before several major currencies went up in value and the dollar went down. The charts show how four U.S. cities compared with 16 other major cities.

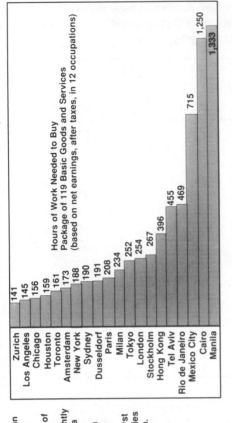

Hours of Work Needed to Buy Package of 119 Basic Goods and Services (based on net earnings, after taxes, in 12 occupations)

Zurich	141
Los Angeles	145
Chicago	156
Houston	159
Toronto	161
Amsterdam	173
New York	188
Sydney	190
Dusseldorf	191
Paris	208
Milan	234
Tokyo	252
London	254
Stockholm	267
Hong Kong	396
Tel Aviv	455
Rio de Janeiro	469
Mexico City	715
Cairo	1,250
Manila	1,333

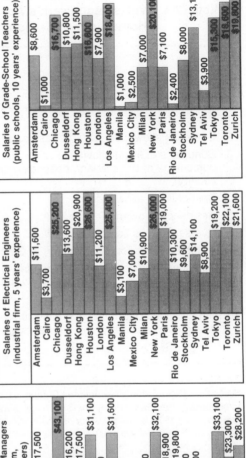

Salaries of Grade-School Teachers (public schools, 10 years' experience)

City	Salary
Amsterdam	$8,600
Cairo	$1,000
Chicago	$16,700
Dusseldorf	$10,800
Hong Kong	$11,500
Houston	$15,600
London	$7,900
Los Angeles	$18,400
Manila	$1,000
Mexico City	$2,500
Milan	$7,000
New York	$20,100
Paris	$7,100
Rio de Janeiro	$2,400
Stockholm	$8,000
Sydney	$13,100
Tel Aviv	$3,900
Tokyo	$15,500
Toronto	$18,600
Zurich	$19,800

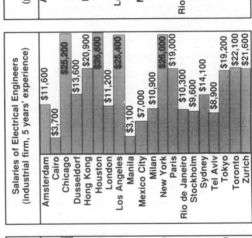

Salaries of Electrical Engineers (industrial firm, 5 years' experience)

City	Salary
Amsterdam	$11,600
Cairo	$3,700
Chicago	$25,200
Dusseldorf	$13,600
Hong Kong	$20,900
Houston	$28,600
London	$11,200
Los Angeles	$25,400
Manila	$3,100
Mexico City	$7,000
Milan	$10,900
New York	$26,000
Paris	$19,000
Rio de Janeiro	$10,300
Stockholm	$9,600
Sydney	$14,100
Tel Aviv	$8,900
Tokyo	$19,200
Toronto	$22,100
Zurich	$21,600

Salaries of Department Managers (metal-working firm, managing 100 workers)

City	Salary
Amsterdam	$17,500
Cairo	$3,700
Chicago	$43,100
Dusseldorf	$16,200
Hong Kong	$17,500
Houston	$31,100
London	$10,000
Los Angeles	$31,600
Manila	$8,200
Mexico City	$5,900
Milan	$10,300
New York	$32,100
Paris	$18,900
Rio de Janeiro	$19,800
Stockholm	$11,600
Sydney	$12,300
Tel Aviv	$6,500
Tokyo	$33,100
Toronto	$23,300
Zurich	$28,200

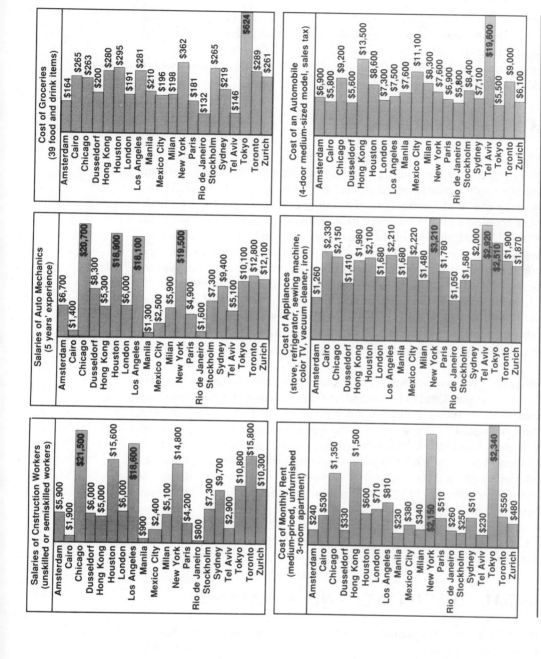

Cost of Groceries
(39 food and drink items)

City	Cost
Amsterdam	$164
Cairo	$265
Chicago	$263
Dusseldorf	$200
Hong Kong	$280
Houston	$295
London	$191
Los Angeles	$281
Manila	$210
Mexico City	$196
Milan	$198
New York	$362
Paris	$181
Rio de Janeiro	$132
Stockholm	$265
Sydney	$219
Tel Aviv	$146
Tokyo	$624
Toronto	$289
Zurich	$261

Cost of an Automobile
(4-door medium-sized model, sales tax)

City	Cost
Amsterdam	$6,900
Cairo	$5,800
Chicago	$9,200
Dusseldorf	$5,600
Hong Kong	$13,500
Houston	$8,600
London	$7,300
Los Angeles	$7,500
Manila	$7,600
Mexico City	$11,100
Milan	$8,300
New York	$7,600
Paris	$6,900
Rio de Janeiro	$5,800
Stockholm	$8,400
Sydney	$7,100
Tel Aviv	$19,600
Tokyo	$5,500
Toronto	$9,000
Zurich	$6,100

Salaries of Auto Mechanics
(5 years' experience)

City	Salary
Amsterdam	$6,700
Cairo	$1,400
Chicago	$20,700
Dusseldorf	$8,300
Hong Kong	$5,300
Houston	$6,000
London	$18,900
Los Angeles	$18,100
Manila	$1,300
Mexico City	$2,500
Milan	$5,900
New York	$19,500
Paris	$4,900
Rio de Janeiro	$1,600
Stockholm	$7,300
Sydney	$9,400
Tel Aviv	$5,100
Tokyo	$10,100
Toronto	$12,800
Zurich	$12,100

Cost of Appliances
(stove, refrigerator, sewing machine, color TV, vacuum cleaner, iron)

City	Cost
Amsterdam	$1,260
Cairo	$2,330
Chicago	$2,150
Dusseldorf	$1,410
Hong Kong	$1,980
Houston	$2,100
London	$1,680
Los Angeles	$2,210
Manila	$1,680
Mexico City	$2,220
Milan	$1,480
New York	$3,210
Paris	$1,780
Rio de Janeiro	$1,050
Stockholm	$1,580
Sydney	$2,000
Tel Aviv	$2,920
Tokyo	$2,510
Toronto	$1,900
Zurich	$1,870

Salaries of Cnstruction Workers
(unskilled or semiskilled workers)

City	Salary
Amsterdam	$5,900
Cairo	$1,900
Chicago	$21,500
Dusseldorf	$6,000
Hong Kong	$5,000
Houston	$15,600
London	$6,000
Los Angeles	$18,600
Manila	$900
Mexico City	$2,400
Milan	$5,100
New York	$14,800
Paris	$4,200
Rio de Janeiro	$800
Stockholm	$7,300
Sydney	$9,700
Tel Aviv	$2,900
Tokyo	$10,800
Toronto	$15,800
Zurich	$10,300

Cost of Monthly Rent
(medium-priced, unfurnished 3-room apartment)

City	Cost
Amsterdam	$240
Cairo	$530
Chicago	$1,350
Dusseldorf	$330
Hong Kong	$1,500
Houston	$600
London	$710
Los Angeles	$810
Manila	$230
Mexico City	$380
Milan	$340
New York	$2,150
Paris	$510
Rio de Janeiro	$260
Stockholm	$250
Sydney	$510
Tel Aviv	$230
Tokyo	$2,340
Toronto	$550
Zurich	$480

SOURCE: Pictogram, "Paycheck Power—From Houston to Hong Kong," *U.S. News & World Report*, October 28, 1985. Copyright, 1985, U.S. News & World Report. Reprinted from issue of October 28, 1985.

tend to encourage moves, thereby making it easier for the company to staff new or upgraded positions across the globe. Permanent additions to income tend to discourage all but the initial move, thereby decreasing the probability that a competent executive will be willing to move to a new location where the "perks" are not at the same level or even better.

EMPLOYEE DEVELOPMENT

Even the most carefully chosen employees may not be perfectly suited to the job requirements or the country conditions. Employee development aims at aligning employee aspirations and capabilities with organizational goals. The process usually goes under the rubric of Training and Development. The basic objective of training and development for international assignments is to cultivate *cultural sensitivity*. In other words, training and development must develop employees' awareness of their own cultural assumptions and cultural conditioning and give them a special kind of intellectual and emotional "radar" which alerts them to situations where cultural assumptions come into play.[10] Exhibit 12-6 lists the top training needs of Americans working abroad, as determined both by Americans themselves and by host-country nationals. The fact that these training needs are ranked differently by Americans and by foreign nationals in itself reveals different cultural assumptions and perceptions about work.

Educating, training, and developing management is a multibillion-dollar business. In the United States and in Europe, most training is done by the companies themselves in their in-house development programs. Such in-house training may be supplemented by services provided by various organizations and universities. In the United States organizations such as the American Management Association and the Center for Creative Leadership offer a variety of courses on management skills and techniques. In Europe the European Foundation for Management Development (EFMD), in Brussels, provides guidance to the training directors of its member companies. The services offered by European universities, such as the London Business School, IMEDE/IMI in Switzerland, and the Center of Management in Europe in Brussels, are similar to those offered by universities in the United States.[11]

APPRAISAL, DISCIPLINE, AND ASSISTANCE

The appraisal of overseas managers is part of the appraisal of a subsidiary's contributions to the attainment of the MNC's short- and long-term goals. Most

---

[10]S. H. Robock and K. Simmonds, *International Business and Multinational Enterprises* (Homewood, IL: R. D. Irwin, 1983), 562.

[11]Leo Steverink, (ed.), *The European Management Education Guide,* Second Edition (The Netherlands: International Management Education Consultancy, 1988) lists seventy-one European institutions offering some 285 programs for senior-, middle-, and lower-level management.

Exhibit 12-6   Training Needs of Americans Working Overseas

Training Need	Ranking by Americans (403 responses)	Ranking by Nationals (131 responses)
Human relations skills	1	1
Understanding of other culture	2	2
Ability to adapt	3	3
Technical competence	4	6.5[a]
Sensitivity training	5	6.5[a]
A sense of politics	6	12.5[b]
Language ability	7	9
Understanding of mission	8	5
Understanding of American culture	9	15
Orientation for service	10	4

[a]The two training needs that tied for sixth place are both ranked 6.5.
[b]The two training needs that tied for twelfth place are ranked as 12.5.
SOURCE: M. B. Johnston and G. L. Carter, Jr., "Training Needs of Americans Working Abroad," *Social Change*, June 1972, 23

MNCs use their domestic employee appraisal system, adapted to fit the legal and cultural requirements of the host country. As a rule, host countries allow MNCs a relatively high degree of freedom in choosing an appropriate appraisal method, except when termination of the employment contract is at issue. Even then, the government is not likely to intervene if the number of employees fired is less than a certain percentage of the company's work force. The issue of termination becomes extremely sticky, however, when the closing of a plant is involved. Most European countries and almost all developing countries prohibit "massive dismissals" of personnel and penalize MNCs that circumvent these prohibitions.[12]

One issue that has received a lot of attention in the developed world in recent years is employee assistance following a termination decision, better

[12]In January 1977, Badger Belgium Naamloze Vennootschap (BBNV), a subsidiary of Raytheon's Badger Company, Inc., went out of business. It dismissed its 250 employees and left behind net assets of approximately $2.8 million, roughly half the indemnification due the discharged workers under Belgian law. The Belgian government, responding to trade union and other pressures, contended that BBNV's parent was liable for this shortfall and legitimized this contention by citing the OECD's Guidelines for Multinational Enterprises, which states that "the entities of a multinational enterprise located in various countries are subject to the laws of these countries."

Exhibit 12-7   Outplacement Services in Europe

Country	First Year Service Appeared	Number of Companies Involved in 1988	Total Turnover in 1986	Number of People Counseled in 1986			Among Sponsored Individuals		
				Paid for Selves	Sponsored in Groups	Sponsored as Individuals	Average Age	Average Pay (pounds)	Average No. of Months Needed to Find Job
United Kingdom	1971	16	18,760,000	980	20,700	2,100	45	26,800	4.4
France	1973	12	6,793,000	—	2,850	1,280	45	32,300	5.0
Netherlands	1978	4	2,680,000	—	150	582	46	30,000	4–5
Scandinavia	1978	3	754,000	—	—	133	49	35,500	4.5
West Germany	1979	3	792,000	—	50	122	48	45,600	5.0
Switzerland	1980	5	1,356,000	—	177	171	48	50,000	4.3
Belgium	1982	9	1,184,000	—	201	296	45	30,000	4.4
Italy	1986	2	17,000	—	—	10	—	—	5.0
Spain	1986	1	17,000	—	—	10	—	—	—
Overall		55	32,353,000	980	24,128	4,704	47	35,800	4.8

SOURCE: "U.K. Leads Europe's Outplacement Market," *Financial Times* (London), July 16, 1987, 8.

known as outplacement assistance. Outplacement assistance generally takes the form of counseling geared toward helping a person establish a new career path, after his or her old path has become defunct as a result of a company's restructuring plan. Invented in the United States in the 1960s, outplacement assistance has spread to most European nations. Exhibit 12-7 gives an overview of European outplacement services.

Exhibit 12-7 shows that the average age of individuals receiving outplacement assistance in Europe is 47 years. Scandinavian countries lead the list with the oldest average age (49 years); workers in Britain, France, and Belgium tend to lose their jobs earlier, at the age of 45. Exhibit 12-8 provides some information on the types of executives most likely to be in need of outplacement assistance.

LABOR RELATIONS

Handling labor relations, sometimes called labor-management relations or union-management relations, is often an extremely thorny task. Collective bargaining is the process of negotiation through which representatives of a company's management and those of its unions determine wages and working conditions for the employees. Issues usually covered in such negotiations are wages and salaries, including fringe benefits; industrial relations (that is, rules and regulations governing the relationship between management and labor); and the settlement of disputes or grievances.

Although one would expect a company to resist unionization of its facilities, one would expect every employee to desire unionization, because the union is the only vehicle labor has for negotiating on an equal basis with management. Nevertheless, worker participation in unions has declined drastically in the United States. In 1986 only about 17% of the labor force in the United States was unionized, compared to 48% in the United Kingdom. And public opinion surveys rank organized labor at the bottom of the trustworthiness scale.

In many other countries the situation is similar, leading some observers to declare the union's sovereignty at bay, as they did that of the nation-state. These observers assert that the sheer size and economic power of the MNCs

---

Exhibit 12-8   Individual Assessment

Individuals wondering about their chances of being unlucky enough to experience outplacement consultancy at first-hand might like to try a brief test. All they have to do is compare themselves with company colleagues and others who could be viewed as career-competitors, and then answer the following questions. By comparison with them, would you say you were:

(1) A calmer person?

(2) Less inhibited socially?

(3)   A good deal more imaginative and unconventional?

(4)   More natural and forthright?

(5)   Less inclined to worry about your own performance?

(6)   More relaxed?

Anyone who answered yes in all cases would do well to start looking for another job. The six traits covered by the questions comprise the main ways executives who get sacked differ in personal make-up from those who do not, according to research done by the UK's Cranfield Management School with support from the Pauline Hyde and Associates outplacement company.

Mrs. Hyde's consultancy made personality assessments of 204 discarded executives, of whom about 60% had been in senior positions. Their results were sent to the management school's psychologists who compared them with assessments made by the same method of more than 1,000 comparably ranked people who consistently stayed employed.

The Cranfield staff concluded that the prime reasons for the 204 executives' predicament lay in the six key personality differences. But the fault was not the positive aspects of the attributes as they were listed here. It was more what the sacked contingent lacked in consequence of possessing those positive characteristics.

Their strength in forthrightness left them weak in shrewdness, for example. The gift of imagination left them short of cool realism. As a result, even though they mostly scored high for alertness, intelligence, leadership, and emotional adjustment, they were missing some of the key abilities on which survival, let alone success, in organizations often depends: political and social skills.

The fact that executives missing those abilities tend to lose their jobs does not mean their organizations are wise to fire them. The management school's psychologists report concludes that companies would probably gain more by providing training to develop the skills which are lacking. The reason is that men and women not endowed with them by nature or early upbringing are nevertheless some of the most "energetic, imaginative, creative people" available for employment.

Even so, the 204 showed another characteristic which would appear to distinguish them from the typical person doing well in an executive career in Britain at present. It is that, on the whole, they were relatively old. Their average age was 47. And, while there are numerous cases of older people proving enterprising and creative as well as canny, there is research evidence that most tend to lose their former get-up-and-go.

SOURCE: *Financial Times* (London), July 16, 1987, 8.

---

allows them to cooperate globally among themselves so as to nullify any international cooperative efforts among unions, such as sympathy strikes. According to this view, the MNCs' ability to source globally via subcontracting and other contractual agreements has undermined international cooperation among unions to the point where unions are international in name only.[13] It is the view of this book, however, that unions, like the nation-state, will survive. No MNC, no matter how big and powerful, can prevent its workers around the globe from unionizing. But by the same token, no union, no matter how large and powerful, can dictate its policies globally.

Notwithstanding the current depressed state of organized labor, it is important for managers to understand the basics of the concept of unionized labor. Labor disputes evoke emotional responses and usually make front page news. The media in most countries are eager to show picketing workers and more often than not portray the company's management as the villains. Knowledge of the basic workings of a union can help a unionized company to become more effective in dealing with the union and help a nonunionized company to maintain its nonunion status.

The nature, role, and power of unions will vary from country to country depending on a multitude of factors, including the following:

(1)   The level at which bargaining takes place (enterprise or industry level): In the United States and Japan the local or company level is preferred; in most European countries the employer's representatives bargain with union representatives at a national or regional level.

(2)   The centralization of union management: In the United States the AFL-CIO does not bargain directly with employers. Its role is to act as a coordinating body and resolve disputes among its member unions. In Europe confederations have more decision-making power.

(3)   The scope of bargaining

(4)   The degree to which the government intervenes

(5)   The percentage of the work force represented by unions[14]

These factors in turn will depend on variables such as labor mobility, level of unemployment, homogeneity of the labor force, the political system, and the educational level of the work force.

In most developing countries the Department of Labor (or the equivalent office) is the appropriate place to go for information about labor relations, as

---

[13]M. C. Schnitzer, M. L. Liebrent, and K. W. Kubin, *International Business* (Cincinnati, OH: South-Western Publishing, 1987), 278.

[14]R. Robinson, *Internationalization of Business: An Introduction* (Chicago: The Dryden Press, 1984), 96.

**Exhibit 12-9   Centralization of Union-Management Structure and Unionization
Related to Level of Bargaining**

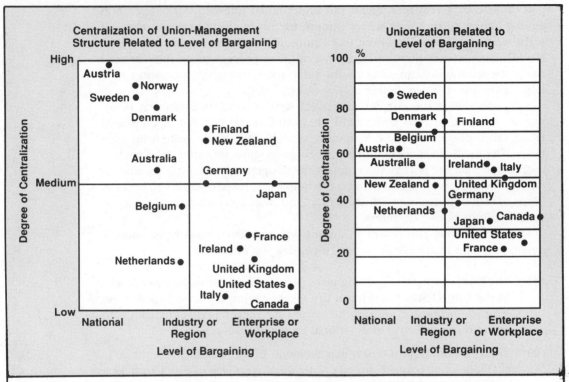

SOURCE: R. D. Robinson, *Internationalization of Business: An Introduction* (Chicago: The Dryden Press, 1984), 96–97.

they are regulated by the federal government. As a result of this power of the government, as a general rule unions in developing countries are supportive of the governing party.

Graph A of Exhibit 12-9 illustrates the relative positions of most of the developed countries with respect to level of bargaining (horizontal axis) and degree of centralization (vertical axis). The United States and Canada are the most "localized" and least "centralized" countries; the Scandinavian countries and Austria are the least "localized" and most "centralized" countries. Graph B shows that the United States, Canada, France, and Japan are the least unionized countries (approximately 20% of the work force is unionized), and the Scandinavian countries are the most unionized. Despite the relatively low levels of union membership in some of the developed countries, "the most important method of establishing conditions of work in the major industrialized countries remains free collective bargaining in a framework of law and customs."[15]

Recently, organized labor has begun to explore additional ways of influencing working conditions. Increasingly labor is demanding the right to participate in what is considered to be management's territory: the decision making that affects the company's operations and performance. In some countries labor's wishes for participation have been met with sympathy and even legislation.[16] This trend goes under many names, the most common one being industrial democracy. Exhibit 12-10 summarizes the characteristics of five of the most common forms of industrial democracy.

Exhibit 12-10   Five Forms of Industrial Democracy

---

(1)   *Codetermination* was introduced in West Germany in 1951 with a law that provided for equal representation of all classes of workers on the supervisory boards of certain corporations. In 1976 codetermination (Mitbestimmung) was extended to all German enterprises employing 2000 or more workers. Similar legislation was attempted in other European countries without much success.

(2)   *Minority board participation* is similar to codetermination. The Shop Constitution Law of 1952 requires that German firms with between 500 and 2000 employees give one-third representation to employees. Most EEC countries, along with Sweden and Norway, have introduced minority board participation with great success. In the United Kingdom and Italy, management resistance to minority board participation has brought repeated labor strikes.

(3)   *Works councils* are bodies through which management-labor relations are institutionalized at the enterprise level. A council may consist of only workers' representatives or of both workers and management, as in the joint works councils in the United Kingdom. These bodies may be mandatory under the law, they may be established at the national level by agreement between trade unions and employers' organizations, or they may be specific to individual companies.

(4)   *Quality circle* (QC) programs organize workers into small groups, through which they can take responsibility for increasing productivity and improving product quality. The unique feature of such programs is the use of statistical and industrial engineering techniques to influence

---

[15]Robinson, *Internationalization of Business.*

[16]T. Mills, "Europe's Industrial Democracy: An American Response," *Harvard Business Review,* November-December 1978, 149.

decision making. In QC programs, employees meet regularly with their supervisors, study quality control and productivity improvement techniques, apply these techniques to identify and solve work-related problems, present their solutions to management for approval, and monitor the implementation of solutions to ensure that they work.

QC programs were conceived and developed in the United States in the 1930s, but they were first implemented in Japan. Their use in the United States appears to be a direct consequence of management's perception that Japanese market successes are due partly to the use of QCs. According to the International Association of Quality Circles (IAQC), 150 American companies were using QCs in 1979; this number had risen to 1500 by 1982.

(5) *Financial participation,* which has traditionally been in the form of profit-sharing, has recently taken on a new dimension with employee stock option plans and management or leveraged buyouts. Although these practices are essentially an American phenomenon, it is expected that they will spread over the globe.

SOURCES: Ronen, *Comparative and Multinational Management,* pp. 367–372; Robinson, *Internationalization of Business,* pp. 76–88; Robock and Simmonds, *International Business and Multinational Enterprises,* pp. 577–580; Scarpello and Ledvinka, *Personnel/Human Resource Management,* pp. 627–628.

One conclusion that can be drawn from the study of labor relations is that under most circumstances unions play a positive role in society. Thus outright declaration of an "antiunion" or a "nonunion" policy is not in the best interests of any MNC anywhere. Exhibit 12-11 gives the OECD guidelines for industrial relations. By following these guidelines, a company can reduce the risks of strikes, confrontations, and direct government intervention.

TRANSFERABILITY OF MANAGEMENT PRACTICES

As in the case of the other functions of management, so with the human resource function: the manager must ask, "How much of the management systems that have already been developed, applied, and evaluated at home can be transferred overseas without change; how much should be adapted to fit local conditions; and how much should be developed from scratch?" Obviously, the MNC would like to transfer as much as possible. Hiring, compensating, training, evaluating and appraising, developing career paths, and other human resource management tasks consume considerable management time and cost significant sums of money. Much money can be saved if a package developed at home for home managers can be generalized to subsidiaries across the globe.

Exhibit 12-11   OECD Employment and Industrial Relations Guidelines

Enterprises should, within the framework of law, regulations and prevailing labour relations and employment practices, in each of the countries in which they operate,

(1)   respect the right of their employees to be represented by trade unions and other bona fide organisations of employees, and engage in constructive negotiations, either individually or through employer's associations, with such employee organisations with a view to reaching agreements on employment conditions, which should include provisions for dealing with disputes arising over the interpretation of such agreements, and for ensuring mutually respected rights and responsibilities;

(2)   **(a)**   provide such facilities to representatives of the employees as may be necessary to assist in the development of effective collective agreements,

     (b)   provide to representatives of employees information which is needed for meaningful negotiations on conditions of employment;

(3)   provide to representatives of employees where this accords with local law and practice, information which enables them to obtain a true and fair view of the performance of the entity or, where appropriate, the enterprise as a whole;

(4)   observe standards of employment and industrial relations not less favourable than those observed by comparable employers in the host country;

(5)   in their operations, to the greatest extent practicable, utilise, train and prepare for upgrading members of the local labour force in co-operation with representatives of their employees and, where appropriate, the relevant governmental authorities;

(6)   in considering changes in their operations which would have major effects upon the livelihood of their employees, in particular in the case of the closure of an entity involving collective lay-offs or dismissals, provide reasonable notice of such changes to representatives of their employees, and where appropriate to the relevant governmental authorities, and co-operate with the employee representatives and appropriate governmental authorities so as to mitigate to the maximum extent practicable adverse effects;

(7)   implement their employment policies including hiring, discharge, pay, promotion and training without discrimination unless selectivity in respect of employee characteristics is in furtherance of established governmental policies which specifically promote greater equality of employment opportunity;

(8) in the context of bona fide negotiations* with representatives of employees on conditions of employment, or while employees are exercising a right to organise, not threaten to utilise a capacity to transfer the whole or part of an operating unit from the country concerned nor transfer employees from the enterprises' component entities in other countries in order to influence unfairly those negotiations or to hinder the exercise of a right to organise;

(9) enable authorised representatives of their employees to conduct negotiations on collective bargaining or labour management relations issues with representatives of management who are authorised to take decisions on the matters under negotiation.

---

*Bona fide negotiations may include labor disputes as part of the process of negotiation. Whether or not labour disputes are so included will be determined by the law and prevailing employment practices of particular countries.

SOURCE: OECD, *Declaration on International Investment and Multinational Enterprises* (Paris: Organization for Economic Cooperation and Development, June 21, 1976).

The degree of transferability of management systems and techniques is a function not only of the host country's culture but also of the company's *corporate culture,* as the corporate culture is the vehicle through which management systems are transferred from the headquarters. Corporate culture has been variously defined as "a cohesion of values, myths, heroes, and symbols that has come to mean a great deal to the people who work [in a company]" and "the way we do things around here."[17] Whatever corporate culture is, it affects employees' attitudes. These attitudes influence behavior, which in turn affects people's performance and their contributions to organizational performance. Although some aspects of the corporate culture are shaped by the country culture (the macroculture) and for this reason are the same for all organizations in a country, corporate culture is largely company-specific.

Though attitudes vary from person to person, an awareness of some generalizations about different countries' cultures can spare the international manager considerable pain. Exhibit 12-12 depicts six key concepts gleaned from theoretical and empirical cross-cultural research. These concepts relate to people's attitudes toward conformity, achievement, sex roles, time, space, and ethnocentrism.[18]

---

[17]T. E. Deal and A. K. Kennedy, *Corporate Cultures: The Rites and Rituals of Corporate Life* (Reading, MA: Addison-Wesley Publishing Co., 1984), 4.

[18]This section draws heavily on Ronen, *Comparative and Multinational Management*, pp. 129–186.

Exhibit 12-12   Generalizations from Cross-Cultural Research Attitudes

Issues	Examples
Conformity: The degree to which individuals are expected to comply with societal goals and aspirations rather than "do their own thing" varies from culture to culture.	Americans are considered to be very individualistic; Japan is often cited as an example of a country in which conformity is valued.
Achievement: Most humans want to accomplish tasks and gain material things. A high need for achievement results in a tendency to take personal responsibility, a desire to receive concrete feedback, and a tendency to take calculated risks. These are entrepreneurial characteristics which are needed for industrialization to occur.	Americans are high achievers, and their society encourages achievement. In some other countries the prevailing attitude is that "the nail that sticks up gets hit."
Sex Roles: Societies have very diverse notions of the proper roles of men and women.	Americans and most Western Europeans cannot legally discriminate between men and women. In Japan female managers are a rarity; in Saudi Arabia they are nonexistent.
Time: People have different attitudes toward time. The traditional view of time is as a cyclical phenomenon: things that cannot be done today will be done tomorrow. The modern view holds that time is linear: once today is gone, it is lost forever.	Americans operate in linear time. Most non-Westerners take a longer view of time. The tendency of the Japanese to take a long view of time may account for their success in making implementable decisions; in an effort to make decisions in a short time, U.S. managers may overlook important factors.
Space: Every society ingrains in its members a notion of the "correct" physical distance between people. These attitudes can have repercussions in the workplace, but identifying them is not as easy as it seems.	The fact that Americans need space leads others to think of them as "standoffish" people.
Ethnocentrism: Most societies believe that their own way is the best way.	Most people place their own country at the center of their conceptual map.

Barrett and Bass[19] suggest the following guidelines for developing an understanding of the world of work in another culture:

(1)   Study national *socialization patterns*. If the nation in question is highly fragmented, a number of socialization patterns may be operating at the same time; each must be addressed.

(2)   Examine *institutions* peculiar to the country. For example, educational institutions may concentrate on preparation of a technical elite, or, alternatively, they may promote universal literacy.

(3)   Consider *individual traits* that distinguish the nation from others. Included here would be distinct perceptual styles, intellectual reasoning, educational qualifications, and values.

(4)   Focus on the *predominant technology*—for example, handicraft or unit, batch or mechanized, automated or process. This information should suggest viable organization objectives, predominant compensation policies, and other management considerations.

There have been any number of attempts to pinpoint specific cultural variables that explain cross-cultural variances. The empirical approach, developed by Hofstede, involves deriving salient dimensions empirically from attitudinal differences. The main assumption underlying Hofstede's landmark longitudinal research[20] is that cultural differences influence management and restrict the generalizability of certain organizational theories and management practices. In other words, culture—or what he calls "collective mental programming"— is a circular and self-reinforced determinant of attitudes and behavior. This collective mental programming that people carry inside their heads tends to be incorporated into the institutions they build to assist them in their survival. These institutions, in turn, tend to promote and reinforce that culture.

From his massive study covering fifty countries and some 116,000 employees of a major MNC, Hofstede distilled four basic dimensions of culture: power distance, uncertainty avoidance, individualism vs. collectivism, and masculinity vs. femininity. He then scored each country on the four dimensions; indices and ranks for all the countries are given in Exhibit 12-13.

Power distance is defined as the degree to which power in organizations is equally distributed. It is associated with the extent to which authority is centralized and leadership is autocratic. Malaysia, Guatemala, Panama, and the Philippines received the highest scores on this dimension (104, 95, 95, and 94, respectively).

---

[19]Quoted in Ronen, *Comparative and Multinational Management*, p. 135.

[20]G. Hofstede, "National Cultures in Four Dimensions," *International Studies of Management and Organizations* 13, No. 2 (1983): 54; also, "The Cultural Relativity of Organizational Practices and Theories," *Journal of International Business Studies,* Fall 1983, 80.

Exhibit 12-13   Indices and Ranks of Fifty Countries and Three Regions on Four Dimensions of Culture

Country	Power Distance		Uncertainty Avoidance		Individualism		Masculinity	
	Index	Rank	Index	Rank	Index	Rank	Index	Rank
Argentina	49	18–19	86	36–41	46	28–29	56	30–31
Australia	36	13	51	17	90	49	61	35
Austria	11	1	70	26–27	55	33	79	49
Belgium	65	33	94	45–46	75	43	54	29
Brazil	69	39	76	29–30	38	25	49	25
Canada	39	15	48	12–13	80	46–47	52	28
Chile	63	29–30	86	36–41	23	15	28	8
Colombia	67	36	80	31	13	5	64	39–40
Costa Rica	35	10–12	86	36–41	15	8	21	5– 6
Denmark	18	3	23	3	74	42	16	4
Equador	78	43–44	67	24	8	2	63	37–38
Finland	33	8	59	20–21	63	34	26	7
France	68	37–38	86	36–41	71	40–41	43	17–18
Germany (F.R.)	35	10–12	65	23	67	36	66	41–42
Great Britain	35	10–12	35	6– 7	89	48	66	41–42
Greece	60	26–27	112	50	35	22	57	32–33
Guatemala	95	48–49	101	48	6	1	37	11
Hong Kong	68	37–38	29	4– 5	25	16	57	32–33
Indonesia	78	43–44	48	12–13	14	6– 7	46	22
India	77	42	40	9	48	30	56	30–31
Iran	58	24–25	59	20–21	41	27	43	17–18
Ireland	28	5	35	6– 7	70	39	68	43–44
Israel	13	2	81	32	54	32	47	23
Italy	50	20	75	28	76	44	70	46–47
Jamaica	45	17	13	2	39	26	68	43–44
Japan	54	21	92	44	46	28–29	95	50
Korea (S.)	60	26–27	85	34–35	18	11	39	13
Malaysia	104	50	36	8	26	17	50	26–27
Mexico	81	45–46	82	33	30	20	69	45
Netherlands	38	14	53	18	80	46–47	14	3
Norway	31	6– 7	50	16	69	38	8	2
New Zealand	22	4	49	14–15	79	45	58	34
Pakistan	55	22	70	26–27	14	6– 7	50	26–27
Panama	95	48–49	86	36–41	11	3	44	19
Peru	64	31–32	87	42	16	9	42	15–16

Country	Power Distance		Uncertainty Avoidance		Individualism		Masculinity	
	Index	Rank	Index	Rank	Index	Rank	Index	Rank
Philippines	94	47	44	10	32	21	64	39–40
Portugal	63	29–30	104	49	27	18–19	31	9
South Africa	49	18–19	49	14–15	65	35	63	37–38
Salvador	66	34–35	94	45–46	19	12	40	14
Singapore	74	40	8	1	20	13–14	48	24
Spain	57	23	86	36–41	51	31	42	15–16
Sweden	31	6– 7	29	4– 5	71	40–41	5	1
Switzerland	34	9	58	19	68	37	70	46–47
Taiwan	58	24–25	69	25	17	10	45	20–21
Thailand	64	31–32	64	22	20	13–14	34	10
Turkey	66	34–35	85	34–35	37	24	45	20–21
Uruguay	61	28	100	47	36	23	38	12
U.S.A.	40	16	46	11	91	50	62	36
Venezuela	81	45–46	76	29–30	12	4	73	48
Yugoslavia	76	41	88	43	27	18–19	21	5– 6
Regions:								
East Africa	64	(31–32)	52	(17–18)	27	(18–19)	41	(14–15)
West Africa	77	(42)	54	(18–19)	20	(13–14)	46	(22)
Arab Ctrs.	80	(44–45)	68	(24–25)	38	(25)	53	(28–29)

SOURCE: G. Hofstede, "National Cultures in Four Dimensions," *International Studies of Management and Organization* 13, No. 2 (1983): 52. Reprinted with permission.

Uncertainty avoidance reflects the degree to which the society considers itself threatened by uncertain and ambiguous situations. The more threatened a society feels by uncertainty, the more formal rules it will set up and the less tolerance it will have for deviant behavior or new ideas. Greece, Guatemala, Uruguay, and Portugal are examples of countries with high indices of uncertainty avoidance.

Individualism vs. collectivism is an index of cultural perceptions of the relationship between the individual and the society as a whole. Hofstede ranked countries according to the degree to which they respect individualism. Not surprisingly, the wealthier countries tended to have more respect for individualism than did the poorer countries.

Masculinity vs. femininity is Hofstede's term for an index that expresses the degree to which a society values assertiveness and the acquisition of wealth ("masculinity") over compassion toward others ("femininity"). Hofstede argues that countries closer to the equator tend to be more "masculine," whereas those closer to the poles are more "feminine."

Hofstede's findings have implications for the design of systems for hiring, training, educating, compensating, appraising, disciplining, and even dismissing overseas employees. A manager can ill afford to ignore a host country's attitudes as revealed by the various indices. For example, whereas motivation, conflict resolution, industrial democracy, and careers for women and disadvantaged people are all important issues in the United States, serious discussion of them is likely to raise eyebrows in societies where formality and obedience are virtues, where women are thought to belong in the kitchen, and where a person's life work ends with his fifty-first birthday.

RECAPITULATION

Corporate executives who pay serious attention to the human resource factor concur that it seems to be joining the list of endangered species. The human element is being squeezed out of global business enterprises by three developments. One is the preoccupation with rationalization, or restructuring, that seems to characterize contemporary management. A new breed of manager has evolved—the minimalist. In the United States a prime example is General Electric's CEO Jack Welch, who, in his first five years as CEO, downsized G.E. by one half, from 200,000 to 100,000 employees worldwide. The minimalists of the world are beginning to gobble up "anachronistic" companies, which they "turn around" by rationalizing their operations, starting with corporate staff and line workers.

The other developments contributing to the human resource dilemma are automation and cybernization. Machines seem to be taking over most of the work that humans once performed; computer-based expert systems and other decision support systems are even beginning to trespass in the domain of the middle manager. Cybernetics, the science of control and communication, has made possible the creation of control and communications systems that collect, organize, and evaluate data from around the globe and use these data to make decisions. Applied cybernetics, or information technology, has led to the development of computers that allow the manager to perform control and communication tasks in virtually zero time and at a fraction of the cost of merely ten years ago.

Human resource management is thus at a crossroads. Some fifteen years ago, in *Global Reach,* Barnet and Muller proposed that "the obsolescence of American labor must be seen as a part of a world problem. In the Global Factory [which is built by the World Managers] there is a steadily declining need for human hands." To the last phrase we might now add "and human brains."

REVIEW QUESTIONS

(1) Define "human resource management."

(2) List the functions of a human resource/personnel department in an MNC.

(3) Most European managers look at the United States as the human resource manager's paradise. They are especially impressed with the freedom managers have to hire and fire as they please. Yet U.S. managers complain that they are terribly constrained by the restrictions imposed on them by the government and the unions. Write an essay comparing personnel management in the United States and Europe. On balance, who has an easier job, in your opinion—European managers or U.S. ones?

(4) Zukunft Manufacturing of Hamburg, West Germany, has recently taken over the only textile mill in your home city. Most of your friends and relatives work in this mill, and you yourself have spent some summers working there. Everyone knows that takeovers are often followed by "rationalization," and if there is something that characterizes Germans, it is that they are extremely rational. So there is a groundswell of suspicion in town that something big—and not good—is going to happen at the mill.

One day the mayor of the city calls you up and says, "I guess you've heard about the mill. Some folks around here are extremely nervous. Would it be possible for you to give me and the city council an inkling of what we might expect and what we can do to minimize the negative impact on our folks who make a living working at the mill?" Prepare a short presentation in which you summarize the kinds of assistance that might be made available to people who lose their jobs as a result of the restructuring/rationalization of the mill. (Look in the indexes of major newspapers for stories about similar incidents that have occurred over the last two or three years.)

(5) The president of Zukunft was very impressed with the local newspaper's coverage of your talk to the city council. Over dinner he explains to you that he *is* going to do some rationalization. But he thinks that if the employees will accept some job reassignments and reclassifications, he might not have to fire a single person. He too wants to minimize the negative impact of rationalization. He would like you to advise him on how best to approach the unions. Prepare a preliminary list of concessions the president might request and guarantees he might offer in return.

(6) Jack Jackson is furious. He has just returned from picking up his new boss, Pierre Perriou, at the airport. The MNC that bought his company sent over a "kid," he tells his friends at a dinner. "Heck, I don't even think he is old enough to drink. And his English—by gosh, they could at least send somebody who can speak English." Over the next few days Jack goes around the offices and the shops complaining.

Your professor meets Mr. Perriou at a social and tells him that he must find a way to get to know Jack and the other employees better. "Any suggestions?" asks Perriou. Excited about the opportunity to apply some of her ideas, your professor forms a new consulting firm whose first project is to advise Mr. Perriou on "coping with the American corporate culture." Develop a plan for Mr. Perriou.

(7)   Greg Greenko has just been chosen to go to Brussels, Belgium, to work on the installation of a new computerized logistics system which his company developed for its plant in Montgomery, Alabama. The system is a money saver; its installation in Alabama and at other affiliates in the United States has been a cinch. Although the computer system takes certain responsibilities away from managers, it saves them a great deal of time. Write a report on the problems Greg may encounter in installing such a system at a plant in a foreign country whose language Greg does not speak. Suggest ways to address these problems.

SUGGESTED READINGS

Austin, Clyde (ed.). *Cross-Cultural Reentry.* Yarmouth, ME: Intercultural Press, 1987.

Blanspain, R. *The Badger Case and the OECD Guidelines for Multinational Enterprises.* Denventer, The Netherlands: Kluwer, 1977.

Cohen, R. B. "The New International Division of Labor and Multinational Corporations." In Frank Hearn (ed.), *The Transformation of Industrial Organization: Management, Labor and Society in the United States* Belmont, CA: Wadsworth Publishing Company, 1988.

Copeland, Lennie, and Lewis Griggs. *Going International: How to Make Friends and Deal Effectively in the Global Marketplace.* New York: Random House, 1985.

Dalton, D. R., and I. F. Kesner. "Composition and CEO Quality in Boards of Directors: An International Perspective." *Journal of International Business Studies,* Fall 1987, 15–32.

"Detroit's New Mentors in Managing Americans—The Japanese." *International Management,* September 1986, 81–87.

Dymsza, William. "The Education of Managers for Future Decades," *Journal of Business Studies,* Winter 1982, 9–18.

Enderwick, Peter. *Multinational Business and Labor.* New York: St. Martin's Press, 1985.

Farh, Jiinglih, P. M. Podsakoff, and Bar-Shiuan Cheng. "Culture-Free Leadership Effectiveness Versus Moderators of Leadership Behavior: An Extension and Test of Kerr and Jamier's Substitutes for Leadership Model in Taiwan." *Journal of International Business Studies,* Fall 1986, 43–60.

Grimaldi, Antonio. "Interpreting Popular Culture: The Missing Link Between Local Labor and International Management." *The Columbia Journal of World Business,* Winter 1986, 67–72.

Grub, P. D., F. Ghadar, and D. Khambata (eds.) *The Multinational Enterprise in Transition.* Princeton, NJ: The Darwin Press, 1986.

Harris, P. R., and R. T. Moran. *Managing Cultural Differences.* Houston, TX: Gulf Publishing Co., 1986.

"Is Profit-Sharing the Way to Get Europe Back to Work?" *International Management,* September 1985, 93–96.

Journal of International Business Studies, Special issue on cross-cultural management, Fall 1983.

Kujawa, Duane (ed.). *International Labor and Multinational Enterprise.* New York: Praeger Publishers, 1975.

Mendelhall, M., and G. Oddou. "Acculturation Profiles of Expatriate Managers: Implications for Cross Cultural Training Programs." *The Columbia Journal of World Business,* Winter 1986, 73–80.

Mitchell, Russell, and Judith H. Dobrzynski. "GE's Jack Weltch: How Good a Manager Is He?" *Business Week,* December 14, 1987, 92–103.

Moore, T. "Goodbye Corporate Staff." *Fortune,* December 21, 1987, 65–76.

Ondrack, D. A. "International Transfer of Managers in North American and European MNEs." *Journal of International Business Studies* 16, No. 3 (Fall 1983): 1–20.

Phillips, Dennis. "How VW Builds Worker Loyalty Worldwide." *Management Review,* June 1987, 37–40.

"Poking and Prodding Japanese Managers into Better Performance." *International Management,* January 1985, 27–31.

Powell, B., B. Martin, D. Lewis, B. Turque, G. Raine, and B. Cohn, "Your Next Boss May Be Japanese." *Newsweek,* February 2, 1987, 42–48.

Ronen, Simcha. *Comparative and Multinational Management.* New York: John Wiley and Sons, 1986.

Scarpello, Vida, and James Ledvinka. *Personnel/Human Resource Management: Environments and Functions.* Boston, MA: Kent Publishing Co., 1987.

Skinner, Wickham. "Wanted: Managers for the Factory of the Future." *The Annuals of the American Academy of Political Science* 470 (November 1983): 102–114.

Vandamme, Jacques (ed.). *Employee Consultation and Information in Multinational Corporations.* London: The Group for European Policy Studies, 1986.

Wysocki, Bernard. "Prior Adjustment: Japanese Executives Going Overseas Take Anti-Shock Course." *The Wall Street Journal,* January 12, 1987, 1.

Zamet, J. M., and M. E. Bonarnick. "Employee Relations for Multinational Companies in China." *The Columbia Journal of World Business,* Spring 1986, 13–20.

CASE ● How to Win Over a Japanese Boss: Eat Sushi, Work Long Hours, Be Patient

You want a job? The Japanese are hiring. So put on your sincere outfit, blot the coffee off your résumé and read this handy, no-results-guaranteed guide on how to find and hold a job at a U.S. subsidiary of a Japanese company.

MANAGERS

Don't be inscrutable. Americans think the Japanese are very formal people and often worry whether they should bow when introducing themselves. The best advice on hitting it off with the Japanese executive is just to be American—within limits. The Japanese are not enthusiastic handshakers, so don't pump their arms off. Just because their manners are better than ours doesn't mean they lack warmth. Mark Hand, then a lab manager, thought he'd blown his shot at a production-supervisor job at the new Denon Digital Industries compact-disc plant in Madison, Ga.: he took his two-year-old along when he couldn't find a babysitter. The Japanese dandled her on their knees, and Hand got the job.

Mention your 12 kids. Job interviews go to great depth in Japanese companies. That's because they operate on a consensus basis: many executives get to take a look. Besides, the Japanese like to go beyond an applicant's résumé and poke into character. "There are a good many things the Japanese would like to know about a person that are not lawful to ask in our culture," says Eric Fossum, vice president of Denon. Like family status. So volunteer the information. The Japanese look on the corporation as a sort of extended family and can be picky about whom they let into the clan. They want to know if a job seeker has the proper group-oriented spirit to fit in. Also be prepared for a detailed inquiry into your professional knowledge. Fred Seitz knew cigarette-packing machinery. Even so, Japanese engineers at the new Canon copier plant in Newport News, Va., took apart a copier and asked him where he would procure nearly every part before recommending him as a purchasing manager.

Shoot for number two. So now you've got the job. The options for mobility are terrific. The chances to learn a new style of management are intriguing. But what about climbing to the top of the corporate ladder? Sorry. It's a rare Japanese subsidiary that, like Pilot Corp., the pen maker, has an American president who reports only to the chairman in Tokyo. More often, the vice presidential level is as far as locals go, frequently in sales and personnel, which need American face men. Finance is almost always a Japanese preserve, as it requires close contact with Tokyo. "You can work for a company for 20 years and never be part of the inner circle," says Bob Spence, who works for a Japanese developer in Los Angeles.

The problem is that strong Japanese sense of corporation as family—their family. "A position given up to a foreigner is one taken from a member of the tribe," says an American executive with a Japanese trading company in New York. And since Japanese companies work on lifetime employment, there's no rush to promote. At Mitsui, the big trading company, assistants spend 10 years before they become traders. "Not so many American young people are patient enough to stay," says Mitsui & Co. (U.S.A.) vice president Yoshitaka Sajima. Japanese executives often swear all this will change: "Someday I hope the CEO of Mitsui U.S.A. will be an American," says Sajima.

Women have it worse. The Japanese know all about the equality that women expect in the American job market. [The 1987] settlement of a sex-discrimination case against the Sumitomo Corp. of America trading company in New York should refresh their memories. Still, "the unwritten rule is that the professional staff is all male," says an American about his trading company. On a gut level, equality is still an acquired taste. In Japan, women often serve tea at the office. Hiroki Kato, associate professor of Japanese at Northwestern University and a consultant to Japanese companies, advises women executives not to offer a Japanese colleague a friendly cup of coffee—he might mistake you for one of the unassertive ladies from home.

Curb your yen for raises. When you ask for a raise, remember three reasons why your Japanese boss may hate you. One, you probably already earn more than he does; Japanese executive salaries are on a lower scale than American. Two, he can never ask for a raise because seniority alone determines his salary. Three, if you mention you could earn more elsewhere, you play into his worst suspicions that Americans lack loyalty to the company. Japanese executives in big companies have signed up for lifetime employment and American job hopping doesn't sit well.

Meetings, meetings. Details, details. The Japanese are great ones for study. They love detailed reports and long-range plans. They use consensus management, a painstaking system of soliciting opinion from all levels before action. "The decision takes longer, but implementing the program is shorter because people are in support of it," says Dick Brown, vice president of Daihatsu, seller of a four-wheel-drive vehicle. Howard Gottlieb, senior executive with NEC America Inc., a telephone maker in Irving, Texas, describes how it works: "At a morning meeting I'd make my presentation and everybody would nod, and in the afternoon I'd go over it with new people and the next day do the same thing with the general manager." Patience is not high on the list of American virtues. But only patience carries the day in a Japanese company. Help is on the way: increasingly, Japanese managers speed up the system to keep pace with American business.

Learn hand signals. Communication is the biggest problem. Few Americans speak Japanese; those who do say the Japanese can be disconcerted by a foreigner who seems to know them too well. The executives sent to the United

States speak English in varying degrees. An engineer at the Stauffer-Meiji plant in York, Pa., calls it the first chocolate-biscuit factory ever built "completely using hand signals." At the Nissin Foods plant nearby in Lancaster, Japanese executives carry dictionaries; one has a sheet of bizarre American phrases such as "You're in hot water."

Never say never. The Japanese shun confrontation; if you can't keep your cool, perhaps you should work for the Italians. Ira Perlman, vice president at Matsushita Electric Corp. of America, interprets: "A yes is a maybe. A maybe is a no. And no is you better not come back."

Take your eye off the clock. Japanese work long hours. Then they may go out and drink for another shift. You probably can't match them on desk time but it's smart to observe one rule: never leave before the president. Much of the real business of the day will be conducted at the bar—so tag along. As the night goes on, the Japanese turn into real party animals. Remember, even after hours, an American "can be one of the boys, but only up to a point," says Bob Spence.

LABOR

Move to a small town. Big Japanese plants were built in small towns in the Midwest and middle South in recent years, and not only for financial reasons. The Japanese perceive a willingness in those places to work hard and show corporate loyalty. "Norman, Okla., is similar to the old days in Japan," says Shiro Takemura, president of a Hitachi computer plant under construction there. "People make a lot of self-sacrifices."

Eat raw fish. Yes, your worst fears are true. If you work for the Japanese, they will make you eat raw fish. And learn some other new tricks. The Japanese like training. They send production staff to Japan to learn at their factories. The Japanese also believe that to understand their work ethic it helps to sample their culture. That's why a group of Denon Digital employees spent a day with an associate professor of Japanese in Atlanta. It included an authentic lunch. "This is the filet mignon of Japan," said Prof. Donald L. Smith, holding up a piece of raw sashimi. "This tastes like boiled fatback," said supervisor Mike Moon.

Keep your union card in your wallet. In Japan, most unions represent only companies, not entire industries, so they are weak by American standards. In the United States, the Japanese go nonunion wherever they can—so chances are you'll have to also. They like to call American employees "associates" to take some of the sting out of labor-management relations. Sanyo took a bitter walkout [in 1986] after it tried to change the seniority system at its Forrest City, Ark., TV facility.... The United Auto Workers organized the Toyota-General Motors plant in Fremont, Calif., but had to agree to strict hiring controls by the company. In return, the company promised a virtual no-layoff policy. That's unusual. U.S. attorneys advise the Japanese not to promise the sort of lifetime employment they offer at home. Americans might sue if fired.

Zero your defects. The Japanese are nuts about quality control. On the line, that means "complete attention to the work the whole seven and a half hours," says Jim Burch, who works for Topy Corp., an autowheel maker in Frankfort, Ky. Many Americans like the change. When Matsushita Electric Corp. of America bought the Motorola television plant in Franklin Park, Ill., it eliminated the conveyor belt to give workers time to do the job right. Mary Howaniec likes controlling the line with a pedal: "You can work at your own pace and not the pace of the belt," she says. Americans can and do rise to the quality challenge. The Honda plant in Marysville, Ohio, has a defect rate similar to the plants in Japan. One tip: the Japanese seem to associate quality with cleanliness. At the Sumitomo transmission plant in Teterboro, N.J., the last 15 minutes of a shift is "housekeeping." So sweep up.

Get out of the rut. A big Japanese complaint is that "American workers tend to do what they're told and no more," says Takeshi Kondo, senior vice president for NEC America in Texas. To counter that, Japanese plants rotate workers through many jobs, hoping that Americans will take on more responsibility. Workers respond favorably, saying it keeps them fresh. The only complaint at the Toyota-GM factory is that rotation requests take too long to be approved. Be flexible in what you'll do.

Talk it out. The Japanese like communication to bubble up through "quality circles," in which workers pool ideas on productivity in their departments (sometimes the old suggestion box is used). At Matsushita's television plant, the president attends each circle's presentation to management; at a recent one, a circle suggested a way to cut one step from picture-tube assembly. "The Japanese want you to have an influence on the end result," says Jim Ballengee, an employee of NEC America. It helps to be a busybody in a Japanese factory.

Lead your team. The high sense of responsibility to employees can help promotion in a Japanese company. At the Nissin Foods plant in Pennsylvania, the American office manager was reprimanded for trying to hire a secretary outside; a worker was taken off the line and sent to typing school for the job. At many plants, a worker can aspire to be a "team leader"—like a foreman but with wider responsibility. The Toyota-GM plant has no time clocks; the leaders are supposed to motivate their crews of six to eight. So be nice to your leader— although some criticize the system as another name for cronyism. "The only way to get a promotion at Honda is if you're the team leader's buddy," says Ron Griffith, a wax sprayer.

Get with the 250-year plan. The Japanese like to see employees as a big, happy family. Do the morning exercises that are routine at a number of plants. Wear the company uniform—the Japanese managers will wear it, too, when they're on the factory floor. At Matsushita, new hires are shown a film about the life of founder Konosuke Matsushita, including an old clip in which he announces that the company's 250-year plan is to eliminate world poverty by producing limitless numbers of products. The film then shows Japanese employees jumping up revival style. The Toyota-GM plant has a more modest way to build group identity—employees each get $30 a year to party with colleagues. If they should happen to cook up a 250-year plan over beers, the next quality-circle meeting can take it up.

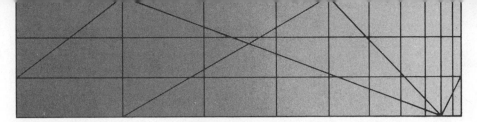

CHAPTER 13

COMMUNICATION AND CONTROL

In the end, management's ability to formulate and execute integrated global strategy requires effective information, planning and control systems.

D. Rutenberg

Multinational Management (Boston: Little, Brown and Co., 1982), 65.

LEARNING OBJECTIVES

After studying the material in this chapter, the student should be familiar with the following concepts:

(1) The basic elements of a control system

(2) Feedback and feedforward

(3) Control objects

(4) Profitability decision trees

(5) Information, information technology, information systems

(6) Global information systems: EXGLOBIS and INGLOBIS

(7) Transborder data flows

(8) The privacy principles

(9) Managing a GLOBIS: diagnosis, policies, and integration

(10) The vision-policy-architecture planning sequence

(11) INFOstructure and INFRAstructure

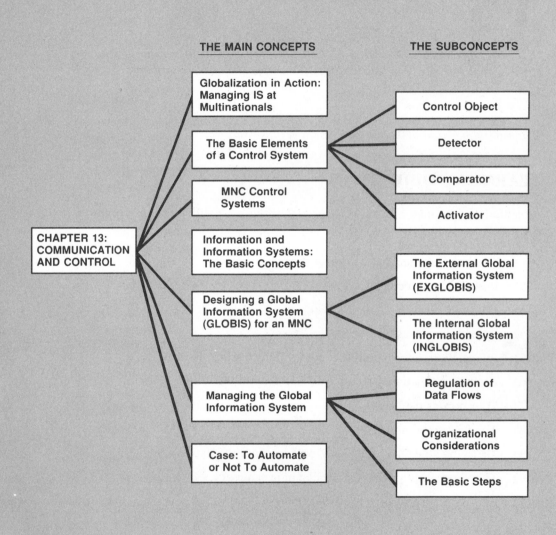

THE MAIN CONCEPTS

THE SUBCONCEPTS

Globalization in Action: Managing IS at Multinationals

The Basic Elements of a Control System

MNC Control Systems

CHAPTER 13: COMMUNICATION AND CONTROL

Information and Information Systems: The Basic Concepts

Designing a Global Information System (GLOBIS) for an MNC

Managing the Global Information System

Case: To Automate or Not To Automate

Control Object

Detector

Comparator

Activator

The External Global Information System (EXGLOBIS)

The Internal Global Information System (INGLOBIS)

Regulation of Data Flows

Organizational Considerations

The Basic Steps

GLOBALIZATION IN ACTION
Managing IS at Multinationals

On the congested data highways of multinational corporations, the problems of getting the right data in the right amount to the right people at the right time are multiplying daily as global markets emerge. "It's a battleground," says Ron Ponder, Senior VP of Information Systems at Federal Express, Memphis. [In 1987] the $3.2 billion company dramatically increased its overseas operations to the point where it services 89 countries and employs nearly 5,000 workers (10% of its work force) outside of the U.S.

The problems are amplified if you are a large multinational with diverse product families, such as 185-year-old E.I. du Pont de Nemours & Co. The chemical giant generates a third of its $27 billion in revenue overseas, employing 35,000 people abroad in some 150 plants and offices. "When remote corporate clients as far apart as Rio, Tokyo, or Rome get 'gobbledygook' on their PCs, the situation is especially frustrating," says Lee Foote, manager of Du Pont's Electronic Data Interchange Section at Wilmington, Delaware. "There are many misconceptions about what this right stuff—information—actually is."

Whatever the scale, getting the right stuff—the stuff that executive decisions are made from—comes down to one thing: getting your data house in order. The need to do so, moreover, never has been more pressing—particularly for manufacturing companies that purport to be world class.

If Europe's instrument makers, Japan's machine tool producers, America's automakers, and the thousands of other manufacturers and service companies worldwide are to survive in this new era of globalization—a time when no supplier is too distant, no customer too foreign—they must rid themselves of the informational chaos endemic to international operations. But how? The answers may be the following: enlightened management, effective use of information technology tools and standards, such as electronic data interchange (EDI) and structured query language (SQL), and enterprisewide alliances.

Although many will insist that computers and information are inseparable, data spewed out by legions of mainframes should not be confused with information. "Properly structured data will result in information, but only in the minds of individuals and under certain contexts and time frames," Du Pont's Foote explains. IS [information system] groups that don't understand this distinction and haven't found out what data client organizations really need will simply print everything out. And the result? Data overload.

User managers—division and department heads who bear functional (as opposed to IS) titles—are already attempting to protect themselves from a torrent of useless data (not just from their own systems organizations) by

---

SOURCE: Ralph Emmett Carlyle, "Managing IS at Multinationals," *Datamation,* March 1, 1988, 41–62.

erecting specially designed software screens and filters. These programs take the form of preference profiles, which rank incoming data and voice messages by order of importance. Such programs are the forerunners of future expert systems and currently are being embedded in computer networks so that they function automatically.

For their part, IS managers are embracing EDI and SQL as the means by which to create information. EDI describes a standardized way of using computers to transmit and receive business documents, such as purchase orders. SQL, on the other hand, is a standard means of accessing database management systems that are shared by different architectures.

Du Pont's customers in the U.S. and elsewhere, for example, can use EDI to conduct more of their business chores with the company electronically. "Any company that's tried EDI has become an apostle of effective data management," Foote says, "but getting the message over has been tough." He says his section had to sell the EDI concept both to top management at Du Pont and to information technology vendors.

"We've pretty much had to educate the vendors, lead them by the nose," echoes George Higgins, a colleague of Foote's and a data resource management (DRM) consultant for Du Pont. Higgins stresses that too many vendors forget that technology is simply a means to an end, not an end in itself. "You've got to show them what the end state is," Higgins feels, "that, for example, you've got this database in Geneva and another in Wilmington that you want to link together if the right technical means can be found."

The education of vendors has been only part of the problem of moving to new data architectures. "We have to get the data in shape to make use of new technologies," says Higgins. "This will take time and a great deal of money. It will also require major changes in the organization." He says that this message wasn't always sympathetically received by top management. "They are coming around by degrees," Higgins says, adding that he no longer feels like a missionary.

Once corporate executives perceive their companies as global entities, they begin to wonder why they don't have worldwide inventory data on their desks. Why, for example, do they have to have U.S. and European data in different forms and for different time periods? By trying to get answers to these questions, decision-makers begin to understand the need for effective data management; perhaps they begin to wonder whether DRM shouldn't be handled by the business side of the house rather than the IS professionals.

Usually, though, changes in volatile world markets force the nation's corporate leaders to focus on DRM issues. "In the steel business, we generally credit the Japanese with dragging us into the twentieth, even the twenty-first, century," says George T. Fugere, VP of Information Services at Bethlehem Steel, Bethlehem, Pa. Major work force reductions have forced Bethlehem Steel and other steel companies to turn to technology to remain productive. These companies have also turned inward, subjecting their organizations to the same intense scrutiny as the steel making process itself, as they search for flaws.

[In 1987] a management SWAT team from Bethlehem Steel and 15 hand-picked experts from across the IBM organization went over the $4.3 billion steel maker with a fine-tooth comb. After interviewing 238 workers from the top to the bottom of the company, one compelling fact was inescapable. "There was too much data and too little information," Fugere says.

OVERVIEW

Chapters 7–12 have covered six of the main functions of international management: choice of an entry strategy, design of an organization structure, and planning and implementation of financial, production, marketing, and human resource development strategies. Management's ability to choose appropriate objectives and goals and to devise appropriate strategies for reaching them is a necessary condition for success, but not a sufficient one. In addition, management must devise appropriate systems for ensuring that the right outcomes emerge. Making sure that all subsidiaries accomplish the desired goals—controlling their performance—is essential. *Control,* the maintenance of certain key variables within certain predetermined limits, is another one of the main functions of management. Control is achieved through communication of information among the various parts of the system.

INTRODUCTION

Managerial competence is not measured by the quality of the strategies chosen and implemented. Rather, the yardstick of managerial performance is the end result—the degree of stakeholder satisfaction achieved. Thus MNC managers find themselves in a bind: they must plan under conditions of uncertainty and incomplete information about future events, yet they are judged by their performance as it is reflected in historical data. Management would like to guarantee that the outcomes reached in the future will be more or less what they planned for. This is the function of control: to guarantee that the difference between actual outcomes and desired outcomes is at its theoretical minimum. The task of MNC managers is to design the appropriate control system to keep certain variables within certain predetermined limits.

Since its inception in the early forties, the science of cybernetics has made many contributions to the field of international management, including a methodology for designing sophisticated systems that allow a manager to deal with uncertainty. Cybernetics is the study of control and communication in animals and machines. What is communicated is *feedback information*—that is, information about the difference between the system's desired outcome and its actual performance. Information technology (IT) is the application of cybernetics to the management of complex multinational and multipurpose global enterprises.

This chapter begins with a general description of a control system. Next the subject of information systems is explored, and the possibility of extending the use of management information systems (MIS), which are designed to provide the information needed to control domestic operations, to the global arena is investigated. Finally, the design and management of a global information system is briefly outlined.

THE BASIC ELEMENTS OF A CONTROL SYSTEM

Control systems can take any number of forms, depending on the business. They can be simple—the local bakery that is producing chocolate chip cookies does not need a computer to keep track of whether the cookies are coming up to standards. The bakers can *see* when cookies are burned, and they adjust the production process based on what they observe. But an MNC is a widespread and complex enterprise; it must have control systems for hundreds of processes of all kinds. The modern MNC could not survive without the help of a computerized control system; what follows is a description of the parts of such a system.

The main function of a control system is to keep some behavioral variables of the focal, or operating, system within predetermined limits. Control systems consist of four basic elements, which are themselves subsystems:[1]

(1)   A control object, or variable to be controlled

(2)   A detector, or scanning subsystem

(3)   A comparator

(4)   An activator, or action-taking subsystem

Exhibit 13-1 depicts these four basic subsystems of a control system, showing their functional interrelationships and their relationship with the operating system.

Control Object

The control object is the variable of the system's behavior chosen for monitoring and control. Variations in the control object are the stimuli that trigger the functioning of the control system. Without these variations, the system would have no reason to exist. Since in reality there is never a perfect match between desired and actual outcomes, variations will always exist—thus the need for control.

Careful thought ought to be given to which of the system's output variables

---

[1]This section is taken from P. P. Schoderbeck, C. G. Schoderbeck, and A. G. Kefalas, *Management Systems: Conceptual Consideration,* Third Edition (Plano, TX: Business Publications, 1985).

Exhibit 13-1   The Major Elements of a Control System

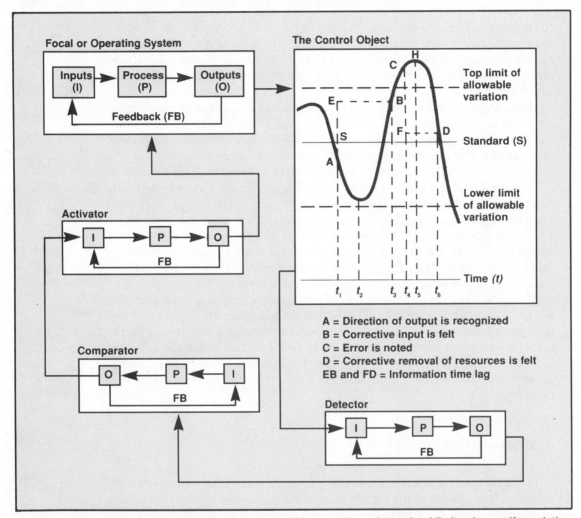

A = Direction of output is recognized
B = Corrective input is felt
C = Error is noted
D = Corrective removal of resources is felt
EB and FD = Information time lag

The control system keeps the system's output within certain predetermined limits via a self-regulating mechanism consisting of *the control object;* the *detector,* which monitors the changes in output over time; a *comparator,* which compares the sensed output against a set of standards; and an *activator,* which decides whether deviations recorded by the comparator warrant taking corrective action against the operating system's input function.

should be controlled. In most cases it is best to include both quantitative and qualitative attributes of the system's output among the control variables.

Detector

A detector system is another name for a management information system (MIS). The detector operates on the principle of selective acquisition, evaluation, and transmission of information.

Comparator

The output from the detector, or scanning system, constitutes the input to the comparator, whose function is to compare the state of the control object against the predetermined standard, or norm. The results of this comparison are then tabulated, and this record of deviations becomes the input to the activating system.

The control object's behavior can be either stable or unstable. Both of these states are necessary for system survival. Although stability is the ultimate long-run goal, short-term and periodic instability is necessary for system adaptation and learning. The system, in other words, pursues long-run stability via short-run changes in its behavior manifested in its output's deviations from a standard.

In general terms, stability is defined as the tendency for a system to return to its original position after a disturbance is removed. In systems nomenclature, a control object is stable if, once an input disturbance has been removed, it exhibits a return to the initial state exhibited at time t_0. Were the control object not able to return to or recover the initial state, the system would be said to exhibit instability. The input disturbance may be initiated by the feedback loop, or it may be a direct input from the system's environment.

When there are significant differences between the output and the goal, the system is said to be out of control. A lack of control generally implies that the goal formulated is unrealistic and/or unsuitable for the system being monitored, in which case either the goal or the system must be altered. For example, if a production goal cannot be met, either the goal must be altered, more people must be put on the production line, or more equipment must be employed.

Activator

The activator is a decision maker. It evaluates alternative courses of corrective action in light of the significance of the deviations transmitted by the comparator. Once the system has been determined to be out of control, the benefits of bringing it under control are compared with the estimated cost of implementing the proposed corrective actions. Corrective actions can include examining the accuracy of the detector and of the comparator, reevaluating the feasibility of the goal being pursued, or investigating the optimal combination of the inputs to the system—that is, the efficiency of the process employed by the operating system. In other words, the output of the activating system can be a corrective action aimed at investigating the controllability of the operating system and/or the controllability of the controller itself.

The particular behavior pattern exhibited by a control system is dependent on the sensitivity and accuracy of the feedback loop (detector, comparator, and activator) as well as on the time required to transmit the error message from the detector to the activator. Oversensitive feedback control systems may contribute as much to instability as do inert and sluggish ones.

Time delay is the most important contributor to instability in social systems such as business enterprises and governments. Although information technology has considerably accelerated the transmission of information from the detector to the activator and has expedited the comparison and evaluation of information inside the comparator, still the impact of a corrective action on the control object's behavior is felt only after a considerable time lag.

Continuous oscillations of the kind shown in the upper right-hand portion of Exhibit 13-1 are the result of two characteristics of feedback systems: (1) the length of the time delays and (2) the size of the feedback effect. This particular graph illustrates the behavior of a system controlled by a feedback system characterized by a one-half-cycle time delay. When there is that large a time delay, the impact of the corrective action designed to counteract a deviation is felt at a time when this deviation is of a considerably different magnitude, although it has the same direction. This time lag causes the system to overcorrect. In Exhibit 13-1, a deviation of magnitude SA is detected at time t_1. At time t_2, new imputs are added to bring the output back to the standard, S. The impact of this corrective action on the system's output is not felt until t_3. By that time the system's actual output is at point B. At time t_4 the detector senses this new deviation. But because of the one-half-cycle time lag, the system's actual output has oscillated above the upper limits to point H by the time new corrective action is initiated. This new corrective action, aimed at bringing the output back to the standard, will be felt at time t_6.

MNC CONTROL SYSTEMS

The basic premise that should underlie the design of a control system for an MNC's subsidiary is that the control objects must be factors over which the subsidiary exerts influence. Once the system has been designed, the exact nature of the control objects—as well as the method and units of measurement and the acceptable level of deviations—must be clearly communicated by the MNC to its subsidiary.

Managers need very specific knowledge of evaluation criteria in order to choose strategies that maximize performance. There are basically two means at their disposal for reducing the uncertainty associated with a specific variable. The first is to prevent variety from arising through better planning of systems and procedures and better selection and acculturation of key personnel. The second is to better detect variety through more accurate and timely data gathering, organization, processing, and evaluation.

Most companies focus on a mixture of financial and nonfinancial control objects. Some companies choose control objects from a set of factors developed by the association to which they belong; others develop their own. General

Electric's system for measuring and evaluating profit center performance focuses on the following eight key areas:[2]

(1)   Profitability

(2)   Market position

(3)   Productivity

(4)   Product leadership

(5)   Personnel development

(6)   Employee attitudes

(7)   Public responsibility

(8)   Balance between short-range and long-range goals

Management Foresight, Inc., a consulting company in Columbus, Ohio, suggests that the very specific set of performance factors listed in Exhibit 13-2 be used to arrive at an overall judgment of management performance and firm value.

Exhibit 13-2   Performance Summary

Performance Overview

Net profit before tax to net sales (adj; %)
Total asset turnover (adj; X)
Net profit before tax to total assets (adj; %)
Total assets to net worth (adj; %)
Net profit before tax to net worth (adj; %)
Operating profit to total assets (adj; %)

Sales Performance

Dollars of net sales ($000)
Percent sales change over prior year (%)

Profitability Performance

Gross margin to net sales (adj; %)

---

[2]C. W. Hofer, E. A. Murray, Jr., R. Chanan, and R. A. Pitts, *Strategic Management: A Casebook in Policy Planning,* Second Edition (St. Paul, MN: West Publishing Co., 1984), 747–748.

Operating Expense Control

Total operating expense % of net sales
Total operating expense to gross margin (adj; %)
Non-people expense to gross margin (adj; %)
Total compensation as % of gross margin (adj; %)

Functional Area Expense Control

Selling expense as % of net sales
Delivery expense as % of net sales
Warehouse & occupancy expense as % of net sales
General and administrative expense as % of net sales

Personnel Productivity

Net sales volume per person ($000)
Net sales volume per outside salesperson ($000)
Gross margin per person (adj; $000)
Average compensation per employee ($000)
Personnel productivity index (all emp; adj; X)

Inventory Management Performance

Average inventory turnover rate (X; adj)
Turnover and earning profitability index (adj; %)

Accounts Receivable Management

Days sales in accounts receivable (days)

Financial Management Performance

Net worth to total indebtedness (adj; %)
Current ratio (current assets/current liabilities) (X)
Accounts receivable to accounts payable (X)

SOURCE: Management Foresight, Inc., Columbus, Ohio.

Most companies use some variation of the basic profitability model depicted in Exhibit 13-3 as the framework for selecting the appropriate control objects for each MNC subsidiary and for the company as a whole. The following generalizations can be made about MNC control systems:

(1)   The nature of the system used to control the foreign operations is generally similar to that used to control the company's domestic operations.

Exhibit 13-3   Profitability Decision Tree

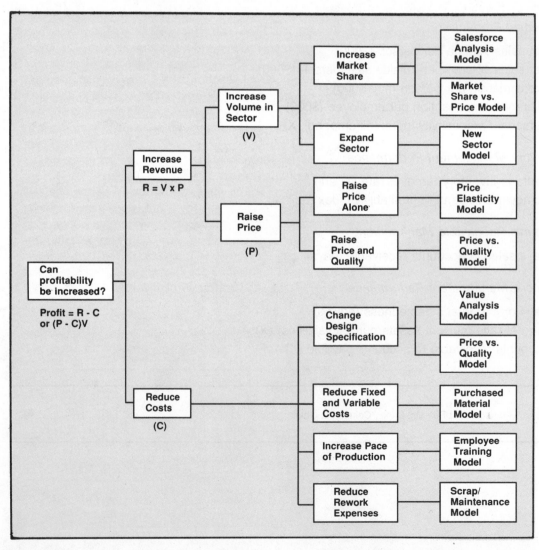

Statistical controls and standards developed for appraising domestic operations are generally imposed on foreign subsidiaries.

(2) There is a heavy emphasis on budgeting and financial controls.

(3) There is a tendency to treat foreign subsidiaries as profit centers and to use profits and return-on-investment as criteria for evaluating their performance.

(4) Top management at the headquarters is far more involved in the control of foreign operations than it is in the control of domestic operations.[3]

INFORMATION AND INFORMATION SYSTEMS: THE BASIC CONCEPTS

Managers learn very early in their careers that information is the key to making good decisions and that making good decisions is the key to success. Thus a causal relationship between success and information is established. What actually constitutes information, how it is measured, and when the point of diminishing returns in information acquisition is reached, however, are subjects seldom considered by most people. They assume that because having information is good, the more information one has, the better.

More than two decades ago, Russell Ackoff exposed some of the most popular myths on information and information systems. In a landmark article entitled "Management Misinformation Systems," Ackoff asserted that more information is not necessarily better.[4] There is a point at which the mind simply goes blank when bombarded with huge amounts of information. Psychologists had introduced the concept of "information overload," and information theorists such as Claude Shannon and Warren Weaver had developed the calculus for the measurement of information and information overload.[5] Later Alvin Toffler popularized the concept of information overload and its consequences in his book *Future Shock.*[6]

Although scientific definitions of information are too abstract for practical use, they emphasize the fact that information *relates to the concept of uncertainty and represents the key to its reduction.* In relating information to uncertainty reduction, one must distinguish between *data* (the raw material in the information-creation process) and *information* (the end result of that process). Information is in turn distinct from *knowledge,* which is the outcome of the use of information in a specific situation of uncertainty reduction. Finally,

---

[3]A. V. Phatak, *Managing Multinational Corporations* (New York: Praeger, 1974), 266.

[4]Russell L. Ackoff, "Management Misinformation Systems," *Management Science,* December 1967, 147–156.

[5]Claude E. Shannon and Warren Weaver, *The Mathematical Theory of Communication* (Urbana, IL: The University of Illinois Press, 1964).

[6]Alvin Toffler, *Future Shock* (New York: Random House, 1970).

wisdom is defined as the "appropriate" (that is, right for the purpose) use of knowledge.[7]

Exhibit 13-4 is a schematic representation of the information-creation process. The process takes place in the mind of the person confronted with an uncertain situation. By bringing into one's mind the problem and a set of data, one begins a selection process that eventually leads to the selection of appropriate data out of a given set of available data.

Business use of information technology—electronic devices (hardware) combined with the appropriate instructions (software)—has gone through several phases. During the data processing era, the technology was used mainly for the acquisition and processing of data. The entire process was controlled by the EDP (electronic data processing) professional; very little freedom was given to the manager user. An increase in the manager's ability to use the technology directly, without the intervention of the EDP professional, ushered in the present-day era of management information systems (MIS). The fact that a manager confronted wth a problem can relate it to a set of data and create information without having to go through the EDP professional has greatly enhanced managerial effectiveness. Even now, however, we are witnessing the beginning of the era of information and knowledge, when the user will have almost total control over the use of the technology. Direct linkages to large databases thousands of miles away will give the user tremendous opportunity to create information in a fraction of the time required before.

Exhibit 13-5 shows how the people in an organization might interact with a computerized information system. The people (left side of the diagram) are the input providers and the output users of the system. The organization is assumed to be a hierarchical structure. The left side of the diagram describes the tasks performed by the three layers of management. These tasks are the uncertainty generators. The right side of the diagram lists the databases (reports) that are used in the information-creation process. Note that as a general rule people at the top of the organization primarily *synthesize* information from the databases, whereas people at the bottom of the hierarchy *analyze* information from the databases. Databases contain basically two types of data: historical and evaluative. The shaded area in Exhibit 13-5 indicates the amount of evaluative data used by different levels of management; the white area represents the amount of historical data. As the exhibit shows, top management uses mostly evaluative data; its use of historical data is minimal. Lower management's role is just the opposite.

---

[7]Harlan Cleveland, *The Knowledge Executive* (New York: E. P. Dutton, 1985).

Exhibit 13-4 Information Formulation and Knowledge Acquisition

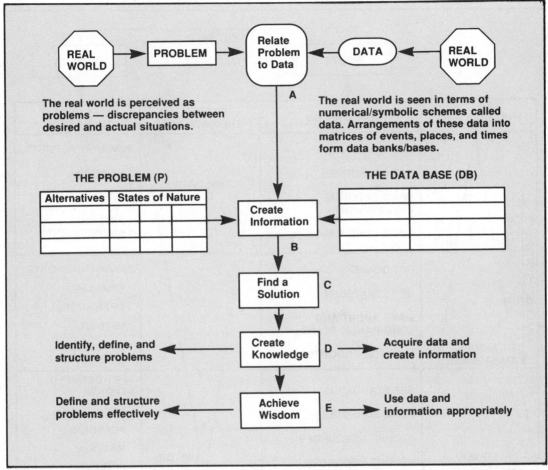

The *decision maker* confronted with a *problem* must relate the problem to the available *data* (A). Selection of certain data from the data base creates *information* (B). This information is used to arrive at a *solution* (C), the use of which results in *knowledge* (D). Appropriate use of this knowledge leads to *wisdom* (E). Step E relates to *effectiveness* (doing the right *thing*)—steps A, B, C, and D relate to *efficiency* (doing the thing *right*).

DESIGNING A GLOBAL INFORMATION SYSTEM (GLOBIS) FOR AN MNC

The diverse activities of a typical MNC create vast amounts of data that are gathered, stored, and transmitted in many different forms and languages. A

Exhibit 13-5 Managers and Information Systems

WHO THEY ARE	WHAT THEY DO	HOW THEY USE THE DATA BASE	WHAT OUTPUT THEY NEED
TOP MANAGEMENT	CLARIFY MISSION SET OBJECTIVES SCAN EXTERNAL ENVIRONMENT MAKE LONG-RANGE PLANS	EVALUATIVE DATA	SUMMARY REPORTS FINANCIAL OPERATIONAL EXTERNAL ENVIRONMENT
MIDDLE MANAGEMENT	SET GOALS SET STRATEGIES MAKE SHORT AND LONG-RANGE PLANS MONITOR PROGRESS		DETAILED REPORTS FINANCIAL OPERATIONAL MARKET EXTERNAL ENVIRONMENT
LOWER MANAGEMENT	SET STANDARDS FORM SCHEDULES SECURE RESOURCES REPORT PROGRESS	HISTORI-CAL DATA	VERY DETAILED REPORTS OPERATIONAL PERSONNEL MATERIAL EQUIPMENT

PROCESS — INPUTS → OUTPUTS

ANALYZE / SYNTHESIZE

OUTPUTS ← INPUTS — FEEDBACK

multinational corporation needs a huge information network created by a sophisticated computer and telecommunication system in order both to control its own and its subsidiaries' activities and to comply with a multitude of laws, rules, and regulations around the globe.

Exhibit 13-6 illustrates the parts of a global information system. The left-hand side of the exhibit shows the external global information subsystem (EXGLOBIS). The purpose of this subsystem is to allow the MNC to identify

Exhibit 13-6   The Global Information System (GLOBIS)

The External Global Information Subsystem (EXGLOBIS)	The Internal Global Information Subsystem (INGLOBIS)

I. ENVIRONMENTAL SCANNING: ISSUE MANAGEMENT APPROACH
A. Issue identification: Brainstorm on events, trends, issues, list top ten Issues or megatrends
B. Issue evaluation: Assess magnitude, importance, and meaning of top ten issues
C. Issue incorporation: Develop scenarios using the top five issues identified in previous step
D. Issue translation: Relate chosen strategies to three scenarios: optimistic, pessimistic, and most likely
 	
II. MACROECONOMIC ASSESSMENT
A. Political economy approach
B. External commercial services: BERI, BI, NBI, PSSI, WPRF, Gladwin-Walter, Frost and Sullivan
	III. STRATEGIC MANAGEMENT REQUIREMENTS
	A. Rationalization/restructuring
	B. Internal growth
	   New markets
	   New products
	C. External growth
	   Joint ventures
	   Acquisitions
	   New plants
	D. Strategic Alliances
	   Existing business domain
	   New business domain
	
	IV. OPERATIONAL/TACTICAL MANAGEMENT REQUIREMENTS
	A. Financial management requirements
	   Exposure management
	   Cash management
	   Capital budgeting
	   Investment evaluation and funding
	B. Non–financial management requirements
	   Organizational structure
	   Sourcing/production strategy
	   Marketing strategy
	   Human resource development strategy
	
	V. STATUTORY REQUIREMENTS
	A. Income/profit and loss statement
	B. Balance sheet statement
	C. Changes in financial position statement
	D. Notes on consolidated financial statements

The output of INGLOBIS is fed into the environmental assessment

The output of EXGLOBIS is fed into the strategic planning process

constraints, threats, and opportunities in the external business environment. The right-hand side of the exhibit depicts the internal global information subsystem (INGLOBIS). The subsystems are linked via feedforward and feedback mechanisms to guarantee adequate control.

THE EXTERNAL GLOBAL INFORMATION SUBSYSTEM (EXGLOBIS)

Accurate information about the external environment is exceedingly difficult to acquire. Whereas in internal information-creation processes data sources can be precisely defined, in external information-acquisition processes data sources have to be taken as they are. The lack of uniformity in definitions and measurements makes the trustworthiness of any data that are collected questionable. In some cases it may be difficult to acquire any data at all, particularly in a timely fashion.

In light of the variability in the reliability of the information coming into the EXGLOBIS, it is crucial that managers have a technique for assessing this information. Chapter 3 recommended environmental scanning and introduced the ENSCAN computer package. In a nutshell, the purpose of environmental scanning is to allow the manager to identify and evaluate emerging issues in the external environment that might affect the MNC. The environmental scanning process is summarized in section I of Exhibit 13-6. (See also Exhibit 3-8.) The ultimate result of this process is the creation of a set of scenarios that make potential future events a bit more concrete and thus more manageable.

Environmental scanning provides an initial broad picture of the environment. The next step is to make a more detailed assessment of the major issues identified through environmental scanning. Two traditional approaches used by academicians are shown in section II of Exhibit 13-6: application of the political economy model and use of external commercial sources.

The political economy approach focuses on the risk that arises out of structural (supply-side) elements, demand-side and monetary elements, and external economic and political developments, as well as on the quality of the national economic management team and the political constraints bearing upon decision makers. Incorporated in the analysis are mathematical equations, such as

$$Y + M = A + X$$

representing real flows of goods and services in an economy, where Y is output, M is imports, A is domestic absorption (consumption, investment, and public-sector spending), and X is exports, all in real terms.

To bring the money side into the picture explicitly, an equally simple equation can be used to describe international financial flows:

$$VX - VM - DS + FDI + U - K_0 = DR - NBR$$

where VX and VM are the money value of exports and imports, respectively; DS is debt-service payments to foreigners (usually part of VM in conventional balance-of-payments accounting); FDI is net flows of nonresident foreign direct investments; U is net flows of private and public-sector grants such as foreign aid; K_0 is net capital flows undertaken by residents; DR is the change in international reserves; and NBR is the net borrowing requirement.[8] An overall negative balance on the left-hand side of the equation clearly means that the country will have to increase its foreign borrowing or use up some of its international reserves.

The various commercial sources providing risk analysis services each have their own system. Some of the best-known are the following:[9]

(1)   The Business Environmental Risk Index (BERI)

(2)   The Business International (BI) system

(3)   Nikkei's Business Index (NBI)

(4)   The Political System Stability Index (PSSI)

(5)   World Political Risk Forecasts (WPRF) (the Prince model)

(6)   The Gladwin-Walter model

(7)   The Frost and Sullivan model

THE INTERNAL GLOBAL INFORMATION SUBSYSTEM (INGLOBIS)

The myriad of financial transactions between an MNC's headquarters and its numerous subsidiaries and among the subsidiaries themselves can be a nightmare for the information systems specialist, whose task is to provide the information necessary for the development of the reports required by the company's stakeholders. The need for efficient internal information systems has been intensified by the changes taking place in the international monetary scene, where new and more complicated financial instruments are being created almost daily. The complex task of the information specialist requires an equally complex system for gathering, organizing, processing, storing, and retrieving data from all subsidiaries; converting these data into useful information; and supplying this information to decision-making centers all over the globe. A firm that has an efficient international financial information management system most definitely has a competitive advantage in this extremely competitive world.[10]

---

[8]Ingo Walter (ed.), *Handbook of International Business* (New York: John Wiley and Sons, 1984).

[9]Charles R. Kennedy, Jr., *Political Risk Management: International Lending and Investing Under Environmental Uncertainty* (New York: Quorum Books, 1987), 41.

[10]Karen Pennon and G. David Wallace, "The Economy: Uncertainty Isn't About to Go Away," *Business Week*, February 22, 1988, 52–53.

The input needs of an efficient MIS are determined by many factors such as organizational structure, product and geographical diversification, management philosophy, and management's attitude toward computerized databases and the use of computers in managerial decision making. Input needs are further shaped by three kinds of requirements to which every MNC is subject.

STATUTORY REQUIREMENTS

Most countries treat private, for-profit organizations as "citizens" subject to taxation and other regulations. An MNC must comply with both its own government's requirements and the requirements of the governments of every one of its subsidiaries. In addition, the company's other stakeholders, such as investors (shareholders), bankers, and employees, are entitled to information about management's handling of their stake in the firm.

Requirements with respect to the information that must be provided to the government and other stakeholders vary considerably from country to country, but there are enough similarities that it is possible to build a system to handle all reporting requirements globally. All stakeholders want to know what resources a firm has, who owns these resources, how the resources are used in the process of wealth creation, and, finally, what share of this wealth is due to them. A firm satisfies these needs of its stakeholders by creating and making available four documents:

(1)   Income statement (P&L statement)

(2)   Balance sheet

(3)   Statement of changes in financial position

(4)   Notes on consolidated financial statements

All four of these documents are contained in the annual report that a company makes available to its stakeholders and to the public.

OPERATIONAL/TACTICAL MANAGEMENT REQUIREMENTS

Statutory reporting requirements are designed to satisfy the demands of the company's external stakeholders. Operational/tactical management requirements, on the other hand, reflect the informational needs of individuals or departments within the MNC. Unlike the statutory requirements, which apply to all of the corporations operating in a particular country, tactical management requirements vary from company to company and from case to case within the company. In general, the purpose of mandating subsidiary inputs to the corporate INGLOBIS is to facilitate planning, following up of plans, detecting deviations from plans, evaluating these deviations, taking corrective actions, and adjusting plans. But the magnitude and frequency of reporting by the subsidiaries to the parent company can be a hidden battleground in an MNC. Frequent reporting keeps headquarters informed, but it can prevent subsidiary management from making the most efficient use of organizational resources.

Frequently smaller subsidiaries complain of being asked to report on matters that are completely strange to them. One managing director of a subsidiary in a small country confided:

> I think I am going crazy. I just finished a monthly report on leasing private aircraft by my executives. . . . I put all zeroes or NA everywhere . . . that's what they told me to do when I called up and told them that over here there is no such thing as private aircraft. Nobody leases airplanes to go and do business or attend a meeting, which is a very common practice in Chicago. You have no idea how much time I spend doing things like that. Our turnover (sales) is barely over $10 million a year and yet we have to report on things that pertain to hundreds of millions of dollars. Every time I do this kind of thing my whole day is shot. I just go home and play with the kids.

As section IV of Exhibit 13-6 shows, there are two types of tactical management requirements. Financial management requirements relate to information used in exposure management, cash management, and project evaluation and funding. Non-financial management requirements cover data pertinent to the designing and updating of the organizational structure, sourcing and production strategy, marketing strategy, and human resource development strategy.

STRATEGIC MANAGEMENT REQUIREMENTS

The strategic management requirements of an MNC call for a global information system that allows managers to chart the company's long-range plans. Again, as discussed in Chapter 3, the basic task is to relate the firm's strengths and weaknesses (X) to the environment's constraints, threats, and opportunities (Y) and set the organization's objectives and goals (Z). These goals fall into four categories:

(1)   Rationalization/restructuring of existing activities

(2)   Internal growth options

(3)   External growth options

(4)   Strategic alliances

To summarize: Designing a global information system involves identifying the informational needs of the MNC and then devising an appropriate system for creating, organizing, and disseminating this information. An effective global information system brings together all the information required for both strategic and tactical management. After the firm's external business environment has been assessed via the EXGLOBIS, the output of the EXGLOBIS becomes the input to the INGLOBIS. The INGLOBIS focuses on the MNC's internal requirements, continuously monitoring and evaluating the MNC's progress toward its goals.

MANAGING THE GLOBAL INFORMATION SYSTEM

Managing a global information system is a major challenge. This inherently complex task involving new technology can seem virtually unmanageable when the international dimension is added (the social, technical, ecological, political, and economic differences among countries). For this reason most MNCs choose, in the words of Martin D. J. Buss, to "let sleeping dogs lie where information processing is concerned"[11]—an understandable but unwise attitude.

Determining which of the various data-processing operations should be carried out by the individual subsidiaries and which by the headquarters would be no easy matter even if cost and efficiency were the only considerations. But the issue is further complicated by the many constraints that must be taken into consideration. The next few pages highlight some of these constraints. Industry-, firm-, and technology-specific constraints are treated in detail in the fast increasing literature.[12]

REGULATION OF DATA FLOWS

Legislative attempts to regulate the flow of data have created a multitude of problems for some MNCs, particularly in service industries such as banking, transportation and shipping, and construction, where data processing and information creation and use are essential. Even though new technological developments have or may soon render some legislative constraints obsolete, it behooves the MNC manager to keep them in mind when designing a global information system.

Political and legislative interest in data processing and transmission of data across national borders began with the recognition that information is a vital ingredient in corporate and government decision making. In the words of Louis Joinet, French Magistrate of Justice,

> Information is power, and economic information is economic power. Information has an economic value, and the ability to store and process certain types of data may well give one country political and technological advantage over other countries. This, in turn, leads to a loss of national sovereignty through supranational data flows.[13]

---

[11]Martin D. J. Buss, "Managing International Information Systems," *Harvard Business Review*, September-October 1982, 153–162.

[12]For example, see Warren McFarlan and J. L. McKenney, *Corporate Information Systems Management: The Issues Facing Senior Executives* (Homewood, IL: R. D. Irwin, 1983), 165–182.

[13]Quoted in P. D. Grub and S. R. Settle, "Transborder Data Flows: An Endangered Species?" in P. D. Grub, F. Ghadan, and D. Khambata (eds.), *The Multinational Enterprise in Transition*, Third Edition (Princeton, NJ: The Darwin Press, 1986), 280–281.

Legislative efforts were first directed toward ensuring personal privacy and safeguarding the rights of individuals regarding the collection, processing, storage, dissemination, and use of personal data. Grub and Settle recommend that the ten essential principles of privacy listed in Exhibit 13-7 govern an MNC's treatment of data on private citizens.

At the nation-state level, privacy has become a national sovereignty issue. Many countries attribute a loss of the ability to set their own policies and laws to their lack of control over the inflow and outflow of information.

Exhibit 13-7   Principles of Privacy

(1) *The Social Justification Principle.* The collection of personal data should be for a general purpose and specific uses which are socially acceptable.

(2) *The Collection Limitation Principle.* The collection of personal data should be restricted to the minimum necessary and such data should not be obtained by unlawful or unfair means but only with the knowledge or consent of the data subject or with the authority of law.

(3) *The Information Quality Principle.* Personal data should, for the purposes for which they are to be used, be accurate, complete and kept up to date.

(4) *The Purpose Specification Principle.* The purpose for which personal data are collected should be specified to the data subject not later than at the time of data collection and the subsequent use limited to those purposes or such others as are not incompatible with those purposes and as are specified on each occasion of change of purpose.

(5) *The Disclosure Limitation Principle.* Personal data should not be disclosed or made available except with the consent of the data subject, the authority of law, or pursuant to a publicly known usage of common and routine practice.

(6) *The Security Safeguards Principle.* Personal data should be protected by security safeguards which are reasonable and appropriate to prevent the loss of, destruction of, or unauthorized use, modification, or disclosure of the data.

(7) *The Openness Principle.* There should be a general policy of openness about developments, practices, and policies with respect to personal data. In particular, means should be readily available to establish the existence, purposes, policies, and practices associated with personal data as well as the identity and residence of the data controller.

(8) *The Time Limitation Principle.* Personal data in a form that permits identification of the data subject should, once their purposes have expired, be destroyed, archived, or de-identified.

(9) *The Accountability Principle.* There should be, in respect of any personal data record, an identifiable data controller who should be accountable in law for giving effect to these principles.

(10) *The Individual Participation Principle.* An individual should have the right (a) to obtain from a data controller, or otherwise, confirmation of whether or not the data controller has data relating to him; (b) to have communicated to him, data relating to him (i) within a reasonable time, (ii) at a charge, if any, that is not excessive, (iii) in a reasonable manner, and (iv) in a form that is readily intelligible to him; (c) to challenge data relating to him and (i) during such challenge to have the record annotated concerning the challenge, and (ii) if the challenge is successful, to have the data corrected, completed, amended, annotated, or if appropriate, erased; and (d) to be notified of the reasons if a request made under paragraphs (a) and (b) is denied and to be able to challenge such denial.

SOURCE: P. D. Grub and S. R. Settle, "Transborder Data Flows: An Endangered Species?" in P. D. Grub, F. Ghadan, and D. Khambata (eds.), *The Multinational Enterprise in Transition*, Third Edition (Princeton, NJ: The Darwin Press, 1986), 280–281. Reprinted by permission.

Closely linked to national sovereignty is the issue of vulnerability to foreign influence. This concern is more acute in the developing countries, which may perceive an MNC's ability to collect and transmit vast amounts of data about the country's economic and political performance as a threat to their national security. The fear is that an unsolicited change agent is undermining the country's pursuit of self-reliant development. But developed countries are not invulnerable, either. France recognized very early the importance of information technology. In a clear expression of economic nationalism, a report to the French government made the following points:

(1) The "informatization" of society will have serious consequences for France, socially, economically, and culturally.

(2) Foreign firms must not be allowed to be instruments of foreign (primarily U.S.) dominance.

(3) Post, Telephone, and Telegraph (PTT) administration should be restructured so that the telecommunications portion can be redirected to work more closely with other high-technology agencies.

(4) Mastery of component technology is as important as nuclear mastery for national independence.[14]

---

[14]Grub and Settle, "Transborder Data Flows," p. 520.

Some other reasons for regulating transborder data flow are as follows:

(1) Expenditures for expensive foreign-made communications equipment have a negative effect on the country's balance of payments.

(2) Allowing data to be processed outside the country "exports" jobs.

(3) Lack of data-processing opportunities within the country deters hardware and software development, thereby making the country dependent on foreign technology.

(4) The national and cultural values of the country may be undermined by cultural and political messages coming from other countries.

(5) Allowing other countries easy and quick access to information could give the enemy an advantage in time of war.[15]

Legislative constraints on the flow of data have tremendous implications for MNC management, as they affect every management function from choosing the appropriate entry strategy to managing human resources.[16] Exhibit 13-8 outlines some of the potential effects of data-flow regulations.

ORGANIZATIONAL CONSIDERATIONS

Organizational considerations in managing a global information system relate primarily to (1) issues of cost and technology and (2) operational changes. Costs for such items as payroll, hardware, and software are considerably higher in most parts of the world than they are in the United States. Wages and fringe benefits for information-processing personnel in West Germany, for example, are twice what they are in the United States, and hardware costs are about 60% higher. Transmission of a line of data in Spain costs six times more than it does in the United States.

Operational changes may be mandated by such developments as the growing interdependence of overseas affiliates, the introduction of the microcomputer and the acceleration of end-user computing and telecommunication, and the unionization of data-processing personnel.

---

[15]Saeed Samiee, "Transnational Data Flow Constraints: A New Challenge for Multinational Corporations," *Journal of International Business Studies*, Spring/Summer 1984, 141–150; Steven W. Baker, "Importing Information: Current U.S. Customs Control," *American Import-Export Bulletin*, March 1981, 50–54; Robert P. Burton, "Transnational Data Flows: International Status, Impact and Accommodation," *Data Management*, June 1980, 27–34.

[16]Arthur A. Bushkin, "The Threat to International Data Flows," *Business Week*, August 3, 1981, 10–11; Jake Kirchner, "TDF Barriers Seen Hitting U.S. Firms in Pocket: Executives Tell Congress," *Computerworld*, August 3, 1981, 5; Burt Nanus, "Business, Government and the Multinational Computer," *Columbia Journal of World Business*, Spring 1978, 19–26; "New OECD Guidelines on Privacy," *OECD Observer*, November 1980, 26–41; United National, *Transnational Corporations and Transborder Data Flows: A Technical Paper* (New York: United Nations Centre on Transnational Corporations, 1982); "We Don't Worry, We're British," *The Economist*, October 25, 1981, 81.

Exhibit 13-8   Potential Impact of Data Flow Legislation

With the advent of more and more complex and sometimes conflicting new laws governing data files and the confusion that is developing, we are experiencing delays in system design. Planning is becoming increasingly difficult and administrative costs are starting to increase. . . . The increased difficulty of managing the company, increased delays in reporting vital operating data, reduced market information, less effective means of evaluating personnel for promotion—all will be far more disruptive to productivity and effective operation than the added out-of-pocket costs.

Multinational computer/communications systems must often be redesigned or restructured in accordance with the new nationally imposed procedures for handling information. Requirements may include all or some combination of the following: (1) the registration of personal data files with a central regulatory authority; (2) limits on data collection to clearly defined purposes; (3) access to data files by subjects and/or governmental authorities for purposes of inspection and (4) sufficient security precautions to prevent unauthorized access to data bases.

While some firms may already have a mechanism in place, others may need to establish "an effective arm of organization to set and implement data security and privacy policy."

Multinational firms generally accept the central objective of data privacy protection legislation, which many feel is simply an extension of existing corporate policy. Their major concern involves the effects of overlapping (and often conflicting) national laws, as well as the wider impact the new regulations will have on corporate information flows. Because multinationals operate on a global basis, they are highly visible and, as a consequence, feel more vulnerable for the following reasons:

(1) MNCs operating in *any* country with data protection laws may be obliged to extend compliance to *every* country where they have operations, resulting in communications with a much higher degree of transparency than would otherwise be normal or acceptable for the firm.

(2) Licensing or registration requirements legitimize government supervision and scrutiny of corporate information systems. Further, registering the patterns and destinations of flows within their organizations to comply with private rules may expose much wider corporate policies and practices.

(3) The right of access by data authorities to corporate data processing operations for security safeguards checks may lead to disclosure of nonpersonal data, since name-linked data may not be segregated from other types of data; even the disclosure of personal information may involve a great deal of related collateral information of a proprietary nature.

SOURCE: Grub and Settle, "Transborder Data Flows," p. 285. Reprinted by permission.

THE BASIC STEPS

STEP 1: DIAGNOSIS

The first step in managing a GLOBIS is to assess the capability of the existing information system at the headquarters and its ability to relate to the numerous systems used by affiliates. Exhibit 13-9 lists some questions a senior executive might ask to get a quick overview of the situation.[17] In most cases the outcome of this diagnostic exercise is the discovery that the MNC is an archipelago of EDP and MIS departments with varying abilities to communicate with each other and with the MNC.

STEP 2: POLICY SETTING

The second step is to establish policies that ensure the uniform use of information technology by all subsidiaries around the globe. Such information technology policies must be in line with the overall policies of the MNC on the use of its conventional resources, such as people, money, material, and equipment. Exhibit 13-10 offers some guidelines for policy setting and suggests some areas that should be covered by such policies.

STEP 3: INTEGRATION

The third step—integration—is designed to enable the MNC to begin conceptualizing information as a "strategic weapon." The purpose of integration is to create an INFOstructure that can accommodate the MNC's need to communicate and control the complex INFRAstructure of physical, human, and monetary resources around the globe. In the words of James L. McKenney and Warren McFarlan, the goal of this step is to "bring the islands that make up an archipelago of information—office automation, telecommunications, and data processing—under integrated control."[18]

Before these islands of information technology can be merged into a coherent whole, the MNC must merge data processing (DP) and office automation, at both the headquarters and subsidiary levels, into an integrated information system. Once this task has been accomplished, the MNC must link the numerous resident ISs into a global information system. In his book *Competing in Time*, Peter Keen describes the process as a movement "from vision to policy to architecture."[19]

Vision is a picture of the future—an easily understood statement about a practical and desirable (though not necessarily fully predictable) goal. It

---

[17]A more complete nontechnical primer for executives is William E. Perry, *The Manager's Survival Guide to Computer Systems* (New York: CBI Publishing Co., 1982).

[18]James L. McKenney and E. Warren McFarlan, "The Information Archipelago—Steps and Bridges," *Harvard Business Review*, September-October 1982, 109–119.

[19]Peter G. W. Keen, *Competing in Time: Using Telecommunications for Competitive Advantage* (Cambridge, MA: Ballinger Publishing Co., 1986), 113–115.

Exhibit 13-9   Rating the Data Processing Operation

Nature of the Information Provided

(1)   Can I compare operating results across affiliates in a way that helps me form conclusions on relative product costs, margins, and sales volumes?   YES   NO

(2)   Do I know whether my subordinates are satisfied with their information resources?   YES   NO

(3)   Do I know whether my competitors have better information systems than I do?   YES   NO

Business and Data Processing Planning

(4)   Have I approved a long-range information systems plan?   YES   NO

(5)   Do I know whether the data processing plan supports my business plans for the key regions?   YES   NO

(6)   Has data processing been on the agenda of high-level operations reviews in the past 6 months?   YES   NO

(7)   In the past 12 months have I been involved in any major decisions on an information processing issue?   YES   NO

(8)   Have I been briefed in the past 12 months on the implications of new information processing technology for my business?   YES   NO

Organization of Data Processing

(9)   Do I know how international data processing responsibilities are organized?   YES   NO

(10) Do I have the authority and responsibility to get the information processing I want?   YES   NO

(11) Do I have a source that keeps me informed as to how well data processing is working?   YES   NO

Cost of Information Processing

(12) Do I know how much I am spending on data processing in my key regions?   YES   NO

(13)   Do I know whether these regions are spending
enough, too much, or too little?   YES   NO

(14)   Do I know on which functions data processing
emphasis is being placed for the current levels of
expenditure?   YES   NO

(15)   Do I think this emphasis is in the right place?   YES   NO

A total of 12 or more yeses indicates that information processing operations
are sound and well coordinated. A total of six to eleven yeses suggests that
management intervention is needed in some areas. Fewer than six yeses
indicates serious problems; senior international managers should almost certainly take action in the following three ways: (1) orchestrate the process by
which the organization plans its approach to international data processing;
(2) create the right organizational framework for the international information
system activity; and (3) define the roles of the key players.

SOURCE: Martin D. J. Buss, "Managing International Information Systems," p. 158.

---

evolves from answers to such questions as

What is happening in our industry and around its edges?

What makes us special? What must we do to remain so?

Who is our competition now?

What style of organization do we want to be?

How can we run our business better?

Policy is a set of mandates and directives from the top of the firm, specifying
"how we do things around here." It addresses questions of authority and
accountability. The following policy questions have to be answered explicitly:

What pace and degree of change—business, organizational, and
technical—are we ready to accept?

What is our planning horizon?

How should the business case for building the long-term infrastructure
be made? How should it be funded?

What range of future business services should be anticipated in the
technical architecture?

What are the criteria for selecting vendors, given the relative importance
of integrating some, most, or all of the components of the information
technology base?

Who defines, coordinates, and monitors standards?

Exhibit 13-10   Policy Guidelines for MNC Information Processing

Issues	Content of policy
A. Hardware: CPU and peripherals	*Central Hardware Concurrence or Approval*: Avoid mistakes in vendor viability and lack of compatibility; pursue economies of scale in purchasing decisions; patronize local vendors.
B. Software: systems, applications, headquarters transfer, in-house development, outside purchase	*Central Software Development and Standards*: Uniform standards must be set for software documentation, maintenance, compatibility and economy; software transferability must be maximized. Development and updating must take into consideration the local needs, availability of well-trained personnel, costs and willingness of the headquarters staff to support and update programs made by the affiliates. Feasibility studies for the development of new software or upgrading of old ones must follow uniform procedures. Purchases of software from outside vendors must adhere to the same rules as the purchase of hardware (compatibility and economy).
C. Data: gathering, processing, transmission	*Data Gathering, Processing and Communication*: Instruments for gathering data such as forms, questionnaires, terminals must be uniform to avoid duplication, confusion and incompatibility. Naming, labeling and classifying data must be done so as to lead to the develoment of an international corporate data dictionary. Storage of data in terms of both form and medium must also follow a corporate model to allow the use of tapes, discs, and other storage devices by data processing equipment across the globe.
D. Organization and personnel	*Organization and Staffing*: Selection, hiring, training, appraising and career development procedures must be uniform to avoid "job hopping" and "brain drain" from subsidiary to headquarters and from developing to developed countries. Job rotation, visitations, conferences, schools and joint educational programs must be encouraged across the globe. Particular attention must be given to nationals in promotions.
E. Consulting services	*Corporate and Outside Consultation*: Corporate and regional headquarters personnel are usually more aware of leading-edge hardware and software developments. Policies and procedures must be set up for both requesting and accepting unsolicited headquarters assistance. In some cases, outside consulting might be preferable.
F. TBDF and other legal matters	*Legal and Transborder Data Transfer*: Care must be taken to assure compliance with local regional and

Issues	Content of policy
	international restrictions on data transfer across national boundaries, in particular where name-carrying data transmission is concerned.

SOURCE: Warren McFarlan and James L. McKenney, *Corporate Information Systems Management: The Issues Facing Senior Executives* (Homewood, IL: Richard D. Irwin, 1983), 165–182.

Architecture is the corporate telecommunications network that links the IS departments of the numerous affiliates of an MNC. Exhibit 13-11 is a sketch of an MNC telecommunications network. The history of modern telecommunications reveals a trend away from separate facilities and incompatibility toward integration. The logical endpoint (which is already technically feasible though not yet available for everyday operation) is an integrated system that includes the following elements:

Multiservice workstations that can access any available remote service

A worldwide set of transmission facilities, some leased by the firm (private networks) and others used on an as-needed basis (public data networks), that can deliver all standard types of information to the workstation: telephone calls, images of documents, memos and messages, computer data and transactions, and pictures

Switches that make this integrated services network "transparent" to the user, so that the person need have no knowledge of the network in order to use it

A *set of standards*, accepted by all manufacturers of computer and communications equipment and providers of communications services, that eliminates incompatibility by defining the interfaces between facilities, not the facilities themselves[20]

Once the three tasks of vision clarification, policy setting, and architecture design have been accomplished, the organizational design must be sketched out. The most efficient way of implementing a GLOBIS is to set up a Global Information Council, to oversee the MNC's creation and use of information

[20]Keen, *Competing in Time*, pp. 14–24.

Exhibit 13-11   Components of a Telecommunications Network

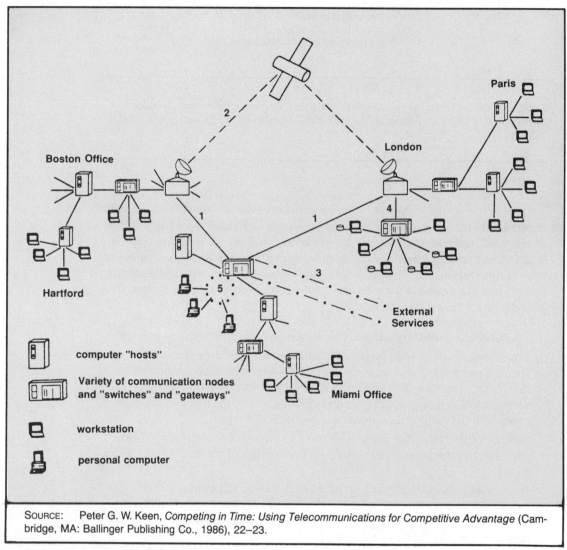

SOURCE: Peter G. W. Keen, *Competing in Time: Using Telecommunications for Competitive Advantage* (Cambridge, MA: Ballinger Publishing Co., 1986), 22–23.

Transmission Links: 1, high-speed leased link; 2, satellite; 3, public data network; 4, fiber optics short link; 5, intrapremise local area network

globally.[21] The place for such a council in the organizational hierarchy is within the MNC's International Division, the head of which reports directly to the CEO. The GLOBIS division should have a line relationship to both affiliate and

---

[21]Buss, "Managing International Information Systems," pp. 158–162.

corporate information system heads. Its mandate and purpose should be similar to those of the domestic computer steering committee. The council might consist of representatives from key regions, from corporate data processing, and from corporate planning.

RECAPITULATION

The subject of communication and control in a MNC has traditionally been dealt with in terms of stakeholder requirements and organizational, managerial, and decision-making requirements. Under the assumption that information is an MNC's most important strategic weapon, this chapter approached the subject of control and communication from the cybernetic viewpoint.

The issue of information systems design and management is an orphan in both international business and management information systems literature. Writers of international business textbooks believe that the subject is too specialized and too complex to be understood by the typical international business student or manager. Writers of MIS textbooks, on the other hand, believe that there is no reason to address the use of information technology in MNCs because differences between domestic and transnational procedures are insignificant. As this chapter pointed out, that is not the case. In addition to environmentally imposed constraints on transborder data transmission, there are numerous other impediments that must be overcome. The literature on these impediments is extremely scarce.

The panoply of technology—both hardware and software—is the INFO-structure, which is superimposed on the MNC's INFRAstructure of land, people, material, equipment, and money. Individual information systems, when integrated into a global information system, form a powerful managerial tool that enables MNC managers to identify and exploit business opportunities across the globe.

An MNC's ability to compete in future global markets will depend on the speed with which its management begins building an organizational strategy and structure that facilitate the movement of information across the globe. A modern GLOBIS integrates electronic data processing (EDP), office automation (word processing, spreadsheets, databases, and expert systems/artificial intelligence software packages), and telecommunications systems, thereby opening up entirely new ways of thinking about customers, markets, productivity, coordination, service, competition, products, and organization.

REVIEW QUESTIONS

(1)   Define the concept of control.

(2)   MNC, AG, a large German car manufacturer in the United States, has been experiencing severe profitability problems. The company's profit has been negative for the last two years. The company's management has come to you for advice. Design a profitability decision tree (as

depicted in Exhibit 13-3) for MNC, AG, indicating the sources of the information you will need to arrive at a specific recommendation for improving the company's profitability.

(3)   In designing a profitability decision tree for MNC, AG, you discover that the firm's management is confused as to what data are needed by managers at different levels. Top management is bombarded with tons of computer printouts, while operational executives are starving for the same data. Apparently, data-processing people are trying to impress top managers by giving them more and more information. Using the framework shown in Exhibit 13-5, list the *specific* kinds of information on the profitability problem that might be of use to executives at each level in the corporation.

(4)   Using questions similar to those in Exhibit 13-9, interview some executives of a local company to determine whether the firm's existing information system is providing them with the information they need to function in the most efficient manner. Then write a report in which you analyze your findings and make recommendations for improving the firm's information management.

SUGGESTED READINGS

Brightman, Harvey J., and Sidney E. Harris. "A Comparison of Modeling Practices in Domestic and Foreign Firms." *Managerial Planning*, September-October 1987, 30–34.

Bruns, William J., and E. Warren McFarlan. "Information Technology Puts Power in Control Systems." *Harvard Business Review*, September-October 1987, 89–94.

Buss, Martin D. J. "Legislative Threat to Transborder Data Flow." *Harvard Business Review*, May-June 1984, 111–118.

Cleveland, Harlan. "Educating for the Information Society." *Change*, July/August 1985, 13–21.

"The Information Edge." *Financial Times*, February 2, 1988, 7.

Jenster, Per V. "Using Critical Success Factors in Planning." *Long Range Planning*, February 1987, pp. 102–109.

Keen, Peter G. W. *Competing in Time: Using Telecommunications for Competitive Advantage*. Cambridge, MA: Ballinger Publishing Co., 1986.

McFarlan, Warren E. "Information Technology Changes the Way You Compete." *Harvard Business Review*, May-June 1984, 98–103.

McFarlan, Warren E., and James L. McKenney. *Corporate Information Systems: Text and Cases*. Homewood, IL: Richard D. Irwin, 1987.

Narchal, R. M., K. Kittappa, and P. Bhattcharya. "An Environmental Scanning System for Business Planning." *Long Range Planning* 20, No. 6 (1987): 96–105.

Nigh, D., and P. L. Cochran. "Issues Management and the Multinational Enterprise." *Management International Review* 27, No. 1 (1987): 4–12.

Porter, Michael E., and Victor E. Miller. "How Information Gives You Competitive Advantage." *Harvard Business Review*, July-August 1985, 149–160.

Radhakrishnan, K. S., and L. A. Soenen. "Why Computerized Financial Reporting and Consolidation Systems?" *Managerial Planning*, July/August 1987, 32–36.

Richman, Louis S. "Software Catches the Team Spirit." *Fortune*, June 8, 1987, 125–136.

Vitro, Robert A. "The Information Engine." *Managing International Development*, January-February 1984, 24–39.

Wallace, W. A. "International Accounting and Likely Approaches to Future Inquiry: An Overview of Research." *Management Information Review* 27, No. 2 (1987): 4–25.

CASE ● To Automate or Not To Automate?

When Pierre Lesparre, chief executive of a Paris-based insurance company, convened a meeting early [one] September to consider plans for automating the head office, he became aware that deep-seated differences among some of his senior managers, which had previously become apparent, had not been resolved.

In August, before the start of the summer vacation, a similar meeting had revealed marked disagreements on how far and fast to automate and indeed, whether to proceed any further in that direction at all. Lesparre had asked his managers to give some further idle thought to the question while skin-diving or lying on the beach. "I'm a great believer in letting the subconscious mind take over, where thorny problems are involved," he had said. "Maybe you will all come back with your views substantially modified."

Now Lesparre sighed as he realized that the summer sun had not, in fact, worked miracles.

First he asked the finance director, Max Robinet, whether he was still opposed to the company installing a local area network along lines suggested by the data processing manager, Daniel Merten.

"I see no reason to modify my original position," Robinet replied. "As you all know, I am a firm believer in the principle of automation. I certainly agree that we cannot afford to fall too far behind our larger competitors in this respect.

SOURCE: *The Best of Dilemma and Decision from International Management* (London: McGraw-Hill International, 1985), 49–50.

"I am fully aware that in his submission in July, Merten favoured a comprehensive local area network of the kind already used by about 20, mainly Anglo-Saxon, companies. But I remain convinced that a more cost-effective solution would be to use our existing PABX, which after all has only recently been installed.

"Incidentally I have since learned that there is a dealer just around the corner who is well qualified to connect our existing equipment to the telephone network. He would provide us with all the support we need."

Lesparre turned to Merten, a younger man who had been hired to manage a small minicomputer the company had purchased three years previously. Since then, many different machines had been purchased and used for different purposes. They included two word processors and several microcomputers all of which had been used to handle particular problems at various times.

At an early stage Merten had mentioned to Lesparre the need for some kind of long-range commitment to link up all these machines so that each could communicate with the others. With the approval of Robinet, to whom Merten reported, Lesparre had asked the data processing manager to look at the market and come up with recommendations.

The result had been Merten's July report, in which he had advocated installing a local area network which would, in effect, mean buying or leasing a number of fairly expensive little black boxes to plug into the devices the insurance company already possessed.

It was the expenditure that Robinet now objected to. But Merten made it plain that despite the opposition of his immediate boss, and notwithstanding the mellowing effects of his recent holiday in Corsica, he had not changed his mind on the issue. "I remain as convinced as ever of the need to go the whole hog and choose an industry standard as our system," he said. "It will pay off in the long run, even if it means more expenditure now."

Finally Lesparre invited the comments of personnel manager Emile Sergent, who all along had been most opposed to the very idea of what he called "reckless automation."

"I want to put it to you," said Sergent, "that until this whole idea cropped up and became common knowledge, morale in this company was sky high. It is still fairly high. But there is this element of uncertainty, which is not helping things at all. Now the logical conclusion to the process suggested by Merten, by his own admission, is that we shall have to make quite large redundancies. Not only will typists not be needed but many professionals also will have to go. Morale is going to suffer heavily."

"With due respect," said Merten, "that is an argument commonly used by personnel departments looking for an easy life. The fact is that despite increasing turnover we have suffered declining profits in recent years. This has led to lower wage increases which in turn have done more than anything else to cause discontent among the staff. What I am proposing is to end the uncertainty. Of course we will have to work out progressive personnel policies to soften the blow. But that is another problem."

"I resent the suggestion that we just seek an easy life," Sergent replied.

"Rather, we are being realistic. Whatever we do to soften the blow, some of the better qualified staff will leave. It can be incredibly boring using computers, or hadn't you noticed?"

"As a technical man you want the very latest equipment—industry standard, as you put it. But I would suggest that as yet there is no such standard. There is no such thing as a fully functioning management information system and there is no such thing as a fully automated office. So I suggest it would be better to wait and do some research, while watching other companies make the mistakes."

"If we do that we shall fall too far behind," Merten said. "Competitors are making progress now."

"Which is an argument for compromising, and using the PABX we already have," Robinet interposed.

All along, Lesparre had said that the final decision would be his. Now he realized, the moment of decision was fast approaching. Maybe he should be a bit wary about supporting a data processing manager who had been brought in, originally, just to manage a minicomputer, and whose recommendation was not favoured by his immediate boss.

On the other hand, could the company afford to dither, using as an excuse the question of staff morale? Faced with internal dissension, what should Lesparre do next, and how could staff morale be maintained?

ISSUES FOR DISCUSSION

(1)   Prepare a 15-minute presentation for Mr. Lesparre on the latest in integrated management information systems and automated offices.

(2)   How would you advise Mr. Lesparre to handle the dilemma of supporting a data processing manager "whose recommendation was not favoured by his boss"?

(3)   In view of the current emphasis on "information as a strategic weapon," can the company afford to dither?

(4)   Are the personnel manager's fears about the impact of computerization on personnel morale well founded? Weigh the positive strategic impact of the use of the latest information technology on the company's performance against its potentially negative impact on personnel morale.

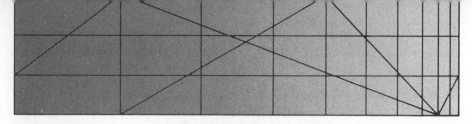

CHAPTER 14

CONSORTIA AND STRATEGIC ALLIANCES

"Traditional multinationals have tried to do everything on their own as they entered each market. They can't do that any more because the skills and products required to compete worldwide have increased greatly.... The future key factor for success for multinationals will be their ability to develop and enhance company-to-company relationships, particularly across national and cultural boundaries."

Kenichi Ohmae

Triad Power: The Coming Shape of Global Competition (New York: Macmillan, 1988).

LEARNING OBJECTIVES

After studying the material in this chapter, the student should be familiar with the following concepts:

(1) Global consortia

(2) Restructuring and rationalization

(3) Macroengineering projects

(4) Commercialization and industrialization of space

(5) The four paramount traits of the twenty-first-century executive

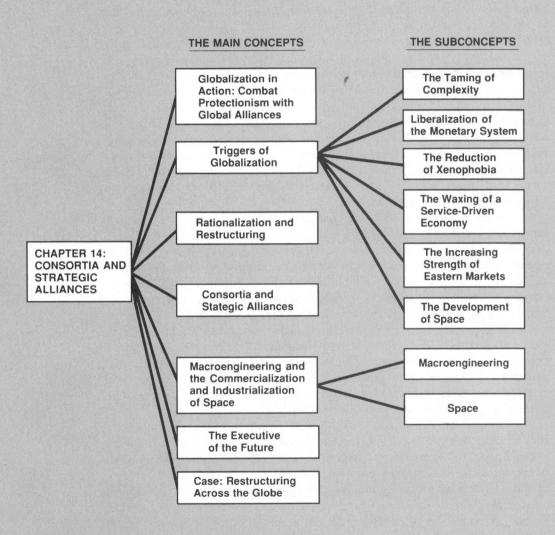

THE MAIN CONCEPTS

THE SUBCONCEPTS

CHAPTER 14: CONSORTIA AND STRATEGIC ALLIANCES

Globalization in Action: Combat Protectionism with Global Alliances

Triggers of Globalization

Rationalization and Restructuring

Consortia and Stategic Alliances

Macroengineering and the Commercialization and Industrialization of Space

The Executive of the Future

Case: Restructuring Across the Globe

The Taming of Complexity

Liberalization of the Monetary System

The Reduction of Xenophobia

The Waxing of a Service-Driven Economy

The Increasing Strength of Eastern Markets

The Development of Space

Macroengineering

Space

GLOBALIZATION IN ACTION
Combat Protectionism with Global Alliances

A new pattern of corporate alliances is emerging around the world, creating unprecedented challenges and opportunities for U.S. companies and U.S. government policy. To be competitive, U.S. corporations must join "networks of international coalitions" and learn how to manage them. Otherwise, erosion of our markets—both international and domestic—could further threaten our world influence and standard of living.

While corporate alliances are not new, their pattern has changed significantly in the past few years. The number of corporate marriages is accelerating, with more than 1,000 such arrangements springing up between U.S. and European firms alone in the past two years. They are found especially in high-technology and information-technology industries, such as office equipment, electronics, automobiles and banking. Previously, industry leaders such as IBM, General Motors, Europe's N.V. Philips and Japan's Nippon Telegraph & Telephone marched to the macho "go it alone" tune. But there is no company now large enough to be truly competitive globally on its own, so the giants are joining forces with many other companies, often including major competitors, in various niches of their product lines.

Why is this happening? Dramatic changes in the external business environment have accelerated the need for global strategic alliances. The world has gone beyond interdependence to an international market in many sectors operating within one global financial system. Yet the protectionist and nationalistic policies of many governments threaten the global market. In response, corporations are using alliances to help head off or jump over protectionist barriers (e.g., the many new Japanese investments in the U.S.).

Converging technologies require companies to integrate a full line of products, rather than, as in the past, selling one stand-alone machine. The Xerox copier, for example, is now part of an integrated office-information system that processes documents from creation to transmission, including storage and retrieval as well as reproduction. No company can cover the complete line competitively without help from other companies.

The increased power of these new alliances is putting even greater pressure on corporations to join, since a company outside the network is barred from selling into it. To become truly competitive, U.S. corporations have two urgent new requirements. First, they must quickly join the right team—or network of alliances. It is no longer enough to pick the right partner. Now companies must assess the networks of each prospective partner for their competitiveness. Second, companies must develop sufficient numbers of senior managers who combine a knowledge of their own companies with the ability to work with foreign partners who have different goals, values, customs and languages.

SOURCE: Daniel A. Sharp, "Combat Protectionism with Global Alliances," *The Wall Street Journal,* June 1, 1987, 22. Reprinted with permission of *The Wall Street Journal* © 1988 Dow Jones & Co., Inc. All rights reserved.

Whether the trend toward alliances helps or hurts U.S. competitiveness is a controversial issue. Robert Reich of Harvard argues that we are giving away our technology, particularly to the Japanese, who will use it to dominate us in industries in which we were once the leaders, such as aeronautics, just as they have done in microcircuits. Mr. Reich and others argue that the U.S. must maintain its strength in such industries—not only for reasons of national security, but also for the economic health of the industries themselves, which depend on domestic U.S. markets for a major part of their revenue.

Mr. Reich's critics counter that by being more competitive globally through strategic alliances, U.S.-based companies are actually preserving jobs in the U.S. and contributing to increased competitiveness at home. One recent study appears to show that U.S. corporations, measured globally rather than just in terms of local U.S. production, are competitive. In any event, without such alliances the international strength of many U.S. companies might rapidly decline.

And there are broader possible advantages to transnational corporate links:

Countries can be brought closer together by combining business and financial institutions. This can help build confidence to overcome our trade fights with Japan and Europe and lay a much needed foundation for the new U.S. role in shared management of the world economy.

Corporations can help preserve an open trading system by jointly lobbying their multiple host governments against protectionism.

Corporate alliances often facilitate finding components at lower cost, in Asia and Latin America, for example. U.S. companies can thus become more efficient short-term and can invest more to improve competitiveness of other aspects of their business.

By joining with foreign companies, U.S. firms can acquire global marketing and extra technological expertise.

If U.S. companies are to be able to participate fully in this new game, some U.S. government impediments to such cooperation may have to be removed. Antitrust laws are already being interpreted more gently. However, new industrial associations are under development in the U.S. that will test that antitrust flexibility as they move into co-production and other forms of cooperation. New laws permitting such actions may be necessary. And tax laws may have to be revised to facilitate U.S. personnel working overseas in their new partnerships, and [to define] how to tax these transnational entities.

National security issues also arise. The U.S. government does not want to support foreign companies or become dependent upon them for its defense technology. The Defense Department already views this as an issue.... Yet Defense is farming out strategic defense initiative contracts to our allies, including Japan.

Inevitably, national governments, beholden to their domestic electorates, will continue to think along the vertical dimension of the nation state when making decisions about taxation, antitrust, industrial, economic and other policies to protect the national interest. However, new economic realities force corporations increasingly to think and act along horizontal, global dimensions. Narrow-minded nationalist loyalties may be eroded as both shareholding and corporate alliances become increasingly global.

OVERVIEW

The global business environment is in a turbulent state. Slow economic growth in the developed world (caused primarily by the low population growth rates and high market saturation rates), in combination with equally slow economic growth in the developing world (caused by the high population growth rates and the lack of financial liquidity), has given rise to commercial protectionism amidst political liberalism. On the positive side, the political liberalization of the planned economies of China and the USSR and the opening of space to commercialization and industrialization provide a ray of hope of future growth and prosperity.

Faced with a changing business environment, MNCs are coming to the realization that cooperation for competition is the best strategy. Thus, as we have seen, many firms are undergoing an internal restructuring in an effort to make themselves leaner and more flexible. Externally, MNCs are forming strategic alliances to promote cooperation in R&D, production, marketing, financing, and new venture development.

Consortia and global alliances are clearly the most appropriate means for tackling the commercialization and industrialization of outer space. In the not-too-distant future, consortia of MNCs are likely to begin exploring the advantages of zero-gravity production of pharmaceuticals, computer chips, and other products whose manufacture depends on either rapid transmission of data around the globe or a trouble-free physical environment.

INTRODUCTION

One of the main theories underlying this book is that MNCs have evolved via a process of *creeping incrementalism.* This process begins with a limited commitment of resources to exporting and importing, primarily of goods and raw materials. Such involvement enables the management of the firm to become familiar with the intricacies of international business and to get a feel for doing business in more than one country. The benefits of spreading business risk over many countries and hedging against unfavorable conditions in one country trigger further expansion into more risky (albeit more lucrative) modes of operation, such as licensing and direct foreign investment.

The 1970s found the world's MNCs diversifying into many far-flung fields unrelated to their core businesses. This rash of expansions and conglomerations was motivated by the prevailing managerial philosophy that in order to service a local market efficiently a firm had to have a complete presence in that market, including a manufacturing plant in the case of a manufacturing firm or a large, full-service office in the case of a service firm.

The 1980s ushered in an awareness that this multidomestic international business strategy had led to the establishment of too many small plants in too many places, which not only robbed the MNC of economies of scale but also created some distinct diseconomies. These diseconomies arose from the need for increasingly complex and costly control and communication systems to keep the numerous affiliates under control.

The strategy currently being implemented in an effort to recoup some of the benefits of the past goes by many different names; here it will be called *globalization.* Globalization involves rationalization or restructuring and the development of strategic alliances with traditional competitors. This last chapter provides a glimpse into the process of building a strategy of cooperation with organizations that thus far have been competitors.

TRIGGERS OF GLOBALIZATION

In an interdependent relationship, such as the one between an MNC and its environment, changes in the behavior of one system lead to changes in the behavior of the other. Although it is difficult to pinpoint when or where a change is initiated, we can determine the *impact* of one system's change in behavior on the other. A review of global events and trends reveals a number of megatrends in the global business environment that have spurred the drive toward globalization. Some of these developments have surfaced only recently; others represent natural trends that have been long in the making and have been discussed elsewhere in this book. The emerging megatrends include

(1) The taming of complexity via information technology

(2) The liberalization of the international monetary system

(3) The reduction of xenophobia

(4) The waxing of a service-driven economy

(5) The increasing strength of Eastern markets

(6) The move toward the development of space

THE TAMING OF COMPLEXITY

The most important change triggering globalization on the part of MNCs has been the advent of information technology. Handling the avalanche of data required to effectively coordinate the operations of affiliates around the globe is a task too complicated for the average manager to cope with alone. Advances in information and telecommunications technologies (Chapter 13) have provided the necessary tools for tackling this formerly almost-unmanageable task.

LIBERALIZATION OF THE MONETARY SYSTEM

With the collapse of the gold standard came fluctuations in international exchange rates, which created opportunities for foreign investors. During the seventies, the overvalued dollar would buy 50% more overseas, making overseas investments very profitable. Thus, for example, Ford Motor Company, which was experiencing tremendous losses in the United States, was able to use the profits from its European subsidiary to develop the models that five years later would bring Ford to the top of the pack. Now the reversal of the dollar's relationship to other major currencies has put the shoe on the other foot, making expansion into U.S. markets attractive to foreign investors.

THE REDUCTION OF XENOPHOBIA

By eliminating barriers to trade, the trend toward political convergence is making it easier for corporations to globalize. In 1957 the six major countries of Europe agreed to cooperate in the struggle for economic survival. Thirty years later the number of countries in the Common Market had doubled, and by 1992 the European community will be the largest market in the world under one economic policy and using one currency.

Japan has made similar efforts to close war wounds via economic, political, and cultural friendships with its former enemies in the Pacific Basin. China, too, is trading and doing business with almost everyone in the world, including its neighboring enemies.[1]

Even the leaders of the USSR are attempting to lessen that country's isolation from the world through policies of *perestroika* and *glasnost.* Such policies are first steps toward full participation in the increasingly global economy.

The contemporary scene on the American continents is also marked by greater cooperative efforts both among the Latin American countries and between the United States and its northern and southern neighbors.[2] It thus appears that by the time the EEC becomes a true economic union in 1992, the Pacific Basin and the Americas will also have reached a level of economic cooperation unprecedented in human history.

THE WAXING OF A SERVICE-DRIVEN ECONOMY

Particularly in developed countries, where the basic needs of the majority of the citizens have been met, the demand is increasing for all kinds of services. Whereas in a product-oriented market the most important commodity is en-

---

[1]Louis Kraar, "Taiwan: Trading with the Enemy," *Fortune,* February 17, 1986, 89–90; Louis Kraar, "Pepsi's Pitch to Quench Chinese Thirsts," *Fortune,* March 17, 1986, 58–64; Louis Kraar, "The China Bubble Bursts," *Fortune,* July 16, 1987, 86–89.

[2]David Peterson, "U.S. and Canadian Relations: The Free Trade Agreement," *Vital Speeches of the Day,* January 1, 1988, 179–182.

ergy, in today's service-oriented markets it is knowledge.[3] The specialized knowledge that different countries have gives them a substantial competitive advantage in providing particular services. Some of these services—in such fields as information processing—relate to the latest scientific developments. Others reflect the new interest in leisure and entertainment. For example, the United States has taken fast food to Japan, and Japan has brought sushi to America.

THE INCREASING STRENGTH OF EASTERN MARKETS

The Japanese success story is by now well documented. A country with a single resource—people—has literally flooded the globe with products, services, and money.[4] Japanese portfolio investment has skyrocketed, and Japanese factories, offices, and entertainment centers are flourishing all across the globe.

Japan's neighbors are also reaping the benefits of the Japanese effect. Today, under Japanese leadership, the Pacific Basin is the manufacturing center of the world. Singapore, South Korea, Taiwan, and Hong Kong have transformed themselves into "little tigers," which are becoming stronger in the global economic kingdom so long dominated by the lions of the West.[5]

Western companies, faced with excess production capacity and saturated markets,[6] see in the newly prosperous East the market they need in order to grow and prosper.

THE DEVELOPMENT OF SPACE

If the East represents the marketing manager's dream, space is the production manager's dream. In space production can take place free of natural impediments, such as gravity, and man-made constraints, such as pollution and legislation. MNCs are looking to the skies with great anticipation.

Given these trends in the external business environment, all of which call for increased globalization, MNCs are beginning to realize that "Porternomics" is bad for business. Managers are turning away from the conventional cutthroat

---

[3]Peter F. Drucker, "The Coming of the New Organization," *Harvard Business Review,* January–February 1988, 45–53; Yoneji Masuda, *The Information Society as Post Industrial Society* (Washington, DC: World Future Society, 1981).

[4]Claudia Rosett, "Japan: So Much Yen, So Little Else," *The Wall Street Journal,* April 29, 1987, 32.

[5]Claudia Rosett, "Taiwan's Perilous Midas Touch," *The Wall Street Journal,* June 2, 1987, 33.

[6]James B. Treece, Mark Maremont, and Larry Armstrong, "Will the Auto Glut Choke Detroit?" *Business Week,* March 7, 1988, 54–62; Louis Uchitelle, "Economic Scene: A Worldwide Glut Crisis," *New York Times,* December 17, 1987, D2.

competitive strategy preached by Michael Porter at Harvard,[7] which involved improving one's own effectiveness while eroding that of one's competitors. Instead, they are opting for the Wharton model of Perlmutter and Heenan, which calls for collaborative strategic partnerships in which cooperation and competition are balanced.[8] MNCs are realizing that cooperation and competition are not antithetical concepts. Rather, they can be complimentary concepts. The competitive zero-sum strategy taught in the leading business schools and practiced by most MNCs has almost certainly outlived its usefulness. In this new information-driven world, there is room for both competitive and cooperative behavior. Indeed, cooperative behavior is imperative, especially in the case of space-based projects, which no single MNC could accomplish alone. Information, unlike mineral and other resources, is not a finite commodity. Thus the sharing of information, unlike the sharing of physical resources, can leave all parties better off.[9]

RATIONALIZATION AND RESTRUCTURING

It has been pointed out repeatedly in this work that the eighties ushered in the age of rationalization. Worldwide, managers realized that conglomeration was not the road to excellence. The promised synergy simply had not materialized. As Martin S. Davis, CEO and chairman of Gulf + Western, put it, "Two plus two doesn't equal five."[10] Thus firms across the globe began the long and tedious process of becoming leaner and more efficient—streamlining, merging, reorganizing, scaling down the size of their assets and the number of activities they are involved in, and in general going back to what they know best.[11] A study by *The Wall Street Journal* and the consulting firm of Booze-Allen & Hamilton Inc. concluded that through restructuring and refocusing on global markets, European business has found a way to meet the challenge from Japan and America.[12]

---

[7]M. E. Porter, *Competitive Strategy: Techniques for Analyzing Industries and Competitors* (New York: Macmillan, 1980); M. E. Porter, *Competitive Advantage: Creating and Sustaining Superior Performance* (New York: Macmillan, 1985).

[8]Howard V. Perlmutter and David A. Heenan, "Cooperate to Compete Globally," *Harvard Business Review,* March–April 1986, 136–152; Howard V. Perlmutter, "Building the Symbiotic Social Enterprise: A Social Architecture for the Future," *World Futures* 19 (1984): 271–284.

[9]Peter F. Drucker, "The Transnational Economy," *The Wall Street Journal,* August 25, 1987, 22.

[10]Martin S. Davis, "Two Plus Two Doesn't Equal Five," *Fortune,* December 9, 1985, 171–172.

[11]T. Peters and R. Waterman, *In Search of Excellence* (New York: Harper and Row, 1982).

[12]Mark M. Nelson and Stephen D. Moore, "Shaping Up: Industries in Europe Take on a New Look Through Restructuring," *The Wall Street Journal,* February 2, 1987, 1, 5.

CONSORTIA AND STRATEGIC ALLIANCES

Despite shifts toward a more cooperative business world, governmental policies on international trade in most developed countries have not kept up with this "collapsing of walls." In most developed countries, pressure to "buy national" and attempts to pass protectionist legislation are still prevalent. The joint communiques in which participants in economic summits proclaim the abolition of trade and investment barriers are often juxtaposed against national legislative actions aimed at shielding domestic economies from "unfair" external competition. Indeed, the United States and Europe have both erected new nontariff barriers against imports of manufactured goods during the eighties. The barriers include outright prohibitions, quotas, voluntary export restrictions, and burdensome licensing requirements. (See Exhibit 14-1.) The United States' nontariff barriers cover some 15% of the manufactured goods imported from developed countries and 17% of those from the developing world. The EEC and Japanese barriers cover, respectively, 13% and 29% of the manufactured goods coming from developed countries and 23% and 22% of those coming from the developing countries.[13]

On another front, businesses are seeing substantial increases in the cost of researching and developing new products and processes. In addition, the returns on money invested in R&D are decreasing because of the short life span of new inventions. To increase its return on investment, a firm must either find access to cheap new production technologies, develop them itself inexpensively (that is, lower the initial investment), or increase the expected cash flows by making its products accessible to a large number of users.

These developments all point in one direction: collaborate to compete. Strategic alliances do not provide immunity against protectionism—the contract for an extension to the District of Columbia subway system was denied to a 70%–30% joint venture of Kiewit Construction of Omaha and Kajima Engineering & Construction of Japan, on the basis of the Murkowski-Brooks amendment, which bans Japanese firms from federally funded public works projects.[14] They do minimize the effects, however. And the benefits of cooperation in R&D are obvious.

The new strategic responses that are being tried by MNCs these days are completely different from the hostile takeovers or mergers of the past. Strategic alliances include global partnerships, link-ups, joint projects, cross-border ties, and collaborative agreements. The aim of all such alliances is to allow MNCs to cooperate and compete. Exhibit 14-2 defines global strategic partnerships,

---

[13]"Coping with the 'New Protection': How the Multinationals Are Learning to Use It and Learning to Love It," *International Management,* September 1986, 20–26; "Can Asia's Four Tigers Be Tamed?" *Business Week,* February 15, 1988, 46–50.

[14]"Protectionism: Japanese Need Not Apply," *Time,* March 14, 1988, 31.

Exhibit 14-1   A Roster of Protectionist Moves

High Technology

United States has secured "voluntary" restraint by Japanese of sales of numerically controlled machine tools.

United States is demanding antidumping action against Japanese semiconductors.

EEC raises duty on video tape recorders from 8% to 14%.

EEC drops semiconductor duty from 17% to 14% to compensate for VCR tariff increase, but is contemplating anti-dumping action against Japan's semiconductor manufacturers.

Brazil imposes import restrictions on a wide range of electronics equipment, spanning computers and all digital instruments.

India insists on special local content rules to protect its domestic computer sector.

Electromechanical Technology

EEC requires "export forecasting" by Japanese producers of automobiles, television sets, quartz watches, and machine tools.

United States moves against imports of South Korean TV sets.

Italy secures special protection against Japanese motorcycle imports and also has protection against hi-fi tuners.

France has special protection against quartz watches and radios.

Australia takes anti-dumping action against imports of dishwashers from West Germany, Italy, and France.

Traditional "Smokestack" Industries

United States imposes special protection against steel imports from the EEC, Japan, Brazil, and Mexico.

Japan imposes special import restrictions on textiles and clothing from Pakistan, South Korea, Taiwan, and China.

United States restricts textile imports from Japan and from Portugal.

EEC has special measures on textiles favoring local producers in Britain, France, Ireland, Italy, and the Benelux countries.

Canada has special import restrictions on steel from South Korea and the EEC, and on shoes from the EEC.

SOURCE: *International Management*, September 1986, 21.

---

and Exhibit 14-3 lists some companies that have formed such alliances. True, most of the alliances shown in the exhibit give credence to the popular notion that in most cases giants are teaming with giants. But for small firms, especially in the new high-tech industries, strategic alliances can represent the best strategy for growth—a chance to team up with a giant without being gobbled up by it.

Exhibit 14-2   What Is a Global Strategic Partnership?

Not all the efforts to mold international coalitions are either global or strategic; some are mere extensions of traditional joint ventures—localized partnerships with a focus on a single national market. One example of a localized partnership is GM's venture with China to coproduce diesel engines and transmissions in that country. Neither the product nor the market is global. Other partnerships are loose amalgams of companies from different countries with little intention of attacking world markets systematically; these alliances usually want a short-term, tactical edge in manufacturing or marketing. A few partnerships widen their scope in order to focus their energies on a geographic region, such as the European Economic Community.

More important, but still not global, are those ventures aimed at the tri-centers of economic power: the United States, Western Europe, and Japan. Even these ventures, however, are not global strategic partnerships by our definition. GSPs are those alliances in which:

(1)   Two or more companies develop a common, long-term strategy aimed at world leadership as low-cost suppliers, differentiated marketers, or both, in an international arena.

(2)   The relationship is reciprocal. The partners possess specific strengths that they are prepared to share with their colleagues.

(3)   The partners' efforts are global, extending beyond a few developed countries to include nations of the newly industrializing, less developed, and socialist world.

(4)   The relationship is organized along horizontal, not vertical lines; technology exchanges, resource pooling, and other "soft" forms of combination are the rule.

(5)   The participating companies retain their national and ideological identities while competing in those markets excluded from the partnership.

SOURCE: H. V. Perlmutter and David Heenan, "Cooperate to Compete Globally," *Harvard Business Review*, March–April 1986, 137.

Exhibit 14-3   A Sample of Global Strategic Partnerships and Alliances

Companies Involved	Focus of Alliance
Philips-AT&T, Holland AT&T, United States	Advanced telephone systems
Sony, Japan Bull, France	Compact disks; electronic credit cards
Matsushita, Japan Electronic Devices, Hong Kong	Lighting and electronic components
Bull, France ICL PLC, Britain Siemens, West Germany Nixdorf Computer, West Germany Olivetti, Italy	Minicomputer software
CIT-Alcatel, France Thomson, France Siemens, West Germany	Mobile communications
Control Data, United States Corona Data Systems, United States Siemens, West Germany	Personal computers
Intel, United States Siemens, West Germany Advanced Semiconductor Materials Int., Holland	Semiconductors and microchips
Grundig, West Germany Victor Company, Japan	Video recorders
Enidata, Italy Selenia-Elsag Spa, Italy IBM, United States	Videotex software and systems; joint-venture production of industrial electronics
Ing. Olivetti and Co., Italy AT&T, United States	Rejuvenation of AT&T's computer systems
Hitachi, Japan GM, United States	Joint R&D and production in five high-tech areas
Bull, France Siemens, West Germany	Agreement to work on 30-gigaflop computer data storage system
Siemens, West Germany CIT Actel, France Plessey, Britain Italtel, Italy	Five-year agreement to join initial research and design work on a new generation of telecommunication switches
Thomson, France GEC, Philips, Holland Siemens, West Germany	Declaration of intent to produce flat-screen technology and 64-megabit chip
SEAT, Spain Volkswagen, West Germany	Joint production of automobiles
Marta, France SGS-ATES, Italy	Agreement to cooperate on robotizing the assembly of integrated circuits

Companies Involved	Focus of Alliance
Marta, France Norsk As, Norway	Collaboration on the production of 32-bit computer
Unisys, United States AT&T, United States SGN, United States	Joint effort to develop new standards for high-performance companies and UNIX
Olivetti, Italy Toshiba, Japan	Sales agreement for Olivetti Corp. products in Japan
Boeing, United States Japan	Joint production of 7J7 aircraft
General Motors, United States Toyota, Japan	Joint production of automobiles in the United States and Europe

MACROENGINEERING AND THE COMMERCIALIZATION AND INDUSTRIALIZATION OF SPACE

In cases where protectionism and rising R&D costs do not provide the impetus for a company to reach out and find a strategic ally, the opportunities provided by macroengineering projects and the commercialization and industrialization of space make such alliances irresistible. In fact, the costs for late-comers and followers are absolutely prohibitive.

MACROENGINEERING

Even though countries may exhibit provincial attitudes when it comes to conventional business, they can bind together closely when the design and implementation of a huge project is at stake. In the past, individual countries were able to build the Great Pyramids of Egypt, the Grand Canal and the Great Wall of China, and the Palace of Knossos in Crete, using their own natural and human resources exclusively. In modern times the construction of megaprojects from the Panama Canal to the Aswan Dam has required the cooperation of a large number of private corporations and public agencies.

A great number of macroengineering projects are currently under way, and an even greater number are in the planning stages. For example, the famous English Channel tunnel ("chunnel") project is currently being tackled again, previous attempts in 1884 and 1975 having failed. France and Britain have considerable experience in collaborative work: they are the producers of the Concorde, the only supersonic commercial airplane. The two countries have been joined by West Germany in the production of a conventional airplane, the Airbus, which is giving U.S. aircraft producers considerable competition.

Several other megatunnels, megabridges, megahighways, and even megacities are in the planning stages.[15]

SPACE

The macroengineering projects mentioned above represent bold attempts to solve earthbound problems. Space commercialization and industrialization is an attempt to get around some of the earth's physical and human constraints and avoid problems. Exhibit 14-4 lists useful attributes of space. Despite the tragedy of the spaceshuttle Challenger in January 1986, commercial exploitation of space seems to be an idea whose time has come. It is estimated that in the next few decades, commercial ventures in space could provide information services, unique space-derived products, and perhaps up to 20% of

---

Exhibit 14-4   Useful Attributes of Space

The following attributes of space make it attractive for various types of industrialization:

Easy gravity control

Absence of atmosphere

Comprehensive overview of the earth's surface and atmosphere

Isolation from earth's biosphere (for hazardous processes)

Freely available light, heat, and power

Infinite natural reservoir for disposal of waste products and safe storage of radioactive products

Super-cold temperatures (heat sink)

Large, three-dimensional volumes (storage, structures)

Variety of non-diffuse (directed) radiation

Magnetic field

Availability of extraterrestrial raw materials

SOURCE: E. Cornish (ed.), *Global Solutions: Innovative Approaches to World Problems* (Bethesda, MD: World Future Society, 1984), 81.

---

[15]Frank P. Davidson, L. J. Giacoletto, and Robert Salked (eds.), *Macroengineering and Infrastructure of Tomorrow* (Boulder, CO: Westview Press, 1978); Frank P. Davidson, "Macroengineering: Appropriate Technology on a Planetary Scale," *The Futurist,* December 1980, in E. Cornish (ed.), *Global Solutions: Innovative Approaches to World Problems* (Bethesda, MD: World Future Society, 1984), 69–75; Ralph E. Hamil, "Macroengineering: Big Is Beautiful," in Cornish, *Global Solutions,* pp. 61–68.

America's electrical energy; in the long run, the commercialization of space could also be a stepping-stone to large-scale colonization of space.[16]

Essentially there are three areas in which the commercialization of space holds promise. One is the operation of satellites for communications, and for a variety of other practical applications involving observation of the earth from orbit. A second is provision of services to satellite operators—building space systems, launching them, and processing and analyzing the data they supply. The third and perhaps the most exciting is the manufacture in orbit of products that cannot be made on the earth, products that promise societal and economic benefits of immense order.[17]

The appeal of manufacturing certain products in space is twofold. First, the absence of gravity and atmosphere allows particles to grow uniformly in size and shape. Second, certain wastes could be disposed of cheaply. Space production has become both technologically and economically feasible only very recently, thanks to the convergence of developments in artificial intelligence and robotics, on one hand, and telecommunications, on the other. Together these developments have made it possible for the private sector to embark on a project to establish a self-sufficient manufacturing facility.[18] (See Exhibit 14-5.)

The U.S. government is determined to get the business community involved in the exploration of space. In the words of a former Secretary of Commerce, C. William Verity, "Space is just a place to do business, just another place where business can thrive." In keeping with this philosophy, the administration in 1988 asked Congress for $10.97 billion for the commercial exploration of space.[19]

If space factories seem to be a bit farfetched, spacebound information stations are real. The use of space as a data, information, and knowledge connection is already a multibillion-dollar enterprise. According to projections made at Rockwell International, "By the year 2000, a new system of communicating via space [Skynet 2000] will distribute the benefits of the information revolution around the globe, making productivity jumps possible even in isolated areas of the Third World."[20]

THE EXECUTIVE OF THE FUTURE

The new trends in global business call for a refocusing of managers' thinking about business enterprises. In addition, they require a reorientation of the

---

[16]Jesco von Putthamer, "The Industrialization of Space: Transcending the Limits to Growth," *The Futurist,* June 1979, in *Global Solutions,* pp. 76–84.

[17]L. B. Taylor, *Commercialization of Space* (New York: Franklin Watts, 1987).

[18]Leland A. C. Weaver, "Factories in Space: The Role of Robots," *The Futurist,* May–June 1987, 29–34.

[19]Warren Strobel, "U.S. Will Make Space for Business," *Insight,* March 7, 1988, 26.

[20]Charles L. Gould and C. R. Gerber, "Skynet 2000: Raising Global Productivity Through Space Communications," *The Futurist,* February 1983, in Cornish, *Global Solutions,* pp. 85–89.

Exhibit 14-5   Manufacturing Facility in Space

The first Industrial Space Facility (ISF) will be ready to launch by the end of 1990. This privately owned, human-tended, orbiting space facility will provide rental space for manufacturing materials in a microgravity environment.

The ISF, being developed by Space Industries, Inc., of Houston and Westinghouse Electric Corporation, is expected to be used first as a materials research laboratory and power source for a docked space shuttle, which will thus be able to remain longer in orbit. But many other uses are anticipated. Business opportunities aboard the facility are expected to include:

Purification of both pharmaceutical and biological products

Growth of large protein crystals to improve the quality and speed of engineering new drugs

Growth of large ultra-pure semiconductor crystals for high-speed computers and advanced electronic devices

Development of new polymers and catalysts

Containerless processing of improved fiber optics

Creation of metal alloys and other composites that cannot be produced on Earth

The microgravity environment of the ISF will eliminate heat convection and hydrostatic pressure. It will also eliminate sedimentation and buoyancy, enabling the fusion of mixed particles or immiscible liquids into homogeneous composites impossible to make on Earth.

The ISF will not be permanently manned, but it is designed to be habitable and will provide a "shirt sleeve" work environment for astronauts when docked with the NASA space shuttle. The ISF is designed to work in tandem with the shuttle and will be in permanent orbit 200 miles above the Earth. NASA has already agreed to deliver two ISFs into space via the space shuttle.

As a major private-sector component of the space program, the industrial space facility will provide a critical bridge between the resumption of shuttle flights and the launching of the NASA space station. The facility could also serve as a "construction shack" for building up the station and, once the space station is operational, provide it with special purpose buildings and production facilities.

SOURCE: Space Industries, Inc., 711 West Bay Area Boulevard, Suite 320, Webster, Texas 77598; in Leland A. C. Weaver, "Factories in Space: The Role of Robots," *The Futurist,* May–June 1987, 33.

---

education of future business managers. Exhibit 14-6 lists some of the trends that will shape the executive of the future.

How well are U.S. executives mastering the management styles demanded by these trends? Not very well. In a scathing report released in 1988, the Massachusetts Institute of Technology's Commission on Productivity pinpointed corporate management's persistent weaknesses: preoccupation with short-term financial results, parochialism, lack of cooperation within and among U.S. firms, failure to train and motivate workers, and a chronic inability to rapidly convert innovations into reliable, well-priced products. "The typical company is just fire fighting, day to day," laments Duane Feeley, a Vice President of Arthur D. Little. "They're not doing any long-term career planning." Nor are enough leaders with the necessary skills being trained. Says Harvard Business School professor John Kotter, coaxing others to accept new work styles "demands skills and approaches that most managers simply did not need" in an earlier age.

To survive in the twenty-first century, future CEOs will have to "have an understanding of how to manage in an international environment.... To be trained as an *American* manager is to be trained for a world that is no longer there," proclaims Lester Thurow, economist and dean of the Sloan School of Management at MIT.

After interviewing scores of executives, management consultants, and business school professors, and after studying the managerial styles of some of the most successful U.S. executives, the editors of *U.S. News & World Report*

Exhibit 14-6   Future Trends in Management

---

(1)   A shift from an ethnocentric or regiocentric viewpoint to a geocentric viewpoint

(2)   A shift from sequential to synchronous operations

(3)   A shift from a centralized or a decentralized approach to a strategy of unity-in-diversity

(4)   A shift from a view of management as an economic activity to a view of management as a political activity

(5)   A shift from cutthroat competition to cooperative competition

---

SOURCES: Patricia Sanders and Andrzej K. Kozminski, "Emerging Global Management Styles," Proceedings of the Second International Conference of the Eastern Academy of Management, Athens, Greece, June 14–18, 1987, 107–111; Kenichi Ohmae, *Triad Power: The Coming Shape of Global Competition* (New York: Macmillan, 1985).

---

concluded that to be successful in the twenty-first century, chief executives will have to overhaul their thinking as well as their factories. The researchers identified the following four paramount traits of the ideal future executive:

Trait One: Global strategist
Trait Two: Master of technology
Trait Three: Politician par excellence
Trait Four: Leader/motivator

Consultants at Arthur D. Little predict that the future will belong to the megacorporations—global federations whose senior managers will concern themselves chiefly with balancing the firm's economic interests with those of the local culture.[21]

RECAPITULATION

The material in this chapter was aimed at sensitizing students to the intricacies and complexities of today's business environment, which is being shaped by important scientific and technological accomplishments. Six megatrends have had a particularly profound effect on the evolution of MNCs in recent years. Information technology has provided the tools needed to coordinate global operations. The liberalization of the monetary system has created opportunities for corporations to benefit from exchange rate fluctuations. The reduction of xenophobia has opened up new markets and permitted new alliances. The waxing of the service-driven economy has elevated knowledge to one of the most important export commodities. The increasing economic strength of the Pacific Basin has created a valuable new market. Finally, the exploration of space has opened up a new frontier for business.

In order to survive in this new environment, multinational corporations must rationalize and restructure, paring down and streamlining operations. These streamlined MNCs, each one doing what it knows best, can then effectively band together in a strategic alliance to tackle megaprojects. Such alliances have the added advantages of minimizing the effects of protectionist legislation and reducing the costs of R&D.

Managing these megacorporations will require a new, more forward-looking management style. The executive of the future will need to be a global strategist, a master of technology, a politician, and a motivator.

REVIEW QUESTIONS

(1)   What is protectionism? In your opinion, what motivates governments to pass protectionist legislation? How do global alliances lessen the effects of such legislation?

---

[21]"Twenty-first Century Executive," *U.S. News and World Report*, March 7, 1988, 48–51.

(2)   Discuss some of the potential disadvantages of corporate strategic alliances.

(3)   Glasnostamericanski, a newly formed Russian company, is negotiating the formation of a strategic alliance with Gigaflop, Inc., a small but progressive computer manufacturer in Atlanta, Georgia. The alliance calls for the two companies to pool resources in R&D in order to design a new superprinter. Authorities in the United States are refusing to grant the necessary permit on the grounds that the alliance represents "trading with the enemy in national security–sensitive business." Defend or refute the argument.

(4)   Defend or refute the statement that the idea of "cooperative competition" is contrary to the basic Western business philosophy.

(5)   Write a short memo explaining to your boss, who graduated from business school before such arguments had any credibility, the merits of getting an early start in the race to commercialize outer space.

(6)   Write a short essay on the traits that you believe executives will need in the year 2000 and the ways you think business schools must change to facilitate the cultivation of these traits.

SUGGESTED READINGS

Anderla, Georges, and Anthony Dunning. *Computer Strategies 1990–9*. New York: John Wiley and Sons, 1987.

Botkin, J., D. Dimancesu, and Ray Strata. *Global Stakes: The Future of High Technology in America*. Cambridge, MA: Ballinger Publishing Co., 1982, 37–38.

Dicken, Peter. *Global Shift: Industrial Change in a Turbulent World*. New York: Harper & Row, 1986.

Feigenbaum, E. A., and P. McCorduck. *The Fifth Generation: Artificial Intelligence and Japan's Computer Challenge to the World*. Reading, MA: Addison-Wesley Publishing Co., 1983.

Huppes, Tjerk. *The Western Edge: Work and Management in the Information Age*. Dordrecht, Holland: Kluwer Academic Publishers, 1987.

Lewis, John S., and Ruth A. Lewis. *Space Resources: Breaking the Bond of Earth*. New York: Columbia University Press, 1987.

Masuda, Yoneji. *The Information Society as Post-Industrial Society*. Washington, DC: World Future Society, 1981.

Ohmae, Kenichi. *The Mind of the Strategist: Business Planning for Competitive Advantage*. New York: Penguin Books, 1982.

———. *Triad Power: The Coming Shape of Global Competition*. New York: Macmillan, 1985.

Prahalad, C. K., and Yves L. Doz. *The Multinational Mission: Balancing Local Demands and Global Vision*. New York: Macmillan, 1987.

Rose, Frank. *Into the Heart of the Mind: An American Quest for Artificial Intelligence*. New York: Harper & Row, 1984.

Snyder, David, and Gregg Edwards. *Future Forces: An Association Executive Guide to a Decade of Change and Choice.* Washington, DC: The American Society of Association Executives, 1984.

Taylor, L. B. *Commercialization of Space.* New York: Franklin Watts, 1987.

Toffler, A. *The Third Wave.* New York: Bantam Books, 1984.

Tomasko, R. M. *Downsizing: Reshaping the Corporation for the Future.* New York: AMACOM, 1987.

Vignault, Walter L. *Worldwide Telecommunications Guide for the Business Manager.* New York: John Wiley and Sons, 1987.

CASE ● Restructuring Across the Globe

UNITED STATES

Over the past few years, managers of a number of U.S. companies looked inward and did not like what they saw. They realized that if they wanted to achieve excellence, they had to trim, shift, twist, and even dispose of under-utilized assets.

Exxon

In the case of Exxon, restructuring meant selling off or discontinuing unprofitable businesses. Exxon's serious attempt to break into the lucrative business of office automation, which had been spoiled by IBM's dominant position in that market, was abandoned. Its equally unsuccessful nuclear business venture was sold to Kraftwerk Union of West Germany. Although Exxon's downsizing earned chairman A. G. Rawl a reputation as an axman, it put Exxon in the enviable position of having so much cash that it had to spend $3 million an hour (over $20 billion a year) on ever-harder-to-find oil.[22]

General Electric

General Electric's success is attributed to the company's "unloading" of the RCA television and audio equipment business to France's Thomson, for a sum estimated to be between $500 million and $1 billion. Another factor was controversial CEO Jack Welch's slicing of the human resource factor by one half, from 200,000 to 100,000 employees worldwide.[23]

Coca-Cola

Coca-Cola Company approached restructuring from another angle. By maneuvering its various lines of business and clearing its balance sheet of the

---

[22]Max Milkinson, "Flush with Cash, but Nowhere to Spend It," *Financial Times,* July 21, 1987, 24; James Cook, "Exxon Proves That Big Doesn't Mean Rigid," *Forbes,* April 29, 1985, 66–74.

[23]Russell Mitchell and Judith H. Dobrzyski, "Jack Welch: How Good a Manager?" *Business Week,* December 14, 1987, 92–103.

entertainment and bottling business and more than $3 billion in debt, it trans-
formed itself into what the analysts call a "quasi-conglomerate." Goizueta, Coca-
Cola's Cuban-born CEO and chairman, has determined that "Coca-Cola will
remain, above all else, a soft drink company."[24] Part of Coca-Cola's new strategy
is to milk the international market, which generates some 63% of the company's operating income and more than 60% of its soft drink revenues. Through
its minority joint ventures with bottling companies in Great Britain (Cadbury
Scheweppes PLC), the Philippines, Thailand, Taiwan, and Indonesia, Coca-
Cola's management hopes to reach its target of a 40% increase in per capita
consumption by 1990.

IBM

In an effort to reverse the first downslide in the Big Blue's profits, Chairman
Akers instituted a process of reinventing IBM through a massive restructuring
and refocusing of the firm's activities. Dubbed "perpetual reorganization" in
industry circles, this strategy is based on instilling in managers what Walton
E. Burdick, Vice President of personnel, calls a "hiring-avoidance mentality."
Between 1985 and 1988, the work force was trimmed from 405,500 to 389,300
employees. In addition, the firm launched a career opportunity plan, aimed at
giving employees the opportunity to change from engineering and administration to sales through a training program known as "backfilling." Some 45,000
employees went through this informal training, which takes a few months.[25]

JAPAN

In Japan, restructuring has taken a different form: internal diversification at
home combined with wholly owned direct foreign investment overseas. This
strategy is reminiscent of the U.S. MNC's conglomeration fever of the sixties.
Japanese firms are leveraging their core skills to branch out into wholly new
businesses. Consider these cases.

> Suntory Ltd. had been known for decades as the top whisky distiller in
> Japan. Faced with slowing growth, the firm opened a biomedical research
> institute six years ago. Now it is the leading biotechnology firm in Japan
> and is licensing its technology for producing gamma interferon, a
> promising anticancer drug, to the U.S. pharmaceutical company Schering-
> Plough Corporation.
>
> Kawasaki Steel Corporation and Nippon Steel Corporation are among
> several Japanese mills moving into the production of silicon wafers, using
> licensed technology.
>
> Nippon Gakki Company, whose Yamaha brands have made it the world's
> largest producer of musical instruments, is today one of Japan's premier
> makers of integrated circuits, all developed on its own.

---

[24]Melissa Turner, "Coke Gets Back to Its Basics," *Atlanta Journal/Constitution*, September 27, 1987, E1–3.

[25]"IBM: Big Changes at Big Blue," *Business Week*, February 15, 1988, 92–98.

Minebea, a miniature-bearing and precision-parts maker, has launched its own semiconductor memory business.

Kao Corporation, Japan's largest detergent maker, is starting to make floppy disks for computer memories. About ten years ago, as part of its long-term research into surface reactive agents, Kao put a small team to work experimenting with magnetic powder, the key component of floppy disks.[26]

EUROPE

Although the executing force behind restructuring is planned and sober management strategies, in Europe the real "driver" is the bargains that the weakening dollar has created since 1985. Europeans, primarily Britons, are beginning to see the fulfillment of their lifelong dream of securing a permanent and equity-based foothold in the U.S. market.

Hanson Trust, the London-based conglomerate, created an empire in the United States by taking over run-of-the-mill companies, selling off the most unprofitable divisions, and using the cash to buy other companies. As Lord Hanson put it, "We're fond of many of our businesses, but we're not in love with them." In the summer of 1987, Hanson beat U.S. experts in a $1.7 billion deal for Kiddle.[27]

EMI added a link to its global chain with the purchase of Rent-A-Car.[28]

NatWest bid $820 million for the First Jersey National Corporation, to take advantage of "the gradual relaxation of American interstate banking laws and to realize its strategy of creating a 'super-regional' bank in the north-eastern U.S."[29]

Britain's whiz kids, Charles and Maurice Saatchi, built the world's biggest ad agency by gobbling up Ted Bates for $450 million. By 1986 the Saatchi brothers' empire had billings of $7.5 billion and pretax profits of some $103 million.[30]

In continental Europe, Bertelsmann spent $330 million to acquire RCA's music business, with which it already had a joint venture. Then the company bought the lackluster Doubleday for $475 million.[31]

---

[26]"Don't Stick to Your Knitting," *International Management,* March 1986, 20–24.

[27]Andrew C. Brown, "Hanson Trust's U.S. Thrust," *Fortune,* October 14, 1985, 47–54.

[28]Terry Dodsworth, "The U.S. Link in a Global Chain," *Financial Times,* July 30, 1987, 19.

[29]Hugo Dixon and James Buchan, "NatWest Makes $820 Million Bid for New Jersey Bank," *Financial Times,* August 6, 1987, 1.

[30]Myron Magnet, "Saatchi & Saatchi Will Keep Gobbling," *Fortune,* June 23, 1987, 36–40; Marck Maremeont, "And Now, the Saatchi & Saatchi Bank?" *Business Week,* September 28, 1987, 92.

[31]Andrew Fisher, "Bertelsmann Is Going for the Biggest Step in U.S.," *Financial Times,* July 6, 1987, 14.

A WIN-WIN SITUATION

The global dealmakers see this global restructuring of the last few years as a win-win situation for everybody involved. The U.S. MNCs cleared their balance sheets of unprofitable investments, and the Japanese and Western Europeans were able to invest their excess cash in assets made cheaper by the ailing dollar.

ISSUE FOR DISCUSSION

Critics have accused Lord Hanson of deliberately destroying good relationships among a business, its employees, and its community just to make a pile of money. They say that his strategy of buying U.S. companies, reselling them, and then buying some more hurts the poor workers, their families, and the stockholders. Refute or support this argument.

GLOSSARY OF SELECTED FINANCIAL TERMS

Absolute Advantage:
A theory, first presented by Adam Smith, that holds that because different countries can produce certain goods more efficiently than others, each should specialize in exporting those it can produce efficiently in exchange for those it cannot produce efficiently

Acquisition:
When one company buys, and therefore controls, another company

Ad Valorem Duty:
A duty (tariff) that represents a percentage of the value of the item

American Depository Receipt (ADR):
A security issued in the United States to represent shares of a foreign stock, which allows that stock to be traded in the United States. Foreign companies use ADRs, which are issued in U.S. dollars, to expand the pool of potential U.S. investors.

Arb or Arbitrageur:
A professional stock trader who invests in stocks of companies that are take-over candidates, or are rumored to be takeover candidates, in the hope of making profits on price movements

Arbitrage:
The simultaneous or near-simultaneous purchase of assets in one market and sale of the same assets in another market to take advantage of price differences between the two markets. Such operations usually involve currencies or securities.

Aussie:
The Australian dollar

Balance of Payments:
A summary of all economic transactions between a country and the rest of the world during a given period of time

Bankers' Acceptance:
A time draft that matures in six months or less, across the face of which a bank has written the word "accepted" to indicate that it will honor the draft upon presentation at maturity

Bear Hug:
An offer by one company to buy the stock of another company at so large a premium over the market price and under such favorable terms that the second company has no choice but to accept the offer

Belgian Dentist:

A stereotype of the traditional Eurobond investor. This self-employed professional must report income, has a disdain for tax authorities, and likes investing in foreign currencies. "Anonymous bearer" Eurobonds fit the bill nicely because they are unregistered and, therefore, untraceable.

Bid/Asked Spread:

The difference between the bid and asked prices on securities or on the foreign exchange market. The spread is reconciled by traders, called market makers, who quote a price at which they will buy or sell, effectively setting the price. Brokers, in contrast, merely match up the two sides.

Big Bang:

The nickname for October 27, 1987, when the London markets in equities and government securities were liberalized through the elimination of fixed commissions on debt and equity dealings

Big Four:

The nickname given to Japan's major brokerages, Nomura Securities Ltd., Nikko Securities Ltd., Daiwa Securities Ltd., and Yamaichi Securities Ltd. These firms dominate equity and bond trading in Japan and are seeking to expand their international presence, particularly in New York and London.

BIS (Bank of International Settlements):

An international organization of central banks and financial institutions, based in Basel, Switzerland, that serves two distinct but related functions. It provides a forum for the discussion of international monetary issues, and it acts as a central bank for central banks. In its second role, BIS holds deposits, keeps gold reserves, and clears central bank deposits and withdrawals.

Cable:

A slang expression for sterling/dollar trade, dating from the days when deals were made by cablegram. Hence those in the financial world talk about the "cable desk," the "cable rate," and so on.

Cedel S.A.:

One of the two main clearing systems for internationally traded securities—mostly Eurobonds, but also some equities. (See Euroclear Clearance System Ltd.)

Chartists:

Financial analysts who believe that the best way to determine which currencies should be traded for profit is by charting ebbs and flows in their values and looking for patterns

Clearing House Interbank Payment System (CHIPS):

An international electronic check transfer system that moves money between major U.S. banks, branches of foreign banks, and other institutions

Cockdate:

To schedule settlement for some date between a week and a month after the deal is made

Common Market:

In general, a form of regional economic integration in which countries abolish internal tariffs, use a common external tariff, and abolish restrictions on factor mobility. The term "Common Market" is also used to refer specifically to the European Economic Community.

Comparative Advantage:

The theory that gains from trade may still be realized if a country specializes in those products that it can produce more efficiently than other products, even if the country does not have an absolute advantage relative to other countries

Confirmed Letter of Credit:

A letter of credit to which a bank in the exporter's country adds its guarantee of payment

Convertible Note:

One of the two main equity-related debt issues (the other being warrants) commonly available overseas. Convertibles allow bondholders to exchange the debt for a fixed amount of equity (stock) within a certain period.

Copey:

The Danish kroner, named after the city of Copenhagen

Corporate Receivables:

The amounts owed to a firm by its clients

Council for Mutual Economic Assistance (COMECON):

A regional economic association made up of countries considered to be within the Soviet bloc of influence

Countertrade:

A sale that involves obligations by the seller to generate foreign exchange for the buying country

Creeping Tender Offer:

The gradual accumulation of a company's stock through purchases on the open market. U.S. law does not require disclosure of holdings of a company's stock until 5% has been acquired; then disclosure of each change in holdings is required.

Cross Rate:

The exchange rate between two foreign currencies

Culture:

The norms of behavior in a society, which are based on attitudes, values, and beliefs

Currency Swap:

A transaction in which two parties exchange specific amounts of two different currencies at the outset and then repay them, over time, according to a predetermined schedule that reflects interest payments and amortization of principal

Current Rate Method:

A method of translating financial statements into a different currency. All assets and liabilities are translated using the exchange rate in effect on the balance sheet date (the current exchange rate). Income statement accounts are translated using the average exchange rate for the period.

Customs Union:
A form of regional economic integration that eliminates tariffs among member nations and establishes common external tariffs

Devaluation:
A formal reduction in the value of a currency in relation to another currency, which causes the foreign currency equivalent of the devalued currency to decrease

Dual Currency Bonds:
Bonds that are denominated in one currency but pay interest in another currency at a fixed rate of exchange. Dual currency bonds can be redeemed in a currency different from the currency of denomination.

Dumping:
The underpricing of exports (usually below cost or below the home country price)

Duty:
A governmental tax (tariff) levied on goods shipped internationally

Economic Exposure:
The extent to which the value of a firm is sensitive to changes in the exchange rate

Economic Integration:
The lessening or abolition of economic discrimination between national economies by means of free trade areas, common markets, economic unions, and the like

Edge Act:
An act that allows banks to set up offices in U.S. money centers other than those where the bank is legally allowed to operate, for the purpose of performing international banking activities. An Edge Act corporation is a banking corporation set up under the provisions of the Edge Act.

Ethnocentrism:
The belief that what works at home should work abroad

Eurobonds:
Long-term bonds marketed internationally in countries other than the country of the currency in which they are denominated. These issues are not subject to national restrictions. In recent years, some Eurobonds have been designed as dual currency bonds that pay interest in one currency and are redeemable in another. For many multinational companies and governments, Eurobonds have become the primary way to raise capital.

Euroclear Clearance System Ltd.:
One of the two main clearing systems for internationally traded securities. (See Cedel S.A.)

Eurocommercial Paper:
A short-term unsecured note issued by a nonbank in the Euromarkets

Eurocurrency:

Money deposited in a financial center outside of the country that issued the currency. For instance, Eurodollars—the most widely used Eurocurrency—are U.S. dollars deposited outside the United States.

Eurodollars:

Dollars held in the form of time deposits in banks outside of the United States. These banks can be foreign-owned or overseas branches of U.S. banks.

European Community (EC):

A regional economic association comprising twelve countries in Europe. It most closely resembles the economic union form of regional integration. The EC is also known as the European Economic Community (EEC).

European Currency Unit (ECU):

A currency composed of specific quantities of the currencies of European Monetary System members. This "basket" of ten European currencies, devised in 1979, is intended to serve as a monetary unit for the European Monetary System (EMS). The ECU is used as part of the system's divergence indicator (for measuring relative movements of member currencies) and as a unit of account to value members' exchange reserve assets. By charter, EMS members reevaluate the composition of the ECU every five years or when there has been a shift of 25% or more in the value of any currency in relation to other currencies in the "basket."

European Free Trade Association (EFTA):

A regional economic association that includes European countries that are not members of the EC. These countries have established a free trade area.

European Monetary System:

A cooperative foreign exchange arrangement involving most of the members of the EC and designed to promote exchange stability within the EC

European Terms:

The quotation of currencies on an indirect basis

Exchange Rate:

The price of one currency in terms of another currency

Exit Bond:

A bond issued by a debtor country to a creditor bank in place of a bank credit that exempts the creditor bank from future requests for new money and restructuring

Experience Curve:

A graph depicting the percentage reduction in production costs as output increases

Export Management Company:

A firm that buys merchandise from manufacturers for international distribution or acts as an agent for manufacturers

Export Trading Company:

A trading company authorized by law to become involved in international commerce. The law that established ETCs in the United States was designed to eliminate some of the antitrust barriers to cooperation.

Financial Accounting Standards Board (FASB):

The private-sector organization in the United States that sets financial accounting standards

Fisher Effect:

A theory of the relationship between inflation and interest rates in two countries: if the nominal interest rate in the home country is lower than that of the foreign country, the home country's inflation rate can be expected to be lower, so real interest rates are equal

Floating Rate Bonds:

The most commonly issued bonds, whose interest coupons are adjusted regularly according to the level of some base interest rate plus a fixed spread

Floating Rate Notes:

Debt instruments with variable interest rates. The notes are pegged to a fluctuating interest rate, such as the six-month Libor rate, and move along with that rate.

Footsie 100:

The Financial Times Stock Index (FT-SE 100), based on the 100 largest British companies. it was introduced on January 1, 1984 with a set value of 1000.0 because there was no suitable index on which to base futures and options contracts.

Foreign Bonds:

Bonds issued by foreign borrowers in a nation's capital market and traditionally denominated in that nation's currency. Yankee bonds, for example, are mostly issued in the United States by foreign countries, banks, or companies.

Foreign Currency Swap:

The trading of one currency for another, with the agreement that the transaction will be reversed at some point in the future

Foreign Sales Corporation:

A special corporation established by U.S. tax law that can be used by a U.S. exporter to shelter some of its income from taxation

Foreign Trade Zone:

Special physical sites in the United States where the U.S. government allows firms to delay or avoid paying tariffs on imports

Forward Contract:

An agreement to exchange currencies at a specified exchange rate (the forward rate) on a specified future date

Forward Cover:

An agreement to purchase or sell a fixed amount of a particular foreign currency on a future date at an agreed-upon price, in order to ensure against exchange rate movements' having a negative impact on the domestic value of the foreign currency

Forward Exchange Market:

The market in contracts for the purchase or sale of currency at some date in the future. Involvement in this market is a way for companies to hedge against major swings in foreign-exchange rates.

Forward Rate:

The exchange rate, established by contract between a foreign exchange trader and a customer, for foreign currency to be delivered at a specific date in the future

Franchising:

A way of doing business in which one party (the franchisor) gives another party (the franchisee) (1) the use of a trademark that is an essential asset in the franchisee's business and (2) continual assistance in the operation of the business

Friendly Takeover:

An acquisition of one company by another company that is supported by the management and directors of the target company

Fundamentalists:

Financial analysts who argue that currencies ought to be valued according to the economic fundamentals of a country

Futures Contract:

A highly standardized foreign exchange contract written for the delivery of a fixed number of foreign currency units on a fixed date; a forward contract

Gilt-edged Market:

A phrase used mainly in the United Kingdom to mean all marketable government securities except Treasury bills

Gilts:

Technically, British and Irish government securities, although the term also is used to refer to issues of local British authorities and some overseas public sector offerings. Like U.S. Treasury issues, gilts have a primary market (for money raised by the government) and a secondary market.

Glider:

A not-so-affectionate name for the Dutch guilder

Golden Parachute:

Provisions in executives' employment contracts with their companies that guarantee substantial severance benefits if the executives lose their jobs or authority in a takeover

Greenmail:

When a company buys its own shares from a suitor for more than the going market price to stop the threat of a hostile takeover

Group of Seven:

The recently enlarged version of the Group of Five. The original five—the United States, France, Japan, West Germany, and Britain—meet several times a year to discuss economic issues. G-7, which includes the Netherlands and Italy, convenes at an annual economic summit.

Hard Currency:

A currency that is freely traded without many restrictions and for which there is usually strong demand. Hard currencies are often called freely convertible currencies.

Hedge or Hedging:

A method of buying and selling commodities, securities, or currencies to reduce the risk of negative price movements that might reduce a trader's profits. (See Forward Cover.)

Infant Industry Argument:

An argument in favor of the imposition of tariffs on goods imported into a country. The argument holds that tariffs raise the prices of foreign products, in effect lowering the prices of domestic goods and allowing young industries of the country to compete successfully with more established foreign firms.

In Play:

A term used by Wall Street deal makers to indicate that a company is on the auction block and will be acquired, whether or not it wants to be. For example, analysts would say that "the ABC Corporation is in play."

Interest Rate Swap:

A transaction in which two parties exchange interest payment streams based on an underlying principal amount. The three main types of swaps are coupon swaps (fixed rate and floating rate in the same currency), basis swaps (two floating rate indexes in the same currency), and cross-currency swaps (fixed rate in one currency and floating rate in the other).

International Fisher Effect:

A theory of the relationship between interest rates and exchange rates that implies that the currency of the country with the lower interest rate will strengthen in the future

Investment Climate:

Those external conditions in a host country that could significantly affect the success or failure of a foreign enterprise

Joint Venture:

An arrangement in which two or more organizations share in the ownership of a direct investment

Junk Bond:

Formerly, bonds of corporations down on their luck. Now the name describes very high-yield, below-investment-grade bonds issued by many corporations to finance acquisitions and other activities. Corporate raiders have used junk bonds to finance hostile takeovers, but the Federal Reserve Board recently limited their use.

Just-in-Time Inventory Management:

An inventory control system perfected by Japanese manufacturing companies that controls the inflow and outflow of parts, components, and finished goods so that very little inventory is kept on hand

Kiwi:

A nickname for the New Zealand dollar

Leontief Paradox:

A surprising finding by Wassily Leontief that overall, U.S. exports are less capital intensive and more labor intensive than U.S. imports

Letter of Credit:
A document by which an importer's bank extends credit to the importer and agrees to pay the exporter

Leveraged Buy-Out:
An acquisition of a public company by a small group of investors, typically including the company's management, which then turns the company into a private corporation. Most of the purchase price is borrowed, and the debt is repaid from the company's profits or by selling assets.

Libor (London Interbank Offered Rate):
The rate the most creditworthy banks charge one another for overnight loans of Eurodollars in the London market

Licensing Agreement:
An agreement whereby one firm, for a fee, gives another rights to use such assets as trademarks, patents, copyrights, or know-how

Lock-Up:
An agreement between two companies designed to thwart a third-party suitor in a merger or acquisition. A typical lock-up involves the acquirer's receiving an option to buy the target's most valuable operations.

Management Contract:
An arrangement whereby one firm assists another by providing personnel to perform general or specialized management functions for a fee

Maquiladora Industry:
Also known as the in-bond industry, an industry developed by the Mexican government in which components from the United States are shipped duty-free to Mexico for assembly and are reexported to the United States

Mark:
The German currency

Market Maker:
An institution that stands willing to buy or sell an asset at some price, or an institution that deals in an asset so frequently and in such volume that others can buy or sell that asset at almost any time

Menu Approach:
The introduction of a broad range of financing modes—the "menu"—into a debt-restructuring process

Merchant Bank:
A bank involved primarily in placing and managing securities, activities not permitted U.S. banks in the United States

Merger:
The combining of the operations of two companies to create, in effect, a third company

Newly Industrialized Countries (NICS):
Developing countries that are importers of oil but are major exporters of manufactured goods

New Money/Concerted Money:

A new loan package for a country that has lost access to external financial resources, created by equiproportional increases in the exposure of several banks and arranged through a bank advisory committee

Note Issuance Facility:

A medium-term arrangement enabling borrowers to issue short-term paper, typically of three or six months' maturity, in their own names. A group of underwriting banks may guarantee the availability of funds to the borrower by purchasing any unsold notes on each rollover date, or by providing standby credit

Organization for Economic Cooperation and Development (OECD):

A multilateral organization of twenty-four countries that helps its member countries formulate social and economic policies. All but three of the OECD countries (Greece, Portugal, and Turkey) are industrial market economies, also known as First World countries, as defined by the World Bank.

Organization for European Economic Cooperation (OEEC):

A sixteen-nation organization established in 1948 to facilitate the distribution of aid from the Marshall Plan. It evolved into the EEC and the EFTA, both regional economic associations.

Outsourcing:

A domestic company's use of foreign suppliers for components or finished products

Pac-Man Defense:

A tactic whereby the target company in a hostile takeover bid becomes the aggressor and tries to take over the would-be acquirer

Paris:

An affectionate name for the French franc

Poison Pill:

An issue of securities by a target company, often in the form of preferred stock granted to holders of common stock, designed to thwart a hostile takeover. The shares are initially worthless, but their "poison" takes effect when a hostile bidder acquires a specified percentage of the target company's stock. Then the shareholders can convert the preferred shares into the target's common stock, forcing the bidder to extend an offer to a much larger number of shares and increasing the cost of the takeover so much that the bidder ends the takeover try

Portfolio Investment:

An investment in either debt or equity that does not bring with it control

Position:

A company's or other investor's holdings of currencies

Premium (in foreign exchange):

The difference between the spot and forward exchange rate in the forward market, when the forward rate exceeds the spot rate and the domestic currency is quoted on the direct basis

Prioritization of Debt:
According one or more categories of claims preference over other claims

Product Life Cycle Theory:
The theory that certain kinds of products go through a cycle consisting of four stages (introduction, growth, maturity, and decline), and that the location of production and consumption will shift from one nation to another depending on the stage of the cycle

Pull:
A product promotion method that relies on mass media

Push:
A product promotion method that relies on direct selling techniques

Quota:
In the IMF, the payment made by each country that joins. The quota is determined by a formula based on the national income, gold and dollar balances, imports, and exports of a country. Twenty-five percent is paid in dollars, SDRs, or other reserve assets, and the remainder is paid in the member's currency.

Quoted Currency:
In exchange rate quotations, the currency whose numerical value is not one. For example, if the exchange rate between the pound and dollar were quoted at $1.40 per pound, the pound would be the base currency and the dollar would be the quoted currency.

Raider:
An investor who buys a big block of a company's stock in the hope either of accomplishing a hostile takeover or being bought out at a premium by the target company—a practice called greenmail

Rationalized Production:
The production of different components or different portions of a product line in different parts of the world to take advantage of varying costs of labor, capital, and raw materials

Revaluation:
A formal change in an exchange rate in which the foreign currency value of the reference currency rises. A revaluation strengthens the reference currency.

Royalties:
Payments for use of assets abroad

Sections:
The divisions of Japan's three largest stock exchanges (Tokyo, Osaka, and Nagoya). The first section includes the stocks of established companies, which are subject to strict requirements on dividends and per-share earnings; the second section is less restricted and includes the stocks of smaller or new companies.

Securitization:
Narrowly, the process by which traditional bank assets, mainly loans or mortgages, are converted into negotiable securities. More broadly, the term refers to the development of markets for a variety of new negotiable instruments.

Self-tender Offer:

A company's offer to buy back its own shares, a move often used to keep the shares out of unfriendly hands

Settlement Date:

The date on which an exchange of money and securities actually takes place

Shark Repellent:

Provisions in a company's bylaws designed to reduce the odds of a hostile takeover bid. These include staggering the terms of directors so that a proxy fight cannot result in the takeover of an entire board and requiring that takeovers be approved by "super majorities"—75% or 80% of stockholders.

Short:

Lacking in a commodity required to satisfy contractual arrangements. For example, you're short in sterling when you don't have enough to cover your obligations and have to sell other currencies to acquire pounds.

Sogo Sosha:

Japanese trading companies that import and export merchandise

Special Drawing Right (SDR):

A unit of account issued to governments by the International Monetary Fund

Spot:

Denotes a deal to be settled within two working days. Such deals are used to establish a position.

Spot-a-Month:

Denotes a deal to be settled within a month

Spot-a-Week:

Denotes a deal to be settled within a week

Spotnext:

Denotes a deal to be settled within three days

Square:

Being neither short nor long in the commodities being handled. Junior dealers in many banks often start and end each day square, ideally having made a profit in between. (Overnight positions are decided by senior managers, who assess what is likely to happen to the value of currency holdings before the next dealing day.)

Standstill Agreement:

An agreement between a bidder and the target company that the bidder will stop buying the target's stock or leave the target alone for a specified period of time

Stock Buyback:

A company's repurchase of its own stock, which reduces the number of shares outstanding. With earnings spread over fewer shares, the earnings per share increase, and so should the price of the company's stock. The move can deter a hostile takeover.

Stocky:

The Swedish kroner—named after Stockholm, the capital of Sweden

Swap:

A market tactic that has revolutionized the way companies raise money overseas. There are two basic kinds of swaps: interest rate and currency. When currency holdings are mismatched with settlement dates, swaps are used to roll a position over from one day to the next. For example, a dealer who is long in dollars and short in deutsche marks due for settlement on the next day would sell the dollars to buy back tomnext and do the opposite with the marks. Interest rates would be paid on each holding currency based on the interest rate prevailing in the appropriate country. Spotnext and tomnext deals are, in effect, forms of swaps.

Swissie:

The Swiss franc

Target Company:

A company that is a takeover candidate

Tariff:

A governmental tax levied on goods shipped internationally (usually imports); a duty. It is the most common type of trade control.

Tax Haven Country:

A country with low income taxes or no taxes on income from a foreign source

Ten-Day Window:

The ten working days a company has to make public a major stock purchase. U.S. law and the Securities and Exchange Commission require that if 5% or more of a company's stock is bought by an individual or a company, the purchase must be made public within ten working days after the stock changes hands, so that the company and investors will be aware of a possible change in control of the company.

Tender Offer:

A public offer to buy a company's stock. The offer is usually priced at a premium above the market price to get shareholders to sell their shares to the bidder. By law the offer must remain open for twenty working days.

Terms of Trade:

The quantity of imports that can be bought with a given quantity of a country's exports

Theory of Country Size:

The theory that larger countries are generally more nearly self-sufficient than smaller countries

Third-Country Nationals:

Employees of a company who are citizens neither of the country where they are working nor of the country where the firm is headquartered

Tomnext:

Denotes a deal to be settled on the next working day

Transaction Exposure:

The extent to which the value of a firm's domestic currency cash flows are affected by changes in the values of foreign currencies used by its subsidiaries

Transfer Price:

The price charged for goods exchanged between entities that are related to each other through stock ownership, such as a parent company and its subsidiaries or subsidiaries owned by the same parent

Translation:

The rerendering of a financial statement in terms of a different currency

Transnational Corporation:

A company owned and managed by nationals in different countries. The term is synonymous with multinational corporation.

Turnkey Contract:

A contract for the construction of an operating facility, which is then turned over to the owner when it is ready to begin operations

Two-Tiered Tender Offer:

An offer to pay cash for part of a company's shares, usually enough to give the bidder control. The bidder then offers a lower price, often in bonds, for the rest of the shares. The idea is to get shareholders to "stampede" their holdings into the cash offer.

United Nations Conference on Trade and Development (UNCTAD):

A U.N. organization that helps to establish and monitors economic relations between developing and industrial countries

Unlisted Securities Market:

The second tier of the London Stock Exchange

Value Added Tax:

A form of tax in which each firm that contributes something to the manufacture of a product is taxed only on the value it has added to the product

Vertical Integration:

A form of corporate organization in which the various subsidiaries of the MNC are either suppliers or customers of each other. This structure allows the MNC to maintain control of different stages of production as the product moves toward final distribution.

Warrant:

An option that allows the holder to buy a company's stock or debt in the future at a specified price, usually above the current value of the debt or equity

White Knight:

A third party who takes over the target of a hostile takeover on a friendly basis, usually at the target's invitation, to avoid a hostile bid from another suitor

Yard:

A billion dollars

Zero Coupon Bonds:

Bonds that pay no periodic interest (hence their name), so the entire yield is obtained as a capital gain on the final maturity date

INDEX

WORLD VALUE OF THE DOLLAR

Country (Currency)	Value 4/7/89	Value 3/31/89	Country (Currency)	Value 4/7/89	Value 3/31/89	Country (Currency)	Value 4/7/89	Value 3/31/89
Afghanistan			Congo, Ppls Rep of			Guinea Rep		
(Afghani)	50.60	50.60	(CFA Franc)	315.4574	316.7544	(Franc)	440.00	440.00
Albania(Lek)	5.929	5.9781	Costa Rica(Colon)	79.15	79.15	Guyana		
Algeria(Dinar)	6.8815	6.8815	Cote d'Ivoire			(Dollar)	33.00	10.00
Andorra(Fr Franc)	6.309	6.395	(CFA Franc)	315.4574	319.7544	Haiti(Gourde)	5.00	5.00
(Sp. Peseta)	115.95	117.835	Cuba(Peso)	0.7616	0.7616	Honduras Rep		
Angola(Kwanza)	29.918	29.918	Cyprus(Pound)	2.05	2.0395	(Lempira)	2.00	2.00
Antigua			Czechoslovakia			Hong Kong(Dollar)	7.784	7.7888
(E. Caribbean $)	2.70	2.70	(Koruna)	15.37	14.31	Hungary(Forint)	56.9431	57.2071
Argentina			Denmark(Krone)	7.26	7.3625	Iceland(Krona)	52.81	53.14
(Austral)	20.08	15.64	Djibouti, Rp of			India(Rupee)	15.66	15.63
Aruba(Florin)	1.79	1.79	(Franc)	170.00	170.00	Indonesia(Ruplah)	1756.00	1755.00
Australia(Dollar)	1.2371	1.2213	Dominica			Iran(Rial)	70.9569	71.3932
Austria(Schilling)	13.1575	13.3175	(E Caribbean $)	2.70	2.70	Iraq(Dinar)	0.3109	0.3217
Azores			Domin. Rp(Peso)	6.35	6.35	Irish Rep(Punt)	1.4269	1.4103
(Port. Escudo)	154.35	155.90	Ecuador(Sucre)	525.00	525.00	Israel(New		
Bahamas(Dollar)	1.00	1.00	Egypt			Shekel)	1.813	1.823
Bahrain(Dinar)	0.377	0.377	(Pound)	0.70	0.70	Italy(Lira)	1372.15	1388.75
Balearic Islands			El Salvador			Jamaica(Dollar)	5.50	5.50
(Sp. Peseta)	115.95	117.835	(Colon)	5.00	5.00	Japan(Yen)	132.00	132.58
Bangladesh(Taka)	30.05	30.05	Eq'tl Guinea			Jordan(Dinar)	0.55	0.5475
Barbados(Dollar)	2.0113	2.0113	(CFA Franc)	315.4574	319.7544	Kampuchea(Riel)	100.00	100.00
Belgium(Franc)	39.13	39.60	Ethiopia(Birr)	2.07	2.07	Kenya(Shilling)	19.2191	18.3704
Belize(Dollar)	2.00	2.00	Faeroe Isl			Kiribati		
Benin(CFA Franc)	315.4574	319.7544	(Danish Krone)	7.26	7.3625	(Aust Dollar)	1.2371	1.2213
Bermuda(Dollar)	1.00	1.00	Falkland Islands			Korea, North(Won)	0.97	0.97
Bhutan(Ngultrum)	15.6593	15.6299	(Pound)	1.7035	1.6895	Korea, South(Won)	667.40	671.90
Bolivia			Fiji(Dollar)	1.4457	1.4492	Kuwait(Dinar)	0.2896	0.2908
(Boliviano)	2.54	2.54	Finland(Markka)	4.209	4.249	Laos, Ppls D. Rep		
Botswana(Pula)	2.0397	2.0525	France(Franc)	6.309	6.395	(Kip)	430.00	430.00
Brazil(Cruzado)	0.9975	0.9975	Fr. C'ty in Af			Lebanon(Pound)	506.00	495.00
Brunei(Dollar)	1.9486	1.9605	(CFA Franc)	315.4574	319.7544	Lesotho(Maloti)	2.5461	2.5608
Bulgaria(Lev)	0.827	0.827	Fr. Guiana(Franc)	6.309	6.395	Liberia(Dollar)	1.00	1.00
Burkina Faso			Fr. Pacific Isl			Libya(Dinar)	0.2952	0.297
(CFA Franc)	315.4574	319.7544	(CFP Franc)	114.7117	116.2742	Liechtenst'n		
Burma(Kyat)	5.0354	5.0664	Gabon(CFA Franc)	315.4574	319.7544	(Sw Franc)	1.6421	1.6575
Burundi(Franc)	151.3696	151.1183	Gambia(Dalasi)	6.50	6.50	Luxembourg		
Cameroun Rp			Germany, East			(Lux Franc)	39.1236	39.604
(CFA Franc)	315.4574	319.7544	(Ostmark)	1.869	1.892	Macao(Pataca)	8.0408	8.0458
Canada(Dollar)	1.193	1.1942	Germany, West			Madagascar D.R.		
Canary Islands			(Mark)	1.869	1.892	(Franc)	1410.87	1430.0883
(Sp Peseta)	115.95	117.835	Ghana(Cedi)	230.00	230.00	Maderia		
Cape Verde Isl			Gibralter(Pound)	1.7035	1.6895	(Port. Escudo)	154.35	155.90
(Escudo)	76.425	76.425	Greece(Drachma)	158.90	159.94	Malawi(Kwacha)	2.708	2.7114
Cayman Isl(Dollar)	0.83	0.83	Greenland			Malaysia(Ringgit)	2.7485	2.7435
Central Africa Rep			(Danish Krone)	7.26	7.3625	Maldive(Rufiyaa)	8.71	8.71
(CFA Franc)	315.4574	319.7544	Grenada			Mali Rep		
Chad(CFA Franc)	315.4574	319.7544	(E Caribbean $)	2.70	2.70	(CFA Franc)	315.4574	319.7544
Chile(Peso)	252.00	252.29	Guadeloupe(Franc)	6.309	6.395	Malta(Lira)	2.907	2.8896
China			Guam(US $)	1.00	1.00	Martinique(Franc)	6.309	6.395
(Renminbi Yuan)	3.7221	3.7221	Guatemala			Mauritania		
Colombia(Peso)	359.33	357.33	(Quetzal)	2.70	2.70	(Ougulya)	75.00	75.00
Comeros			Guinea Bissau			Mauritius(Rupee)	14.96	14.9469
(CFA Franc)	315.4574	319.7544	(Peso)	650.00	650.00	Mexico(Peso)	2396.00	2389.00

SOURCE: Bank of America Global Trading, London.